ROTHMANS
RUGBY LEAGUE
YEARBOOK 1987-88

**Raymond Fletcher
and David Howes**

ROTHMANS

Queen Anne Press

A *Queen Anne Press* **BOOK**

© **Rothmans Publications Ltd 1987**

First published in Great Britain in 1987 by
Queen Anne Press, a division of
Macdonald & Co (Publishers) Ltd
3rd Floor
Greater London House
Hampstead Road
London NW1 7QX

A BPCC plc Company

Front Cover: Halifax's Australian centre Grant Rix is subjected to a Widnes double tackle by fellow countryman Phil McKenzie (left) and Great Britain prop Mike O'Neill. In support in the 1987 Silk Cut Challenge Cup semi-final is Halifax player-coach Chris Anderson.

Back Cover: Wigan's New Zealand Test star import, centre Dean Bell, falling to a Castleford twin tackle during the 1986-87 Stones Bitter Championship fixture at Central Park.

ACKNOWLEDGEMENTS
Our thanks to Robert Gate, for research into material for the *RU to RL* section. The compilers would also like to acknowledge the assistance of the Rugby League Record Keepers' Club, club secretaries and individuals in providing material as a further source of reference for accuracy.

PHOTOGRAPHS
Modern day domestic photographs in this *Rothmans Rugby League Yearbook* are from the files of the *Rugby Leaguer,* the only weekly newspaper dedicated solely to the 13-a-side code. The compilers acknowledge the co-operation of Chief Photographer Gerald Webster and his staff.
The colour photographs on the front and back covers, plus a number of black-and-white contributions, are by freelance photographer Andrew Varley.

British Library Cataloguing in Publication Data
Rothmans Rugby League Yearbook — 1987-88
  1. Rugby football — Great Britain —
  Periodicals
  796.33.3.0941 GV945.9.G7

ISBN 0 356 14620 0

Photoset by New Rush Filmsetters, London

Reproduced, printed and bound in Great Britain by
Hazell Watson & Viney Ltd., Aylesbury, Bucks.
Member of the BPCC Group

Rothmans Rugby League Yearbook 1987-88

CONTENTS

EDITORIAL PREFACE

Our aim since the first edition of the *Rothmans Rugby League Yearbook* in 1981 has been to make each one better than the previous year's. We believe we have always achieved that and are particularly proud of this edition.

A prime reason for our satisfaction is the chapter on Rugby Union internationals who have switched to Rugby League. This first-ever compilation of more than 200 players who have switched games will fascinate lovers of both codes. We are indebted to Robert Gate, who was mainly responsible for the chapter. It is the first time we have used another contributor and he maintained the high standard we set ourselves in research. To those who would like to know the stories behind the facts in RU to RL we recommend Robert's book *Gone North* which deals with Welsh RU converts.

Another feature is a section on Papua New Guinea, whose tour this year is the first including matches against professional English teams. This has been the most difficult section to compile because records of their early Test teams are sketchy. In the main we have relied on details supplied from official Papua New Guinea sources. But if anyone knows, for instance, if it was Arebo Taumaku and not Ati Lomutopa who went on as a last minute substitute in a Test, we would be pleased to hear about it!

We have also found difficulty in compiling records in the lower regions of Division Two. It is obvious some clubs are playing unregistered players and abusing the use of trialists. We know of instances where the same name is used for different players. We have again tried to comply with clubs' wishes where they do not want to identify trialists, but question whether there is any real reason why all players should not be named. The only exception should be Rugby Union trialists who would be banned by the 15-a-side code if they wished to return.

In thanking club secretaries and the Record Keepers' Club for help in cross checking our facts, we would like to make special mention of George Bennison, who has assisted with comprehensive details of all 34 clubs.

Thanks, once again, to our understanding house editor, Celia Kent, and to our wives who remain sympathetic.

● Facts and figures in this Yearbook as at 1st June 1987.

RAYMOND FLETCHER, of the *Yorkshire Post*
DAVID HOWES, Rugby League Public Relations Officer

FOREWORD

For the seventh time the *Rothmans Rugby League Yearbook* chronicles facts and expresses opinions about a sport which continues to enjoy the healthy respect of other sports, and which continues to provide trouble-free family entertainment, while others struggle to survive against a mounting tide of hooliganism.

So it is with pride that we associate ourselves once again with the game's finest reference publication.

As ever the authors have laboured long and hard for the benefit of the game which they love and once again their care shines through the pages of another *Rothmans Rugby League Yearbook*.

Jubilant Doncaster eliminate Hull KR

Wigan romp to title success

Australia show us way ahead

Reilly named as new Great Britain coach

League closes door on Bishop

MEMORIES

1986-87 HEADLINES
Behind the facts and figures of the 1986-87 season were a selection of stories which made big headlines:

TEST HISTORY
For the first time, a Rugby League Test was staged at Manchester United's Old Trafford soccer stadium. The first Whitbread Trophy Bitter encounter between Great Britain and Australia on 25th October attracted a British Test record crowd of 50,583, despite day-long rain and live national television coverage. The previous top gate was 42,680 for the third Test with New Zealand at Bradford in 1947. The bold move to hire the world famous stadium — proposed by Rugby League PRO David Howes — met with pockets of criticism and scepticism but all 24,000-plus seats were sold out before the day and the receipts of over £251,000 were a Test record.

PREMIERSHIP DOUBLEHEADER
The Rugby League boosted the introduction of a top-eight Second Division Premiership by deciding to stage the new final as a doubleheader with the 12-year-old Premiership Trophy final. The new style twin event was further upgraded by the selection of Manchester United's soccer stadium as the venue for the last showpiece of the season. The double bill was backed by a massive promotional campaign — featuring a television advertising campaign — funded by Stones Bitter in their inaugural season of Championship and Premiership sponsorship. The adventurous event attracted a Premiership record crowd of 38,756 who paid more than £165,000 — three times the previous highest receipts. The 'two for the price of one' promotion provided a crowd of over 22,000 for the kick off of the Second Division encounter, plus an entertainment programme featuring inflatable giant wrestlers, cheerleaders and a military band.

WIGAN DOMINANCE
Big-spending Wigan fell one trophy short of Rugby League's Grand Slam. The Riversiders lifted the Championship Trophy for the first time in 27 years, the Premiership Trophy for the first time, the John Player Special Trophy for a second successive season and the Lancashire Cup for a record 18th time. The Stones Bitter Championship success, with a record £20,000 prize, was marked by the establishment of a host of league records. The ambitious club also swept the board in the Greenalls Man of Steel awards. Ellery Hanley, the game's top try scorer for the second time in three years, was named Man of Steel for a record second time, while ex-New Zealand Test supremo Graham Lowe was judged to be Coach of the Year in his first season on the British club scene, Shaun Edwards retaining his Young Player title and scrum half Andy Gregory being chosen as First Division Player of the Year by his fellow professionals. The cherry-and-whites provided Great Britain captains at all three levels. Hanley led his country in the two French Tests, Edwards skippered the Under-21s and hooker Martin Dermott was captain of the Colts in Toulouse. Wigan continued their spending spree by creating a cash transfer record by paying £130,000 to Warrington for Gregory.

PLAYERS' CONTRACTS
The season ended with a series of special meetings to consider the scrapping of the traditional retain and transfer system of employing players. A sub-committee, chaired by Bramley council member Ron Teeman, a solicitor, recommended the introduction of a contract system, with any transfer disputes being dealt with by a new independent tribunal. The long-standing policy of players being signed for life by a club was felt to be out-dated, the contract system being designed to bring the code into line with other major sports.

BLACKPOOL SWITCH

Faced with a six-figure ground safety bill and an average league gate of less than 500, Blackpool Borough decided to relocate the club. Formed in 1954, Borough were forced to quit their Borough Park ground at the start of February and seek temporary refuge at the Blackpool FC soccer stadium in Bloomfield Road. A newly constituted board of directors agreed terms to share Wigan FC's soccer ground at Springfield Park and their application to the League for permission to relocate aroused a storm of protest from Wigan RLFC, and to a lesser extent, neighbours Leigh. After two lengthy debates, the Rugby League Council meeting of 15th May gave permission for the relocation by 22 votes to 11. Blackpool Borough argued that the switch to Wigan would keep the club alive, the move being enforced by crippling ground safety costs coupled with dwindling support, the terms of lease at Springfield Park being extremely attractive.

GROUND SAFETY EFFECTS

The second season of the implementation of stringent ground safety measures following the Bradford City fire tragedy of May 1985, had an even greater impact on the structure of the 13-a-side code. Rugby League's biggest-ever financial burden took the League's special loans fund past the £1 million mark as nearly every club faced major repair work. Stands were closed or demolished at several grounds, including Wakefield Trinity, Huddersfield Barracudas, Batley, Blackpool Borough and Keighley. The top clubs were badly hit, too, with Wigan, Hull, Hull K.R., Halifax and Oldham facing ground capacity limits. Blackpool were forced out of Borough Park while Hull K.R. and Keighley were both planning new grounds. Local councils also came to the fore to take over grounds on a community basis, following the purchase of Wakefield Trinity and Bradford Northern stadia.

RECORD TRANSFER

The record transfer fee soared to £130,000 when Wigan captured Test scrum-half Andy Gregory from Warrington on 11th January.

A year earlier Wigan had paid the previous cash record of £100,000 when signing utility Test back Joe Lydon from Widnes. The world record deal remains the £150,000 involved when Wigan signed Test back Ellery Hanley from Bradford Northern in September 1985. They paid £85,000 cash, with Test backs Steve Donlan and Phil Ford moving to Bradford.

AMATEUR RECORD

A record inducement of more than £40,000 was offered to a junior player when Halifax captured Simon Longstaff, a 17-year-old schoolboy from Wakefield. The centre or loose forward signed amateur forms in March but was promised £28,000 in trust over 12 months with extra incentives that would eventually take his fee past £40,000.

The previous record deal for a junior was the £35,000 contract Shaun Edwards received when the utility back signed for Wigan on his 17th birthday in 1983.

AMATEURS SHOCK PROS

Amateur clubs achieved two notable feats in Cup-ties against professional clubs. Myson of Hull won 8-2 at Batley in the preliminary round of the John Player Special Trophy and Kells of Cumbria drew 4-4 against Fulham in a preliminary round of the Silk Cut Challenge Cup at Whitehaven, before losing the replay 22-14.

Myson's victory was only the second by an amateur club over professional opposition in the John Player competition, Cawoods, also of Hull, having won 9-8 at Halifax in 1977-78. Myson lost 18-11 to Swinton at Hull K.R.'s ground in the second round.

Kells went near to becoming the first amateurs to knock out professionals from the Challenge Cup since 1908-09.

AUSTRALIA MARCH ON

The 1986 Australian tourists had a hard act to follow, but they matched the 1982 'Invincibles' by winning all their matches in Britain and France.

They made another clean sweep of the Test series and attracted record crowds. The Kangaroos began with the biggest-ever tour crowd for a club match when 30,642 saw the opening game against Wigan and then the first Test drew a record for an international in Britain with 50,583 at Old Trafford, Manchester.

OVERSEAS IMPORTS

With the quota system being restricted to three overseas players per club in 1987-88 and thereafter, the League gained permission from the Department of Employment to introduce three exemptions. Overseas players would not be counted in the quota system if they possessed an EEC passport, a British passport which did not require a work permit, or if they had been resident in Britain for five or more years. Meanwhile, the overseas stars continued to make an impact on the British club scene. Former New Zealand Test coach Graham Lowe arrived at Wigan to collect four winners medals and the Greenalls Coach of the Year title, while Australian player-coach Chris Anderson ended his playing career with a Challenge Cup winners medal. Ex-Kangaroo full back Graham Eadie came out of a three-year retirement to enjoy victory at Wembley with Halifax and take home the coveted Lance Todd Trophy, while Runcorn Highfield's John Cogger was named Greenalls Second Division Player of the Year.

NEW FIXTURE FORMATS

The 1986-87 season featured a one-off promotion and relegation formula of two-up, four-down, in order to produce a 14-club Stones Bitter Championship for 1987-88. While Hunslet and Swinton established themselves as pacesetters for promotion, the battle to avoid the drop was not settled until the last match of the league campaign. Leigh and Salford rounded off survival runs with victories at Warrington and Leigh respectively, leaving Hull and Oldham poised for the final relegation place, joining already doomed Featherstone Rovers, Barrow and Wakefield Trinity. Hull beat a weakened Widnes side at the Boulevard to sentence Oldham to lower grade football, having lost their last six matches of the season.

In line with recent Rugby League policy, the 1987-88 Second Division clubs each play 28 matches, the following fixture formula applying with the 20 clubs being divided into two groups of 10, listed below, as Groups One and Two.

Group One 1. Featherstone Rovers, 2. Wakefield Trinity, 3. Doncaster, 4. Sheffield Eagles, 5. Bramley, 6. York, 7. Batley, 8. Mansfield Marksman, 9. Fulham, 10. Dewsbury.

Group Two 11. Oldham, 12. Barrow, 13. Whitehaven, 14. Rochdale Hornets, 15. Carlisle, 16. Blackpool Borough, 17. Runcorn Highfield, 18. Workington Town, 19. Huddersfield Barracudas, 20. Keighley.

Clubs 1 - 10 play each other home and away.
Clubs 11 - 20 play each other home and away.
Clubs 1 - 5 play clubs 11 - 15 home and away.
Clubs 6 - 10 play clubs 16 - 20 home and away.

June... Alan Platt moved from Fulham to Hunslet.

JUNE

On holiday in Sydney, Hull K.R. loose forward Gavin Miller coaxed to join struggling Cronulla.... Wigan axe joint coaches Colin Clarke and Alan McInnes to make way for New Zealand supremo Graham Lowe on a three-year contract.... A first-ever Premiership competition approved for the Second Division clubs who are to play 28 fixtures instead of the previous 34.... Oldham committee beats off a takeover bid and launches plan to introduce a limited company.... Leigh list winger Phil Fox at £30,000.... Swinton appoint Bill Holliday and Mike Peers as joint coaches.... Wakefield Trinity show interest in £65,000-rated Oldham packman Mick Worrall.... Hull chase Australian Les Boyd as player-coach.... Warrington take £120,000 Andy Gregory off the transfer list, while offering forward Tommy Gittins at £10,000.... Silk Cut Challenge Cup-winning Castleford coach Malcolm Reilly agrees to a 13th season in charge at Wheldon Road.... Warrington offer veteran winger Steve Hesford at £8,000 and back row man Dave Allen at £10,000....

Free agent Terry Webb, formerly with Leeds, joins neighbours Hunslet.... Salford refuse permission for £2,000-rated Clive Griffiths to join St. Helens as trainer.... Featherstone Rovers receive fourth transfer request from scrum half Deryck Fox.... Batley end a three-year wait by signing former amateur international John McGowan.... Hull join the chase for Oldham's Mick Worrall.... Geoff Fletcher quits as coach of Runcorn Highfield and moves up to general manager.... Second row man Alan Platt moves from Fulham to Hunslet.... Mansfield Marksman invited to enter the preliminary round of the John Smiths Yorkshire Cup.... Castleford list want-away full back David Roockley at £40,000.... Len Casey leaves Wakefield Trinity to take over as coach of Hull.... Fulham list nine Northern-based players at a total £46,000.... Oldham recruit Australians, stand off Gary Bridge and prop Bruce Clark.... League AGM reduces First Division from 16 to 14 from start of 1987-88 season.

JULY

Australian centre Tony Currie rejects a return to Leeds in favour of a contract with Sydney club Canterbury Bankstown.... Wakefield Trinity promote Tony Dean to coach.... Hull K.R. pursue experienced Australian centre Brian Hetherington.... Leeds prop Jeff Grayshon, 37, advised to retire because of a back injury.... Halifax sign Brisbane Valleys centre Grant Rix.... Keighley player-coach Peter Roe quits.... Oldham sign Warrington's Dave Allen for £5,000.... Leeds utility back Neil Hague turns down a move to Wakefield Trinity.... Salford list full back Paul Fletcher at £50,000.... Rochdale Hornets succeed in staving off liquidation.... David Ward's bid to become coach of Hunslet blocked by Leeds' demand for him to continue playing.... Great Britain management duo Les Bettinson and Maurice Bamford travel Down Under to view the Australia-New Zealand Tests.... Halifax coax Australian full back Graham Eadie out of retirement, having spent nearly three years on the sidelines.... Keighley appoint Colin Dixon as coach.... St. Helens sign 1985-86 top try scorer Steve Halliwell.... Having agreed terms with Leeds, New Zealand Test centre Dean Bell joins Wigan.... Hull K.R. line up winger Kerry Boustead, holder of 25 Australian Test caps.... Wakefield Trinity recruit packman Tommy Gittins from Warrington.... Hunslet hand over £5,000 for Dewsbury prop Keith Mason.... Bradford Northern sign amateur stars, second row man Karl Fairbank and centre Phil Hellewell.... Leigh clinch deal for Australians Ian Schubert and Gary Howell.... Neil Hague moves from Leeds to Halifax for £12,000.... Hull utility back Steve Evans signs for Wakefield Trinity.... A shoulder injury rules out Cronulla prop Craig Dimond joining St. Helens.... Hull K.R. coach Roger Millward visits grid iron outfit Chicago Bears on a two-week fact finding mission.... John Holmes comes out of retirement at Leeds.... Carlisle appoint Roy Lester as coach.... Former Welsh international centre Frank Wilson joins Runcorn Highfield as coach.... Steve Nash named as new assistant coach of Rochdale Hornets.

AUGUST

Injury rules Australian vice-captain Wayne Pearce out of the Kangaroo visit to Britain.... Oldham stand off Ian Birkby joins Doncaster for £5,000.... Hull offer prop Trevor Skerrett at £40,000 and scrum half Andy Gascoigne at £10,000.... Leeds recruit Australian forwards Peter Smith, from Illawara, and NSW Country hooker Bob Morris.... Salford sign Australian utility back Mark Wakefield from Cronulla.... Barrow bring over Australian veteran Kevin Hastings from Eastern Suburbs.... Swinton hooker Rod Haslam forced to quit with knee trouble.... Special meeting of the League decides to relegate four clubs and promote two in order to reduce the First Division to 14 clubs in 1987-88.... Widnes sign Australians Les Cleal, brother of Test star Noel, and scrum half Craig Coleman.... Keith Hepworth returns to Hull as assistant coach.... Hull's bid to sign Australian scrum half Brett Clark falls through.... Loose forward Stuart Raper, son of Australian Test star Johnny, joins Oldham.... BARLA sanction the postponement of amateur matches on the day of the first Test at Old Trafford in October.... Hunslet fined £200 for employing David Ward as coach without the permission of his club, Leeds.... York offer forwards Steve Crooks, at £17,000, and Gary Price, at £60,000.... Leeds agree terms with Brisbane South's centre Peter Jackson.... Batley's main stand condemned to closure by the local council.... Salford list centre Nigel Lamb at £12,000 for missing pre-season training.... Fulham declare a cash crisis only two weeks before the opening of the season.... Oldham reduce Mick Worrall's asking price by £20,000 to £45,000.... St. Helens clinch a double Australian signing in St. George prop Pat Jarvis and Wests half back Brett Clark.... Widnes full back David Lyon breaks a leg in three places in pre-season sevens tournament.... New Stones Bitter Championship campaign highlighted by a first-ever Division One and Two Premiership double header and a record £20,000 prize for the 1986-87 Champions.... Castleford recruit Australian backs Colin Scott and Chris Johns, plus the return of packman Brett Atkins.... Fulham withdraw only 11 days before the start of the Second Division season.... Doncaster, Carlisle and Workington Town protest at new fixture formula which gives four points to the 14 clubs who would have met Fulham.... Castleford pay £2,000 to Oldham for veteran prop Mick Morgan.... Halifax beat Castleford in Okells Charity Shield match at Douglas, Isle of Man.... Hull K.R. list hooker Chris Rudd at £40,000.... St. Helens severely reprimanded for considering the appointment of Salford winger Clive Griffiths as trainer.... Western Suburbs forward Gerry Byron joins Rochdale Hornets.... Doncaster hand over a club record £10,000 fee for Castleford half back Kevin Jones.... Des Drummond returns from a summer's stay in Sydney to enter a new dispute with Leigh.

SEPTEMBER

Former Wales RU skipper Terry Holmes returns after injury to set up two tries in his first 80-minute appearance for Bradford Northern.... Great Britain take 31 players to a four-day preparation camp at Lilleshall, minus injured stars Harry Pinner and Mick Burke.... Australian centre Andrew Ettingshausen joins Leeds.... Oldham scrum half Paddy Kirwan turns down move to Hull.... £17,000-rated York skipper Steve Crooks joins Hull in exchange for Paul Prendiville and Carl Arnett, plus cash.... Hull K.R. forward Phil Hogan ruled out for several months with broken arm.... The League gives go-ahead for a re-launch of Fulham....

Hull protest as Garry Schofield continues to play for Balmain without their permission.... Australian Test winger Kerry Boustead signs for Hull K.R. after Manly drop demands for £20,000 fee.... Leigh ask £22,000 for scrum half Phil Johnson.... Andy Ruane priced at £15,000 by Widnes.... Four top Yorkshire clubs chase Bramley centre Andy Mason.... Huddersfield Barracudas recruit Fulham skipper Tony Kinsey in £10,000 deal.... Warrington sign New Zealand Test winger Joe Ropati.... Broken thumb rules Hull K.R. second row man Chris Burton out of the first Test.... Yorkshire make it 2-0 in the Rodstock War of the Roses series with a 26-14 success over Lancashire at Headingley.... Leeds scrum half Kevin Dick joins Hull in £50,000 exchange deal for Boulevard duo Trevor Skerrett and Andy Gascoigne.... Widnes reject £35,000 Wigan offer for Test forward John Fieldhouse.... Wakefield Trinity call off their home league encounter with Leeds because of non-completion of £200,000 ground improvement scheme.... Oldham list centre Mick Parrish at £25,000 for not attending training.... Warrington offer Great Britain forward Alan Rathbone at £45,000.... The League introduce a declaration of retirement, settling the David Ward and Clive Griffiths disputes.... Record breaking Llanelli back Gary Pearce signs for Hull in £65,000 deal.... Swinton offer £18,000 for Oldham's Mick Worrall.... Great Britain coach Maurice Bamford adds Featherstone Rovers duo Peter Smith and Paul Lyman, Bradford Northern full back Keith Mumby and Wigan winger Henderson Gill to training squad.... Bradford Northern hooker Brian Noble ruled out of Great Britain consideration with a broken thumb.... Leigh fail with a £25,000 bid for Mick Worrall.... Widnes put John Fieldhouse on offer at £75,000.... Carlisle recruit free agent Peter Subritzky, Blackpool Borough's top points scorer the previous season.... The Disciplinary Committee hand out a total of 28 matches to five players, headed by Workington Town's Neil Fraser with 10.... Hull chase Australian forward Geoff Robinson who spent the previous season with Halifax.... Wally Lewis chosen to captain the 1986 Australian tourists, one of only six who visited Britain with the all-conquering 1982 Kangaroos.... Leeds fail in double Australian bid for Wayne Pearce and Greg Alexander, both omittted from the touring party.

OCTOBER

Leigh receive a transfer request from Test winger Des Drummond.... St. Helens consider swap deal between Harry Pinner and Leigh's Des Drummond.... Injury rules winger Eric Grothe out of the Australian touring party, scrum half Greg Alexander being called up.... The League bans any club signing Welsh RU scrum half David Bishop until his 11-month suspension has been served.... Leeds pull out of deal for Bramley threequarter Andy Mason.... St. Helens reject Warrington proposal for the exchange of Harry Pinner for Test forward Alan Rathbone.... Leeds recruit Cronulla centre Mark McGaw.... Leigh ask £100,000 for Des Drummond.... Great Britain Under-21 prop Brendan Hill offered at £35,000 by Leeds.... Plans relaunched for new club based at Stockport.... Hull K.R. list prop Asuquo Ema at £80,000.... Australia open their 13-match tour with hard earned 26-18 victory at Wigan, watched by over 30,000 fans.... Castleford defeat Hull 31-24 to lift the John Smiths Yorkshire Cup.... Wigan's Andy Goodway recalled in Great Britain's 17-man squad, which includes Second Division centre Andy Mason.... Frenchman Julien Rascagneres appointed referee for the Anglo-Aussie Test series.... The Kangaroos dispose of Hull K.R. 46-10.... Wigan extend their Lancashire Cup final record to 18 wins with 27-6 defeat of Oldham.... Australia march on with 40-0 hammering of Leeds.... Leigh hand over £20,000 for Carlisle's Milton Huddart.... New Zealander Kurt Sorensen ap-

pointed to the Widnes coaching staff.... Shock Great Britain call up at full back for Joe Lydon.... Cumbria crash 48-12 to Australia at Barrow.... Wakefield Trinity ask £40,000 for Tracey Lazenby and £20,000 for Dean Williams.... Leigh sign Hull's Kiwi centre James Leuluai for the season.... The Adidas Golden Boot for the international player of the year awarded to Australia's Brett Kenny.... Former Wigan coaches Colin Clarke and Alan McInnes sue the club for unfair dismissal.... Bradford Northern sign Australian hooker Mario Fenech, while Sheffield Eagles recruit Manly's Cliff Lyons, both subject to four-match bans.... A British Test record 50,583 crowd pay a record £251,061 to witness Great Britain crash 38-16 in the first Whitbread Trophy Bitter Test at Old Trafford, Manchester.... Featherstone Rovers sign Castleford third-choice hooker Martin Slater for £8,000.... Former BBC TV commentator Eddie Waring dies at 76.... Wakefield Trinity beat off a host of fellow Yorkshire clubs to sign loose forward Gary Price in a 17th birthday £30,000 deal.... French champions Le Pontet call off their challenge match with English counterparts Halifax with only four days' notice.... Australia run in seven tries in 36-2 rout of Halifax.

NOVEMBER

Leeds sign Bramley centre Andy Mason in near-£60,000 deal, with £12,000-rated David Healey set to move to McLaren Field in part exchange.... Oldham list hooker Ian Sanderson at £25,000.... St. Helens swap £95,000 Harry Pinner for £75,000-rated John Fieldhouse.... Australia beat current league leaders St. Helens 32-8.... Kangaroo Test stars Steve Roach and Les Kiss ruled out with injury.... Four players sent to the sin bin — two apiece — as Australia scrape home 22-16 at Oldham.... Featherstone Rovers sack coach George Pieniazek.... Great Britain's Ellery Hanley ruled out of the final two Tests by a knee operation.... Britain crash 34-4 in the second Test at Elland Road, Leeds.... Paul Daley returns for a second spell as coach of Featherstone Rovers.... Runcorn Highfield sack Frank Wilson as coach and appoint Arthur Daley and Paul Woods on a caretaker basis.... Hull sign Wakefield Trinity's £40,000-rated loose forward Tracey Lazenby.... Oldham increase Mick Worrall's asking price by £30,000 to £75,000.... Swinton offer winger Ken Jones at £10,000.... Australia beat Widnes 20-4.... Great Britain coach Maurice Bamford makes several changes for third Test and brings in John Basnett, Ronnie Duane, Andy Gregory, Chris Burton and Harry Pinner.... Hull go down 48-0 to Australia in a bruising encounter.... Hull amateur side Myson knock Second Division Batley out of the John Player Special Trophy.... Australia's scrum half Peter Sterling promises a return to Hull should he decide to play again in Britain.... Wally Lewis signs for Wigan.... Oldham join in the chase for Leeds prop forward Brendan Hill.... Halifax stand off John Crossley joins Featherstone Rovers.... Australia rout Bradford Northern 38-0 in fog and rain.... Hull rap Garry Schofield for missing the tour match against Australia and list him at £150,000.... Australia announce shock selection of centre Mal Meninga as second row replacement for the injured Noel Cleal.... Controversial penalty try helps Australia to a 24-15 third Test victory over a recharged British side.... Mick Worrall asks to come off the Oldham transfer list.... The Whitbread Trophy Bitter Man of the Series awards presented to Wally Lewis (Australia) and Britain's Kevin Ward.... Tour gates up 33 per cent as Australia make a £115,000 profit in Britain.... Leeds cancel Australian prop Peter Smith's contract.... Bramley ask £10,000 for want-away full back Shaun Kilner.... Wakefield referee Fred Lindop appointed for the two France-Australia Tests.... St. Helens send New Zealand Test centre Mark Elia back home after arriving with a long-term hamstring injury.... Barrow join Wakefield Trinity, Halifax and Leigh in pursuit of Salford's John Pendlebury.

DECEMBER

Hull K.R., John Player Special Trophy finalists for the past two years, knocked out of the tournament by Second Division Doncaster.... Struggling Leeds stage a public clear-the-air meeting.... In a bid to replace centre Mark Elia, St. Helens sound out Australian tourists Mal Meninga, Gene Miles and Greg Alexander.... Warrington lead the chase for Kangaroo hooker Ben Elias.... Test centre Garry Schofield makes his peace with Hull.... Hull K.R. back coach Roger Millward.... Ground safety restrictions force Blackpool Borough to concede home advantage to Hull in John Player Special Trophy second round tie.... Castleford list centre Phil Payne at £20,000.... Ellery Hanley puts in shock transfer request at Wigan.... Great Britain scrum half Andy Gregory fined £250 and suspended for two weeks by Warrington for missing two training sessions.... Gregory refuses to pay and is listed at world record £150,000 after requesting transfer .... Wigan have their ground capacity cut from 30,000 to 12,000 under the Ground Safety Act .... Ellery Hanley settles his differences with Wigan .... St. Helens sign Welsh centre Steve Bayliss, four years after selling him to Fulham for £40,000 .... Salford forward Steve Dickens moves to Dewsbury for £3,000 .... Leeds move for Warrington's Andy Gregory .... Oldham offer Australian tour full back Gary Belcher a one-year contract .... Barrow and Leigh chase Warrington packman Alan Rathbone .... Mansfield Marksman replace Steve Dennison with Jim Crellin as coach ....Lifesaving on-the-pitch treatment for Widnes winger John Basnett after swallowing his tongue in the John Player tie at Barrow .... Great Britain coach Maurice Bamford decides not to seek renewal of his contract because of his wife's multiple sclerosis .... Hunslet sign a 20-year lease to stay at Elland Road .... Hull K.R. annual meeting reveals a cash crisis and the threat of having to sell Craven Park to stay in business .... Alan Rathbone asks to come off the Warrington transfer list .... Bradford Northern offer loose forward Mark Fleming at £40,000 .... Wakefield Trinity sack Tony Dean and appoint Trevor Bailey as coach .... Whitehaven's former Great Britain centre Vince Gribbin joins Barrow on loan, in preference to Oldham .... Wally Lewis announces in Brisbane that a shoulder injury will prevent him from joining Wigan .... Bolton Wanderers' Burnden Park chosen to stage the John Player Special Trophy Final .... Warrington tell Andy Gregory to pay his £250 fine or stay away .... Leeds sack coach Peter Fox and bring Maurice Bamford back for a second spell at Headingley .... Wigan list want-away scrum half Mick Ford at £50,000 .... Chris Forster quits as coach of Huddersfield Barracudas after they concede more than 100 points in two Christmas fixtures .... Swinton chairman Ian Clift slams trial by video .... Leigh sack coach Tommy Dickens after a 13-month stint and appoint Billy Benyon .... Oldham ask Widnes about £25,000-rated prop Fred Whitfield.

JANUARY

St. Helens inquire about Warrington's Andy Gregory as Wigan withdraw their offer .... Jack Addy resigns as coach of Dewsbury to take over at Huddersfield Barracudas.... Bradford Northern sign Leeds prop forward Brendan Hill for £30,000 .... Leeds give Oldham permission to speak to Jeff Grayshon .... Dewsbury appoint Dave Busfield as coach .... Australian referee Mick Stone appointed to take charge of the Great Britain-France Tests .... St. Helens make a move for Wigan's Shaun Edwards .... Wigan respond by bidding for St. Helens second row man Roy Haggerty .... Stay-away winger Des Drummond turns down new coach Billy Benyon's plea to return to Hilton Park .... Rochdale Hornets rejected in approach for Leeds stand off John Holmes .... Widnes offer full back Mick Burke at £40,000 .... Rugby League's Board of Appeal lower Andy Gregory's fee by £20,000 to £130,000 .... Leigh make a move for Warrington's Tony Worrall .... Warrington list forward Roy Campbell at £10,000 .... Bradford Northern call off the signing of Hunslet packman Kelvin Skerrett .... Castleford's Malcolm Reilly appointed coach of Great Britain .... Warrington scrum half Paul Bishop ruled out of the John Player Special Trophy final with a two-match ban, despite an appeal .... Leeds hand over £40,000 for Oldham scrum half Ray Ashton .... Wigan retain the John Player Special Trophy by beating Warrington 18-4 at Bolton Wanderers' soccer ground .... Warrington's Andy Gregory moves to Wigan for a record £130,000 .... Oldham recruit Mick Burke from Widnes, and Blackpool Borough prop forward Hugh Waddell .... Warrington winger Rick Thackray moves to Widnes for £25,000 .... Rugby League Secretary-General David Oxley blasts BBC TV for their coverage of the John Player Special Trophy .... Leigh's Test winger Des Drummond threatens to retire .... Development talks between the League and BARLA break down because of the amateur game's insistence on the scrapping of the Colts League .... Oldham and Warrington both hire Manchester City's Maine Road soccer ground for the staging of Championship fixtures on successive nights .... Workington Town forgo home advantage and switch their Silk Cut preliminary round tie to Wigan .... Wales RU star Jonathan Davies announces his future plans to switch to Rugby League after the summer's World Cup tournament .... St. Helens and Bradford Northern join Leeds and Warrington in the chase for Jonathan Davies' signature .... Workington Town list Steve Maguire at £28,000 as a disciplinary measure .... Oldham deny reports of a £75,000 offer to Swansea RU flanker Paul Moriarty .... Blackpool Borough refused £65,000 ground safety grant aid from the local council, forcing the closure of their ground and a switch to Blackpool Town's soccer ground .... Bradford Northern's Mark Fleming asks to come off the transfer list .... Leigh reduce Des Drummond's fee from £85,000 to £65,000 .... Wigan knock £10,000 off the asking price for scrum halves Mick Ford, down to £40,000, and Keith Holden, to £10,000 .... Castleford reserve hooker Stuart Horton requests to be taken off the list after 18 months on offer at £40,000 .... Mansfield Marksman reject a £500 offer from amateur opponents Heworth to switch their first round Silk Cut Challenge Cup tie to York .... Former Featherstone Rovers and Hull utility back Steve Evans moves from Wakefield Trinity to Bradford Northern in exchange for Test forward Dick Jasiewicz .... Wakefield Trinity also recruit Northern's Ian Sheldon and Batley's Ian Douglas .... Britain's John Holdsworth, Fred Lindop and Robin Whitfield appointed to the international panel of referees .... Wigan's Andy Gregory and Runcorn Highfield's John Cogger halfway stage leaders in the Greenalls Man of Steel player of the year award ballots .... St. Helens break with tradition and offer coach Alex Murphy a two-year contract .... St. Helens sign Wigan Colts product Sean Devine .... Widnes offer Geoff Sephton at £15,000 and Paul Houghton at £10,000 .... The League announce the formation of a Development Foundation with an initial investment of £50,000 .... Hull forward Les Crooks ruled out of selection for Great Britain's return Test in France by a two-match ban .... Castleford forward Barry Higgins banned for 12 matches by the League's Disciplinary Committee.

FEBRUARY

Manchester United's Old Trafford soccer stadium selected as the venue for the Stones Bitter Premiership final doubleheader .... Dewsbury forced to install temporary floodlighting in order to stage their home Challenge Cup tie with St. Helens .... Great Britain players released for club duty in the week of the return Test in France as only four of the 16 first round Challenge Cup ties are staged at the frostbound weekend .... Kiwi Dean Bell signs a new three-year contract with Wigan .... Leeds show interest in Leigh's stay-away winger Des Drummond .... Wembley favourites Wigan crash out of the Challenge Cup at Oldham in a first round 10-8 shock defeat .... Billy Benyon awarded a three-year coaching contract at Leigh after only five weeks in charge .... Warrington hand over £40,000-plus for Leigh's Des Drummond .... Leigh spend £27,500 of the Drummond fee on Wigan scrum half Mick Ford .... Wigan's Andy Goodway pulls out of the Caracassonne Test through injury, Halifax's Paul Dixon stepping up for his Test debut .... Widnes list centre John Gilbert at £30,000 .... Coach Malcolm Reilly brands the French as 'animals' as Great Britain record a 20-10 victory in Carcassonne .... Papua New Guinea referee Graham Ainui appointed for the Anglo-French Under-21 internationals .... St. Helens chosen to stage an international doubleheader in March with both the Colts and Under-21 fixture at Knowsley Road .... St. Helens reject a transfer request from packman Paul Round, a target for Leigh .... Kiwi centre Mark Elia returns to St. Helens fully recovered from a serious hamstring injury .... Local council proposes that Dewsbury and Batley share Crown Flatt while refusing grant aid towards ground safety repairs .... Wigan move Ellery Hanley to loose forward .... Hull centre Garry Schofield chased by Balmain and Manly for a third successive season Down Under .... Hull teammate Lee Crooks pursued by Parramatta, Manly and St. George for a Sydney contract .... Halifax turn down ground sharing plan at Thrum Hall with cash crisis soccer club Halifax Town .... Bradford Northern express willingness to house Halifax Town at Odsal .... Doncaster veteran David Noble celebrates a year of playing and scoring in every match for the Dons .... Whitehaven forward Paul McDermott joins Wakefield Trinity for the fourth time .... Barrow sack coach Ivor Kelland and appoint Dennis Jackson .... Wakefield Trinity and Barrow chase St. Helens centre Steve Halliwell .... Halifax list Neil Hague at £12,000 .... Warrington forward Mike Gregory threatens to sue the French League after sustaining a broken nose and cheekbone in the British Test in Carcassonne .... League Secretary-General David Oxley hits out at local authorities' handling of ground safety measures .... Shaun Edwards, of Wigan, named as captain of Great Britain Under-21s .... Dewsbury offer Paul Jennings at £20,000 .... A knee injury forces Featherstone Rovers half back Ian Slater to retire at 29 .... Eight-match Papua New Guinea itinerary announced for the autumn, with a 24 October Test at Wigan .... Wakefield Trinity make a double swoop for St. Helens centre Steve Halliwell and Rochdale Hornets full back Kevin Harcombe .... Leeds City Council tell Rugby League Development Officer Maurice Bamford that he must choose between the job and that of coaching Leeds .... Leigh approach Rochdale Hornets for forwards Brian Dunn and David Evans .... France threaten to cancel a summer tour Down Under, putting the new style World Cup in jeopardy .... The Sunday Mirror Rugby League Roadshow passes the £100,000 fund raising landmark with its 71st show.

MARCH

Workington Town, fourth from the bottom of the Second Division, sack coach Keith Davies and appoint Barrow's Norman Turley as player-coach .... Hull K.R. assistant coach John Moore decides to leave after 25 years' service at Craven Park .... Leigh fail in bid to fly back Australian import Ian Schubert for the Challenge Cup semi-final .... Bradford Northern players offer to play for nothing after a 60-6 hammering at Wigan, their ninth successive defeat .... Oldham vice-chairman Keith Potter severely reprimanded by the League after publicly criticising referees .... Oldham second row man Tom Nadiole rejects a move to Barrow .... Hull's Test forward Lee Crooks signs a summer contract with Sydney club Balmain .... French Test prop Jean-Luc Rabot suspended for two weeks for striking Great Britain loose forward Mike Gregory .... Police chief Graham Ainui becomes the first Papua New Guinea referee at international level as Great Britain Under-21s beat France 40-7 in St. Jean de Luz .... Warrington turn down a transfer request from Great Britain winger Mark Forster .... Sydney clubs Manly and St. George chase Castleford prop Kevin Ward .... Warrington list Great Britain Under-21 winger Brian Carbert at £60,000 and sign Great Britain amateur hooker Mark Roskell .... Leeds offer prop Keigh Rayne at £35,000 .... Whitehaven list David Lightfoot at £40,000 and Gary Hetherington at £35,000 after refusing permission for the duo to set off Down Under before the end of the British season .... Hull K.R. allow loose forward Gavin Miller to return to Australia two months early .... Phil Lowe quits as coach of York .... Hull deputation travels to Australia to sign up Balmain pair Scott Gale and David Brooks .... Kiwi centre Mark Elia signs a three-year contract with St. Helens .... Batley reject proposals for ground sharing with neighbours Dewsbury .... Keighley threatened with winding up by

Inland Revenue .... Hull recruit Australian tourist scrum half Greg Alexander from Penrith .... Halifax pursue Hull K.R. scrum half Paul Harkin, on offer at £60,000 .... Hull K.R. prop Zook Ema ruled out for the rest of the season by fire service training .... Wakefield Trinity list full back Gary Spencer at £110,000 .... Hull Test centre Garry Schofield signs up for a third season with Sydney club Balmain .... Leigh extend new coach Billy Benyon's contract to five years .... Swinton put £75,000 price tag on want-away loose forward Les Holliday .... Kippax referee John Holdsworth appointed for the Silk Cut Challenge Cup final .... Featherstone Rovers pay £7,000 for Wakefield Trinity second row man Paul Geary .... Bradford Northern turn down a transfer plea from hooker Gary Brentley .... Great Britain Under-21s complete the double over France with record breaking 54-6 rout at St. Helens .... Veteran Jeff Grayshon leaves Leeds to rejoin Bradford Northern .... Greg Alexander pulls out of deal with Hull .... Warrington sign Wigan scrum half Keith Holden for £10,000 .... Sydney club Wests give Brett Clark permission to play for St. Helens at Wembley .... Full back Phil Veivers agrees a new one-year contract with St. Helens .... Halifax duo Paul Dixon and Colin Whitfield sign summer contracts with Sydney club Canterbury Bankstown .... Warrington loose forward Mike Gregory agrees to short-term stay with Sydney outfit Cronulla .... Hull K.R. scrum half Paul Harkin returns to Bradford Northern in £40,000 deal, former Welsh RU skipper Terry Holmes switching to loose forward .... Castleford upgrade Dave Sampson to first team coach to replace new Great Britain boss Malcolm Reilly .... Halifax win the chase for 17-year-old loose forward Simon Longstaff .... Defeat of Widnes 12-8 provides Halifax with their first Wembley appearance for 31 years .... Rochdale Hornets sign full back Steve Rule two years after his retirement at

Salford .... Halifax player-coach Chris Anderson has an operation on a fractured cheekbone suffered in the Challenge Cup semi-final victory .... Oldham sign former England RU Colts international Wayne Grix on loan from Mansfield .... Sydney club Canberra join the race for Castleford's Kevin Ward .... Silk Cut extend sponsorship of the Challenge Cup in new two-year £330,000 deal.

APRIL
Leigh pay around £20,000 for Rochdale Hornets prop forward David Evans .... Leeds create a new football division under the chairmanship of banker Bernard Coulby .... Featherstone Rovers list hooker Mark Campbell at £5,000 .... Bradford Northern sign Great Britain forward David Hobbs from Oldham in part exchange for Oldham-based prop Ian Sherratt .... Featherstone Rovers snap up 19-year-old Ian Smales, son of former club loose forward and coach Tommy .... Wigan romp to their first Championship title success for 27 years, plus Stones Bitter £20,000 prize .... Warrington offer Bob Eccles for £27,500 .... Dave Busfield quits as coach of Dewsbury, who appoint Terry Crook within 24 hours .... Widnes reduce £25,000 fee on full back David Lyon by £5,000 .... General manager Frank Myler to leave Oldham at the end of the season .... Fulham supporter Bob Evans chosen as Traveleads Top Fan 1987 .... Runcorn Highfield appoint Bill Ashurst as coach .... Hunslet clinch the Second Division title .... Wakefield Trinity to advertise for a new coach .... Broken wrist and hand rules Les Boyd out of Warrington's bid to retain the Premiership Trophy .... Castleford's Test prop Kevin Ward signs a summer contract with Sydney club Manly, rejecting a counter offer from St. George .... Hull list Neil Puckering at £45,000 .... Blackpool Borough sign a five-year contract to play at Wigan Football Club ....

Wakefield Trinity fail in a bid to tempt Australian skipper Wally Lewis with a lucrative three-year player-coach job .... Six consecutive defeats send Oldham into Division Two along with Featherstone Rovers, Barrow and Wakefield Trinity .... Swinton promoted for the second time in three years .... Oldham face cash crisis and make appeal to the local council .... Allan Agar leaves Bramley after clinching a top-eight Second Division Premiership place .... Peter Fox linked with vacant coaching posts at Bramley and York .... Champions Wigan blast Blackpool Borough's proposed move to Wigan FC .... Leigh decide not to renew contracts with New Zealand centre James Leuluai and Australian half back Mike Davis .... Leeds make shock double bid for Hull Test duo Lee Crooks and Garry Schofield.

MAY

Halifax lift the Rugby League Challenge Cup for the first time in 48 years after 19-18 thriller with St. Helens .... Oldham announce plans for the formation of a limited company and the takeover of Watersheddings by the local council .... St. Helens face competition from Leigh, Canberra and newly-formed Brisbane for centre Mal Meninga .... Leigh's Shaun Fairhurst named Slalom Lager Alliance Player of the Year .... Peter Fox appointed coach of Featherstone Rovers, replacing Paul Daley .... David Topliss given free transfer by Oldham .... Great Britain tourist Wayne Proctor asks for a move from Hull and is listed at £50,000 .... the League introduce new exemptions to the quota system including EEC passport holders and overseas players resident in Britain for five or more years .... Leeds offer Gary Price at £42,500 only seven months after his signing from York .... Rochdale Hornets chase Australian Test forward Noel Cleal .... Wakefield Trinity appoint former captain David Topliss as coach .... Blackpool Borough

given permission by the Rugby League Council by 22 votes to 11 to move to Wigan FC's Springfield Park despite protests from Wigan and Leigh .... Wigan collect their fourth major trophy of the season by lifting the Stones Bitter Premiership for the first time, beating Warrington 8-0 .... Division Two title runners-up Swinton beat champions Hunslet 27-10 in the first-ever Second Division Premiership final .... Sydney Premiership pacesetters Balmain offer a summer contract to Wigan's Shaun Edwards .... Halifax agree to new one-year contract with coach Chris Anderson .... Australian packman Mal Graham applies for the player-coach job at Oldham .... Warrington duo Paul Bishop and Mike Gregory join Sydney club Cronulla for the summer .... Wigan issue a public statement denouncing the introduction of Blackpool Borough into the town .... Great Britain scrum half Deryck Fox has a transfer plea rejected by Featherstone Rovers .... Bradford Northern sign Hunslet's Kelvin Skerrett .... Oldham's former Test forward Mick Worrall resubmits a demand for a move .... Garry Schofield's summer stay with Balmain put in jeopardy by Hull insisting on a 31st August return .... Swinton skipper Les Holliday asks to come off the transfer list .... Local council consider buying Featherstone Rovers' ground for £100,000 .... Leeds coach Maurice Bamford quits as Leeds City Council Development Officer .... Knee injury prevents Wigan's Shaun Edwards from joining Balmain for the summer.

Widnes hooker Phil McKenzie, scorer of 11 tries in 37 games in his first season at Naughton Park.

Hull K.R.'s Kiwi prop Mark Broadhurst, brought out of retirement to make 24 appearances.

CLUBS

The following is a focus on the 34 professional Rugby League clubs, the section providing each club with a profile and an analysis of their 1986-87 campaign on a match by match basis with a summary for each first team player.

KEY

In the individual club profiles the following headings are featured:

First season refers to when the club gained senior league status. In some instances clubs have disbanded and re-formed, sometimes under different titles. For record purposes these changes are ignored except where there has been a break of more than one full season.

Honours. Until they were scrapped in 1970, the Yorkshire and Lancashire Leagues were among the honours in the professional game. Before 1903 they operated under the title of the Yorkshire and Lancashire Senior Competitions. Winners of these senior competitions are listed under Yorkshire and Lancashire League Champions. The pre-1903 Yorkshire Senior Competition should not be confused with the league operating for A-teams in Yorkshire which had the same title.

Coaches. Changes in the appointment of a club's coach during 1986-87 are shown in brackets.

Attendances. Crowds in brackets are at neutral venue.

Appearances. Players' totals are based on official teamsheets submitted to the League after each first team match. + indicates playing substitute appearance.

In the match by match review for each club the following abbreviations are used:

YC	—	Yorkshire Cup	A	—	Away
LC	—	Lancashire Cup	W	—	Won
SBC	—	Stones Bitter Championship	L	—	Lost
SD	—	Second Division	D	—	Drawn
JPS	—	John Player Special Trophy	dg	—	Drop goal
CC	—	Challenge Cup	Fr	—	France
PT	—	Premiership Trophy	Aus	—	Australia
SDP	—	Second Division Premiership	NZ	—	New Zealand
P	—	Preliminary Round	PNG	—	Papua New Guinea
H	—	Home	Pr	—	Probationer

BARROW

Ground:	Craven Park
Colours:	Royal blue jerseys
First Season:	1900-01
Nickname:	Shipbuilders
Chairman:	Bob Brady
Secretary:	Wilf Livingstone
Coach:	Ivor Kelland (May 1985-Feb 1987), Dennis Jackson (Feb 1987-)

Honours: **Challenge Cup** Winners, 1954-55
Beaten finalists, 1937-38, 1950-51, 1956-57, 1966-67
John Player Trophy Beaten finalists 1980-81
Lancashire Cup Winners, 1954-55, 1983-84
Beaten finalists, 1937-38
Division Two Champions, 1975-76, 1983-84

Records: Attendance: 21,651 v. Salford (League) 15 Apr, 1938
Season
Goals: 135 by J. Ball, 1956-57
Tries: 50 by J. Lewthwaite, 1956-57
Points: 305 by I. Ball, 1979-80
Match
Goals: 12 by F. French v. Maryport, 19 Feb, 1938; W. Horne v. Cardiff, 8 Sep, 1951; S. Tickle v. Kent Invicta, 8 Apr, 1984
Tries: 6 by V. Cumberbatch v. Batley, 21 Nov, 1936; J. Thornburrow v. Maryport, 19 Feb, 1938; F. Castle v. York, 29 Sep, 1951
Points: 28 by K. Jarrett v. Doncaster, 25 Aug, 1970; S. Tickle v. Kent Invicta, 8 Apr 1984
Highest score: 83-3 v. Maryport, 1937-38
Highest against: 71-15 v. St. Helens, 1958-59

1986-87 PLAYERS' SUMMARY

	App	Tries	Goals	Dr	Pts
Blacker, Brian	25 + 2	7	—	—	28
Burns, Paul	2 + 1	—	—	—	—
Cairns, David	37	9	—	—	36
Carter, Dane	7	—	—	—	—
Carter, Steve	8	3	—	—	12
Creary, Paul	4	—	—	—	—
Du Toit, Nick	12	4	—	—	16
Flynn, Malcolm	6	—	—	—	—
Gittins, Tommy	10	1	—	—	4
Hastings, Kevin	23	1	—	2	6
Hewer, Gary	0 + 1	—	—	—	—
Irving, Paul	16 + 1	9	29	—	94
James, Mick	25 + 2	3	—	—	12
Kay, Tony	22 + 2	10	2	—	44
Kendall, David	16	1	—	—	4
Kendall, Gary	7 + 7	1	—	—	4
Lightfoot, John	21	1	—	—	4
Livesey, Dave	1 + 4	—	—	—	—
Lowden, Syd	6	1	9	—	22
Maguire, Steve	5	—	—	—	—
McNichol, Tony	27 + 4	9	—	—	36
Meskell, Mark	27	7	—	—	28
Miles, Steve	1	—	—	—	—
Moore, Terry	0 + 3	—	—	—	—
Morrison, Steve	6 + 5	—	—	—	—
Moses, Alan	0 + 1	—	—	—	—
Mossop, Steve	17 + 7	1	—	—	4
Muir, Nick	3 + 1	—	—	—	—
Naidole, Tom	2 + 1	—	—	—	—
Quirk, Les	32 + 1	13	—	—	52
Rea, Steve	2	—	—	—	—
Richardson, Dave	8 + 3	1	—	—	4
Tickle, Steve	32	7	27	1	83
Turley, Norman	17 + 5	4	19	2	56
Walker, Russ	22 + 2	5	—	—	20
Wilkinson, Chris	6	1	—	—	4
Wilkinson, Stuart	6 + 2	1	—	—	4
Williams, Stewart	16 + 10	9	—	—	36
Woods, David	4	—	—	—	—

TOTALS:
39 players		109	86	5	613

Four tries in 12 games for ex-Wigan forward Nick Du Toit.

1986-87 MATCH ANALYSIS

Date	Com-petition	H/A	Opponent	Rlt	Score	Tries	Goals	Atten-dance	Referee
31.8.86	SBC	H	Hull K.R.	W	24-6	McNichol, James, Meskell, Blacker	Tickle (3), Turley (2 dg)	2460	McDonald
3.9.86	SBC	A	Wigan	L	6-18	Meskell	Tickle	—	—
7.9.86	SBC	A	Widnes	L	14-26	Cairns, McNichol, Blacker	Tickle	—	—
14.9.86	LC (1)	A	Blackpool B.	W	30-6	S. Wilkinson, Williams, James, Turley, Tickle, Kay	Tickle (3)	—	—
21.9.86	SBC	H	Castleford	L	14-24	James, Quirk, Walker	Tickle	2930	Mean
24.9.86	LC (2)	H	Widnes	L	10-12	Cairns, McNichol	Turley	3315	McDonald
28.9.86	SBC	A	Salford	W	24-12	Irving (2), Turley, Quirk	Tickle (4)	—	—
5.10.86	SBC	H	Halifax	L	12-23	Kay, Walker	Tickle (2)	4019	Kendrew
12.10.86	SBC	H	St Helens	L	12-34	Irving (2)	Tickle (2)	3809	Beaumont
19.10.86	SBC	A	Bradford N.	L	20-36	Walker, Quirk, Tickle, Kay	Tickle (2)	—	—
26.10.86	SBC	H	Hull	L	16-17	Quirk (2), Cairns	Tickle (2)	2459	Bowman
2.11.86	SBC	A	Oldham	L	20-32	Du Toit (2), McNichol	Turley (4)	—	—
9.11.86	SBC	H	Widnes	L	16-18	G. Kendall, S. Carter	Turley (4)	2857	Haigh
19.11.86	SBC	A	Wakefield T.	D	14-14	Tickle	Turley (5)	—	—
23.11.86	SBC	H	Wigan	L	8-16	Meskell	Tickle (2)	4542	Volante
30.11.86	JPS (1)	H	Runcorn H.	W	36-10	Kay (3), Du Toit, S. Carter, Turley, Blacker, Meskell	Turley (2)	1771	Tenant
7.12.86	JPS (2)	A	Sheffield E.	W	14-8	Blacker, Hasting, Cairns	Turley	—	—
14.12.86	JPS (3)	H	Widnes	L	6-16	Williams	Tickle	3199	Houghton
21.12.86	SBC	H	Leeds	L	16-23	Quirk (2), Walker	Tickle (2)	2541	Carter
26.12.86	SBC	A	Leigh	D	9-9	Tickle, Meskell	Tickle (dg)	—	—
4.1.87	SBC	H	Bradford N.	W	18-14	Irving, McNichol, Quirk	Tickle (3)	2558	Fox
19.1.87	SBC	A	Warrington (at Manchester C. FC)	L	20-24	Cairns, Meskell, Mossop	Irving (4)	—	—
25.1.87	SBC	H	Wakefield T.	W	38-13	Du Toit, Gittins, McNichol, Tickle, Lightfoot, Cairns	Irving (7)	2201	Mean
28.1.87	SBC	A	Halifax	L	14-40	Quirk (2)	Irving (3)	—	—
3.2.87	CC(1)	H	Batley	W	54-2	Tickle (2), Irving, Walker, Turley, S. Carter, Williams, C. Wilkinson, Quirk, Meskell	Irving (7)	1708	Tickle
8.2.87	SBC	A	Hull	L	18-41	Kay (2), McNichol, Irving	Irving	—	—
15.2.87	CC(2)	A	Leeds	L	7-26	Williams	Irving, Hastings (dg)	—	—
22.2.87	SBC	H	Warrington	W	9-6	Cairns	Irving (2), Hastings (dg)	2628	Beaumont
8.3.87	SBC	H	Leigh	L	16-27	Williams (2), Kay	Kay (2)	2499	McDonald
15.3.87	SBC	H	Salford	L	20-26	Williams (2), Kay	Lowden (4)	2030	Houghton
22.3.87	SBC	A	Castleford	L	10-70	Cairns, Blacker	Lowden	—	—
25.3.87	SBC	A	Hull K.R.	L	8-26	Williams, Lowden	—	—	—
29.3.87	SBC	A	Leeds	L	4-14	Richardson	—	—	—
5.4.87	SBC	H	Oldham	W	24-22	McNichol (2), Cairns, Irving, Quirk	Irving (2)	1310	Allatt
8.4.87	SBC	A	St Helens	L	4-26	Blacker	—	—	—
12.4.87	SBC	A	Featherstone R.	L	14-66	Quirk, Blacker	Lowden (3)	—	—
20.4.87	SBC	H	Featherstone R.	W	14-2	D. Kendall, Irving	Irving (2), Lowden	1123	Volante

BATLEY

Ground:	Mount Pleasant
Colours:	Cerise and fawn jerseys
First Season:	1895-96
Nickname:	Gallant Youths
Chairman:	Michael Lumb
Secretary:	Les Hardy
Coach:	Brian Lockwood (Nov 1985-)
Honours:	**Championship** Winners, 1923-24
	Challenge Cup Winners, 1896-97, 1897-98, 1900-01
	Yorkshire League Winners, 1898-99, 1923-24
	Yorkshire Cup Winners, 1912-13
	Beaten finalists, 1909-10, 1922-23, 1924-25, 1952-53
Records:	Attendance: 23,989 v. Leeds (RL Cup) 14 Mar, 1925
	Season
	Goals: 120 by S. Thompson, 1958-59
	Tries: 29 by J. Tindall, 1912-13
	Points: 281 by J. Perry, 1950-51
	Match
	Goals: 9 by W. Davies v. Widnes, 27 Mar, 1909; S. Thompson v. Keighley, 20 Sep, 1958
	Tries: 5 by J. Oakland v. Bramley, 19 Dec, 1908; T. Brannan v. Swinton, 17 Jan, 1920; J. Wale v. Bramley, 4 Dec, 1926 and v. Cottingham, 12 Feb, 1927
	Points: 26 by J. Perry v. Liverpool C., 16 Sep, 1951
	Highest score: 52-0 v. Widnes, 1908-09
	Highest against: 78-9 v. Wakefield T., 1967-68

1986-87 PLAYERS' SUMMARY

	App	Tries	Goals	Dr	Pts
Arnold, Derek	4 + 1	—	—	—	—
Austin, Tony	15 + 4	4	—	—	16
Bartle, Phil	8 + 1	—	—	—	—
Carroll, John	13 + 2	—	—	—	—
Cousins, Kevin	0 + 2	—	—	—	—
Davies, Tom	16 + 6	5	—	—	20
Davis, Alan	4	—	—	—	—
Douglas, Ian	4 + 3	—	—	—	—
Durham, Steve	14	1	—	—	4
Harris, Billy	8	—	—	—	—
Hartley, Neil	6 + 2	—	—	—	—
Hemingway, Neil	17 + 2	—	—	—	—
Illingworth, Neil	27 + 1	4	1	—	18
Ineson, David	0 + 1	—	—	—	—
James, Kevin	12 + 1	—	—	—	—
Madden, Shaun	13 + 2	4	—	—	16
McCleary, Jack	23 + 2	4	—	—	16
McGowan, John	3 + 2	—	—	—	—
McGrath, Damian	3 + 1	2	4	—	16
Oulton, Henry	15	3	19	—	50
Pickerill, Neil	29 + 1	4	—	4	20
Ratcliffe, Paul	6 + 3	—	—	—	—
Reed, Steve	24 + 1	6	—	—	24
Riggs, Keith	2	—	—	—	—
Roberts, Carl	1	1	—	—	4
Scott, Mark	3 + 2	—	—	—	—
Shaw, Alan	3	—	—	—	—
Sheridan, Mark	0 + 1	—	—	—	—
Snell, Graham	0 + 3	—	—	—	—
Sowden, Russ	20	—	—	—	—
Speight, Mark	9 + 3	—	—	—	—
Spendler, Mark	17 + 1	—	—	—	—
Stainburn, John	4 + 2	—	—	1	1
Storey, Paul	17	—	1	—	2
West, Brian	4	2	—	—	8
Williams, Andy	21 + 4	9	—	—	36
Wilson, Mick	3 + 2	1	—	—	4
Wilson, Simon	26 + 2	10	17	—	74
Wray, David	9 + 1	1	9	—	22
TOTALS: 39 players		61	51	5	351

Batley coach Brian Lockwood.

1986-87 MATCH ANALYSIS

Date	Com-petition	H/A	Opponent	Rlt	Score	Tries	Goals	Atten-dance	Referee
31.8.86	SD	A	Swinton	L	0-42	—	—	—	—
3.9.86	SD	A	York	W	30-0	Williams (2), Madden, Pickerill, S. Wilson	S. Wilson (5)	—	—
14.9.86	YC(1)	H	Wakefield T.	L	12-14	Davies, Durham	S. Wilson (2)	1502	Tennant
21.9.86	SD	A	Huddersfield B.	W	25-20	Reed (2), S. Wilson (2), Davies	S. Wilson, Wray, Pickerill (dg)	—	—
28.9.86	SD	H	Whitehaven	W	26-2	Reed, West, Wray, McCleary, Davies	Wray (2), S. Wilson	748	Tickle
5.10.86	SD	A	Hunslet	L	10-36	S. Wilson, Williams	Wray	—	—
12.10.86	SD	H	Runcorn H.	L	6-10	—	Wray (3)	817	Cross
19.10.86	SD	A	Fulham	W	24-23	Madden (2), Davies, Pickerill, S. Wilson	Wray (2)	—	—
26.10.86	SD	H	Huddersfield B.	L	12-14	S. Wilson (2), Madden	—	807	Mean
2.11.86	SD	A	Rochdale H.	L	6-34	M. Wilson	S. Wilson	—	—
9.11.86	SD	A	Keighley	W	18-17	Austin (2), McCleary	S. Wilson (3)	—	—
16.11.86	JPS(P)	H	Myson (Hull)	L	2-8	—	S. Wilson	687	Lindop
23.11.86	SD	A	Sheffield E.	L	4-24	West	—	—	—
14.12.86	SD	H	Rochdale H.	L	12-15	S. Wilson, Illingworth	S. Wilson (2)	884	Holdsworth
26.12.86	SD	A	Dewsbury	W	8-6	McCleary, S. Wilson	—	—	—
1.1.87	SD	H	Dewsbury	L	13-18	Davies, Pickerill	Oulton (2), Pickerill (dg)	1218	Tennant
4.1.87	SD	A	Mansfield M.	L	6-14	S. Wilson	Oulton	—	—
25.1.87	SD	H	Keighley	W	16-8	Williams, Oulton	Oulton (2)	663	Bowman
3.2.87	CC(1)	A	Barrow	L	2-54	—	Oulton	—	—
8.2.87	SD	H	Mansfield M.	L	6-15	Williams	Oulton	563	Whitfield
15.2.87	SD	H	Blackpool B.	L	10-18	Oulton, Illingworth	Oulton	507	Kendrew
22.2.87	SD	A	Whitehaven	L	6-40	Austin	Storey	—	—
1.3.87	SD	A	Runcorn H.	L	8-26	Illingworth	Oulton (2)	—	—
8.3.87	SD	H	York	W	29-2	Oulton, Austin, Reed, Illingworth, Pickerill	Oulton (4), Pickerill (dg)	633	Beaumont
15.3.87	SD	A	Bramley	L	6-16	Reed	Oulton	—	—
22.3.87	SD	H	Sheffield E.	L	7-28	—	Oulton (3), Pickerill (dg)	605	Mean
29.3.87	SD	H	Swinton	L	0-8	—	—	864	Spencer
5.4.87	SD	H	Fulham	L	8-15	Reed	S. Wilson, Oulton	502	Bowman
12.4.87	SD	H	Hunslet	L	4-34	Williams	—	1115	Smith
14.4.87	SD	H	Bramley	W	17-9	Williams (2), McGrath	McGrath (2), Stainburn (dg)	491	Spencer
20.4.87	SD	A	Blackpool B.	L	18-34	McCleary, McGrath, Roberts	McGrath (2), Illingworth	—	—

BLACKPOOL BOROUGH

Ground: Springfield Park, Wigan
Colours: Tangerine jerseys with black and white broad bands
First Season: 1954-55
Chairman: Mike Marsland
Secretary: Deryk Brown
Coach: Stan Gittins (Nov 1985-)
Honours: **John Player Trophy** Beaten finalists, 1976-77
Records: Attendance: 7,614 v. Castleford (RL Cup) 14 Mar, 1964. There was an attendance of 21,000 in an RL Cup-tie against Leigh on Blackpool FC ground on 9 Mar, 1957
Season
Goals: 89 by J. Maughan, 1958-59
Tries: 30 by T. Frodsham, 1985-86
Points: 201 by P. Fearis, 1957-58
Match
Goals: 11 by N. Turley v. Carlisle, 26 Apr, 1984;
Tries: 4 by T. Wilkshire v. Bradford N, 14 Jan, 1961;
J. Stockley v. Doncaster, 1 Apr, 1984
T. Frodsham v. Bridgend, 14 Apr, 1985 and v. Mansfield M., 30 Nov, 1986
Points: 27 by N. Turley v. Carlisle, 26 Apr, 1984
Highest score: 54-0 v. Carlisle, 1985-86
Highest against: 77-8 v. Wigan, 1963-64

● Blackpool Borough were given Rugby League Council permission to relocate at Wigan F.C. on 15 May, 1987.

1986-87 PLAYERS' SUMMARY

	App	Tries	Goals	Dr	Pts
Bacon, David	22	11	—	—	44
Brennan, Steve	27	10	—	—	40
Briscoe, Carl	25 + 2	5	—	—	20
Colwell, Tim	2 + 2	—	—	—	—
Crawshaw, Carl	5 + 3	—	—	—	—
Frodsham, Tommy	26	19	—	—	76
Frost, Steve	3	—	—	—	—
Gadaskie, Alan	0 + 1	—	—	—	—
Gamble, Paul	26	1	—	—	4
Ganley, Chris	17 + 1	2	—	—	8
Garner, Steve	6	1	—	—	4
Glover, Mick	4 + 5	1	—	—	4
Green, Jimmy	2	—	—	—	—
Grundy, Tracy	19 + 9	2	—	—	8
Hindley, Alan	1 + 1	—	—	—	—
Hoare, Shaun	4	—	—	—	—
Howarth, Roy	24	2	29	—	66
Lowe, Kevin	4 + 1	1	—	—	4
McLoughlin, Brendan	2 + 1	—	—	—	—
Melling, Steve	20 + 2	5	—	—	20
Meyrick, Martin	19 + 8	7	—	—	28
Moore, Brent	4 + 5	2	—	—	8
Muir, Nick	1 + 2	1	—	—	4
Nanyn, Mick	28 + 2	16	—	—	64
O'Hara, Mick	12 + 1	—	—	—	—
Price, Billy	30 + 2	5	58	4	140
Riddell, Mark	0 + 2	—	—	—	—
Roberts, Paul	19	7	—	—	28
Sanderson, Mark	16 + 1	—	—	—	—
Scott, Alan	4 + 1	—	—	—	—
Sivori, Martin	17 + 3	7	—	—	28
Subritzky, Peter	0 + 1	1	—	—	4
Tabern, Ray	4	—	—	—	—
Waddell, Hugh	17	2	—	—	8
Waldken, Gary	3 + 1	—	—	—	—
Wilkinson, Stuart	3	—	—	—	—

TOTALS:					
36 players		108	87	4	610

1986-87 MATCH ANALYSIS

Date	Com-petition	H/A	Opponent	Rlt	Score	Tries	Goals	Atten-dance	Referee
31.8.86	SD	A	Dewsbury	W	16-14	Briscoe, Bacon	Howarth (4)	—	—
3.9.86	SD	A	Carlisle	W	36-5	Roberts (2), Lowe, Subritzky, Price, Nanyn	Howarth (6)	—	—
7.9.86	SD	H	Workington T.	W	17-14	Brennan, Briscoe	Howarth (4), Price (dg)	592	Whitfield
14.9.86	LC(1)	H	Barrow	L	6-30	Bacon	Howarth	1112	Simpson
21.9.86	SD	A	Bramley	W	26-8	Sivori (2), Frodsham, Brennan, Meyrick	Howarth (3)	—	—
28.9.86	SD	H	Runcorn H.	L	16-19	Meyrick (2), Grundy	Howarth (2)	484	Kendrew
5.10.86	SD	H	York	W	14-13	Price	Price (5)	453	Allatt
12.10.86	SD	A	Mansfield M.	W	30-16	Melling (3), Bacon, Nanyn, Sivori	Howarth (3)	—	—
19.10.86	SD	H	Keighley	W	26-10	Bacon (3), Frodsham (2), Sivori	Howarth	490	Bowman
26.10.86	SD	A	Workington T.	W	32-17	Nanyn, Waddell, Price, Frodsham, Roberts, Brennan	Price (4)	—	—
2.11.86	SD	H	Doncaster	L	20-22	Brennan, Meyrick, Moore	Price (4)	573	Haigh
9.11.86	SD	A	Runcorn H.	W	21-12	Roberts, Briscoe, Meyrick	Price (4, 1dg)	—	—
16.11.86	SD	A	Whitehaven	L	10-26	Brennan, Roberts	Price	—	—
23.11.86	SD	H	Mansfield M.	W	20-14	Nanyn (2), Muir, Garner	Price (2)	230	Hodgson
30.11.86	JPS(1)	H	Mansfield M.	W	42-12	Frodsham (4), Ganley, Nanyn, Roberts	Price (7)	376	Smith
7.12.86	JPS(2)	H (at Hull)	Hull	L	22-48	Price, Gamble, Nanyn	Price (5)	(3723)	Volante
14.12.86	SD	A	Fulham	L	12-30	Frodsham, Moore	Price (2)	—	—
26.12.86	SD	H	Rochdale H.	L	6-18	Frodsham	Price	908	Spencer
1.1.87	SD	A	Keighley	L	2-10	—	Price	—	—
4.1.87	SD	W	Whitehaven	L	5-8	Waddell	Price (dg)	386	Beaumont
8.2.87	SD	*H	Fulham	W	48-28	Nanyn (3), Frodsham (2), Bacon (2), Brennan, Briscoe	Price (6)	401	Carter
10.2.87	CC(1)	H	Wakefield T.	L	10-15	Nanyn	Price (3)	823	McDonald
15.2.87	SD	A	Batley	W	18-10	Howarth, Nanyn, Price, Melling	Price	—	—
1.3.87	SD	A	Doncaster	L	12-18	Sivori, Glover	Price (2)	—	—
15.3.87	SD	A	Swinton	L	8-22	Frodsham	Price (2)	—	—
25.3.87	SD	H	Swinton	L	10-25	Ganley, Howarth	Price	610	Carter
29.3.87	SD	H	Bramley	L	18-22	Nanyn, Frodsham, Brennan, Sivori	Howarth	373	Tickle
5.4.87	SD	A	Rochdale H.	L	16-24	Sivori, Grundy, Nanyn	Howarth (2)	—	—
12.4.87	SD	A	York	L	14-24	Nanyn, Frodsham, Bacon	Howarth	—	—
14.4.87	SD	H	Dewsbury	W	32-12	Bacon, Nanyn, Brennan, Roberts, Frodsham, Briscoe	Price (4)	301	Bowman
20.4.87	SD	H	Batley	W	34-18	Frodsham (3), Brennan (2), Meyrick, Bacon	Price (2), Howarth	301	Houghton
22.4.87	SD	H	Carlisle	L	11-18	Meyrick, Melling	Price (1, 1dg)	553	Lindop

*From 8.2.87 all home games staged at Blackpool FC.

BRADFORD NORTHERN

Ground: Odsal Stadium
Colours: White jerseys with red, amber and black hoops
First Season: 1895-96 as "Bradford". Disbanded and became Bradford Northern in 1907-08. Disbanded during 1963-64 and re-formed for start of 1964-65
Nickname: Northern
Chairman: Jack Bates
Secretary: Rita Winter
Coach: Barry Seabourne (May 1985-)
Honours: **Challenge Cup** Winners, 1905-06, 1943-44, 1946-47, 1948-49
Beaten finalists, 1897-98, 1944-45, 1947-48, 1972-73
Championship Beaten finalists, 1947-48, 1951-52
Division One Champions, 1903-04, 1979-80, 1980-81
Division Two Champions, 1973-74
War-time Emergency League Championship winners, 1939-40, 1940-41, 1944-45
Beaten finalists, 1941-42
Yorkshire League Winners, 1899-1900, 1900-01, 1939-40, 1940-41, 1947-48
Yorkshire Cup Winners, 1906-07, 1940-41, 1941-42, 1943-44, 1945-46, 1948-49, 1949-50, 1953-54, 1965-66, 1978-79
Beaten finalists, 1913-14, 1981-82, 1982-83
Premiership Winners, 1977-78
Beaten finalists, 1978-79, 1979-80
John Player Trophy Winners, 1974-75, 1979-80
Records: Attendance: 102,569 Warrington v. Halifax (RL Cup Final replay) 5 May, 1954
Home: 69,429 v. Huddersfield (RL Cup) 14 March, 1953
Season
Goals: 173 by E. Tees, 1971-72
Tries: 63 by J. McLean, 1951-52
Points: 364 by E. Tees, 1971-72

Match
Goals: 14 by J. Phillips v. Batley, 6 Sep, 1952
Tries: 7 by J. Dechan v. Bramley, 13 Oct, 1906
Points: 36 by J. Woods v. Swinton, 13 Oct, 1985
Highest score: 72-9 v. Doncaster, 1973-74; 72-12 v. Hunslet, 1984-85
Highest against: 75-18 v. Leeds, 1931-32

1986-87 PLAYERS' SUMMARY

	App	Tries	Goals	Dr	Pts
Bond, Steve	8 + 8	1	—	—	4
Brentley, Gary	7 + 1	2	—	—	8
Crawford, Adrian	0 + 1	1	—	—	4
Donlan, Steve	32 + 2	8	—	—	32
Evans, Steve	7 + 2	2	—	—	8
Fairbank, Karl	32	7	—	—	28
Fenech, Mario	2	—	—	—	—
Fleming, Mark	10 + 2	1	—	—	4
Ford, Phil	38	30	—	7	127
Godfrey, Heath	6 + 3	1	—	—	4
Graham, Mal	40	12	—	1	49
Grayshon, Jeff	6 + 1	—	—	—	—
Hamer, Jon	12 + 3	—	—	—	—
Harkin, Paul	7	2	—	4	12
Hellewell, Phil	29 + 3	5	—	—	20
Heron, Wayne	1 + 2	1	—	—	4
Hill, Brendan	16	—	—	—	—
Hobbs, David	5	—	—	1	1
Holmes, Terry	32	8	—	—	32
Howcroft, Ian	3 + 3	—	—	—	—
Jasiewicz, Dick	22	5	—	—	20
Mallinder, Paul	4 + 4	1	—	—	4
Moulden, Darren	2 + 3	—	—	—	—
Mumby, Keith	38 + 1	1	43	—	90
Noble, Brian	29 + 2	1	—	—	4
Parrish, Steve	1	—	—	—	—
Potts, Martin	4 + 1	—	9	—	18
Preece, Chris	2	—	—	—	—
Race, Wayne	24	5	—	—	20
Redfearn, David	9 + 6	3	—	—	12
Robinson, Andy	1 + 1	—	—	—	—
Roebuck, Neil	1	—	—	—	—
Sherratt, Ian	26 + 1	4	—	—	16
Sidebottom, Gary	16 + 2	5	—	—	20
Simpson, Roger	19 + 4	8	—	—	32
Spurr, Bob	2	—	—	—	—
White, Brendan	11 + 9	1	—	—	4
Woods, John	29	8	70	2	174
TOTALS:					
38 players		123	122	15	751

1986-87 MATCH ANALYSIS

Date	Com-petition	H/A	Opponent	Rlt	Score	Tries	Goals	Atten-dance	Referee
31.8.86	SBC	H	Widnes	W	27-14	Donlan, Woods, Noble, White, Graham	Woods (3), Ford (dg)	4755	Holdsworth
3.9.86	SBC	A	Hull K.R.	W	30-12	Ford (2), Jasiewicz, Donlan	Woods (7)	—	—
7.9.86	SBC	A	Salford	W	22-12	Graham, Redfearn, Woods, Race	Woods (3)	—	—
14.9.86	YC (1)	A	Hunslet	W	40-12	Woods (3), Fairbank (2), Ford, Jasiewicz	Woods (6)	—	—
21.9.86	SBC	H	Wigan	L	10-20	Graham	Woods (3)	11277	Berry
24.9.86	YC (2)	H	Dewsbury	W	42-10	Fairbank (2), Simpson (2), Hellewell, Sherratt, Graham, Crawford	Mumby (5)	2682	Tennant
28.9.86	SBC	A	Wakefield T.	W	32-22	Sidebottom (2), Holmes, Donlan, Ford, Jasiewicz	Woods (4)	—	—
1.10.86	YC (SF)	H	Hull	L	12-16	Donlan (2)	Woods (2)	4727	Holdsworth
5.10.86	SBC	H	Castleford	W	12-7	Ford (2)	Mumby (2)	5604	Volante
14.10.86	SBC	A	Hull	L	22-27	Graham, Ford, Simpson	Woods (5)	—	—
19.10.86	SBC	H	Barrow	W	36-20	Mumby, Simpson, Graham, Hellewell, Fairbank, Jasiewicz	Woods (6)	2361	Spencer
26.10.86	SBC	A	Leeds	W	12-4	Redfearn, Holmes	Woods (2)	—	—
2.11.86	SBC	H	Featherstone R.	W	41-2	Ford (2), Simpson, Woods, Holmes, Bentley, Graham, Hellewell	Woods (4), Ford (dg)	4791	Simpson
16.11.86	SBC	A	Widnes	W	36-14	Ford (3), Holmes, Fairbank, Sherratt	Woods (5), Ford (dg), Graham (dg)	—	—
18.11.86	Tour	H	Australia	L	0-38	—	—	10663	Fox
23.11.86	SBC	A	Oldham	L	10-18	Ford, Holmes	Woods	4060	Bowman
30.11.86	JPS (1)	A	Oldham	W	22-12	Jasiewicz, Ford, Holmes, Redfearn	Woods (3)	—	—
7.12.86	JPS (2)	A	Featherstone R.	W	19-12	Ford (2), Sherratt	Woods (2, 1 dg), Ford (2 dg)	—	—
13.12.86	JPS (3)	H	Hull	L	8-20	Brentley	Woods (2)	3545	Berry
26.12.86	SBC	A	Halifax	L	4-20	Ford	—	—	—
28.12.86	SBC	H	Halifax	L	8-12	Simpson	Mumby (2)	6427	Mean
1.1.87	SBC	A	Castleford	L	18-46	Race (2), Simpson	Mumby (3)	—	—
4.1.87	SBC	A	Barrow	L	14-18	Ford, Donlan, Woods	Woods	—	—
25.1.87	SBC	H	Leigh	L	18-26	Holmes (2), Ford	Woods (3)	2832	Carter
1.2.87	CC(1)	A	Warrington	W	21-17	Woods, Sherratt, Graham	Woods (4, 1dg)	—	—
8.2.87	SBC	A	Warrington	L	10-31	Ford, Graham	Mumby	—	—
15.2.87	CC(2)	H	Widnes	D	6-6	Ford	Woods	7318	Haigh
18.2.87	CC(2) Replay	A	Widnes	L	12-29	Heron, Ford	Woods (2)	—	—
22.2.87	SBC	A	St Helens	L	14-40	Fleming, Hellewell, Simpson	Woods	—	—
1.3.87	SBC	A	Wigan	L	6-60	Bond	Mumby	—	—
11.3.87	SBC	H	Hull	D	20-20	Donlan, Sidebottom, Fairbank	Mumby (4)	1669	Allatt
15.3.87	SBC	A	Oldham	L	8-12	Mallinder	Mumby (2)	—	—
18.3.87	SBC	H	Hull K.R.	W	24-6	Ford (2), Sidebottom, Godfrey	Mumby (4)	1674	Whitfield
22.3.87	SBC	H	Wakefield T.	W	15-12	Ford	Mumby (5), Ford (dg)	3262	Ainui (PNG)
29.3.87	SBC	A	Leigh	L	16-18	Ford, Evans	Mumby (4)	—	—
31.3.87	SBC	A	Featherstone R.	W	26-10	Sidebottom, Graham, Evans	Potts (6), Ford (dg), Harkin (dg)	—	—
5.4.87	SBC	H	Warrington	W	11-10	Graham	Potts (3), Harkin (dg)	3272	Lindop
12.4.87	SBC	H	St Helens	W	18-4	Ford, Hellewell, Graham	Mumby (2), Harkin (2dg)	3953	McDonald
17.4.87	SBC	H	Leeds	W	23-10	Ford (2), Race, Donlan	Mumby (3), Hobbs (dg)	4710	Cross
21.4.87	SBC	H	Salford	L	12-23	Ford, Harkin	Mumby (2)	4040	Smith
26.4.87	PT(1)	A	St Helens	L	14-46	Harkin, Race	Mumby (3)	—	—

33

BRAMLEY

Ground: McLaren Field
Colours: Amber and black jerseys
First Season: 1896-97
Nickname: Villagers
Chairman: Jeff Wine
Secretary: Lynda Thomas
Coach: Allan Agar (Dec 1985-Apr 1987)
Honours: **BBC2 Floodlit Trophy** Winners, 1973-74
Records: Attendance: 12,600 v. Leeds (League) 7 May, 1947
Season
Goals: 130 by J. Wilson, 1961-62
Tries: 34 by P. Lister, 1985-86
Points: 276 by G. Langfield, 1956-57
Match
Goals: 11 by B. Ward v. Doncaster, 1 Sep, 1974
Tries: 7 by J. Sedgewick v. Normanton, 16 Apr, 1906
Points: 28 by B. Ward v. Doncaster, 1 Sep, 1974
Highest score; 52-17 v. Doncaster, 1974-75
Highest against: 92-7 v. Australia, 1921-22

1986-87 PLAYERS' SUMMARY

	App	Tries	Goals	Dr	Pts
Agar, Allan	1	—	—	—	—
Barraclough, Glen	0 + 2	1	—	—	4
Beale, Graham	29 + 1	3	1	—	14
Beddis, Chris	1	—	—	—	—
Bibb, Trevor	32	6	—	—	24
Binder, Tony	5	1	—	—	4
Bowman, Chris	17 + 2	5	—	—	20
Burgoyne, Paddy	14	2	1	—	10
Carroll, Steve	24 + 2	6	—	—	24
Clarkson, Allan	2 + 1	—	—	—	—
Clayton, Peter	10	—	—	—	—
Coldwell, Tim	0 + 1	—	—	—	—
Coventry, Paul	10 + 2	1	—	—	4
Duckworth, Ken	1 + 2	—	—	—	—
Edmondson, Stephen	1	—	—	—	—
Fletcher, Paul	25 + 1	4	—	—	16
Gibson, Mark	16 + 2	—	—	—	—
Green, Karl	22 + 1	3	—	—	12
Heeds, Mark	5	1	—	—	4
Hobbs, Gary	5 + 5	4	—	—	16
Howard, Les	13 + 2	3	—	—	12
Idle, Graham	9	—	—	—	—
Kilner, Shaun	25	2	53	—	114
Lister, Peter	18 + 4	11	—	2	46
Lonergan, Dean	6 + 2	—	—	—	—
Loynes, Dean	0 + 1	—	—	—	—
Lund, Steve	2 + 2	—	—	—	—
Marsh, Richard	7	4	—	—	16
Mason, Andy	6	6	—	—	24
Payne, Phil	7	2	—	—	8
Porter, Craig	5 + 4	—	—	—	—
Pudsey, Adrian	15	3	—	—	12
Rhodes, Chris	1 + 1	—	—	—	—
Robinson, Graeme	11 + 7	—	13	1	27
Savage, Dave	5 + 5	—	—	—	—
Schaumkell, Kevin	23	4	—	—	16
Sheldon, Ian	0 + 1	—	—	—	—
Shipley, Jon	11	—	—	—	—
Tennant, Jeff	32	6	—	—	24
TOTALS:					
39 players		78	68	3	451

Six tries in six games for Andy Mason before his move to neighbours, Leeds.

1986-87 MATCH ANALYSIS

Date	Competition	H/A	Opponent	Rlt	Score	Tries	Goals	Attendance	Referee
31.8.86	SD	H	Whitehaven	W	20-12	Barraclough, Mason, Lister	Kilner (4)	648	Carter
7.9.86	SD	A	Rochdale H.	L	12-30	Mason (2), Heeds	—	—	—
14.9.86	YC(1)	A	Hull	L	22-29	Carroll, Mason, Fletcher, Howard	Kilner (3)	—	—
21.9.86	SD	H	Blackpool B.	L	8-26	Bibb	Kilner (2)	644	Fox
28.9.86	SD	A	York	L	8-16	Tennant	Kilner (2)	—	—
5.10.86	SD	A	Dewsbury	W	18-16	Hobbs, Mason, Carroll	Kilner (3)	—	—
12.10.86	SD	H	Huddersfield B.	W	24-19	Mason, Burgoyne, Carroll, Schaumkell	Kilner (4)	820	Whitfield
19.10.86	SD	A	Swinton	L	12-54	Lister (2)	Kilner (2)	—	—
26.10.86	SD	A	Mansfield M.	W	13-8	Howard (2)	Robinson (2), Lister (dg)	—	—
2.11.86	SD	H	Sheffield E.	W	24-14	Lister (2), Bibb (2)	Robinson (4)	742	Bowman
16.11.86	SD	A	Keighley	W	18-12	Lister, Bibb, Bowman	Robinson (3)	—	—
23.11.86	SD	H	Fulham	W	18-10	Carroll, Fletcher, Schaumkell	Robinson (3)	641	Houghton
30.11.86	JPS(1)	A	Sheffield E.	L	6-14	Burgoyne	Robinson	—	—
14.12.86	SD	A	Whitehaven	L	10-24	Lister, Binder	Beale	—	—
26.12.86	SD	H	Hunslet	L	2-16	—	Kilner	1431	Berry
1.1.87	SD	A	Hunslet	L	8-34	Beale	Kilner (2)	—	—
4.1.87	SD	H	Runcorn H.	W	20-6	Bibb, Green, Bowman, Fletcher	Kilner (2)	495	Kershaw
18.1.87	SD	A (at Leeds)	Sheffield E.	W	14-12	Schaumkell, Bibb	Kilner (3)	—	—
25.1.87	SD	A	Runcorn H.	L	12-14	Beale, Lister, Coventry	—	—	—
4.2.87	CC(1)	H	Hull	L	2-10	—	Kilner	1561	Bowman
8.2.87	SD	H	Dewsbury	W	18-3	Pudsey, Kilner, Green	Kilner (2), Burgoyne	757	Allatt
15.2.87	SD	A	Fulham	L	20-24	Lister (2), Fletcher, Pudsey	Kilner (2)	—	—
22.2.87	SD	H	Mansfield M.	W	12-3	Carroll, Lister	Kilner (2)	550	Kendrew
1.3.87	SD	H	Rochdale H.	L	1-5	—	Lister (dg)	637	Smith
8.3.87	SD	A	Huddersfield B.	L	10-20	Kilner, Green	Kilner	—	—
15.3.87	SD	H	Batley	W	16-6	Tennant, Marsh, Payne	Kilner (2)	699	Tennant
22.3.87	SD	H	Swinton	W	14-13	Bowman, Tennant	Kilner (3)	997	Simpson
29.3.87	SD	A	Blackpool B.	W	22-18	Schaumkell, Bowman, Tennant, Hobbs	Kilner (3)	—	—
5.4.87	SD	H	York	W	10-4	Marsh, Beale	Kilner	616	Hodgson
14.4.87	SD	A	Batley	L	9-17	Carroll	Kilner (2), Robinson (dg)	—	—
17.4.87	SD	H	Keighley	W	34-4	Hobbs (2), Tennant (2), Marsh, Pudsey	Kilner (5)	640	Drinkwater (Pr)
26.4.87	SDP(1)	A	Swinton	L	14-59	Bowman, Payne, Marsh	Kilner	—	—

CARLISLE

Ground: Brunton Park
Colours: Blue jerseys with red and white band
First Season: 1981-82. A Carlisle City team entered the League in 1928-29 but withdrew after 10 matches, winning one
Chairman: Alan Tucker
Secretary: Bob Taylor
Coach: Alan Kellett (Feb-May 1986)
    Roy Lester (June 1986-)
Records: Attendance: 5,903 v. Workington T. (Div. 2) 6 Sep, 1981

Season
Goals: 113 by S. Ferres, 1981-82
Tries: 25 by M. Morgan, 1981-82; G. Peacham, 1984-85
Points: 242 by S. Ferres, 1981-82

Match
Goals: 9 by D. Carroll v. Mansfield M., 16 Mar, 1986
Tries: 4 by G. Peacham v. Workington T., 25 Jan, 1987 and K. Pape v. Rochdale H., 11 Feb, 1987
Points: 21 by D. Carroll v. Mansfield M., 16 Mar, 1986 and v. Fulham, 2 May, 1986
Highest score:
47-18 v Fulham, 1984-85
Highest against: 112-0 v. St. Helens, 1986-87

1986-87 PLAYERS' SUMMARY

	App	Tries	Goals	Dr	Pts
Armstrong, Colin	26 + 2	—	5	—	10
Bond, Gary	2 + 3	1	—	—	4
Bowness, Chris	0 + 1	—	—	—	—
Brierley, Steve	3 + 2	—	—	—	—
Carroll, Dean	8 + 1	—	18	2	38
Duffy, Don	29	2	—	1	9
Duncanson, Mark	0 + 1	—	—	—	—
Elliott, David	5	—	—	—	—
Graham, John	19 + 1	—	—	—	—
Green, Jimmy	1 + 3	1	—	—	4
Green, Ken	15 + 2	—	—	—	—
Henney, Harold	3	—	—	—	—
Huddart, Milton	7	1	—	2	6
Kirkby, Steve	30	12	—	—	48
Langton, Steve	35	7	—	—	28
Leck, Gary	6 + 2	—	—	—	—
Lithgow, Paul	16 + 7	3	—	—	12
Loynes, Dean	1 + 1	—	—	—	—
McAvoy, Brian	15 + 1	5	—	—	20
McMullen, Alan	3 + 2	—	—	—	—
Miller, Craig	2	1	—	—	4
Pape, Kevin	34	22	—	—	88
Peacham, Gary	21	7	—	—	28
Peacham, Tony	5	—	—	—	—
Phillips, Graham	1 + 1	—	—	—	—
Portz, Karl	2 + 2	—	—	—	—
Rampling, Darren	1	—	—	—	—
Robinson, Kevin	3	—	—	—	—
Schubert, Garry	23	5	—	—	20
Scott, Tony	12 + 9	1	—	—	4
Smith, David	1 + 3	—	—	1	1
Smith, Joe	0 + 1	—	—	—	—
Stafford, Peter	0 + 2	—	—	—	—
Stockley, John	32	6	—	—	24
Subritzky, Peter	24 + 1	6	14	1	53
Thomason, Malcolm	35	6	—	—	24
Tunstall, Brian	21	—	38	—	76
Wi Hongi, Heemi	9	1	—	—	4
Wilkinson, Chris	5	3	—	—	12
TOTALS:					
39 players		90	75	7	517

1986-87 MATCH ANALYSIS

Date	Competition	H/A	Opponent	Rlt	Score	Tries	Goals	Attendance	Referee
31.8.86	SD	A	York	L	14-20	Pape, Thomason, McAvoy	Armstrong	—	—
3.9.86	SD	H	Blackpool B.	L	5-36	Pape	D. Smith (dg)	504	Spencer
7.9.86	SD	H	Runcorn H.	D	12-12	Stockley, Langton	Tunstall (2)	516	Simpson
10.9.86	SD	A	Workington T.	L	24-31	Bond, Stockley, Kirkby, Langton	Tunstall (4)	—	—
14.9.86	LC (1)	A	St Helens	L	0-112	—	—	—	—
21.9.86	SD	H	Doncaster	W	16-12	Thomason, Huddart, Miller	Tunstall (2)	443	Tickle
28.9.86	SD	A	Keighley	L	6-16	Kirkby	Tunstall	—	—
5.10.86	SD	H	Rochdale H.	W	22-2	Lithgow (2), Pape, Wihongi	Tunstall (2), Huddart (2 dg)	518	Bowman
12.10.86	SD	A	Sheffield E.	L	10-24	Pape (2)	Tunstall	—	—
19.10.86	SD	H	Mansfield M.	W	22-16	Kirkby (2), Langton, Stockley	Tunstall (3)	438	Holdsworth
26.10.86	SD	A	Hunslet	L	8-20	Thomason	Tunstall (2)	—	—
2.11.86	SD	H	Keighley	L	16-26	Subritzky, Schubert	Tunstall (4)	507	Beaumont
9.11.86	SD	H	Huddersfield B.	W	18-10	Langton (2), Wilkinson	Tunstall (3)	481	Berry
16.11.86	SD	A	Mansfield M.	W	28-16	Wilkinson (2), Subritzky, Pape	Tunstall (6)	—	—
23.11.86	SD	A	Doncaster	L	2-30	—	Tunstall	—	—
4.12.86	JPS (1)	H (at Penrith)	Keighley	W	8-2	Kirkby	Tunstall, Subritzky	300	Houghton
7.12.86	JPS (2)	A	Widnes	L	6-36	G. Peacham	Subritzky	—	—
14.12.86	SD	H	Hunslet	W	11-8	Pape (2)	Tunstall, Subritzky (dg)	322	Kershaw
4.1.87	SD	H (at Penrith)	Sheffield E.	W	17-6	Kirkby, Duffy, Lithgow	Armstrong (2), Duffy (dg)	500	McDonald
25.1.87	SD	H	Workington T.	W	42-6	G. Peacham (4), Pape (2), Kirkby, Subritzky	Subritzky (5)	813	Simpson
4.2.87	CC(1)	A	Rochdale H.	D	4-4	Stockley	—	—	—
8.2.87	SD	A	Swinton	L	20-23	Kirkby (3), Thomason	Subritzky, Carroll	—	—
11.2.87	CC(1) Replay	H	Rochdale H.	W	30-22	Pape (4), Kirkby	Carroll (5)	788	Hodgson
15.2.87	CC(2)	A	Leigh	L	6-18	Pape	Carroll	—	—
22.2.87	SD	H	York	W	30-16	Pape (3), Schubert, Kirkby, Thomason	Carroll (3)	800	Bowman
1.3.87	SD	A	Huddersfield B.	W	19-8	McAvoy, Subritzky, Pape	Carroll (3, 1dg)	—	—
8.3.87	SD	A	Rochdale H.	L	1-11	—	Carroll (dg)	—	—
15.3.87	SD	A	Runcorn H.	W	26-4	McAvoy (2), Duffy, Schubert, Pape	Carroll (3)	—	—
22.3.87	SD	H	Dewsbury	W	24-14	G. Peacham (2), Langton, Subritzky	Carroll (2), Subritzky (2)	1000	Kendrew
5.4.87	SD	A	Dewsbury	W	12-6	Stockley, Schubert	Armstrong (2)	—	—
12.4.87	SD	H	Swinton	L	16-35	Subritzky, Pape, Schubert	Subritzky (2)	1200	Tickle
17.4.87	SD	H	Whitehaven	W	16-11	Stockley, Scott, McAvoy	Subritzky (2)	3000	Carter
20.4.87	SD	A	Whitehaven	L	8-16	Langton	Tunstall (2)	—	—
22.4.87	SD	A	Blackpool B.	W	18-11	Thomason, Pape, J. Green	Tunstall (3)	—	—
26.4.87	SDP(1)	A	Hunslet	L	0-54	—	—	—	—

CASTLEFORD

Ground: Wheldon Road
Colours: Yellow and black jerseys
First Season: 1926-27. There was also a
Castleford team from 1896-97 to
1905-06, inclusive
Nickname: Glassblowers
Chairman: David Poulter
Secretary: Denise Cackett
Coach: Mal Reilly (Dec 1974-May 1987)
David Sampson (May 1987-)
Honours: **Championship** Beaten finalists,
1938-39, 1968-69
Challenge Cup Winners, 1934-35,
1968-69, 1969-70, 1985-86
Yorkshire League Winners,
1932-33, 1938-39, 1964-65
Yorkshire Cup Winners, 1977-78,
1981-82, 1986-87
Beaten finalists, 1948-49, 1950-51,
1968-69, 1971-72, 1983-84, 1985-86
Eastern Division Championship
Beaten finalists, 1963-64
BBC2 Floodlit Trophy Winners,
1965-66, 1966-67, 1967-68, 1976-77
John Player Trophy Winners,
1976-77
Premiership Beaten finalists,
1983-84
Charity Shield Beaten finalists
1986-87
Records: Attendance: 25,449 v. Hunslet
(RL Cup) 3 Mar, 1935
Season
Goals: 158 by S. Lloyd, 1976-77
Tries: 36 by K. Howe, 1963-64
Points: 334 by R. Beardmore,
1983-84
Match
Goals: 17 by S. Lloyd v. Millom,
16 Sep, 1973

Tries: 5 by D. Foster v. Hunslet,
10 Nov, 1972; J. Joyner v. Millom,
16 Sep, 1973; S. Fenton v.
Dewsbury, 27 Jan, 1978; I. French
v. Hunslet, 9 Feb, 1986
Points: 43 by S. Lloyd v. Millom,
16 Sep, 1973
Highest score: 88-5 v. Millom,
1973-74
Highest against: 62-12 v. St.
Helens, 1985-86

1986-87 PLAYERS' SUMMARY

	App	Tries	Goals	Dr	Pts
Anderson, Grant	9	3	—	—	12
Atkins, Brett	28 + 1	9	—	—	36
Beardmore, Bob	37	14	62	3	183
Beardmore, Kevin	28	9	—	—	36
Blackburn, John	5 + 2	1	—	—	4
Chapman, Chris	3	1	—	—	4
England, Keith	38	7	—	—	28
Fenton, Steve	2	1	—	—	4
Fletcher, Ian	1 + 5	1	—	—	4
Horton, Stuart	11	2	—	—	8
Hyde, Gary	20 + 7	9	—	—	36
Irwin, Sean	21 + 2	3	—	—	12
Johns, Chris	18	7	—	—	28
Johnson, Barry	38	2	1	—	10
Jones, Keith	0 + 3	—	—	—	—
Joyner, John	37	13	—	—	52
Kear, John	3	3	—	—	12
Ketteridge, Martin	36	2	80	—	168
Lindner, Bob	9	5	—	—	20
Lord, Gary	15 + 6	7	—	—	28
Marchant, Tony	29	8	—	—	32
Mountain, Dean	4 + 12	1	—	—	4
Plange, David	34 + 1	21	—	—	84
Roockley, David	16 + 6	6	—	—	24
Scott, Colin	25	10	8	1	57
Shillito, Alan	16 + 10	2	—	—	8
Slater, Martin	1	—	—	—	—
Southernwood, Roy	3 + 3	1	—	—	4
Spears, Tony	8 + 1	—	—	—	—
Thornton, Wayne	1	—	—	—	—
Ward, Kevin	24 + 2	3	—	—	12

TOTALS:
31 players		150	151	4	906

1986-87 MATCH ANALYSIS

Date	Competition	H/A	Opponent	Rlt	Score	Tries	Goals	Attendance	Referee
24.8.86	Charity Shield	Isle of Man	Halifax	L	8-9	Lord	Ketteridge (2)	(3276)	Lindop
31.8.86	SBC	A	Warrington	W	26-20	Ketteridge, Marchant, Ward, R. Beardmore	Ketteridge (5)	—	—

MATCH ANALYSIS (continued)

Date	Comp	H/A	Opponent	W/L	Score	Try scorers	Goal scorers	Att	Referee
3.9.86	SBC	H	Hull	W	16-6	Plange, Joyner, Marchant	Ketteridge (2)	4032	Haigh
7.9.86	SBC	H	Wakefield T.	W	42-16	Shillito, Roockley, Lord, Hyde, Mountain, R. Beardmore, Joyner	Ketteridge (7)	4683	Beaumont
14.9.86	YC (1)	H	Halifax	W	16-10	K. Beardmore, Johns	Ketteridge (4)	7594	Lindop
21.9.86	SBC	A	Barrow	W	24-14	K. Beardmore, R. Beardmore, Hyde, Johns	Ketteridge (3), R. Beardmore	—	—
24.9.86	YC (2)	H	Leeds	W	38-16	Johns, Roockley, R. Beardmore, Hyde, Joyner, Plange, England, Atkins	Ketteridge (3)	7198	Fox
28.9.86	SBC	H	Featherstone R.	W	16-7	Hyde (2), K. Beardmore	R. Beardmore (2)	5593	McDonald
1.10.86	YC (SF)	A	Featherstone R.	W	30-2	Irwin, Ward, K. Beardmore, Plange, R. Beardmore	R. Beardmore (3), Ketteridge (2)	—	—
5.10.86	SBC	A	Bradford N.	L	7-12	Hyde	Scott, R. Beardmore (dg)	—	—
11.10.86	YC (F)	Leeds	Hull	W	31-24	K. Beardmore (2), Atkins, Ward, Ketteridge	Ketteridge (5), R. Beardmore (dg)	(10590)	McDonald
15.10.86	SBC	A	Widnes	L	20-29	Plange (2), Scott, Joyner	Ketteridge (2)	—	—
26.10.86	SBC	A	Halifax	W	16-12	England, Scott	Ketteridge (4)	—	—
29.10.86	SBC	H	Wigan	L	6-12	—	Ketteridge (3)	6686	Tickle
2.11.86	SBC	H	Leigh	W	19-8	Fenton, Fletcher	Scott (5, 1 dg)	3954	Smith
16.11.86	SBC	H	Salford	L	20-21	R. Beardmore, Joyner, Atkins, Plange	Scott (2)	3225	Bowman
23.11.86	SBC	A	Featherstone R.	W	18-16	Scott (2), Hyde	Ketteridge (3)	—	—
30.11.86	JPS (1)	A	Fulham	W	34-24	Lord (3), Johns, R. Beardmore, Scott	Ketteridge (5)	—	—
6.12.86	JPS (2)	H	St Helens	L	22-26	Johns (2), Horton, Scott	Ketteridge (3)	4808	Whitfield
21.12.86	SBC	A	Wakefield T.	W	40-12	Atkins (2), Lord, Horton, Hyde, Shillito, Irwin	R. Beardmore (5), Johnson	—	—
26.12.86	SBC	H	Hull K.R.	W	16-10	K. Beardmore, Joyner	Ketteridge (4)	4707	Whitfield
1.1.87	SBC	H	Bradford N.	W	46-18	Plange (3), R. Beardmore (2), Lord, Lindner, Southernwood	Ketteridge (7)	5834	McDonald
4.1.87	SBC	A	Leigh	W	12-6	Scott, Joyner	Ketteridge (2)	—	—
17.1.87	CC (P)	H (at Leeds)	Blackbrook (St Helens)	W	74-6	Kear (3), Plange (3), England (2), Atkins, (2), Johnson, Roockley, Marchant	Ketteridge (11)	—	Stone (Aus)
25.1.87	SBC	H	Warrington	L	18-24	Lindner (2), Scott, Hyde	Ketteridge	5828	Volante
31.1.87	CC(1)	H	Widnes	L	16-24	Joyner, Lindner, Johns	R. Beardmore (2)	4416	Lindop
8.2.87	SBC	L	Leeds	L	12-14	Lindner	R. Beardmore (4)	6345	Houghton
15.2.87	SBC	A	Wigan	L	6-16	Plange	R. Beardmore	—	—
20.2.87	SBC	A	Salford	L	10-36	Atkins	R. Beardmore (3)	—	—
1.3.87	SBC	H	Oldham	W	22-18	Marchant (2), Joyner, Chapman	R. Beardmore (3)	3960	Holdsworth
4.3.87	SBC	H	St Helens	W	12-10	Plange	R. Beardmore (4)	4067	Berry
18.3.87	SBC	H	Widnes	W	44-8	Anderson (2), Plange (2), Scott, Joyner, Roockley, Marchant	R. Beardmore (6)	3247	Simpson
22.3.87	SBC	H	Barrow	W	70-10	R. Beardmore (4), England (2), Joyner (2), Scott, Atkins, Plange, Johnson	R. Beardmore (11)	3137	Bowman
29.3.87	SBC	A	Oldham	W	29-6	Plange (2), Joyner, Anderson, Marchant	R. Beardmore (4, 1dg)	—	—
1.4.87	SBC	A	St Helens	W	10-8	Roockley	R. Beardmore (3)	—	—
5.4.87	SBC	H	Halifax	W	26-14	Roockley, Plange, K. Beardmore, Irwin	R. Beardmore (5)	6079	Berry
7.4.87	SBC	A	Hull	L	6-18	R. Beardmore	R. Beardmore	—	—
12.4.87	SBC	A	Leeds	W	16-8	K. Beardmore, Marchant	R. Beardmore (4)	—	—
20.4.87	SBC	A	Hull K.R.	L	6-20	Plange	Ketteridge	—	—
26.4.87	PT(1)	H	Halifax	L	6-18	England	Ketteridge	6927	Lindop

DEWSBURY

Ground: Crown Flatt
Colours: Red, amber and black jerseys
First Season: 1901-02
Chairman: Rodney Hardcastle
Secretary: Geoff Parrish
Coach: Jack Addy (Feb 1984-Jan 1987)
Dave Busfield (Jan-Apr 1987)
Terry Crook (Apr 1987-)
Honours: **Championship** Winners, 1972-73
Beaten finalists, 1946-47
Division Two Champions, 1904-05
Challenge Cup Winners, 1911-12,
1942-43
Beaten finalists, 1928-29
Yorkshire League Winners,
1946-47
Yorkshire Cup Winners, 1925-26,
1927-28, 1942-43
Beaten finalists, 1918-19, 1921-22,
1940-41, 1972-73
BBC2 Floodlit Trophy Beaten
finalists, 1975-76
War League Championship
Winners, 1941-42. (1942-43 won
final but championship declared
null and void because Dewsbury
played an ineligible player.)
Beaten finalists, 1943-44
Records: Attendance: 26,584 v. Halifax
(Yorkshire Cup) 30 Oct, 1920
Season
Goals: 145 by N. Stephenson,
1972-73
Tries: 40 by D. Thomas, 1906-07
Points: 368 by N. Stephenson,
1972-73
Match
Goals: 10 by J. Ledgard v.
Yorkshire Amateurs, 13 Sep, 1947;
N. Stephenson v. Blackpool B,
28 Aug, 1972
Tries: 8 by D. Thomas v. Liverpool
C, 13 Apr, 1907
Points: 29 by J. Lyman v. Hull,
22 Apr, 1919
Highest score: 72-0 v. Doncaster,
1984-85
Highest against: 82-0 v. Widnes,
1986-87

1986-87 PLAYERS' SUMMARY

	App	Tries	Goals	Dr	Pts
Bailey, Dennis	12 + 4	3	—	—	12
Bates, Phil	6	—	—	—	—
Booth, Dean	5	—	—	—	—
Broxholme, Paul	16 + 1	—	—	—	—
Burgess, Mark	8	—	—	—	—
Cairncross, Chris	3	—	—	—	—
Charlton, Mark	1 + 1	—	—	—	—
Clarke, Phil	2 + 2	1	—	—	4
Collins, Mick	7 + 2	1	—	—	4
Cooper, Andy	13 + 2	1	—	—	4
Cooper, Paul	2 + 2	2	—	—	8
Cornell, Paul	0 + 2	—	—	—	—
Dickens, Steve	2	—	—	—	—
Diskin, Tony	32	1	—	1	5
Dunford, Shaun	12	2	13	1	35
Garforth, David	4 + 5	1	—	—	4
Garner, Peter	9 + 2	—	—	—	—
Hawksworth, Mick	2	—	—	—	—
Holden, Barry	1 + 3	—	—	—	—
Howley, Pat	9 + 1	1	6	—	16
Janicwiez, Paul	25 + 3	1	—	—	4
Jennings, Paul	15	3	—	—	12
Keyworth, Mark	13 + 2	1	—	—	4
Marsden, Graham	10 + 5	—	—	—	—
Mook, Graham	8 + 3	—	—	—	—
Moore, John	26	5	—	—	20
Morris, Stuart	6 + 2	1	—	—	4
Ramsden, Andrew	24	5	—	—	20
Richardson, Don	26 + 2	2	—	—	8
Sharp, Greg	5	—	—	—	—
Shuttleworth, Paul	32	5	—	2	22
Spooner, Chris	5	3	—	—	12
Squires, Chris	25	12	—	—	48
Toole, Tim	13 + 5	1	—	—	4
Vasey, Chris	23 + 1	6	41	—	106
Westbury, Mark	1 + 3	1	—	—	4
Womersley, Shaun	13 + 1	—	—	—	—

TOTALS:
37 players		59	60	4	360

1986-87 MATCH ANALYSIS

Date	Competition	H/A	Opponent	Rlt	Score	Tries	Goals	Attendance	Referee
31.8.86	SD	H	Blackpool B.	L	14-16	Squires (2), Collins	Vasey	680	Beaumont
7.9.86	SD	A	Hunslet	L	12-22	Toole, Squires	Howley (2)	—	—
14.9.86	YC(1)	A	Sheffield E.	W	10-9	Shuttleworth, Howley	Howley	—	—
21.9.86	SD	H	Rochdale H.	W	19-14	Squires, Moore, Ramsden	Howley (3), Shuttleworth (dg)	657	Lindop
24.9.86	YC(2)	A	Bradford N.	L	10-42	Bailey, Ramsden	Vasey	—	—
28.9.86	SD	A	Sheffield E.	L	10-31	Squires (2)	Vasey	—	—
5.10.86	SD	H	Bramley	L	16-18	Moore, Shuttleworth, Squires	Vasey (2)	641	Smith
12.10.86	SD	A	York	L	16-25	Vasey, Ramsden, Richardson	Vasey (2)	—	—
19.10.86	SD	H	Workington T.	W	18-0	Squires (2), Keyworth	Vasey (3)	327	Fox
26.10.86	SD	A	Doncaster	L	12-34	Moore, Shuttleworth	Vasey (2)	—	—
2.11.86	SD	H	Swinton	W	8-6	Moore	Vasey (2)	1021	Whitfield
16.11.86	SD	A	Fulham	L	6-16	Jennings	Vasey	—	—
23.11.86	SD	H	Whitehaven	L	16-24	Jennings (2), Richardson	Vasey (2)	501	Kendrew
30.11.86	JPS(1)	A	Widnes	L	0-82	—	—	—	—
7.12.86	SD	H	Fulham	W	30-26	Shuttleworth (2), Vasey, Ramsden, Bailey	Vasey (5)	522	Spencer
14.12.86	SD	A	Swinton	L	0-40	—	—	—	—
26.12.86	SD	H	Batley	L	6-8	—	Dunford (3)	1492	Cross
1.1.87	SD	A	Batley	W	18-13	Clarke, Bailey, A. Cooper	Dunford (3)	—	—
4.1.87	SD	H	York	L	4-8	Westbury	—	620	Simpson
25.1.87	SD	H	Hunslet	L	8-36	Ramsden	Dunford (2)	832	Fox
5.2.87	CC(1)	H	St Helens	L	12-48	Squires, Vasey	Dunford (2)	1998	Houghton
8.2.87	SD	A	Bramley	L	3-18	—	Dunford (1, 1dg)	—	—
15.2.87	SD	A	Rochdale H.	W	12-10	Vasey, Morris	Dunford (2)	—	—
22.2.87	SD	H	Doncaster	L	10-16	Vasey	Vasey (3)	911	Lindop
1.3.87	SD	A	Workington T.	L	1-10	—	Shuttleworth (dg)	—	—
15.3.87	SD	H	Sheffield E.	L	6-28	Squires	Vasey	422	Smith
22.3.87	SD	A	Carlisle	L	14-24	Moore, Squires	Vasey (3)	—	—
5.4.87	SD	H	Carlisle	L	6-12	Spooner	Vasey	616	Kershaw
12.4.87	SD	A	Whitehaven	L	12-50	Dunford, Janicweiz	Vasey (2)	—	—
14.4.87	SD	A	Blackpool B.	L	12-32	Vasey, Spooner	Vasey (2)	—	—
18.4.87	SD	A	Huddersfield B.	W	21-14	P. Cooper (2), Spooner	Vasey (4), Diskin (dg)	—	—
20.4.87	SD	H	Huddersfield B.	W	18-12	Diskin, Garforth, Dunford	Vasey (3)	424	Allatt

DONCASTER

Ground: Tatters Field
Colours: Blue and yellow jerseys
First Season: 1951-52
Nickname: Dons
Chairman: John Desmond
Coach: John Sheridan (June 1984-)
Records: Attendance: 4,793 v. Wakefield T. (League) 7 Apr, 1962. There was an attendance of 10,000 for a Challenge Cup tie against Bradford N. at York Road Stadium on 16 Feb, 1952

Season
Goals: 118 by D. Noble, 1985-86
Tries: 20 by N. Turner, 1985-86
Points: 250 by D. Noble, 1986-87

Match
Goals: 9 by D. Towle v. York, 9 Sep, 1967
Tries: 4 by V. Grace v. Rochdale H, 4 Oct, 1952; B. Tasker v. Leeds, 26 Oct, 1963; J. Buckton v. Rochdale H., 30 Aug, 1981; T. Kemp v. Carlisle, 23 Nov, 1986
Points: 18 by D. Towle v. York, 9 Sep, 1967; I. Fortis v. Blackpool B., 5 Sep, 1970; D. Noble v. Keighley, 22 Mar, 1987
Highest score: 50-6 v. Keighley, 1986-87
Highest against: 75-3 v. Leigh, 1975-76

1986-87 PLAYERS' SUMMARY

	App	Tries	Goals	Dr	Pts
Barrett, Dale	3 + 1	—	—	—	—
Bell, David	28 + 1	5	—	—	20
Birkby, Ian	21 + 8	2	6	—	20
Carr, Alan	20 + 5	2	—	—	8
Chapman, Tony	0 + 1	—	—	—	—
Crooks, Martin	2	1	—	—	4
Ellis, David	0 + 4	—	—	—	—
Ellis, Kevin	1	—	—	—	—
Gibbon, Mark	33	8	—	—	32
Green, John	27 + 1	2	—	—	8
Hartley, Iain	11 + 5	2	—	—	8
Hulme, Tony	6 + 5	—	—	—	—
Hutchinson, Alan	5 + 1	1	—	—	4
Jackson, Alan	1	—	—	—	—
Jones, Kevin	33	9	—	—	36
Kemp, Tony	19 + 1	15	—	—	60
Kilkelly, Boyd	3	1	—	—	4
Kupe, Darren	1	—	—	—	—
Lane, Gary	24	6	—	—	24
Moore, Gary	3 + 5	—	—	—	—
Morrell, Wayne	5	3	—	—	12
Morris, Geoff	9 + 3	4	—	—	16
Noble, David	33	6	112	2	250
Parkhouse, Kevin	26 + 1	13	—	—	52
Pennant, Audley	23 + 2	2	—	—	8
Pickett, John	10	2	—	—	8
Roache, Mark	14 + 3	6	—	—	24
Smith, Stuart	11	1	—	—	4
Timson, Andrew	22 + 2	5	—	—	20
Turner, Neil	32	12	—	—	48
Walker, Mark	2 + 2	—	—	—	—
Winter, Martin	1 + 1	—	—	—	—
Trialist	0 + 4	—	—	—	—
TOTALS:					
33 players		108	118	2	670

Mark Gibbon, eight tries in 33 appearances, collared by Hull K.R.'s Chris Burton.

1986-87 MATCH ANALYSIS

Date	Competition	H/A	Opponent	Rlt	Score	Tries	Goals	Attendance	Referee
31.8.86	SD	A	Workington T.	W	16-15	Turner, Roache	Noble (4)	—	—
3.9.86	YC(P)	A	Sheffield E.	L	20-22	Gibbon, Crooks, Morris, Turner	Noble (2)	—	—
7.9.86	SD	H	Swinton	L	6-18	Gibbon	Noble	1352	Cross
21.9.86	SD	A	Carlisle	L	12-16	Roache, Green	Noble (2)	—	—
28.9.86	SD	H	Hunslet	L	18-22	Roache, Morris	Noble (5)	1050	Tennant
5.10.86	SD	A	Huddersfield B.	W	24-14	Bell (2), Parkhouse, Morris	Noble (4)	—	—
12.10.86	SD	H	Whitehaven	W	28-12	Parkhouse (3), Lane, Turner	Noble (4)	743	Allatt
19.10.86	SD	A	York	W	24-23	Pickett (2), Jones, Turner	Noble (3), Birkby	—	—
26.10.86	SD	H	Dewsbury	W	34-12	Turner (2), Green, Parkhouse, Noble, Jones	Noble (5)	1032	Houghton
2.11.86	SD	A	Blackpool B.	W	22-20	Kemp (2), Morris	Noble (4), Birkby	—	—
9.11.86	SD	H	Rochdale H.	D	28-28	Kemp, Noble, Birkby, Roache	Noble (4), Birkby (2)	1572	Kendrew
16.11.86	SD	A	Swinton	L	9-20	Timson	Noble (2, 1dg)	—	—
23.11.86	SD	H	Carlisle	W	30-2	Kemp (4), Bell	Noble (5)	850	Fox
30.11.86	JPS(1)	H	Hull K.R.	W	18-14	Gibbon, Jones, Parkhouse	Noble (3)	3084	Bowman
7.12.86	JPS(2)	A	Leigh	L	14-26	Lane, Bell	Noble (3)	—	—
14.12.86	SD	A	Keighley	W	24-6	Kemp (2), Parkhouse, Lane, Hartley	Noble (2)	—	—
26.12.86	SD	A	Runcorn H.	W	24-14	Birkby, Kemp, Roache, Timson, Turner	Noble (2)	—	—
4.1.87	SD	A	Rochdale H.	W	14-6	Kemp, Parkhouse	Noble (3)	—	—
25.1.87	SD	A	Whitehaven	L	7-26	Jones	Noble (1, 1dg)	—	—
3.2.87	CC(1)	A	Hull K.R.	L	14-29	Kemp, Timson	Noble (3)	—	—
8.2.87	SD	H	Runcorn H.	W	32-12	Jones, Kemp, Roache, Turner, Lane	Noble (5), Birkby	1248	Smith
22.2.87	SD	A	Dewsbury	W	16-10	Jones, Gibbon	Noble (4)	—	—
1.3.87	SD	H	Blackpool B.	W	18-12	Parkhouse, Gibbon, Noble	Noble (3)	1501	Allatt
8.3.87	SD	H	Sheffield E.	W	14-8	Lane, Jones	Noble (3)	2336	Volante
15.3.87	SD	H	Workington T.	W	30-0	Parkhouse, Smith, Bell, Noble, Turner	Noble (5)	1809	Spencer
22.3.87	SD	H	Keighley	W	50-6	Parkhouse (2), Pennant (2), Kemp, Noble, Kilkelly, Gibbon, Turner	Noble (7)	1913	Whitfield
29.3.87	SD	H	York	W	20-10	Turner, Lane, Timson, Kemp	Noble (2)	2616	Cross
5.4.87	SD	A	Hunslet	L	10-16	Jones	Noble (3)	—	—
12.4.87	SD	H	Huddersfield B.	W	36-18	Carr (2), Morrell, Noble, Turner, Hartley	Noble (6)	1743	Houghton
15.4.87	SD	H	Mansfield M.	W	22-11	Morrell, Gibbon, Parkhouse	Noble (5)	1835	Berry
17.4.87	SD	A	Mansfield M.	L	2-17	—	Noble	—	—
19.4.87	SD	A	Sheffield E.	W	16-14	Jones, Hutchinson	Noble (3), Birkby	—	—
26.4.87	SDP(1)	H	Rochdale H.	L	18-30	Timson, Gibbon, Morrell	Noble (3)	2543	Carter

FEATHERSTONE ROVERS

Ground: Post Office Road
Colours: Blue and white hooped jerseys
First Season: 1921-22
Nickname: Colliers
Chairman: Richard Evans
Secretary: Terry Jones
Coach: George Pieniazek
(Nov 1985-Nov 1986)
Paul Daley (Nov 1986 — May 1987)
Peter Fox (May 1987-)
Honours: **Challenge Cup** Winners, 1966-67, 1972-73, 1982-83
Beaten finalists, 1951-52, 1973-74
Championship Beaten finalists, 1927-28
·**Division One** Champions, 1976-77
Division Two Champions, 1979-80
Yorkshire Cup Winners, 1939-40, 1959-60
Beaten finalists, 1928-29, 1963-64, 1966-67, 1969-70, 1970-71, 1976-77, 1977-78
Captain Morgan Trophy Beaten finalists, 1973-74
Records: Attendance: 17,531 v. St. Helens (RL Cup) 21 Mar, 1959
Season
Goals: 163 by S. Quinn, 1979-80
Tries: 31 by C. Woolford, 1958-59
Points: 375 by S. Quinn, 1979-80
Match
Goals: 12 by D. Fox v. Stanningley, 8 Feb, 1964
Tries: 6 by M. Smith v. Doncaster, 13 Apr, 1968
Points: 29 by S. Quinn v. Doncaster, 4 Nov, 1979
Highest score: 66-14 v. Barrow, 1986-87
Highest against: 70-2 v. Halifax, 1940-41

1986-87 PLAYERS' SUMMARY

	App	Tries	Goals	Dr	Pts
Bamforth, Mick	0 + 1	—	—	—	—
Banks, Alan	23	7	—	—	28
Barker, Alan	5 + 3	—	—	—	—
Barker, Nigel	15 + 6	4	—	—	16
Bell, Keith	29 + 2	2	—	4	12
Bibb, Chris	18 + 1	5	—	—	20
Bradford, Patrick	0 + 1	—	—	—	—
Campbell, Mark	7 + 1	—	—	1	1
Clarkson, Peter	6 + 3	1	—	—	4
Crossley, John	23	12	—	—	48
Dakin, Alan	8 + 3	—	—	—	—
Fox, Deryck	36	14	33	5	127
Gearey, Paul	9 + 1	1	—	—	4
Gibbins, Mick	2	—	—	—	—
Hall, Gary	0 + 1	—	—	—	—
Harrison, Karl	31 + 4	4	—	—	16
Heselwood, David	10 + 3	1	—	—	4
Hinchcliffe, Mark	1 + 4	—	—	—	—
Hird, Adrian	1 + 2	—	—	—	—
Hopkins, Calvin	6 + 1	—	—	—	—
Jones, David	16	3	—	—	12
Kellett, Brian	9 + 6	2	—	—	8
Kellett, Lee	5	—	—	—	—
Kelly, Neil	0 + 1	—	—	—	—
Langton, Terry	5	1	—	—	4
Lyman, Paul	28 + 2	10	—	—	40
Marsh, Richard	21 + 1	1	—	—	4
O'Byrne, Mick	1	—	—	—	—
O'Toole, Tony	7 + 1	—	—	—	—
Quinn, Steve	24	1	77	—	158
Siddall, Gary	0 + 1	—	—	—	—
Slater, Martin	6 + 2	1	—	—	4
Slater, Tim	24 + 4	3	—	—	12
Smith, Peter	36	10	—	—	40
Spedding, Paul	0 + 1	—	—	—	—
Spurr, Bob	6 + 1	—	—	—	—
Staniforth, Tony	6	1	—	—	4
Steadman, Graham	28	12	1	1	51
Storey, Peter	0 + 1	—	—	—	—
Sykes, Andy	9	1	—	—	4
Ward, Sean	1	—	—	—	—
Wild, Paul	11 + 2	2	—	—	8
Woolford, Neil	8	—	—	—	—

TOTALS:
43 players		99	111	11	629

New Great Britain Under-21 cap, Chris Bibb.

1986-87 MATCH ANALYSIS

Date	Competition	H/A	Opponent	Rlt	Score	Tries	Goals	Attendance	Referee
31.8.86	SBC	H	Halifax	D	16-16	Steadman, Lyman, Banks	Quinn (2)	4693	Fox
3.9.86	SBC	A	Leeds	L	12-33	Lyman	Quinn (4)	—	—
7.9.86	SBC	A	Hull K.R.	L	14-36	Steadman, Quinn	Quinn (3)	—	—
14.9.86	YC(1)	H	York	W	40-13	Steadman (2), Fox (2), Banks (2), Lyman	Quinn (6)	1732	Haigh
21.9.86	SBC	H	Widnes	L	14-48	Steadman, N. Barker	Quinn (3)	2115	Kershaw
24.9.86	YC(2)	A	Hull K.R.	D	20-20	Smith, Langton, Clarkson	Quinn (4)	—	—
26.9.86	YC(2) Replay	H	Hull K.R.	W	23-12	Lyman (2), Smith	Quinn (4), Fox (2 dg), Steadman (dg)	2385	Berry
28.9.86	SBC	A	Castleford	L	7-16	—	Quinn (3), Fox (dg)	—	—
1.10.86	YC(SF)	H	Castleford	L	2-30	—	Quinn	5523	Lindop
5.10.86	SBC	H	Leigh	W	50-16	Steadman (2), Banks (2), Sykes, N. Barker, Fox, Lyman, Heselwood	Quinn (7)	2239	Beaumont
12.10.86	SBC	H	Warrington	L	22-29	Smith (2), Banks, Lyman	Quinn (3)	2586	Volante
26.10.86	SBC	H	Salford	W	16-6	Steadman, Fox	Fox (3), Steadman	1801	Allatt
2.11.86	SBC	A	Bradford N.	L	2-41	—	Fox	—	—
9.11.86	SBC	H	St Helens	L	8-44	B. Kellett	Fox (2)	2477	Whitfield
23.11.86	SBC	H	Castleford	L	16-18	Crossley (2)	Fox (4)	3407	Lindop
30.11.86	JPS(1)	H	Workington T.	W	22-18	Smith, Fox, Lyman, B. Kellett	Fox (3)	1521	Mean
7.12.86	JPS(2)	H	Bradford N.	L	12-19	Slater, Crossley	Fox (2)	3907	Hodgson
14.12.86	SBC	A	Wakefield T.	W	29-2	Slater, Staniforth, Fox, Bell, Banks	Fox (4, 1dg)	—	—
26.12.86	SBC	A	Hull	L	6-26	Fox	Fox	—	—
28.12.86	SBC	H	Hull	W	18-12	Bibb, Smith, Marsh	Fox (3)	2935	Haigh
4.1.87	SBC	H	Hull K.R.	L	0-14	—	—	2524	Tickle
18.1.87	SBC	A	Oldham (at Manchester C. FC)	L	16-20	Fox, Bibb	Fox (4)	—	—
25.1.87	SBC	A	St Helens	L	14-43	Smith, Steadman	Fox (3)	—	—
4.2.87	CC(1)	H	Hunslet	L	12-26	Crossley, Bibb	Quinn (2)	2537	Smith
8.2.87	SBC	A	Halifax	L	8-34	Fox	Quinn (2)	—	—
15.2.87	SBC	A	Salford	L	16-26	Jones, Fox, Steadman	Quinn (2)	—	—
22.2.87	SBC	H	Wakefield T.	W	27-10	N. Barker, Smith, Jones, Lyman	Quinn (5), Bell (dg)	2007	Hodgson
1.3.87	SBC	A	Warrington	L	15-32	Crossley, Slater	Fox (2), Quinn, Bell (dg)	—	—
8.3.87	SBC	H	Oldham	W	24-6	Slater, Jones, N. Barker, Steadman	Quinn (4)	2239	Lindop
18.3.87	SBC	A	Leigh	L	18-20	Fox, Crossley, Smith	Quinn (3)	—	—
22.3.87	SBC	H	Leeds	W	29-14	Crossley (3), Lyman	Quinn (6), Bell (dg)	2736	McDonald
25.3.87	SBC	H	Wigan	L	0-36	—	—	4073	Holdsworth
31.3.87	SBC	H	Bradford N.	L	10-26	Bibb, Gearey	Quinn	2143	Houghton
5.4.87	SBC	A	Wigan	L	7-62	Fox	Quinn, Fox (dg)	—	—
12.4.87	SBC	H	Barrow	W	66-14	Harrison (3), Wild (2), Crossley (2), Bibb, Bell, Steadman	Quinn (9)	1123	Simpson
14.4.87	SBC	A	Widnes	L	16-62	Smith, Harrison, Crossley	Quinn, Fox	—	—
19.4.87	SBC	A	Barrow	L	2-14	—	Campbell (dg), Bell (dg)	—	—

FULHAM

Ground:	Polytechnic of Central London Stadium, Chiswick
Colours:	Black jerseys with red and white chevron
First Season:	1980-81
Chairman:	Mrs Barbara Close
Secretary:	Tim Lamb
Coach:	Bill Goodwin (Apr 1986-)
Honours:	**Division Two** Champions, 1982-83
Records:	Attendance: 15,013 v. Wakefield T. (RL Cup) 15 Feb, 1981 at Fulham FC

Season
Goals: 136 by S. Diamond, 1982-83
Tries: 27 by J. Crossley, 1982-83
Points: 308 by S. Diamond, 1982-83

Match
Goals: 8 by I. MacCorquodale v. Huddersfield, 12 Oct, 1980
Tries: No player has scored more than 3
Points: 22 by A. Platt, v. Mansfield M., 10 May, 1986
Highest score: 50-5 v. Huyton, 1982-83
Highest against: 72-6 v. Whitehaven, 1986-87

1986-87 PLAYERS' SUMMARY

	App	Tries	Goals	Dr	Pts
Bibby, Neil	1 + 5	1	—	—	4
Birmingham, Mark	0 + 1	—	—	—	—
Bowen, Karl	5 + 1	—	—	—	—
Bridge, Russ	28 + 2	5	—	—	20
Cambriani, Adrian	14 + 1	1	—	—	4
Collier, Andy	1	—	—	—	—
Cooper, Dominic	12 + 1	—	—	1	1
Dean, Martin	1	—	—	—	—
Feighan, Frank	17 + 2	2	—	—	8
Fenn, Colin	22 + 2	1	65	—	134
Fisoh, John	1 + 1	1	—	—	4
Flashman, Brian	4	1	—	—	4
Gibson, Russ	6 + 5	1	6	—	16
Gillan, Dave	20 + 1	7	—	—	28
Goyer, Steve	6	1	—	—	4
Green, Gavin	1	—	—	—	—
Grimaldi, Mick	8 + 2	—	—	—	—
Haggath, Glen	18	3	2	—	16
Herdman, Martin	3	—	—	—	—
Hutchinson, Mick	4 + 1	—	—	—	—
Jones, Charlie	27 + 1	6	—	—	24
Knight, Bob	24	1	—	—	4
Lawrie, Geordie	10 + 2	1	—	—	4
Mayo, John	6	—	—	—	—
Miller, Craig	6	3	—	—	12
Millington, Wayne	2	1	—	—	4
Mills, Steve	28 + 1	12	3	—	54
Mitchell, Simon	3 + 2	—	—	—	—
Murphy, Keiron	23	8	—	3	35
O'Brien, Gary	3	2	—	—	8
O'Doherty, Pat	18 + 1	7	—	—	28
Pratt, Greg	16	1	—	—	4
Rampling, Darren	2 + 6	—	—	—	—
Rees, Huw	25	8	7	2	48
Rendell, Brian	11 + 5	2	—	—	8
Scott, Gary	1 + 1	—	—	—	—
Taylor, Craig	17	1	—	—	4
White, Peter	22 + 1	7	—	—	28
Wilkinson, Chris	10	1	6	3	19
Trialists (2)	3 + 3	—	—	—	—
TOTALS:					
41 players		85	89	9	527

1986-87 MATCH ANALYSIS

Date	Competition	H/A	Opponent	Rlt	Score	Tries	Goals	Attendance	Referee
14.9.86	LC(1)	A	Whitehaven	L	6-72	Millington	Wilkinson	—	—
21.9.86	SD	H	Sheffield E.	L	14-68	Feighan, Mills	Fenn (3)	680	Smith
28.9.86	SD	A	Mansfield M. (at Notts C. FC)	L	18-32	O'Brien, Jones, Gillan	Fenn (3)	—	—
5.10.86	SD	H	Keighley	W	44-12	Jones (2), Rees (2), Haggath, O'Brien, O'Doherty, Flashman	Fenn (6)	658	Spencer
12.10.86	SD	A	Rochdale H.	L	12-20	Gillan, Murphy	Fenn (2)	—	—
19.10.86	SD	H	Batley	L	23-24	Mills (3), Bridge	Fenn (3), Cooper (dg)	812	Kendrew
2.11.86	SD	H	Hunslet	L	4-16	—	Fenn (2)	867	Cross
9.11.86	SD	A	Sheffield E	L	8-17	Bridge	Fenn (2)	—	—
16.11.86	SD	H	Dewsbury	W	16-6	Jones, Gillan	Fenn (4)	647	Kershaw
23.11.86	SD	A	Bramley	L	10-18	Bridge, Jones	Rees	—	—
30.11.86	JPS(1)	H	Castleford	L	24-34	Mills (3), Haggath	Fenn (4), Rees (2)	1374	Carter
7.12.86	SD	A	Dewsbury	L	26-30	O'Doherty (2), White, Taylor, Gillan	Haggarth, Mills, Gibson	—	—
14.12.86	SD	H	Blackpool B.	W	30-12	Murphy (2), Mills, O'Doherty	Fenn (7)	678	Tennant
21.12.86	SD	H	York	W	18-16	White, Fenn, Pratt	Fenn (3)	625	Beaumont
26.12.86	SD	A	Swinton	L	10-50	Mills (2)	Fenn	—	—
4.1.87	SD	H	Huddersfield B.	L	12-18	Lawrie, Bridge	Fenn (2)	578	Hodgson
22.1.87	CC(P)	A	Kells	D	4-4	Rees	—	—	—
25.1.87	SD	A	Huddersfield B.	W	24-16	Knight, Rees, Gillan, White, O'Doherty	Fenn (2)	—	—
27.1.87	CC(P) Replay	H	Kells	W	22-14	Jones, Mills, Haggath, Murphy	Rees (3)	370	Berry
1.2.87	CC(1)	H	Halifax	L	10-38	Rees, O'Doherty	Gibson	1575	Simpson
8.2.87	SD	A	Blackpool B.	L	28-48	White (2), Rees, Gibson, Rendell	Gibson (4)	—	—
15.2.87	SD	H	Bramley	W	24-20	Murphy (2), O'Doherty, Rees, Mills	Rees, Haggarth	661	Lindop
22.2.87	SD	H	Swinton	D	15-15	Fisoh, Mills	Fenn (3), Rees (dg)	745	Houghton
1.3.87	SD	A	York	L	19-21	Rendell, Cambriani, Gillan	Fenn (3), Rees (dg)	—	—
8.3.87	SD	H	Runcorn H.	W	19-2	Murphy, White	Fenn (5), Wilkinson (dg)	572	Mean
15.3.87	SD	A	Hunslet	L	4-30	—	Fenn (2)	—	—
22.3.87	SD	H	Whitehaven	D	8-8	Miller	Fenn, Murphy (dg), Wilkinson (dg)	668	Haigh
29.3.87	SD	A	Whitehaven	L	14-32	Bibby, Feighan	Wilkinson (3)	—	—
4.4.87	SD	A	Keighley	L	9-22	Murphy	Wilkinson (2), Murphy (dg)	—	—
5.4.87	SD	A	Batley	W	15-8	Bridge, Wilkinson	Fenn (3), Wilkinson (dg)	—	—
12.4.87	SD	H	Mansfield M.	L	12-20	White, Gillan	Fenn (2)	625	Kendrew
17.4.87	SD	H	Rochdale H.	L	16-33	Miller, Rees, Goyer	Fenn (2)	766	Tickle
20.4.87	SD	A	Runcorn H.	L	9-18	Miller	Mills (2), Murphy (dg)	—	—

HALIFAX

Ground: Thrum Hall
Colours: Blue and white hooped jerseys
First Season: 1895-96
Nickname: Thrum Hallers
Chairman: Stan Ackroyd
General
  Manager: Tony Beevers
Coach: Chris Anderson (Nov 1984-)
Honours: **Championship** Winners, 1906-07, 1964-65
Beaten finalists, 1952-53, 1953-54, 1955-56, 1965-66
Division One Champions, 1902-03, 1985-86
War League Beaten finalists, 1942-43, 1944-45
Challenge Cup Winners, 1902-03, 1903-04, 1930-31, 1938-39, 1986-87
Beaten finalists, 1920-21, 1940-41, 1941-42, 1948-49, 1953-54, 1955-56
Yorkshire League Winners, 1908-09, 1920-21, 1952-53, 1953-54, 1955-56, 1957-58
Eastern Division Championship Winners, 1963-64
Yorkshire Cup Winners, 1908-09, 1944-45, 1954-55, 1955-56, 1963-64
Beaten finalists, 1905-06, 1907-08, 1941-42, 1979-80
John Player Trophy Winners, 1971-72
Premiership Trophy Beaten finalists, 1985-86
Charity Shield Winners, 1986-87
Records: Attendance: 29,153 v. Wigan (RL Cup) 21 Mar, 1959
Season
Goals: 147 by T. Griffiths, 1955-56

Tries: 48 by J. Freeman, 1956-57
Points: 298 by C. Whitfield, 1986-87
Match
Goals: 14 by B. Burton v. Hunslet, 27 Aug, 1972
Tries: 8 by K. Williams v. Dewsbury, 9 Nov, 1957
Points: 31 by B. Burton v. Hunslet, 27 Aug, 1972
Highest score: 76-8 v. Hunslet, 1972-73
Highest against: 64-0 v. Wigan, 1922-23

1986-87 PLAYERS' SUMMARY

	App	Tries	Goals	Dr	Pts
Anderson, Chris	34	9	—	—	36
Anderson, Tony	7	3	—	—	12
Bailey, Jimmy	1	—	—	—	—
Beevers, Graham	22 + 1	—	—	—	—
Bell, Peter	8 + 6	2	—	—	8
Cerchione, Mario	0 + 1	—	—	—	—
Dickinson, Roy	17 + 1	2	—	—	8
Dixon, Paul	41	14	—	—	56
Dobek, David	1	—	—	—	—
Eadie, Graham	36	20	4	—	88
Fairbank, Dick	10 + 2	3	—	—	12
Finn, Brendan	2	—	—	—	—
George, Wilf	38	15	—	—	60
Hague, Neil	26 + 2	3	—	2	14
James, Neil	19 + 14	1	—	—	4
Juliff, Brian	17 + 19	6	—	—	24
Longstaff, Simon	0 + 1	—	—	—	—
McCallion, Seamus	34	7	—	—	28
Neller, Keith	36 + 1	3	—	—	12
Parkinson, Andy	1	—	—	—	—
Pendlebury, John	24	6	1	1	27
Preece, Chris	6	2	—	—	8
Riddlesden, Eddie	15	3	—	—	12
Rix, Grant	29	11	—	—	44
Scott, Mick	23 + 2	—	—	—	—
Simpson, Andy	3	1	—	—	4
Smith, Steve	14 + 4	6	13	—	50
Stephens, Gary	36	9	—	2	38
Whitfield, Colin	39 + 1	21	105	4	298
Wilson, Scott	33 + 1	8	—	—	32
TOTALS:					
30 players		155	123	9	875

1986-87 MATCH ANALYSIS

Date	Competition	H/A	Opponent	Rlt	Score	Tries	Goals	Attendance	Referee
17.8.86	YC(P)	H	Mansfield M.	W	56-0	George (2), Fairbank (2), Smith, Stephens, McCallion, Dixon, Whitfield, Juliff	Smith (8)	2962	Fox
24.8.86	Charity Shield	Isle of Man	Castleford	W	9-8	Whitfield, George	Hague (dg)	3276	Lindop
31.8.86	SBC	A	Featherstone R.	D	16-16	Whitfield (2), Fairbank	Whitfield (2)	—	—
3.9.86	SBC	H	Oldham	W	20-14	Stephens (2), Dixon	Whitfield (4)	4396	Holdsworth
7.9.86	SBC	H	Hull	W	28-16	Whitfield (2), Riddlesden, Hague, C. Anderson	Whitfield (4)	4693	Tickle

(continued)

MATCH ANALYSIS (continued)

Date	Comp		Opponent		Score	Tries	Goals	Att	Referee
14.9.86	YC(1)	A	Castleford	L	10-16	Whitfield, Eadie	Whitfield	—	—
21.9.86	SBC	A	St Helens	L	16-38	Dixon (2), Eadie	Whitfield, Eadie	—	—
28.9.86	SBC	H	Warrington	L	13-16	Eadie (2)	Whitfield (2, 1dg)	5507	Berry
5.10.86	SBC	A	Barrow	W	23-12	Riddlesden, C. Anderson, Eadie	Whitfield (5, 1dg)	—	—
12.10.86	SBC	H	Leeds	W	23-8	George (2), Stephens	Whitfield (5, 1dg)	6057	Fox
19.10.86	SBC	A	Hull	L	23-28	Stephens, Dickinson, Dixon, Smith	Whitfield (3), Stephens (dg)	—	—
26.10.86	SBC	H	Castleford	L	12-16	Preece, C. Anderson	Whitfield (2)	4862	Simpson
29.10.86	Tour	H	Australia	L	2-36	—	Whitfield	7193	Beaumont
9.11.86	SBC	A	Leigh	W	28-20	George, Bell, Preece, Wilson, Whitfield	Whitfield (4)	—	—
12.11.86	JPS(P)	H	York	W	38-23	George (3), Eadie, Hague, Dickinson, Juliff	Whitfield (5))	2962	Spencer
16.11.86	SBC	H	Hull K.R.	W	24-18	Dixon, Rix, Whitfield, Eadie, Wilson	Whitfield (2)	4413	Houghton
23.11.86	SBC	A	Warrington	L	10-18	Dixon, Eadie	Whitfield	—	—
30.11.86	JPS(1)	H	Wakefield T.	W	36-22	Smith, McCallion, Whitfield, Bell, Juliff	Whitfield (8)	4076	Cross
7.12.86	JPS(2)	A	Warrington	L	10-44	Eadie, George	Eadie	—	—
14.12.86	SBC	A	Oldham	W	20-18	Smith, Rix, Eadie, Pendlebury	Eadie (2)	—	—
21.12.86	SBC	H	Salford	W	18-8	Neller, Stephens, C. Anderson	Whitfield (3)	3410	Tennant
26.12.86	SBC	H	Bradford N.	W	20-4	Whitfield, Rix, McCallion, Pendlebury	Whitfield (2)	6135	Holdsworth
28.12.86	SBC	A	Bradford N.	W	12-8	Juliff, Stephens	Whitfield (2)	—	—
1.1.86	SBC	A	Hull K.R.	L	0-14	—	—	—	—
4.1.86	SBC	H	St Helens	W	20-19	George, Smith, Whitfield	Whitfield (4)	4359	Bowman
28.1.87	SBC	H	Barrow	W	40-14	Pendlebury, Whitfield, James, George, Neller, Eadie, Rix	Whitfield (6)	3002	Hodgson
1.2.87	CC(1)	A	Fulham	W	38-10	Rix (2), George, Eadie, Neller, C. Anderson, Whitfield	Whitfield (5)	—	—
8.2.87	SBC	H	Featherstone R.	W	34-8	Pendlebury (2), Eadie, Whitfield, C. Anderson, McCallion	Whitfield (5)	4271	Mean
15.2.87	CC(2)	H	Hunslet	W	29-10	Eadie (2), Dixon, Whitfield, C. Anderson	Whitfield (3), Pendlebury, Stephens (dg)	6112	Kershaw
22.2.87	SBC	H	Leigh	W	43-24	Dixon (2), McCallion (2), Whitfield, Stephens, Smith, Rix	Smith (3), Whitfield (2, 1dg)	4056	Simpson
28.2.87	CC(3)	H	Hull K.R.	W	35-7	C. Anderson (2), Whitfield, Wilson, Eadie, Dixon, Rix	Whitfield (3), Hague (dg)	7052	Holdsworth
8.3.87	SBC	A	Widnes	W	10-6	Dixon, Rix	Whitfield	—	—
15.3.87	SBC	H	Wigan	L	8-12	Rix	Whitfield (2)	10000	Allatt
22.3.87	SBC	A	Salford	L	8-16	Eadie	Whitfield (2)	—	—
28.3.87	CC(SF)	Leeds	Widnes	W	12-8	Pendlebury, Rix	Whitfield (2)	(16064)	Allatt
1.4.87	SBC	A	Wigan	L	2-42	—	Whitfield	—	—
5.4.87	SBC	A	Castleford	L	14-26	Eadie, Wilson, Dixon	Smith	—	—
12.4.87	SBC	H	Widnes	W	20-0	Whitfield (2), George, Dixon	Whitfield (2)	4124	Tennant
14.4.87	SBC	A	Wakefield T.	L	14-18	Wilson, Juliff, Simpson	Smith	—	—
17.4.87	SBC	H	Wakefield T.	L	10-18	T. Anderson	Whitfield (3)	4080	Mean
20.4.87	SBC	A	Leeds	W	24-12	Stephens, Juliff, Hague, Whitfield, Wilson	Whitfield (2)	—	—
26.4.87	PT(1)	A	Castleford	W	18-6	T. Anderson (2), Wilson, Riddlesden	Whitfield	—	—
2.5.87	CC(F)	Wembley	St. Helens	W	19-18	George, Eadie, McCallion	Whitfield (3), Pendlebury (dg)	(91267)	Holdsworth
10.5.87	PT(SF)	A	Wigan	L	10-18	Eadie, Wilson	Whitfield	—	—

HUDDERSFIELD BARRACUDAS

Ground: Arena 84
Colours: Claret and gold jerseys
First Season: 1895-96; added Barracudas to title
               1984-85
Nickname: Barracudas
Chairman: John Bailey
Secretary: Stuart Greaves
Coach: Chris Forster (Feb 1985-Dec 1986)
               Jack Addy (Jan 1987-)
Honours: **Championship** Winners, 1911-12,
               1912-13, 1914-15, 1928-29,
               1929-30, 1948-49, 1961-62
               Beaten finalists, 1913-14, 1919-20,
               1922-23, 1931-32, 1945-46, 1949-50
               Division Two Champions, 1974-75
               Challenge Cup Winners, 1912-13,
               1914-15, 1919-20, 1932-33, 1944-45,
               1952-53
               Beaten finalists, 1934-35, 1961-62
               Yorkshire League Winners,
               1911-12, 1912-13, 1913-14, 1914-15,
               1919-20, 1921-22, 1928-29, 1929-30,
               1948-49, 1949-50, 1951-52
               Eastern Division Beaten finalists,
               1962-63
               Yorkshire Cup Winners, 1909-10,
               1911-12, 1913-14, 1914-15, 1918-19,
               1919-20, 1926-27, 1931-32, 1938-39,
               1950-51, 1952-53, 1957-58
               Beaten finalists, 1910-11, 1923-24,
               1925-26, 1930-31, 1937-38, 1942-43,
               1949-50, 1960-61
Records: Attendance: 35,136 Leeds v.
               Wakefield T. (RL Cup SF)
               19 April 1947. Home: 32,912 v.
               Wigan (League) 4 Mar, 1950
               Season
               Goals: 147 by B. Gronow, 1919-20
               Tries: 80 by A. Rosenfeld, 1913-14
               Points: 330 by B. Gronow, 1919-20

Match
Goals: 18 by M. Holland v.
Swinton Park, 28 Feb, 1914
Tries: 10 by L. Cooper v. Keighley,
17 Nov, 1951
Points: 39 by M. Holland v.
Swinton Park, 28 Feb, 1914
Highest score: 119-2 v. Swinton
Park, 1913-14
Highest against: 64-17 v. Leeds,
1958-59

1986-87 PLAYERS' SUMMARY

	App	Tries	Goals	Dr	Pts
Ashe, Jeff	18 + 1	2	—	—	8
Boothroyd, Alan	26	4	—	—	16
Brooke, Kevin	11 + 1	1	—	—	4
Campbell, Mark	28	10	—	—	40
Cockerham, Paul	18 + 5	7	—	—	28
Cook, Billy	3 + 1	1	—	—	4
Dickinson, Andy	5 + 1	—	—	—	—
Edwards, Tony	30	11	—	—	44
Farrell, Carlton	0 + 1	—	—	—	—
Farrell, Tony	4 + 6	1	—	—	4
Finekifolau, Tisi	5 + 1	—	—	—	—
Fitzpatrick, Dennis	4 + 2	—	—	—	—
Fortis, Mark	3	—	—	—	—
Harris, Colin	7	—	—	—	—
Hesford, Steve	2	—	7	—	14
Hirst, Bob	19	1	35	—	74
Huck, Phil	8 + 1	2	—	—	8
Johnson, Jimmy	10 + 2	1	—	—	4
Johnson, Phil	9	2	—	—	8
Johnson, Willie	10 + 1	1	—	—	4
Kenworthy, Simon	10 + 5	—	5	—	10
Kenniff, Damien	7	5	—	—	20
Kinsey, Tony	3	—	—	—	—
Knight, Glen	2	—	—	—	—
Marshall, Nigel	15 + 4	7	—	2	30
Meehan, Gary	7	—	—	1	1
Munro, Geoff	18 + 1	10	—	—	40
Nelson, David	14 + 6	1	—	—	4
O'Brien, Kenny	8 + 2	1	—	—	4
Platt, Billy	20	3	21	7	61
St Hilaire, Lee	4	—	—	—	—
Schofield, David	2	—	—	—	—
Sedgwick, Peter	29	4	—	—	16
Simpson, Frank	0 + 4	—	—	—	—
Thomas, Ian	15 + 5	8	10	—	52
Unsworth, Martin	5 + 1	—	—	—	—
Wills, Steve	21 + 3	1	—	—	4
Wood, Neil	0 + 2	—	—	—	—
Wroe, Derek	3	—	—	—	—
TOTALS:					
39 players		84	78	10	502

1986-87 MATCH ANALYSIS

Date	Com-petition	H/A	Opponent	Rlt	Score	Tries	Goals	Atten-dance	Referee
31.8.86	SD	H	Keighley	W	27-16	Munro (2), Marshall, P. Johnson, Sedgwick	Hesford (3), Platt (dg)	731	Kershaw
7.9.86	SD	A	Mansfield M.	W	36-31	Munro, J. Johnson, P. Johnson, Campbell, Boothroyd, Thomas, Edwards	Hesford (4)	—	—
14.9.86	YC(1)	A	Hull K.R.	L	30-52	Campbell (3), Marshall, Sedgwick	Kenworthy (4), Platt	—	—
21.9.86	SD	H	Batley	L	20-25	Campbell, Edwards, Sedgwick, Boothroyd	Platt (2)	896	Spencer
28.9.86	SD	A	Workington T.	W	22-20	Munro (2), Cockerham, Platt	Platt (1, 1 dg), Kenworthy, Meehan (dg)	—	—
1.10.86	SD	A	Sheffield E.	L	9-12	Cockerham	Platt (2, 1 dg)	—	—
5.10.86	SD	H	Doncaster	L	14-24	Cook, Munro	Platt (3)	710	Simpson
12.10.86	SD	A	Bramley	L	19-24	Marshall, Munro, Boothroyd	Platt (2, 2 dg), Marshall (dg)	—	—
19.10.86	SD	H	Hunslet	L	10-26	Huck, W. Johnson	Platt	689	Haigh
26.10.86	SD	A	Batley	W	14-12	Marshall, A. Farrell	Hirst (2), Marshall (dg), Platt (dg)	—	—
2.11.86	SD	H	Mansfield M.	W	29-18	Marshall (2), Platt (2), Edwards	Hirst (4), Platt (dg)	561	Fox
9.11.86	SD	A	Carlisle	L	10-18	Munro	Hirst (3)	—	—
16.11.86	JPS(P)	A	Workington T.	L	6-16	Hook	Hirst	—	—
20.11.86	SD	H	Sheffield E.	L	8-12	Marshall	Hirst (2)	336	Lindop
23.11.86	SD	A	Runcorn H.	L	10-14	Munro, Edwards	Platt	—	—
30.11.86	SD	H	York	L	16-32	Edwards (2), Nelson	Hirst (2)	535	Volante
14.12.86	SD	H	Workington T.	L	12-20	Edwards, Cockerham	Platt (2)	341	McDonald
21.12.86	SD	A	Hunslet	L	6-52	Cockerham	Platt	—	—
26.12.86	SD	A	York	L	22-54	Campbell (2), Munro	Platt (5)	—	—
1.1.87	SD	H	Swinton	L	12-34	Kenniff, Edwards	Hirst (2)	656	Volante
4.1.87	SD	A	Fulham	W	18-12	O'Brien, Kenniff, Campbell	Hirst (3)	—	—
18.1.87	SD	A	Swinton (at Bolton W. FC)	L	10-48	Thomas	Hirst (3)	—	—
25.1.87	SD	H	Fulham	L	16-24	Thomas, Campbell, Brooke	Hirst (2)	379	Holdsworth
8.2.87	CC(1)	H	Whitehaven	L	10-32	Kenniff, Thomas	Thomas	859	Kershaw
22.2.87	SD	A	Keighley	L	18-29	Thomas (2), Kenniff	Hirst (3)	—	—
1.3.87	SD	H	Carlisle	L	8-19	Kenniff	Thomas, Hirst	324	Whitfield
8.3.87	SD	H	Bramley	W	20-10	Ashe (2), Sedgwick	Hirst (4)	374	Berry
29.3.87	SD	H	Runcorn H.	W	26-12	Edwards (2), Hirst, Cockerham, Boothroyd	Hirst (3)	362	Volante
12.4.87	SD	A	Doncaster	L	18-36	Cockerham (2), Campbell	Thomas (3)	—	—
18.4.87	SD	H	Dewsbury	L	14-21	Edwards, Mills	Thomas (3)	435	Holgate (Pr)
20.4.87	SD	A	Dewsbury	L	12-18	Thomas (2)	Thomas (2)	—	—

HULL

Ground: The Boulevard
Colours: Irregular black and white hooped
            jerseys
First Season: 1895-96
Nickname: Airlie Birds
Chairman: John Rawlings
Secretary: Geoff Lythe
Coach: Len Casey (June 1986-)
Honours: **Championship** Winners, 1919-20,
            1920-21, 1935-36, 1955-56, 1957-58
            Beaten finalists, 1956-57
            Division One Champions, 1982-83
            Division Two Champions, 1976-77,
            1978-79
            Challenge Cup Winners, 1913-14,
            1981-82
            Beaten finalists, 1907-08, 1908-09,
            1909-10, 1921-22, 1922-23,
            1958-59, 1959-60, 1979-80,
            1982-83, 1984-85
            Yorkshire League Winners,
            1918-19, 1922-23, 1926-27, 1935-36
            Yorkshire Cup Winners, 1923-24,
            1969-70, 1982-83, 1983-84, 1984-85
            Beaten finalists, 1912-13, 1914-15,
            1920-21, 1927-28, 1938-39,
            1946-47, 1953-54, 1954-55,
            1955-56, 1959-60, 1967-68, 1986-87
            John Player Trophy Winners
            1981-82
            Beaten finalists, 1975-76, 1984-85
            BBC2 Floodlit Trophy Winners,
            1979-80
            Premiership Beaten finalists,
            1980-81, 1981-82, 1982-83
Records: Attendance: 28,798 v. Leeds
            (RL Cup) 7 Mar, 1936
            Season
            Goals: 170 by S. Lloyd, 1978-79
            Tries: 52 by J. Harrison, 1914-15
            Points: 369 by S. Lloyd, 1978-79

Match
Goals: 14 by J. Kennedy v.
Rochdale H., 7 Apr, 1921; S. Lloyd
v. Oldham, 10 Sep, 1978
Tries: 7 by C. Sullivan v.
Doncaster, 15 Apr, 1968
Points: 36 by J. Kennedy v.
Keighley, 29 Jan, 1921
Highest score: 86-0 v. Elland,
1898-99
Highest against: 57-14 v. St.
Helens, 1985-86

1986-87 PLAYERS' SUMMARY

	App	Tries	Goals	Dr	Pts
Ah Kuoi, Fred	34 + 6	5	—	—	20
Brand, Mike	11	3	—	—	12
Brown, Dave	9	1	—	—	4
Crane, Mick	13 + 5	2	—	—	8
Crooks, Lee	35 + 2	7	46	5	125
Crooks, Steve	18 + 1	—	—	—	—
Dannatt, Andy	28	3	—	—	12
Dick, Kevin	21 + 5	5	3	1	27
Divorty, Gary	10 + 11	4	—	1	17
Eastwood, Paul	39	19	—	—	76
Edmonds, Phil	1	—	—	—	—
Elgar, Nicky	9 + 2	2	—	—	8
Gibbins, Mick	3 + 1	—	—	—	—
Hick, Steve	7 + 1	—	1	—	2
James, Kevin	2	—	—	—	—
Kemble, Gary	34	5	—	—	20
Kerman, Richard	0 + 1	—	—	—	—
Kirkwood, John	0 + 1	—	—	—	—
Lazenby, Tracy	13 + 3	2	—	—	8
Mallinson, Billy	8	2	—	—	8
McCoid, Carl	15	5	—	—	20
Norfolk, Carl	1	—	—	—	—
Norton, Steve	22 + 4	—	—	1	1
O'Hara, Dane	40	17	—	—	68
Patrick, Shaun	32	1	—	—	4
Pearce, Gary	23 + 2	11	51	2	148
Portz, Jimmy	0 + 2	—	—	—	—
Proctor, Wayne	13 + 8	3	—	—	12
Puckering, Neil	5 + 10	1	—	—	4
Schofield, Garry	31 + 1	32	1	—	130
Sharp, Jon	18 + 9	6	—	—	24
Sutton, Mick	1	—	—	—	—
Tomlinson, Alan	12	1	—	—	4
Vass, Stuart	9 + 1	1	—	—	4
Welham, Paul	7 + 1	1	—	—	4
Windley, Phil	22 + 3	5	—	—	20
TOTALS:					
36 players		144	102	10	790

1986-87 MATCH ANALYSIS

Date	Competition	H/A	Opponent	Rlt	Score	Tries	Goals	Attendance	Referee
31.8.86	SBC	H	Wakefield T.	W	12-6	Windley, Ah Kuoi	L. Crooks (2)	5318	Berry
3.9.86	SBC	A	Castleford	L	6-16	Welham	L. Crooks	—	—
7.9.86	SBC	A	Halifax	L	16-28	Dannatt, Proctor, Eastwood	L. Crooks, Hick	—	—

MATCH ANALYSIS (continued)

Date	Competition	H/A	Opponent	Rlt	Score	Tries	Goals	Attendance	Referee
14.9.86	YC(1)	H	Bramley	W	29-22	Windley, L. Crooks, Divorty, Patrick, Sharp	L. Crooks (4, 1dg)	3580	Kershaw
21.9.86	SBC	H	Leigh	W	31-26	O'Hara, Brand, Crane, McCoid, Eastwood, Sharp	Pearce (3), L. Crooks (dg)	5721	Holdsworth
24.9.86	YC(2)	H	Wakefield T.	W	21-12	McCoid (2), Mallinson, O'Hara	L. Crooks (2), Divorty (dg)	3737	Smith
28.9.86	SBC	A	Wigan	L	7-34	Ah Kuoi	Pearce, L. Crooks (dg)	—	—
1.10.86	YC(SF)	A	Bradford N.	W	16-12	McCoid, Sharp, Ah Kuoi	L. Crooks (2)	—	—
5.10.86	SBC	A	Hull K.R.	L	6-29	Schofield	L. Crooks	—	—
11.10.86	YC(F)	Leeds	Castleford	L	24-31	O'Hara (2), Brand (2)	L. Crooks (4)	(10590)	McDonald
14.10.86	SBC	H	Bradford N.	W	27-22	Mallinson, Schofield, L. Crooks, O'Hara	L. Crooks (5), Dick (dg)	4198	Houghton
19.10.86	SBC	H	Halifax	W	28-23	Eastwood (2), O'Hara, Pearce, Schofield	Pearce (4)	6439	Kershaw
26.10.86	SBC	A	Barrow	W	17-16	O'Hara, Brown, Divorty	Pearce (2, 1dg)	—	—
2.11.86	SBC	H	Leeds	L	10-32	Schofield, Dick	Pearce	6202	Volante
9.11.86	SBC	A	Warrington	L	10-42	Eastwood	Pearce (3)	—	—
16.11.86	Tour	H	Australia	L	0-48	—	—	8216	Smith
23.11.86	SBC	A	St Helens	L	10-50	O'Hara, Eastwood	Pearce	—	—
30.11.86	JPS(1)	A	Salford	W	27-12	Schofield (2), Windley, Eastwood	Pearce (5, 1dg)	—	—
7.12.86	JPS(2)	A (at Hull)	Blackpool B.	W	48-22	O'Hara (3), Kemble (2), Schofield (2), Pearce, Lazenby, Puckering	Pearce (4)	(3723)	—
13.12.86	JPS(3)	A	Bradford N.	W	20-8	Schofield (3), Lazenby	Pearce (2)	—	—
20.12.86	JPS(SF)	Leeds	Wigan	L	11-12	Windley, Pearce	L. Crooks, Pearce (dg)	(5245)	Holdsworth
26.12.86	SBC	H	Featherstone R.	W	26-6	Schofield, Pearce, O'Hara, Eastwood, Crooks	Pearce (3)	4850	Beaumont
28.12.86	SBC	A	Featherstone R.	L	12-18	Schofield, Eastwood, Windley	—	—	—
4.1.87	SBC	H	Oldham	W	20-16	Schofield (2), Crane	Pearce (4)	5110	Mean
25.1.87	SBC	A	Salford	L	18-29	Eastwood (2), Kemble, Pearce	Pearce	—	—
4.2.87	CC(1)	A	Bramley	W	10-2	Sharp (2)	Schofield	—	—
8.2.87	SBC	H	Barrow	W	41-18	Pearce (3), L. Crooks (2), McCoid, Kemble	Pearce (6), L. Crooks (dg)	4219	Tennant
15.2.87	CC(2)	A	Mansfield M.	W	38-7	Schofield (2), Eastwood (2), Tomlinson, Pearce, Proctor	Pearce (5)	—	—
22.2.87	SBC	A	Oldham	L	18-24	O'Hara (2), Schofield, Eastwood	Pearce	—	—
1.3.87	CC(3)	H	Leigh	L	8-12	O'Hara, Dannatt	—	7329	Volante
11.3.87	SBC	A	Bradford N.	D	20-20	Vass, Schofield, Elgar, Pearce	Pearce (2)	—	—
15.3.87	SBC	A	Leeds	L	22-28	Schofield (2), Dick, Sharp	Pearce (2), Dick	—	—
17.3.87	SBC	H	St Helens	W	36-22	Eastwood (2), Schofield, Ah Kuoi, Dick, Divorty, Proctor	L. Crooks (4)	3904	Lindop
22.3.87	SBC	A	Leigh	L	10-22	O'Hara, Elgar	L. Crooks	—	—
25.3.87	SBC	H	Salford	L	8-14	Schofield	L. Crooks (2)	3664	Kershaw
29.3.87	SBC	H	Warrington	L	12-46	Schofield, Divorty	L. Crooks (2)	4183	McDonald
5.4.87	SBC	A	Widnes	W	18-10	Schofield (2), Dannatt	L. Crooks (3)	—	—
7.4.87	SBC	H	Castleford	W	18-6	Schofield, L. Crooks, Dick	L. Crooks (3)	4021	Beaumont
12.4.87	SBC	H	Wigan	L	12-18	Schofield, Eastwood	L. Crooks (2)	8583	Allatt
17.4.87	SBC	H	Hull K.R.	L	8-21	Dick	L. Crooks, Dick	9216	Whitfield
20.4.87	SBC	A	Wakefield T.	W	38-4	Schofield (4), Eastwood, Ah Kuoi, Pearce	L. Crooks (5)	—	—
22.4.87	SBC	H	Widnes	W	21-4	Eastwood, L. Crooks, O'Hara, Kemble	L. Crooks, Dick, Norton (dg)	7446	Berry

53

HULL KINGSTON ROVERS

Ground: Craven Park
Colours: White jerseys with red yoke
First Season: 1899-1900
Nickname: Robins
Chairman: Colin Hutton
Secretary: Ron Turner
Coach: Roger Millward MBE (Mar 1977-)
Honours: **Championship** Winners, 1922-23, 1924-25
               Beaten finalists, 1920-21, 1967-68
               First Division Champions, 1978-79, 1983-84, 1984-85
               Challenge Cup Winners, 1979-80
               Beaten finalists, 1904-05, 1924-25, 1963-64, 1980-81, 1985-86
               John Player Trophy Winners, 1984-85, Beaten finalists, 1981-82, 1985-86
               Premiership Winners, 1980-81, 1983-84, Beaten finalists, 1984-85
               Yorkshire League Winners, 1924-25, 1925-26
               Yorkshire Cup Winners, 1920-21, 1929-30, 1966-67, 1967-68, 1971-72, 1974-75, 1985-86
               Beaten finalists, 1906-07, 1911-12, 1933-34, 1962-63, 1975-76, 1980-81, 1984-85
               BBC2 Floodlit Trophy Winners, 1977-78
               Beaten finalists, 1979-80
               Eastern Division Championship Winners, 1962-63
               Charity Shield Beaten finalists, 1985-86
Records: Attendance: 22,282 v. Hull, 7 October, 1922. There was a crowd of 27,670 for a League match v. Hull at Hull City FC's Boothferry Park on 3 April, 1953

Season
Goals: 166 by G. Fairbairn, 1981-82
Tries: 45 by G. Prohm, 1984-85
Points: 366 by S. Hubbard, 1979-80
Match
Goals: 14 by A. Carmichael v. Merthyr Tydfil, 8 Oct, 1910
Tries: 11 by G. West v. Brookland R., 4 Mar, 1905
Points: 53 by G. West v. Brookland R., 4 Mar, 1905
Highest score: 73-5 v. Brookland R., 1904-05
Highest against: 68-0 v. Halifax, 1955-56

1986-87 PLAYERS' SUMMARY

	App	Tries	Goals	Dr	Pts
Beall, Malcolm	16 + 1	—	—	—	—
Boustead, Kerry	19 + 1	7	—	—	28
Broadhurst, Mark	24	1	—	—	4
Burton, Chris	24	1	—	—	4
Busby, Dave	5 + 2	2	—	—	8
Clark, Garry	25	10	—	—	40
Dorahy, John	29 + 1	11	51	—	146
Ema, Asuquo	26	3	—	—	12
Fairbairn, George	31	7	51	—	130
Fletcher, Mike	5 + 5	—	2	—	4
Harkin, Paul	14	2	—	6	14
Harrison, Des	22 + 4	—	—	—	—
Hogan, Phil	1	—	—	—	—
Kelly, Andy	31 + 7	8	—	—	32
Laws, David	22	4	—	—	16
Lydiat, John	22 + 4	4	—	—	16
Marchant, Billy	1 + 1	—	—	—	—
Miller, Gavin	14	2	—	—	8
Needler, Tony	0 + 1	—	—	—	—
Parker, Wayne	27 + 3	15	—	4	64
Rudd, Chris	14 + 10	2	—	—	8
Sims, Gary	2 + 2	—	—	—	—
Smith, Gordon	27 + 4	7	—	1	29
Smith, Mike	26	4	—	1	17
Smith, Steve	12 + 2	6	—	—	24
Speckman, Paul	12 + 3	1	—	—	4
Stead, Ray	25 + 9	7	—	—	28
Thompson, Andy	3 + 1	—	—	—	—
Watkinson, David	28 + 2	2	—	—	8

TOTALS:
29 players 106 104 12 644

1986-87 MATCH ANALYSIS

Date	Competition	H/A	Opponent	Rlt	Score	Tries	Goals	Attendance	Referee
31.8.86	SBC	A	Barrow	L	6-24	Laws	Fairbairn	—	—
3.9.86	SBC	H	Bradford N.	L	12-30	Fairbairn	Fairbairn (4)	4146	Lindop
7.9.86	SBC	H	Featherstone R.	W	36-14	Lydiat, Laws, Ema, Stead, Parker, Rudd, Kelly	Fairbairn (4)	4427	Smith
14.9.86	YC(1)	H	Huddersfield B.	W	52-30	Parker (2), Busby (2), Clark (2), Dorahy (2), Burton, Kelly	Fairbairn (6)	3736	Volante
21.9.86	SBC	A	Oldham	L	12-28	Clark, Laws	Fairbairn (2)	—	—
24.9.86	YC(2)	H	Featherstone R.	D	20-20	Ema, Watkinson, Kelly	Fairbairn (4)	3841	Berry
26.9.86	YC(2) replay	A	Featherstone R.	L	12-23	Stead (2)	Fairbairn, Dorahy	—	—
28.9.86	SBC	H	St Helens	L	4-36	—	Dorahy (2)	5208	Holdsworth
5.10.86	SBC	H	Hull	W	29-6	G. Smith, Parker, Dorahy, Kelly	Dorahy (6), M. Smith (dg)	7980	Fox
12.10.86	SBC	A	Salford	W	34-14	Boustead (2), Clark, M. Smith, Dorahy, Parker	Dorahy (4), Fairbairn	—	—
15.10.86	Tour	H	Australia	L	10-46	Boustead	Dorahy (3)	6868	Kershaw
26.10.86	SBC	H	Leigh	W	35-20	Fairbairn (2), Dorahy, Ema, G. Smith, Boustead, Rudd	Fairbairn (3), W. Parker (dg)	4186	Tennant
2.11.86	SBC	A	Widnes	L	8-26	Parker	Dorahy (2)	—	—
9.11.86	SBC	H	Oldham	W	6-4	—	Dorahy (2), Harkin (2 dg)	4481	Spencer
16.11.86	SBC	A	Halifax	L	18-24	Boustead, Lydiat, Fairbairn	Fairbairn (2), Dorahy	—	—
23.11.86	SBC	H	Wakefield T.	W	22-11	Clark (2), Dorahy, M. Smith	Dorahy (3)	3536	McDonald
30.11.86	JPS(1)	A	Doncaster	L	14-18	Kelly, G. Smith, Dorahy	Dorahy	—	—
14.12.86	SBC	A	Leeds	L	7-42	Broadhurst	Dorahy, Harkin (dg)	—	—
21.12.86	SBC	H	Widnes	W	18-0	Fairbairn (2)	Fairbairn (4), G. Smith (dg), Parker (dg)	3861	Fox
26.12.86	SBC	A	Castleford	L	10-16	Parker	Fairbairn (3)	—	—
1.1.87	SBC	H	Halifax	W	14-0	Fairbairn, S. Smith, Miller	Fairbairn	5402	Kendrew
4.1.87	SBC	A	Featherstone R.	W	14-0	Dorahy, S. Smith	Fairbairn (3)	—	—
25.1.87	SBC	H	Wigan	L	6-23	S. Smith	Fairbairn	7693	Allatt
3.2.87	CC(1)	H	Doncaster	W	29-14	Harkin, Dorahy, M. Smith, S. Smith, Miller	Fairbairn (3), Dorahy, Harkin (dg)	3826	Kendrew
8.2.87	SBC	A	Leigh	W	12-8	Stead, S. Smith	Dorahy (2)	—	—
15.2.87	CC(2)	H	Keighley	W	42-4	Dorahy (2), Lydiat (2), Parker, Kelly, Harkin	Dorahy (7)	4543	Volante
22.2.87	SBC	H	Leeds	W	10-6	Parker	Dorahy (2), Harkin (2dg)	4847	Tennant
28.2.87	CC(3)	A	Halifax	L	7-35	Stead	Dorahy, Parker (dg)	—	—
15.3.87	SBC	H	Warrington	W	14-10	G. Smith, Parker	Dorahy (3)	4152	Lindop
18.3.87	SBC	A	Bradford N.	L	6-24	Laws	Fairbairn	—	—
22.3.87	SBC	A	Wigan	L	0-26	—	—	—	—
25.3.87	SBC	H	Barrow	W	26-8	Kelly, Parker, G. Smith, Watkinson	Dorahy (5)	2343	Berry
29.3.87	SBC	A	St Helens	L	22-44	Clark, Parker, Stead, Speckman	Fletcher (2), Fairbairn	—	—
1.4.87	SBC	A	Wakefield T.	L	4-19	Clark	—	—	—
5.4.87	SBC	H	Salford	W	20-16	G. Smith, Stead, Kelly, Clark	Dorahy (2)	3084	Carter
12.4.87	SBC	A	Warrington	L	0-38	—	—	—	—
17.4.87	SBC	A	Hull	W	21-8	Clark, Boustead, Parker	Fairbairn (4), Parker (dg)	—	—
20.4.87	SBC	H	Castleford	W	20-6	Parker (2), M. Smith, Boustead	Fairbairn (2)	4421	McDonald
26.4.87	PT(1)	A	Warrington	L	12-24	S. Smith, G. Smith	Dorahy (2)	—	—

HUNSLET

Ground: Elland Road
Colours: Myrtle, flame and white jerseys
First Season: 1895-96. Disbanded at end of 1972-73. Re-formed as New Hunslet in 1973-74. Retitled Hunslet from start of 1979-80
Chairman: Jerry Mason
Secretary: John Moses
Coaches: Peter Jarvis (Nov 1985-) and David Ward (July 1986-)
Honours: **Challenge Cup** Winners, 1907-08, 1933-34
Beaten finalists, 1898-99, 1964-65
Championship Winners, 1907-08, 1937-38
Beaten finalists, 1958-59
Division Two Champions, 1962-63, 1986-87
Second Division Premiership Beaten finalists, 1986-87
Yorkshire Cup Winners, 1905-06, 1907-08, 1962-63
Beaten finalists, 1908-09, 1929-30, 1931-32, 1944-45, 1956-57, 1965-66
Yorkshire League Winners, 1897-98, 1907-08, 1931-32
Records: Attendance: 54,112 v. Leeds (Championship final) 30 Apr, 1938
Season
Goals: 181 by W. Langton, 1958-59
Tries: 34 by A. Snowden, 1956-57
Points: 380 by W. Langton, 1958-59
Match
Goals: 12 by W. Langton v. Keighley, 18 Aug, 1959

Tries: 7 by G. Dennis v. Bradford N., 20 Jan, 1934
Points: 27 by W. Langton v. Keighley, 18 Aug, 1959
Highest score: 75-5 v. Broughton Rec., 1896-97
Highest against: 76-8 v. Halifax, 1972-73

1986-87 PLAYERS' SUMMARY

	App	Tries	Goals	Dr	Pts
Arnold, Bob	13 + 1	4	—	—	16
Bateman, Andy	25	12	—	—	48
Bell, Mick	33	17	4	—	76
Bowden, Chris	10 + 24	3	—	—	12
Coates, Ged	33	10	—	—	40
Dufton, Steve	1	—	—	—	—
Gibson, Phil	17 + 2	2	—	—	8
Irvine, Jimmy	19 + 5	6	—	—	24
Jennings, Graeme	33 + 1	15	—	1	61
Kay, Andy	34	12	8	—	64
King, Graham	12 + 2	6	—	—	24
Lay, Steve	1	1	—	—	4
Marson, Andy	7 + 3	3	—	—	12
Mason, Keith	19 + 1	—	—	—	—
Milton, Roy	24 + 2	5	—	—	20
Mitchell, Keith	1 + 5	—	—	—	—
Morgan, Paul	1 + 3	—	—	—	—
Murrell, Bryan	2 + 1	1	—	—	4
Nicholson, Steve	7 + 1	3	—	—	12
Nickle, Sonny	1	1	—	—	4
Penola, Colin	13 + 3	7	—	—	28
Platt, Alan	33 + 1	9	102	—	240
Rowse, Gary	1 + 3	—	1	—	2
Senior, Gary	24 + 8	8	—	—	32
Skerrett, Kelvin	13	6	—	—	24
Sykes, Andy	9	—	—	—	—
Tate, Phil	23 + 2	11	—	—	44
Warrener, Stan	0 + 2	—	—	—	—
Webb, Terry	33	10	1	—	42
Wilkinson, Shaun	1	1	—	—	4
Wilson, Warren	24	11	—	—	44
Trialist	1	—	—	—	—

TOTALS:
32 players		164	116	1	889

1986-87 MATCH ANALYSIS

Date	Competition	H/A	Opponent	Rlt	Score	Tries	Goals	Attendance	Referee
31.8.86	SD	A	Runcorn H.	W	36-0	Skerrett (2), Marson, Bell, Platt (4) Platt, Wilson, Morrell		—	—
7.9.86	SD	H	Dewsbury	W	22-12	Skerrett, Webb, Kay, Wilson	Platt (3)	1220	Kendrew

MATCH ANALYSIS (continued)

14.9.86	YC(1)	H	Bradford N.	L	12-40	Milton	Platt (4)	3101	Berry
21.9.86	SD	H	Workington T.	W	38-5	Wilson (2), Coates (2), Tate, Webb, Platt	Platt (5)	636	Volante
28.9.86	SD	A	Doncaster	W	22-18	Kay (2), Marson	Platt (5)	—	—
5.10.86	SD	H	Batley	W	36-10	Platt, Bell, Bateman, Tate, Jennings, Coates	Platt (6)	1155	Whitfield
12.10.86	SD	A	Keighley	W	24-1	Arnold, Platt, Webb, Jennings	Platt (4)	—	—
19.10.86	SD	A	Huddersfield B.	W	26-10	Arnold, Bateman, Kay, Bowden, Penola	Platt (3)	—	—
26.10.86	SD	H	Carlisle	W	20-8	Milton, Jennings, Kay	Platt (4)	772	Hodgson
2.11.86	SD	A	Fulham	W	16-4	Bowden, Nicholson, Coates	Platt (2)	—	—
9.11.86	SD	A	York	W	26-13	Bell (2), Skerrett (2), Senior	Platt (3)	—	—
16.11.86	SD	H	Runcorn H.	W	22-14	Nicholson, Platt, Coates, Jennings	Platt (2), Bell	747	Mean
23.11.86	SD	H	Swinton	W	12-4	Webb, Nicholson	Platt (2)	1635	Allatt
30.11.86	JPS(1)	A	Warrington	L	10-11	Coates, Irvine	Platt	—	—
7.12.86	SD	A	Mansfield M.	W	42-2	Senior (3), Platt, Irvine, Skerrett, Webb, Bell, Milton	Bell (3)	—	—
14.12.86	SD	A	Carlisle	L	8-11	Marson, Kay	—	—	—
21.12.86	SD	H	Huddersfield B.	W	52-6	Arnold (2), Senior (2), Kay, Platt, Coates, Webb, Penola, King	Platt (6)	950	Houghton
26.12.86	SD	A	Bramley	W	16-2	Kay, Penola, Tate	Platt (2)	—	—
1.1.87	SD	H	Bramley	W	34-8	Jennings (2), Bell (2), Penola, Webb, Bateman	Platt (3)	1113	Carter
11.1.87	SD	H	Mansfield M.	W	12-6	Bell, Kay	Platt (2)	743	Bowman
18.1.87	CC(P)	H	York	W	13-0	Tate, Kay	Platt (2), Jennings (dg)	1351	Whitfield
25.1.87	SD	A	Dewsbury	W	36-8	Tate (2), Jennings, Wilson, Bateman, Irvine, King	Platt (4)	—	—
4.2.87	CC(1)	A	Featherstone R.	W	26-12	Jennings (2), Coates, Bateman, Bell	Platt (3)	—	—
8.2.87	SD	H	Keighley	W	24-6	Bell (2), Gibson, Webb, Coates	Platt (2)	920	Hodgson
15.2.87	CC(2)	A	Halifax	L	10-29	Bell, Tate	Kay	—	—
22.2.87	SD	H	Sheffield E.	W	18-10	Bateman (2), Milton, Wilson	Kay	923	Tickle
1.3.87	SD	A	Swinton	L	12-14	Bateman, Bell	Kay (2)	—	—
15.3.87	SD	H	Fulham	W	30-4	Bell (3), Jennings, King, Wilson	Platt (3)	754	Ainui (PNG)
22.3.87	SD	A	Workington T.	W	34-2	Tate (2), Bell, Webb, Jennings, King	Platt (5)	—	—
29.3.87	SD	A	Sheffield E.	L	12-16	Jennings, Bowden	Platt (2)	—	—
5.4.87	SD	H	Doncaster	W	16-10	Platt, Irvine, Gibson	Platt (2)	1946	McDonald
12.4.87	SD	A	Batley	W	34-4	Coates, Senior, King, Webb, Bateman, Jennings	Kay (4), Webb	—	—
20.4.87	SD	H	York	W	42-10	Tate (2), Lay, Wilkinson, Milton, Irvine, Wilson, Nickle	Platt (4), Rowse	1186	Mean
26.4.87	SDP(1)	H	Carlisle	W	54-0	Wilson (2), Kay (2), Penola (2), Bateman, Jennings, Senior	Platt (9)	1135	McDonald
10.5.87	SDP(SF)	H	Rochdale H.	W	32-8	King, Jennings, Platt, Penola, Irvine, Wilson	Platt (4)	1953	Spencer
17.5.87	SDP(F)	Man U. FC	Swinton	L	10-27	Bateman (2)	Platt	(—)	McDonald

KEIGHLEY

Ground:	Lawkholme Lane
Colours:	Green, scarlet and white jerseys
First Season:	1901-02
Nickname:	Lawkholmers
Chairman:	Colin Farrar
Secretary:	Betty Spencer
Coach:	Peter Roe (Sep 1985-July 1986)
	Colin Dixon and Les Coulter (July 1986-)
Honours:	**Division Two** Champions, 1902-03
	Challenge Cup Beaten finalists, 1936-37
	Yorkshire Cup Beaten finalists, 1943-44, 1951-52
Records:	Attendance: 14,500 v. Halifax (RL Cup) 3 Mar, 1951

Season
Goals: 155 by B. Jefferson, 1973-74
Tries: 30 by J. Sherburn, 1934-35
Points: 331 by B. Jefferson, 1973-74

Match
Goals: 11 by R. Walker v. Castleford, 13 Jan, 1906; H. Cook v. Hull K.R., 31 Oct, 1953
Tries: 5 by I. Jagger v. Castleford, 13 Jan, 1906; S. Stacey v. Liverpool C., 9 Mar, 1907
Points: 24 by J. Phillips v. Halifax, 5 Oct, 1957
Highest score: 67-0 v. Castleford, 1905-06
Highest against: 92-2 v. Leigh, 1985-86

1986-87 PLAYERS' SUMMARY

	App	Tries	Goals	Dr	Pts
Anderson, Tony	5	3	—	—	12
Atkinson, Colin	18	4	—	—	16
Barrett, David	9	—	—	—	—
Bragger, Ian	24	6	—	—	24
Butterfield, Jeff	27	5	—	—	20
Cerchione, Mario	1	—	—	—	—
Dixon, Keith	21	7	40	1	109
Dwyer, Mark	5 + 1	—	—	—	—
Ellis, Kevin	2 + 1	1	—	—	4
Fairbank, Andy	7 + 8	2	—	—	8
Fairbank, Mark	1	—	—	—	—
Fairhurst, Ian	2 + 1	1	—	—	4
Fogerty, Adam	0 + 1	—	—	—	—
Goodier, Frank	15 + 4	—	—	—	—
Gorman, Mick	1	—	—	—	—
Greenwood, Brett	0 + 1	—	—	—	—
Gregoire, Don	5 + 3	—	—	—	—
Gudor, Mark	4	—	—	—	—
Hawksworth, Mick	6	3	—	—	12
Kelly, Mick	0 + 5	—	—	—	—
McCaffrey, David	7 + 1	2	—	—	8
McCaffrey, Mick	1 + 4	—	—	—	—
McInerney, Mark	27 + 1	1	—	—	4
McLaren, Guy	1	—	—	—	—
Moses, Paul	17 + 1	2	—	4	12
Page, Steve	3	—	3	—	6
Perrett, Haydn	0 + 1	—	—	—	—
Pitts, John	23 + 6	2	1	—	10
Proctor, Rob	24 + 1	2	—	—	8
Ragan, Mark	23 + 6	6	3	—	30
Raiterie, Rob	2 + 4	1	—	—	4
Richardson, Peter	32	8	—	—	32
Robinson, Kevan	19	—	—	1	1
Roe, Peter	16 + 1	—	—	—	—
Sharkey, John	0 + 1	—	—	—	—
Townsley, Paul	0 + 1	—	—	—	—
Turner, Fred	6	—	—	—	—
Tyrers, Andy	5	1	—	—	4
Waller, Vin	5	3	—	—	12
Walsh, Tim	15 + 1	—	—	—	—
Welsh, Paul	4 + 5	1	—	—	4
White, Steve	6 + 1	3	6	—	24
Winterbottom, Ricky	27	4	—	—	16

TOTALS:
43 players .... 68 | 53 | 6 | 384

| | | 68 | 53 | 6 | 384 |

1986-87 MATCH ANALYSIS

Date	Com-petition	H/A	Opponent	Rlt	Score	Tries	Goals	Atten-dance	Referee
31.8.86	SD	A	Huddersfield B.	L	16-27	Butterfield, Ellis, White	Page (2)	—	—
2.9.86	SD	A	Runcorn H.	L	6-20	White	Page	—	—
7.9.86	SD	H	Sheffield E.	L	16-29	Hawksworth, Atkinson, Richardson	Pitts, White	448	Volante
12.9.86	YC(1)	A	Leeds	L	4-40	Hawksworth	—	—	—
21.9.86	SD	A	Whitehaven	L	6-44	Pitts	Ragan	—	—
28.9.86	SD	H	Carlisle	W	16-6	Atkinson (2), White	White (2)	387	Lindop
5.10.86	SD	A	Fulham	L	12-44	Richardson, Hawksworth	White (2)	—	—
12.10.86	SD	H	Hunslet	L	1-24	—	Moses (dg)	827	Tickle
19.10.86	SD	A	Blackpool B.	L	10-26	Bragger, Richardson	White	—	—
26.10.86	SD	H	Whitehaven	L	4-26	Richardson	—	299	Cross
2.11.86	SD	A	Carlisle	W	26-16	Moses, Winterbottom, Raiteri, Proctor	Dixon (5)	—	—
9.11.86	SD	H	Batley	L	17-18	Richardson, Winterbottom, Bragger	Dixon (2), Moses (dg)	551	Carter
16.11.86	SD	H	Bramley	L	12-18	Richardson, Bragger	Dixon, Moses (2 dg)	492	Simpson
23.11.86	SD	A	Rochdale H.	L	8-28	Butterfield	Dixon (2)	—	—
4.12.86	JPS(1)	A (at Penrith)	Carlisle	L	2-8	—	Dixon	—	—
14.12.86	SD	H	Doncaster	L	6-24	Proctor	Dixon	661	Smith
21.12.86	SD	H	Runcorn H.	W	22-10	Richardson, Butterfield, D. McCaffrey, Ragan	Dixon (3)	347	McDonald
1.1.87	SD	H	Blackpool B.	W	10-2	Dixon, Butterfield	Dixon	366	Fox
25.1.87	SD	A	Batley	L	8-16	Ragan	Dixon (2)	—	—
5.2.87	CC(1)	A	Sheffield E.	W	8-6	Dixon, D. McCaffrey	—	—	—
8.2.87	SD	A	Hunslet	L	6-24	Welsh	Dixon	—	—
15.2.87	CC(2)	A	Hull K.R.	L	4-42	Pitts	—	—	—
22.2.87	SD	H	Huddersfield B.	W	29-18	Anderson (2), Bragger, Winterbottom, McInerney	Dixon (4), Robinson (dg)	474	Cross
1.3.87	SD	A	Sheffield E.	L	15-18	Ragan, Atkinson, Butterfield	Dixon (1, 1dg)	—	—
8.3.87	SD	A	Workington T.	L	22-34	Bragger (2), Ragan, Anderson	Dixon (2), Ragan	—	—
15.3.87	SD	H	Mansfield M.	L	6-12	Dixon	Dixon	322	Tickle
22.3.87	SD	A	Doncaster	L	6-50	Fairhurst	Dixon	—	—
29.3.87	SD	H	Rochdale H.	L	18-30	Dixon (2), Ragan	Dixon (3)	576	Kendrew
4.4.87	SD	H	Fulham	W	22-9	Moses, Dixon, Waller, A. Fairbank	Dixon (3)	216	Lindop
15.4.87	SD	H	Workington T.	W	32-22	Waller (2), Richardson, Dixon, Winterbottom	Dixon (6)	262	Simpson
17.4.87	SD	A	Bramley	L	4-34	A. Fairbank	—	—	—
20.4.87	SD	A	Mansfield M.	L	10-12	Ragan, Tyers	Ragan	—	—

LEEDS

Ground:	Headingley
Colours:	Blue and amber jerseys
First Season:	1895-96
Nickname:	Loiners
Chairman:	Bernard Coulby
General Manager:	Joe Warham
Coach:	Peter Fox (May 1985-Dec 1986)
	Maurice Bamford (Dec 1986-)

Honours: **Championship** Winners, 1960-61, 1968-69, 1971-72
Beaten finalists, 1914-15, 1928-29, 1929-30, 1930-31, 1937-38, 1969-70, 1972-73
League Leaders Trophy Winners, 1966-67, 1967-68, 1968-69, 1969-70, 1971-72
Challenge Cup Winners, 1909-10, 1922-23, 1931-32, 1935-36, 1940-41, 1941-42, 1956-57, 1967-68, 1976-77, 1977-78
Beaten finalists, 1942-43, 1946-47, 1970-71, 1971-72
Yorkshire League Winners, 1901-02, 1927-28, 1930-31, 1933-34, 1934-35, 1936-37, 1937-38, 1950-51, 1954-55, 1956-57, 1960-61, 1966-67, 1967-68, 1968-69, 1969-70
Yorkshire Cup Winners, 1921-22, 1928-29, 1930-31, 1932-33, 1934-35, 1935-36, 1937-38, 1958-59, 1968-69, 1970-71, 1972-73, 1973-74, 1975-76, 1976-77, 1979-80, 1980-81
Beaten finalists, 1919-20, 1947-48, 1961-62, 1964-65
BBC2 Floodlit Trophy Winners, 1970-71
John Player Trophy Winners, 1972-73, 1983-84
Beaten finalists, 1982-83
Premiership Winners, 1974-75, 1978-79

Records: Attendance: 40,175 v. Bradford N. (League) 21 May, 1947
Season
Goals: 166 by B.L. Jones, 1956-57
Tries: 63 by E. Harris, 1935-36
Points: 431 by B.L. Jones, 1956-57

Match
Goals: 13 by B.L. Jones v. Blackpool B., 19 Aug, 1957
Tries: 8 by F. Webster v. Coventry, 12 Apr, 1913; E. Harris v. Bradford N., 14 Sep, 1931
Points: 31 by B.L. Jones v. Bradford N., 22 Aug, 1956
Highest score: 102-0 v. Coventry, 1912-13
Highest against: 71-0 v. Wakefield T., 1945-46

1986-87 PLAYERS' SUMMARY

	App	Tries	Goals	Dr	Pts
Armitage, Des	1	—	—	—	—
Ashton, Ray	15	1	—	2	6
Butt, Kurshid (Tony)	4 + 2	—	—	—	—
Clark, Trevor	7 + 7	2	—	—	8
Conway, Mark	17 + 5	10	27	—	94
Cooper, Colin	2 + 2	—	—	—	—
Creasser, David	29 + 1	13	48	—	148
Dick, Kevin	4	4	—	—	16
Ettingshausen, Andrew	20	17	—	—	68
Fox, Phil	18	6	—	—	24
Francis, Norman	19 + 1	3	—	—	12
Gascoigne, Andy	6	—	—	—	—
Gibson, Carl	26	13	—	—	52
Gill, Paul	4 + 1	—	4	—	8
Grayshon, Jeff	8	—	—	—	—
Gunn, Richard	2 + 6	—	—	—	—
Healy, David	4 + 1	1	—	—	4
Heron, David	31	5	—	—	20
Hill, Brendan	5 + 1	1	—	—	4
Holmes, John	28 + 3	3	—	2	14
Johnson, Erroll	2	—	—	—	—
Maskill, Colin	25 + 1	1	4	—	12
Mason, Andy	17	5	—	—	20
McGaw, Mark	16	6	—	—	24
Medley, Paul	22 + 4	11	—	—	44
Moorby, Gary	5 + 5	—	—	—	—
Morris, Bob	10	1	—	—	4
Owen, Phil	3	—	—	—	—
Powell, Roy	20 + 1	6	—	—	24
Pratt, Richard	3	—	—	—	—
Price, Gary	14 + 6	2	—	—	8
Rayne, Keith	7 + 4	1	—	—	4
Rayne, Kevin	25 + 5	4	—	—	16
Sharp, Henry	5	—	—	—	—
Skerrett, Trevor	27 + 2	1	—	—	4
Smith, Andy	5	—	—	—	—
Smith, Peter	7 + 2	—	—	—	—
Staniland, Andrew	1	—	—	—	—
Turner, Phil	2 + 1	—	—	—	—
Wilkes, Mark	1	—	2	—	4
Wilkinson, Ian	14	6	1	—	26
Wilson, Mark	0 + 1	—	—	—	—
TOTALS: 42 players		123	86	4	668

1986-87 MATCH ANALYSIS

Date	Competition	H/A	Opponent	Rlt	Score	Tries	Goals	Attendance	Referee
31.8.86	SBC	A	Oldham	L	12-14	Medley, Dick	Creasser, Conway	—	—
3.9.86	SBC	H	Featherstone R.	W	33-12	Gibson (2), Medley (2), Hill, Conway	Gill (4), Holmes (dg)	5496	Whitfield
7.9.86	SBC	H	St Helens	L	20-40	Gibson (2), Dick, Medley	Creasser (2)	7675	Carter
12.9.86	YC(1)	H	Keighley	W	40-4	Dick (2), Creasser (2), Morris, Heron, Gibson, Medley	Creasser (4)	2862	Cross
24.9.86	YC(2)	A	Castleford	L	16-38	Kevin Rayne, Creasser, Gibson	Conway (2)	—	—
28.9.86	SBC	A	Widnes	L	10-35	Kevin Rayne, Holmes	Creasser	—	—
5.10.86	SBC	H	Salford	W	46-10	Wilkinson (3), Creasser (2), Francis, Ettingshausen, Skerrett	Creasser (7)	6346	Kershaw
12.10.86	SBC	A	Halifax	L	8-23	Ettingshausen (2)	—	—	—
19.10.86	Tour	H	Australia	L	0-40	—	—	11389	Whitfield
26.10.86	SBC	H	Bradford N.	L	4-12	Ettingshausen	—	7514	McDonald
2.11.86	SBC	A	Hull	W	32-10	Ettingshausen (2), Conway (2), Heron, Mason	Creasser (4)	—	—
9.11.86	SBC	A	Wakefield T.	W	28-14	Creasser (2), Mason (2), Heron	Creasser (4)	—	—
16.11.86	SBC	H	Warrington	L	16-54	Wilkinson, Price, Mason	Conway (2)	6993	Beaumont
23.11.86	SBC	A	Leigh	L	8-20	Price	Creasser (2)	—	—
29.11.86	JPS(1)	A	Wigan	L	10-32	Wilkinson, McGaw	Conway	—	—
14.12.86	SBC	H	Hull K.R.	W	42-7	Ettingshausen, Medley, Kevin Rayne, Conway, McGaw, Francis, Fox	Conway (7)	5853	Simpson
21.12.86	SBC	A	Barrow	W	23-16	Fox (2), Holmes, Francis	Conway (3), Holmes (dg)	—	—
26.12.86	SBC	H	Wakefield T.	W	46-4	Ettingshausen (3), Conway (2), Creasser, Gibson, Powell	Conway (5), Creasser (2)	8616	Tennant
1.1.87	SBC	H	Oldham	L	20-26	Ettingshausen (2), Conway, McGaw	Conway (2)	7925	Haigh
4.1.87	SBC	A	Warrington	L	6-20	Creasser	Conway	—	—
11.1.87	SBC	H	Leigh	W	26-12	Ettingshausen (2), Creasser, Fox, Kevin Rayne, Powell	Creasser	5675	Tickle
25.1.87	SBC	H	Widnes	W	35-6	Fox (2), Holmes, Clark, McGaw, Gibson	Creasser (5), Ashton (dg)	6252	Kershaw
1.2.87	CC(1)	A	Salford	W	4-0	Gibson	—	—	—
8.2.87	SBC	A	Castleford	W	14-12	Mason, Ashton, Powell	Maskill	—	—
15.2.87	CC(2)	H	Barrow	W	26-7	McGaw (2), Ettingshausen (2), Powell	Maskill (3)	7849	Carter
18.2.87	SBC	A	Wigan	L	8-30	Ettingshausen, Medley	—	—	—
22.2.87	SBC	A	Hull K.R.	L	6-10	Gibson	Wilkinson	—	—
1.3.87	CC(3)	H	Widnes	L	7-14	Heron	Creasser, Ashton (dg)	14791	Lindop
8.3.87	SBC	A	Salford	W	14-12	Wilkinson, Creasser, Keith Rayne	Creasser	—	—
11.3.87	SBC	H	Wigan	L	0-30	—	—	8309	Smith
15.3.87	SBC	H	Hull	W	28-22	Medley (2), Clark, Maskill, Gibson	Conway (3), Creassor	5563	Whitfield
22.3.87	SBC	A	Featherstone R.	L	14-29	Powell (2), Gibson	Creasser	—	—
29.3.87	SBC	H	Barrow	W	14-4	Medley (2)	Wilkes (2), Creasser	4517	Lindop
5.4.87	SBC	A	St Helens	L	22-24	Heron, Creasser, Conway	Creasser (5)	—	—
12.4.87	SBC	H	Castleford	L	8-16	Gibson	Creasser (2)	5936	Haigh
17.4.87	SBC	A	Bradford N.	L	10-23	Conway, Creasser	Creasser	—	—
20.4.87	SBC	H	Halifax	L	12-24	Healey, Conway	Creasser (2)	6386	Beaumont

LEIGH

Ground:	Hilton Park
Colours:	Red and white jerseys
First Season:	1895-96
Chairman:	Brian Sharples
General Manager:	John Stringer
Coach:	Tommy Dickens (Nov 1985-Dec 1986). Billy Benyon (Dec 1986-)
Honours:	**Championship** Winners, 1905-06
	Division One Champions, 1981-82
	Division Two Champions, 1977-78, 1985-86
	Challenge Cup Winners, 1920-21, 1970-71
	Lancashire Cup Winners, 1952-53, 1955-56, 1970-71, 1981-82
	Beaten finalists, 1905-06, 1909-10, 1920-21, 1922-23, 1949-50, 1951-52, 1963-64, 1969-70
	BBC2 Trophy Winners, 1969-70, 1972-73
	Beaten finalists, 1967-68, 1976-77
Records:	Attendance: 31,324 v. St. Helens (RL Cup) 14 Mar, 1953
	Season
	Goals: 173 by C. Johnson, 1985-86
	Tries: 49 by S. Halliwell, 1985-86
	Points: 400 by C. Johnson, 1985-86
	Match
	Goals: 15 by M. Stacey v. Doncaster, 28 Mar, 1976
	Tries: 6 by J. Wood v. York, 4 Oct, 1947
	Points: 38 by J. Woods v. Blackpool B., 11 Sep, 1977
	Highest score: 92-2 v. Keighley, 1985-86
	Highest against: 60-8 v. Salford, 1940

1986-87 PLAYERS' SUMMARY

	App	Tries	Goals	Dr	Pts
Atherton, Wayne	9 + 1	1	14	—	32
Bentley, Keith	4	1	—	—	4
Collier, Andy	20 + 10	3	—	—	12
Cottrell, Tony	33 + 4	1	—	—	4
Davis, Mike	25 + 6	10	—	—	40
Dean, Mike	23 + 4	3	—	—	12
Evans, David	5	2	—	—	8
Ford, Mike	10	5	—	—	20
Fox, Phil	10	3	—	—	12
Gelling, Bryan	13	2	—	—	8
Gormally, Joe	1	—	—	—	—
Hardman, Paul	0 + 1	—	—	—	—
Henderson, John	29	27	—	—	108
Howell, Garry	6 + 2	1	—	—	4
Huddart, Milton	24 + 1	1	—	1	5
Hughes, Gary	8 + 4	—	—	—	—
Jeffrey, Ian	14 + 3	6	2	—	28
Johnson, Chris	28	1	84	2	174
Johnson, Phil	11 + 7	4	9	1	35
Kerr, John	33 + 1	8	—	—	32
Leuluai, James	25	6	—	—	24
Manfredi, Tony	7 + 3	1	—	—	4
McCulloch, Neil	38	13	—	—	52
Mellor, Sean	4 + 2	1	—	—	4
Owen, Ivor	10	1	—	—	4
Pyke, Derek	30 + 1	2	—	—	8
Ramsdale, Darren	6	—	—	—	—
Riding, Colin	12 + 1	2	1	—	10
Robinson, Nigel	0 + 2	—	—	—	—
Round, Mike	1	—	—	—	—
Schubert, Ian	21	3	3	—	18
Tabern, Ray	8 + 1	2	—	—	8
Thomas, Mark	4 + 1	—	—	—	—
Walkden, Gary	2	—	—	—	—
Westhead, John	20 + 3	6	—	—	24
TOTALS:					
35 players		116	113	4	694

Six tries in 25 games for James Leuluai, on extended loan from Hull.

1986-87 MATCH ANALYSIS

Date	Competition	H/A	Opponent	Rlt	Score	Tries	Goals	Attendance	Referee
31.8.86	SBC	A	St Helens	L	18-50	Henderson (2)	C. Johnson (3), P. Johnson (2)	—	—
4.9.86	SBC	H	Warrington	W	22-17	Fox, Riding, McCulloch, Davis, Manfredi	Riding	4434	Kershaw
7.9.86	SBC	H	Wigan	L	0-35	—	—	12391	Fox
14.9.86	LC(1)	A	Oldham	L	22-29	Henderson (2), Fox, Kerr	Schubert (3)	—	—
21.9.86	SBC	A	Hull	L	26-31	Cottrell, Henderson, Gelling, Fox	C. Johnson (5)	—	—
28.9.86	SBC	H	Oldham	W	40-12	Davis, Gelling, Pyke, McCulloch, Collier, Kerr	Atherton (5), C. Johnson (3)	4571	Carter
5.10.86	SBC	A	Featherstone R.	L	16-50	Tabern, Kerr, Atherton	Atherton (2)	—	—
12.10.86	SBC	A	Wakefield T.	W	12-6	Howell, Tabern	Atherton (2)	—	—
19.10.86	SBC	H	Widnes	L	18-20	Kerr, Davis, Henderson	Atherton (3)	3466	Allatt
26.10.86	SBC	A	Hull K.R.	L	20-35	McCulloch, Davis, Dean, Henderson	Atherton (2)	—	—
2.11.86	SBC	A	Castleford	L	8-19	Henderson (2)	—	—	—
9.11.86	SBC	H	Halifax	L	20-28	Leuluai, C. Johnson, Owen	C. Johnson (4)	4889	Cross
16.11.86	SBC	A	Wigan	L	0-31	—	—	—	—
23.11.86	SBC	H	Leeds	W	20-8	Henderson, Westhead, Dean	C. Johnson (4)	2626	Mean
30.11.86	JPS(1)	H	Rochdale H.	W	32-10	Henderson (2), Huddart, Schubert, Miller, Davis	C. Johnson (4)	2754	McDonald
7.12.86	JPS(2)	H	Doncaster	W	26-14	Henderson (2), Collier, Davis	C. Johnson (5)	3363	Tickle
14.12.86	JPS(3)	A	Wigan	L	2-6	—	C. Johnson	—	—
26.12.86	SBC	H	Barrow	D	9-9	McCulloch	C. Johnson (2, 1dg)	2690	Bowman
1.1.87	SBC	A	Salford	L	12-20	McCulloch (2)	C. Johnson (2)	—	—
4.1.87	SBC	H	Castleford	L	6-12	McCulloch	C. Johnson	2732	Spencer
11.1.87	SBC	A	Leeds	L	12-26	Riding, Pyke	C. Johnson (2)	—	—
25.1.87	SBC	A	Bradford N.	W	26-18	Westhead (2), Bentley, Schubert	C. Johnson (5)	—	—
4.2.87	CC(1)	A	Runcorn H.	W	25-6	Schubert, Westhead, Leuluai	C. Johnson (6), P. Johnson (dg)	—	—
8.2.87	SBC	H	Hull K.R.	L	8-12	Westhead, P. Johnson	—	2516	Haigh
15.2.87	CC(2)	H	Carlisle	W	18-6	Dean, Leuluai, Jeffrey	P. Johnson (3)	3062	Bowman
22.2.87	SBC	A	Halifax	L	24-43	Henderson (2), McCulloch, Jeffrey	C. Johnson (4)	—	—
1.3.87	CC(3)	A	Hull	W	12-8	Kerr, Davis	C. Johnson (2)	—	—
8.3.87	SBC	A	Barrow	W	27-16	Jeffrey (2), Davis, P. Johnson, Leuluai	C. Johnson (3, 1dg)	—	—
14.3.87	CC(SF)	Wigan	St Helens	L	8-14	McCulloch	C. Johnson (2)	(13105)	Whitfield
18.3.87	SBC	H	Featherstone R.	W	20-18	Henderson (2), P. Johnson	C. Johnson (4)	2509	Spencer
22.3.87	SBC	H	Hull	W	22-10	Henderson (3), McCulloch (2)	C. Johnson	2919	Carter
25.3.87	SBC	H	St Helens	L	8-16	Kerr	Jeffrey (2)	5276	Allatt
29.3.87	SBC	H	Bradford N.	W	18-16	Westhead, Davis, Ford	C. Johnson (3)	3855	Hodgson
1.4.87	SBC	A	Widnes	W	10-8	Henderson, Collier	C. Johnson	—	—
5.4.87	SBC	H	Wakefield T.	W	46-8	Jeffrey (2), Ford (2), McCulloch, Evans, Leuluai, Henderson, Kerr	C. Johnson (5)	3163	Beaumont
9.4.87	SBC	H	Salford	L	10-14	Henderson	C. Johnson (3)	5441	Mean
12.4.87	SBC	A	Oldham	W	54-12	Ford (2), Henderson, McCulloch, Evans, Leuluai, Davis, Kerr, P. Johnson	C. Johnson (5), P. Johnson (4)	—	—
20.4.87	SBC	A	Warrington	W	17-10	Henderson (2)	C. Johnson (4), Huddart (dg)	—	—

MANSFIELD MARKSMAN

Ground: Alfreton Sports Stadium
Colours: Green and yellow
First Season: 1984-85
Chairman: Paul Tomlinson
General
  Manager: David Parker
Coach: Steve Dennison (Apr-Dec 1986)
  Jim Crellin (Dec 1986-)
Records: Attendance: 2,291 v. Wakefield T.
  (Div. 2) 9 Sep, 1984
  Season
  Goals: 63 by C. Sanderson, 1984-85
  Tries: 13 by S. Nicholson,
      K. Whiteman, 1984-85
  Points: 136 by C. Sanderson,
  1984-85
  Match
  Goals: 7 by B. Holden v. Keighley,
  10 Mar, 1985
  Tries: 4 by K. Whiteman v.
  Doncaster, 4 Nov, 1984
  Points: 18 by B. Holden v.
  Keighley, 10 Mar, 1985
  Highest score: 54-10 v. Doncaster,
  1984-85
  Highest against: 76-6 v. Leigh,
  1985-86

John Buckton, 22 points in 22 games.

1986-87 PLAYERS' SUMMARY

	App	Tries	Goals	Dr	Pts
Barrett, Mark	5 + 1	—	—	—	—
Blackmore, Peter	11 + 1	—	—	—	—
Buckton, John	16 + 6	2	7	—	22
Chadwick, Darren	5	—	—	—	—
Chadwick, Les	4	—	—	—	—
Cochrane, Tony	15	1	—	—	4
Crossingham, Mark	7	1	15	—	34
Deakin, Chris	2	—	—	—	—
Dennison, Steve	4 + 2	—	—	—	—
Duffy, Andy	27 + 1	—	—	—	—
Edginton, Dave	23 + 4	—	—	—	—
Fletcher, Andrew	22 + 1	6	—	—	24
Fletcher, Colin	9 + 2	—	—	—	—
Gentle, Peter	10	4	—	—	16
Gillespie, Steve	1	—	—	—	—
Grix, Wayne	19 + 5	5	—	—	20
Holden, Barry	4 + 1	—	—	—	—
Hooper, Mick	11 + 1	4	—	—	16
Hough, Mick	8 + 3	—	—	—	—
Humphries, Lee	2	—	—	—	—
Jackson, Robert	3	—	—	—	—
Kellett, Neil	17 + 1	4	—	—	16
King, Craig	6 + 1	1	—	—	4
Langton, Terry	14 + 2	6	—	—	24
Lawrence, Steve	5	—	—	—	—
Leary, Simon	3	—	—	—	—
Lord, Mark	1	—	—	—	—
Loynes, Dean	0 + 1	—	—	—	—
McRohon, Dave	1	—	—	—	—
Morrell, Wayne	1	—	—	—	—
Oates, David	14	1	16	—	36
Ogburn, John	5	1	—	—	4
O'Grady, Gerry	10 + 4	1	—	1	5
Pflaster, George	1 + 1	1	—	—	4
Platt, Billy	10	2	8	11	35
Portz, Karl	2 + 1	—	—	—	—
Robinson, George	0 + 3	—	—	—	—
Sanderson, Carl	7 + 1	—	2	2	6
Sealey, Camrul	1	—	—	—	—
Simpson, Colin	5	—	8	—	16
Smith, Keith	5 + 5	1	2	—	8
Stevens, Darren	15	3	—	—	12
Thompson, Courtney	25	7	—	—	28
Topping, Paul	6	—	13	4	30
Tupaea, Shane	23 + 1	4	—	—	16
Westbury, Mark	3	1	—	—	4
Whitehead, Craig	4 + 3	—	—	—	—
Williams, Tony	7	—	—	—	—
Willis, Chris	17 + 4	2	3	1	15

TOTALS:
49 players		58	74	19	399

1986-87 MATCH ANALYSIS

Date	Competition	H/A	Opponent	Rlt	Score	Tries	Goals	Attendance	Referee
17.8.86	YC(P)	A	Halifax	L	0-56	—	—	—	—
31.8.86	SD	A	Sheffield E.	L	5-40	Kellett	Sanderson (dg)	—	—
7.9.86	SD	H	Huddersfield B.	L	31-36	A. Fletcher (2), O'Grady, Grix	Buckton (5), Sanderson (2), O'Grady (dg)	256	Holdsworth
21.9.86	SD	A	Runcorn H.	L	8-54	Smith	Oates (2)	—	—
28.9.86	SD	H (at Notts C. FC)	Fulham	W	32-18	Willis, Hooper, Kellett, Westbury, Pflaster	Oates (5), Willis	950	Haigh
5.10.86	SD	A	Whitehaven	L	18-22	Hooper, A. Fletcher, Grix	Smith (2), Willis	—	—
12.10.86	SD	H	Blackpool B.	L	16-30	Grix, Hooper	Crossingham (4)	282	Lindop
19.10.86	SD	A	Carlisle	L	16-22	Thompson, Gentle, Tupaea	Crossingham (2)	—	—
26.10.86	SD	H	Bramley	L	8-13	Stevens	Crossingham (2)	312	Volante
2.11.86	SD	A	Huddersfield B.	L	18-29	Oates, Stevens, Gentle	Crossingham (2), Oates	—	—
9.11.86	SD	A	Workington T.	L	4-20	—	Oates (2)	—	—
16.11.86	SD	H	Carlisle	L	16-28	Kellett, Crossingham, Buckton	Oates (2)	236	Cross
23.11.86	SD	A	Blackpool B.	L	14-20	Thompson, Hooper	Crossingham (3)	—	—
30.11.86	JPS(1)	A	Blackpool B.	L	12-42	Thompson, Gentle	Crossingham (2)	—	—
7.12.86	SD	H	Hunslet	L	2-42	—	Buckton	415	Tennant
14.12.86	SD	H	Runcorn H.	W	27-26	A. Fletcher, Stevens, Grix, Gentle	Oates (4), Buckton, Sanderson (dg)	277	Allatt
21.12.86	SD	A	Rochdale H.	L	8-22	Langton, Tupaea	—	—	—
28.12.86	SD	H	Sheffield E.	L	10-26	Cochrane	Topping (3)	392	Houghton
4.1.87	SD	H	Batley	W	14-6	Kellett, Langton, Buckton	Topping	307	Carter
11.1.87	SD	A	Hunslet	L	6-12	Grix	Topping	—	—
25.1.87	SD	H	Rochdale H.	L	9-26	Langton	Topping (2, 1 dg)	366	Spencer
5.2.87	CC(1)	H	Heworth (York)	W	14-7	Fletcher (2)	Topping (2, 2dg)	701	Mean
8.2.87	SD	A	Batley	W	15-6	King	Topping (4, 1dg), Platt (2dg)	—	—
15.2.87	CC(2)	H	Hull	L	7-38	Thompson	Willis (1, 1dg)	1579	Simpson
22.2.87	SD	A	Bramley	L	3-12	—	Simpson, Platt (dg)	—	—
15.3.87	SD	A	Keighley	W	12-6	Langton, Tupaea	Simpson, Platt (2dg)	—	—
29.3.87	SD	H	Workington T.	L	7-8	Thompson	Simpson, Platt (dg)	179	Berry
5.4.87	SD	H	Whitehaven	L	7-22	Platt	Simpson, Platt (dg)	244	Tennant
12.4.87	SD	A	Fulham	W	20-12	Thompson, Tupaea, Ogburn	Platt (3, 2dg)	—	—
15.4.87	SD	A	Doncaster	L	11-22	Willis	Platt (3, 1dg)	—	—
17.4.87	SD	H	Doncaster	W	17-2	Langton (2), Platt	Platt (2, 1dg)	723	Dockray (Pr)
20.4.87	SD	H	Keighley	W	12-10	Thompson	Simpson (4)	208	Whitelam (Pr)

OLDHAM

Ground: Watersheddings
Colours: Red and white hooped jerseys
First Season: 1895-96
Nickname: Roughyeds
Chairman: Harvey Ashworth
Secretary: Eddie Bayliss
Coach: Frank Myler (June 1984-Apr 1987)
Honours: **Championship** Winners, 1909-10, 1910-11,1956-57
              Beaten finalists, 1906-07, 1907-08, 1908-09, 1921-22, 1954-55
              Division One Champions, 1904-05
              Division Two Champions, 1963-64, 1981-82
              Challenge Cup Winners, 1898-99, 1924-25, 1926-27
              Beaten finalists, 1906-07, 1911-12, 1923-24, 1925-26
              Lancashire League Winners, 1897-98, 1900-01, 1907-08, 1909-10, 1921-22, 1956-57, 1957-58
              Lancashire Cup Winners, 1907-08, 1910-11, 1913-14, 1919-20, 1924-25, 1933-34, 1956-57, 1957-58, 1958-59
              Beaten finalists, 1908-09, 1911-12, 1918-19, 1921-22, 1954-55, 1966-67, 1968-69, 1986-87
Records: Attendance: 28,000 v. Huddersfield (League) 24 Feb, 1912
              Season
              Goals: 200 by B. Ganley, 1957-58
              Tries: 49 by R. Farrar, 1921-22
              Points: 412 by B. Ganley, 1957-58
              Match
              Goals: 14 by B. Ganley v. Liverpool C., 4 Apr, 1959
              Tries: 7 by Miller v. Barry, 31 Oct, 1908
              Points: 30 by A. Johnson v. Widnes, 9 Apr, 1928
              Highest score: 67-6 v. Liverpool C., 1958-59
              Highest against: 67-11 v. Hull K.R., 1978-79

1986-87 PLAYERS' SUMMARY

	App	Tries	Goals	Dr	Pts
Ashton, Ray	16 + 2	3	—	3	15
Atkinson, Keith	7 + 1	3	2	—	16
Bardsley, Mike	0 + 1	—	—	—	—
Bridge, Gary	18	8	—	—	32
Burke, Mick	13	1	35	—	74
Casey, Leo	0 + 1	—	—	—	—
Clark, Bruce	28	4	—	—	16
Clawson, Neil	18 + 8	2	—	—	8
Edwards, Jeff	10 + 6	1	—	—	4
Fairbank, Mark	1 + 1	—	—	—	—
Flanagan, Terry	35	3	—	—	12
Foy, Des	28	16	—	—	64
Hall, Martin	3 + 2	—	—	—	—
Hawkyard, Colin	16 + 11	6	—	—	24
Hobbs, David	27 + 1	7	47	2	124
Jones, Wally	5 + 2	—	—	—	—
Kirwan, Paddy	16 + 3	2	—	—	8
Lord, Paul	1 + 1	—	—	—	—
Lowndes, Paul	0 + 2	—	—	—	—
Marsden, Robert	0 + 1	—	—	—	—
M'Barki, Hussein	26	5	—	—	20
Morrison, Tony	0 + 5	—	—	—	—
Nadiole, Tom	8 + 8	1	—	—	4
Ogburn, John	0 + 1	—	—	—	—
Raper, Stuart	27 + 4	11	—	—	44
Sanderson, Ian	16	2	—	—	8
Saunders, Eddie	2	—	—	—	—
Sherman, Paul	30 + 2	6	—	—	24
Sherratt, Ian	5	2	—	—	8
Taylor, Michael	31	11	—	—	44
Topliss, David	33 + 1	6	—	—	24
Waddell, Hugh	16	—	—	—	—
Warnecke, Gary	27 + 3	13	—	—	52
Worrall, Mike	30	4	31	—	78
Wright, Steve	1	—	—	—	—
TOTALS:					
35 players		117	115	5	703

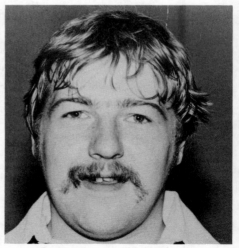

Cup deadline signing Mick Burke, scorer of 74 points in 13 games.

1986-87 MATCH ANALYSIS

Date	Competition	H/A	Opponent	Rlt	Score	Tries	Goals	Attendance	Referee
31.8.86	SBC	H	Leeds	W	14-12	Atkinson, Foy	Atkinson, Hobbs, Ashton (2 dg)	4621	Lindop
3.9.86	SBC	A	Halifax	L	14-20	Atkinson, Taylor	Hobbs (3)	—	—
7.9.86	SBC	A	Warrington	L	18-22	Hawkyard, Clark, M'Barki	Hobbs (3)	—	—
14.9.86	LC(1)	H	Leigh	W	29-22	Nadiole, M'Barki, Sherman, Hobbs	Worrall (6), Hobbs (dg)	4566	Whitfield
21.9.86	SBC	H	Hull K.R.	W	28-12	Raper, Hobbs, Warnecke, Clawson, Taylor	Worrall (3), Hobbs	4069	Beaumont
24.9.86	LC(2)	H	Workington T.	W	46-13	Warnecke (2), Raper (2), M'Barki, Worrall, Hobbs, Clark	Hobbs (7)	3412	Houghton
28.9.86	SBC	A	Leigh	L	12-40	Warnecke, M'Barki	Hobbs (2)	—	—
1.10.86	LC(SF)	H	Widnes	W	16-14	Hobbs, Sherman	Hobbs (4)	5601	Hodgson
5.10.86	SBC	H	Widnes	W	22-16	Hobbs, Clark, Atkinson, Warnecke	Worrall (3)	3875	Houghton
19.10.86	LC(F)	St Helens	Wigan	L	6-27	Bridge	Hobbs	(20180)	Smith
26.10.86	SBC	A	Wakefield T.	W	54-10	Foy (3), Warnecke (2), Sherman, Raper, Topliss, Ashton, Worrall	Hobbs (6), Worrall	—	—
2.11.86	SBC	H	Barrow	W	32-20	Hobbs, Worrall, Ashton, Taylor, Sherman	Hobbs (6)	3306	Tickle
4.11.86	Tour	H	Australia	L	16-22	Hawkyard, Foy	Worrall (3), Hobbs	5678	Allatt
9.11.86	SBC	A	Hull K.R.	L	4-6	—	Worrall (2)	—	—
16.11.86	SBC	H	St Helens	L	17-18	Hawkyard, Sherman, Foy	Worrall (2), Ashton (dg)	5719	Berry
23.11.86	SBC	A	Bradford N.	W	18-10	Foy, Raper, Worrall	Worrall (3)	—	—
30.11.86	JPS(1)	H	Bradford N.	L	12-22	Foy, Warnecke	Worrall (2)	5642	Whitfield
14.12.86	SBC	H	Halifax	L	18-20	Raper, Bridge, Taylor, Foy	Worrall	4995	Beaumont
21.12.86	SBC	A	St Helens	L	6-28	Sherman	Worrall	—	—
26.12.86	SBC	H	Salford	W	34-18	Bridge (2), M'Barki, Foy, Raper, Ashton	Worrall (4), Hobbs	4011	Hodgson
1.1.87	SBC	A	Leeds	W	26-20	Flanagan (2), Warnecke, Raper, Taylor	Hobbs (3)	—	—
4.1.87	SBC	A	Hull	L	16-20	Taylor, Bridge, Foy	Hobbs (2)	—	—
18.1.87	SBC	H	Featherstone R. (at Manchester C. FC)	W	20-16	Foy, Sanderson, Burke, Bridge	Hobbs (2)	2719	Berry
21.1.87	SBC	A	Widnes	L	10-44	Bridge, Taylor	Burke	—	—
4.2.87	CC(1)	H	Wigan	W	10-8	Kirwan	Burke (3)	11906	Spencer
14.2.87	CC(2)	H	St Helens	L	14-24	Foy, Raper	Burke (3)	7699	Allatt
22.2.87	SBC	H	Hull	W	24-18	Taylor, Topliss, Hawkyard	Burke (5), Hobbs	3504	Berry
1.3.87	SBC	A	Castleford	L	18-22	Taylor, Topliss, Bridge	Burke (2), Hobbs	—	—
8.3.87	SBC	A	Featherstone R.	L	6-24	Kirwan	Hobbs	—	—
11.3.87	SBC	H	Warrington	W	15-14	Topliss, Warnecke	Burke (3), Hobbs (dg)	3108	Tickle
15.3.87	SBC	H	Bradford N.	L	12-8	Hobbs	Burke (4)	3589	Volante
25.3.87	SBC	H	Wakefield T.	W	38-20	Foy (2), Taylor, Hawkyard, Raper, Clark, Clawson	Burke (5)	2682	Smith
29.3.87	SBC	H	Castleford	L	6-29	Raper	Hobbs	3659	Whitfield
5.4.87	SBC	A	Barrow	L	22-24	Taylor, Topliss, Hawkyard, Flanagan	Burke (3)	—	—
8.4.87	SBC	A	Wigan	L	2-54	—	Burke	—	—
12.4.87	SBC	H	Leigh	L	12-54	Warnecke (2)	Burke (2)	3531	Holdsworth
17.4.87	SBC	A	Salford	L	30-36	Sherratt (2), Foy, Warnecke, Topliss, Edwards	Burke (3)	—	—
20.4.87	SBC	H	Wigan	L	6-24	Sanderson	Atkinson	5432	Simpson

67

ROCHDALE HORNETS

Ground:	Athletic Ground
Colours:	White jerseys with blue and red band
First Season:	1895-96
Nickname:	Hornets
Chairman:	Len Stansfield
Secretary:	Paul Reynolds
Coach:	Eric Fitzsimons (June 1986-)
Honours:	**Challenge Cup** Winners, 1921-22 **Lancashire League** Winners, 1918-19 **Lancashire Cup** Winners, 1911-12, 1914-15, 1918-19 Beaten finalists, 1912-13, 1919-20, 1965-66 **John Player Trophy** Beaten finalists 1973-74 **BBC2 Floodlit Trophy** Beaten finalists 1971-72
Records:	Attendance: 41,831 Wigan v. Oldham (RL Cup Final) 12 Apr 1924 Home: 26,664 v. Oldham (RL Cup) 25 Mar, 1922

Season

Goals: 115 by K. Harcombe, 1985-86
Tries: 30 by J. Williams, 1934-35
Points: 235 by G. Starkey, 1966-67

Match

Goals: 10 by H. Lees v. Glasshoughton, 19 Feb, 1938
Tries: 5 by J. Corsi v. Barrow, 31 Dec, 1921 and v. Broughton Moor, 25 Feb, 1922; J. Williams v. St Helens, 4 Apr, 1933; N. Brelsford v. Whitehaven, 3 Sep, 1972
Points: 27 by F. Blincow v. Normanton, 17 Oct, 1903
Highest score: 75-13 v. Broughton M., 1914-15
Highest against: 79-2 v. Hull, 1920-21

1986-87 PLAYERS' SUMMARY

	App	Tries	Goals	Dr	Pts
Aspey, Steve	1 + 1	—	—	—	—
Brown, David	16 + 3	3	—	—	12
Byron, Gerry	33	6	7	2	40
Caffery, Brian	3 + 1	—	—	—	—
Cartwright, Phil	17 + 2	5	—	—	20
Causey, Mark	34	6	—	—	24
Clucas, Geoff	1	—	—	—	—
Connell, Chris	1	—	—	—	—
Cowie, Neil	7 + 9	1	—	—	4
Davies, Warren	0 + 1	—	—	—	—
Deakin, Chris	2 + 3	—	—	—	—
Dobson, Mark	13 + 2	4	—	—	16
Duane, Ian	14 + 1	5	—	—	20
Dunn, Brian	30 + 2	23	—	—	92
Dwyer, Mark	2 + 6	—	—	—	—
Edge, Phil	8	—	—	—	—
Evans, David	26 + 1	5	—	—	20
Fairhurst, Alan	2	—	—	—	—
Fellows, Paul	0 + 2	2	—	—	8
Geldard, David	5	1	—	—	4
Harcombe, Kevin	6 + 2	—	10	—	20
Harrigan, Mark	23 + 1	4	—	—	16
Hitchen, Gary	14 + 2	2	1	4	14
Hughes, Eric	9	1	—	—	4
Idle, Graham	15	—	—	—	—
Johnson, Willie	12	1	—	—	4
Jones, Glen	4 + 1	—	—	—	—
Lowe, Kevin	18 + 1	—	—	—	—
Meachin, Colin	1 + 2	—	—	—	—
Munro, Geoff	4	—	—	—	—
Nash, Steve	3 + 2	—	—	—	—
Purcell, Craig	20 + 6	2	—	—	8
Roe, Peter	2	—	—	—	—
Round, Mike	4	1	—	—	4
Rule, Steve	4	—	—	—	—
Sanby, Tony	4	—	—	—	—
Sanderson, Mark	4 + 1	—	—	—	—
Stapleton, John	13 + 6	9	—	—	36
Thomson, Darren	25	9	—	—	36
Williams, Dean	16 + 1	2	—	—	8
Wood, David	26 + 3	6	79	1	183

TOTALS:

	App	Tries	Goals	Dr	Pts
41 players		98	97	7	593

Second row man Brian Dunn, 23 tries in 31 appearances.

1986-87 MATCH ANALYSIS

Date	Competition	H/A	Opponent	Rlt	Score	Tries	Goals	Attendance	Referee
7.9.86	SD	H	Bramley	W	30-12	Stapleton (2), Dunn, Round, Harrigan	Byron (5)	774	Houghton
10.9.86	SD	H	Whitehaven	W	6-0	Stapleton	Byron	822	Simpson
14.9.86	LC(1)	A	Wigan	L	0-52	—	—	—	—
21.9.86	SD	A	Dewsbury	L	14-19	Evans, Dunn	Harcombe (3)	—	—
28.9.86	SD	H	Swinton	L	8-19	Byron	Harcombe (2)	1429	Spencer
5.10.86	SD	A	Carlisle	L	2-22	—	Harcombe	—	—
12.10.86	SD	H	Fulham	W	20-12	Dunn, Causey, Dobson	Harcombe (4)	871	Mean
19.10.86	SD	A	Whitehaven	L	4-20	Wood	—	—	—
2.11.86	SD	H	Batley	W	34-6	Stapleton (2), Dunn (2), Evans, Thompson	Wood (5)	969	Kershaw
9.11.86	SD	˙A	Doncaster	D	28-28	Causey (2), Hughes, Dunn, Wood	Wood (4)	—	—
16.11.86	SD	A	York	W	26-17	Dunn (2), Dobson, Thompson, Byron	Wood (3)	—	—
23.11.86	SD	H	Keighley	W	28-8	Causey (2), Wood, Dunn	Wood (6)	810	Berry
30.11.86	JPS(1)	A	Leigh	L	10-32	Cowie, Dobson	Wood	—	—
14.12.86	SD	A	Batley	W	15-12	Harrigan, Thompson	Wood (3), Byron (dg)	—	—
21.12.86	SD	H	Mansfield M.	W	22-8	Dunn (2), Harrigan, Thompson	Wood (3)	865	Tickle
26.12.86	SD	A	Blackpool B.	W	18-6	Thompson (2), Dunn	Wood (3)	—	—
4.1.87	SD	H	Doncaster	L	6-14	Cartwright	Wood	1023	Cross
25.1.87	SD	A	Mansfield M.	W	26-9	Thompson (2), Wood, Cartwright, Harrigan	Wood (3)	—	—
4.2.87	CC(1)	H	Carlisle	D	4-4	Dunn	—	746	Hodgson
8.2.87	SD	H	York	W	12-8	Dunn (2)	Byron, Wood	875	Volante
11.2.87	CC(1) Replay	A	Carlisle	L	22-30	Evans, Dunn, Causey, Duane	Wood (3)	—	—
15.2.87	SD	H	Dewsbury	L	10-12	Duane, Fellows	Wood	881	Beaumont
22.2.87	SD	H	Workington	W	28-12	Cartwright, Johnson, Byron, Dunn, Williams	Wood (3)	694	Whitfield
1.3.87	SD	A	Bramley	W	5-1	Fellows	Hitchen	—	—
8.3.87	SD	H	Carlisle	W	11-1	Stapleton	Wood (3), Hitchen (dg)	782	Allatt
22.3.87	SD	H	Runcorn H.	W	32-2	Duane, Evans, Stapleton, Dunn, Brown	Wood (6)	765	Tennant
29.3.87	SD	A	Keighley	W	30-18	Stapleton (2), Byron, Evans	Wood (7)	—	—
5.4.87	SD	H	Blackpool B.	W	24-16	Duane (2), Wood, Byron	Wood (3, 1dg), Byron (dg)	829	Cross
8.4.87	SD	A	Runcorn H.	W	15-14	Purcell, Hitchen	Wood (3), Hitchen (dg)	—	—
12.4.87	SD	A	Workington T.	L	18-25	Cartwright (2), Williams, Hitchen	Wood	—	—
17.4.87	SD	A	Fulham	W	33-16	Dunn (2), Wood, Brown, Geldard	Wood (6), Hitchen	—	—
20.4.87	SD	A	Swinton	L	14-32	Purcell, Dobson	Wood (3)	—	—
26.4.87	SDP(1)	A	Doncaster	W	30-18	Dunn (3), Byron, Brown	Wood (5)	—	—
10.5.87	SDP(SF)	A	Hunslet	L	8-32	Thompson	Wood (2)	—	—

69

RUNCORN HIGHFIELD

Ground: Canal Street
Colours: Black jerseys
First Season: 1922-23 as Wigan Highfield.
Became London Highfield in
1933-34. Became Liverpool Stanley
in 1934-35 and changed to
Liverpool City in 1951-52. Became
Huyton in 1968-69 and changed to
Runcorn Highfield in 1984-85.
There was also a Liverpool City in
1906-07
Chairman: Terry Hughes
Secretary: Tony Almond
Coach: Geoff Fletcher (Aug 1977-June 1986),
Frank Wilson (July-Nov 1986),
Paul Woods and Arthur Daley
(Nov 1986-Apr 1987),
Bill Ashurst (Apr 1987-)
Honours: **Lancashire League** Winners,
1935-36
Records: Attendance: 14,000 v. Widnes
(Championship semi-final) 2 May,
1936 at Prescott Road
Season
Goals: 126 by P. Wood, 1984-85
Tries: 28 by J. Maloney, 1930-31
Points: 240 by P. Wood, 1984-85
Match
Goals: 11 by P. Wood v. Batley,
21 Oct, 1984
Tries: 5 by J. Maloney v. Bramley,
25 Apr, 1931
Points: 20 by Barnes v.
Featherstone Jnrs, 7 Feb, 1931;
S. Oakley v. Bramley, 4 May, 1934;
P. Twiss v. Warrington, 20 Aug,
1958
Highest score: 59-11 v. Bramley,
1933-34
Highest against: 73-0 v.
Warrington, 1950-51

1986-87 PLAYERS' SUMMARY

	App	Tries	Goals	Dr	Pts
Alati, Mark	0 + 1	—	—	—	—
Ashcroft, Keith	23 + 2	2	—	—	8
Ball, Jimmy	6	1	—	—	4
Barrow, Norman	3	—	8	—	16
Blackwood, Bob	6 + 5	1	—	—	4
Berry, John	7 + 3	1	—	—	4
Blythin, Kevin	13 + 1	7	—	—	28
Booth, John	24 + 2	2	—	—	8
Campbell, Danny	26 + 1	1	—	—	4
Cogger, John	23	18	—	—	72
Connor, Sean	11 + 1	2	2	—	12
Crompton, David	15	2	—	—	8
Daley, Arthur	10	1	—	—	4
Davies, Dave	1	—	1	—	2
Dooley, Jim	8	—	—	—	—
Durnin, Paul	25 + 1	—	—	—	—
Egan, Martin	1	—	—	—	—
Fairhurst, Jimmy	2	—	—	—	—
Fitzpatrick, Paul	6 + 1	2	—	—	8
Fraser, Paul	18 + 2	4	13	2	44
Garritty, Brian	12 + 1	6	—	—	24
Gauchwin, Steve	22 + 1	3	27	1	67
Geldard, Steve	11	1	—	—	4
Gilmore, John	2 + 1	—	—	—	—
Henney, Harold	3 + 2	1	—	—	4
Hunt, David	1	—	—	—	—
Hunter, Clive	24 + 1	3	—	—	12
Jackson, Tony	14 + 7	1	7	—	18
McCabe, James	2	—	—	—	—
McCallister, Sam	0 + 1	—	—	—	—
McCrohn, David	0 + 1	—	—	—	—
McGrath, Joe	1	—	—	—	—
O'Connell, Seamus	20	5	—	—	20
Prescott, Eric	8 + 7	—	—	—	—
Rawlinson, Tommy	20 + 1	2	—	—	8
Sallent, Paul	4	—	—	—	—
Simm, Steve	4 + 1	—	—	—	—
Smith, Glen	2	—	—	—	—
Smith, Ian	8 + 1	3	1	—	14
Tabern, John	3	1	—	—	4
Walters, Graham	5	1	—	—	4
Wilson, Frank	0 + 1	—	—	—	—
Wood, Peter	1	—	1	—	2
Woods, Paul	1 + 2	—	1	—	2
Trialists (4)	7 + 2	2	—	—	8
TOTALS: 48 players		73	61	3	393

Eric Prescott, 15 appearances.

1986-87 MATCH ANALYSIS

Date	Competition	H/A	Opponent	Rlt	Score	Tries	Goals	Attendance	Referee
31.8.86	SD	H	Hunslet	L	0-36	—	—	402	Bowman
2.9.86	SD	H	Keighley	W	20-6	Booth, Ball, I. Smith, Henney	Jackson (2)	—	—
7.9.86	SD	A	Carlisle	D	12-12	Connors, Hunter	Jackson, Gauchwin	—	—
14.9.86	LC(1)	H	Widnes	L	10-48	Blythen	Jackson (3)	2338	Spencer
21.9.86	SD	H	Mansfield M.	W	54-8	Blythen (3), Gauchwin (2), Garrity (2), I. Smith, Fitzpatrick, Blackwood, O'Connell	Gauchwin (4), I. Smith	338	Whitfield
28.9.86	SD	A	Blackpool B.	W	19-16	Cogger (2), Blythen	Gauchwin (3, 1 dg)	—	—
5.10.86	SD	H	Workington T.	W	30-14	Garrity (3), Cogger (2), Booth	Connors (2), Gauchwin	312	Holdsworth
12.10.86	SD	A	Batley	W	10-6	I. Smith, O'Connell	Gauchwin	—	—
19.10.86	SD	H	Sheffield E.	W	22-4	Connors, Fraser, Cogger, O'Connell	Gauchwin (3)	454	Hodgson
2.11.86	SD	A	Whitehaven	L	2-26	—	Gauchwin	—	—
9.11.86	SD	H	Blackpool B.	L	12-21	Jackson, Blythen	Gauchwin (2)	644	Tickle
16.11.86	SD	A	Hunslet	L	14-22	Fraser, Cogger	Gauchwin (3)	—	—
23.11.86	SD	H	Huddersfield B.	W	14-10	Gauchwin, Blythen, O'Connell	Gauchwin	271	Smith
30.11.86	JPS(1)	A	Barrow	L	10-36	Cogger (2)	Gauchwin	—	—
14.12.86	SD	A	Mansfield M.	L	26-27	Cogger (3), Fitzpatrick	Fraser (5)	—	—
21.12.86	SD	A	Keighley	L	10-22	O'Connell, Garrity	Fraser	—	—
26.12.86	SD	H	Doncaster	L	14-24	Rawlinson, Ashcroft	Gauchwin (3)	335	Simpson
4.1.87	SD	A	Bramley	L	6-20	Campbell	Wood	—	—
25.1.87	SD	H	Bramley	W	14-12	Daley, Crompton	Barrow (3)	282	Haigh
4.2.87	CC(1)	H	Leigh	L	6-25	—	Barrow (3)	964	Cross
8.2.87	SD	A	Doncaster	L	12-32	Crompton, Cogger	Barrow (2)	—	—
15.2.87	SD	A	Workington T.	L	6-20	Fraser	Jackson	—	—
1.3.87	SD	H	Batley	W	26-8	Cogger (3), Fraser, Berry	Fraser (3)	258	Simpson
8.3.87	SD	A	Fulham	L	2-19	—	Fraser	—	—
15.3.87	SD	H	Carlisle	L	4-26	Cogger	—	224	Holdsworth
22.3.87	SD	A	Rochdale H.	L	2-32	—	Davies	—	—
29.3.87	SD	A	Huddersfield B.	L	12-26	Jones, Cogger	Gauchwin (2)	—	—
1.4.87	SD	H	Whitehaven	L	4-8	Hunter	—	287	Hodgson
8.4.87	SD	H	Rochdale H.	L	14-15	Geldard, Rawlinson, Walters	Woods	287	McDonald
12.4.87	SD	A	Sheffield E.	L	12-52	Tabern, Trialist	Fraser (1, 2dg)	—	—
20.4.87	SD	H	Fulham	W	18-9	Hunter, Ashcroft, Cogger	Fraser (2), Gauchwin	202	Burke (Pr)

71

ST. HELENS

Ground: Knowsley Road
Colours: White jerseys with red V
First Season: 1895-96
Nickname: Saints
Chairman: Lawrie Prescott
Secretary: Geoff Sutcliffe
Coach: Alex Murphy (Nov 1985-)
Honours: **Championship** Winners, 1931-32, 1952-53, 1958-59, 1965-66, 1969-70, 1970-71
Beaten finalists, 1964-65, 1966-67, 1971-72
Division One Champions, 1974-75
League Leaders Trophy Winners, 1964-65, 1965-66
Club Championship (Merit Table) Beaten finalists, 1973-74
Challenge Cup Winners, 1955-56, 1960-61, 1965-66, 1971-72, 1975-76
Beaten finalists, 1896-97, 1914-15, 1929-30, 1952-53, 1977-78, 1986-87
Lancashire Cup Winners, 1926-27, 1953-54, 1960-61, 1961-62, 1962-63, 1963-64, 1964-65, 1967-68, 1968-69, 1984-85
Beaten finalists, 1932-33, 1952-53, 1956-57, 1958-59, 1959-60, 1970-71, 1982-83
Lancashire League Winners, 1929-30, 1931-32, 1952-53, 1959-60, 1964-65, 1965-66, 1966-67, 1968-69
Premiership Winners, 1975-76, 1976-77, 1984-85
Beaten finalists, 1974-75
Western Division Championship Winners, 1963-64
BBC2 Trophy Winners, 1971-72, 1975-76
Beaten finalists, 1965-66, 1968-69, 1970-71, 1977-78, 1978-79
Records: Attendance: 35,695 v. Wigan (League) 26 Dec, 1949
Season
Goals: 214 by K. Coslett, 1971-72
Tries: 62 by T. Van Vollenhoven, 1958-59
Points: 452 by K. Coslett, 1971-72

Match
Goals: 16 by P. Loughlin v. Carlisle, 14 Sep, 1986
Tries: 6 by A. Ellaby v. Barrow, 5 Mar, 1932; S. Llewellyn v. Castleford, 3 Mar, 1956 and v. Liverpool C., 20 Aug, 1956; T. Vollenhoven v. Wakefield T., 21 Dec, 1957 and v. Blackpool B., 23 Apr, 1962; F. Myler v. Maryport, 1 Sep, 1969
Points: 40 by P. Loughlin v. Carlisle, 14 Sep, 1986
Highest score: 112-0 v. Carlisle, 1986-87
Highest against: 78-3 v. Warrington, 1908-09

1986-87 PLAYERS' SUMMARY

	App	Tries	Goals	Dr	Pts
Allen, Shaun	13 + 16	3	—	—	12
Arkwright, Chris	34 + 1	20	—	—	80
Bailey, Mark	3 + 1	1	—	—	4
Bayliss, Steve	7 + 3	—	—	—	—
Burke, Tony	35 + 5	5	—	—	20
Clark, Brett	36	19	—	—	76
Dainteth, Ian	1	—	—	—	—
Devine, Sean	1	—	—	—	—
Doherty, Paul	7 + 1	1	—	1	5
Dwyer, Bernard	7 + 6	1	4	1	13
Elia, Mark	13	7	—	—	28
Fieldhouse, John	20 + 4	2	—	—	8
Forber, Paul	25 + 16	11	—	—	44
Gavin, Neil	0 + 1	—	—	—	—
Haggerty, Roy	33 + 1	9	—	—	36
Halliwell, Steve	22	16	—	—	64
Harrison, David	18	2	—	—	8
Holding, Neil	36	20	1	4	86
Hopkins, Paul	2 + 1	—	—	—	—
Jarvis, Pat	17 + 1	2	—	—	8
Large, David	1	—	—	—	—
Ledger, Barry	44	23	18	3	131
Lee, Mark	1	—	—	—	—
Liptrot, Graham	25	1	—	—	4
Litherland, Dennis	6	5	—	—	20
Loughlin, Paul	39	9	178	—	392
McCormack, Kevin	40	20	—	—	80
Parkes, Brian	2 + 3	1	—	—	4
Pinner, Harry	3	1	—	—	4
Platt, Andy	34 + 2	11	—	—	44
Price, Phil	1	1	—	—	4
Round, Paul	15 + 14	8	—	—	32
Southward, Phil	1 + 1	—	—	—	—
Veivers, Phil	43	14	—	—	56
TOTALS:					
34 players		213	201	9	1,263

1986-87 MATCH ANALYSIS

Date	Competition	H/A	Opponent	Rlt	Score	Tries	Goals	Attendance	Referee
31.8.86	SBC	H	Leigh	W	50-18	Arkwright (2), Veivers (2), McCormack (2), Haggerty (2), Forber, Ledger	Loughlin (5)	6594	Spencer
3.9.86	SBC	A	Salford	W	38-4	Veivers (2), Holding, Pinner, Arkwright, McCormack	Loughlin (7)	—	—
7.9.86	SBC	A	Leeds	W	40-20	Halliwell (3), Clark, Haggerty, Ledger	Loughlin (8)	—	—
14.9.86	LC(1)	H	Carlisle	W	112-0	Holding (4), Ledger (4), Halliwell (3), Loughlin (2), Arkwright (2), McCormack, Clark, Liptrot, Veivers, Burke	Loughlin (16)	4068	McDonald
21.9.86	SBC	H	Halifax	W	38-16	Forber, Holding, Ledger, Platt, Round, Clark	Loughlin (6), Holding (dg), Ledger (dg)	8489	Allatt
24.9.86	LC(2)	H	Warrington	W	19-15	Ledger, Haggerty, Round	Loughlin (3), Ledger (dg)	9750	Whitfield
28.9.86	SBC	A	Hull K.R.	W	36-4	Halliwell (2), Harrison, Arkwright, Clark, Loughlin	Loughlin (6)	—	—
1.10.86	LC(SF)	A	Wigan	L	16-22	Holding (2), Loughlin	Loughlin (2)	—	—
5.10.86	SBC	H	Wakefield T.	W	32-11	Clark (2), Loughlin, Allen, Haggerty	Loughlin (6)	5700	Mean
12.10.86	SBC	A	Barrow	W	34-12	Halliwell (3), Platt, Holding, Clark, Ledger	Loughlin (2), Holding	—	—
17.10.86	SBC	H	Salford	W	32-14	Ledger, Haggerty, McCormack, Clark, Platt	Loughlin (6)	5712	Smith
2.11.86	Tour	H	Australia	L	8-32	—	Loughlin (4)	15381	Lindop
9.11.86	SBC	A	Featherstone R.	W	44-8	Platt (2), Ledger, Holding, Forber, Halliwell, Round, Veivers	Loughlin (6)	—	—
16.11.86	SBC	A	Oldham	W	18-17	Arkwright (2), Platt	Ledger (2), Loughlin	—	—
23.11.86	SBC	H	Hull	W	50-10	Holding (2), Burke (2), Jarvis, Ledger, Halliwell, McCormack, Forber	Ledger (7)	5380	Holdsworth
30.11.86	JPS(1)	A	Whitehaven	W	10-8	Veivers, Jarvis	Ledger	—	—
6.12.86	JPS(2)	A	Castleford	W	26-22	Clark, Halliwell, Holding, Platt, McCormack	Ledger (3)	—	—
14.12.86	JPS(3)	H	Warrington	L	20-22	Halliwell (2), Haggerty	Ledger (4)	11571	Fox
21.12.86	SBC	H	Oldham	W	28-6	McCormack (2), Clark, Haggerty, Forber	Loughlin (4)	6821	Simpson
26.12.86	SBC	H	Wigan	L	4-12	—	Loughlin (2)	21214	Kershaw
1.1.87	SBC	A	Widnes	L	10-16	McCormack	Loughlin (3)	—	—
4.1.87	SBC	A	Halifax	L	19-20	McCormack, Haggerty, Platt	Loughlin (3), Holding (dg)	—	—
21.1.87	CC(P)	H	Swinton	W	18-16	Clark, Platt, Burke	Loughlin (3)	4455	Allatt
25.1.87	SBC	H	Featherstone R.	W	43-14	Arkwright (3), McCormack (2), Veivers (2)	Loughlin (7), Holding (dg)	4827	Whitfield
5.2.87	CC(1)	A	Dewsbury	W	48-12	Arkwright (2), Ledger, Holding, McCormack, Clark, Veivers, Loughlin	Loughlin (8)	—	—
8.2.87	SBC	A	Wakefield T.	W	30-6	Ledger, Loughlin, Clark, Arkwright, McCormack	Loughlin (5)	—	—
14.2.87	CC(2)	A	Oldham	W	24-14	McCormack (2), Forber, Holding	Loughlin (4)	—	—
18.2.87	SBC	H	Warrington	W	42-22	Elia (2), Forber, Holding, Ledger, Veivers	Loughlin (9)	9468	Mean
22.2.87	SBC	H	Bradford N.	W	40-14	Elia (2), Holding, Clark, Ledger, Allen, Forber	Loughlin (6)	6988	Spencer

(continued on page 95)

73

SALFORD

Ground: The Willows
Colours: Red jerseys
First Season: 1896-97
Nickname: Red Devils
Chairman: John Wilkinson
Secretary: Graham McCarty
Coach: Kevin Ashcroft (May 1984-)
Honours: **Championship** Winners, 1913-14, 1932-33, 1936-37, 1938-39
Beaten finalists, 1933-34
Division One Champions, 1973-74, 1975-76
Challenge Cup Winners, 1937-38
Beaten finalists, 1899-1900, 1901-02, 1902-03, 1905-06, 1938-39, 1968-69
Lancashire League Winners, 1932-33, 1933-34, 1934-35, 1936-37, 1938-39
Lancashire Cup Winners, 1931-32, 1934-35, 1935-36, 1936-37, 1972-73
Beaten finalists, 1929-30, 1938-39, 1973-74, 1974-75, 1975-76
Premiership Beaten finalists, 1975-76
John Player Trophy Beaten finalists 1972-73
BBC2 Trophy Winners, 1974-75
Records: Attendance: 26,470 v. Warrington (RL Cup) 13 Feb, 1937
Season
Goals: 221 by D. Watkins, 1972-73
Tries: 46 by K. Fielding, 1973-74
Points: 493 by D. Watkins, 1972-73
Match
Goals: 13 by A. Risman v. Bramley, 5 Apr, 1933 and v. Broughton R., 18 May, 1940; D. Watkins v. Keighley, 7 Jan, 1972; S. Rule v. Doncaster, 4 Sep, 1981
Tries: 6 by F. Miles v. Lees, 5 Mar, 1898; E. Bone v. Goole, 29 Mar, 1902; J. Hilton v. Leigh, 7 Oct, 1939
Points: 39 by J. Lomas v. Liverpool C., 2 Feb, 1907
Highest score: 78-0 v. Liverpool C., 1906-07

Highest against: 63-5 v. Wigan, 1924-25

1986-87 PLAYERS' SUMMARY

	App	Tries	Goals	Dr	Pts
Austin, Greg	31 + 1	17	24	1	117
Barrett, Mark	0 + 1	—	—	—	—
Beckett, Adrian	1	—	—	—	—
Bentley, Keith	4	1	—	—	4
Blease, Ian	5 + 1	1	—	—	4
Bloor, Darren	23 + 1	7	—	1	29
Brownbill, Paul	0 + 2	—	—	—	—
Bullough, David	7	—	—	—	—
Burgess, David	0 + 1	—	—	—	—
Byrne, Gerard	23	10	—	—	40
Disley, Gary	13 + 7	—	—	—	—
Fazackerley, John	7	—	11	—	22
Fletcher, Paul	28	6	—	—	24
Foy, Martin	3 + 1	1	—	—	4
Glynn, Peter	25 + 3	3	—	1	13
Groves, Paul	15 + 7	1	—	—	4
Herbert, Steve	31 + 2	3	—	—	12
Major, David	30 + 1	2	—	—	8
Makin, John	1	—	—	—	—
Marsh, Ian	13	2	—	—	8
McTigue, Mick	25 + 1	6	—	—	24
Moran, Mark	16 + 1	1	—	—	4
Morris, Steve	2	1	—	—	4
Moylan, Steve	2 + 1	1	—	—	4
Needham, David	1 + 2	—	—	—	—
O'Loughlin, Keiron	33	7	—	—	28
O'Shea, Terry	19 + 1	9	49	—	134
Pendlebury, John	7	—	1	—	2
Ruddy, David	8 + 4	2	—	—	8
Schubert, Garry	5 + 2	—	—	—	—
Selby, Geoff	19	6	—	—	24
Smith, Ron	2 + 2	—	—	—	—
Wakefield, Mark	15 + 5	2	—	—	8
Whiteley, Chris	0 + 1	—	—	—	—
Wiltshire, Roy	15	3	—	—	12
TOTALS:					
35 players		92	85	3	541

Great Britain Under-21 debutant Gary Disley.

1986-87 MATCH ANALYSIS

Date	Com-petition	H/A	Opponent	Rlt	Score	Tries	Goals	Atten-dance	Referee
31.8.86	SBC	A	Wigan	L	12-42	Moylan, Fletcher	Austin (2)	—	—
3.9.86	SBC	H	St Helens	L	4-38	—	Austin (2)	2817	Berry
7.9.86	SBC	H	Bradford N.	L	12-22	Austin, Bentley	Austin (2)	2396	Mean
14.9.86	LC(1)	A	Warrington	L	20-28	Bloor (2), Fletcher	Fazackerley (4)	—	—
21.9.86	SBC	A	Warrington	L	14-42	McTigue (2), Austin	Fazackerley	—	—
28.9.86	SBC	H	Barrow	L	12-24	McTigue, Ruddy	Fazackerley (2)	1328	Fox
5.10.86	SBC	A	Leeds	L	10-46	Groves, Wakefield	Fazackerley	—	—
12.10.86	SBC	H	Hull K.R.	L	14-34	Morris, Foy	Fazackerley (3)	1759	Haigh
17.10.86	SBC	A	St Helens	L	14-32	Wiltshire, Ruddy, Selby	Austin	—	—
26.10.86	SBC	A	Featherstone R.	L	6-16	Wiltshire	Pendlebury	—	—
2.11.86	SBC	H	Warrington	L	10-25	McTigue, Byrne	O'Shea	2546	Holdsworth
9.11.86	SBC	H	Wigan	L	0-34	—	—	5391	Beaumont
16.11.86	SBC	A	Castleford	W	21-20	Bloor, O'Loughlin, Glynn	O'Shea (4), Austin (dg)	—	—
23.11.86	SBC	H	Widnes	W	22-16	O'Shea (2), Austin, Fletcher	O'Shea (3)	1414	Tickle
30.11.86	JPS(1)	H	Hull	L	12-27	Bloor (2)	O'Shea (2)	2100	Kendrew
21.12.86	SBC	A	Halifax	L	8-18	Selby	O'Shea (2)	—	—
26.12.86	SBC	A	Oldham	L	18-34	Blease, Glynn, Byrne	O'Shea (3)	—	—
1.1.87	SBC	H	Leigh	W	20-12	Selby, O'Loughlin, Austin	O'Shea (3), Austin	2502	Kershaw
4.1.87	SBC	A	Wakefield T.	W	16-10	O'Shea (2), Moran	O'Shea (2)	—	—
25.1.87	SBC	H	Hull	W	29-18	Austin (2), Byrne, O'Shea, Wiltshire	O'Shea (4), Glynn (dg)	1858	Lindop
1.2.87	CC(1)	H	Leeds	L	0-4	—	—	4534	Beaumont
8.2.87	SBC	A	Widnes	L	12-13	McTigue, Selby	O'Shea, Austin	—	—
15.2.87	SBC	H	Featherstone R.	W	26-16	O'Loughlin, O'Shea, Byrne, Fletcher	O'Shea (4), Austin	1967	Cross
20.2.87	SBC	H	Castleford	W	36-10	O'Shea (2), Herbert, Austin, Selby, Marsh	O'Shea (6)	2024	Smith
1.3.87	SBC	H	Wakefield T.	W	36-12	O'Loughlin (2), Selby, Byrne, Herbert, Wakefield, Major	O'Shea (4)	1530	Bowman
8.3.87	SBC	H	Leeds	L	12-14	Austin, Glynn	O'Shea (2)	2152	Simpson
15.3.87	SBC	A	Barrow	W	26-20	Austin (2), Major, Fletcher, McTigue	O'Shea (3)	—	—
22.3.87	SBC	H	Halifax	W	16-8	O'Shea, Byrne, Bloor	O'Shea (2)	4192	Holdsworth
25.3.87	SBC	A	Hull	W	14-8	Austin (2)	O'Shea (3)	—	—
5.4.87	SBC	A	Hull K.R.	L	16-20	O'Loughlin, Herbert, Austin	Austin (2)	—	—
9.4.87	SBC	A	Leigh	W	14-10	Byrne, Bloor	Austin (3)	—	—
17.4.87	SBC	H	Oldham	W	36-30	Byrne (3), Austin (2), O'Loughlin	Austin (6)	4222	Kendrew
21.4.87	SBC	A	Bradford N.	W	23-12	Austin (2), Marsh, Fletcher	Austin (3), Bloor (dg)	—	—

SHEFFIELD EAGLES

Ground: Owlerton Stadium
Colours: White, claret and gold jerseys, white shorts
First Season: 1984-85
Nickname: Eagles
Managing Director: Gary Hetherington
Coach: Alan Rhodes (May 1984-May 1986)
Gary Hetherington (July 1986-)
Records: Attendance: 2,022 v. Doncaster (Div.2) 19 Apr, 1987

Season
Goals: 79 by R. Rafferty, 1985-86
Tries: 17 by S. Lidbury, 1986-87
Points: 186 by R. Rafferty, 1985-86

Match
Goals: 12 by R. Rafferty at Fulham, 21 Sep, 1986
Tries: No player has scored more than 3
Points: 32 by R. Rafferty at Fulham, 21 Sep, 1986
Highest score: 68-14 at Fulham, 1986-87
Highest against: 62-11 v. Warrington, 1985-86

1986-87 PLAYERS' SUMMARY

	App	Tries	Goals	Dr	Pts
Aston, Mark	22	7	26	—	80
Blazey, John	3 + 1	—	—	—	—
Brennan, Peter	4	—	—	—	—
Bridgeman, Derek	30 + 3	10	—	—	40
Cholmondeley, David	14 + 2	1	2	2	10
Close, David	13	4	—	—	16
Crowther, Ian	0 + 1	—	—	—	—
Dickinson, Andy	30	15	—	—	60
Farrell, Kevin	16 + 12	4	—	—	16
Gamson, Mark	28 + 3	6	—	—	24
Glancy, John	30	6	—	—	24
Harris, Billy	1 + 3	1	—	—	4
Hetherington, Gary	8 + 1	—	—	—	—
Kellett, Neil	8 + 1	3	—	—	12
Kuhnemann, Paul	22 + 7	2	1	—	10
Lane, Steve	11	—	—	—	—
Lidbury, Steve	33	17	—	—	68
Lyons, Cliff	6	3	3	—	18
Midgley, Trevor	1	—	—	—	—
Miller, Craig	22 + 6	7	—	—	28
Muir, Nick	1	—	—	—	—
Nason, Kevin	9 + 1	2	—	—	8
Parkes, Steve	12 + 2	4	—	—	16
Powell, Daryl	28 + 1	8	—	1	33
Rafferty, Roy	20	11	70	—	184
Sarsfield, Sean	3 + 1	—	—	—	—
Sheridan, Greg	3 + 4	—	—	—	—
Sherwood, Mitch	0 + 3	—	—	—	—
Smith, Gary	27 + 1	9	—	1	37
Taylor, Malcolm	1	—	—	—	—
Wilders, Peter	21 + 5	—	—	—	—
Wilson, Andy	15 + 2	5	—	—	20
TOTALS:					
32 players		125	102	4	708

New club record try scorer Steve Lidbury.

1986-87 MATCH ANALYSIS

Date	Com-petition	H/A	Opponent	Rlt	Score	Tries	Goals	Atten-dance	Referee
31.8.86	SD	H	Mansfield M.	W	40-5	Dickinson (3), Lidbury (2), Smith, Rafferty	Rafferty (6)	594	Kendrew
3.9.86	YC(P)	H	Doncaster	W	22-20	Rafferty (2), Lidbury, Glancy	Rafferty (2), Cholmondeley	654	Beaumont
7.9.86	SD	A	Keighley	W	29-16	Glancy, Powell, Dickinson, Bridgeman	Rafferty (6), Smith (dg)	—	—
14.9.86	YC(1)	H	Dewsbury	L	9-10	Bridgeman, Rafferty	Cholmondeley (dg)	641	Kendrew
21.9.86	SD	A	Fulham	W	68-14	Dickinson (3), Rafferty (2), Glancy, Nason, Miller, Smith, Lidbury, Cholmondeley	Rafferty (12)	—	—
28.9.86	SD	H	Dewsbury	W	31-10	Lidbury (2), Miller, Powell, Nason, Rafferty	Rafferty (3), Powell (dg)	522	Kershaw
1.10.86	SD	H	Huddersfield B.	W	12-9	Bridgeman (2)	Rafferty (2)	686	Cross
5.10.86	SD	A	Swinton	L	26-46	Miller, Harris, Lidbury, Smith, Kuhnemann	Rafferty (3)	—	—
12.10.86	SD	H	Carlisle	W	24-10	Smith, Lidbury, Gamson	Rafferty (6)	412	Tennant
19.10.86	SD	A	Runcorn H.	L	4-22	Dickinson	—	—	—
26.10.86	SD	H	York	L	14-32	Miller (2)	Rafferty (3)	507	Berry
2.11.86	SD	A	Bramley	L	14-24	Gamson, Farrell, Smith	Rafferty	—	—
9.11.86	SD	H	Fulham	W	17-8	Dickinson, Bridgeman, Smith	Rafferty (2), Cholmondeley (dg)	564	Allatt
20.11.86	SD	A	Huddersfield B.	W	12-8	Rafferty, Powell	Rafferty (2)	—	—
23.11.86	SD	H	Batley	W	24-4	Parkes, Lyons, Powell, Bridgeman	Lyons (3), Rafferty	567	Simpson
30.11.86	JPS(1)	H	Bramley	W	14-6	Aston, Parkes, Miller	Kuhnemann	415	Haigh
7.12.86	JPS(2)	H	Barrow	L	8-14	Smith, Lidbury	—	513	Lindop
14.12.86	SD	A	York	W	28-18	Parkes (2), Bridgeman, Lyons, Lidbury	Rafferty (4)	—	—
21.12.86	SD	A	Workington T.	L	16-28	Powell, Lidbury, Miller	Aston (2)	—	—
28.12.86	SD	A	Mansfield M.	W	26-10	Dickinson (2), Lidbury, Lyons, Kuhnemann	Aston (3)	—	—
4.1.87	SD	A (at Penrith)	Carlisle	L	6-17	Powell	Aston	—	—
8.1.87	SD	H (at Leeds)	Bramley	L	12-14	Powell, Bridgeman	Aston, Cholmondeley	709	Beaumont
25.1.87	SD	H	Swinton	L	14-17	Smith, Lidbury, Gamson	Aston	880	Cross
5.2.87	CC(1)	H	Keighley	L	6-8	Aston	Aston	375	Tennant
8.2.87	SD	H	Workington T.	W	34-14	Gamson, Aston, Close, Farrell, Lidbury, Wilson	Aston (5)	341	Berry
22.2.87	SD	A	Hunslet	L	10-18	Dickinson, Wilson	Aston	—	—
1.3.87	SD	H	Keighley	W	18-15	Farrell (2), Lidbury, Aston	Aston	393	McDonald
8.3.87	SD	A	Doncaster	L	8-14	Glancy	Aston (2)	—	—
15.3.87	SD	A	Dewsbury	W	28-6	Bridgman (2), Dickinson, Gamson, Kellett	Aston (4)	—	—
22.3.87	SD	A	Batley	W	28-7	Aston, Gamson, Glancy, Lidbury, Wilson	Aston (4)	—	—
29.3.87	SD	H	Hunslet	W	16-12	Rafferty (2), Wilson	Rafferty (2)	1211	Haigh
12.4.87	SD	H	Runcorn H.	W	52-12	Aston (2), Close (2), Kellett, Lidbury, Wilson, Rafferty, Smith	Rafferty (8)	609	Lindop
19.4.87	SD	H	Doncaster	L	14-16	Dickinson, Close	Rafferty (3)	1922	Bowman
26.4.87	SDP(1)	A	Whitehaven	L	24-29	Glancy, Dickinson, Powell, Kellett	Rafferty (4)	—	—

SWINTON

Ground: Station Road
Colours: Blue jerseys with white V
First Season: 1896-97
Nickname: Lions
Chairman: Ian Clift
Secretary: Steve Moyes
Coaches: Bill Holliday and Mike Peers
              (June 1986-)
Honours: **Championship** Winners, 1926-27,
              1927-28, 1930-31, 1934-35
              Beaten finalists, 1924-25, 1932-33
              War League Beaten finalists,
              1939-40
              Division One Champions, 1962-63,
              1963-64
              Division Two Champions, 1984-85
              Second Division Premiership
              Winners 1986-87
              Challenge Cup Winners, 1899-1900,
              1925-26, 1927-28
              Beaten finalists, 1926-27, 1931-32
              Lancashire League Winners,
              1924-25, 1927-28, 1928-29, 1930-31,
              1960-61
              Lancashire War League Winners,
              1939-40
              Lancashire Cup Winners, 1925-26,
              1927-28, 1939-40, 1969-70
              Beaten finalists, 1910-11, 1923-24,
              1931-32, 1960-61, 1961-62, 1962-63,
              1964-65, 1972-73
              BBC Trophy Beaten finalists,
              1966-67
              Western Division Championship
              Beaten finalists, 1963-64
Records: Attendance: 44,621 Wigan v.
              Warrington (RL Cup SF) 7 Apr,
              1951
              Season
              Goals: 128 by A. Blan, 1960-61
              Tries: 42 by J. Stopford, 1963-64
              Points: 283 by A. Blan, 1960-61

Match
Goals: 12 by K. Gowers v.
Liverpool C., 3 Oct, 1959
Tries: 5 by T. Bevan v.
Morecambe, 10 Sep, 1898; W.
Wallwork v. Widnes, 15 Dec, 1900;
J. Evans v. Bradford N., 30 Sep,
1922; H. Halsall v. St. Helens, 24
Jan, 1925; R. Cracknell v.
Whitehaven Rec., 11 Feb, 1928; R.
Lewis v. Keighley, 12 Jan, 1946; J.
Stopford v. Bramley, 22 Dec, 1962;
A. Buckley v. Salford, Apr 8, 1964
Points: 29 by B. McMahon v.
Dewsbury, 15 Aug, 1959
Highest score: 76-4 v. Pontefract,
1906-07
Highest against: 76-3 v.
Huddersfield, 1945-46

1986-87 PLAYERS' SUMMARY

	App	Tries	Goals	Dr	Pts
Ainsworth, Gary	19	13	—	—	52
Allen, John	19 + 2	—	—	—	—
Bate, Derek	33	31	—	—	124
Bourneville, Mark	3	1	—	—	4
Brown, Jeff	20 + 3	8	—	—	32
Cassidy, Frank	2 + 1	2	—	—	8
Derbyshire, Alan	18 + 1	2	—	—	8
Evans, Tex	12	8	—	—	32
Grima, Joe	18	5	—	—	20
Hewitt, Tony	14	8	—	—	32
Holliday, Les	28 + 3	10	—	6	46
Holliday, Mike	20 + 6	6	—	—	24
Horrocks, John	2 + 3	—	—	—	—
Jones, Ken	15 + 2	2	3	—	14
Lee, Martin	21	9	—	—	36
Lomax, Bill	2 + 1	—	—	—	—
Meadows, Mark	7 + 5	3	—	—	12
Melling, Alex	16	2	—	—	8
Mooney, Frank	17	—	—	—	—
Muller, Roby	28 + 1	5	—	—	20
Ratcliffe, Alan	8 + 11	3	—	—	12
Rippon, Andy	19 + 4	4	44	—	104
Rowbottom, Mark	3 + 2	—	—	—	—
Scott, Terry	6	3	—	—	12
Sheals, Mark	12 + 4	2	—	—	8
Snape, Steve	28	4	—	—	16
Topping, Paul	23	10	80	3	203
Viller, Mark	22 + 1	7	2	—	32
Wilson, Danny	20 + 2	2	—	8	16
Wright, Terry	0 + 2	—	—	—	—
TOTALS:					
30 players		150	129	17	875

1986-87 MATCH ANALYSIS

Date	Competition	H/A	Opponent	Rlt	Score	Tries	Goals	Attendance	Referee
31.8.86	SD	H	Batley	W	42-0	Evans (2), Bate (2), Lee, Wilson	Topping (9)	1242	Hodgson
7.9.86	SD	A	Doncaster	W	18-6	Lee, Evans, Bate	Topping (2), Wilson (2dg)	—	—

MATCH ANALYSIS (continued)

Date	Comp	H/A	Opponent	Res	Score	Tries	Goals	Att	Man
14.9.86	LC(1)	A	Workington T.	L	16-25	Lee, Bate	Topping (3), L. Holliday (dg), Wilson (dg)	—	—
21.9.86	SD	H	York	W	22-9	Lee, Evans, Bate, Melling	Jones (3)	1307	Bowman
28.9.86	SD	A	Rochdale H.	W	19-8	Bate, M. Holliday, Hewitt	Topping (2, 2 dg), Wilson (dg)	—	—
5.10.86	SD	H	Sheffield E.	W	46-26	Viller (2), Topping, Muller, M. Holliday, Hewitt, Ratcliffe, Bate	Topping (7)	1664	Carter
12.10.86	SD	A	Workington T.	W	33-18	Scott (2), Derbyshire, M. Holliday, Hewitt, Bate	Topping (4), Wilson (dg)	—	—
19.10.86	SD	H	Bramley	W	54-12	Bate (3), Cassidy (2), L. Holliday (2), M. Holliday, Hewitt	Topping (9)	1460	Lindop
2.11.86	SD	A	Dewsbury	L	6-8	Hewitt	Topping	—	—
9.11.86	SD	H	Whitehaven	W	14-8	Bourneville, Topping, Wilson	Topping	1651	Kershaw
16.11.86	SD	H	Doncaster	W	20-9	M. Holliday (2), Rippon, Hewitt	Viller (2)	1684	Volante
23.11.86	SD	A	Hunslet	L	4-12	Scott	—	—	—
30.11.86	JPS(1)	A	Myson (Hull) (at Hull K.R.)	W	18-11	Bate, Ratcliffe, Hewitt	Rippon (3)	—	—
7.12.86	JPS(2)	A	Wigan	L	14-20	Muller, Bate	Rippon (3)	—	—
14.12.86	SD	H	Dewsbury	W	40-0	Snape (2), Ainsworth, Rippon, Sheals, Bate, Ratcliffe	Rippon (6)	1483	Mean
26.12.86	SD	H	Fulham	W	50-10	Bate (2), L. Holliday (2), Viller, Grima, Brown, Snape, Hewitt	Rippon (7)	1700	Tickle
1.1.87	SD	A	Huddersfield B.	W	34-12	Bate (2), Evans (2), Ainsworth	Rippon (7)	—	—
18.1.87	SD	H	Huddersfield B. (at Bolton W. FC)	W	48-10	Bate (2), Evans (2), Meadows, Melling, Rippon, Snape	Rippon (8)	1162	Allatt
21.1.87	CC(P)	A	St Helens	L	16-18	Lee (2), Grima	Rippon (2)	—	—
25.1.87	SD	A	Sheffield E.	W	17-14	Bate, Meadows	Rippon (4), L. Holliday (dg)	—	—
8.2.87	SD	H	Carlisle	W	23-20	Bate, Meadows, Muller, Rippon, Brown	Rippon, Wilson (dg)	1515	Beaumont
15.2.87	SD	A	York	W	15-10	Bate (2), L. Holliday	Topping, L. Holliday (dg)	—	—
22.2.87	SD	A	Fulham	D	15-15	Bate, Lee	Topping (3), Wilson (dg)	—	—
1.3.87	SD	H	Hunslet	W	14-12	Jones, L. Holliday, Topping	Topping	2562	Tennant
8.3.87	SD	A	Whitehaven	L	12-22	Jones, Ainsworth	Topping (2)	—	—
15.3.87	SD	H	Blackpool B.	W	22-8	Brown (2), Sheals, Topping	Topping (3)	1622	Hodgson
22.3.87	SD	A	Bramley	L	13-14	L. Holliday, Ainsworth	Topping (2), Wilson (dg)	—	—
25.3.87	SD	A	Blackpool B.	W	25-10	Topping (2), Ainsworth (2)	Topping (4), L. Holliday (dg)	—	—
29.3.87	SD	A	Batley	W	8-0	Brown	Topping (2)	—	—
5.4.87	SD	H	Workington T.	W	32-20	Ainsworth (2), Bate, Topping, Lee, Muller	Topping (4)	1605	Mean
12.4.87	SD	A	Carlisle	W	35-16	L. Holliday (2), Bate (2), Ainsworth, Viller	Topping (5), L. Holliday (dg)	—	—
20.4.87	SD	H	Rochdale H.	W	32-14	Topping (2), Viller, Ainsworth, Brown, L. Holliday	Topping (4)	2055	Berry

(continued on page 95)

WAKEFIELD TRINITY

Ground:	Belle Vue
Colours:	White jerseys with red and blue band
First Season:	1895-96
Nickname:	Dreadnoughts
Chairman:	Rodney Walker
Secretary:	Alan Pearman
Coach:	Len Casey (Apr 1985-June 1986)
	Tony Dean (June-Dec 1986)
	Trevor Bailey (Dec 1986-Apr 1987)
	David Topliss (May 1987-)

Honours: **Championship** Winners, 1966-67, 1967-68
Beaten finalists, 1959-60, 1961-62
Division Two Champions, 1903-04
Challenge Cup Winners, 1908-09, 1945-46, 1959-60, 1961-62, 1962-63
Beaten finalists, 1913-14, 1967-68, 1978-79
Yorkshire League Winners, 1909-10, 1910-11, 1945-46, 1958-59, 1959-60, 1961-62, 1965-66
Yorkshire Cup Winners, 1910-11, 1924-25, 1946-47, 1947-48, 1951-52, 1956-57, 1960-61, 1961-62, 1964-65
Beaten finalists, 1926-27, 1932-33, 1934-35, 1936-37, 1939-40, 1945-46, 1958-59, 1973-74, 1974-75
John Player Trophy Beaten finalists, 1971-72

Records: Attendance: 37,906 Leeds v. Huddersfield (RL Cup SF) 21 March, 1936
Home: 28,254 v. Wigan (RL Cup) 24 Mar, 1962
Season
Goals: 163 by N. Fox, 1961-62
Tries: 38 by F. Smith, 1959-60, D. Smith, 1973-74
Points: 407 by N. Fox, 1961-62
Match
Goals: 12 by N. Fox v. Workington T., 19 Sep, 1970 and v. Batley, 26 Aug, 1967; B. Ward v. Hunslet, 6 Feb, 1971
Tries: 7 by F. Smith v. Keighley, 25 Apr, 1959; K. Slater v. Hunslet, 6 Feb, 1971
Points: 33 by N. Fox v. Batley, 26 Aug, 1967
Highest score: 78-9 v. Batley, 1967-68
Highest against: 72-6 v. Wigan, 1986-87

1986-87 PLAYERS' SUMMARY

	App	Tries	Goals	Dr	Pts
Bell, Nigel	23 + 5	5	—	—	20
Brennan, Rowan	15	1	—	—	4
Cartwright, Phil	7	1	—	—	4
Cocks, Gary	16	2	—	—	8
Conway, Billy	31 + 1	5	—	—	20
Cowie, Bob	9 + 3	—	—	—	—
Diamond, Steve	20 + 1	1	31	2	68
Douglas, Ian	10 + 3	—	—	—	—
Eden, Phil	22	4	—	—	16
Evans, Steve	15	4	2	—	20
Gittins, Tom	16	1	—	—	4
Green, Jimmy	12	—	—	—	—
Haggerty, Gary	1 + 2	—	—	—	—
Halliwell, Steve	5	1	—	—	4
Harcombe, Kevin	11	1	33	—	70
Hendry, Paul	9 + 4	1	—	—	4
Hickman, Kevin	4	—	—	—	—
Hopkinson, Ian	23 + 12	2	—	—	8
Hughes, Ian	4	—	—	—	—
Jasiewicz, Dick	3	—	—	—	—
Jowitt, Ian	20 + 4	5	—	—	20
Kelly, Neil	13 + 3	2	1	—	10
Klein, Russell	18 + 3	5	—	—	20
Lazenby, Tracy	7	2	—	—	8
Lyons, John	25 + 6	15	1	3	65
Mallinder, Paul	7	—	—	—	—
Moll, David	3	3	—	—	12
Parrish, Mick	3	—	4	—	8
Potts, Steve	0 + 2	—	—	—	—
Rotherforth, Lindsay	12	—	—	—	—
Shaw, Alan	2 + 1	—	—	—	—
Sheldon, Ian	14	3	—	—	12
Smith, Stuart	10 + 3	1	—	—	4
Spencer, Gary	15	6	—	—	24
Stanton, Glen	19	6	—	—	24
Sygrove, Andy	1	—	—	—	—
Thompson, John	15 + 9	1	—	—	4
Thornton, Gary	11 + 2	1	—	—	4
Tosney, Andy	0 + 1	—	—	—	—
Van Bellen, Gary	8	—	—	—	—
Walker, Andy	2	—	—	—	—
Whiteman, Keith	4	1	—	—	4
Wild, Mark	1	—	—	—	—
Williams, Dean	1 + 2	—	—	—	—
Zelei, Tony	1 + 2	—	—	—	—
TOTALS:					
45 players		80	72	5	469

1986-87 MATCH ANALYSIS

Date	Competition	H/A	Opponent	Rlt	Score	Tries	Goals	Attendance	Referee
31.8.86	SBC	A	Hull	L	6-12	Jowitt	Diamond	—	—
3.9.86	SBC	A	Widnes	L	14-48	Jowitt, Spencer, Gittins	Diamond	—	—
7.9.86	SBC	A	Castleford	L	16-42	Whiteman, Spencer, Brennan	Evans (2)	—	—
14.9.86	YC(1)	A	Batley	W	14-12	Lazenby, Jowitt, Evans	Diamond	—	—
24.9.86	YC(2)	A	Hull	L	12-21	Conway, Evans	Diamond (2)	—	—
28.9.86	SBC	H	Bradford N.	L	22-32	Hopkinson, Eden, Jowitt, Bell	Diamond (3)	3666	Hodgson
5.10.86	SBC	A	St Helens	L	11-32	Lazenby, Evans	Diamond (1, 1 dg)	—	—
12.10.86	SBC	H	Leigh	L	6-12	Stanton	Diamond	2435	Simpson
19.10.86	SBC	A	Warrington	L	18-28	Conway (2), Spencer	Diamond (3)	—	—
26.10.86	SBC	H	Oldham	L	10-54	Stanton, Evans	Diamond	2738	Smith
2.11.86	SBC	A	Wigan	L	10-62	Lyons, Stanton	Diamond	—	—
9.11.86	SBC	H	Leeds	L	14-28	Diamond, Lyons, Cartwright	Diamond	3798	Houghton
15.11.86	JPS(P)	A	Millom (Cumbria)	W	18-4	Lyons (2), Hopkinson, Klein	Diamond	—	—
19.11.86	SBC	H	Barrow	D	14-14	Stanton, Smith	Diamond (3)	1470	Whitfield
23.11.86	SBC	A	Hull K.R.	L	11-22	Lyons, Jowitt	Diamond (1, 1 dg)	—	—
30.11.86	JPS(1)	A	Halifax	L	22-36	Klein, Bell, Conway, Stanton	Diamond (3)	—	—
14.12.86	SBC	H	Featherstone R.	L	2-29	—	Lyons	2890	Bowman
21.12.86	SBC	H	Castleford	L	12-40	Eden, Lyons	Diamond (2)	3234	Allatt
26.12.86	SBC	A	Leeds	L	4-46	Cocks	—	—	—
4.1.87	SBC	H	Salford	L	10-16	Spencer, Thompson	Parrish	1600	Volante
25.1.87	SBC	A	Barrow	L	13-38	Spencer (2)	Parrish (2), Lyons (dg)	—	—
8.2.87	SBC	H	St Helens	L	6-30	Kelly	Parrish	2444	Kendrew
10.2.87	CC(1)	A	Blackpool B.	W	15-10	Stanton, Cocks	Diamond (3), Lyons (dg)	—	—
15.2.87	CC(2)	H	Whitehaven	L	2-25	—	Diamond	2779	Spencer
22.2.87	SBC	A	Featherstone R.	L	10-27	Thornton, Lyons	Diamond	—	—
1.3.87	SBC	A	Salford	L	12-36	Harcombe, Hendry	Harcombe (2)	—	—
8.3.87	SBC	H	Warrington	L	22-38	Conway, Sheldon, Lyons	Harcombe (5)	1847	Kershaw
15.3.87	SBC	H	Widnes	W	38-20	Klein (2), Halliwell, Bell, Sheldon, Eden	Harcombe (7)	1613	Cross
22.3.87	SBC	A	Bradford N.	L	12-15	Klein	Harcombe (4)	—	—
25.3.87	SBC	A	Oldham	L	20-38	Sheldon, Lyons, Kelly, Bell	Harcombe (2)	—	—
29.3.87	SBC	H	Wigan	L	6-72	Lyons	Harcombe	5400	Carter
1.4.87	SBC	H	Hull K.R.	W	19-4	Lyons (2), Bell	Harcombe (3), Lyons (dg)	1281	Tennant
5.4.87	SBC	A	Leigh	L	8-46	Lyons	Harcombe, Kelly	—	—
14.4.87	SBC	H	Halifax	W	18-14	Lyons, Eden	Harcombe (5)	2386	Houghton
17.4.87	SBC	A	Halifax	W	18-10	Moll (2), Lyons	Harcombe (3)	—	—
20.4.87	SBC	H	Hull	L	4-38	Moll	—	2750	Kendrew

WARRINGTON

Ground: Wilderspool
Colours: White jerseys with primrose and blue hoop
First Season: 1895-96
Nickname: Wire
Chairman: Peter Higham
General
  Manager: Mike Harvey
Coach: Tony Barrow (Mar 1986-)
Honours: **Championship** Winners, 1947-48, 1953-54, 1954-55
Beaten finalists, 1925-26, 1934-35, 1936-37, 1948-49, 1950-51, 1960-61
League Leaders Trophy Winners, 1972-73
Club Championship (Merit Table) Winners, 1973-74
Challenge Cup Winners, 1904-05, 1906-07, 1949-50, 1953-54, 1973-74
Beaten finalists, 1900-01, 1903-04, 1912-13, 1927-28, 1932-33, 1935-36, 1974-75
Lancashire League Winners, 1937-38, 1947-48, 1948-49, 1950-51, 1953-54, 1954-55, 1955-56, 1967-68
Lancashire Cup Winners, 1921-22, 1929-30, 1932-33, 1937-38, 1959-60, 1965-66, 1980-81, 1982-83
Beaten finalists, 1906-07, 1948-49, 1950-51, 1967-68, 1985-86
John Player Trophy Winners, 1973-74, 1977-78, 1980-81
Beaten finalists, 1978-79, 1986-87
Premiership Trophy Winners, 1985-86
Beaten finalists 1976-77, 1986-87
Captain Morgan Trophy Winners, 1973-74
BBC2 Trophy Beaten finalists, 1974-75
Records: Attendance: 35,000 Wigan v. Leigh (Lancs. Cup Final) 29 Oct, 1949
Home: 34,304 v. Wigan (League) 22 Jan, 1949

Season
Goals: 170 by S. Hesford, 1978-79
Tries: 66 by B. Bevan, 1952-53
Points: 363 by H. Bath, 1952-53
Match
Goals: 14 by H. Palin v. Liverpool C., 13 Sep, 1950
Tries: 7 by B. Bevan v. Leigh, 29 Mar, 1948 and v. Bramley, 22 Apr, 1953
Points: 33 by G. Thomas v. St. Helens, 12 Apr, 1909
Highest score: 78-3 v. St. Helens, 1908-09
Highest against: 68-14 v. Hunslet, 1927-28

1986-87 PLAYERS' SUMMARY

	App	Tries	Goals	Dr	Pts
Abram, Darren	0 + 1	—	—	—	—
Bishop, Paul	34 + 3	12	99	17	263
Boyd, Les	26	5	—	—	20
Campbell, Roy	0 + 1	—	—	—	—
Capewell, Philip	3 + 1	—	—	—	—
Carbert, Brian	5	3	12	—	36
Crompton, Martin	3 + 2	—	—	—	—
Cullen, Paul	21	9	—	—	36
Drummond, Des	17	8	—	—	32
Duane, Ronnie	24 + 3	7	—	—	28
Eccles, Bob	4 + 8	1	—	—	4
Ford, Paul	3 + 1	—	4	—	8
Forster, Mark	27 + 1	10	—	—	40
Gleave, Mark	0 + 1	—	—	—	—
Gregory, Andy	13 + 1	3	4	—	20
Gregory, Mike	27 + 1	5	—	—	20
Harmon, Neil	2	—	—	—	—
Hodson, Tony	16	1	—	—	4
Holden, Keith	9	2	—	—	8
Humphries, Tony	8 + 10	2	—	—	8
Jackson, Bob	38	10	7	1	55
Johnson, Brian	39	25	—	—	100
Kelly, Ken	16 + 9	4	—	—	16
Lowndes, Paul	0 + 1	—	—	—	—
McGinty, Billy	4 + 7	—	—	—	—
Meadows, Kevin	27	12	—	—	48
Mossop, Andy	3 + 1	1	—	—	4
Peters, Barry	3	1	—	—	4
Peters, Steve	8 + 2	—	—	—	—
Rathbone, Alan	10 + 4	3	—	—	12
Roberts, Mark	29 + 2	15	—	—	60
Ropati, Joe	32 + 1	19	—	—	76
Roskell, Mark	11	1	—	—	4
Sanderson, Gary	22 + 6	1	—	—	4
Tamati, Kevin	28 + 4	1	—	—	4
Thackray, Rick	14	6	—	—	24
Thorniley, Tony	0 + 1	—	—	—	—
Webb, Carl	5	1	—	—	4
Worrall, Tony	2	1	—	—	4

TOTALS:
| 39 players | | 169 | 126 | 18 | 946 |

1985-86 MATCH ANALYSIS

Date	Competition	H/A	Opponent	Rlt	Score	Tries	Goals	Attendance	Referee
31.8.86	SBC	H	Castleford	L	20-26	Bishop (2)	Bishop (6)	4009	Whitfield
4.9.86	SBC	A	Leigh	L	17-22	Thackray, Hodson, Worrall	Bishop (2, 1 dg)	—	—
7.9.86	SBC	H	Oldham	W	22-18	Duane, Eccles, Humphries	Bishop (5)	4393	McDonald
14.9.86	LC(1)	H	Salford	W	28-20	Johnson, Webb, Duane, Eccles, Thackray	Gregory (4)	3617	Allatt
21.9.86	SBC	H	Salford	W	42-14	Forster (3), Johnson (2), Thackray (2), Roberts	Bishop (5)	2981	Tennant
24.9.86	LC(2)	A	St Helens	L	15-19	Bishop, Boyd, Roberts	Bishop (1, 1 dg)	—	—
28.9.86	SBC	A	Halifax	W	16-13	Roberts, Thackray, Cullen	Bishop (2)	—	—
5.10.86	SBC	H	Wigan	W	23-12	Johnson, Boyd, M. Gregory, Cullen	Bishop (3, 1 dg)	8561	Lindop
12.10.86	SBC	A	Featherstone R.	W	29-22	Roberts, Jackson, Bishop, Cullen, Johnson	Bishop (4, 1 dg)	—	—
19.10.86	SBC	H	Wakefield T.	W	28-18	Meadows (2), Kelly, Roberts, Bishop	Bishop (4)	3233	Carter
2.11.86	SBC	A	Salford	W	25-10	Boyd, Bishop, Duane, A. Gregory	Bishop (4, 1 dg)	—	—
9.11.86	SBC	H	Hull	W	42-10	M. Gregory, Roberts, Bishop, Forster, A. Gregory, Jackson, Ropati, Kelly	Bishop (5)	3774	Hodgson
16.11.86	SBC	A	Leeds	W	54-16	Roberts (3), Duane (2), Johnson (2), M. Gregory, A. Gregory, Meadows, Bishop, Jackson	Bishop (3)	—	—
23.11.86	SBC	H	Halifax	W	18-10	Ropati, Meadows, Forster	Bishop (3)	4683	Haigh
30.11.86	JPS(1)	H	Hunslet	W	11-10	Thackray	Bishop (3, 1 dg)	3680	Simpson
7.12.86	JPS(2)	H	Halifax	W	44-10	Johnson (3), Ropati, Jackson, Meadows, Bishop	Bishop (8)	5804	Kershaw
14.12.86	JPS(3)	A	St Helens	W	22-20	Johnson, Forster, Ropati, Meadows	Bishop (4, 2 dg)	—	—
27.12.86	JPS(SF)	Wigan	Widnes	W	35-4	Johnson (2), Cullen (2), Roberts, Boyd, Forster, Meadows	Jackson, Bishop (dg)	(6409)	McDonald
1.1.87	SBC	A	Wigan	W	6-4	Cullen	Bishop	—	—
4.1.87	SBC	H	Leeds	W	20-6	Ropati (2), Bishop, Roberts	Bishop (2)	4718	Allatt
10.1.87	JPS(F)	Bolton W. FC	Wigan	L	4-18	Forster	—	(21,144)	Holdsworth
19.1.87	SBC	H (at Manchester C. FC)	Barrow	W	24-20	Roberts (2), Cullen, Johnson	Ford (4)	2215	McDonald
25.1.87	SBC	A	Castleford	W	24-18	Cullen (2), Kelly, Meadows, Johnson	Bishop (1, 2 dg)	—	—
1.2.87	CC(1)	H	Bradford N.	L	17-21	Meadows, Kelly, Boyd	Bishop (2, 1dg)	5148	Holdsworth
8.2.87	SBC	H	Bradford N.	W	31-10	Jackson, Rathbone, Drummond, Humphries, Johnson	Bishop (5), Jackson (dg)	4038	Lindop
18.2.87	SBC	A	St Helens	L	22-42	Meadows (2), Drummond, Roberts	Bishop (3)	—	—
22.2.87	SBC	A	Barrow	L	6-9	Ropati	Bishop	—	—
1.3.87	SBC	H	Featherstone R.	W	32-15	Ropati (3), Duane, Jackson, Tamati	Bishop (3, 2dg)	3104	Carter
8.3.87	SBC	A	Wakefield T.	W	38-22	Ropati (2), Johnson (2), Forster, Duane, Meadows	Jackson (5)	—	—
11.3.87	SBC	A	Oldham	L	14-15	Jackson, Ropati, M. Gregory	Bishop	—	—
15.3.87	SBC	A	Hull K.R.	L	10-14	Ropati, Bishop	Jackson	—	—
22.3.87	SBC	H	St Helens	D	17-17	Drummond (2), Ropati	Bishop (2, 1dg)	5523	Allatt

(continued on page 95)

83

WHITEHAVEN

Ground:	Recreation Ground
Colours:	Chocolate, blue and gold jerseys
First Season:	1948-49
Nickname:	Haven
Chairman:	David Wigham
Secretary:	Eppie Gibson
Coach:	Phil Kitchin (June 1985-)
Records:	Attendance: 18,500 v. Wakefield T. (RL Cup) 19 Mar, 1960

Season

Goals: 141 by J. McKeown, 1956-57
Tries: 29 by W. Smith, 1956-57
Points: 291 by J. McKeown, 1956-57

Match

Goals: 11 by W. Holliday v. Hunslet, 31 Mar, 1962
Tries: 6 by V. Gribbin v. Doncaster, 18 Nov, 1984
Points: 25 by W. Holliday v. Hunslet, 31 Mar, 1962
Highest score: 72-6 v. Fulham, 1986-87
Highest against: 74-6 v. Wigan, 1986-87

1986-87 PLAYERS' SUMMARY

	App	Tries	Goals	Dr	Pts
Ackerman, Rob	35	14	—	—	56
Banks, Alan	5 + 3	1	—	—	4
Beckwith, Mark	8 + 8	6	—	—	24
Bottell, Gary	8 + 1	2	—	—	8
Burney, Steve	28	9	—	—	36
Cameron, Graham	27	7	35	1	99
Crossingham, Mark	0 + 1	—	—	—	—
Dalton, Jimmy	10 + 2	7	—	—	28
Fearon, Neal	10 + 3	3	—	—	12
Fisher, Billy	34 + 1	13	—	—	52
Fryer, Mark	0 + 1	—	—	—	—
Gorley, Peter	2	—	—	—	—
Hall, Colin	4	—	—	—	—
Hetherington, Gary	36	4	—	—	16
Howse, Steve	24 + 5	4	—	—	16
Johnston, Frank	2 + 9	—	—	—	—
Lightfoot, David	25 + 1	3	3	—	18
Lofthouse, Norman	31	13	53	—	158
McCartney, Duncan	10 + 7	—	—	—	—
McConnell, Ralph	9 + 2	5	—	—	20
McCurrie, Alan	29 + 3	2	—	—	8
McFarlane, Gary	18	8	—	—	32
Richardson, Willie	8 + 4	4	19	—	54
Ritson, Dave	0 + 1	—	—	—	—
Rose, Tony	27	1	—	—	4
Shuttleworth, Greg	31 + 2	6	—	2	26
Simpson, Jeff	17 + 3	1	—	—	4
Solarie, Tony	25 + 5	21	—	—	84
Tomlinson, Brian	5 + 2	2	—	—	8
Weiss, Steve	0 + 1	—	—	—	—

TOTALS:

	App	Tries	Goals	Dr	Pts
30 players		136	110	3	767

1986-87 MATCH ANALYSIS

Date	Competition	H/A	Opponent	Rlt	Score	Tries	Goals	Attendance	Referee
31.8.86	SD	A	Bramley	L	12-20	Lofthouse, Bottell	Cameron (2)	—	—
7.9.86	SD	H	York	W	30-10	Lofthouse, Ackerman, McConnell, Tomlinson, Fisher	Richardson (4), Lightfoot	1928	Hodgson
10.9.86	SD	A	Rochdale H.	L	0-6	—	—	—	—
14.9.86	LC(1)	H	Fulham	W	72-6	Ackerman (3), Fearon (2), McCurrie, Fisher, Shuttleworth, Dalton, Banks, Lofthouse, Rose	Lofthouse (10), Lightfoot (2)	1602	Carter

MATCH ANALYSIS (continued)

21.9.86	SD	H	Keighley	W	44-6	Dalton (2), Tomlinson, Howse, Shuttleworth, Bottell, Lofthouse	Lofthouse (8)	1554	Haigh
24.9.86	LC(2)	A	Wigan	L	6-74	Fisher	Lofthouse	—	—
28.9.86	SD	A	Batley	L	2-26	—	Lofthouse	—	—
5.10.86	SD	H	Mansfield M.	W	22-18	McConnell (2), Dalton, Hetherington	Lofthouse (3)	1514	McDonald
12.10.86	SD	A	Doncaster	L	12-28	Burney, Shuttleworth	Lofthouse (2)	—	—
19.10.86	SD	H	Rochdale H.	W	20-4	Ackerman, Dalton, Howse, Lofthouse	Lofthouse (2)	1441	Tennant
26.10.86	SD	A	Keighley	W	26-4	Ackerman (2), Dalton (2), Fisher	Lofthouse (3)	—	—
2.11.86	SD	H	Runcorn H.	W	26-2	Cameron, Lofthouse, Burney, Shuttleworth, Ackerman	Cameron (2), Lofthouse	1585	Houghton
9.11.86	SD	A	Swinton	L	8-14	Fisher, Solarie	—	—	—
16.11.86	SD	H	Blackpool B.	W	26-10	McFarlane (2), Solarie, Lofthouse	Cameron (5)	1426	Holdsworth
23.11.86	SD	A	Dewsbury	W	24-16	Lightfoot, Burney, Lofthouse, Solarie, Cameron	Cameron, Lofthouse	—	—
30.11.86	JPS(1)	H	St Helens	L	8-10	Lightfoot	Cameron (2)	3678	Spencer
14.12.86	SD	H	Bramley	W	24-10	McFarlane, Fisher, Cameron, Lofthouse	Cameron (4)	1688	Cross
26.12.86	SD	A	Workington T.	W	22-14	Lightfoot, Solarie, Ackerman, McFarlane	Cameron (2), Lofthouse	—	—
1.1.87	SD	H	Workington T.	W	16-2	Solarie, Ackerman, Cameron	Cameron, Lofthouse	2801	Smith
4.1.87	SD	A	Blackpool B.	W	8-5	Solarie	Cameron (2)	—	—
25.1.87	SD	H	Doncaster	W	26-7	Fisher, Ackerman, Solarie, Hetherington	Lofthouse (5)	1822	Tickle
8.2.87	CC(1)	A	Huddersfield B.	W	32-10	McFarlane (2), Solarie (2), Burney, Beckwith	Lofthouse (4)	—	—
15.2.87	CC(2)	A	Wakefield T.	W	25-2	Fisher, McCurrie, Beckwith, Lofthouse	Lofthouse (4), Cameron (dg)	—	—
22.2.87	SD	H	Batley	W	40-6	Cameron (2), Burney (2), Solarie, Shuttleworth, McFarlane, Beckwith	Lofthouse (4)	1508	McDonald
1.3.87	CC(3)	A	St Helens	L	12-41	Fisher, Lofthouse	Cameron, Lofthouse	—	—
8.3.87	SD	H	Swinton	W	22-12	Howse, Cameron, Ackerman, Lofthouse	Cameron (3)	2432	Cross
15.3.87	SD	A	York	W	20-15	Shuttleworth, Ackerman, Fisher, McFarlane	Cameron (2)	—	—
22.3.87	SD	A	Fulham	D	8-8	Solarie	Cameron (2)	—	—
29.3.87	SD	H	Fulham	W	32-14	Solarie (3), Burney, Ackerman, Fisher	Cameron (4)	1712	Smith
1.4.87	SD	A	Runcorn	W	8-4	Beckwith	Cameron (2)	—	—
5.4.87	SD	A	Mansfield M.	W	22-7	Solarie (2), Beckwith, Fisher, Lofthouse	Lofthouse	—	—
12.4.87	SD	H	Dewsbury	W	50-12	Solarie (3), Richardson (2), Howse, Burney, Hetherington, Fearon	Richardson (7)	1522	Whitfield
17.4.87	SD	A	Carlisle	L	11-16	Solarie (2)	Richardson, Shuttleworth (dg)	—	—
20.4.87	SD	H	Carlisle	W	16-8	Fisher, Richardson, McConnell	Richardson (2)	2236	Spencer
26.4.87	SDP(1)	H	Sheffield E.	W	29-24	Beckwith, Simpson, Richardson, Burney, McConnell	Richardson (4), Shuttleworth (dg)	2602	Kendrew
10.5.87	SDP(SF)	A	Swinton	L	6-12	Hetherington	Richardson	—	—

WIDNES

Ground:	Naughton Park
Colours:	White jerseys with black trim
First Season:	1895-96
Nickname:	Chemics
Chairman:	Tom Smith
Secretary:	Ron Close
Coach:	Doug Laughton (Jan 1986-)
Honours:	**Division One** Champions, 1977-78
	Championship Beaten finalists, 1935-36
	Challenge Cup Winners, 1929-30, 1936-37, 1963-64, 1974-75, 1978-79, 1980-81, 1983-84
	Beaten finalists, 1933-34, 1949-50, 1975-76, 1976-77, 1981-82
	Lancashire League Winners, 1919-20
	Lancashire Cup Winners, 1945-46, 1974-75, 1975-76, 1976-77, 1978-79, 1979-80
	Beaten finalists, 1928-29, 1939-40, 1955-56, 1971-72, 1981-82, 1983-84
	John Player Trophy Winners, 1975-76, 1978-79
	Beaten finalists, 1974-75, 1977-78, 1979-80, 1983-84
	Premiership Winners, 1979-80, 1981-82, 1982-83
	Beaten finalists, 1977-78
	BBC2 Floodlit Trophy Winners, 1978-79
	Beaten finalists, 1972-73, 1973-74
	Western Division Championship Beaten finalists, 1962-63
Records:	Attendance: 24,205 v. St. Helens (RL Cup) 16 Feb, 1961
	Season
	Goals: 140 by M. Burke, 1978-79
	Tries: 34 by F. Myler, 1958-59
	Points: 316 by M. Burke, 1978-79
	Match
	Goals: 11 by R. Whitfield v. Oldham, 28 Oct, 1965

Tries: 5 by E. Cunningham v. Doncaster, 15 Feb, 1981; J. Basnett v. Hunslet, 17 Oct, 1981 and v. Hull K.R., 2 Nov, 1986; D. Hulme v. Dewsbury, 30 Nov, 1986
Points: 27 by H. Dawson v. Liverpool C., 22 Apr, 1957
Highest score: 82-0 v. Dewsbury, 1986-87
Highest against: 60-5 v. Oldham, 1927-28

1986-87 PLAYERS' SUMMARY

	App	Tries	Goals	Dr	Pts
Basnett, John	36	20	—	—	80
Burke, Mick	20	3	21	1	55
Cleal, Les	9 + 2	2	—	—	8
Coleman, Craig	3	1	—	1	5
Currier, Andy	4 + 1	1	9	—	22
Dowd, Barry	22 + 2	6	33	1	91
Eyres, Andrew	3 + 1	—	—	—	—
Eyres, Richard	21 + 7	6	—	—	24
Fieldhouse, John	3 + 2	—	—	—	—
Gilbert, John	16 + 1	5	—	—	20
Gormley, Ian	13 + 1	5	—	—	20
Haughton, Paul	1 + 1	—	—	—	—
Hulme, David	38 + 3	19	—	—	76
Hulme, Paul	24 + 6	3	—	—	12
Lamb, David	0 + 2	—	—	—	—
Linton, Ralph	10 + 2	6	—	—	24
Lyon, David	0 + 1	—	—	—	—
McKenzie, Phil	36 + 1	11	—	—	44
McMannion, Phil	0 + 1	—	—	—	—
Moran, David	8 + 1	—	—	—	—
Myler, John	11 + 3	3	32	2	78
Myler, Tony	22	11	—	—	44
Newton, Keith	13 + 4	—	—	—	—
O'Neill, Mike	37 + 2	9	—	—	36
O'Neill, Steve	36 + 3	4	—	2	18
Pinner, Harry	23 + 2	2	—	—	8
Platt, Duncan	14 + 4	7	26	—	80
Rigby, Colin	1	—	—	—	—
Ruane, Andrew	11 + 1	2	4	—	16
Ruane, David	5 + 2	—	—	—	—
Rutter, Philip	1	—	—	—	—
Schmidt, Darrel	2	—	—	—	—
Sephton, Geoff	1	—	—	—	—
Sorensen, Kurt	33	11	—	—	44
Stockley, Trevor	11 + 13	5	—	—	20
Sullivan, Andy	18 + 1	2	—	—	8
Thackray, Rick	18	5	—	—	20
Worgan, Graham	3 + 1	—	—	—	—
Wright, Darren	40	15	—	—	60
Wright, Stuart	5	—	—	—	—
TOTALS:					
40 players		164	125	7	913

1986-87 MATCH ANALYSIS

Date	Competition	H/A	Opponent	Rlt	Score	Tries	Goals	Attendance	Referee
31.8.86	SBC	A	Bradford N.	L	14-27	Sorensen, S. O'Neill	Burke (3)	—	—
3.9.86	SBC	H	Wakefield T.	W	48-14	Gormley (2), D. Wright (2), Dowd, Basnett, Sorensen, D. Hulme, Stockley, Gilbert	Currier (4)	2414	McDonald
7.9.86	SBC	H	Barrow	W	26-14	Sorensen, McKenzie, P. Hulme, Gilbert, M. O'Neill	Currier (3)	2923	Lindop
14.9.86	LC(1)	A	Runcorn H.	W	48-10	Burke (2), Sorensen (2), S. O'Neill (2), Currier, M. O'Neill, D. Wright, D. Hulme	Platt (3), Currier	—	—
21.9.86	SBC	A	Featherstone R.	W	48-14	Platt (2), Gormley (2), Basnett (2), D. Hulme, Gilbert	Platt (7), Dowd (dg), S. O'Neill (dg)	—	—
24.9.86	LC(2)	A	Barrow	W	12-10	Platt, Sorensen	Platt (2)	—	—
28.9.86	SBC	H	Leeds	W	35-10	Stockley (2), D. Hulme (2), A. Ruane, M. O'Neill, Gormley	Burke (2), Currier, Coleman (dg)	3748	Smith
1.10.86	LC(SF)	A	Oldham	L	14-16	Basnett, Platt, Gilbert	Platt	—	—
5.10.86	SBC	A	Oldham	L	16-22	Coleman, R. Eyres, Platt	A. Ruane (2)	—	—
15.10.86	SBC	H	Castleford	W	29-20	D. Wright (2), Cleal, A. Myler	J. Myler (6), Burke (dg)	3349	Hodgson
19.10.86	SBC	A	Leigh	W	20-18	Basnett, D. Hulme, Sorensen, Gilbert	J. Myler (2)	—	—
2.11.86	SBC	H	Hull K.R.	W	26-8	Basnett (5)	Burke (3)	3460	Mean
9.11.86	SBC	A	Barrow	W	18-16	Basnett, D. Hulme, R. Eyres	Burke (3)	—	—
12.11.86	Tour	H	Australia	L	4-20	—	Burke (2)	10268	Berry
16.11.86	SBC	H	Bradford N.	L	14-36	D. Wright, McKenzie	Burke (3)	4157	Tennant
23.11.86	SBC	A	Salford	L	16-22	P. Hulme, McKenzie, Basnett	Burke (2)	—	—
30.11.86	JPS(1)	H	Dewsbury	W	82-0	D. Hulme (5), Basnett (3), McKenzie (2), Dowd (2), R. Eyres, Sorensen, Burke, D. Wright, Pinner	Dowd (7)	2138	Allatt
8.12.86	JPS(2)	H	Carlisle	W	36-6	Cleal, Dowd, A. Myler, Basnett, Sorensen, J. Myler, D. Hulme	J. Myler (2), Burke, Dowd	2016	Holdsworth
14.12.86	JPS(3)	A	Barrow	W	16-6	D. Wright, Dowd, McKenzie	Burke (2)	—	—
21.12.86	SBC	A	Hull K.R.	L	0-18	—	—	—	—
27.12.86	JPS(SF)	Wigan	Warrington	L	4-35	P. Hulme	—	(6409)	McDonald
1.1.87	SBC	H	St Helens	W	16-10	A. Ruane, S. O'Neill	Platt (4)	5981	Lindop
4.1.87	SBC	H	Wigan	L	16-22	Sullivan, M. O'Neill	Platt (3), A. Ruane	7628	Houghton
21.1.87	SBC	H	Oldham	W	44-10	A. Myler (2), J. Myler (2), Linton (2), D. Hulme, Sullivan	J. Myler (6)	2798	Beaumont
25.1.87	SBC	A	Leeds	L	6-35	Linton	J. Myler	—	—
31.1.87	CC(1)	A	Castleford	W	24-16	D. Hulme, A. Myler, Sorensen, Basnett	J. Myler (4)	4416	—
8.2.87	SBC	H	Salford	W	13-12	D. Wright, M. O'Neill	J. Myler (2, 1dg)	3101	McDonald
15.2.87	CC(2)	A	Bradford N.	D	6-6	—	J. Myler	—	—
18.2.87	CC(2) Replay	H	Bradford N.	W	29-12	A. Myler (2), McKenzie, R. Eyres, D. Wright	J. Myler (4, 1dg)	11118	Haigh
22.2.87	SBC	A	Wigan	L	4-40	M. O'Neill	—	—	—
1.3.87	CC(3)	A	Leeds	W	14-7	M. O'Neill, Thackray	J. Myler (3)	—	—
8.3.87	SBC	H	Halifax	L	6-10	Basnett	J. Myler	5182	Kendrew

(continued on page 96)

WIGAN

Ground: Central Park
Colours: Cherry and white hooped jerseys
First Season: 1895-96
Nickname: Riversiders
Chairman: Jack Hilton
Coach: Graham Lowe (Aug 1986-)
Honours: **Championship** Winners, 1908-09, 1921-22, 1925-26, 1933-34, 1945-46, 1946-47, 1949-50, 1951-52, 1959-60
Beaten finalists, 1909-10, 1910-11, 1911-12, 1912-13, 1923-24, 1970-71
League Leaders Trophy Winners, 1970-71
Division One Champions 1986-87
Challenge Cup Winners, 1923-24, 1928-29, 1947-48, 1950-51, 1957-58, 1958-59, 1964-65, 1984-85
Beaten finalists, 1910-11, 1919-20, 1943-44, 1945-46, 1960-61, 1962-63, 1965-66, 1969-70, 1983-84
Lancashire League Winners, 1901-02, 1908-09, 1910-11, 1911-12, 1912-13, 1913-14, 1914-15, 1920-21, 1922-23, 1923-24, 1925-26, 1945-46, 1946-47, 1949-50, 1951-52, 1958-59, 1961-62, 1969-70
Lancashire War League Winners, 1940-41
Lancashire Cup Winners, 1905-06, 1908-09, 1909-10, 1912-13, 1922-23, 1928-29, 1938-39, 1946-47, 1947-48, 1948-49, 1949-50, 1950-51, 1951-52, 1966-67, 1971-72, 1973-74, 1985-86, 1986-87
Beaten finalists, 1913-14, 1914-15, 1925-26, 1927-28, 1930-31, 1934-35, 1935-36, 1936-37, 1945-46, 1953-54, 1957-58, 1977-78, 1980-81, 1984-85
John Player Trophy Winners, 1982-83, 1985-86, 1986-87
Premiership Winners 1986-87
BBC2 Floodlit Trophy Winners, 1968-69
Beaten finalists, 1969-70
Charity Shield Winners, 1985-86
War League Championship Winners, 1943-44
Beaten finalists, 1940-41

Records: Attendance: 47,747 v. St. Helens (League) 27 Mar, 1959
Season
Goals: 176 by F. Griffiths, 1958-59
Tries: 62 by J. Ring, 1925-26
Points: 394 by F. Griffiths, 1958-59
Match
Goals: 22 by J. Sullivan v. Flimby & Fothergill, 14 Feb, 1925
Tries: 7 by J. Ring v. Flimby & Fothergill, 14 Feb, 1925; v. Salford, 13 Apr, 1925 and v. Pemberton R., 12 Feb, 1927; W. Boston v. Dewsbury, 20 Aug, 1955 and v. Salford, 30 Apr. 1962; G. Vigo v. St. Helens, 21 Aug, 1976
Points: 44 by J. Sullivan v. Flimby & Fothergill, 14 Feb, 1925
Highest score: 116-0 v. Flimby & Fothergill, 1924-25
Highest against: 58-3 v. Leeds, 1972-73

1986-87 PLAYERS' SUMMARY

	App	Tries	Goals	Dr	Pts
Bell, Dean	42	22	—	—	88
Beswick, Dave	1 + 1	—	—	—	—
Betts, Dennis	0 + 2	1	—	—	4
Case, Brian	44	2	—	—	8
Dermott, Martin	25 + 2	3	—	—	12
Du Toit, Nick	0 + 4	—	—	—	—
Edwards, Shaun	41	24	6	—	108
Ford, Mike	9 + 6	6	—	1	25
Gildart, Ian	1	—	—	—	—
Gill, Henderson	37 + 1	30	72	—	264
Goodway, Andy	44 + 1	11	—	—	44
Gregory, Andy	21	4	—	—	16
Hampson, Steve	40 + 2	11	—	—	44
Hanley, Ellery	38 + 1	59	1	—	238
Holden, Keith	0 + 1	1	—	—	4
Kiss, Nicky	19	2	—	—	8
Louw, Rob	15 + 7	2	—	—	8
Lucas, Ian	0 + 7	—	—	—	—
Lydon, Joe	42 + 1	22	36	3	163
Mayo, John	0 + 3	—	—	—	—
Mordt, Ray	16 + 4	15	—	—	60
Potter, Ian	39 + 3	2	—	—	8
Roberts, Ian	19 + 1	3	—	—	12
Russell, Richard	7 + 8	5	—	—	20
Stephenson, David	37 + 4	13	64	—	180
Stott, Phil	2	1	—	—	4
Wane, Shaun	18 + 5	1	—	—	4
West, Graeme	28 + 5	6	—	—	24
TOTALS:					
28 players		246	179	4	1,346

1986-87 MATCH ANALYSIS

Date	Com-petition	H/A	Opponent	Rlt	Score	Tries	Goals	Atten-dance	Referee
31.8.86	SBC	H	Salford	W	42-12	Gill (3), Hanley (2), Louw, Case	Stephenson (7)	10671	Houghton
3.9.86	SBC	H	Barrow	W	18-6	Stott, West, Louw	Stephenson (3)	9189	Allatt
7.9.86	SBC	A	Leigh	W	35-0	Lydon (2), Gill (2), Hanley, Bell, Goodway	Stephenson (2), Lydon (1, 1 dg)	—	—
14.9.86	LC(1)	H	Rochdale H.	W	52-0	Bell (2), Hanley (2), Gill (2), Stephenson (2), Lydon, Hampson	Stephenson (6)	10230	Bowman
21.9.86	SBC	A	Bradford N.	W	20-10	Lydon, Gill, Hampson, Potter	Stephenson, Lydon	—	—
24.9.86	LC(2)	H	Whitehaven	W	74-6	Mordt (4), Hanley (4), Gill (2), Wane, Goodway, Ford, Lydon	Gill (8), Lydon	9099	Spencer
28.9.86	SBC	H	Hull	W	34-7	Hanley (4), West	Gill (7)	12526	Whitfield
1.10.86	LC(SF)	H	St Helens	W	22-16	Goodway, Dermott, Hanley	Gill (5)	28252	Allatt
5.10.86	SBC	A	Warrington	L	12-23	Ford, Holden	Lydon, Gill	—	—
12.10.86	Tour	H	Australia	L	18-26	Bell, Edwards, Lydon	Gill (3)	30622	Holdsworth
19.10.86	LC(F)	St Helens	Oldham	W	27-6	Edwards (2), Ford, Lydon	Gill (5), Lydon (dg)	(20180)	Smith
29.10.86	SBC	A	Castleford	W	12-6	Edwards, Hanley	Gill (2)	—	—
2.11.86	SBC	H	Wakefield T.	W	62-10	Hanley (3), Bell (2), Edwards (2), Ford, Goodway, Hampson, Roberts, Gill	Stephenson (4), Gill (2), Hanley	9918	Spencer
9.11.86	SBC	A	Salford	W	34-0	Gill (2), Lydon, West, Ford	Gill (7)	—	—
16.11.86	SBC	H	Leigh	W	31-0	Bell (2), Roberts, West, Edwards, Stephenson	Stephenson (2), Gill, Ford (dg)	12839	Hodgson
23.11.86	SBC	A	Barrow	W	16-8	Ford, Lydon, Mordt	Gill (2)	—	—
29.11.86	JPS(1)	H	Leeds	W	32-10	Hanley (2), Goodway (2), Case, Edwards	Gill (4)	9112	Fox
7.12.86	JPS(2)	H	Swinton	W	20-14	Roberts, Dermott, Bell	Gill (4)	9874	Berry
14.12.86	JPS(3)	H	Leigh	W	6-2	Hanley	Stephenson	11573	Haigh
20.12.86	JPS(SF)	Leeds	Hull	W	12-11	Hanley (2)	Gill, Stephenson	(5245)	Holdsworth
26.12.86	SBC	A	St Helens	W	12-4	Stephenson, Gill	Stephenson, Gill	—	—
1.1.87	SBC	H	Warrington	L	4-6	—	Stephenson, Lydon	17106	Whitfield
4.1.87	SBC	A	Widnes	W	22-16	Hanley (2), Lydon, Mordt	Lydon (3)	—	—
10.1.87	JPS(F)	Bolton W. FC	Warrington	W	18-4	Gill (2), Goodway, Bell	Gill	(21144)	Holdsworth
18.1.87	CC(P)	A (at Wigan)	Workington T.	W	68-0	Edwards (3), Hanley (3), West (2), Dermott, Bell, Betts, Lydon	Lydon (7), Gill (3)	—	—
25.1.87	SBC	A	Hull K.R.	W	23-6	Mordt (2), Edwards, Hanley	Lydon (3, 1 dg)	—	—
4.2.87	CC(1)	A	Oldham	L	8-10	Bell	Lydon (2)	—	—
15.2.87	SBC	H	Castleford	W	16-6	Gill (2), Goodway, Edwards	—	12977	Whitfield
18.2.87	SBC	H	Leeds	W	30-8	Stephenson (2), Kiss, Lydon, Edwards, Potter	Lydon (2), Edwards	11118	Berry
22.2.87	SBC	H	Widnes	W	40-4	Hanley (2), Bell (2), Gill, Edwards, Hampson, Russell	Lydon (4)	13084	Mean
1.3.87	SBC	H	Bradford N.	W	60-6	Hanley (5), Lydon (2), Bell, Russell, Edwards, Mordt	Lydon (7), Edwards	11683	Haigh
11.3.87	SBC	A	Leeds	W	30-0	Russell (3), Mordt (3), Edwards	Stephenson	—	—
15.3.87	SBC	A	Halifax	W	12-8	Hanley, Gregory	Edwards (2)	—	—

(continued on page 96)

89

WORKINGTON TOWN

Ground:	Derwent Park
Colours:	White jerseys with blue band
First Season:	1945-46
Nickname:	Town
Chairman:	George Graham
Secretary:	John Bell
Coach:	Keith Davies (Feb 1986-Mar 1987), Norman Turley (Mar 1987-)
Honours:	**Championship** Winners, 1950-51
	Beaten finalists, 1957-58
	Challenge Cup Winners, 1951-52
	Beaten finalists, 1954-55, 1957-58
	Lancashire Cup Winners, 1977-78
	Beaten finalists, 1976-77, 1978-79, 1979-80
	Western Division Championship Winners, 1962-63
Records:	Attendance: 17,741 v. Wigan (RL Cup) 3 Mar, 1965. There was a crowd of 20,403 at Borough Park for a RL Cup-tie v. St. Helens on 8 Mar, 1952
	Season
	Goals: 186 by L. Hopkins, 1981-82
	Tries: 49 by J. Lawrenson, 1951-52
	Points: 438 by L. Hopkins, 1981-82
	Match
	Goals: 11 by I. MacCorquodale v. Blackpool B., 6 Jan, 1973
	Tries: 7 by I. Southward v. Blackpool B., 17 Sep, 1955
	Points: 33 by I. Southward v. Blackpool B., 17 Sep, 1955
	Highest score: 62-15 v. Hunslet, 1963-64
	Highest against: 68-0 at Wigan, 1986-87

1986-87 PLAYERS' SUMMARY

	App	Tries	Goals	Dr	Pts
Bailey, Stephen	4 + 2	—	—	—	—
Banks, John	3	—	—	—	—
Beattie, John	32	7	—	—	28
Beck, David	32	8	—	—	32
Bond, Gary	2 + 1	4	—	—	16
Bower, Ian	19	7	—	—	28
Burgess, Glen	15 + 1	2	1	1	11
Burns, Howard	6 + 2	2	—	—	8
Courty, Dave	33	3	—	—	12
Denny, Ian	4 + 2	1	—	—	4
Falcon, Colin	13 + 4	1	—	—	4
Higgins, Michael	0 + 3	1	—	—	4
Hillier, Errol	19	3	—	—	12
Hurst, Phil	14 + 1	7	1	—	30
Key, Andy	2 + 1	—	—	—	—
Law, Andrew	10	1	—	—	4
Law, Michael	0 + 5	—	—	—	—
Lewis, Ray	4 + 1	1	—	—	4
Lowden, Dave	28 + 1	3	66	—	144
Lynch, Keith	10 + 3	—	—	—	—
Maguire, Steve	22	1	1	7	13
Mawson, Mark	3 + 1	1	—	—	4
Mounsey, Gary	11	1	—	—	4
Newall, John	1	1	—	—	4
Nixon, Gary	25 + 2	6	—	—	24
Pattinson, Bill	16 + 1	1	—	—	4
Rea, Geoff	20 + 2	2	—	—	8
Rooney, Neil	9 + 3	2	—	—	8
Roper, Tony	0 + 1	—	—	—	—
Smith, Gary	28 + 1	4	7	—	30
Stafford, Peter	2	—	—	—	—
Sullivan, Joe	12 + 1	—	—	—	—
Tubman, Keith	8 + 4	—	—	—	—
Turley, Norman	7	—	8	1	17
Walker, Cliff	3 + 1	2	—	—	8
Wilkes, Mark	4 + 2	3	—	—	12
Woods, David	7	—	—	—	—
Trialists (2)	1 + 1	—	—	—	—
TOTALS:					
39 players		75	84	9	477

1986-87 MATCH ANALYSIS

Date	Competition	H/A	Opponent	Rlt	Score	Tries	Goals	Attendance	Referee
31.8.86	SD	H	Doncaster	L	15-16	Bower, Smith	Smith (3), Maguire (dg)	480	Mean
7.9.86	SD	A	Blackpool B.	L	14-17	Nixon (2), Pattinson	Smith	—	—
10.9.86	SD	H	Carlisle	W	31-24	Hurst (2), Bower (2)	Lowden (7), Maguire (dg)	704	Houghton
14.9.86	LC(1)	H	Swinton	W	25-16	Bower, Nixon, Rea	Lowden (5), Smith, Maguire (dg)	710	Tickle
21.9.86	SD	A	Hunslet	L	5-38	Beck	Maguire (dg)	—	—
24.9.86	LC(2)	A	Oldham	L	13-46	Falcon, Bower	Lowden (2), Maguire (dg)	—	—
28.9.86	SD	H	Huddersfield B.	L	20-22	Rooney (2), Bower, Beattie	Lowden (2)	527	Allatt
5.10.86	SD	A	Runcorn H.	L	14-30	Lowden, Burns	Lowden (3)	—	—
12.10.86	SD	H	Swinton	L	18-33	Burns, Hillier, Courty	Lowden (3)	776	Berry
19.10.86	SD	A	Dewsbury	L	0-18	—	—	—	—
26.10.86	SD	H	Blackpool B.	L	17-32	Smith, Hurst, Beck	Lowden (2), Maguire	490	Carter
2.11.86	SD	A	York	L	10-60	Wilkes, Newall	Smith	—	—
9.11.86	SD	H	Mansfield M.	W	20-4	Nixon (2), Beck	Lowden (4)	325	Tennant
16.11.86	JPS(P)	H	Huddersfield B.	W	16-6	Beattie (2), Beck	Lowden, Hurst	420	Kendrew
23.11.86	SD	H	York	L	4-6	Beattie	—	385	Cross
30.11.86	JPS(1)	A	Featherstone R.	L	18-22	Beattie, Hillier	Lowden (4), Maguire	—	—
14.12.86	SD	A	Huddersfield B.	W	20-12	Hurst, Burgess, Lowden, Hillier	Lowden (2)	—	—
21.12.86	SD	H	Sheffield E.	W	28-16	Maguire, Mounsey	Lowden (9), Maguire (dg), Burgess (dg)	528	Spencer
26.12.86	SD	H	Whitehaven	L	14-22	Hurst, Bower	Lowden (3)	2891	Volante
1.1.87	SD	A	Whitehaven	L	2-16	—	Lowden	—	—
18.1.87	CC(P)	H	Wigan (at Wigan)	L	0-68	—	—	(12046)	Stone (Aus)
25.1.87	SD	A	Carlisle	L	6-42	Lewis	Lowden	—	—
8.2.87	SD	H	Sheffield E.	L	14-34	Mawson, Beck, Beattie	Smith	—	—
15.2.87	SD	H	Runcorn H.	W	20-6	Hurst (2), Beck, Beattie	Burgess, Lowden	341	Tennant
22.2.87	SD	A	Rochdale H.	L	12-28	Wilkes, Courty	Lowden	—	—
1.3.87	SD	H	Dewsbury	W	10-1	Smith	Lowden (3)	347	Tickle
8.3.87	SD	H	Keighley	W	34-22	Wilkes, Beck, Rea, Smith, Lowden, Courtey	Lowden (5)	392	Holdsworth
15.3.87	SD	A	Doncaster	L	0-30	—	—	—	—
22.3.87	SD	H	Hunslet	L	2-34	—	Lowden	553	Houghton
29.3.87	SD	A	Mansfield M.	W	8-7	Denny	Lowden (2)	—	—
5.4.87	SD	A	Swinton	L	20-32	Burgess, A. Law, Walker	Lowden (3), Turley	—	—
12.4.87	SD	H	Rochdale H.	W	25-18	Bond (2), Walker, Beck	Turley (4, 1dg)	286	Beaumont
15.4.87	SD	A	Keighley	L	22-32	Bond (2), Nixon, Higgins	Turley (3)	—	—

YORK

Ground:	Wigginton Road
Colours:	Amber and black jerseys
First Season:	1901-02
Nickname:	Wasps
Chairman:	Ted Tebbutt
Secretary:	Ian Clough
Coach:	Phil Lowe (Mar 1983-Mar 1987), Danny Sheehan (Mar 1987-)
Honours:	**Division Two** Champions, 1980-81 **Challenge Cup** Beaten finalists, 1930-31 **Yorkshire Cup** Winners, 1922-23, 1933-34, 1936-37 Beaten finalists, 1935-36, 1957-58, 1978-79
Records:	Attendance: 14,689 v. Swinton (RL Cup) 10 Feb, 1934 **Season** Goals: 146 by V. Yorke, 1957-58 Tries: 35 by J. Crossley, 1980-81 Points: 318 by G. Steadman, 1984-85 **Match** Goals: 11 by V. Yorke v. Whitehaven, 6 Sep, 1958; C. Gibson v. Dewsbury, 28 Sep, 1980 Tries: 6 by R. Hardgrave v. Bramley, 5 Jan, 1935 Points: 26 by G. Steadman v. Batley, 25 Nov, 1984 Highest score: 60-0 v. Barrow, 1971-72; 60-10 v. Workington T., 1986-87 Highest against: 75-3 v. Warrington 1950-51

1986-87 PLAYERS' SUMMARY

	App	Tries	Goals	Dr	Pts
Arnett, Carl	25	2	—	—	8
Atkin, Gary	9 + 2	2	—	—	8
Blackburn, Steve	3 + 2	1	2	—	8
Carlyle, Brendan	0 + 4	—	—	—	—
Carr, John	1	—	—	—	—
Clancey, Robert	1	—	—	—	—
Clark, Trevor	8 + 1	6	—	—	24
Colley, Mick	12 + 7	5	—	—	20
Crooks, Steve	1	1	—	—	4
Deighton, Carl	3	—	—	—	—
Diamond, Steve	2	—	3	—	6
Dobson, Steve	15	9	2	10	50
Ellis, St John	14	10	15	—	70
Hagan, Mick	1	—	—	—	—
Hammerton, Chris	1 + 1	1	2	—	8
Harrison, Chris	26 + 2	4	—	—	16
Hooper, Trevor	19 + 1	—	—	—	—
Hughes, Mick	6 + 1	—	—	—	—
Kerr, Mick	9	2	—	—	8
Kirkwood, John	4	—	—	—	—
Long, Mark	8 + 1	3	—	—	12
Maxwell, Paul	10	1	—	—	4
Mercer, Andy	4	1	—	—	4
Midgley, Trevor	2	—	—	—	—
Miles, Paul	7 + 1	—	—	—	—
Morrell, Wayne	10	2	—	—	8
Olsen, Steve	9 + 9	1	—	—	4
Phillippo, Peter	19 + 2	—	—	—	—
Prendiville, Paul	19 + 2	5	50	3	123
Price, Gary	6	2	—	—	8
Proctor, Paul	2	—	—	—	—
Pryce, Dennis	13 + 1	—	—	—	—
Pryce, Geoff	5 + 2	—	—	—	—
Rhodes, Chris	9 + 3	2	—	—	8
Richmond, Mark	1	—	—	—	—
Stephenson, Nigel	25	7	—	1	29
Strutt, Darren	6 + 2	—	—	—	—
Sutton, Mick	2	—	—	—	—
Tansley, Ian	10 + 2	2	—	—	8
Turner, Paul	6	—	—	—	—
Waites, Brian	2 + 1	—	—	—	—
White, Paul	23	6	—	—	24
Wigglesworth, Iain	20 + 5	4	3	—	22
Willey, Sean	24	11	—	—	44
Wilson, Ian	1 + 1	—	—	—	—

TOTALS:					
45 players		90	77	14	528

New recruit from Hull, Paul Prendiville, scorer of 123 points in 21 matches.

1986-87 MATCH ANALYSIS

Date	Competition	H/A	Opponent	Rlt	Score	Tries	Goals	Attendance	Referee
31.8.86	SD	H	Carlisle	W	20-14	Harrison, Crooks, Hammerton	Blackburn (2), Hammerton (2)	1674	Cross
3.9.86	SD	H	Batley	L	0-30	—	—	1221	Smith
7.9.86	SD	A	Whitehaven	L	10-30	Wigglesworth, Price	Prendiville	—	—
14.9.86	YC(1)	A	Featherstone R.	L	13-40	Price, Long	Prendiville (2), Dobson (dg)	—	—
21.9.86	SD	A	Swinton	L	9-22	Dobson	Prendiville (2), Dobson	—	—
28.9.86	SD	H	Bramley	W	16-8	Arnett, Mercer	Prendiville (3, 1 dg), Dobson (dg)	1308	Simpson
5.10.86	SD	A	Blackpool B.	L	13-14	Long, Dobson	Prendiville (2), Dobson (dg)	—	—
12.10.86	SD	H	Dewsbury	W	25-16	Dobson (2), Harrison, Stephenson	Prendiville (2), Wigglesworth (2), Dobson (dg)	1582	McDonald
19.10.86	SD	H	Doncaster	L	23-24	Rhodes, Tansley, Harrison, Long	Dobson (2, 1 dg), Wigglesworth	1572	Beaumont
26.10.86	SD	A	Sheffield E.	W	32-14	Dobson (2), Clark (2), Tansley	Prendiville (6)	—	—
2.11.86	SD	H	Workington T.	W	60-10	Willey (3), Stephenson (3), Morrell (2), White (2), Prendiville	Prendiville (7), Dobson (2 dg)	1478	Kendrew
9.11.86	SD	H	Hunslet	L	13-26	Clark, Colley	Prendiville (2), Dobson (dg)	2697	Fox
12.11.86	JPS(P)	A	Halifax	L	23-38	Clark, White, Willey, Wigglesworth	Prendiville (3, 1 dg)	—	—
16.11.86	SD	H	Rochdale H.	L	17-26	White (2), Clark, Prendiville	Dobson (dg)	1617	Carter
23.11.86	SD	A	Workington T.	W	6-4	Harrison	Prendiville	—	—
30.11.86	SD	A	Huddersfield B.	W	32-16	Dobson (2), Willey, Clark, Wigglesworth	Prendiville	—	—
14.12.86	SD	H	Sheffield E.	L	18-28	Prendiville, Dobson, Stephenson	Prendiville (3)	1414	Whitfield
21.12.86	SD	A	Fulham	L	16-18	Willey, Atkins, White	Ellis (2)	—	—
26.12.86	SD	H	Huddersfield B.	W	54-22	Willey (2), Prendiville (2), Ellis (2), Colley (2), Wigglesworth, Atkins, Kerr	Prendiville (5)	1373	Lindop
4.1.87	SD	A	Dewsbury	W	8-4	Stephenson	Ellis (2)	—	—
18.1.87	CC(P)	A	Hunslet	L	0-13	—	—	—	—
8.2.87	SD	A	Rochdale H.	L	8-12	Arnett	Ellis (2)	—	—
15.2.87	SD	H	Swinton	L	10-15	Ellis, Rhodes	Ellis	1877	Holdsworth
22.2.87	SD	A	Carlisle	L	16-30	Colley, Ellis, Willey	Prendiville (2)	—	—
1.3.87	SD	H	Fulham	W	21-19	Ellis (3), Blackburn	Prendiville (2, 1dg)	1183	Spencer
8.3.87	SD	A	Batley	L	2-29	—	Prendiville	—	—
15.3.87	SD	H	Whitehaven	L	15-20	Ellis, Colley	Diamond (3), Stephenson (dg)	1257	Berry
29.3.87	SD	A	Doncaster	L	10-20	Willey, Kerr	Ellis	—	—
5.4.87	SD	A	Bramley	L	4-10	—	Ellis (2)	—	—
12.4.87	SD	H	Blackpool B.	W	24-14	Olsen, Willey, Maxwell, Ellis	Ellis (4)	1030	Berry
20.4.87	SD	A	Hunslet	L	10-42	Stephenson, Ellis	Ellis	—	—

93

Veteran Whitehaven hooker Alan McCurrie in action at St. Helens in the Silk Cut third round tie.

Kiwi Kurt Sorensen releases a pass despite a three man Halifax tackle in Widnes's 1987 Silk Cut Challenge Cup semi-final at Leeds.

ST. HELENS MATCH ANALYSIS (continued)

Date	Com-petition	H/A	Opponent	Rlt	Score	Tries	Goals	Atten-dance	Referee
1.3.87	CC(3)	H	Whitehaven	W	41-12	Arkwright (3), Loughlin, Holding, Clark, Fieldhouse	Loughlin (6), Holding (dg)	10788	Berry
4.3.87	SBC	A	Castleford	L	10-12	Clark, Round	Dwyer	—	—
14.3.87	CC(SF)	Wigan	Leigh	W	14-8	McCormack, Arkwright, Platt	Loughlin	(13105)	Whitfield
17.3.87	SBC	A	Hull	L	22-36	Clark (2), Allen, Forber	Loughlin (3)	—	—
22.3.87	SBC	A	Warrington	D	17-17	Elia, Veivers	Loughlin (4), Dwyer (dg)	—	—
25.3.87	SBC	A	Leigh	W	16-8	Litherland (2), Clark	Loughlin (2)	—	—
29.3.87	SBC	H	Hull K.R.	W	44-22	Ledger (2), Bailey, Fieldhouse, Forber, Harrison, Litherland, Parkes	Loughlin (5), Dwyer	6194	Holdsworth
1.4.87	SBC	H	Castleford	L	8-10	Ledger	Loughlin, Doherty (dg), Ledger (dg)	5570	Carter
5.4.87	SBC	H	Leeds	W	24-22	Arkwright, Litherland, Doherty, Platt	Loughlin (4)	5887	Houghton
8.4.87	SBC	H	Barrow	W	26-4	Litherland, Veivers, Dwyer, Ledger	Loughlin (5)	4311	Haigh
12.4.87	SBC	A	Bradford N.	L	4-18	Ledger	—	—	—
17.4.87	SBC	A	Wigan	L	12-42	Forber, Price	Dwyer (2)	—	—
20.4.87	SBC	H	Widnes	L	24-30	McCormack, Ledger, Burke, Round	Loughlin (4)	7559	Hodgson
26.4.87	PT(1)	H	Bradford N.	W	46-14	Holding (2), Round (2), Elia, Veivers, McCormack, Arkwright	Loughlin (7)	7112	Kershaw
2.5.87	CC(F)	Wembley	Halifax	L	18-19	Elia, Loughlin, Round	Loughlin	91267	Holdsworth
10.5.87	PT(SF)	H	Warrington	L	8-18	Ledger	Loughlin, Ledger	12828	Whitfield

SWINTON MATCH ANALYSIS (continued)

Date	Com-petition	H/A	Opponent	Rlt	Score	Tries	Goals	Atten-dance	Referee
26.4.87	SDP(1)	H	Bramley	W	59-14	Grima (2), Ainsworth (2), Bate (2), Viller (2), Topping, Brown	Topping (9, 1dg)	1521	Whitfield
10.5.87	SDP(SF)	H	Whitehaven	W	12-6	Brown, Muller	Topping (2)	2605	Lindop
17.5.87	SDP(F)	Man. U. FC	Hunslet	W	27-10	Bate, Derbyshire, Grima, Lee, Ainsworth	Rippon (3), L. Holliday (dg)	(—)	McDonald

WARRINGTON MATCH ANALYSIS (continued)

Date	Com-petition	H/A	Opponent	Rlt	Score	Tries	Goals	Atten-dance	Referee
29.3.87	SBC	A	Hull	W	46-12	Jackson (2), Johnson (2), Roberts, M. Gregory, Ropati, Bishop	Bishop (7)	—	—
5.4.87	SBC	A	Bradford N.	L	10-11	Roskell	Bishop (3)	—	—
8.4.87	SBC	H	Widnes	W	26-16	Carbert, Mossop, Holden, Johnson	Carbert (5)	3166	Smith
12.4.87	SBC	H	Hull K.R.	W	38-0	Ropati (2), Drummond (2), Sanderson, Johnson, Rathbone	Carbert (5)	3355	Hodgson
17.4.87	SBC	A	Widnes	L	18-25	Carbert (2), Jackson	Carbert (2), Bishop	—	—
20.4.87	SBC	H	Leigh	L	10-17	Holden	Bishop (3)	4829	Tennant
26.4.87	PT(1)	H	Hull K.R.	W	24-12	Johnson (2), Rathbone, B. Peters, Drummond	Bishop (2)	3250	Allatt
10.5.87	PT(SF)	A	St. Helens	W	18-8	Ropati, Drummond, Johnson	Bishop (2, 2dg)	—	—
17.5.87	PT(F)	Man. U. FC	Wigan	L	0-8	—	—	(38756)	Allatt

WIDNES MATCH ANALYSIS (continued)

Date	Competition	H/A	Opponent	Rlt	Score	Tries	Goals	Attendance	Referee
15.3.87	SBC	A	Wakefield T.	L	20-38	Platt, D. Wright, Linton, Dowd	Platt (2)	—	—
18.3.87	SBC	A	Castleford	L	8-44	Thackray (2)	—	—	—
28.3.87	CC(SF)	Leeds	Halifax	L	8-12	McKenzie	Platt (2)	(16064)	Allatt
1.4.87	SBC	H	Leigh	L	8-10	R. Eyres	Platt (2)	2701	Kendrew
5.4.87	SBC	H	Hull	L	10-18	McKenzie, R. Eyres	A. Ruane	2229	Holdsworth
8.4.87	SBC	A	Warrington	L	16-26	Thackray, Stockley	Dowd (4)	—	—
12.4.87	SBC	A	Halifax	L	0-20	—	—	—	—
14.4.87	SBC	H	Featherstone R.	W	62-16	A. Myler (2), D. Hulme (2), M. O'Neill (2), D. Wright, Linton, McKenzie, Thackray, Platt	Dowd (9)	2183	Lindop
17.4.87	SBC	H	Warrington	W	25-18	D. Wright, McKenzie, A. Myler, D. Hulme	Dowd (4), S. O'Neill (dg)	5746	Volante
20.4.87	SBC	A	St Helens	W	30-24	Stockley, D. Hulme, Sorensen, D. Wright, A. Myler	Dowd (5)	—	—
22.4.87	SBC	A	Hull	L	4-21	Linton	—	—	—
26.4.87	PT(1)	A	Wigan	L	18-22	Basnett, D. Wright, Pinner	Dowd (3)	—	—

WIGAN MATCH ANALYSIS (continued)

Date	Competition	H/A	Opponent	Rlt	Score	Tries	Goals	Attendance	Referee
22.3.87	SBC	H	Hull K.R.	W	26-0	Hanley (2), Hampson (2), Stephenson, Lydon	Edwards	11939	Beaumont
25.3.87	SBC	A	Featherstone R.	W	36-0	Hanley (2), Gill (2), Bell, Mordt, Lydon	Gill (2), Lydon (2)	—	—
29.3.87	SBC	A	Wakefield T.	W	72-6	Hanley (3), Gill (3), Edwards (2), Hampson (2), Stephenson, Mordt, Goodway, Bell	Stephenson (5), Gill (2), Edwards	—	—
1.4.87	SBC	H	Halifax	W	42-2	Hanley (3), Edwards (2), Stephenson, Goodway, Gill	Stephenson (5)	13154	Spencer
5.4.87	SBC	H	Featherstone R.	W	62-7	Hanley (4), Gill (3), Lydon (2), Gregory, Bell, Stephenson	Stephenson (6), Gill	13317	Whitfield
8.4.87	SBC	H	Oldham	W	54-2	Hanley (2), Hampson, Gregory, Edwards, Stephenson, Mordt, Lydon, Gill	Stephenson (5), Gill (4)	11108	Lindop
12.4.87	SBC	A	Hull	W	18-12	Edwards (2), Hanley	Stephenson (2), Gill	—	—
17.4.87	SBC	H	St Helens	W	42-12	Hanley (2), Bell (2), Gill, Gregory, Kiss	Stephenson (6), Gill	20355	Lindop
20.4.87	SBC	A	Oldham	W	24-6	Hanley (3), Stephenson	Stephenson (4)	—	—
26.4.87	PT(1)	H	Widnes	W	22-18	Bell (2), Hampson, Lydon	Gill (3)	14746	Holdsworth
10.5.87	PT(SF)	H	Halifax	W	18-10	Goodway, Lydon, Hampson, Stephenson	Lydon	22457	Kershaw
17.5.87	PT(F)	Man. U. FC	Warrington	W	8-0	Lydon	Stephenson, Gill	(38756)	Allatt

Top goals and points scorer Paul Loughlin.

RECORDS

LEADING SCORERS FOR 1986-87

TOP TEN TRIES

1. Ellery Hanley (Wigan) 63
2. Garry Schofield (Hull) 37
3. Henderson Gill (Wigan) 32
4. Derek Bate (Swinton) 31
5. Phil Ford (Bradford N.) 30
6. John Henderson (Leigh) 27
7. Shaun Edwards (Wigan) 26
8. Brian Johnson (Warrington) 25
9. Joe Lydon (Wigan) 24
10. Brian Dunn (Rochdale H.) 23
    Barry Ledger (St. Helens) 23
    Kevin McCormack (St. Helens) 23

● Others with 20 or more: Dean Bell (Wigan), Kevin Pape (Carlisle) 22; John Basnett (Widnes), Paul Eastwood (Hull), David Plange (Castleford), Tony Solarie (Whitehaven), Colin Whitfield (Halifax) 21; Chris Arkwright (St. Helens), Graham Eadie (Halifax), Neil Holding (St. Helens) 20.

TOP TEN GOALS
(Including drop goals)

1. Paul Loughlin (St. Helens) 190
2. Paul Bishop (Warrington) 117
3. David Noble (Doncaster)........................... 114
4. Colin Whitfield (Halifax) 109
5. Alan Platt (Hunslet) 102
6. Paul Topping (Swinton) 100
7. Chris Johnson (Leigh) 86
8. Martin Ketteridge (Castleford) 80
   David Wood (Rochdale H.) 80
10. Steve Quinn (Featherstone R.) 77

TOP FIVE DROP GOALS

1. Billy Platt (Mansfield M./Huddersfield B.) 18
2. Paul Bishop (Warrington) 17
3. Steve Dobson (York) 10
   Paul Harkin (Bradford N./Hull K.R.) 10
5. Danny Wilson (Swinton) 8

TOP FIVE POINTS

	T	G	DG	Pts
1. Paul Loughlin (St. Helens).	11	190	0	424
2. Colin Whitfield (Halifax) ...	21	105	4	298
3. Henderson Gill (Wigan).....	32	74	0	276
4. Paul Bishop (Warrington) ..	12	100	17	265
5. Ellery Hanley (Wigan).......	63	1	0	254

Key:
SBC	Stones Bitter Championship
SD...............	Second Division
SDP.............	Second Division Premiership
LC...............	Lancashire Cup
YC...............	Yorkshire Cup
JPS	John Player Special Trophy
CC...............	Challenge Cup
PT...............	Premiership Trophy
NA	Non-appearance

OUTSTANDING SCORING FEATS IN 1986-87

INDIVIDUAL

Most tries in a match:
5 by Terry Lamb (Australia) v. Hull K.R. .... Tour
John Basnett (Widnes) v. Hull K.R. .... SBC
David Hulme (Widnes) v. Dewsbury .... JPS(1)
Ellery Hanley (Wigan) v. Bradford N. ...... SBC

Most goals in a match:
16 by Paul Loughlin (St. Helens) v. Carlisle ..... LC(1)
12 by Roy Rafferty (Sheffield E.) at Fulham .... SD
11 by Martin Ketteridge (Castleford) v. Blackbrook
.... CC(P)
Bob Beardmore (Castleford) v. Barrow ...... SBC
10 by Paul Topping (Swinton) v. Bramley ...... SDP(1)
Norman Lofthouse (Whitehaven) v. Fulham
.... LC(1)

Most points in a match:
40 by Paul Loughlin (St. Helens) v. Carlisle ..... LC(1)
38 by Bob Beardmore (Castleford) v. Barrow ...... SBC
32 by Roy Rafferty (Sheffield E.) at Fulham .... SD
26 by Terry Lamb (Australia) at Hull K.R....... Tour

TEAM

Highest score:
St. Helens 112 v. Carlisle 0 .... LC(1)
● There was a total of 36 matches in which a team scored 50 points or more compared with 26 in the previous season. The other 60-plus scores were:

Home:
Widnes 82 v. Dewsbury 0 .... JPS(1)
Wigan 74 v. Whitehaven 6........................ LC(1)
Castleford 74 v. Blackbrook 6................... CC(P)
Whitehaven 72 v. Fulham 6 .... LC(1)
Castleford 70 v. Barrow 10..................... SBC
Wigan 68 v. Workington T. 0 .... CC(P)
Featherstone R. 66 v. Barrow 14............... SBC
Wigan 62 v. Wakefield T. 10................... SBC
Wigan 62 v. Featherstone R. 7................. SBC
Widnes 62 v. Featherstone R. 16.............. SBC
Wigan 60 v. Bradford N. 6 .... SBC
York 60 v. Workington T. 10 .... SD

Away:
Wakefield T. 6 v. Wigan 72 .... SBC
Fulham 14 v. Sheffield E. 68 .... SD

Highest score by losing team:
Mansfield M. 31 v. Huddersfield B. 36 .... SD

● There was a total of 59 matches in which a team scored 20 points or more and lost compared with 61 in the previous season.

High-scoring draws:
Doncaster 28 v. Rochdale H. 28 .... SD
Hull K.R. 20 v. Featherstone R. 20 .... YC(2)
Bradford N. 20 v. Hull 20 .... SBC

● From the start of the 1983-84 season, the value of a try was raised from three points to four points. It was officially decided that records for most points in a match, season or career would subsequently include the four-point try and that no attempt would be made to adjust existing records featuring the three-point try.
● Substitute appearances do not count towards players' full appearance records.

RECORD-BREAKING FEATS 1986-87

NEW RECORDS AT A GLANCE . . .

ELLERY HANLEY of Wigan scored a Division One record 44 tries in a season, including a record-equalling five in a match. His total of 63 in all matches was the most ever by a non-winger in a season.

DAVID NOBLE scored a Doncaster club record 250 points in a season, including scoring in every match. He also equalled Doncaster's 18 points in a match record.

COLIN WHITFIELD scored a Halifax club record 298 points in a season.

STEVE LIDBURY scored a Sheffield Eagles club record 17 tries in a season.

JOHN WOODS, of Bradford Northern, amassed a record Division One career points total of 1,760.

NIGEL STEPHENSON, of York, totalled a career record-equalling 79 one-point drop goals.

JOHN BASNETT, of Widnes, equalled the club record of five tries in a match which also equalled the Division One record.

DAVID HULME equalled the Widnes club record of five tries in a match.

TONY KEMP equalled the Doncaster club record of four tries in a match.

TOMMY FRODSHAM equalled the Blackpool Borough club record of four tries in a match.

GARY PEACHAM broke the Carlisle club record with four tries in a match.

KEVIN PAPE equalled the Carlisle club record of four tries in a match.

BOB BEARDMORE, of Castleford, scored a Division One record 38 points in a match.

PAUL LOUGHLIN scored a St. Helens club record 16 goals and 40 points in a match.

ROY RAFFERTY scored a Sheffield Eagles club record 12 goals and 32 points in a match.

MARTIN KETTERIDGE, of Castleford, scored a Yorkshire Cup final record 14 points, including a record-equalling five goals.

WIGAN smashed a host of Division One records in taking the Stones Bitter Championship. Most tries, 174; most points, 941; least tries conceded, 29; fewest points conceded, 193; most wins and points, 28 wins and 56 points; highest score, 72-6, also being the biggest away win.

ST. HELENS completed a Division One record run of 25 successive wins and had a club record 112-0 victory which was also a Lancashire Cup high.

CARLISLE went down to a club record 112-0 defeat.

DONCASTER had a club record 50-6 win.

WIDNES ran up a club record 82-0 victory, which was also DEWSBURY'S biggest defeat.

SHEFFIELD EAGLES scored a club record 68-14 win.

WHITEHAVEN had a club record 72-6 victory which was FULHAM'S biggest defeat, but suffered a record 74-6 defeat.

YORK equalled the club record with a 60-10 win.

FEATHERSTONE ROVERS scored a club record 66-14 victory.

WAKEFIELD TRINITY went down to a club record 72-6 defeat.

WORKINGTON TOWN crashed to a club record 68-0 defeat.

GREAT BRITAIN gained a record 52-4 victory over France.

NEW RECORDS IN DETAIL . . .

ELLERY HANLEY of Wigan scored a Division One record 44 tries in a season, including a record-equalling five in a match. His total of 63 in all matches was the most ever by a non-winger in a season.

Hanley had set the previous Division One record for a season with 40 tries for Bradford Northern in 1984-85. He passed that total with the second of his two tries in Wigan's 42-12 home defeat of St. Helens on 17 April.

Hanley equalled the Division One match record with five tries in the 60-6 home win over his old club, Bradford Northern, on 1 March. It was only his fourth match since the Test back's switch to loose forward and the only time any forward had scored five tries in a Division One match since the reintroduction of two divisions in 1973.

The backs who have scored five are wingers: Roy Mathias (St. Helens) twice, Steve Fenton (Castleford), Kevin Meadows (Oldham), Peter Glynn (St. Helens), and John Basnett (Widnes); stand off John Woods (Bradford N.); scrum half Parry Gordon (Warrington); and centre Steve Hartley (Hull K.R.).

Hanley also held the previous record for most tries by a non-winger in a season when he scored 55 in 1984-85, mostly at stand off, with the occasional game at centre. Last season his total of 63 featured 59 for Wigan made up of 30 in 17 matches at loose forward; 25 in 19 at standoff; one in two matches at centre; and even three after going on as a substitute.

He played twice in the centre for Great Britain, scoring one try, and once at stand off when he touched down twice. Hanley also scored one try at centre for Yorkshire.

Hanley scored three tries or more in a match on nine occasions including four three times and five once.

His match-by-match record was as follows:

For Wigan

		Tries
Salford	(H)	2
Barrow	(H)	0
Leigh	(A)	1
Rochdale H. (LC)	(H)	2
Bradford N.	(A)	0
Whitehaven (LC)	(H)	4
Hull	(H)	4
St. Helens (LC)	(H)	1
Warrington	(H)	NA
Australia	(H)	NA
Oldham (LC)	(St. Helens)	0
Castleford	(A)	1
Wakefield T.	(H)	3
Salford	(A)	NA
Leigh	(H)	NA
Barrow	(A)	NA
Leeds (JPS)	(H)	2
Swinton (JPS)	(H)	NA
Leigh (JPS)	(H)	1
Hull (JPS)	(Leeds)	2
St. Helens	(A)	0
Warrington	(H)	0
Widnes	(A)	2
Warrington (JPS)	(Bolton)	0
Workington T. (CC)	(H)	3 sub.
Hull K.R.	(A)	1
Oldham (CC)	(A)	0
Castleford	(H)	0
Leeds	(H)	0
Widnes	(H)	2
Bradford N.	(H)	5
Leeds	(A)	0
Halifax	(A)	1
Hull K.R.	(H)	2
Featherstone R.	(A)	2
Wakefield T.	(A)	3
Halifax	(H)	3
Featherstone R.	(H)	4
Oldham	(H)	2
Hull	(A)	1
St. Helens	(H)	2
Oldham	(A)	3
Widnes (PT)	(H)	0
Halifax (PT)	(H)	0
Warrington (PT)	(Man U. FC)	0

For Great Britain

Australia	(H)	0
France	(H)	2
France	(A)	1

For Yorkshire

Lancashire	(H)	1

Totals	Wigan	59
	Great Britain	3
	Yorkshire	1

GRAND TOTAL 63

Division One tries in a season record breaker, Ellery Hanley.

DAVID NOBLE achieved a Doncaster club record 250 points in scoring in every match throughout the season, a feat that had been achieved only 11 times previously. He also equalled the club record of 18 points in a match.

He broke the Doncaster points in a season record for a third time with the last of his three goals in the 16-14 win at Sheffield Eagles on 19 April. His season's total was made up of 112 goals, two drop goals and six tries.

Noble first broke the record with 188 points in 1982-83 from 80 goals, 10 drop goals and six tries. He followed that with a record 242 points (112 goals, six drop goals and three tries) in 1985-86.

Noble scored in all 33 of Doncaster's matches to become only the second forward to score in each match for his club throughout a season. Jim Hoey, a Widnes second row forward, was the first player to achieve the score-a-match feat back in 1932-33.

Noble played 15 times in the second row, 15 at prop and three at loose forward. He was at prop when he equalled Doncaster's match record of 18 points with a try and seven goals in a 50-6 home league win over Keighley on 22 March.

Others to have scored 18 are David Towle (nine goals) v. York on 9 September 1967, and Ian Fortis (six goals, two tries) v. Blackpool Borough on 5 September 1970.

Noble's match-by-match figures for 1986-87 are as follows:

	T	G	DG	Pts
Workington T. .... (A)	0	4	0	8
Sheffield E. (YC) .... (A)	0	2	0	4
Swinton .... (H)	0	1	0	2
Carlisle........................... (A)	0	2	0	4
Hunslet............................ (H)	0	5	0	10
Huddersfield B. .... (A)	0	4	0	8
Whitehaven .... (H)	0	4	0	8
York.............................. (A)	0	3	0	6
Dewsbury........................ (H)	1	5	0	14
Blackpool B. .... (A)	0	4	0	8
Rochdale H. .... (H)	1	4	0	12
Swinton........................... (A)	0	2	1	5
Carlisle .... (H)	0	5	0	10
Hull K.R. (JPS) .... (H)	0	3	0	6
Leigh (JPS)...................... (A)	0	3	0	6
Keighley.......................... (A)	0	2	0	4
Runcorn H. .... (A)	0	2	0	4
Rochdale H....................... (A)	0	3	0	6
Whitehaven .... (A)	0	1	1	3
Hull K.R. (CC) .... (A)	0	3	0	6
Runcorn H. .... (H)	0	5	0	10
Dewsbury......................... (A)	0	4	0	8
Blackpool B. .... (H)	1	3	0	10
Sheffield E. .... (H)	0	3	0	6
Workington T. .... (H)	1	5	0	14
Keighley .... (H)	1	7	0	18
York .... (H)	0	2	0	4
Hunslet........................... (A)	0	3	0	6
Huddersfield B................. (H)	1	6	0	16
Mansfield M. .... (H)	0	5	0	10
Mansfield M. .... (A)	0	1	0	2
Sheffield E....................... (A)	0	3	0	6
Rochdale H. (SDP) .... (H)	0	3	0	6

Totals

	T	G	DG	Pts
Division Two	6	98	2	222
Second Division Premiership	0	3	0	6
Yorkshire Cup	0	2	0	4
John Player Special Trophy	0	6	0	12
Challenge Cup	0	3	0	6
GRAND TOTALS	**6**	**112**	**2**	**250**

COLIN WHITFIELD scored a Halifax record of 298 points in a season. He broke the record with his last goal of the campaign, his only score in Halifax's 18-10 Stones Bitter Premiership semi-final defeat at Wigan on 10 May.

The centre's total was made up of 105 goals, four drop goals and 21 tries. When Welsh full back Tysul Griffiths set the previous record of 297 in 1955-56 he scored a club record 147 goals and a try.

Halifax centre Colin Whitfield,
new points in a season record holder at Thrum Hall.

Whitfield played in 40 matches during the season, including the first as substitute, and his total was made up as follows:

		T	G	DG	Pts
Mansfield M. (YC)	(H)	1	0	0	4
Castleford (Charity Shield)	(IOM)	1	0	0	4
Featherstone R.	(A)	2	2	0	12
Oldham	(H)	0	4	0	8
Hull	(H)	2	4	0	16
Castleford (YC)	(A)	1	1	0	6
St. Helens	(A)	0	1	0	2
Warrington	(H)	0	2	1	5
Barrow	(A)	0	5	1	11
Leeds	(H)	0	5	1	11
Hull	(A)	0	3	0	6
Castleford	(H)	0	2	0	4
Australia	(H)	0	1	0	2
Leigh	(A)	1	4	0	12
York (JPS)	(H)	0	5	0	10
Hull K.R.	(H)	1	2	0	8
Warrington	(A)	0	1	0	2
Wakefield T. (JPS)	(H)	1	8	0	20
Warrington (JPS)	(A)	NA			
Oldham	(A)	NA			
Salford	(H)	0	3	0	6
Bradford N.	(H)	1	2	0	8
Bradford N.	(A)	0	2	0	4
Hull K.R.	(A)	0	0	0	0
St. Helens	(H)	1	4	0	12
Barrow	(H)	1	6	0	16
Fulham (CC)	(A)	1	5	0	14
Featherstone R.	(H)	1	5	0	14
Hunslet (CC)	(H)	1	3	0	10
Leigh	(H)	1	2	1	9
Hull K.R. (CC)	(H)	1	3	0	10
Widnes	(A)	0	1	0	2
Wigan	(H)	0	2	0	4
Salford	(A)	0	2	0	4
Widnes (CC)	(Leeds)	0	2	0	4
Wigan	(A)	0	1	0	2
Castleford	(A)	NA			
Widnes	(H)	2	2	0	12
Wakefield T.	(A)	NA			
Wakefield T.	(H)	0	3	0	6
Leeds	(A)	1	2	0	8
Castleford (PT)	(A)	0	1	0	2
St. Helens (CC)	(Wembley)	0	3	0	6
Wigan (PT)	(A)	0	1	0	2

Totals

		T	G	DG	Pts
Division One		14	72	4	204
Premiership		0	2	0	4
Challenge Cup		3	16	0	44
John Player Special Trophy		1	13	0	30
Yorkshire Cup		2	1	0	10
Tour match		0	1	0	2
Charity Shield		1	0	0	4
GRAND TOTALS		**21**	**105**	**4**	**298**

STEVE LIDBURY scored a club record 17 tries for Sheffield Eagles in his first season as a professional. The winger broke the record of 16 with a try in Sheffield's 52-12 home league defeat of Runcorn Highfield on 12 April.

Loose forward Paul McDermott set the old record in the club's inaugural campaign of 1984-85.

Lidbury signed from Castleford amateurs Lock Lane and scored two tries on his debut in the opening match of the season, a 48-5 home league defeat of Mansfield Marksman on 31 August.

His record-breaking season went as follows:

		Tries
Mansfield M.	(H)	2
Doncaster (YC)	(H)	1
Keighley	(A)	0
Dewsbury (YC)	(H)	0
Fulham	(A)	1
Dewsbury	(H)	2
Huddersfield B.	(H)	0
Swinton	(A)	1
Carlisle	(H)	1
Runcorn H.	(A)	0
York	(H)	0
Bramley	(A)	0
Fulham	(H)	NA
Huddersfield B.	(A)	0
Batley	(H)	0
Bramley (JPS)	(H)	0
Barrow (JPS)	(H)	1
York	(A)	1
Workington T.	(A)	1
Mansfield M.	(A)	1
Carlisle	(At Penrith)	0
Bramley	(At Leeds H)	0
Swinton	(H)	1
Keighley (CC)	(H)	0
Workington T.	(H)	1
Hunslet	(A)	0
Keighley	(H)	1
Doncaster	(A)	0
Dewsbury	(A)	0
Batley	(A)	1
Hunslet	(H)	0
Runcorn H.	(H)	1
Doncaster	(H)	0
Whitehaven (SDP)	(A)	0

Totals		
	Division Two	15
	Second Division Premiership	0
	Yorkshire Cup	1
	John Player Special Trophy	1
	Challenge Cup	0
GRAND TOTAL		**17**

JOHN WOODS, the Bradford Northern and former Leigh Test stand off, finished the season with a record Division One career total of 1,760 points. His total was made up of 111 tries, 695 goals, including 10 drop goals.

The former record holder was utility back Steve Hesford, who amassed 1,756 points with Warrington from 1975 until his departure to Second Division Huddersfield Barracudas at the start of last season. Hesford's total comprised a Division One record 845 goals, including 35 drop goals, and 32 tries.

Five of Hesford's tries were worth four points, while Woods scored 47 four-pointers.

Woods broke the record with the last of his three goals in a 26-18 home defeat on 25 January against Leigh — the club with whom he scored the majority of his points.

Woods made a tryscoring debut for Leigh in a Division One 18-8 home victory over Barrow on 5 September 1976. Leigh were relegated to Division Two the following season, but returned after one season and Woods has since remained a Division One player.

Woods also holds the Division One record of 295 points in a season with Leigh in 1983-84 and equalled the division's match record of five tries for Bradford Northern at home to Swinton on 13 October 1984. He added eight goals in that match for a then record 36 points which was beaten last season by Castleford's Bob Beardmore with 38.

Woods scored 1,440 Division One points for Leigh before being transferred to Bradford Northern for £65,000 — a record for both clubs — in 1985. He kicked one goal on his debut for Northern in a 32-7 league defeat at Warrington on 1 September 1985.

Woods is the only player to have totalled more than 100 tries and 500 goals in Division One since the reintroduction of two divisions in 1973.

His totals, which do not include six goals scored in two abandoned matches, are as follows:

For Leigh	T	G	DG	Pts
1976-77	5	60	2	137
1977-78	In Division Two			
1978-79	7	71	1	164
1979-80	18	53	2	162
1980-81	10	61	1	153
1981-82	14	109	1	261
1982-83	10	43	1	117
1983-84	23	101	1	295
1984-85	10	55	1	151
Bradford N.				
1985-86	10	84	0	208
1986-87	4	48	0	112
Totals				
Leigh	97	553	10	1,440
Bradford N.	14	132	0	320
GRAND TOTALS	**111**	**685**	**10**	**1,760**

NIGEL STEPHENSON equalled the career record of 79 one-point drop goals with his only one of the season in York's 20-15 home league defeat against Whitehaven on 15 March.

It took the veteran level with Harry Pinner, the Widnes and former St. Helens loose forward, who did not add to his total last season.

The record refers to the period since the start of 1974-75 when the drop goal was halved to one point in Britain. Stephenson had kicked a drop goal for Dewsbury against Australia in 1973 which was worth one point under international rules but does not count towards the record.

Pinner's total is made up as follows:

St. Helens

1975-76	1	
1976-77	2	+ 1 GB Under-24
1977-78	6	
1978-79	10	
1979-80	9	+ 2 Lancashire, 2 England
1980-81	6	
1981-82	4	
1982-83	13	
1983-84	14	
1984-85	8	
1985-86	0	+ 1 GB
1986-87	0	

Widnes

1986-87	0

Totals

St. Helens	73
GB Under-24	1
Great Britain	1
England	2
Lancashire	2
Widnes	0

GRAND TOTAL 79

Stephenson's total is made up as follows:

Dewsbury

1974-75	9
1975-76	7
1976-77	16
1977-78	2
1978-79	4

Bradford N.

1978-79	4
1979-80	9
1980-81	4

Carlisle

1981-82	5

(continued)

Wakefield T.

1982-83	....	3
1983-84	....	7
1984-85	....	3

Dewsbury

1984-85	....	5
1985-86	....	0

York

1986-87	....	1

Totals

Dewsbury	....	43
Bradford N.	....	17
Carlisle	....	5
Wakefield T.	....	13
York	....	1

GRAND TOTAL **79**

JOHN BASNETT and DAVID HULME both equalled the Widnes record of five tries in a match, with Basnett's feat also equalling the Division One best.

Basnett scored all five tries in Widnes's 26-8 home defeat of Hull K.R. on 2 November. The winger also scored five tries away to Hunslet on 17 October 1981 in a John Player Trophy 44-8 victory to equal the club record set by centre Eddie Cunningham in a home Challenge Cup-tie against Doncaster on 15 February 1981.

Soon after Basnett's feat, scrum half David Hulme equalled the record again with five tries in an 82-0 home defeat of Dewsbury in the John Player Special Trophy on 30 November.

TONY KEMP equalled the Doncaster club match record with four tries in a 30-2 home league victory over Carlisle on 23 November. The young New Zealand centre became the fourth Doncaster player to achieve the feat.

The others were centre Vernon Grace v. Rochdale Hornets, 4 October 1952; winger Brian Tasker at Leeds, 26 October 1963; and stand off John Buckton v. Rochdale Hornets, 30 August 1981.

TOMMY FRODSHAM equalled the Blackpool Borough match record for a second time with four tries in a John Player Special Trophy first round 42-12 home defeat of Mansfield Marksman on 30 November. He was stand off then and in the centre when scoring four at Bridgend on 14 April 1985.

Other Blackpool players to score four tries were wingers Tony Wilkshire at Bradford Northern on 14 January 1961 and John Stockley at home to Doncaster on 1 April 1984.

GARY PEACHAM and KEVIN PAPE both scored a club record four tries in a match for Carlisle after the previous record had been three, achieved on 14 occasions.

Centre Peacham, who had shared the record with six hat-tricks, set a new figure with four in a 42-6 home league defeat of Workington Town on 25 January.

Three matches later co-centre Pape, who also shared the previous record with a hat-trick, scored four in a 30-22 Silk Cut Challenge Cup first round home replay win over Rochdale Hornets on 11 February.

BOB BEARDMORE, the Castleford scrum half, regained the Division One points in a match record with 38 from four tries and 11 goals in the 70-10 home defeat of Barrow on 22 March.

The previous record was held by Bradford Northern stand off John Woods with 36 points from eight goals and five tries in a 48-20 home win over Swinton on 13 October 1985.

Woods had taken the record from Beardmore who scored 34 points (11 goals, three tries) in Castleford's 54-4 home defeat of Leeds on 2 October 1983.

Division One points in a match record breaker Bob Beardmore.

PAUL LOUGHLIN scored a St. Helens record of 16 goals and 40 points in a 112-0 home defeat of Carlisle in the first round of the Grunhalle Lager Lancashire Cup on 14 September. The centre's total included two tries. They were also the best individual feats by any player against professional opposition.

Three players had shared the St. Helens record of 13 goals in a match — George Lewis v. Wardley amateurs on 16 February 1924; Peter Fearis v. Barrow on 14 February 1959; and Geoff Pimblett v. Bramley on 5 March 1978.

Fearis also added a try to set the previous St. Helens points record of 29.

The old record for goals in a match against professionals was 15 by Leigh's Mick Stacey against Doncaster on 28 March 1976. The record in any match remains with Jim Sullivan who kicked 22 in Wigan's 116-0 Challenge Cup defeat of Flimby and Fothergill amateurs on 14 February 1925.

The previous highest points tally against a professional club was 39 (five tries, 12 goals) by Salford centre Jim Lomas against Liverpool City on 2 February 1907. The highest total in any match was 53 (11 tries, 10 goals) by Hull K.R. winger George West against Brookland Rovers amateurs 4 March 1905.

ROY RAFFERTY doubled Sheffield Eagles match records with 12 goals and 32 points in the 68-14 league win at Fulham on 21 September, when he also scored two tries.

The winger had equalled the old records with six goals and 16 points in the 40-5 home league defeat of Mansfield Marksman on the opening day of the season, 31 August.

Rafferty had also kicked six goals in a 36-6 home league defeat of Huddersfield Barracudas on 30 March 1986. David Cholmondeley had set the old points record when the hooker scored 16 (two tries, four goals) in a 32-22 league win at Huddersfield on 9 March 1986.

MARTIN KETTERIDGE, the Castleford second row forward, broke a long-standing Yorkshire Cup final record with 14 points, which included a record-equalling five goals, in the 31-24 defeat of Hull at Leeds on 11 October.

The points record of 12 was set by winger Stan Moorhouse with four tries for Huddersfield in the 24-5 defeat of Leeds in 1919-20.

It was then equalled by Bradford Northern winger Alan Edwards with three goals and two tries in the 18-9 defeat of Castleford in 1948 and Wakefield Trinity centre Neil Fox with three goals and two tries in the 18-2 defeat of Leeds in 1964.

Ketteridge's five goals equalled the Yorkshire Cup final record achieved on 11 other occasions.

WIGAN won the Stones Bitter Championship with the following Division One records since the reintroduction of two divisions in 1973-74.

Most tries — 174, beating the 156 by St. Helens in 1984-85.

Most points — 941, beating the 920 by St. Helens in 1984-85.

Least tries conceded — 29, beating the 36 against St. Helens in 1974-75.

Least points conceded — 193, beating the 229 against St. Helens in 1974-75.

Most wins and points — 56 points from 28 wins, beating the 53 points from 26 wins plus a draw by St. Helens in 1974-75.

Winning margin as leaders — 15 points clear of second-placed St. Helens, beating St. Helens' 11-point gap above Wigan in 1974-75.

Highest score, widest winning margin and biggest away win — 72-6 at Wakefield Trinity on 29 March. It equalled Bradford Northern's 72 points at home to Hunslet (12) on 7 October 1984. Northern scored 12 tries, compared with Wigan's 14.

Wigan's winning margin beat that of St. Helens' 15-try 71-7 home defeat of Bramley on 5 March 1978.

Previous biggest away wins were Carlisle 8 v. Castleford 66 (played at Wakefield on 8 April 1985) and Workington T. 18 v. Hull 64 on 20 April 1985. Castleford scored 14 tries and Hull 11.

ST. HELENS completed a Division One record run of 25 successive wins and had a club record 112-0 victory which was also a Lancashire Cup high and the most scored against professional opposition.

The Saints won their last 13 league matches of 1985-86 and the first 12 of 1986-87. The run began with a 44-14 home win over Featherstone Rovers on 2 February 1986 and ended with a 12-4 home defeat against Wigan on 26 December 1986.

Widnes set the record by winning their first 13 matches of 1981-82.

St. Helens' 25-match winning run also included the longest unbeaten sequence, beating the 16 by Widnes, who won their last 12 matches of 1973-74, then drew the first and won the next three of the following season.

The longest winning league run of all was 31 by Wigan under the old one-league system between February 1970 and February 1971.

St. Helens ran up a club record score with their 112-0 home defeat of Carlisle in the first round of the Grunhalle Lancashire Cup on 14 September. The 20-try romp beat the 73-0 home defeat of Wardley amateurs in the first round of the Challenge Cup on 16 February 1924 when they scored 15 tries.

The 112 points were also the most scored against professional opposition, beating Leeds' 102-0 league defeat of Coventry on 12 April 1913. Leeds scored 24 tries against a club which quit soon after, having lasted only three seasons.

There have been only two scores higher than St. Helens' 112 and they were against amateur opposition in the first round of the Challenge Cup. Huddersfield beat Swinton Park 119-2 on 28 February 1914 and Wigan beat Flimby and Fothergill 116-0 on 14 February 1925.

CARLISLE'S 112-0 defeat was 40 points more than they had conceded in their previous biggest defeat, 72-8, also against St. Helens in the first round of the Lancashire Cup on 15 September 1985 when the Saints scored 13 tries.

DONCASTER scored a club record victory with their 50-6 home league defeat of Keighley on 22 March. It beat the previous best of 43-5 at home to Batley in a league match on 17 April 1965 when they scored 11 tries compared with nine in their first half-century score.

WIDNES scored a club record 82-0 victory with their home defeat of Dewsbury in the first round of the John Player Special Trophy on 30 November. It was DEWSBURY'S biggest defeat.

Widnes' previous highest score was a 59-0 home league defeat of Bramley on 4 October 1952 when they scored 15 tries compared with the new record of 17.

Dewsbury's previous defeat was 62-5 at Hull on 5 October 1957 and 62-2 at Halifax on 9 November 1957. Both were league matches and Dewsbury conceded 16 tries each time.

SHEFFIELD EAGLES twice beat their record highest score. The new record is the 68-14 win at Fulham on 21 September when they scored 11 tries.

It beat the record set in the opening match of the season when winning 40-5 at home to Mansfield Marksman in a league match on 31 August. They scored seven tries.

Previously, their biggest victory was 36-6 at home to Huddersfield Barracudas in a league match on 30 March 1986 when they scored six tries.

WHITEHAVEN had a club record 72-6 victory in the first round of the Grunhalle Lager Lancashire Cup and then crashed to a record 74-6 defeat in the second round.

Their 12-try home win also meant a record defeat for FULHAM. Whitehaven's previous highest score was the 64-0 defeat of Doncaster in the first round of the John Player Special Trophy on 11 November 1984 when they scored 11 tries.

Fulham's record defeat came in their first match after a delayed start to the season when the club was re-formed to save it from extinction. Previously, the most points the Londoners had conceded came in the 58-32 league defeat at home to Warrington on 15 April 1984 when they let in 10 tries.

Whitehaven's record 74-6 defeat against Wigan on 24 September saw them concede 14 tries. The Cumbrians' previous worst defeat was 68-14 in a Division One match at Leigh, who scored 13 tries.

YORK equalled their record highest score with the 60-10 Division Two home league defeat of Workington Town on 2 November. They scored 11 tries compared with the 14 when they beat Barrow 60-0 in a home league victory on 3 April 1972.

FEATHERSTONE ROVERS had a club record 66-14 victory with their home league defeat of Barrow on 12 April. It included 12 tries compared with the 15 when they set the previous record with a 65-5 home league victory over Whitehaven on 17 April 1971.

WAKEFIELD TRINITY went down to a club record 72-6 home defeat against Wigan on 29 March which was also a record Division One score. Trinity's 14-try defeat beat the 69-11 at Hull who scored 15 tries on 15 January 1920 and the 69-17 at St. Helens, also 15 tries, on 7 March 1953.

WORKINGTON TOWN suffered their worst defeat when they crashed 68-0 at Wigan who scored 12 tries in the Silk Cut Challenge Cup preliminary round on 18 January. The tie had been switched to Wigan because Town's ground was frostbound.

Workington's previous highest score conceded was 64 points – twice – in 1984-85. They lost 64-4 in a Challenge Cup second round tie at Castleford who scored 12 tries on 24 February 1985 and 64-18 at home to Hull who scored 11 tries in a Division One match on 20 April 1985.

GREAT BRITAIN'S nine-try 52-4 defeat of France in a World Cup-rated Whitbread Trophy Bitter Test at Leeds on 24 January was a record score and winning margin for a match between the two countries.

The previous widest margin was Britain's 50-4 victory at Leeds on 1 March 1985 when they scored eight tries. They also reached the half century with a 12-try 50-15 win at Leeds on 14 March 1959.

Britain's 52-4 win was also their widest winning margin against any country. They just failed to beat their highest score which remains the 53-19 World Cup defeat of New Zealand at Pau in France, on 4 November 1972.

MILESTONES . . .

ELLERY HANLEY'S record-breaking season also included two career milestones . . . 100 Division One tries and 200 tries in all club and representative matches.

The Test star's century of Division One tries came with the third of four touchdowns in Wigan's 34-7 home defeat of Hull on 28 September.

At the end of the season Hanley had taken his league total to 138, putting him into fourth place in the all-time list of Division One tryscorers behind leader Keith Fielding (Salford), who scored 165.

Hanley's total included a record 44 in a season, beating the 40 he scored for Bradford Northern in 1984-85. He also equalled the Division One match record with five against his old club Bradford in a 60-6 home victory on 1 March.

He finished the season by scoring at least one try in each of Wigan's last 10 league matches, leaving him one short of the Division One record 11 successive tryscoring matches by Hull K.R.'s Gary Prohm. The New Zealand centre touched down in the last nine matches of 1984-85 and the first two of 1985-86.

Hanley scored his 200th career try in all matches with the first of two in Wigan's 54-2 home league defeat of Oldham on 8 April. His total at the end of the season was 207 tries made up of 94 for Wigan, 90 for Bradford and 23 in representative matches.

After playing most of his career at either stand off or centre, Hanley moved to loose forward in February 1987 with devastating effect, scoring 30 tries in 17 matches.

He turned professional as a 17-year-old with Bradford on 2 June 1978 from amateurs Corpus Christi, Leeds. The youngster made his debut as a substitute, scoring one try in the 30-18 home league defeat of Rochdale Hornets on 26 November 1978.

He was then absent for a period and did not make his full debut until 16 August 1981 when he scored a try in the centre in a 33-5 Yorkshire Cup first round win at Halifax.

Wigan signed him in a world record £150,000 deal on 16 September 1985. They paid a then record £85,000 plus the transfer of Phil Ford (valued at £40,000) and Steve Donlan (£25,000).

He made his Wigan debut in the centre in a 32-10 home league victory over Widnes on 22 September 1985.

His career total includes three or more tries in a match on 21 occasions, including 14 hat-tricks, six four-try feats and five once.

Hanley's season-by-season totals are as follows:

Bradford N.

	T	G	DG	Pts
1978-79........	1	0	0	3
1979-80........	NA			
1980-81........	NA			
1981-82........	15	41	0	127
1982-83........	10	2	1	35
1983-84........	12	2	1	53	1t GB Under-24
1984-85........	52	36	0	280	2t GB, 1t England

Wigan

1985-86........	35	8	0	156	2t GB, 1t + 1dg Yorks
1986-87........	59	1	0	238	3t GB, 1t Yorks

Totals

Bradford N. .	90	81	2	498	
Wigan	94	9	0	394	
Britain.........	11	0	0	44	
England	1	0	0	4	
GB Under-24	1	0	0	4	
Yorkshire.....	2	0	1	9	
1984 tour	8	3	0	38	(Not inc. Tests)

GRAND TOTALS

207	93	5	991

Included in the above totals are Hanley's 138 Division One tries made up as follows:

Bradford N.

1978-79........	1
1979-80........	0
1980-81........	0
1981-82........	12
1982-83........	8
1983-84........	11
1984-85........	40

Wigan

1985-86........	22
1986-87........	44

GEORGE FAIRBAIRN kicked his 500th career goal for Hull Kingston Rovers with the first of his four goals in the 20-20 John Smiths Yorkshire Cup second round home draw against Featherstone Rovers on 24 September.

Rovers signed the Scottish full back from Wigan in June 1981 for a then world record £72,500 and he made an eight-goal debut in a 34-7 Yorkshire Cup first round home defeat of Huddersfield on 14 August 1981.

He finished that first season at Rovers with a club record 166 goals.

Fairbairn's best match tally for the club is nine in a 45-3 home league defeat of Whitehaven on 18 April 1982.

His club total of 533 goals includes 19 drop goals and is made up as follows:

1981-82	166	(Inc. 6 dg)
1982-83	88	(Inc. 5 dg)
1983-84	59	(Inc. 1 dg)
1984-85	141	(Inc. 6 dg)
1985-86	28	(Inc. 1 dg)
1986-87	51	
Total	**533**	**(Inc. 19 dg)**

KEITH MUMBY scored his 1,000th Division One point when his third goal in Bradford Northern's 46-18 defeat at Castleford on 1 January took his total to 1,001.

At the end of the season the Test full back's total stood at 1,057 from 440 goals and 56 tries.

Bradford spent the first season of the 1973-74 reintroduction of two divisions in Division Two, when Mumby made his debut. Since then, Northern have remained in Division One with Mumby building the majority of his points total in the early years when he was their regular goalkicker.

His most prolific Division One season was 1977-78 when he totalled 168 league points. Since giving up the regular kicking role his scoring rate has dropped considerably.

Mumby's season-by-season Division One scoring record is as follows:

	G	T	Pts
1974-75	63	1	129
1975-76	65	3	139
1976-77	61	3	131
1977-78	78	4	168
1978-79	55	9	137
1979-80	7	4	26
1980-81	33	13	105
1981-82	8	4	28
1982-83	29	6	76
1983-84	5	7	38
1984-85	1	0	2
1985-86	0	1	4
1986-87	35	1	74
Totals	**440**	**56**	**1,057**

STEVE QUINN passed the 3,000 career points mark during the season, including his 1,000th goal for Featherstone Rovers.

He scored his 1,000th goal for Rovers with the last of three in a 48-14 home league defeat against Widnes on 21 September.

His 3,000th career point came with the last of four goals in Rovers' 23-12 home defeat of Hull K.R. in a John Smiths Yorkshire Cup second round replay on 26 September.

Quinn's points total at the end of the season was 3,102, made up of 2,311 for Featherstone, 763 for York and 28 for Yorkshire.

York-born, he made his first team debut for his home town team in the centre on 18 October 1970 when he kicked four goals in a 17-19 home defeat against Halifax.

He moved to Featherstone in an exchange deal with forward Barry Hollis, making his debut at centre and kicking another four goals in a 23-9 Challenge Cup first round home win over Wakefield Trinity on 15 February 1976.

Quinn set up a succession of club records at Featherstone as follows:

Most points in a match: 29 (10g,3t) v. Doncaster on 4 November 1979
Most goals in a season: 163 in 1979-80
Most points in a season: 375 in 1979-80
Most career goals: 1,059
Most career points: 2,311

The 1979-80 season was clearly Quinn's best. In addition to the above records, he joined the elite band who have scored in each of his club's matches in a season and raced to a record-equalling fastest century of goals in 18 matches. He finished as the game's top goals and points scorer and was voted Trumanns Steel Division Two Player of the Year.

Quinn has finished among the top 10 goalkickers in eight seasons, heading the list once. His best match feats are 11 goals twice, against Wakefield Trinity on 2 January 1977 and Workington Town on 31 August 1980. Both were Division One matches. He has also kicked 10 goals in a match twice.

Quinn's career totals are made up as follows:

York	T	G	DG	Pts	
1970-71	1	22	0	47	
1971-72	2	0	0	6	
1972-73	6	107	0	232	
1973-74	7	112	0	245	
1974-75	3	112	0	233	
Featherstone R.					
1975-76	3	39	0	87	
1976-77	8	152	0	328	
1977-78	11	54	0	141	+ 6g Yorks
1978-79	2	30	0	66	
1979-80	17	161	2	375	
1980-81	4	115	1	243	+ 7g Yorks
1981-82	4	119	0	250	+ 1g Yorks
1982-83	5	98	0	211	
1983-84	4	74	3	167	
1984-85	3	77	2	168	
1985-86	2	54	1	117	
1986-87	1	77	0	158	
Totals					
York	19	353	0	763	
Featherstone R.	64	1,050	9	2,311	
Yorkshire	0	14	0	28	

GRAND TOTALS

	83	1,417	9	3,102

NIGEL STEPHENSON scored the 200th try of his long career with a touchdown in York's 42-10 league defeat at Hunslet on 20 April.

He signed for Dewsbury while still a 16-year-old schoolboy, moving from the local Shaw Cross Under-17 team for a then sensational club record four-figure sum for a junior.

The youngster made his debut for Dewsbury on 17 February 1968 at full back in a home league game against Hull K.R. when he kicked the goal in a 15-2 defeat.

Stephenson had 12 seasons at Dewsbury before returning to them briefly after spells at Bradford Northern, Carlisle and Wakefield Trinity.

His total of 131 tries for Dewsbury is a club career record. Another club record is a run of 13 successive try-scoring matches from April to September in 1973.

Stephenson played most of his early rugby at centre before moving to stand off and much later to loose forward.

His most prolific tryscoring season was 1972-73 when he scraped into the top 10 for the only time with 26. He has scored three tries in a match on four occasions and his career total includes nine tries for Yorkshire.

Following his first move from Dewsbury in 1978, Stephenson's debuts for various clubs were:

● For Bradford Northern at Leigh on 19 November 1978. He played stand off in the 13-7 league victory.

● Carlisle at home to Wigan on 16 August 1981. Playing at stand off, he dropped a goal in the 9-6 Lancashire Cup first round defeat.

● Wakefield Trinity at Dewsbury on 22 August 1982. Playing at stand off he scored a try in the 16-10 league win.

● Dewsbury at Workington Town on 17 February 1985. He went on as a substitute in the 28-6 defeat.

● York at Blackpool Borough on 5 October 1986. He was at loose forward as York lost 14-13.

Stephenson's total of 200 tries is made up as follows:

Dewsbury

1967-68	2	
1968-69	2	
1969-70	5	
1970-71	17	+ 4 Yorkshire
1971-72	16	+ 3 Yorkshire
1972-73	26	
1973-74	16	
1974-75	8	
1975-76	9	
1976-77	19	+ 1 Yorkshire
1977-78	1	
1978-79	3	+ 1 Yorkshire

Bradford N.

1978-79	3
1979-80	4
1980-81	7

Carlisle

1981-82	14

Wakefield T.

1982-83	15
1983-84	9
1984-85	1

Dewsbury

1984-85	3
1985-86	4

York

1986-87	7

Totals

Dewsbury	131
Bradford N.	14
Carlisle	14
Wakefield T.	25
York	7
Yorkshire	9
GRAND TOTAL	**200**

PHIL FOX scored the 100th try of his career with a touchdown in Leigh's 22-29 home league defeat against Oldham in the first round of the Grunhalle Lager Lancashire Cup on 14 September.

The winger's total at the end of the season stood at 107 with five for Widnes, 96 for Leigh and six for Leeds.

Fox made his first team debut with a try in Widnes' 34-6 Lancashire Cup first round home victory over Huyton on 20 August 1978.

He played only a few first team matches for Widnes before transferring to Leigh to make a tryscoring debut with a touchdown in the 22-18 home league defeat of Castleford on 28 September 1980.

After adding only one to his career century of tries, Fox moved to Leeds and made his debut in a 32-10 defeat at Wigan in the first round of the John Player Special Trophy on 29 November 1986.

Fox has scored three hat-tricks, including one five-try feat, in his total of 107 tries which is made up as follows:

Widnes

1978-79	2
1979-80	0
1980-81	3

Leigh

1980-81	9
1981-82	13
1982-83	10
1983-84	19
1984-85	13
1985-86	29
1986-87	3

Leeds

1986-87	6

Totals

Widnes	5
Leigh	96
Leeds	6
GRAND TOTAL	**107**

PHIL FORD scored the 100th try of his career with the second of three touchdowns in Bradford Northern's 36-14 league win at Widnes on 16 November.

The Welsh winger's total at the end of the season was 119 made up of 57 for Warrington, 16 for Wigan, 44 for Bradford and two for Great Britain.

A former Cardiff RU player, Ford made his professional debut as an unnamed trialist when he scored Warrington's only try in the 10-9 home league defeat of Featherstone Rovers on 11 January 1981.

He made another vital tryscoring debut when he moved to Wigan for a winger's record transfer fee of £40,000. Ford's two tries included the last minute match winner in the 20-16 home league defeat of Hull K.R. on 3 March 1985.

Ford scored 16 tries in only 15 appearances for Wigan before moving to Bradford early the next season. He was exchanged along with Steve Donlan, plus cash, for Ellery Hanley in a world record £150,000 deal.

The two Bradford signings made their debuts in a 17-12 home league defeat against Hull K.R. on 22 September 1985.

Ford has played once for Great Britain, scoring two tries in the 24-16 defeat against France at Perpignan in 1984-85. He has also played once for Wales.

He has scored only four hat-tricks but they include a Premiership record four touchdowns in Wigan's first round 46-12 home win over Hull on 28 April 1985.

Ford's total of 119 is made up as follows:

Warrington

1980-81	4
1981-82	9
1982-83	20
1983-84	20
1984-85	4

Wigan

1984-85	13 + 2 GB
1985-86	3

Bradford N.

1985-86	14
1986-87	30

Totals

Warrington................	57
Wigan	16
Bradford N.	44
Gt Britain	2

GRAND TOTAL **119**

DAVID STEPHENSON reached a century of career tries with the first of two touchdowns in Wigan's 30-8 home league victory over Leeds on 18 February.

He finished the season with 108 made up of 66 for Wigan, 36 for Salford, and six in representative matches.

A former England Schools RU international, Stephenson joined Salford as a 20-year-old from Fylde RU in December 1978 for a reported £10,000.

He made his first team professional debut in a 13-4 league home defeat against Rochdale Hornets on 23 January 1979.

Stephenson moved to Wigan for £60,000 in February 1982 and made a two-try debut in a 20-12 first round Challenge Cup-tie win at St. Helens on 13 February 1982.

The Test centre has scored two tries for Great Britain Under-24s and four for Lancashire. Despite scoring 108 tries, his total does not include a hat-trick or more.

His season-by-season totals are as follows:

Salford

1978-79	3
1979-80	11 + 1 GB Under-24
1980-81	12
1981-82	10 + 1 GB Under-24

Wigan

1981-82	6 + 3 Lancashire
1982-83	11
1983-84	10
1984-85	8
1985-86	18
1986-87	13 + 1 Lancashire

Totals

Salford	36
Wigan	66
GB Under-24	2
Lancashire	4

GRAND TOTAL **108**

Ton up try scorer David Stephenson.

GARRY SCHOFIELD became one of the youngest players to reach a career century of tries when he passed the milestone last season while still only 21. The Hull centre finished the campaign with a total of 125 in club and representative matches.

He reached 100 in all matches with the first of two tries for Hull in a 48-22 home defeat of Blackpool Borough in the second round of the John Player Special Trophy on 6 December.

His century for Hull came with the first of two tries in the 18-10 league win at Widnes on 5 April.

A former Hunslet Parkside junior, Schofield signed for Hull soon after captaining the Great Britain amateur youth squad to New Zealand in 1983. He made his professional debut in a 22-22 home league draw against Warrington on 21 August 1983.

It was the start of a remarkable first season in which he became the youngest player to finish at the top of the try chart with 38. He was only 18 years 10 months when the season finished.

Schofield's total for Hull includes four hat-tricks, plus a four-try feat. He has also twice scored four tries in representative matches. His four in the second Test 25-6 defeat of New Zealand at Wigan in 1985 equalled the record for a Great Britain player in an international match.

His other four-try feat for Britain was for the 1984 tourists in the 44-12 defeat of North Queensland at Rockhampton.

Schofield's five tries for Britain against the 1986 Kangaroos is a record total for a British player in a home Test series against Australia.

He has also scored tries while playing for Balmain in Australia but these are not included in his totals as a registered British player which are as follows:

Hull

1983-84	37	+ 1 GB Under-24
1984-85	23	
1985-86	15	+ 5 GB
1986-87	32	+ 5 GB

Totals

Hull	107
Gt. Britain	12
GB Under-24	1
1984 tour	5 (not including 2 in in Tests)
GRAND TOTAL	**125**

HENDERSON GILL scored his 100th career try for Wigan with the first of two touchdowns in their 52-0 home defeat of Rochdale Hornets in the first round of the Grunhalle Lager Lancashire Cup on 14 September.

The winger turned professional with Bradford Northern in 1978 before moving to Rochdale Hornets in 1980.

Wigan signed him for a then record £30,000 for a winger and he marked his debut with a try in a 20-15 league defeat at Barrow on 11 October 1981.

At the end of last season the Test winger's total for Wigan stood at 124 including eight three-try feats.

Gill's season-by-season totals for Wigan are as follows:

1981-82	12
1982-83	18
1983-84	16
1984-85	33
1985-86	15
1986-87	30
Total	**124**

JOHN BASNETT, of Widnes, passed a century of career tries in club and representative matches during the season.

The winger reached 100 in all matches with the last of his five tries in Widnes' 26-8 home league defeat of Hull K.R. on 2 November. They accounted for all of his side's tries that day and equalled the club and Division One record.

Basnett scored his 100th try for Widnes in the 24-16 win at Castleford in the first round of the Silk Cut Challenge Cup on 31 January.

A former England RU Under-23 international with New Brighton, Basnett signed for Widnes in April 1981 after scoring five tries in a reserve team trial.

He has twice scored five tries in a match for the first team. In addition to the five against Hull K.R. last season, Basnett went nap against Hunslet at Mount Pleasant, Batley, in a 44-8 first round John Player Trophy victory on 16 October 1981 — then a record for the competition. He has also scored three other hat-tricks for Widnes.

The Test winger's overall total includes six on the 1984 tour of Australasia when he was flown out as a replacement. He has also scored a try for Lancashire. His season-by-season totals are as follows:

Widnes

1981-82	26	
1982-83	5	
1983-84	26	
1984-85	12	
1985-86	14	
1986-87	20	+ 1 Lancashire

Totals

Widnes	103
1984 tour	6
Lancashire	1
GRAND TOTAL	**110**

ROY HAGGERTY scored his 100th career try for St. Helens with a touchdown in the 20-19 league defeat at Halifax on 4 January.

A local product and former Colts international, Haggerty made his first team debut for St. Helens in a John Player Trophy second round tie at Widnes on 30 September 1979 when they lost 31-20. ٭

A strong-running centre turned second row forward, Haggerty maintained a steady tryscoring rate with 1985-86 being his best with 21.

His consistent, rather than spectacular scoring rate, is reflected in a century which does not feature a single hat-trick.

Haggerty's season-by-season totals for St. Helens are as follows:

1979-80	3
1980-81	4
1981-82	12
1982-83	18
1983-84	17
1984-85	16
1985-86	21
1986-87	9
Total	**100**

DANE O'HARA reached a career century of tries for Hull with two touchdowns in the 24-18 league defeat at Oldham on 22 February.

The New Zealand Test back made his debut for Hull on the wing at home to Castleford on 27 September 1981. James Leuluai made his debut at centre while recently signed full back Gary Kemble completed the Kiwi trio as a 16,159 crowd saw Hull's 42-24 league victory.

New Zealander Dane O'Hara, a try centurion for Hull.

O'Hara has never finished in the top 10 and his best season was 1984-85 when he scored 22. His career total includes only two hat-tricks.

At the end of last season his total stood at 103 made up as follows:

1981-82	15
1982-83	17
1983-84	13
1984-85	22
1985-86	19
1986-87	17
Total	**103**

CARL GIBSON scored the 100th try of his career with the only touchdown in Leeds' 4-0 win at Salford in the first round of the Silk Cut Challenge Cup on 1 February. At the end of the season he had taken his total to 104 made up of 81 for Batley, 22 for Leeds and one for Yorkshire.

A former Batley Boys Club amateur, Gibson turned professional with Batley in July 1981. He made his debut for them by scoring a try as a substitute in a 29-19 defeat at Keighley on 18 April 1982 and played his first full game three days later in the centre at Huddersfield, who won 11-0.

His move to Leeds on 18 January 1986 involved a record fee for both clubs of £50,000. Gibson made his debut for Leeds on the left wing at Swinton in a preliminary round of the Silk Cut Challenge Cup on 30 January 1986.

Although Gibson has played many matches on the wing, he is regarded as a promising centre.

While with Batley he scored three tries in a match on six occasions and has achieved one hat-trick with Leeds.

Gibson's century was one of the quickest of recent times. After scoring one try from three appearances in his first season with Batley he maintained a high scoring rate and finished in the top 10 in three successive seasons.

His best season's totals were 26 in 1983-84 and 1984-85 when he finished fifth and seventh respectively. His season-by-season totals are as follows:

Batley

1981-82	1
1982-83	15
1983-84	26
1984-85	26
1985-86	13 + 1 Yorkshire

Leeds

1985-86	9
1986-87	13

Totals

Batley	81
Leeds	22
Yorkshire	1
GRAND TOTAL	**104**

LEADING SCORERS 1895-1970

	TRIES	GOALS	POINTS
1895-96	Hurst (Oldham) 28	Lorimer (Manningham) 35	Cooper (Bradford)..........106
			Lorimer (Manningham)...106
1896-97	Hannah (Hunslet)............19	Goldthorpe (Hunslet) 26	Rigg (Halifax) 112
		Sharpe (Liversedge) 26	
1897-98	Hoskins (Salford) 30	Goldthorpe (Hunslet) 66	Goldthorpe (Hunslet)......135
1898-99	Williams (Oldham) 39	Goldthorpe (Hunslet) 67	Jaques (Hull) 169
1899-00	Williams (Oldham) 36	Cooper (Bradford) 39	Williams (Oldham).........108
1900-01	Williams (Oldham) 47	Goldthorpe (Hunslet) 44	Williams (Oldham).........141
1901-02	Wilson (Broughton R.) 38	James (Broughton R.) 75	Lomas (Salford).............172
1902-03	Evans (Leeds).................27	Goldthorpe (Hunslet) 48	Davies (Batley)..............136
1903-04	Hogg (Broughton R.) 34	Lomas (Salford) 66	Lomas (Salford).............222
1904-05	Dechan (Bradford)...........31	Ferguson (Oldham)..........50	Lomas (Salford).............146
1905-06	Leytham (Wigan) 40	Ferguson (Oldham)..........49	Leytham (Wigan)............160
1906-07	Eccles (Halifax)...............41	Lomas (Salford) 86	Lomas (Salford).............280
1907-08	Leytham (Wigan) 44	Goldthorpe (Hunslet)......101	Goldthorpe (Hunslet)......217
1908-09	Miller (Wigan)................49	Lomas (Salford) 88	Lomas (Salford).............272
	Williams (Halifax) 49		
1909-10	Leytham (Wigan) 48	Carmichael (Hull K.R.) 78	Leytham (Wigan)............232
1910-11	Kitchen (Huddersfield).....40	Carmichael (Hull K.R.)...129	Carmichael (Hull K.R.)...261
	Rosenfeld (Huddersfield) ..40		
	Miller (Wigan)................40		
1911-12	Rosenfeld (Huddersfield) ..78	Carmichael (Hull K.R.)...127	Carmichael (Hull K.R.)...254
1912-13	Rosenfeld (Huddersfield) ..56	Carmichael (Hull K.R.) 93	Thomas (Wigan)............198
1913-14	Rosenfeld (Huddersfield) ..80	Holland (Huddersfield) ...131	Holland (Huddersfield) ...268
1914-15	Rosenfeld (Huddersfield) ..56	Gronow (Huddersfield) ...136	Gronow (Huddersfield) ...284
● Competitive matches suspended during war years			
1918-19	Francis (Hull).................25	Kennedy (Hull) 54	Kennedy (Hull) 135
1919-20	Moorhouse (Huddersfield).39	Gronow (Huddersfield) ...148	Gronow (Huddersfield) ...332
1920-21	Stone (Hull) 41	Kennedy (Hull) 108	Kennedy (Hull) 264
1921-22	Farrar (Oldham) 49	Sullivan (Wigan)............100	Farrar (Oldham) 213
1922-23	Ring (Wigan) 41	Sullivan (Wigan)............161	Sullivan (Wigan)............349
1923-24	Ring (Wigan) 49	Sullivan (Wigan)............158	Sullivan (Wigan)............319
1924-25	Ring (Wigan) 54	Sullivan (Wigan)............138	Sullivan (Wigan)............282
1925-26	Ring (Wigan) 63	Sullivan (Wigan)............131	Sullivan (Wigan)............274
1926-27	Ellaby (St. Helens) 55	Sullivan (Wigan)............149	Sullivan (Wigan)............322
1927-28	Ellaby (St. Helens) 37	Thompson (Leeds)..........106	Thompson (Leeds).........233
1928-29	Brown (Wigan) 44	Sullivan (Wigan)............107	Sullivan (Wigan)............226
	Mills (Huddersfield).........44		
1929-30	Ellaby (St. Helens) 39	Thompson (Leeds) 111	Thompson (Leeds).........243
1930-31	Harris, E. (Leeds) 58	Sullivan (Wigan)............133	Sullivan (Wigan)............278
1931-32	Mills (Huddersfield).........50	Sullivan (Wigan)............117	Sullivan (Wigan)............249
1932-33	Harris, E. (Leeds) 57	Sullivan (Wigan)............146	Sullivan (Wigan)............307
1933-34	Brown (Salford) 45	Sullivan (Wigan)............193	Sullivan (Wigan)............404

	TRIES	GOALS	POINTS
1934-35	Morley (Wigan) 49	Sullivan (Wigan)............165	Sullivan (Wigan)............348
1935-36	Harris, E. (Leeds) 63	Sullivan (Wigan)............117	Sullivan (Wigan)............246
1936-37	Harris, E. (Leeds) 40	Sullivan (Wigan)............120	Sullivan (Wigan)............258
1937-38	Harris, E. (Leeds) 45	Sullivan (Wigan)............135	Sullivan (Wigan)............285
1938-39	Markham (Huddersfield)...39	Sullivan (Wigan)............124	Risman (Salford)............267

● For the next six seasons emergency war-time competitions resulted in a reduction of matches and players were allowed to 'guest' for other clubs

	TRIES	GOALS	POINTS
1939-40	Batten (Hunslet) 38	Hodgson (Swinton)...........98	Hodgson (Swinton) 208
1940-41	Walters (Bradford N.) 32	Lockwood (Halifax) 70	Belshaw (Warrington) 174
1941-42	Francis (Barrow) 29	Lockwood (Halifax) 91	Lockwood (Halifax)........185
1942-43	Batten (Hunslet) 24	Lockwood (Halifax) 65	Lockwood (Halifax)........136
1943-44	Lawrenson (Wigan) 21	Horne (Barrow) 57	Horne (Barrow) 144
1944-45	Batten (Bradford N.)........41	Stott (Wakefield T.).........51	Stott (Wakefield T.) 129

● Normal peace-time rugby resumed

	TRIES	GOALS	POINTS
1945-46	Batten (Bradford N.)........35	Ledgard (Dewsbury)........88	Bawden (Huddersfield) ...239
1946-47	Bevan (Warrington) 48	Miller (Hull).................103	Bawden (Huddersfield) ...243
1947-48	Bevan (Warrington) 57	Ward (Wigan) 141	Ward (Wigan) 312
1948-49	Cooper (Huddersfield) 60	Ward (Wigan) 155	Ward (Wigan) 361
1949-50	Nordgren (Wigan) 57	Gee (Wigan) 133	Palin (Warrington) 290
		Palin (Warrington) 133	
1950-51	Bevan (Warrington) 68	Cook (Leeds) 155	Cook (Leeds) 332
1951-52	Cooper (Huddersfield) 71	Ledgard (Leigh) 142	Horne (Barrow) 313
1952-53	Bevan (Warrington) 72	Bath (Warrington)..........170	Bath (Warrington)..........379
1953-54	Bevan (Warrington) 67	Metcalfe (St. Helens) 153	Metcalfe (St. Helens)......369
		Bath (Warrington)..........153	
1954-55	Cooper (Huddersfield) 66	Ledgard (Leigh) 178	Ledgard (Leigh) 374
1955-56	McLean (Bradford N.) 61	Ledgard (Leigh) 155	Bath (Warrington)..........344
1956-57	Boston (Wigan)...............60	Jones (Leeds).................194	Jones (Leeds).................496
1957-58	Sullivan (Wigan) 50	Ganley (Oldham) 219	Ganley (Oldham) 453
1958-59	Vollenhoven (St. Helens) ..62	Ganley (Oldham) 190	Griffiths (Wigan) 394
1959-60	Vollenhoven (St. Helens) ..54	Rhodes (St. Helens) 171	Fox (Wakefield T.) 453
		Fox (Wakefield T.) 171	
1960-61	Vollenhoven (St. Helens) ..59	Rhodes (St. Helens) 145	Rhodes (St. Helens) 338
1961-62	Boston (Wigan)...............51	Fox (Wakefield T.) 183	Fox (Wakefield T.) 456
1962-63	Glastonbury (Work'ton T.)41	Coslett (St. Helens)........156	Coslett (St. Helens)........321
1963-64	Stopford (Swinton) 45	Coslett (St. Helens)........138	Fox (Wakefield T.) 313
1964-65	Lake (Wigan) 40	Kellett (Hull K.R.) 150	Killeen (St. Helens)........360
1965-66	Killeen (St. Helens) 32	Killeen (St. Helens)........120	Killeen (St. Helens)........336
	Lake (Wigan) 32		
1966-67	Young (Hull K.R.)...........34	Risman (Leeds) 163	Killeen (St. Helens)........353
	Howe (Castleford) 34		
1967-68	Millward (Hull K.R.).......38	Risman (Leeds) 154	Risman (Leeds) 332
1968-69	Francis (Wigan) 40	Risman (Leeds) 165	Risman (Leeds) 345
1969-70	Atkinson (Leeds).............38	Tyrer (Wigan)...............167	Tyrer (Wigan)...............385

LEADING SCORERS 1970-86

TRIES

1970-71
Haigh (Leeds)...40
Jones (St. Helens)...38
Atkinson (Leeds)...36
Sullivan (Hull)..33
Slater (Wakefield T.).......................................33
Wright (Wigan)..33
Wilson (St. Helens)...27
Hynes (Leeds)...25
A. Smith (Leeds)..23
Topliss (Wakefield T.)......................................23
Richards (Salford)..23
Benyon (St. Helens)...23

1971-72
Atkinson (Leeds)...36
Lamb (Bradford N.)..36
Richards (Salford)..35
D. Redfearn (Bradford N.)...................................35
Sullivan (Hull)...33
Watkins (Salford)...29
Hardisty (Leeds)..27
Brown (Widnes)..27
O'Neill (Widnes)..25
Topliss (Wakefield T.)......................................24

1972-73
Atkinson (Leeds)...39
Richards (Salford)..38
Charlton (Salford)..33
Topliss (Wakefield T.)......................................30
Lowe (Hull K.R.)..29
Hardisty (Leeds)..28
A. Smith (Leeds)..28
Dunn (Hull K.R.)..27
D. Redfearn (Bradford N.)...................................27
N. Stephenson (Dewsbury)....................................26
Mathias (St. Helens)..26

1973-74
Fielding (Salford)..49
Mathias (St. Helens)..40
D. Smith (Wakefield T.).....................................38
Eckersley (St. Helens)......................................26
Fleay (Swinton)...26
Jones (St. Helens)..25
Wilson (St. Helens)...25
Watkins (Salford)...24
Atkinson (Leeds)..23
Lamb (Bradford N.)..22
A. Smith (Leeds)..22
Bevan (Warrington)..22
Ayres (Wigan)...22

1974-75
Dunn (Hull K.R.)..42
Fielding (Salford)..35
Bevan (Warrington)..31
A. Smith (Leeds)..30
Millward (Hull K.R.)..30
Atkinson (Leeds)..29
Richards (Salford)..28
Sullivan (Hull K.R.)..28
Mathias (St. Helens)..27
Dyl (Leeds)...26

1975-76
Richards (Salford)..37
Fielding (Salford)..33
Jones (St. Helens)..31
Briggs (Leigh)..27
D. Smith (Wakefield T.).....................................26
Burton (Castleford)...25
Clark (Hull)..23
Wright (Workington T.)......................................22
Barends (York)..21
Boxall (Hull)...21
Holmes (Leeds)..21
Mathias (St. Helens)..21
Butler (Salford)..21

1976-77
Wright (Widnes)...31
Burton (Castleford)...29
D. Smith (Leeds)..28
Fielding (Salford)..27
Dunn (Hull K.R.)..26
Cunningham (St. Helens).....................................26
Topliss (Wakefield T.)......................................24
Richards (Salford)..23
Mathias (St. Helens)..23
Barends (York)..22

1977-78
Wright (Widnes)...33
Fielding (Salford)..31
Cunningham (St. Helens).....................................30
Bevan (Warrington)..30
Fenton (Castleford)...30
Vigo (Wigan)..29
Glynn (St. Helens)..28
D. Smith (Leeds)..28
T. Morgan (York)..27
Burton (Castleford)...27

1978-79
Hartley (Hull K.R.)..35
Wright (Widnes)...28
Barends (Bradford N.)..25
Lowe (Hull K.R.)...25
Prendiville (Hull)...25
Fielding (Salford)...24
D. Redfearn (Bradford N.)....................................23
Mathias (St. Helens)...22
Bray (Hull)..21
O'Loughlin (Wigan)...21
Sullivan (Hull K.R.)...21

1979-80
Fielding (Salford)...30
Hubbard (Hull K.R.)..30
Munro (Oldham)...29
Ball (Barrow)..27
Bentley (Widnes)...27
Glynn (St. Helens)...27
Mathias (St. Helens)...27
Bevan (Warrington)...26
D. Redfearn (Bradford N.)....................................26
D. Smith (Leeds)...24

1980-81
Crossley (York)..35
Richardson (Castleford)......................................28
Hubbard (Hull K.R.)..25
Hartley (Hull K.R.)..23
McDermott (York)...23
Slater (Huddersfield)..23
Drummond (Leigh)...20
Ball (Barrow)..19
Bevan (Warrington)...19
Cramp (Huddersfield)...19
Hyde (Castleford)..19
Ramsdale (Wigan)...19

1981-82
Jones (Workington T.)..31
Drummond (Leigh)...26
Basnett (Widnes)...26
Ashton (Oldham)..26
Morgan (Carlisle)..25
Hartley (Hull K.R.)..23
Hopkins (Workington T.)......................................23
Day (Hull)...23
Evans (Hull)...22
D. Hobbs (Featherstone R.)...................................21
Moll (Keighley)..21

1982-83
Eccles (Warrington)..37
Evans (Hull)...28
Crossley (Fulham)..27
David (Cardiff C.)...26
Topliss (Hull)...24
M'Barki (Fulham)...23
Hyde (Castleford)..22
McDermott (York)...22
Leuluai (Hull)...21
Phil Ford (Warrington).......................................20
Clark (Hull K.R.)..20

1983-84
Schofield (Hull)...38
Lydon (Widnes)...28
King (Hunslet)...28
Woods (Leigh)..27
Basnett (Widnes)...26
Gibson (Batley)..26
Herbert (Barrow)...25
Steadman (York)..25
Prohm (Hull K.R.)..25
Clark (Hull K.R.)..24

1984-85
Hanley (Bradford N.)...55
Prohm (Hull K.R.)..45
Gill (Wigan)...34
Ledger (St. Helens)..30
Meninga (St. Helens)...28
Gibbin (Whitehaven)..27
Gibson (Batley)..26
G. Peacham (Carlisle)..25
Byrne (Salford)..25
Evans (Hull)...24
Ferguson (Wigan)...24

1985-86
Halliwell (Leigh)..49
Hanley (Wigan)...38
Lister (Bramley)...34
Henderson (Leigh)..31
Frodsham (Blackpool B.)......................................30
Fox (Leigh)..29
Williams (Barrow)..27
Garrity (Runcorn H.)...24
Gibson (Leeds)...23
Beck (Workington T.)...23

GOALS
(including drop goals)

1970-71
Coslett (St. Helens) 183
Ferguson (Leigh) 166
Holmes (Leeds) 159
Watkins (Salford) 155
Tyrer (Wigan) 141
Stephenson (Dewsbury) 134
Clawson (Hull K.R.)...114
Fox (Wakefield T.)...110
Davies (Huddersfield) 99
Jefferson (Keighley) 98

1971-72
Coslett (St. Helens) 214
Watkins (Salford) 193
Tees (Bradford N.)...173
Dutton (Widnes)...120
Clawson (Hull K.R., Leeds)..............................120
Gowers (Swinton) 119
Tyrer (Wigan) 117
Larder (Oldham)...114
Whitehead (Warrington) 108
Maloney (York, Hull) 108

1972-73
Watkins (Salford) 221
Coslett (St. Helens) 162
Tees (Bradford N.)...160
Stephenson (Dewsbury) 149
C. Kellett (Featherstone R.) 139
Fox (Wakefield T.)...138
Whitehead (Warrington) 136
Larder (Oldham)...127
Jefferson (Keighley) 120
Quinn (York) 107

1973-74
Watkins (Salford) 183
Whitehead (Warrington) 168
Jefferson (Keighley) 165
Coslett (St. Helens) 134
Mumby (Bradford N.).......................................131
Dutton (Widnes)...129
Lloyd (Castleford) 121
Quinn (York) 112
Fiddler (Leigh)...111
Holliday (Rochdale H.) 107

1974-75
Fox (Hull K.R.)..146
Coslett (St. Helens) 129
Dutton (Widnes)...122
Lloyd (Castleford) 112
Quinn (York) 112
Hartley (Huddersfield) 110
MacCorquodale (Workington T.) 107

Marshall (Leeds)...107
Mumby (Bradford N.)....................................... 96
Fiddler (Salford, Leigh).................................... 85

1975-76
Watkins (Salford) 175
Pimblett (St. Helens) 149
Lloyd (Castleford) 149
Dutton (Widnes)...148
Fairbairn (Wigan)..146
Stacey (Leigh) 137
MacCorquodale (Workington T.) 130
Fox (Hull K.R., York).......................................102
Marshall (Leeds)..101
Gaitley (New Hunslet).......................................100

1976-77
Lloyd (Castleford) 163
Quinn (Featherstone R.) 152
Pimblett (St. Helens) 152
Hesford (Warrington)..132
MacCorquodale (Workington T.) 128
Watkins (Salford) 125
Stephenson (Dewsbury) 106
Fairbairn (Wigan)..105
Dutton (Widnes)... 97
Woods (Leigh)... 90

1977-78
Pimblett (St. Helens) 178
Hesford (Warrington)..158
Woods (Leigh)..149
MacCorquodale (Workington T.) 138
Woods (Widnes) 122
Watkins (Salford) 110
Mumby (Bradford N.).......................................107
Lloyd (Castleford) 104
Fox (Bradford N.)... 95
Oulton (Leeds)... 80

1978-79
Lloyd (Hull) 172
Hesford (Warrington)..170
Burke (Widnes) 140
MacCorquodale (Workington T.) 114
Pimblett (St. Helens) 105
Beale (Keighley)... 96
Woods (Leigh)... 96
Birts (Halifax) 86
Fairbairn (Wigan)... 86
Norton (Castleford)... 82

1979-80
Quinn (Featherstone R.) 163
Hubbard (Hull K.R.) 138
Rule (Salford)..134
Hesford (Warrington)..................................128
Burke (Widnes) 127
Ball (Barrow)..119
Diamond (Wakefield T.)...............................116
Fitzsimons (Oldham)....................................108
Parrish (Hunslet)... 98
Birts (Halifax) 97

1980-81
Hesford (Warrington)..................................147
Quinn (Featherstone R.) 123
Diamond (Wakefield T.)...............................112
Burke (Widnes) 110
Hubbard (Hull K.R.)...................................109
Ball (Barrow)..104
Birts (Halifax)...100
Beale (Keighley)... 97
Parrish (Oldham) 95
Fairbairn (Wigan)....................................... 94

1981-82
Hopkins (Workington T.) 190
Fairbairn (Hull K.R.) 168
Parrish (Oldham) 164
Woods (Leigh)...158
Rule (Salford)...130
Dick (Leeds)...125
Quinn (Featherstone R.) 120
Agar (Halifax) 119
Crooks (Hull) 118
Hesford (Warrington)..................................116

1982-83
Diamond (Fulham)......................................136
Fitzsimons (Hunslet)....................................121
Crooks (Hull) 120
R. Beardmore (Castleford)............................117
Hesford (Warrington)..................................113
Fenwick (Cardiff C.)...................................111
Jones (Swinton)..110
Whitfield (Wigan).......................................104
Kilner (Bramley)..104
Quinn (Featherstone R.) 98

1983-84
Hesford (Warrington)..................................142
R. Beardmore (Castleford)............................142
Hallett (Cardiff C.) 140
Fitzsimons (Hunslet)....................................131
Woods (Leigh)...124
Whitfield (Wigan) 122
Ball (Barrow)..104
Parrish (Oldham) 101
Agar (Halifax) 94
Tickle (Barrow) 91

1984-85
Day (St. Helens)..157
Fairbairn (Hull K.R.) 141
Wood (Runcorn H.) 126
Steadman (York)..122
Griffiths (Salford)......................................118
Parrish (Oldham) 117
Schofield (Hull) 105
Creasser (Leeds)..102
Agar (Halifax) 87
Jones (Swinton) 87

1985-86
C. Johnson (Leigh)......................................173
Stephenson (Wigan).....................................128
Noble (Doncaster)......................................118
Harcombe (Rochdale H.) 115
Kilner (Bramley)..110
Dorahy (Hull K.R.)....................................101
Woods (Bradford N.) 98
Creasser (Leeds).. 84
Carroll (Carlisle)....................................... 83
Smith (Workington T.)................................. 83

DROP GOALS

1974-75 Seabourne (Bradford N.) 10
1975-76 Hancock (Hull)..............................10
1976-77 N. Stephenson (Dewsbury) 16
1977-78 Fiddler (Bramley, Leigh) 10
1978-79 Turley (Blackpool B.) 18
1979-80 Dean (Hunslet)..............................18
1980-81 Walker (Whitehaven) 22
1981-82 Agar (Halifax) 17
        Donlan (Leigh)..............................17
1982-83 Pinner (St. Helens)..........................13
1983-84 Hallett (Cardiff C.) 29
1984-85 Wood (Runcorn H.) 28
1985-86 Bishop (Warrington) 13

POINTS

1970-71 Coslett (St. Helens)........................375
1971-72 Watkins (Salford)...........................473
1972-73 Watkins (Salford)...........................493
1973-74 Watkins (Salford)...........................438
1974-75 Fox (Hull K.R.)............................333
1975-76 Watkins (Salford)...........................385
1976-77 Lloyd (Castleford)..........................341
1977-78 Pimblett (St. Helens)........................381
1978-79 Lloyd (Hull)................................373
1979-80 Quinn (Featherstone R.)....................375
1980-81 Hesford (Warrington).......................310
1981-82 Hopkins (Workington T.)...................446
1982-83 Diamond (Fulham) 308
1983-84 Woods (Leigh)..............................355
1984-85 Day (St. Helens)............................362
1985-86 C. Johnson (Leigh) 400

ALL TIME RECORDS

Most goals in a match:
22 by Jim Sullivan (Wigan) v. Flimby & Fothergill (Challenge Cup), 14th February 1925

Most goals in a season:
DAVID WATKINS holds the record for most goals in a season with 221 — all for Salford — in 1972-73. Watkins played and scored a goal in every match that season as follows:

1972			
Aug. 19	Leeds ....(H)	5
23	Featherstone R. ....(A)	3
26	Whitehaven..............................(A)	4
28	Swinton ....(H)	1
Sept. 1	Oldham ....(LC) (H)	10
9	Leeds...................................(A)	2
15	Rochdale H. ....(LC) (H)	11
17	Leigh......................................(A)	6
24	Barrow................................(JP) (A)	4
29	Huyton ....(H)	10
Oct. 3	Oldham..........................(FT) (A)	4
6	Wigan..............................(LC) (A)	4
8	Blackpool B. ....(A)	5
13	Blackpool B. ....(H)	8
21	Swinton..............................(LCF)	5
Nov. 5	Huyton ....(A)	8
10	Rochdale H. ....(H)	6
17	Warrington..............................(A)	4
19	New Zealand...........................(H)	10
24	Dewsbury ....(JP) (A)	4
26	Workington T. ....(H)	6
Dec. 1	Barrow....................................(H)	9
10	Bradford N. ....(JP) (H)	9
13	Oldham...................................(A)	4
15	Leigh......................................(H)	3
24	Bradford N. ....(A)	5
26	Workington T. ....(A)	3
30	Hull K.R. ....(JP) (A)	5
1973		
Jan. 3	Bradford N..............................(H)	6
7	Rochdale H. ....(A)	2
12	Featherstone R. ....(H)	4
28	Featherstone R...........(RL Cup) (A)	4
Feb. 2	Whitehaven..............................(H)	4
11	Barrow....................................(A)	5
23	St. Helens ....(H)	3
Mar. 7	Widnes....................................(H)	3
9	Dewsbury................................(H)	3
16	St. Helens ....(A)	2
24	Leeds............................(JP Final)	2
30	Warrington...............................(H)	1
Apr. 6	Widnes ....(H)	4
13	Oldham...................................(H)	3
15	Dewsbury................................(A)	2
17	Wigan ....(A)	3
20	Swinton...................................(A)	7
23	Wigan.....................................(H)	3
29	Rochdale H. ....(top 16) (H)	2

	App	Gls
League	34	147
Lancs Cup...................................	4	30
John Player.................................	5	24
Tour match	1	10
RL Cup	1	4
Floodlit Cup	1	4
Top 16	1	2
Totals	**47**	**221**

Fastest goals century:
Three players share the record of scoring the fastest 100 goals from the start of a season in terms of number of matches played. They are Bernard Ganley, David Watkins and Steve Quinn, who achieved the century in 18 matches.

Ganley reached 100 goals on 16 November 1957, after playing 17 matches for Oldham and one for Great Britain.

Watkins scored his 100th goal on 17 November 1972, all for Salford.

Quinn scored his 100th goal on 16 December 1979, all for Featherstone Rovers.

Most goals in a career:
JIM SULLIVAN holds the record for most goals in a career with 2,859 between 1921-22 and 1945-46. He scored a century of goals in every season after leaving Welsh Rugby Union for Wigan until the War interrupted the 1939-40 campaign.

The Test full back played all of his club rugby for Wigan apart from War-time appearances with Bradford Northern, Dewsbury and Keighley.

Sullivan's total includes 441 in representative matches, including three tours of Australasia. These figures are accepted by the Record Keepers' Club following research by James Carter and Malcolm Bentley.

Most one-point drop goals in a match:
5 by Danny Wilson (Swinton) v. Hunslet (John Player Special), 6 November 1983.
Peter Wood (Runcorn H.) v. Batley, 21 October 1984.
Paul Bishop (Warrington) at Wigan (Premiership semi-final), 11 May 1986.

Most one-point drop goals in a season:
29 by Lyn Hallett (Cardiff C.)......................1983-84

Most one-point drop goals in a career:
79 by Harry Pinner (St. Helens, Widnes) 1974-87
Nigel Stephenson (Dewsbury, Bradford N., Carlisle, Wakefield T., York)...............1974-87

Most tries in a match:
11 by George West (Hull K.R.) v Brookland Rovers Challenge Cup ....4 March 1905

119

Most tries in a career:

BRIAN BEVAN holds the record for most tries in a career with 796 between 1946 and 1964. His season-by-season record is:

1946-47	48
1947-48	57
1948-49	56
1949-50	33
1950-51	68
1951-52	51
1952-53	72
1953-54	67
1954-55	63
1955-56	57
1956-57	17
1957-58	46
1958-59	54
1959-60	40
1960-61	35
1961-62	15
1962-63	10
1963-64	7

Totals

Warrington	740
Blackpool Borough	17
Other Nationalities	26
Other representative matches	13
Grand Total	**796**

The Australian winger played his first game for Warrington on 17 November 1945 and his last on 23 April 1962 before having two seasons at Blackpool Borough. His last match for Borough was on 22 February, 1964.

Most tries in a season:

ALBERT ROSENFELD holds the record for most tries in a season with 80 — all for Huddersfield — in 1913-14.

Rosenfeld's match-by-match record:
1913

Sept. 6	York	(A)	4
8	Warrington	(H)	2
13	Leeds	(H)	5
20	Halifax	(A)	1
27	Batley	(A)	0
Oct. 4	Oldham	(H)	2
11	Rochdale H.	(A)	0
18	Bramley	(YC) (H)	2
25	Dewsbury	(A)	4
Nov. 1	Halifax	(YC) (A)	2
8	Wigan	(A)	1
15	Dewsbury	(YC) (H)	3
19	Bradford N.	(H)	3
22	Leeds	(A)	3
29	Bradford N.	(Halifax, YCF)	1

Dec. 3	Halifax	(H)	3
6	Hunslet	(A)	2
13	Rochdale H.	(H)	3
20	Hull K.R.	(A)	2
25	Hull	(A)	1
26	Wakefield T.	(H)	3
27	Hunslet	(H)	0
1914			
Jan. 1	St. Helens	(A)	0
3	Warrington	(A)	0
10	York	(H)	3
17	Keighley	(A)	2
24	Dewsbury	(H)	1
31	Batley	(H)	0
Feb. 7	Oldham	(A)	0
14	Bramley	(H)	5
21	Wigan	(H)	3'
28	Swinton Park R.	(RL Cup) (H)	7
Mar. 7	Wakefield T.	(A)	2
14	Hull K.R.	(RL Cup) (A)	2
18	Bramley	(A)	3
21	Widnes	(RL Cup) (H)	0
25	Keighley	(H)	3
28	Hull K.R.	(H)	1
30	Bradford N.	(A)	1'
Apr. 4	Hull	(Leeds, RL Cup SF)	0
11	Hull	(H) did not play	
13	St. Helens	(H)	0
20	Hull	(Play-off) (H) did not play	
25	Salford	(Leeds, Championship final)	0

	App	Tries
League	33	63
Yorks Cup	4	8
RL Cup	4	9
Play Off	1	0
Totals	**42**	**80**

Most points in a season:

LEWIS JONES holds the record for most points in a season with 496 from 194 goals and 36 tries for Leeds and representative teams in 1956-57.

Jones' match-by-match record:

For Leeds
1956

			Gls	Tries	Pts
Aug. 17	Halifax	(H)	3	0	6
22	Bradford N.	(A)	11	3	31
25	Wigan	(A)	4	0	8
27	Featherstone R.	(H)	4	1	11
Sept. 1	Wakefield	(YC) (A)	3	1	9
8	Dewsbury	(A)	6	0	12
15	Warrington	(H)	7	0	14
22	Huddersfield	(A)	3	0	6
29	York	(H)	6	0	12

Oct.	6	Batley..........................(A)	4	2	14
	13	Australia....................(H)	Did not play		
	20	Hull K.R. ....(A)	Did not play		
	27	Wigan.........................(H)	2	0	4
Nov.	3	Hunslet ....(A)	1	0	2
	10	Barrow ....(H)	3	2	12
	17	Halifax ....(A)	4	0	8
	24	Keighley ....(H)	3	3	15
Dec.	1	Barrow ....(A)	4	0	8
	8	Bramley ....(A)	5	0	10
	15	Doncaster ....(H)	1	2	8
	22	Bradford N (abandoned) (H)	1	1	5
	25	Batley ....(H)	8	1	19
	29	Keighley ....(A)	3	0	6
1957					
Jan.	5	Hull ....(H)	5	2	16
	12	Warrington ....(A)	0	3	9
	19	St. Helens...................(H)	5	1	13
	26	Doncaster....................(A)	Did not play		
Feb.	2	Huddersfield ....(H)	6	0	12
	9	Wigan ....(RL Cup) (H)	2	1	7
	16	York ....(A)	7	1	17
	23	Warrington....(RL Cup) (H)	5	1	13
	27	Castleford ....(H)	4	1	11
Mar.	9	Halifax ....(RL Cup) (A)	5	0	10
	16	Wakefield T. ....(H)	5	1	13
	20	Bradford N ....(H)	5	1	13
	23	Hull...........................(A)	2	0	4
	30	Whitehaven ....(Odsal, RL Cup SF)	1	0	2
Apr.	3	Wakefield T. ....(A)	3	0	6
	6	St. Helens....................(A)	0	0	0
	12	Hull K.R.....................(H)	Did not play		
	13	Dewsbury ....(H)	6	2	18
	19	Hunslet ....(H)	5	2	16
	20	Featherstone R.............(A)	2	0	4
	22	Castleford ....(A)	2	0	4
	23	Bramley.......................(H)	7	1	17
May	4	Oldham ....(Play-off) (A)	3	0	6
	11	Barrow ...(Wembley, RL Cup final)	0	0	0

Representative matches
For Great Britain:

Jan.	26	France..............(at Leeds)	9	1	21
Mar.	3	France...........(at Toulouse)	5	1	13
Apr.	10	France.........(at St. Helens)	7	1	17

For The Rest:

| Oct. | 3 | Britain XIII .....(at Bradford) | 4 | 0 | 8 |

For RL XIII:

| Oct. | 29 | Australia................(Leigh) | 3 | 0 | 6 |

	App	Gls	Tries	Pts
League	36	147	30	384
RL Cup	5	13	2	32
Yorks Cup............................	1	3	1	9
Play-off..............................	1	3	0	6
Representative.....................	5	28	3	65
Totals	**48**	**194**	**36**	**496**

Most points in a match:
53 (11t, 10g) by George West (Hull K.R.) v. Brookland Rovers (RL Cup)..............................4 March, 1905

Most points in a career:
NEIL FOX holds the record for most points in a career with 6,220 between 1956 and 1979. This total does not include points scored during a spell of club rugby in New Zealand.

Fox was a month short of his 17th birthday when he made his debut for Wakefield Trinity on 10 April, 1956. Apart from a brief time at Bradford Northern Fox had 19 seasons at Wakefield before moving to a succession of clubs in later years.

After a long career as an international centre Fox moved into the forwards and played his last professional match for Bradford in their opening fixture of the 1979-80 season, on 19 August. That match enabled him to join the elite few who have played first team rugby at 40 years of age.

Fox's season-by-season tally is as follows:

	Gls	Tries	Pts
1955-56................................	6	0	12
1956-57................................	54	10	138
1957-58................................	124	32	344
1958-59................................	148	28	380
1959-60................................	171	37	453
1960-61................................	94	20	248
1961-62................................	183	30	456
1962 Tour			
Australasia...........................	85	19	227
South Africa	19	4	50
1962-63................................	125	14	292
1963-64................................	125	21	313
1964-65................................	121	13	281
1965-66................................	98	11	229
1966-67................................	144	16	336
1967-68................................	98	18	250
1968-69................................	95	9	217
1969-70................................	17	5	49
1970-71................................	110	12	256
1971-72................................	84	6	186
1972-73................................	138	8	300
1973-74................................	62	8	148
1974-75................................	146(1)	14	333
1975-76................................	102(1)	4	215
1976-77................................	79(1)	6	175
1977-78................................	95(1)	9	216
1978-79................................	50	4	112
1979-80................................	2	0	4

A breakdown of Fox's club and representative totals is as follows:

	App	Gls	Tries	Pts
Wakefield T.	574	1,836	272	4,488
Bradford N.	70	85(1)	12	205
Hull K.R.	59	212(2)	16	470
York........................	13	42	2	90
Bramley.....................	23	73	6	164
Huddersfield..............	21	73(1)	5	160
Club Totals	**760**	**2,321(4)**	**313**	**5,577**

Yorkshire.................	17	60	9	147
Britain v. Australia	8	26	3	61
New Zealand.	4	11	1	25
France.........	17	56	10	142
Other representative games including tour	22	101	22	268
Representative Totals.	**68**	**254**	**45**	**643**
Grand Totals	**828**	**2,575(4)**	**358**	**6,220**

( ) Figures in brackets are one point drop goals included in total.

Score-a-match:
The following players have appeared and scored in all of their club's matches in one season:

Jim Hoey (Widnes) 1932-33
Billy Langton (Hunslet) 1958-59
Stuart Ferguson (Leigh) 1970-71
David Watkins (Salford)............................1972-73
David Watkins (Salford)............................1973-74
John Woods (Leigh)...................................1977-78
Steve Quinn (Featherstone R.) 1979-80
Mick Parrish (Hunslet) 1979-80
John Gorton (Swinton).............................1980-81
Mick Parrish (Oldham) 1981-82
Peter Wood (Runcorn H.) 1984-85
David Noble (Doncaster)............................1986-87

Longest scoring run:
DAVID WATKINS holds the record for the longest scoring run, playing and scoring in 92 consecutive matches for Salford from 19 August 1972 to 25 April 1974. He totalled 403 goals, 41 tries and 929 points.

Longest run of appearances:
KEITH ELWELL holds the record for the longest run of appearances with one club with a total of 239 for Widnes. The consecutive run started at Wembley in the 1977 Challenge Cup final against Leeds on 7 May, and ended after he played in a Lancashire Cup-tie at home to St. Helens on 5 September 1982. He was dropped for the match at Featherstone Rovers a week later. Although he went on as a substitute the record refers to full appearances only.

Elwell played as a substitute in the next match and then made a full appearance before his run of all appearances ended at 242.

Highest score:
Huddersfield 119 v. Swinton Park 2 (RL Cup)
.......28 February 1914

Most points in all matches in a season:
1,436 by Leigh from 43 matches in 1985-86 as follows:
34 Division Two matches 1,156
2 Lancashire Cup 54
4 John Player Special Trophy 161
3 RL Challenge Cup 65

1,000 points in a League season:
1,156 by Leigh from 34 Division Two matches in 1985-86.
1,126 by Barrow from 34 Division Two matches in 1983-84.
1,005 by St. Helens from 38 matches in one-league system in 1958-59.

Longest unbeaten run:
40 Cup and League matches by Huddersfield in 1914-15, including three draws.

Longest winning run in the League:
31 matches by Wigan. Last 8 matches of 1969-70 and first 23 of 1970-71.
● In 1978-79 Hull won all of their 26 Division Two matches, the only time a club has won all its league matches in one season.

Longest League losing run:
40 Division Two matches by Doncaster between November 1975 and April 1977. This period included a run of 37 Cup and League defeats.
● In 1906-07 Liverpool City lost all 30 of their league matches, the only time a team playing more than 12 league matches has lost them all. Liverpool also lost their two cup ties and dropped out after only one season. Liverpool did manage a home league draw against Bramley but when they were unable to fulfil a return fixture the match was expunged from league records.

Halifax player-coach Chris Anderson hoists aloft the Silk Cut Challenge Cup.

CUPS

RUGBY LEAGUE CHALLENGE CUP

1987 Final

Halifax crowned Rugby League's first-ever £1m Wembley by hanging on to a one-point lead for the last 11 minutes of a nailbiting final to lift the coveted Silk Cut Challenge Cup.

Favourites St. Helens, trailing 18-8 after 51 minutes, fought back to 19-18 in the 69th minute. In a nerve-wracking finish, Saints centre Mark Elia twice crossed the Halifax line to be denied the winning touchdown both times.

On the first occasion, the Kiwi Test centre only had to put the ball down. He chose to dive over and while in full flight Halifax loose forward John Pendlebury made a desperate lunge and succeeded in punching the ball from Elia's grasp.

Minutes later, second row man Andy Platt burst through to put Elia over only for his pass to be judged forward by Wembley debutant referee John Holdsworth, a decision fully vindicated by video replays.

Obsessed with playing the ball wide, St. Helens did not try a drop at goal to set up a replay at Old Trafford, Manchester. Ironically, it was a successful one-point effort from Pendlebury in the 64th minute, when Halifax held a six-point lead, that proved vital.

The creation of a try for full back Graham Eadie by Pendlebury put the former Wigan and Salford number 13 in contention for the Lance Todd Trophy, along with scrum half Gary Stephens. The individual match honour went to Eadie, only the second Australian to be awarded the trophy, for a powerful display highlighted by four try-saving tackles and his 51st minute touchdown.

Eadie had been doubtful with a hamstring injury but justified his inclusion even though Elia left him stranded by sheer pace for a try immediately after the interval.

The same could not be said for stand-off, captain-coach and fellow Australian Chris Anderson. His 35th birthday was celebrated with the lifting of the Silk Cut Challenge Cup but the party was almost ruined by his gamble of playing with a rib injury.

The former Test winger had a quiet game and missed a vital tackle when Elia set up Paul Loughlin for a 53rd minute touchdown. He took himself off after 66 minutes with Halifax holding a seven-point lead only to return with three minutes left to steady his charges in the wake of a last desperate assault from St. Helens.

While Anderson did little of note on the day, his pre-match planning was apparent throughout a final which grew in momentum.

Second row men Mick Scott and Paul Dixon led the charges into the Saints' ranks with excellent results, the veteran Scott crashing out of a series of tackles to set up Wilf George's disputed try in the corner after 11 minutes. St. Helens claimed they were obstructed and it appeared George's legs were swept into touch-in-goal before he made the touchdown.

Then Dixon, capped for Great Britain two months earlier, went within inches of the line before Belfast-born hooker Seamus McCallion dived over on the sixth tackle amid a mass of St. Helens defenders to score in the 33rd minute, Colin Whitfield's second of three goals opening a 12-2 half-time lead.

Halifax's triumph was their fifth Challenge Cup haul on their first visit to the stadium since St. Helens inflicted a 13-2 defeat in 1956. They last won there in 1939. The Wembley win rounded off a fairytale revival of Championship and Cup success in a 12-month period, only four years after being on the verge of bankruptcy as a yo-yo club in the promotion and relegation zone.

Saints had to be content with runners-up medals to add to second place in the Stones Bitter Championship stakes, coach Alex Murphy experiencing his third defeat as a coach after a record-equalling four winners medals on the field.

124

The volatile Murphy was involved in two unsavoury after-match incidents which soured an otherwise first class afternoon for the 13-a-side code. He fired an on-the-field broadside at referee Holdsworth for disallowing Elia's two late touchdowns, unaware that television had shown the Kippax match official to be correct in his judgements. The Knowsley Road coach also had to calm down his assistant Dave Chisnall after a scuffle inside the arena with Halifax substitute Brian Juliff, both incidents being in full view of the crowd.

World record receipts of £1,009,206 were taken from a crowd of 91,267 who were thrilled to the final seconds of a nerve tingling encounter, graced by His Royal Highness Prince Philip, the Duke of Edinburgh.

Wembley also provided a fitting finale for the illustrious careers of Eadie and Anderson. Having been tempted out of premature retirement after a three-year break, Eadie fully repaid the faith shown by Halifax president David Brook and coach Anderson, who also announced his retirement as a player at the end of the season.

With the final being broadcast live in Australia, the ex-Kangaroos found the best way of signing off by lifting Britain's two prized trophies . . . Anderson the Challenge Cup, Eadie the Lance Todd Trophy.

Wembley celebrations as the Silk Cut Challenge Cup is flanked by Halifax skipper Chris Anderson (right) and try scoring hooker Seamus McCallion.

125

SILK CUT CHALLENGE CUP FINAL

2nd May   **Wembley**

HALIFAX 19		**ST. HELENS 18**
Graham Eadie	1.	Phil Veivers
Scott Wilson	2.	Barry Ledger
Colin Whitfield	3.	Paul Loughlin
Grant Rix	4.	Mark Elia
Wilf George	5.	Kevin McCormack
Chris Anderson, Capt.	6.	Brett Clark
Gary Stephens	7.	Neil Holding
Graham Beevers	8.	Tony Burke
Seamus McCallion	9.	Graham Liptrot
Keith Neller	10.	John Fieldhouse
Paul Dixon	11.	Andy Platt
Mick Scott	12.	Roy Haggerty
John Pendlebury	13.	Chris Arkwright, Capt.
Brian Juliff	14.	Paul Round
Neil James	15.	Paul Forber

T: George, McCallion, Eadie
G: Whitfield (3), Pendlebury (dg)
Substitutions:
Juliff for Anderson (66 min.)
James for Beevers (70 min.)
Half-time: 12-2
Referee: John Holdsworth (Kippax)

T: Elia, Loughlin, Round
G: Loughlin (3)
Substitution:
Round for Haggerty (50 min.)
Attendance: 91,267
Receipts: £1,009,206

Scorechart

		Scoreline	
Minute	*Score*	*Halifax*	*St. Helens*
11:	George (T)		
	Whitfield (G)	6	0
20:	Loughlin (P)	6	2
33:	McCallion (T)		
	Whitfield (G)	12	2
41:	Elia (T)		
	Loughlin (G)	12	8
51:	Eadie (T)		
	Whitfield (G)	18	8
53:	Loughlin (T)	18	12
64:	Pendlebury (DG)	19	12
69:	Round (T)		
	Loughlin (G)	19	18
	Scrums	10	7
	Penalties	6	10

*Try scoring Lance Todd Trophy winner,
Graham Eadie.*

The vital last ditch tackle by Halifax's John Pendlebury which prevented Mark Elia from claiming the potential match winning try.

St. Helens' substitute Paul Rund dives over for a 69th minute touchdown.

1987 Round by Round

To accommodate the biggest Wembley era Challenge Cup entry of 38 clubs, there were six preliminary round ties, featuring the three amateur county cup winners and the leaders of the new Slalom Lager National Amateur League as at 1 December.

Lancashire Cup winners Blackbrook, of St. Helens, were drawn to meet current Silk Cut Challenge Cup holders Castleford, the tie being switched from frostbound Wheldon Road to underground-heated Headingley. The Championship title contenders ran in 13 tries in a 74-6 triumph, the highest score in the tournament for almost 50 years, wingers David Plange and John Kear both recording hat-tricks of tries. Yorkshire Cup winners Elland, of Halifax, and National League leaders Heworth, of York, met at Thrum Hall, Halifax, Elland losing their unbeaten record with a 10-6 defeat. Heworth player-coach Colin Forsyth, a former England prop, came on halfway through the second half to engineer the winning try by Ian Ellis. Cumbria Cup victors Kells entertained Fulham at Whitehaven's Recreation Ground, holding the Second Division side to a 4-4 draw. The amateurs dominated the match for an hour before Fulham's Huw Rees scored the only try, Kells scoring through two Peter Starkey penalty goals, one after Fulham prop Pat Doherty was sent off. In the replay at Chiswick, Kells moved into an 8-6 lead shortly after half-time before the Londoners notched three tries in eight minutes midway through the second half to seal a 22-14 success. Workington Town conceded home advantage to play Wigan on the underground-heated Central Park pitch. The Riversiders romped home victors by 68-0 with 12 tries and 10 goals in front of 11,970 fans. The landslide was marked by the debut of world record £130,000 scrum half recruit Andy Gregory and hat-tricks for Ellery Hanley and Shaun Edwards. St. Helens scraped home 18-16 against Second Division promotion favourites Swinton at Knowsley Road, a 68th minute penalty attempt by Andy Rippon shaving the post to deny the Lions a replay. Underground heating at Elland Road enabled the Hunslet-York tie to be staged in freezing conditions. Hunslet scored two tries, one at either end of the second half, through Phil Tate and Andy Kay respectively, while York provided the Man of the Match in scrum half Iain Wigglesworth, despite losing 13-0.

In the first round, only four of the 16 ties were staged on the scheduled weekend because of frost and snow. The shock of the round came in a rearranged midweek tie when Oldham knocked out favourites Wigan 10-8 at Watersheddings. The Riversiders looked home and dry with an 8-4 lead and only a minute to go when Joe Lydon knocked on near his own line, Oldham winning the scrum and scrum half Paddy Kirwan forcing his way over for a try to level the scores, new full back recruit Mick Burke hitting the winning goal. Second Division leaders Hunslet also pulled off a surprise victory, disposing of First Division strugglers Featherstone Rovers at Post Office Road. Second row man Alan Platt was the hero of the comfortable 26-12 success, creating three of their five tries and kicking three goals. Fancied Warrington also went out at the first hurdle, losing at home to Bradford Northern, 21-17. Northern shrugged off six successive defeats to rewrite the form book, stand off John Woods outstanding with a 13-point haul from four goals, a drop goal and a try. Leeds travelled to Salford to record a tense 4-0 success, Carl Gibson notching his 100th career touchdown to seal victory. Fulham played hosts to current champions Halifax and went down 38-10 after fully deserving a 10-8 lead before the Thrum Hallers ran in five second half tries without reply.

In the televised tie, holders Castleford fell to Widnes on a frostbound pitch declared playable only 45 minutes before kick off. New

Zealand Test star Kurt Sorensen and Australian hooker Phil McKenzie adapted to the alien conditions to lead Widnes to a convincing 24-16 victory. The turning point came in the 51st minute with Castleford leading 10-6, home scrum half Bob Beardmore kicking crossfield into the hands of Tony Myler who sprinted 85 yards for a try which set the Chemics on the road to success. Hull K.R. gained revenge for their first round John Player Special Trophy defeat at Second Division Doncaster by securing a 29-14 victory at Craven Park. Barrow ran in 10 tries in a 54-2 home defeat of Batley.

Hull struggled at Second Division Bramley, taking the lead only 14 minutes from time, youngster Jon Sharp scoring the first of his two tries in the 10-2 victory. Leigh visited Runcorn Highfield and laid the foundation for a 25-6 victory with a 17-4 half-time lead. Carlisle centre Kevin Pape set up a try for John Stockley against the run of play at Rochdale Hornets, the home side levelling the scores with a Brian Dunn touchdown 10 minutes later, David Woods' goal attempt hitting the upright. In the replay, Pape took the individual honours with a hat-trick of tries in a devastating six-minute spell in the first half, adding a fourth after the break as Carlisle registered a 30-22 victory. New Cup favourites St. Helens took 20 minutes to break the Dewsbury defence in a Crown Flatt tie staged under emergency lighting. The Saints scored eight tries to two, Paul Loughlin amassing 20 points with eight goals and a try in the 48-12 win. Heworth missed a golden chance to become the first amateur side to knock out a professional team since 1909, going down 14-7 to Second Division strugglers Mansfield Marksman at Alfreton. Whitehaven ended a run of 21 consecutive first round Challenge Cup knockouts by beating Huddersfield Barracudas 32-10 at Arena '84, back row forwards Gary McFarlane, Brian Hetherington and Steve Burney outstanding. Wakefield Trinity, bottom of the Championship table without a win, toppled Second Division Blackpool Borough 15-10 at Bloomfield Road soccer ground. Trinity clinched victory with tries from Glen Stanton and Gary Cocks in a three-minute spell midway through the first half. Keighley recorded their first victory, 8-6, at Sheffield Eagles in a dour contest decided by a second half try from Australian Dave McCaffrey, the Eagles' points coming from a try and a goal by Mark Aston.

In the second round, Oldham entertained St. Helens in the televised match, the Saints marching on with a 24-14 victory. The Roughyeds' hopes were dashed by the dismissal of hooker Ian Sanderson after a first half off-the-ball incident, while visiting winger Kevin McCormack boosted his Great Britain Under-21 selection hopes with two well taken tries. Bradford Northern and Widnes drew 6-6 at Odsal after a thrilling finish, Northern full back Keith Mumby hitting the post with a drop goal attempt seven minutes from the end and teammate Woods shaving the post with a penalty shot. In the replay at Naughton Park, Widnes cruised home 29-12 with Great Britain stand off Tony Myler outstanding, scoring crucial tries either side of the interval. Former Australian Test full back Graham Eadie was in brilliant form for Halifax, who disposed of Hunslet's brave challenge, 29-10, at Thrum Hall. Eadie repeatedly broke the Hunslet cover and scored two tries and created another against the new Second Division title favourites, well served by Andy Kay and Roy Milton. Hull K.R.'s resounding 42-4 home success against Keighley was marred by the sending off of captain David Watkinson, along with fellow hooker Rob Proctor. Keighley also had captain Peter Roe dismissed as Man of the Match John Dorahy sealed victory with two tries and seven goals.

Second Division Whitehaven created the shock result of the round with a 25-2 triumph at Division One strugglers Wakefield Trinity. A cheeky try from former Trinity hooker

Alan McCurrie started the scoring for the Cumbrians who rounded off an impressive performance with two touchdowns in the last five minutes, from substitute Mark Beckwith and winger Norman Lofthouse, who also added four goals. Australian centre Mark McGaw marked his farewell Headingley appearance with two tries in a Man of the Match display against Barrow, the Loiners going through 26-7. Leigh swept into a 10-0 lead against visitors Carlisle, who fought back to trail 14-6 before Ian Jeffrey barged over to seal a hard fought 18-6 victory. Hull took 13 minutes to get on the scoresheet at lowly Mansfield Marksman, Great Britain centre Garry Schofield notching the first of the Boulevarders' seven tries in the 38-7 win.

In the third round, Halifax hammered visitors Hull K.R. in the televised tie. Veteran player-coach Chris Anderson was outstanding in the 35-7 rout, showing skill and surprising speed to score two tries in a dominating performance. Leeds led only 7-0 at half-time after dominating the first 40 minutes of the Headingley tie with Widnes, being drawn in Yorkshire for the third successive round. As the home side tired, the Widnes pack took control, prop Steve O'Neill creating a try for brother Mike, two John Myler goals putting the Chemics ahead 8-7 in the 51st minute. Three minutes from time, Widnes made sure of a semi-final place when Leeds' Australian full back Andrew Ettingshausen's attempted chip kick was caught by winger Rick Thackray to secure his first try for the club, Myler adding the goal for a 14-7 scoreline. Leigh sprung the shock result of the round by recording a 12-8 victory at Hull. Veteran Tony Cottrell steered outsiders Leigh into the last four, creating both the visitors' tries, scored by John Kerr and substitute Mike Davis, full back Chris Johnson adding two goals. Cup favourites St. Helens romped home against Second Division Whitehaven at Knowsley Road by 41-12. High speed Saints scored seven tries to two, Silk Cut Award winner Chris Arkwright leading the way with a hat-trick, centre Paul Loughlin contributing a try and six goals.

Leigh coach Billy Benyon — sacked 17 months earlier by St. Helens — came close to spoiling Saints' dream of a return to Wembley after a nine-year absence. Relegation-haunted Leigh shocked the Cup favourites with a magnificent second half semi-final rally, going down only 14-8 in the Central Park, Wigan, thriller. Renowned try scoring winger Barry Ledger saved Saints' embarrassment — with a tackle. Ledger's halting of Leigh's runaway centre John Henderson blunted the Hilton Park challenge. St. Helens had swept to a 14-2 interval lead with tries from McCormack, skipper Arkwright and Andy Platt, before Leigh captain Derek Pyke inspired a comeback, highlighted by a Neil McCulloch touchdown and a superb touchline goal from Chris Johnson.

In the second semi-final, Halifax's celebrations at reaching Wembley for the first time in 31 years were clouded by player-coach Anderson suffering a fractured cheekbone in the final minutes of the Headingley encounter. The Thrum Hall side survived a Widnes second half revival to record a 12-8 victory as the Chemics failed in a bid to reach Wembley for the eighth time in 12 years. Widnes allowed Halifax too much room in the first half, loose forward John Pendlebury opening the Thrum Hall side's try account in the 16th minute by playing the ball to himself a yard from the goal line. Australian centre Grant Rix added a superb solo try eight minutes before the break for Halifax to hold on despite a Harry Pinner-inspired comeback which resulted in hooker Phil McKenzie scooting over to set up a tense final 10 minutes.

1987 RESULTS

Preliminary Round

Castleford	74	Blackbrook	6
Elland	6	Heworth	10
(at Halifax)			
Hunslet	13	York	0
Kells	4	Fulham	4
(at Whitehaven)			
St. Helens	18	Swinton	16
Workington T.	0	Wigan	68
(at Wigan)			

Replay

Fulham	22	Kells	14

First Round

Barrow	54	Batley	2
Blackpool B.	10	Wakefield T.	15
(at Blackpool FC)			
Bramley	2	Hull	10
Castleford	16	Widnes	24
Dewsbury	12	St. Helens	48
Featherstone R.	12	Hunslet	26
Fulham	10	Halifax	38
Huddersfield B.	10	Whitehaven	32
Hull K.R.	29	Doncaster	14
Mansfield M.	14	Heworth	7
Oldham	10	Wigan	8
Rochdale H.	4	Carlisle	4
Runcorn H.	6	Leigh	25
Salford	0	Leeds	4
Sheffield E.	6	Keighley	8
Warrington	17	Bradford N.	21

Replay

Carlisle	30	Rochdale H.	22

Second Round

Bradford N.	6	Widnes	6
Halifax	29	Hunslet	10
Hull K.R.	42	Keighley	4
Leeds	26	Barrow	7
Leigh	18	Carlisle	6
Mansfield M.	7	Hull	38
Oldham	14	St. Helens	24
Wakefield T.	2	Whitehaven	25

Replay

Widnes	29	Bradford N.	12

Third Round

Halifax	35	Hull K.R.	7
Hull	8	Leigh	12
Leeds	7	Widnes	14
St. Helens	41	Whitehaven	12

Semi-Finals

St. Helens	14	Leigh	8
(at Wigan)			
Halifax	12	Widnes	8
(at Leeds)			

Final

Halifax	19	St. Helens	18
(at Wembley)			

1987 PRIZES

Round	Per Round		Total
Preliminary	12 ×	£1,200	£14,400
First	16 ×	£1,200	£19,200
Second	8 ×	£1,650	£13,200
Third	4 ×	£2,750	£11,000
Semi-Finals	2 ×	£4,500	£9,000
Runners-up	1 ×	£9,000	£9,000
Winners	1 ×	£16,000	£16,000
	Total Prize Money		£91,800
	Capital Development Fund		£58,200
	Total		£150,000

St. Helens' Wembley captain, Chris Arkwright.

CHALLENGE CUP ROLL OF HONOUR

Year	Winners		Runners-up		Venue	Attendance	Receipts
1897	Batley	10	St Helens	3	Leeds	13,492	£624.17.7
1898	Batley	7	Bradford	0	Leeds	27,941	£1,586.3.0
1899	Oldham	19	Hunslet	9	Manchester	15,763	£946.16.0
1900	Swinton	16	Salford	8	Manchester	17,864	£1,100.0.0
1901	Batley	6	Warrington	0	Leeds	29,563	£1,644.16.0
1902	Broughton R.	25	Salford	0	Rochdale	15,006	£846.11.0
1903	Halifax	7	Salford	0	Leeds	32,507	£1,834.8.6
1904	Halifax	8	Warrington	3	Salford	17,041	£936.5.6
1905	Warrington	6	Hull K.R.	0	Leeds	19,638	£1,271.18.0
1906	Bradford	5	Salford	0	Leeds	15,834	£920.0.0
1907	Warrington	17	Oldham	3	Broughton	18,500	£1,010.0.0
1908	Hunslet	14	Hull	0	Huddersfield	18,000	£903.0.0
1909	Wakefield T.	17	Hull	0	Leeds	23,587	£1,490.0.0
1910	Leeds	7	Hull	7	Huddersfield	19,413	£1,102.0.0
Replay	Leeds	26	Hull	12	Huddersfield	11,608	£657.0.0
1911	Broughton R.	4	Wigan	0	Salford	8,000	£376.0.0
1912	Dewsbury	8	Oldham	5	Leeds	15,271	£853.0.0
1913	Huddersfield	9	Warrington	5	Leeds	22,754	£1,446.9.6
1914	Hull	6	Wakefield T.	0	Halifax	19,000	£1,035.5.0
1915	Huddersfield	37	St. Helens	3	Oldham	8,000	£472.0.0
1920	Huddersfield	21	Wigan	10	Leeds	14,000	£1,936.0.0
1921	Leigh	13	Halifax	0	Broughton	25,000	£2,700.0.0
1922	Rochdale H.	10	Hull	9	Leeds	32,596	£2,964.0.0
1923	Leeds	28	Hull	3	Wakefield	29,335	£2,390.0.0
1924	Wigan	21	Oldham	4	Rochdale	41,831	£3,712.0.0
1925	Oldham	16	Hull K.R.	3	Leeds	28,335	£2,879.0.0
1926	Swinton	9	Oldham	3	Rochdale	27,000	£2,551.0.0
1927	Oldham	26	Swinton	7	Wigan	33,448	£3,170.0.0
1928	Swinton	5	Warrington	3	Wigan	33,909	£3,158.1.11
1929	Wigan	13	Dewsbury	2	Wembley	41,500	£5,614.0.0
1930	Widnes	10	St. Helens	3	Wembley	36,544	£3,102.0.0
1931	Halifax	22	York	8	Wembley	40,368	£3,908.0.0
1932	Leeds	11	Swinton	8	Wigan	29,000	£2,479.0.0
1933	Huddersfield	21	Warrington	17	Wembley	41,874	£6,465.0.0
1934	Hunslet	11	Widnes	5	Wembley	41,280	£6,686.0.0
1935	Castleford	11	Huddersfield	8	Wembley	39,000	£5,533.0.0
1936	Leeds	18	Warrington	2	Wembley	51,250	£7,070.0.0
1937	Widnes	18	Keighley	5	Wembley	47,699	£6,704.0.0
1938	Salford	7	Barrow	4	Wembley	51,243	£7,174.0.0
1939	Halifax	20	Salford	3	Wembley	55,453	£7,681.0.0
1940	No competition						
1941	Leeds	19	Halifax	2	Bradford	28,500	£1,703.0.0
1942	Leeds	15	Halifax	10	Bradford	15,250	£1,276.0.0
1943	Dewsbury	16	Leeds	9	Dewsbury	10,470	£823.0.0
	Dewsbury	0	Leeds	6	Leeds	16,000	£1,521.0.0
	Dewsbury won on aggregate 16-15						
1944	Bradford	0	Wigan	3	Wigan	22,000	£1,640.0.0
	Bradford	8	Wigan	0	Bradford	30,000	£2,200.0.0
	Bradford won on aggregate 8-3						
1945	Huddersfield	7	Bradford N.	4	Huddersfield	9,041	£1,184.3.7
	Huddersfield	6	Bradford N.	5	Bradford	17,500	£2,050.0.0
	Huddersfield won on aggregate 13-9						

Year	Winners		Runners-up		Venue	Attendance	Receipts
1946	Wakefield T.	13	Wigan	12	Wembley	54,730	£12,013.13.6
1947	Bradford N.	8	Leeds	4	Wembley	77,605	£17,434.5.0
1948	Wigan	8	Bradford N.	3	Wembley	91,465	£21,121.9.9
1949	Bradford N.	12	Halifax	0	Wembley	95,050	£21,930.5.0
1950	Warrington	19	Widnes	0	Wembley	94,249	£24,782.13.0
1951	Wigan	10	Barrow	0	Wembley	94,262	£24,797.19.0
1952	Workington T.	18	Featherstone R.	10	Wembley	72,093	£22,374.2.0
1953	Huddersfield	15	St. Helens	10	Wembley	89,588	£30,865.12.3
1954	Warrington	4	Halifax	4	Wembley	81,841	£29,706.7.3
Replay	Warrington	8	Halifax	4	Bradford	102,569	£18,623.7.0
1955	Barrow	21	Workington T.	12	Wembley	66,513	£27,453.16.0
1956	St. Helens	13	Halifax	2	Wembley	79,341	£29,424.7.6
1957	Leeds	9	Barrow	7	Wembley	76,318	£32,671.14.3
1958	Wigan	13	Workington T.	9	Wembley	66,109	£33,175.17.6
1959	Wigan	30	Hull	13	Wembley	79,811	£35,718.19.9
1960	Wakefield T.	38	Hull	5	Wembley	79,773	£35,754.16.0
1961	St. Helens	12	Wigan	6	Wembley	94,672	£38,479.11.9
1962	Wakefield T.	12	Huddersfield	6	Wembley	81,263	£33,390.18.4
1963	Wakefield T.	25	Wigan	10	Wembley	84,492	£44,521.17.0
1964	Widnes	13	Hull K.R.	5	Wembley	84,488	£44,840.19.0
1965	Wigan	20	Hunslet	16	Wembley	89,016	£48,080.4.0
1966	St. Helens	21	Wigan	2	Wembley	*98,536	£50,409.0.0
1967	Featherstone R.	17	Barrow	12	Wembley	76,290	£53,465.14.0
1968	Leeds	11	Wakefield T.	10	Wembley	87,100	£56,171.16.6
1969	Castleford	11	Salford	6	Wembley	*97,939	£58,848.1.0
1970	Castleford	7	Wigan	2	Wembley	95,255	£89,262.2.0
1971	Leigh	24	Leeds	7	Wembley	85,514	£84,452.15
1972	St. Helens	16	Leeds	13	Wembley	89,495	£86,414.30
1973	Featherstone R.	33	Bradford N.	14	Wembley	72,395	£125,826.40
1974	Warrington	24	Featherstone R.	9	Wembley	77,400	£132,021.05
1975	Widnes	14	Warrington	7	Wembley	85,098	£140,684.45
1976	St. Helens	20	Widnes	5	Wembley	89,982	£190,129.40
1977	Leeds	16	Widnes	7	Wembley	80,871	£241,488.00
1978	Leeds	14	St. Helens	12	Wembley	*96,000	£330,575.00
1979	Widnes	12	Wakefield T.	3	Wembley	94,218	£383,157.00
1980	Hull K.R.	10	Hull	5	Wembley	*95,000	£448,202.90
1981	Widnes	18	Hull K.R.	9	Wembley	92,496	£591,117.00
1982	Hull	14	Widnes	14	Wembley	92,147	£684,500.00
Replay	Hull	18	Widnes	9	Elland Rd., L'ds	41,171	£180,525.00
1983	Featherstone R.	14	Hull	12	Wembley	84,969	£655,510.00
1984	Widnes	19	Wigan	6	Wembley	80,116	£686,171.00
1985	Wigan	28	Hull	24	Wembley	*97,801	£760,322.00
1986	Castleford	15	Hull K.R.	14	Wembley	82,134	£806,676.00
1987	Halifax	19	St. Helens	18	Wembley	91,267	£1,009,206.00

*Indicates a capacity attendance, the limit being fixed annually taking into account variable factors.

RUGBY LEAGUE CHALLENGE CUP ....
A REVIEW
1964-65
Wigan 20 Ashby; Boston, Ashton (1g), Holden
(1t), Lake (2t); C. Hill, Parr; Gardiner, Clarke,
McTigue, Evans, A. Stephens, Gilfedder (3g, 1t)
Hunslet 16 Langton (5g); Griffiths (1t), Shelton
(1t), Preece, Lee; Gabbitas, Marchant; Hartley,
Prior, K. Eyre, Ramsey, Gunney, Ward
Referee: J. Manley (Warrington)
1965-66
St. Helens 21 F. Barrow; Vollenhoven,
Murphy (1g), Benyon, Killeen (5g, 1t); Harvey,
Bishop (1t); Halsall, Sayer, Watson, French,
Warlow, Mantle (1t)
Wigan 2 Ashby; Boston, D. Stephens, Ashton,
Lake; C. Hill, Parr; Gardiner, Woosey, McTigue,
A. Stephens, Gilfedder (1g), Major
Referee: H.G. Hunt (Prestbury)
1966-67
Featherstone R. 17 Wrigglesworth; Thomas (1t),
Cotton, Jordan, Greatorex; M. Smith, Dooler (1g);
Tonks, Harris, Dixon, A. Morgan (1t),
Thompson (1t), Smales (1t, 3g)
Barrow 12 Tees (1g); Burgess, Challinor,
Hughes, Murray; Brophy (1t), G. Smith; Kelland,
Redhead, Hopwood, Sanderson, Delooze (2g),
Watson (1t)
Referee: E. Clay (Leeds)
1967-68
Leeds 11 Risman (4g); Alan Smith, Hynes,
Watson, Atkinson (1t); Shoebottom, Seabourne;
Clark, Crosby, K. Eyre, Ramsey, A. Eyre, Batten
Wakefield T 10 Cooper, Hirst (2t), Brooke,
Coetzer, Batty; Poynton, Owen; Jeanes,
Shepherd, D. Fox (2g), Haigh, McLeod, Hawley
Referee: J.P. Hebblethwaite (York)
1968-69
Castleford 11 Edwards; Briggs, Howe (1t),
Thomas, Lowndes; Hardisty (1t), Hepworth (1t);
Hartley, C. Dickinson, J. Ward, Redfearn (1g),
Lockwood, Reilly
Salford 6 K. Gwilliam; Burgess, Whitehead,
Hesketh, Jackson; Watkins, Brennan; Ogden,
Dickens, Bott, Coulman, Dixon, Hill (3g)
Referee: D.S. Brown (Preston)
1969-70
Castleford 7 Edwards; Briggs, Thomas, Stenton,
Lowndes (1t); Hardisty (Hargrave), Hepworth;
Hartley, C. Dickinson, Redfearn (2g), Kirkbride,
Lockwood, Reilly
Wigan 2 Tyrer (1g) (C. Hill); Jones, Francis,
Rowe, Kevin O'Loughlin; D. Hill, Parr;
Ashcroft, Burdell, Hogan, Ashurst, D. Robinson,
Laughton
Referee: G.F. Lindop (Wakefield)

1970-71
Leigh 24 Eckersley (1t, 1g); Ferguson (5g),
Dorrington (1t), Collins, Walsh; A. Barrow,
Murphy (2g) (L. Chisnall); Watts, Ashcroft,
Fiddler (1g), Grimes, Clarkson, Smethurst
Leeds 7 Holmes (2g); Langley, Hynes, Cowan
(Dyl), Atkinson; Wainwright (1t), Seabourne;
J. Burke, Fisher, Barnard, Hick, Haigh, Ramsey
Referee: W.H. Thompson (Huddersfield)
1971-72
St. Helens 16 G. Pimblett; L. Jones (1t), Benyon,
Walsh, Wilson; K. Kelly, Heaton; Rees (1t),
Greenall, J. Stephens, Mantle, E. Chisnall,
Coslett (5g)
Leeds 13 Holmes; Alan Smith, Hynes (Langley),
Dyl, Atkinson; Hardisty, Hepworth; Clawson
(5g), Fisher, Ramsey, Cookson (1t), Haigh, Batten
Referee: E. Lawrinson (Warrington)
1972-73
Featherstone R. 33 C. Kellett (8g); Coventry,
M. Smith (1t) (Hartley) (1t), Newlove (2t),
K. Kellett; Mason, Nash (1g); Tonks, Bridges,
Farrar (1t), Rhodes (Hollis), Thompson, Stone
Bradford N. 14 Tees (4g); Lamb, Stockwell,
Watson, D. Redfearn (1t); Blacker (Treasure),
Seabourne; Hogan, Dunn, Earl (Long), Joyce,
W. Pattinson, Fearnley (1t)
Referee: M.J. Naughton (Widnes)
1973-74
Warrington 24 Whitehead (7g); M. Philbin,
Noonan, Whittle, Bevan; Murphy (2g) (Pickup),
Gordon; D. Chisnall, Ashcroft (1t), Brady
(Wanbon), Wright, Nicholas (1t), B. Philbin
Featherstone R. 9 Box (3g); Dyas, M. Smith,
Hartley, Bray; Newlove (1t), Nash; Tonks,
Bridges, Harris, Rhodes (Busfield), Thompson
(Stone), Bell
Referee: S. Shepherd (Oldham)
1974-75
Widnes 14 Dutton (5g, 1dg); A. Prescott, George,
Aspey, Anderson; Hughes, Bowden; Mills (1t),
Elwell, Sheridan, Foran, Adams, Laughton
Warrington 7 Whitehead (2g); M. Philbin,
Noonan, Reynolds (W. Briggs), Bevan (1t);
Whittle, Gordon; D. Chisnall, Ashcroft, Wanbon,
Conroy, Martyn (Nicholas), B. Philbin
Referee: P. Geraghty (York)
1975-76
St. Helens 20 G. Pimblett (3g, 2dg); L. Jones,
Cunningham (1t), Noonan, Mathias; Benyon
(Glynn 2t), Heaton (1t); Mantle (James),
A. Karalius, Coslett, Nicholls, E. Chisnall, Hull
Widnes 5 Dutton (2g); A. Prescott (D. O'Neill),
Hughes, George, Jenkins; Eckersley, Bowden;
Nelson, Elwell (1dg), Wood, Foran (Sheridan),
Adams, Laughton
Referee: R. Moore (Wakefield)

1976-77
Leeds 16 Murrell; Alan Smith (D. Smith),
Hague, Dyl (1t), Atkinson (1t); Holmes,
Dick (1t, 3g, 1dg); Harrison, Ward, Pitchford,
Eccles, Cookson, Fearnley (Dickinson)
Widnes 7 Dutton (2g); Wright (George), Aspey
(1t), Eckersley, D. O'Neill; Hughes, Bowden;
Ramsey, Elwell, Mills, Dearden (Foran), Adams,
Laughton
Referee: V. Moss (Manchester)
1977-78
Leeds 14 Oulton (1g); D. Smith (1t), Hague, Dyl,
Atkinson (1t); Holmes (1dg), J. Sanderson (Dick);
Harrison (Dickinson), Ward (2dg), Pitchford,
Cookson (1t), Eccles, Crane
St. Helens 12 G. Pimblett (3g), L. Jones,
Noonan, Glynn, Mathias; Francis (1t),
K. Gwilliam; D. Chisnall, Liptrot (1t), James,
Nicholls, Cunningham, Pinner
Referee: W.H. Thompson (Huddersfield)
1978-79
Widnes 12 Eckersley (1dg); Wright (1t), Aspey,
George (Hull), Burke (2g); Hughes (1t), Bowden;
Mills, Elwell (1dg), Shaw, Adams, Dearden
(M. O'Neill), Laughton
Wakefield T. 3 Sheard; Fletcher (1t), K. Smith,
Diamond, Juliff; Topliss, Lampkowski; Burke,
McCurrie, Skerrett, Ashurst, Keith Rayne, Idle
Referee: J.E. Jackson (Pudsey)
1979-80
Hull K.R. 10 Hall; Hubbard (3g, 1t) (Hogan),
M. Smith, Hartley, Sullivan; Millward (1dg),
Agar; Holdstock, Watkinson, Lockwood, Lowe,
Rose (Millington), Casey
Hull 5 Woods; Bray, Walters, Wilby (1t),
Prendiville; Newlove (Hancock), Pickerill;
Tindall, Wileman, Stone (Farrar), Birdsall,
Lloyd (1g), Norton
Referee: G.F. Lindop (Wakefield)
1980-81
Widnes 18 Burke (4g, 1t); Wright, George (1t),
Cunningham (J. Myler), Bentley; Hughes,
Gregory (1t); M. O'Neill (Shaw), Elwell,
Lockwood, L. Gorley, E. Prescott, Adams (1dg)
Hull K.R. 9 Hall; Hubbard (3g), M. Smith,
Hogan, Muscroft; Hartley, Harkin; Holdstock
(Millington), Watkinson, Crooks (Proctor), Lowe,
Burton (1t), Casey
Referee: D.G. Kershaw (Easingwold)
1981-82
Hull 14 Kemble; O'Hara (1t), Day, S. Evans,
Prendivillle; Topliss, Harkin; Skerrett, Wileman,
Stone, Crane (Crooks), Lloyd (4g), Norton (1t)

Widnes 14 Burke (1g), (A. Myler); Wright (1t),
Keiron O'Loughlin, Cunningham (2t), Basnett;
Hughes, Gregory (1g); M. O'Neill, Elwell (1dg),
Lockwood (S. O'Neill), L. Gorley, E. Prescott,
Adams
Referee: G.F. Lindop (Wakefield)
Replay
Hull 18 Kemble (1t); Sullivan, Leuluai, S. Evans,
Prendiville; Topliss (2t), Dean; Tindall, Duke,
Stone, Skerrett, Crooks (1t, 3g), Norton (Crane)
Widnes 9 Burke (3g); Wright (1t), Keiron
O'Loughlin, Cunningham, Basnett; Hughes,
Gregory; M. O'Neill, Elwell, Lockwood,
L. Gorley, E. Prescott, Adams
Referee: G.F. Lindop (Wakefield)
1982-83
Featherstone R. 14 N. Barker; Marsden,
Quinn (4g), Gilbert (Lyman), K. Kellett;
A. Banks, Hudson; Gibbins, Handscombe,
Hankins, D. Hobbs (2t), Slatter (Siddall), Smith
Hull 12 Kemble; O'Hara, S. Evans, Leuluai (1t),
Prendiville; Topliss, Harkin (Day), (Crane);
Skerrett, Bridges, Stone, Rose, Crooks (1t, 3g),
Norton
Referee: M.R. Whitfield (Widnes)
1983-84
Widnes 19 Burke (3g); Wright, Hughes (Hulme),
Lydon (2t), Basnett; Keiron O'Loughlin (1t),
Gregory; S. O'Neill (1dg), Elwell, K. Tamati,
L. Gorley, M. O'Neill (Whitfield), Adams
Wigan 6 Edwards; Ramsdale, Stephenson,
Whitfield (1g), (Elvin), Gill; Cannon, Stephens;
Hemsley (1t), H. Tamati, Case (Juliff), West,
Scott, Pendlebury
Referee: W.H. Thompson (Huddersfield)
1984-85
Wigan 28 Edwards (1t); Ferguson (2t),
Stephenson (1g), Donlan, Gill (1t, 3g);
Kenny (1t), M. Ford; Courtney, Kiss, Case
(Campbell), West, Dunn, Potter
Hull 24 Kemble; James (1t), S. Evans (1t),
Leuluai (2t), O'Hara (Schofield); Ah Kuoi,
Sterling; Crooks (2g), Patrick, Puckering
(Divorty 1t), Muggleton, Rose, Norton
Referee: R. Campbell (Widnes)
1985-86
Castleford 15 Lord (Roockley); Plange,
Marchant (1t), Hyde, Sandy (1t); Joyner,
R. Beardmore (1t, 1dg); Ward, K. Beardmore
(Horton), Johnson, England, Ketteridge (1g),
French
Hull K.R. 14 Fairbairn; Clark, M. Smith,
Prohm (2t), Laws; Dorahy (1g), Harkin; P.
Johnston, Watkinson, Ema, Kelly (G. Smith),
D. Harrison (Lydiat 1t), Miller
Referee: R. Whitfield (Widnes)

135

THE LANCE TODD TROPHY

The Lance Todd Trophy is presented to the Man of the Match in the Rugby League Challenge Cup Final, the decision being reached by a ballot of members of the Rugby League Writers' Association present at the game.

Lance Todd made his name in Britain as a player with Wigan and as manager of Salford. His untimely death in a road accident on the return journey from a game at Oldham was commemorated by the introduction of the Lance Todd Trophy.

The award was instituted by Australian-born Harry Sunderland, Warrington director Bob Anderton and Yorkshire journalist John Bapty.

Around 1950, the Red Devils' Association at Salford, comprising players and officials who had worked with Todd, raised sufficient funds to provide a trophy and replica for each winner.

The trophy is now sponsored by brewers Greenall Whitley, who help to finance the annual dinner and trophy presentation at the Willows, Salford.

Gerry Helme, of Warrington, is the only player to win the trophy twice; Len Killeen, of St. Helens, is the only winger to earn the title; Hull's Tommy Harris the only hooker; and Ray Ashby and Brian Gabbitas the only players to share the honour.

Following the 1954 replay, it was decided by the Red Devils that in future the trophy would be awarded for the Wembley game. In 1954, Gerry Helme had received the trophy for his performance in the Odsal replay.

The 1987 winner was Halifax full back Graham Eadie, only the second Australian to receive the individual honour, the first being Wigan's Brett Kenny in 1985.

Lance Todd Trophy winner Graham Eadie powers in for his 51st minute touchdown, with a stranded Saints duo Phil Veiver (left) and Mark Elia in the wake.

The Lance Todd Trophy Roll of Honour

Year	Winner	Team	Position
1946	Billy Stott	Wakefield Trinity (v Wigan)	Centre
1947	Willie Davies	Bradford Northern (v Leeds)	Stand off
1948	Frank Whitcombe	Bradford Northern (v Wigan)	Prop
1949	Ernest Ward	Bradford Northern (v Halifax)	Centre
1950	Gerry Helme	Warrington (v Widnes)	Scrum half
1951	Cec Mountford	Wigan (v Barrow)	Stand off
1952	Billy Ivison	Workington T. (v Featherstone R.)	Loose forward
1953	Peter Ramsden	Huddersfield (v St. Helens)	Stand off
1954	Gerry Helme	Warrington (v Halifax)	Scrum half
1955	Jack Grundy	Barrow (v Workington Town)	Second row
1956	Alan Prescott	St. Helens (v Halifax)	Prop
1957	Jeff Stevenson	Leeds (v Barrow)	Scrum half
1958	Rees Thomas	Wigan (v Workington Town)	Scrum half
1959	Brian McTigue	Wigan (v Hull)	Second row
1960	Tommy Harris	Hull (v Wakefield Trinity)	Hooker
1961	Dick Huddart	St. Helens (v Wigan)	Second row
1962	Neil Fox	Wakefield Trinity (v Huddersfield)	Centre
1963	Harold Poynton	Wakefield Trinity (v Wigan)	Stand off
1964	Frank Collier	Widnes (v Hull K.R.)	Prop
1965	Ray Ashby	Wigan	Full back
	Brian Gabbitas	Hunslet	Stand off
1966	Len Killeen	St. Helens (v Wigan)	Winger
1967	Carl Dooler	Featherstone Rovers (v Barrow)	Scrum half
1968	Don Fox	Wakefield Trinity (v Leeds)	Prop
1969	Malcolm Reilly	Castleford (v Salford)	Loose forward
1970	Bill Kirkbride	Castleford (v Wigan)	Second row
1971	Alex Murphy	Leigh (v Leeds)	Scrum half
1972	Kel Coslett	St. Helens (v Leeds)	Loose forward
1973	Steve Nash	Featherstone R. (v Bradford N.)	Scrum half
1974	Derek Whitehead	Warrington (v Featherstone Rovers)	Full back
1975	Ray Dutton	Widnes (v Warrington)	Full back
1976	Geoff Pimblett	St. Helens (v Widnes)	Full back
1977	Steve Pitchford	Leeds (v Widnes)	Prop
1978	George Nicholls	St. Helens (v Leeds)	Second row
1979	David Topliss	Wakefield Trinity (v Widnes)	Stand off
1980	Brian Lockwood	Hull K.R. (v Hull)	Prop
1981	Mick Burke	Widnes (v Hull K.R.)	Full back
1982	Eddie Cunningham	Widnes (v Hull)	Centre
1983	David Hobbs	Featherstone Rovers (v Hull)	Second row
1984	Joe Lydon	Widnes (v Wigan)	Centre
1985	Brett Kenny	Wigan (v Hull)	Stand off
1986	Bob Beardmore	Castleford (v Hull K.R.)	Scrum half
1987	Graham Eadie	Halifax (v St. Helens)	Full back

CHALLENGE CUP RECORDS

ALL ROUNDS

TEAM

Highest score:
Huddersfield 119 v. *Swinton Park 2. 1914

INDIVIDUAL

Most goals in a match:
22 by Jim Sullivan (Wigan) v. *Flimby and Fothergill
. . . . 1925

Most tries in a match:
11 by George West (Hull K.R.) v. *Brookland Rovers
. . . . 1905

Most points in a match:
53 (11t,10g) by George West (Hull K.R.) as above.

*Amateur teams

FINAL RECORDS

TEAM

Most wins: 10 by Leeds

Most finals: 17 by Wigan

Highest score:
Wakefield T. 38 v. Hull 5. 1960

Widest margin:
Huddersfield 37 v. St. Helens 3. 1915

Biggest attendance:
102,569 Warrington v. Halifax (Replay) at Bradford
. . . . 1954

INDIVIDUAL

Most goals:
8 by Cyril Kellett (Featherstone R.) v. Bradford N.
. . . . 1973

Most tries:
3 by Bob Wilson (Broughton R.) v. Salford. . . . 1902
Stan Moorhouse (Huddersfield) v. Warrington. 1913
Tom Holliday (Oldham) v. Swinton. 1927

Most points:
20 (7g,2t) by Neil Fox (Wakefield T.) v. Hull. . . 1960

WEMBLEY FACTS

WIGAN made a record 13th appearance at Wembley in the 1985 final against Hull, recording their seventh victory at the stadium to equal the Widnes record set a year earlier.

A RECORD 10 overseas players trod the Wembley turf in 1985. Hull fielded six — a record for one club. The Airlie Birds sextet were Australians Peter Sterling and John Muggleton, plus New Zealanders Gary Kemble, James Leuluai, Dane O'Hara and Fred Ah Kuoi. Wigan added Australians John Ferguson and Brett Kenny together with New Zealanders Graeme West and Danny Campbell, who went on as substitute. South African Nick Du Toit was substitute back but did not play.

THE 1985 aggregates of 10 tries and 52 points were both record totals for a Challenge Cup final with Hull's 24 points the most by a losing side. There were also 10 tries in the 1915 final when Huddersfield beat St. Helens 37-3, which is the widest margin. Wakefield Trinity ran up the highest Cup final score when they beat Hull 38-5 in 1960.

WORLD RECORD receipts of £1,009,206 were taken at the 1987 Final between Halifax and St. Helens, from a crowd of 91,267.

FIVE players share the record of playing in four Cup-winning sides at Wembley — Alex Murphy, Brian Lockwood, Eric Hughes, Keith Elwell and Mick Adams.
Murphy was in St. Helens' victorious side of 1961 and as captain led St. Helens (1966), Leigh (1971) and Warrington (1974) to victory. He played in three different positions — stand off, centre and scrum half. Murphy was a scorer in each final with a total of five drop goals and a try.
Brian Lockwood was in the winning final teams of Castleford (1969 and 1970), Hull K.R. (1980) and Widnes (1981). He also appeared with Widnes in the drawn final of 1982.
Hughes, Elwell and Adams each played in the Widnes teams that won the Cup in 1975, 1979, 1981 and 1984. They also appeared in the drawn final of 1982.

THE Widnes trio of Eric Hughes, Keith Elwell and Mick Adams also hold the record for most appearances at Wembley ... seven. In addition to the five finals mentioned above they were on the losing side in 1976 and 1977.

ERIC ASHTON captained a record six teams at Wembley — Wigan in 1958, 1959, 1961, 1963, 1965 and 1966. His record of three wins (in 1958, 1959, 1965) is shared with Derek Turner (Wakefield Trinity 1960, 1962, 1963) and Alex Murphy (St. Helens 1966, Leigh 1971 and Warrington 1974).

THE YOUNGEST player to appear in a Wembley Cup final was Shaun Edwards who was 17 years, 6 months and 19 days when he played full back for Wigan against Widnes in 1984.

THE OLDEST at Wembley was Gus Risman, who at 41 years 29 days led Workington Town to victory over Featherstone Rovers in 1952. He played full back.

THE TALLEST player at Wembley was New Zealand Test star Graeme West who captained Wigan in the 1984 and 1985 finals. He measured 6ft. 5in.

SCHOOLBOYS who have appeared in an Under-11 curtain-raiser at Wembley and gone on to play in the major final at the stadium are Joe Lydon, David Hulme, Mike Ford, Neil Puckering and David Plange. Lydon became the first to achieve the feat with Widnes in the 1984 final against Wigan, followed by Hulme who went on as a 72nd minute substitute. Both had played in the first schoolboys' curtain-raiser in 1975 — Lydon for Wigan, and Hulme for Widnes. Ford played scrum half for Wigan in the 1985 final having represented Oldham in the 1977 curtain-raiser. Puckering played for Hull in the 1977 curtain-raiser and for his home town club in the Challenge Cup final of 1985. Plange was in the Hull Schools team of 1976 and played for Castleford in the 1986 final.

CYRIL KELLETT holds the record for most goals in a Challenge Cup final with his eight for Featherstone Rovers in 1973.

In the most remarkable exhibition of kicking seen at Wembley, the veteran full back was successful with every one of his attempts as Bradford Northern crashed 33-14.

Nine years earlier he scored only one for Hull Kingston Rovers in the 13-5 defeat by Widnes.

NEIL FOX — the record aggregate points scorer of all time — piled up the most points in a Challenge Cup final in 1960. His 20 points helped Wakefield Trinity to a 38-5 defeat of Hull. Fox's points came from two tries and seven goals.

His three drop goals for Trinity in the 12-6 victory over Huddersfield two years later was another extraordinary feat in the days when the drop goal was a rarity.

NO player has scored a hat-trick of tries at Wembley, the feat being achieved only three times in the preceding era.

The last to do it was Oldham winger Tom Holliday in the 26-7 defeat of Swinton in 1927.

Bob Wilson, the Broughton Rangers centre and captain, was the first to score three tries, in the 25-0 victory over Salford in 1902.

In between, Stan Moorhouse's three-try feat accounted for all of Huddersfield's points when they beat Warrington 9-5 in 1913. Moorhouse was winger to Harold Wagstaff, recognised as the greatest centre of all time.

MANY great players have gone through an entire career without achieving their ambition of playing at Wembley. Hull's Mike Smith achieved it in his first senior game.

Smith made one of the most remarkable debuts in sporting history when he played in the second row of an injury-hit Boulevard side against Wakefield Trinity in 1960.

In contrast, Freddie Miller signed for Hull in 1932 and did not play at Wembley until 1952 . . . two years after joining Featherstone Rovers.

A NOTABLE Wembley captain was Gus Risman who led two clubs to victory . . . 14 years apart.

He was captain of Salford when they beat Barrow in 1938. At 41, he led Workington Town to their triumph over Featherstone Rovers in 1952.

PROBABLY the unluckiest Challenge Cup finalist was Dai Davies who appeared in four finals and was on the losing side each time.

Three of those occasions were at Wembley with different clubs. He was a loser with Warrington (1933), Huddersfield (1935) and Keighley (1937).

Before the Wembley era he was also in Warrington's beaten team of 1928.

Steve Norton has played at Wembley four times and has yet to be on the winning side. He was in the beaten Hull teams of 1980, 1983 and 1985 in addition to playing in the 1982 drawn final. In 1970 he was a non-playing substitute for Castleford who won the Cup.

Bill Ramsey was on the losing side in four Wembley finals but gained a winner's medal with Leeds in 1968. He picked up losers' medals with Hunslet (1965), Leeds (1971 and 1972) and Widnes (1977).

A TOTAL of 13 current clubs have yet to play at Wembley . . . . Batley, Blackpool Borough, Bramley, Carlisle, Doncaster, Fulham, Mansfield Marksman, Oldham, Rochdale Hornets, Runcorn Highfield, Sheffield Eagles, Swinton and Whitehaven.

Fate seems to be against Swinton and Oldham. In the five years preceding the move to Wembley, one or the other appeared in the final, twice meeting each other.

Oldham played in four successive finals in that period. Swinton's run of three finals ended when the first Wembley took place in 1929.

They did get through to the final again three years later . . . . only for it to be played at Wigan!

Gus Risman, the oldest player at Wembley.

CHALLENGE CUP

Wembley Era Semi-Finals

It is generally felt that it is better to have played at Wembley and lost than never to have played there at all. This makes the semi-final stage of the RL Challenge Cup almost as important as the final with no consolation for the losers.

Of the 13 current clubs who have never appeared at Wembley four have been beaten semi-finalists. They are Oldham (four times), Swinton, Rochdale Hornets (twice) and Whitehaven.

Probably the unluckiest are Oldham. They have reached the penultimate stage four times without being able to realise their ambition. Oldham almost made it in 1964. After drawing 5-5 with Hull K.R. they were winning 17-14 in extra time of the replay when bad light stopped play and they were beaten in the third game.

Swinton did win a semi-final in 1932 but the final that year was switched from Wembley to Wigan!

There have been three occasions when Yorkshire has provided all four semi-finalists in one year — in 1962, 1973 and 1983. Only once have all four semi-finalists come from west of the Pennines — in 1930.

Until 1962 the two semi-finals were always played on the same Saturday, but with four Yorkshire clubs competing for the first time it was decided to play one mid-week. Both matches were played at Odsal Stadium, Bradford. The first was on a Wednesday evening — without floodlights — when 43,625 saw Wakefield Trinity beat Featherstone Rovers and on the following Saturday there were 31,423 to see Huddersfield beat Hull K.R.

The following year both semi-finals were again played on the same Saturday, but since then they have been staged on different Saturdays.

Some semi-final facts during the Wembley era are:

Biggest attendance: 69,898 Warrington v. Leeds at Bradford in 1950

Biggest aggregate: 104,453 in 1939 (Only other six-figure aggregate was 102,080 in 1951)

Record receipts: £113,345 Hull K.R. v. Leeds replay at Elland Road, Leeds in 1986

Lowest attendance: 7,971 Featherstone R. v. Leigh at Leeds in 1974

Highest score and widest margin: Huddersfield 30 v. Leeds 8 in 1933

CHALLENGE CUP SEMI-FINALS

Year	Winners		Runners-up		Venue	Attendance	Receipts
1929	Dewsbury	9	Castleford	3	Huddersfield	25,000	£1,562
	Wigan	7	St. Helens Recs.	7	Swinton	31,000	£2,209
Replay	Wigan	13	St. Helens Recs.	12	Leigh	21,940	£1,437
1930	Widnes	10	Barrow	3	Warrington	25,500	£1,630
	St. Helens	5	Wigan	5	Swinton	37,169	£2,666
Replay	St. Helens	22	Wigan	10	Leigh	24,000	£1,657
1931	Halifax	11	St. Helens	2	Rochdale	21,674	£1,498
	York	15	Warrington	5	Leeds	32,419	£2,329
1932	Leeds	2	Halifax	2	Huddersfield	31,818	£2,456
Replay	Leeds	9	Halifax	2	Wakefield	21,000	£1,417
	Swinton	7	Wakefield T.	4	Rochdale	21,273	£1,369
●	*Final was played at Wigan, not Wembley*						
1933	Huddersfield	30	Leeds	8	Wakefield	36,359	£2,299
	Warrington	11	St. Helens	5	Swinton	30,373	£2,055
1934	Hunslet	12	Huddersfield	7	Wakefield	27,450	£1,797
	Widnes	7	Oldham	4	Swinton	17,577	£1,050

1935	Castleford	11	Barrow	5	Swinton	24,469	£1,534
	Huddersfield	21	Hull	5	Leeds	37,111	£2,753
1936	Leeds	10	Huddersfield	5	Wakefield	37,906	£2,456
	Warrington	7	Salford	2	Wigan	41,538	£2,796
1937	Keighley	0	Wakefield T.	0	Leeds	39,998	£2,793
Replay	Keighley	5	Wakefield T.	3	Huddersfield	14,400	£1,052
	Widnes	13	Wigan	9	Warrington	29,260	£1,972
1938	Barrow	4	Halifax	2	Huddersfield	31,384	£2,431
	Salford	6	Swinton	0	Belle Vue, Manchester	31,664	£2,396
1939	Halifax	10	Leeds	4	Bradford	64,453	£3,645
	Salford	11	Wigan	2	Rochdale	40,000	£2,154
●	*During the war the semi-finals were two-legged and the finals were not played at Wembley*						
1946	Wakefield T.	7	Hunslet	3	Leeds	33,000	£4,991
	Wigan	12	Widnes	5	Swinton	36,976	£4,746
1947	Bradford N.	11	Warrington	7	Swinton	33,474	£4,946
	Leeds	21	Wakefield T.	0	Huddersfield	35,136	£6,339
1948	Bradford N.	14	Hunslet	7	Leeds	38,125	£7,437
	Wigan	11	Rochdale H.	0	Swinton	26,004	£4,206
1949	Bradford N.	10	Barrow	0	Swinton	26,572	£4,646
	Halifax	11	Huddersfield	10	Bradford	61,875	£8,638
1950	Warrington	16	Leeds	4	Bradford	69,898	£9,861
	Widnes	8	Bradford N.	0	Wigan	25,390	£3,936
1951	Barrow	14	Leeds	14	Bradford	57,459	£8,248
Replay	Barrow	28	Leeds	13	Huddersfield	31,078	£5,098
	Wigan	3	Warrington	2	Swinton	44,621	£7,358
1952	Featherstone R.	6	Leigh	2	Leeds	35,621	£6,494
	Workington T.	5	Barrow	2	Wigan	31,206	£4,782
1953	Huddersfield	7	Wigan	0	Bradford	58,722	£10,519
	St. Helens	9	Warrington	3	Swinton	38,059	£7,768
1954	Halifax	18	Hunslet	3	Bradford	46,961	£8,243
	Warrington	8	Leeds	4	Swinton	36,993	£7,596
1955	Barrow	9	Hunslet	6	Wigan	25,493	£4,671
	Workington T.	13	Featherstone R.	2	Leeds	33,499	£7,305
1956	Halifax	11	Wigan	10	Bradford	51,889	£9,054
	St. Helens	5	Barrow	5	Swinton	38,897	£7,793
Replay	St. Helens	10	Barrow	5	Wigan	44,731	£7,750
1957	Barrow	2	Leigh	2	Wigan	34,628	£6,340
Replay	Barrow	15	Leigh	10	Swinton	28,081	£5,695
	Leeds	10	Whitehaven	9	Bradford	49,094	£8,987
1958	Wigan	5	Rochdale H.	3	Swinton	28,597	£6,354
	Workington T.	8	Featherstone R.	2	Bradford	31,517	£6,325
1959	Wigan	5	Leigh	0	Swinton	27,906	£6,068
	Hull	15	Featherstone R.	5	Bradford	52,131	£9,776
1960	Wakefield T.	11	Featherstone R.	2	Bradford	55,935	£10,390
	Hull	12	Oldham	9	Swinton	27,545	£6,093
1961	St. Helens	26	Hull	9	Bradford	42,935	£9,231
	Wigan	19	Halifax	10	Swinton	35,118	£7,557

Year	Winners		Runners-up		Venue	Attendance	Receipts
1962	Wakefield T.	9	Featherstone R.	0	Bradford	43,625	£8,496
	Huddersfield	6	Hull K.R.	0	Bradford	31,423	£6,685
1963	Wakefield T.	5	Warrington	2	Swinton	15,565	£3,530
	Wigan	18	Hull K.R.	4	Leeds	21,420	£6,029
1964	Widnes	7	Castleford	7	Swinton	25,603	£5,541
Replay	Widnes	7	Castleford	5	Wakefield	28,739	£5,313
	Hull K.R.	5	Oldham	5	Leeds	28,823	£7,411
Replay	Hull K.R.	14	Oldham	17	Swinton	27,209	£5,929

● *Score after 80 minutes was 14-14, then bad light caused match to be abandoned after 12 minutes of extra time with Oldham winning 17-14*

Year	Winners		Runners-up		Venue	Attendance	Receipts
Second Replay	Hull K.R.	12	Oldham	2	Huddersfield	28,732	£6,183
1965	Wigan	25	Swinton	10	St. Helens	26,658	£6,384
	Hunslet	8	Wakefield T.	0	Leeds	21,262	£6,090
1966	St. Helens	12	Dewsbury	5	Swinton	13,046	£3,102
	Wigan	7	Leeds	2	Huddersfield	22,758	£5,971
1967	Featherstone R.	16	Leeds	8	Huddersfield	20,052	£6,276
	Barrow	14	Dewsbury	9	Swinton	13,744	£4,560
1968	Leeds	25	Wigan	4	Swinton	30,058	£9,845
	Wakefield T.	0	Huddersfield	0	Bradford	21,569	£6,196
Replay	Wakefield T.	15	Huddersfield	10	Leeds	20,983	£6,425
1969	Castleford	16	Wakefield T.	10	Leeds	21,497	£8,477
	Salford	15	Warrington	8	Wigan	20,600	£7,738
1970	Castleford	6	St. Helens	3	Swinton	18,913	£7,171
	Wigan	19	Hull K.R.	8	Leeds	18,495	£7,862
1971	Leeds	19	Castleford	8	Bradford	24,464	£9,120
	Leigh	10	Huddersfield	4	Wigan	14,875	£5,670
1972	St. Helens	10	Warrington	10	Wigan	19,300	£8,250
Replay	St. Helens	10	Warrington	6	Wigan	32,380	£12,604
	Leeds	16	Halifax	3	Bradford	16,680	£6,851
1973	Featherstone R.	17	Castleford	3	Leeds	15,369	£9,454
	Bradford N.	23	Dewsbury	7	Leeds	14,028	£9,221
1974	Warrington	17	Dewsbury	7	Wigan	11,789	£6,821
	Featherstone R.	21	Leigh	14	Leeds	7,971	£4,461
1975	Widnes	13	Wakefield T.	7	Bradford	9,155	£5,856
	Warrington	11	Leeds	4	Wigan	13,168	£9,581
1976	Widnes	15	Featherstone R.	9	Swinton	13,019	£9,078
	St. Helens	5	Keighley	4	Huddersfield	9,829	£6,113
1977	Leeds	7	St. Helens	2	Wigan	12,974	£11,379
	Widnes	14	Hull K.R.	5	Leeds	17,053	£16,068
1978	Leeds	14	Featherstone R.	9	Bradford	12,824	£11,322
	St. Helens	12	Warrington	8	Wigan	16,167	£13,960
1979	Widnes	14	Bradford N.	11	Swinton	14,324	£16,363
	Wakefield T.	9	St. Helens	7	Leeds	12,393	£14,195
1980	Hull K.R.	20	Halifax	7	Leeds	17,910	£31,650
	Hull	10	Widnes	5	Swinton	18,347	£29,415
1981	Widnes	17	Warrington	9	Wigan	12,624	£20,673
	Hull K.R.	22	St. Helens	5	Leeds	17,073	£30,616
1982	Hull	15	Castleford	11	Leeds	21,207	£41,867
	Widnes	11	Leeds	8	Swinton	13,075	£25,796

Year	Winners		Runners-up		Venue	Attendance	Receipts
1983	Featherstone R.	11	Bradford N.	6	Leeds	10,784	£22,579
	Hull	14	Castleford	7	Elland Rd., L'ds	26,031	£65,498
1984	Wigan	14	York	8	Elland Rd., L'ds	17,156	£52,888
	Widnes	15	Leeds	4	Swinton	14,046	£37,183
1985	Wigan	18	Hull K.R.	11	Elland Rd., L'ds	19,275	£70,192
	Hull	10	Castleford	10	Leeds	20,982	£64,163
Replay	Hull	22	Castleford	16	Leeds	20,968	£65,005
1986	Castleford	18	Oldham	7	Wigan	12,430	£38,296
	Hull K.R.	24	Leeds	24	Elland Rd., L'ds	23,866	£83,757
Replay	Hull K.R.	17	Leeds	0	Elland Rd., L'ds	32,485	£113,345
1987	St. Helens	14	Leigh	8	Wigan	13,105	£48,627
	Halifax	12	Widnes	8	Leeds	16,064	£61,260

NON-LEAGUE CLUBS IN THE CHALLENGE CUP

AMATEUR clubs were invited to compete in the 1986 Rugby League Challenge Cup after a five-year break. The League asked for two of the three county cup competition winners to enter the preliminary round. Cumbria Cup winners Kells were given a bye into the draw for the preliminary round, while Yorkshire victors Dudley Hill met Lancashire winners Simms Cross at Bramley in an eliminator, the White Rose side going through.

The League later decided that in the 1987 Silk Cut Challenge Cup campaign there would be 38 teams, four amateur clubs joining the professionals for a preliminary round of six ties.

In the early years of the Northern Union Challenge Cup — as it was then called — the line between professional and amateur was less clearly defined.

A variety of Leagues also make it difficult to set non-League clubs apart. Fifty-six clubs appeared in the inaugurating first round of 1897 and four others received byes. The complications continued until 1904 when the League format settled down and non-League clubs had to qualify for the first round.

Not since 1909 when BEVERLEY beat Ebbw Vale 7-2 had a senior team been knocked out by a non-League club although amateur teams twice had victories in the two-leg era of 1946-54.

RECORDS OF NON-LEAGUE CLUBS IN THE RUGBY LEAGUE CHALLENGE CUP SINCE 1904
(Excluding preliminary rounds before 1908)
Non-League Clubs in Capitals

Victories over Senior Clubs

1905-06
*FEATHERSTONE ROVERS 23 v. Widnes 2
 (second round)

1907-08
WHITEHAVEN RECREATION 13 v. St. Helens 8
 (Lost 33-5 at Merthyr Tydfil in second round)

1908-09
BEVERLEY 7 v. Ebbw Vale 2
 (Lost 53-2 at Halifax in second round)

1945-46
SHARLSTON 12 v. Workington Town 7
 (1st leg) (Workington Town won 2nd leg 16-2)

1947-48
RISEHOW and GILLHEAD 10 v. Keighley 2 (2nd leg)
 (Keighley won 1st leg 11-0)

*FEATHERSTONE ROVERS are the only non-League club to appear in the third round when they lost 3-0 at Keighley. In the first round they beat BROOKLAND ROVERS 16-5.

There have been several other instances of non-League clubs meeting in the first round. The last occasion was in 1960 when WALNEY CENTRAL beat LOCK LANE 10-5 before losing at Oldham 55-4 in the second round.

In 1964 THAMES BOARD MILLS received a bye when Bradford Northern disbanded, but lost 48-8 at Blackpool Borough in the second round.

Draws against Senior Clubs

1905-06 VICTORIA RANGERS 0 v. Widnes 0
 Widnes won replay 8-3

1906-07 WORKINGTON 3 v. Wakefield Trinity 3
 Wakefield Trinity won replay 16-5

1907-08 WIGAN HIGHFIELD 3 v. Bramley 3
 Bramley won replay 8-6

1911-12 NORMANTON ST. JOHN'S 6 v. Warrington 6
 Warrington won replay 75-0

1921-22 Widnes 5 v. WIGAN HIGHFIELD 5
 Widnes won replay 9-4

1951-52 RYLAND RECS 9 v. Whitehaven 9 (2nd leg)
 Whitehaven won first leg 16-0

1986-87 KELLS 4 v. Fulham 4
 Fulham won replay 22-14

143

RECORD SCORES

Team

Huddersfield 119 v. SWINTON PARK 2 (1913-14)

● This is the highest score in any competitive match in England.

Non-League teams have provided other sides with club records as follows:

Hull K.R.   73 v. BROOKLAND ROVERS 5 (1905)
Rochdale H. 75 v. BROUGHTON MOOR 13 (1915)
Wigan   116 v. FLIMBY & FOTHERGILL 0
                                        (1925)
Barrow   83 v. MARYPORT 3 (1938)

All told, non-League clubs have conceded 50 points or more on 42 occasions but only once after 1973-74 (B.A.R.L.A.'s first season).
The lowest score by a senior club was in the 0-0 draw between VICTORIA RANGERS and Widnes in 1906.

Individual

Most tries and points:
11 tries (10g) 53 points by George West (Hull K.R.) v. BROOKLAND ROVERS (1905)

Most goals:
22 by Jim Sullivan (Wigan) v. FLIMBY & FOTHERGILL (1925)

● All three feats are records for any competitive matches in England.

HIGHEST NON-LEAGUE SCORES

FEATHERSTONE ROVERS 23 v. Widnes 2 (second round 1906)

Only other 20 score:

LATCHFORD ALBION 20 v. Wigan 40 (1st leg 1954) Wigan won second leg 41-2

PILKINGTON RECS. 22 v. Castleford 23 (1978)

NON-LEAGUE CLUBS YEAR-BY-YEAR CUP RECORD FROM 1904

● Non-League clubs in block capitals and all first round ties other than where stated.

1903-04   Broughton R. 26 v. PARTON 0
           Salford 57 v. BROOKLAND ROVERS 0

1904-05   Hull 52 v. LEIGH SHAMROCKS 0
           Hull KR 73 v. BROOKLAND ROVERS 5
           Hunslet 22 v. PARTON 3
           Leeds 20 v. OSSETT 0
           St. Helens 9 v. ROCHDALE R. 2

1905-06   EGERTON 9 v. LEIGH SHAMROCKS 0
           FEATHERSTONE ROVERS 16 v.
               BROOKLAND ROVERS 5
           Keighley 13 v. EGREMONT 0
           VICTORIA RANGERS 0 v. Widnes 0
               Replay
           Widnes 8 v. VICTORIA RANGERS 3
               Second round
           FEATHERSTONE ROVERS 23 v. Widnes 2
           Salford 38 v. EGERTON 5
               Third round
           Keighley 3 v. FEATHERSTONE ROVERS 0

1906-07   Halifax 45 v. MILLOM 0
           Huddersfield 38 v.
               BRIGHOUSE ST. JAMES 0
           Keighley 18 v. BROOKLAND ROVERS 0
           RADCLIFFE RANGERS 0 v. York 13
           WHITEHAVEN REC 10 v.
               SAVILLE GREEN 0
           WORKINGTON 3 v. Wakefield T. 3
               Replay
           Wakefield T. 16 v. WORKINGTON 5
               Second round
           WHITEHAVEN REC 0 v. Keighley 14

1907-08   Barrow 28 v. MILLOM 5
           Batley 32 v. BARROW ST. GEORGE 5
           BEVERLEY 3 v. Merthyr Tydfil 15
           HALF-ACRE TRINITY 2 v. York 7
           WHITEHAVEN REC 13 v. St. Helens 8
           WIGAN HIGHFIELD 3 v. Bramley 3
               Replay
           Bramley 8 v. WIGAN HIGHFIELD 6
               Second round
           Merthyr Tydfil 33 v.
               WHITEHAVEN REC 5

1908-09   Barrow 36 v. BARROW ST. GEORGE 0
           BEVERLEY 7 v. Ebbw Vale 2
           NORMANTON 10 v. Hull 20
           Runcorn 23 v. EGREMONT 5
           PEMBERTON 6 v. Keighley 41
               Second round
           Halifax 53 v. BEVERLEY 2

1909-10   MILLOM 9 v. BROOKLAND ROVERS 4
           PURSTON WHITE HORSE 10 v.
               Halifax 23
           Salford 64 v. YORK IRISH
               NATIONAL LEAGUE 0
           Warrington 31 v. WIGAN HIGHFIELD 3
               Second round
           Warrington 37 v. MILLOM 0

1910-11   BROUGHTON MOOR 6 v. Runcorn 23
          Dewsbury 47 v. YORK GROVE UNITED 0
          NORMANTON ST. JOHN'S 6 v.
              Broughton R. 10
          PEMBERTON 4 v. Bradford N 12
          Widnes 23 v. LANE END UNITED 0

1911-12   BEVERLEY 5 v. Hull KR 34
          Dewsbury 36 v. LANE END UNITED 9
          MILLOM 0 v. Keighley 11
          NORMANTON ST. JOHN'S 6 v.
              Warrington 6
          Replay
          Warrington 75 v.
              NORMANTON ST. JOHN'S 0
          Wigan 35 v. WIGAN HIGHFIELD 10

1912-13   Bradford N 33 v. PEMBERTON 4
          Broughton R 59 v. BARTON 0
          ELLAND 2 v. Wakefield T 15
          Hull 24 v. SEATON 2
          NORMANTON ST. JOHN'S 4 v.
              Oldham 17
          Rochdale H. 15 v.
              FEATHERSTONE ROVERS 3

1913-14   CASTLEFORD 8 v. Wigan 27
          ELLAND 2 v.
              FEATHERSTONE ROVERS 7
          Huddersfield 119 v. SWINTON PARK 2
          Hull KR 62 v. MILLOM 0
          St. Helens 27 v. WIGAN HIGHFIELD 4
          York 45 v. GLASSON RANGERS 0
          Second round
          FEATHERSTONE ROVERS 3 v. Hull 27

1914-15   BRIGHOUSE RANGERS 0 v.
              Salford 26
          BROUGHTON MOOR 6 v. WARDLEY 3
          FEATHERSTONE ROVERS 0 v.
              St. Helens 6
          Keighley 8 v. ASKHAM 5
          WIGAN HIGHFIELD 0 v. Swinton 2
          Second round
          Rochdale H 75 v. BROUGHTON MOOR 13

1919-20   Bramley 13 v. WIGAN HIGHFIELD 0
          FEATHERSTONE ROVERS 2 v.
              Broughton R 17
          Halifax 55 v. BROOKLAND ROVERS 0
          Hull 75 v. BRITISH OIL & CAKE MILLS 2
          Leeds 44 v. MILLOM 5
          Warrington 9 v. ASKHAM-in-FURNESS 0
          Wigan 64 v. HEALEY STREET ADULTS 3

1920-21   ASKHAM 2 v. Bradford N 7
          FEATHERSTONE ROVERS 41 v.
              PENDLEBURY 0
          Oldham 41 v. ELLAND WANDERERS 5
          Swinton 25 v. BRITISH OIL &
              CAKE MILLS 5
          Widnes 41 v. DEARHAM WANDERERS 5
          WIGAN HIGHFIELD 10 v. Broughton R 15
          Second round
          FEATHERSTONE ROVERS 0 v.
              Dewsbury 22

1921-22   ASKHAM 15 v. CADISHEAD 5
          ELLAND WANDERERS 0 v. Oldham 29
          Rochdale H 54 v. BROUGHTON MOOR 2
          Swinton 24 v. BRITISH OIL &
              CAKE MILLS 5
          Widnes 5 v. WIGAN HIGHFIELD 5
          Replay
          WIGAN HIGHFIELD 4 v. Widnes 9
          Second round
          Keighley 15 v. ASKHAM 0

1922-23   NORWOOD 3 v. St. Helens 29
          Salford 16 v. CASTLEFORD 0
          Wakefield T 67 v HENSINGHAM 13
          Wigan Highfield 16 v.
              CADISHEAD & IRLAM 0
          York 40 v. MILLOM 0

1923-24   Barrow 67 v. DEARHAM WANDERERS 3
          Broughton R 34 v. HULL ST. PATRICK'S 0
          WARDLEY 0 v. St. Helens 73
          Warrington 46 v. DALTON 3
          Hull KR 24 v. CASTLEFORD 0

1924-25   BARNSLEY UNITED (Hull) 3 v.
              DALTON 3
          Hunslet 25 v. CASTLEFORD 0
          Leeds 27 v. TWELVE APOSTLES 0
          Wigan 116 v. FLIMBY & FOTHERGILL 0
          Replay
          DALTON 3 v.
              BARNSLEY UNITED (Hull) 2
          Second round
          St. Helens Rec 74 v. DALTON 5

1925-26   Barrow 44 v.
              BARROW CAMBRIDGE ST. 0
          CASTLEFORD 12 v. St. Helens Rec 18
          HENSINGHAM 0 v. Huddersfield 33
          Hull 27 v. PEMBERTON ROVERS 3
          Hull KR 28 v.
              BARNSLEY UNITED (Hull) 0

145

1926-27	Batley 32 v. COTTINGHAM 5	1938-39	Bradford N 37 v. SEATON 7

1926-27   Batley 32 v. COTTINGHAM 5
Dewsbury 20 v.
      DEARHAM WANDERERS 5
Wigan 51 v. PEMBERTON ROVERS 11

1927-28   Batley 31 v. COTTINGHAM 2
Bradford N 17 v. TWELVE APOSTLES 0
Warrington 43 v. KINSLEY 2
WHITEHAVEN REC 0 v. Swinton 44

1928-29   Castleford 31 v. WHITEHAVEN REC 7
Dewsbury 37 v. COTTINGHAM 0
St. Helens 32 v. LINDLEY 2
Wigan Highfield 45 v. UNO's DABS 0

1929-30   Halifax 74 v.
      FEATHERSTONE JUNIORS 9
Hull 44 v. BICKERSHAW HORNETS 10
Keighley 6 v. GREAT CLIFTON 5
Leigh 48 v. COTTINGHAM 0

1930-31   Bramley 7 v. GOLDEN LIONS 3
Huddersfield 60 v.
      BROOKLAND ROVERS 2
LINDLEY 2 v. Rochdale H 13
Wigan Highfield 41 v.
      FEATHERSTONE JUNIORS 3

1931-32   Barrow 65 v. LINDLEY 5
Dewsbury 27 v. UNO's DABS 10
GREAT CLIFTON 2 v. Broughton R 20

1932-33   ASKERN WELFARE 0 v. Wigan 46
Halifax 42 v. UNO's DABS 5
Hull 37 v. HIGGINSHAW 2
York 35 v. BARROW MARSH HORNETS 6

1933-34   Bramley 20 v. DEARHAM WANDERERS 11
Hull KR 18 v. WIGAN RANGERS 2
London Highfield 32 v. HULL ST MARY'S 2
St. Helens Rec 32 v.
      PENDLEBURY JUNIORS 3

1934-35   Barrow 28 v. SHARLSTON 3
Castleford 33 v. ASTLEY &
      TYLDESLEY COLLIERIES 4
MANCHESTER SHIP CANAL 9 v.
      Dewsbury 28
Rochdale H. 28 v.
      BARROW MARSH HORNETS 18

1935-36   Leigh 49 v. SEATON 4
Oldham 38 v. HIGGINSHAW 2

1936-37   GOOLE 2 v. Broughton Rangers 14
Widnes 39 v. HIGGINSHAW 2

1937-38   Rochdale H 50 v. GLASSHOUGHTON 2
St. Helens 39 v. PENDLEBURY 0
Barrow 83 v. MARYPORT 3

1938-39   Bradford N 37 v. SEATON 7
SHARLSTON 5 v. Bramley 23
Hunslet 48 v.
      UNITED GLASS BLOWERS 5
Swinton 46 v. HIGGINSHAW 3

1945-46   HULL JUNIORS 0 v. Bramley 29
Bramley 51 v. HULL JUNIORS 3
Hull KR 18 v.
      LANGWORTHY JUNIORS 0
LANGWORTHY JUNIORS 7 v.
      Hull KR 14
KELLS 0 v. Warrington 3
Warrington 27 v. KELLS 0
HIGHER INCE 3 v. Widnes 30
Widnes 42 v. HIGHER INCE 3
SHARLSTON 12 v. Workington Town 7
Workington Town 16 v. SHARLSTON 2

1946-47   WHELDALE COLLIERY 0 v. Halifax 25
Halifax 20 v. WHELDALE COLLIERY 10
PEMBERTON ROVERS 6 v. Liverpool S 27
Liverpool S 20 v. PEMBERTON ROVERS 5
Warrington 46 v. BROOKLAND ROVERS 3
BROOKLAND ROVERS 3 v. Warrington 32
Workington T 48 v. WIDNES DRAGONS 0
WIDNES DRAGONS 5 v. Workington T 21

1947-48   VINE TAVERN 6 v. Bramley 17
Bramley 10 v. VINE TAVERN 2
Keighley 11 v. RISEHOW & GILLHEAD 0
RISEHOW & GILLHEAD 10 v. Keighley 2
Rochdale H 13 v. PEMBERTON ROVERS 0
PEMBERTON ROVERS 0 v. Rochdale H 11
St. Helens 48 v.
      BUSLINGTHORPE VALE 0
BUSLINGTHORPE VALE 2 v.
      St. Helens 13

1948-49   NORMANTON 4 v. Belle Vue Rangers 9
Belle Vue Rangers 12 v. NORMANTON 0
Oldham 30 v. BROUGHTON MOOR 0
BROUGHTON MOOR 2 v. Oldham 35
VINE TAVERN 4 v. York 11
York 17 v. VINE TAVERN 3

1949-50   WORSLEY BOYS' CLUB 7 v. Hunslet 45
Hunslet 18 v. WORSLEY BOYS' CLUB 9
CARDIFF 10 v. Salford 15
Salford 20 v. CARDIFF 5
BROUGHTON MOOR 5 v. Wakefield T 28
Wakefield T 73 v. BROUGHTON MOOR 3

1950-51　LLANELLY 9 v. Barrow 23
　　　　　Barrow 39 v. LLANELLY 5
　　　　　Batley 41 v. BROUGHTON MOOR 3
　　　　　BROUGHTON MOOR 0 v. Batley 36
　　　　　Leigh 43 v. LATCHFORD ALBION 0
　　　　　LATCHFORD ALBION 0 v. Leigh 19

1951-52　Whitehaven 16 v. RYLANDS RECS 0
　　　　　RYLANDS RECS 9 v. Whitehaven 9

1952-53　ORFORD TANNERY 2 v. Warrington 46
　　　　　Warrington 46 v. ORFORD TANNERY 8
　　　　　Widnes 28 v. HULL DOCKERS (NDLB) 0
　　　　　HULL DOCKERS (NDLB) 3 v. Widnes 22

1953-54　LATCHFORD ALBION 20 v. Wigan 40
　　　　　Wigan 41 v. LATCHFORD ALBION 2
　　　　　Workington T 50 v.
　　　　　　　　　WHELDALE COLLIERY 2
　　　　　WHELDALE COLLIERY 6 v.
　　　　　　　　　Workington T 32

1954-55　Workington T 43 v. DEWSBURY CELTIC 0

1955-56　Keighley 33 v. TRIANGLE VALVE 8
　　　　　Rochdale H 55 v. STANNINGLEY 0

1956-57　Barrow 53 v.
　　　　　　　　　WAKEFIELD LOCOMOTIVE 12
　　　　　Halifax 48 v. WIDNES ST. MARIE'S 0

1957-58　York 50 v. LOCK LANE 5
　　　　　Widnes 51 v. ORFORD TANNERY 2

1958-59　York 54 v. ASTLEY &
　　　　　　　　　TYLDESLEY COLLIERY 2
　　　　　Hunslet 55 v. KELLS REC CENTRE 9

1959-60　WALNEY CENTRAL 10 v.
　　　　　　　　　LOCK LANE 5
　　　　　　　Second round
　　　　　Oldham 55 v. WALNEY CENTRAL 4

1960-61　Hull KR 56 v. PILKINGTON RECS 8
　　　　　DEWSBURY CELTIC 0 v. Castleford 32

1961-62　Hunslet 53 v. OLDHAM ST ANNE'S 10
　　　　　BROOKHOUSE 4 v. Doncaster 7

1962-63　Liverpool C 11 v. ROOSE 0
　　　　　IMPERIAL ATHLETIC 4 v. Bramley 15

1963-64　Featherstone R 60 v. STANNINGLEY 4
　　　　　THAMES BOARD MILLS — a bye
　　　　　　　Second round
　　　　　Blackpool B 48 v.
　　　　　　　　　THAMES BOARD MILLS 8

1964-65　Blackpool B 27 v. CROSSFIELD RECS 4
　　　　　Swinton 48 v. DEWSBURY CELTIC 5

1965-66　Barrow 11 v. CROSSFIELD RECS 2
　　　　　Widnes 23 v. BROOKHOUSE 5

1966-67　BLACKBROOK 12 v. York 23
　　　　　BRITISH OIL & CAKE MILLS 9 v.
　　　　　　　　　Liverpool C 20

1967-68　LEIGH MINERS' WELFARE 7 v.
　　　　　　　　　Halifax 24
　　　　　BRITISH OIL & CAKE OILS 6 v.
　　　　　　　　　Castleford 9

1968-69　Wigan 61 v. LEIGH MINERS'
　　　　　　　　　WELFARE 0
　　　　　Wakefield T 50 v. ACKWORTH 7

1969-70　Doncaster 22 v. GLASSON RANGERS 4
　　　　　Huddersfield 15 v. LOCK LANE 10

1970-71　Dewsbury 25 v. BRITISH OIL &
　　　　　　　　　CAKE MILLS 3
　　　　　Hunslet 49 v. THAMES BOARD MILLS 5

1971-72　Bramley 19 v. PILKINGTON RECS 5
　　　　　DEWSBURY CELTIC 2 v.
　　　　　　　　　Featherstone Rovers 34

1972-73　MILLOM 5 v. Hunslet 18
　　　　　Leigh 27 v. DEWSBURY CELTIC 4

1973-74　LOCK LANE 9 v. Wigan 37
　　　　　Leigh 63 v. KIPPAX WHITE SWAN 7

1974-75　DEWSBURY CELTIC 15 v. Hull KR 31
　　　　　New Hunslet 9 v. MAYFIELD 5

1975-76　Leigh 37 v. POINTER PANTHERS 8
　　　　　Warrington 16 v.
　　　　　　　　　LEIGH MINERS' WELFARE 12

1976-77　BEECROFT & WIGHTMAN 2 v.
　　　　　　　　　Swinton 10
　　　　　PILKINGTON RECS 4 v. Wigan 10

1977-78　DEWSBURY CELTIC 5 v. Wigan 15
　　　　　PILKINGTON RECS 22 v. Castleford 23

1978-79　LEIGH MINERS' WELFARE 10 v.
　　　　　　　　　Leigh 23
　　　　　Oldham 23 v. ACE AMATEURS 5

1979-80　ACE AMATEURS 5 v. Widnes 22
　　　　　Hull 33 v. MILLOM 10

1980-81　PILKINGTON RECS 7 v. York 18

　　　　　　　Preliminary round
1985-86　Hull 38 v. DUDLEY HILL 10
　　　　　Hunslet 20 v. KELLS 8

　　　　　　　Preliminary round
1986-87　Castleford 74 v. BLACKBROOK 6
　　　　　ELLAND 6 v. HEWORTH 10
　　　　　KELLS 4 v. Fulham 4
　　　　　　　Replay
　　　　　Fulham 22 v. KELLS 14
　　　　　　　First Round
　　　　　Mansfield M. 14 v. HEWORTH 7

CHALLENGE CUP PROGRESS CHART

Key: W — Winners. F — Beaten finalists. SF — Semi-final. P — Preliminary round.

	1986-87	1985-86	1984-85	1983-84	1982-83	1981-82	1980-81	1979-80	1978-79	1977-78	1976-77	1975-76	1974-75	1973-74	1972-73	1971-72	1970-71	1969-70	1968-69	1967-68	1966-67	1965-66
BARROW	2	2	P	1	2	2	1	2	3	1	2	1	1	1	1	2	1	2	1	1	F	2
BATLEY	1	1	1	1	1	2	1	1	1	1	1	1	1	1	1	1	1	1	1	1	2	1
BLACKPOOL B.	1	2	1	1	1	1	1	1	1	1	1	1	1	1	1	1	1	1	1	1	1	1
BRADFORD N.	2	3	3	3	SF	3	1	3	SF	3	3	2	3	3	F	2	1	1	2	2	1	3
BRAMLEY	1	2	3	1	1	1	1	1	2	1	1	1	1	2	1	3	3	2	2	2	1	1
CARLISLE	2	1	1	P	1	1																
CASTLEFORD	1	W	SF	3	SF	SF	2	2	3	3	3	1	1	1	SF	2	SF	W	W	3	3	1
DEWSBURY	1	1	1	1	1	1	2	1	2	1	3	1	1	SF	SF	1	2	1	1	1	SF	SF
DONCASTER	1	2	P	2	1	1	1	1	1	1	1	2	1	1	1	1	1	3	1	1	2	1
FEATHERSTONE R.	1	1	P	1	W	P	3	1	1	SF	2	SF	1	F	W	2	2	1	2	3	W	2
FULHAM	1	1	1	2	2	2	1															
HALIFAX	W	1	2	1	2	3	2	SF	1	1	1	1	1	1	1	SF	1	1	1	2	1	1
HUDDERSFIELD B.	1	1	1	1	1	1	1	2	3	3	1	1	1	1	1	2	SF	2	2	SF	1	3
HULL	3	1	F	2	F	W	2	F	3	2	2	1	2	1	2	2	3	1	1	1	3	2
HULL K.R.	3	F	SF	3	1	2	F	W	2	1	SF	2	3	2	2	1	1	SF	1	1	2	3
HUNSLET	2	1	3	2	3	1	1	1	1	2	1	2	3	1	2	1	2	1	1	1	1	1
KEIGHLEY	2	1	1	1	1	2	1	2	1	1	SF	1	1	1	1	2	1	2	3	1	1	
LEEDS	3	SF	1	SF	2	SF	1	2	1	W	W	3	SF	3	1	F	F	3	3	W	SF	SF
LEIGH	SF	3	2	1	1	3	2	1	2	1	1	3	2	SF	2	2	W	3	1	2	1	2
MANSFIELD M.	2	P	1																			
OLDHAM	2	SF	1	2	1	2	3	2	2	2	1	3	3	1	3	1	1	2	2	3	2	1
ROCHDALE H.	1	2	2	1	1	2	1	2	2	1	2	1	2	2	1	1	1	2	3	1	1	1
RUNCORN H.	1	1	2	1	2	1	1	1	1	1	1	2	1	1	1	2	1	1	2	1	2	1
ST. HELENS	F	2	1	3	3	1	SF	2	SF	F	SF	W	2	3	2	W	2	SF	3	1	1	W
SALFORD	1	1	2	1	2	1	3	3	1	2	2	2	2	1	1	3	3	F	2	3	1	
SHEFFIELD E.	1	1	1																			
SWINTON	P	P	1	P	2	1	1	1	1	2	2	1	2	1	3	3	2	1	1	3	2	
WAKEFIELD T.	2	1	2	2	2	3	3	3	F	2	2	1	SF	1	3	3	1	1	SF	F	2	1
WARRINGTON	1	2	2	2	3	1	SF	3	1	SF	1	3	F	W	3	SF	2	2	SF	1	1	3
WHITEHAVEN	3	1	1	1	1	1	1	1	1	1	1	1	1	1	1	1	1	1	1	1	1	1
WIDNES	SF	3	3	W	1	F	W	SF	W	3	F	F	W	2	2	1	2	1	3	2	1	2
WIGAN	1	3	W	F	1	2	1	1	2	2	2	2	3	3	2	2	F	2	SF	2	F	
WORKINGTON T.	P	1	2	2	3	2	2	1	2	3	2	2	2	2	1	1	1	2	2	1	2	2
YORK	P	2	1	SF	1	1	2	2	1	1	1	2	2	1	3	1	1	1	2	2	1	

JOHN PLAYER SPECIAL TROPHY

1986-87 Final

The euphoria surrounding Warrington's installation as pre-match favourites proved to be the perfect motivation ... for Wigan.

The Wire arrived at Bolton Wanderers' soccer ground — staging a major Rugby League occasion for the first time — on the crest of a wave. A winning run of 14 matches, four successive victories against Wigan; the most recent only nine days earlier; two consecutive Team of the Month awards; a superb 35-4 annihilation of Widnes in the semi-finals; and the most highly rated pack of forwards.

Their macho pride dented, Wigan rewrote the record books with an 18-4 victory, scoring four tries to one. The historic Burnden Park triumph signalled the first time a team had retained the John Player Special Trophy, the widest winning margin and equalled Warrington's own record of three final wins.

Wigan's forwards took on the feared Warrington six ... and won. Superbly led by Kiwi skipper Graeme West, the determined spirit of the Riversiders was typified by second row partners Ian Potter, coming straight back from a knee operation, and Australian Ian Roberts, playing on with a split lip which later required 10 stitches.

Warrington were hampered by the unavailability through suspension of half back Paul Bishop, the half-time retirement through injury of their most effective forward, hooker Kevin Tamati, and the ineffectiveness of captain Les Boyd.

Their Australian prop appeared to be carrying an injury which progressively hampered his contribution, until in the last half hour he handled the ball only five times and made just two tackles.

Great Britain wingman Henderson Gill opened the scoring after only eight minutes,

following an orthodox crossfield back movement with centre Dean Bell straightening up to provide the perfect service.

Warrington's riposte was equally effective as Tamati sent loose forward Mike Gregory tearing down the middle to feed scrum half Steve Peters. His long pass was scooped up off the floor by winger Mark Forster for a diving try, the score remaining level 4-4 up to the interval.

With Tamati kept in the dressing room with a hamstring injury, Warrington moved second row man Mark Roberts to hooker, who succeeded in reversing the scrummaging figures to give the Wire a 5-1 second half advantage.

But it was Wigan who took the initiative and 15 minutes after the break, Gill popped up in the centre position, sold an outrageous dummy and swept through virtually unopposed for his second touchdown, his kick bouncing back off an upright.

Midway through the half and only four points adrift, typically adventurous Warrington full back Brian Johnson attempted to chip over Andy Goodway's head. The Great Britain packman plucked the ball out of the air and raced 65 yards for a spectacular touchdown which clinched Wigan's retention of the trophy, especially when Gill added the goal for a 10-point lead.

There was no outstanding individual performance and Goodway's individual try probably swung the vote for the £200 Man of the Match award in his favour, ahead of candidates such as West, scrum half Shaun Edwards, full back Steve Hampson, two-try Gill and Kiwi Test star Bell, who rounded off the scoring with a clean cut 79th minute touchdown.

Burnden Park proved the ideal venue with the underground-heated pitch providing a perfect playing surface on a freezing day and a crowd of 21,144 — the third highest in the tournament's history — paying a record £86,041.

JOHN PLAYER SPECIAL TROPHY FINAL

10th January   **Bolton Wanderers FC**

WARRINGTON 4		WIGAN 18
Brian Johnson	1.	Steve Hampson
Kevin Meadows	2.	David Stephenson
Paul Cullen	3.	Joe Lydon
Joe Ropati	4.	Dean Bell
Mark Forster	5.	Henderson Gill
Ken Kelly	6.	Ellery Hanley
Steve Peters	7.	Shaun Edwards
Les Boyd, Capt.	8.	Graeme West, Capt.
Kevin Tamati	9.	Martin Dermott
Bob Jackson	10.	Brian Case
Gary Sanderson	11.	Ian Roberts
Mark Roberts	12.	Ian Potter
Mike Gregory	13.	Andy Goodway
Ronnie Duane	14.	Mike Ford
Alan Rathbone	15.	Rob Louw

T: Forster

Substitutions:

Rathbone for Tamati (Half-time)

Duane for Peters (63 min.)

Attendance: 21,144

T: Gill (2), Goodway, Bell

G: Gill

Half-time: 4-4

Referee: John Holdsworth (Kippax)

Coach Graham Lowe holds the John Player Special Trophy in the jubilant Wigan dressing room.

Wigan Test winger Henderson Gill scores the first of his two touchdowns.

Veteran Warrington stand-off Ken Kelly hands off Wigan hooker Martin Dermott.

1986-87 Round by Round

Hull amateur side Myson produced the giant-killing act of the four-tie preliminary round, knocking out Second Division Batley at Mount Pleasant. The Humbersiders' 8-2 shock victory was only the second success by an amateur outfit in the 16-year history of the John Player tournament. Half backs Stuart Sawyers and Mark Powley were the Myson heroes, Sawyers opening their account with a penalty goal before hitting the upright for the ball to bounce back and be fed to Powley for the only touchdown of the game, Sawyers adding the goal. The other amateur entrants, Millom, attracted a crowd of around 2,000 for their home tie with First Division Wakefield Trinity, staged on their own pitch on a Saturday afternoon, but damaged their cause by having scrum half O'Brien sent off. Two-try John Beattie was outstanding for Workington Town as the Cumbrians won 16-6 in a hard fought game against Huddersfield Barracudas at Derwent Park. Halifax winger Wilf George scored his first hat-trick for the club in a fast moving 38-23 victory over York at Thrum Hall.

In the first round, Second Division Doncaster sent shock tremors through the 13-a-side code by disposing of the mighty Hull K.R., John Player Special Trophy finalists for the past two years. Two late David Noble penalty goals sealed Doncaster's 18-14 win, each side having scored three tries. A spirited Doncaster display reduced Rovers' star-studded side — featuring 11 Test players — to a bout of nerves, typified by 25-cap Australian Kerry Boustead dropping the ball with the line wide open for what would have been the match-winning try. Hull amateurs Myson earned a standing ovation after holding Second Division pacesetters Swinton to 18-11 at Craven Park after leading the professionals 7-6 at half-time. Holders Wigan opened their try account

after only 22 seconds in the home tie with Leeds without a pass being made. From the kick off, Joe Lydon booted the ball upfield for loose forward Andy Goodway to win the race for the line. Wigan went on to win 32-10 with stand off Ellery Hanley celebrating his return after a knee injury with a brace of tries. Second Division Whitehaven held league leaders St. Helens to a two-point margin in a tight encounter at the Recreation Ground. Level 2-2 at the break, Saints pulled 10-2 ahead with tries from Australian imports Phil Veivers and Pat Jarvis, before a David Lightfoot try and Graham Cameron goal set up a thrilling finish and a 10-8 victory.

Widnes broke a 34-year club record by piling up 82 points without reply in the home tie against troubled Dewsbury. Scrum half David Hulme led the 17-try rout with a club record-equalling five touchdowns, Test winger John Basnett grabbing a hat-trick. Unbeaten Second Division leaders Hunslet travelled to Warrington and gave the title contenders a fright by deservedly leading 10-6 at the interval. The Wire, shorthanded following the dismissal of hooker Kevin Tamati, produced a second half match-winner in half back Paul Bishop, who sent over two goals and a drop goal to clinch an 11-10 success. Hull centre Garry Schofield confirmed his £150,000 rating by snatching two opportunist tries in the last four minutes at Salford to take the Airlie Birds from 15-12 to a comfortable 27-12 victory. Bradford Northern gained quick revenge for a home league defeat by Oldham a week earlier by travelling to the Watersheddings for a 22-12 victory, highlighted by an outstanding performance from Welsh RU scrum half Terry Holmes, the scorer of an early try and creator of a Dick Jasiewicz touchdown which put Northern on the route to success at 16-6.

A hat-trick of tries by local product Tony Kay, including a spectacular 80-yard effort, was the bright spot of Barrow's 36-10 home triumph over Runcorn Highfield. Stand off Tommy Frodsham bagged a club record-equalling four tries in Blackpool Borough's 42-12 victory over visitors Mansfield Marksman, while Leigh centre John Henderson contributed two outstanding touchdowns in their 32-10 home success over Rochdale Hornets. Fulham's never-say-die spirit tested Challenge Cup holders Castleford at Chiswick, the Londoners' chances being rocked by the dismissal of Bob Knight after only 17 minutes. Gary Lord scored a hat-trick of tries in Castleford's 34-24 victory, after being held to 12-apiece at the interval, Fulham having the last word with the final two touchdowns.

First Division strugglers Featherstone Rovers won 22-18 but were matched for all but the last 10 minutes by Second Division visitors Workington Town. At 16-14, the Colliers secured success with a Paul Lyman try and Deryck Fox goal, Town hitting back with an Errol Hillier try. Colin Whitfield was the star of Halifax's 36-22 win over Wakefield Trinity, hitting eight goals from nine attempts and adding a try for a 20-point haul, while Sheffield Eagles were flattered by the 14-6 winning margin over Bramley at Owlerton Stadium. Craig Miller's try and a Paul Kuhnamann goal coming in the final seconds. Second row man Steve Kirkby scored the only try in Carlisle's 8-2 success over Keighley, the match being switched from Carlisle to Penrith because of water-logging.

The second round was highlighted by a magnificent St. Helens comeback in the televised tie at Castleford, Saints winning 26-22. After a scoreless opening 25 minutes, Castleford staged an 11-minute scoring burst to lead 16-0 at the break. A pep talk from the inimitable Alex Murphy inspired the Saints to run in 26 points in a blistering 21-minute spell, with scrum half Neil Holding outstanding. Wigan skipper Graeme

West was sent off after only 11 minutes of the home clash with Swinton, the Second Division battlers, restricting the Riversiders to two Henderson Gill penalties in the second half as they fought back with tries from Roby Muller and Derek Bate. Wigan's 20-14 victory was not convincing. In a battle of the forwards at Post Office Road, Bradford Northern winger Phil Ford proved to be the matchwinner with two tries and two drop goals as Featherstone Rovers crashed 19-12. In their second John Player Special Trophy match in four days, Carlisle went down 36-6 at Widnes. The Chemics led 20-0 at the break, Carlisle opening the second half scoring with a Gary Peacham try and Peter Subritzky goal before a drab home side opened up a 30-point winning margin.

Having been at the receiving end of a series of hammerings, Hull took advantage of Blackpool Borough conceding home territory because of the ground safety restrictions, to win 48-22, led by Kiwi hat-trick merchant Dane O'Hara. Test centre Schofield notched the 100th try of his short career with the first of two touchdowns. Doncaster could not repeat their giant-killing act of the first round, going down 26-14 at Leigh, the home side rapidly opening a 14-2 lead with Doncaster hampering their chances with a succession of handling blunders. Halifax dropped key backs Whitfield and Gary Stephens for the visit to Warrington because of their lateness for training and gave former Salford loose forward John Pendlebury a tough debut at scrum-half. Warrington, who romped to a 44-10 victory, well served by their Australian contingent, skipper Les Boyd and Bob Jackson dominant up front and full back Brian Johnson adding a hat-trick of tries. Despite the absence of four regular players through illness, Second Division Sheffield Eagles proved a threat to First Division visitors Barrow, opening the scoring after only two minutes with a Gary Smith try.

Roy Rafferty was especially missed for his marksmanship, five goal attempts going astray before the Cumbrians clinched a 14-8 victory with a David Cairns try nine minutes from time.

The quarter-final stage saw St. Helens fail yet again in their quest for a John Player final place. The league leaders were thwarted 22-20 by visitors Warrington who built a 14-8 interval lead inspired by skipper Boyd before Saints responded with tries from Steve Halliwell and substitute Roy Haggerty. Back came Warrington to clinch the semi-final spot with a late match winning touchdown from former St. Helens winger Kevin Meadows. Great Britain centre Schofield brightened a dour tie in the Odsal mud as Hull defeated Bradford Northern 20-8 in the televised encounter. A Schofield hat-trick featured two glorious interception tries, the final effort being a 90-yard run across the heavy ground. Wigan kept a grip on the John Player Special Trophy by knocking out neighbours Leigh 6-2 in a defence-orientated contest. Penalty goals from Wigan's David Stephenson and visiting full back Chris Johnson provided a 2-2 scoreline until the 30th minute when Hanley produced a superb 70-yard touchdown which proved to be the match winning effort. Widnes qualified for their ninth John Player semi-final appearance with a 16-6 success at Barrow. Having fought back to trail 10-6 through a Stewart Williams try, Barrow fell for the old trick of a try from acting half back, executed by Australian hooker Phil McKenzie.

In the first semi-final at Leeds, underdogs Hull shook favourites Wigan before losing 12-11, Hanley again providing the match winning difference. The Humbersiders' Hull-born pack outplayed Wigan's United Nations outfit and earned an 11-6 second half lead when Welsh recruit Gary Pearce added the goal to his own try. But Hanley scored his second try for wing partner Gill to add the clinching goal to give Wigan their third final appearance in five years. A week later, Warrington continued their winning run with a 35-4 rout of Widnes at Wigan. Full back Johnson and centre Paul Cullen each touched down twice as Widnes could only muster a Paul Hulme try in reply. A series of melées resulted in a private battle between scrum half rivals Paul Bishop and Paul Hulme developing into a 50th-minute double dismissal.

Warrington half-back Paul Bishop, sent off in the semi-final victory.

1986-87 PRIZES

Round	Per Team	Total
Preliminary	8 × £ 800	£ 6,400
First	16 × £ 800	£12,800
Second	8 × £ 1,100	£ 8,800
Quarter-Finals	4 × £ 1,700	£ 6,800
Semi-Finals	2 × £ 3,000	£ 6,000
Runners-up	1 × £ 6,000	£ 6,000
Winners	1 × £12,000	£12,000

Total Prizes	£58,800
Capital Development Fund	£26,200
Grand Total	£85,000

RESULTS 1986-87

Preliminary Round

Batley	2	Myson	8
Halifax	38	York	23
Millom	4	Wakefield T.	18
Workington T.	16	Huddersfield B.	6

First Round

Barrow	36	Runcorn H.	10
Blackpool B.	42	Mansfield M.	12
Carlisle	8	Keighley	2
(at Penrith)			
Doncaster	18	Hull K.R.	14
Featherstone R.	22	Workington T.	18
Fulham	24	Castleford	34
Halifax	36	Wakefield T.	22
Leigh	32	Rochdale H.	10
Myson	11	Swinton	18
(at Hull K.R.)			
Oldham	12	Bradford N.	22
Salford	12	Hull	27
Sheffield E.	14	Bramley	6
Warrington	11	Hunslet	10
Whitehaven	8	St. Helens	10
Widnes	82	Dewsbury	0
Wigan	32	Leeds	10

Second Round

Blackpool B.	22	Hull	48
		(at Hull)	
Castleford	22	St. Helens	26
Featherstone R.	12	Bradford N.	19
Leigh	26	Doncaster	14
Sheffield E.	8	Barrow	14
Warrington	44	Halifax	10
Widnes	36	Carlisle	6
Wigan	20	Swinton	14

Quarter Finals

Barrow	6	Widnes	16
Bradford N.	8	Hull	20
St. Helens	20	Warrington	22
Wigan	6	Leigh	2

Semi-Finals

Hull	11	Wigan	12
(at Leeds)			
Widnes	4	Warrington	35
(at Wigan)			

Final

Wigan	18	Warrington	4
(at Bolton W. FC)			

JOHN PLAYER SPECIAL TROPHY ROLL OF HONOUR

Season	Winners		Runners-up		Venue	Attendance	Receipts
1971-72	Halifax	22	Wakefield T.	11	Bradford	7,975	£2,545
1972-73	Leeds	12	Salford	7	Huddersfield	10,102	£4,563
1973-74	Warrington	27	Rochdale H.	16	Wigan	9,347	£4,380
1974-75	Bradford N.	3	Widnes	2	Warrington	5,935	£3,305
1975-76	Widnes	19	Hull	13	Leeds	9,035	£6,275
1976-77	Castleford	25	Blackpool B.	15	Salford	4,512	£2,919
1977-78	Warrington	9	Widnes	4	St. Helens	10,258	£8,429
1978-79	Widnes	16	Warrington	4	St. Helens	10,743	£11,709
1979-80	Bradford N.	6	Widnes	0	Leeds	9,909	£11,560
1980-81	Warrington	12	Barrow	5	Wigan	12,820	£21,020
1981-82	Hull	12	Hull K.R.	4	Leeds	25,245	£42,987
1982-83	Wigan	15	Leeds	4	Elland Rd, Leeds	19,553	£49,027
1983-84	Leeds	18	Widnes	10	Wigan	9,510	£19,824
1984-85	Hull K.R.	12	Hull	0	Hull City FC	25,326	£69,555
1985-86	Wigan	11	Hull K.R.	8	Elland Rd, Leeds	17,573	£66,714
1986-87	Wigan	18	Warrington	4	Bolton W. FC	21,144	£86,041

JOHN PLAYER SPECIAL FINAL ....
A REVIEW

1971-72
Halifax 22 Hepworth; Rayner, Davies (1t),
Willicombe (1t), Kelly (1t); Burton (5g), Baker
(Sanderson); Dewhirst, Hawksley, Callon (1t),
(Reeves), Fogerty, J. Martin, Halmshaw
Wakefield T. 11 Wraith (Ward); Slater (1t),
Marston, Hegarty, Major; Topliss (1t), Harkin;
Jeanes, Morgan, Lyons, Harrison (Spencer),
Valentine (1t), N. Fox (1g)
Referee: S. Shepherd (Oldham)
1972-73
Leeds 12 Holmes (1g); Alan Smith, Hynes,
Dyl, Atkinson (2t); Hardisty, Hepworth;
Clawson (2g) (Ward), Fisher (Pickup), Jeanes,
Haigh, Cookson, Eccles
Salford 7 Charlton; Colloby, Watkins (2g),
Hesketh, Richards; Gill (P. Ward), Banner;
Ramshaw, J. Ward, Mackay, Grice (Davies),
Kirkbride, Dixon (1t)
Referee: W.H. Thompson (Huddersfield)
1973-74
Warrington 27 Whitehead (6g, 1t); M. Philbin,
Noonan (2t), Reynolds (Pickup), Bevan (1t);
Whittle, Gordon; D. Chisnall, (Nicholas 1t),
Ashcroft, Brady, Wright, Wanbon, B. Philbin
Rochdale H. 16 Crellin; Brelsford (2t), Brophy
(1t), Taylor (1t), Aspinall; Butler (Wood),
Gartland; Holliday (2g), Harris, Whitehead,
Fogerty, Sheffield, Halmshaw
Referee: D.G. Kershaw (York)
1974-75
Bradford N. 3 Carlton (1t); Francis, Ward,
Gant, D. Redfearn; Blacker, Seabourne; Earl,
Jarvis, Jackson, Joyce, Trotter, Fearnley
Widnes 2 Dutton (1g); A. Prescott, D.O'Neill,
Aspey, Anderson; Hughes, Bowden; Mills,
Elwell, Sheridan, Adams, Blackwood,
Laughton
Referee: G.F. Lindop (Wakefield)
1975-76
Widnes 19 Dutton (3g); A. Prescott, George,
Aspey, Jenkins (2t); Hughes, Bowden (1t, 1dg);
Mills, Elwell, Wood, Foran, Sheridan,
Adams (1t)
Hull 13 Stephenson; A. Macklin, Clark, Portz,
Hunter (1t); Hancock, Foulkes (Davidson);
Ramsey, Flanagan, Wardell, Boxall (2g),
Walker, Crane (2t)
Referee: J.V. Moss (Manchester)
1976-77
Castleford 25 Wraith (1t); Fenton, Joyner (1t),
P. Johnson (1t), Briggs; Burton (1t), Stephens
(1t); Khan, Spurr, A. Dickinson, Reilly, Lloyd
(5g), S. Norton

Blackpool B 15 Reynolds; Robinson, Heritage,
Machen (1t), Pitman; Marsh, Newall;
Hamilton, Allen (1t), Egan (3g, 1t), Gamble,
Groves (Hurst), M. Pattinson
Referee: M. J. Naughton (Widnes)
1977-78
Warrington 9 Finnegan; Hesford (3g), Benyon,
Wilson, Bevan (1t); K. Kelly, Gordon; Lester,
Dalgreen, Nicholas, Martyn, B. Philbin, Potter
Widnes 4 Eckersley; Wright, Aspey, George,
Woods (2g); Hughes, Bowden; Ramsey, Elwell,
Shaw (Dearden), Adams, Hull, Laughton
Referee: W.H. Thompson (Huddersfield)
1978-79
Widnes 16 Eckersley; Wright (1t), Aspey,
Hughes, Burke (3g); Moran, Bowden; Mills,
Elwell (2dg), Shaw, Dearden, Hull (1t), Adams
(2dg)
Warrington 4 Finnegan; M. Kelly, Hesford
(2g), Benyon, Sutton; K. Kelly, (Hunter),
Gordon; Lester, Waller, Nicholas, Case,
Martyn, A. Gwilliam
Referee: G.F. Lindop (Wakefield)
1979-80
Bradford N. 6 Mumby (1g); Barends, D.
Redfearn, D. Parker (1t), Gant; Stephenson
(1dg), A. Redfearn; Thompson, Bridges,
Forsyth (I. Van Bellen), Grayshon, G. Van
Bellen (Ferres), Casey
Widnes 0 Eckersley; Wright, Aspey, George,
Burke; Hughes, Bowden; Hogan (Mills),
Elwell, Shaw, L. Gorley, Hull, Adams
Referee: W.H. Thompson (Huddersfield)
1980-81
Warrington 12 Hesford (2g, 2dg); Thackray,
I. Duane, Bevan (2t), M. Kelly; K. Kelly,
A. Gwilliam; Courtney, Waller, Case, Martyn,
Potter, Hunter (Eccles)
Barrow 5 Elliott; McConnell, French, Ball (1g),
Wainwright; Mason (1t), Cairns; D. Chisnall,
Allen (Szymala), Flynn, K. James, Kirkby,
Hadley
Referee: W.H. Thompson (Huddersfield)
1981-82
Hull 12 Banks; O'Hara, Harrison, Leuluai,
Prendiville; Day, Dean (1dg) (K. Harkin);
Skerrett, Wileman (1t), Stone, Crane, L.
Crooks (4g), Norton
Hull K.R. 4 Fairbairn (2g); Hubbard, M.
Smith, Hogan, Muscroft; Hartley, P. Harkin
(Burton); Holdstock (Millington), Watkinson,
S. Crooks, Lowe, Casey, Hall
Referee: G.F. Lindop (Wakefield)
1982-83
Wigan 15 Williams; Ramsdale, Stephenson,
Whitfield (4g, 1dg), Gill (1t) (Juliff 1t); M.
Foy, Fairhurst; Shaw, Kiss, Campbell, West
(Case), Scott, Pendlebury

Leeds 4 Hague; Campbell, Wilkinson, Dyl, Andy Smith; Holmes, Dick (2g); Dickinson, Ward, Burke, Sykes, W. Heron, D. Heron
Referee: R. Campbell (Widnes)
1983-84
Leeds 18 Wilkinson; Prendiville, Creasser (5g), D. Bell, Andy Smith; Holmes (1t), Dick (1t); Keith Rayne, Ward (Squire), Kevin Rayne, Moorby, Laurie, Webb
Widnes 10 Burke (1g); Wright, Keiron O'Loughlin, Lydon (1t), Linton (1t); Hughes, Gregory; S. O'Neill, Elwell, K. Tamati, L. Gorley, Whitfield, Adams
Referee: W.H. Thompson (Huddersfield)
1984-85
Hull K.R. 12 Fairbairn; Clark (1t), Robinson, Prohm (1t), Laws; M. Smith, Harkin; Broadhurst, Watkinson, Ema, Burton, Hogan (1t), Miller
Hull 0 Kemble (Schofield); Evans, Ah Kuoi, Leuluai, O'Hara; Topliss, Sterling; Edmonds (Dannatt), Patrick, Rose, Crooks, Proctor, Divorty
Referee: S. Wall (Leigh)
1985-86
Wigan 11 Hampson; Mordt, Stephenson (1g), Hanley, Gill (Edwards); Ella, Ford (1t); Dowling (1dg), Kiss, Wane (1t), West, Goodway, Potter (Du Toit)

Hull K.R. 8 Lydiat (1t); Clark, M. Smith, Dorahy, Laws (1t); G. Smith, Harkin; Johnston (Robinson), Watkinson, Ema, Burton, Kelly, Miller
Referee: J. Holdsworth (Kippax)

1987 Man of the Match Andy Goodway.

JOHN PLAYER SPECIAL MAN OF THE MATCH

Season	Winner	Team	Position
1971-72	Bruce Burton	Halifax (v. Wakefield T.)	Stand off
1972-73	Keith Hepworth	Leeds (v. Salford)	Scrum half
1973-74	Kevin Ashcroft	Warrington (v. Rochdale H.)	Hooker
1974-75	Barry Seabourne	Bradford N. (v. Widnes)	Scrum half
1975-76	Reg Bowden	Widnes (v. Hull)	Scrum half
1976-77	Gary Stephens	Castleford	Scrum half
	Howard Allen	Blackpool B.	Hooker
1977-78	Steve Hesford	Warrington (v. Widnes)	Winger
1978-79	David Eckersley	Widnes (v. Warrington)	Full back
1979-80	Len Casey	Bradford N. (v. Widnes)	Loose forward
1980-81	Tommy Martyn	Warrington (v. Barrow)	Second row
1981-82	Trevor Skerrett	Hull (v. Hull K.R.)	Prop
1982-83	Martin Foy	Wigan (v. Leeds)	Stand off
1983-84	Mark Laurie	Leeds (v. Widnes)	Second row
1984-85	Paul Harkin	Hull K.R. (v. Hull)	Scrum half
1985-86	Paul Harkin	Hull K.R. (v. Wigan)	Scrum half
1986-87	Andy Goodway	Wigan (v. Warrington)	Loose forward

JOHN PLAYER SPECIAL TROPHY RECORDS

ALL ROUNDS

TEAM

*Highest score: Castleford 88 v. Millom 5
Biggest attendance: 25,326 Hull v. Hull K.R.
(at Hull C. FC)....... Final 1984-85

INDIVIDUAL

*Most goals: 17 by Sammy Lloyd (Castleford)
Most tries: 6 by Vince Gribbin (Whitehaven) v. Doncaster 1984-85
*Most points: 43 (17g,3t) by Sammy Lloyd (Castleford)
*The above records were achieved in the Castleford v. Millom first round tie in 1973-74.

● *BEFORE 1977-78 the competition was known as the Player's No. 6 Trophy, then the John Player Trophy. In 1983-84 it became the John Player Special Trophy. It was not until 1979-80 that semi-finals were played at neutral venues.*

JOHN PLAYER SPECIAL TROPHY FINAL RECORDS

Most final appearances: 6 by Widnes
Most wins: 3 by Warrington and Wigan
Most tries: No player has scored 3 or more
Most goals: 6 by Derek Whitehead (Warrington) v.
Rochdale H............................. 1973-74
Most points: 15 (6g,1t) by Derek Whitehead (Warrington)
v. Rochdale H........................ 1973-74
Highest score: Warrington 27 v. Rochdale H. 16 1973-74
Widest margin win: Wigan 18 v. Warrington 4 1986-87
Biggest attendance: 25,326 Hull v. Hull K.R.
(at Hull C. FC)............... 1984-85
Biggest receipts: £86,041 Wigan v. Warrington
(at Bolton W. FC)............... 1986-87

Warrington's sole try scorer, winger Mark Forster, with Wigan centre Joe Lydon in pursuit.

NON-LEAGUE CLUBS IN THE
JOHN PLAYER SPECIAL TROPHY

Amateur clubs have entered the John Player tournament in every season apart from a period between 1981 and 1984. Two figured in the first round up to 1979-80 and one the following season. They were then left out from 1981-82 because the number of professional clubs had grown beyond the mathematically suitable 32.

But the amateurs returned in 1984-85 with two clubs joining the professionals in a small preliminary round.

The fate of the amateurs has varied from the record 88-5 hammering Millom received at Castleford to victories by Cawoods and Myson over Halifax and Batley respectively.

The full list of amateur clubs' results — all first round matches except where stated (P) Preliminary (2) Second Round — is:

Season							Attendance
1971-72		Wigan	33	v	Ace Amateurs (Hull)	9	2,678
		Thames Board Mill (Warr.)	7	v	Huddersfield	27	1,175
1972-73		Bramley	26	v	Pilkington Recs. (St. Helens)	5	616
		Dewsbury	22	v	Dewsbury Celtic	4	1,897
1973-74		Whitehaven	26	v	Dewsbury Celtic	3	1,276
		Castleford	88	v	Millom (Cumbria)	5	1,031
1974-75		Whitehaven	32	v	Lock Lane (Castleford)	6	537
		Doncaster	15	v	Kippax White Swan	6	453
1975-76		Salford	57	v	Mayfield (Rochdale)	3	3,449
		Barrow	16	v	Pilkington Recs. (St. Helens)	9	612
1976-77		Halifax	24	v	Ovenden (Halifax)	4	3,680
		Salford	39	v	Ace Amateurs (Hull)	15	3,037
1977-78		N.D.L.B. (Hull)	4	v	New Hunslet	18	3,845
		Halifax	8	v	Cawoods (Hull)	9	1,168
	(2)	Wakefield T.	31	v	Cawoods (Hull)	7	3,380
1978-79		Leigh Miners Welfare	9	v	Halifax	21	1,621
		Milford (Leeds)	5	v	Dewsbury	38	3,129
1979-80		Pilkington Recs. (St. Helens)	9	v	Wigan	18	6,707
		Blackpool B.	6	v	West Hull	3	555
1980-81		Castleford	30	v	Pilkington Recs. (St. Helens)	17	2,823
1984-85	(P)	Myson (Hull)	2	v	Dewsbury	8	1,572
	(P)	Keighley	24	v	Dudley Hill (Bradford)	10	1,570
1985-86	(P)	Keighley	24	v	Jubilee (Featherstone)	6	1,007
	(P)	West Hull	10	v	Castleford	24	2,500
1986-87	(P)	Batley	2	v	Myson (Hull)	8	687
	(P)	Millom (Cumbria)	4	v	Wakefield T.	18	2,000
		Myson (Hull)	11	v	Swinton	18	1,648

JOHN PLAYER SPECIAL TROPHY PROGRESS CHART

Key: W — Winners. F — Beaten finalists. SF — Semi-final. P — Preliminary round.

	1986-87	1985-86	1984-85	1983-84	1982-83	1981-82	1980-81	1979-80	1978-79	1977-78	1976-77	1975-76	1974-75	1973-74	1972-73	1971-72
BARROW	3	2	1	2	3	3	F	1	1	1	1	2	1	1	1	3
BATLEY	P	1	1	P	1	1	1	1	1	1	1	2	1	1	2	1
BLACKPOOL B.	2	1	1	1	2	P	2	2	1	1	F	1	1	1	1	3
BRADFORD N.	3	2	2	1	3	2	1	W	SF	SF	2	1	W	1	3	1
BRAMLEY	1	1	3	*	1	1	1	2	1	1	2	1	2	SF	2	2
BRIDGEND				1	3	1	1									
CARLISLE	2	P	P	2	2	2										
CASTLEFORD	2	1	2	1	1	2	SF	3	3	2	W	SF	1	2	1	2
DEWSBURY	1	1	3	1	1	1	1	1	2	1	1	1	1	3	2	1
DONCASTER	2	2	1	1	1	1	1	1	1	1	1	1	2	1	1	1
FEATHERSTONE R.	2	P	2	3	1	2	2	2	2	3	2	1	1	1	2	1
FULHAM	1	1	1	1	1	1	2									
HALIFAX	2	1	SF	1	1	1	3	1	2	1	2	1	1	2	1	W
HUDDERSFIELD B.	P	1	1	1	2	2	2	1	1	3	1	3	1	1	2	2
HULL	SF	3	F	2	2	W	SF	1	2	1	3	F	1	1	3	3
HULL K.R.	1	F	W	2	3	F	2	1	SF	1	1	3	SF	1	SF	2
HUNSLET	1	2	P	1	1	1	2	1	1	2	1	2	1	1	1	1
KEIGHLEY	1	2	1	2	1	2	1	2	3	2	1	1	2	3	1	2
LEEDS	1	1	SF	W	F	3	1	2	1	1	3	2	3	3	W	SF
LEIGH	3	SF	1	SF	2	1	3	3	3	3	SF	2	1	2	2	1
MANSFIELD M.	1	1	1													
OLDHAM	1	2	2	1	1	SF	1	1	1	2	2	2	2	1	1	1
ROCHDALE H.	1	1	2	1	2	1	1	1	1	1	1	1	1	F	1	2
RUNCORN H.	1	1	2	2	P	1	1	1	1	1	1	1	2	1	1	1
ST. HELENS	3	SF	3	SF	2	1	1	2	2	2	2	3	1	SF	SF	SF
SALFORD	1	2	1	2	3	3	2	SF	2	2	2	SF	3	2	F	1
SHEFFIELD E.	2	1	1													
SOUTHEND I.				P	1											
SWINTON	2	1	1	3	1	SF	1	1	1	1	1	1	3	1	3	1
WAKEFIELD T.	1	2	P	1	1	1	1	SF	3	SF	1	2	2	3	2	F
WARRINGTON	F	3	1	2	SF	2	W	3	F	W	1	1	3	W	1	1
WHITEHAVEN	1	1	2	P	1	1	3	1	1	1	1	1	SF	2	1	2
WIDNES	SF	3	3	F	SF	3	3	F	W	F	SF	W	F	1	3	1
WIGAN	W	W	2	3	W	1	1	2	2	3	2	2	2	2	1	3
WORKINGTON T.	1	1	1	1	1	2	1	3	2	2	3	3	1	2	1	1
YORK	P	3	1	1	2	1	2	2	1	1	3	1	2	2	2	2

*Bramley withdrew from the Trophy while in liquidation, opponents Hull K.R. receiving a bye.

PREMIERSHIP TROPHY

1987 Final

The planned bright end to the season with a first-ever Stones Bitter Premiership Trophy doubleheader was clouded by a dour First Division final at a cold, rainy Old Trafford.

A Premiership record crowd of 38,756 at Manchester United's soccer ground had only a Joe Lydon spectacular try and two top-class defences to warm them as Wigan collected their fourth trophy of the campaign by defeating the holders.

Lydon's 35th minute touchdown not only sealed the match but earned him the Harry Sunderland Trophy as Man of the Match, the first winger to win the award. The Great Britain star also added a series of vital tactical kicks, including an almighty 70-yard effort which ran into touch just before the corner flag.

The former Widnes utility man became only the fourth player to receive both of the code's top match awards, the Lance Todd Trophy — in the 1984 Challenge Cup final — and the Harry Sunderland Trophy.

Scrum half Andy Gregory began the thrilling tryscoring move with a short kick through from within his own 25-yard zone. As Gregory fell to the ground, referee Kevin Allatt allowed advantage for Lydon to show perfect ball control to kick it on three times.

The Wigan winger remained calm under intense pressure from fellow Test player Des Drummond to regather possession and force his way over despite the attentions of two Warrington defenders.

Centre David Stephenson had opened the scoring with a second minute penalty goal while wing partner Henderson Gill closed their account with a penalty goal five minutes from time for Wigan to lift the Premiership Trophy for the first time.

Warrington, lacking key figures in injured hooker Mark Roskell, stand off Keith Holden and skipper Les Boyd, were forced to build a defensive wall in a determined bid to retain the trophy from third place in the final table.

Acting captain Bob Jackson led by example to run Lydon close for the Man of the Match award. Without a specialist hooker, Warrington lost the scrums 12-6, but were given a 19-8 penalty count boost.

Warrington second row man Gary Sanderson touched down shortly after the interval, the score being disallowed.

Wigan failed to find the spark which had set the Stones Bitter Championship trail alight with a record haul of tries and points. Ellery Hanley never looked like scoring the hat-trick of tries he needed to equal Johnny Ring's 61-year-old club record of 62 tries in a season, while Shaun Edwards' lack of full fitness was apparent when he was put clear minutes from the end and had to pass inside with an open line beckoning.

Wigan skipper Hanley collected the Stones Bitter Premiership Trophy to round off a highly successful Old Trafford promotion, the Central Park coffers receiving a further £9,000 prize money. Warrington earned a runners-up consolation prize of £3,500 as both clubs collected £40,000 as their third share from a record £165,166 gate, three times the previous best return.

Warrington's Gary Sanderson, disallowed a second half touchdown.

STONES BITTER PREMIERSHIP FINAL

17th May　　　　　　**Old Trafford, Manchester**

WARRINGTON 0　　　　　　　　　　　**WIGAN 8**

Brian Johnson	1.	Steve Hampson
Des Drummond	2.	Henderson Gill
Joe Ropati	3.	David Stephenson
Barry Peters	4.	Dean Bell
Mark Forster	5.	Joe Lydon
Paul Cullen	6.	Shaun Edwards
Paul Bishop	7.	Andy Gregory
Kevin Tamati	8.	Brian Case
Mark Roberts	9.	Nicky Kiss
Bob Jackson, Capt.	10.	Shaun Wane
Tony Humphries	11.	Andy Goodway
Gary Sanderson	12.	Ian Potter
Ronnie Duane	13.	Ellery Hanley, Capt.
Mike Gregory	14.	Richard Russell
Bob Eccles	15.	Graeme West

Substitutions:　　　　　　　　　　　T: Lydon
Gregory for Humphries (Half-time)　　G: Stephenson, Gill
Eccles for Roberts (54 min.)　　　　　Substitutions:
Half-time: 0-6　　　　　　　　　　　West for Wane (46 min.)
Referee: Kevin Allatt (Southport)　　Russell for Lydon (75 min.)
　　　　　　　　　　　　　　　　　　Attendance: 38,756

1987 Round by Round

Challenge Cup finalists Halifax were the only side to reverse the form guide in the first round. The Thrum Hall side travelled to Castleford and produced a storming second half display to dispose of the fourth-placed club, 18-6. They were 4-0 down at the break but struck a double blow early in the second half with two tries in three minutes from wingers Scott Wilson and Eddie Riddlesden. Castleford reduced the arrears with a Martin Ketteridge penalty goal, only for visiting centre Tony Anderson to seal a semi-final spot with two tries in the final five minutes.

Champions Wigan were given a mighty fright by eighth-placed Widnes before winning 22-18. Widnes secured a shock 14-6 half-time lead through tries by John Basnett and Darren Wright. The Riversiders rallied after the break and their composure was rewarded with a try from full back Steve Hampson, Dean Bell's second touchdown

levelling the scores at 14-apiece. Joe Lydon virtually sealed victory with a try against his former club, although Chemics' loose forward Harry Pinner set up a nail biting finish with a late try.

After a run of three successive defeats, St. Helens received a Wembley confidence booster with a 46-14 success at home to Bradford Northern. Saints secured a semi-final placing in the first half with four tries in 11 minutes to lead 24-2 at the break. Northern trailed 46-2 to a Neil Holding-inspired home side, until late tries from Wayne Race and Paul Harkin brought some consolation.

Holders Warrington entertained sixth-placed Hull K.R. and built a commanding 18-2 interval lead before Rovers rallied with a second half purple patch which brought tries for Gordon and Steve Smith. Any hopes of a shock comeback were dashed when second row man Andy Kelly was sent off after a midfield punch up and Warrington finished convincing 24-12 winners.

In the semi-finals, Wigan left it to the final five minutes to clinch an 18-10 victory over Challenge Cup winners Halifax. Showing no signs of Wembley weariness, the Thrum Hall men had shaken the Wigan section of the 22,443 crowd by taking a 6-0 interval lead. High speed tries from Andy Goodway, Joe Lydon and Steve Hampson put Wigan in front for the first time, before Halifax pulled back to trail only 12-10 with a Scott Wilson touchdown. With Colin Whitfield missing three simple kicks, while hitting one to create a new Halifax points record of 298 in a season, Wigan sealed victory with a David Stephenson try.

Warrington qualified to meet Wigan in a repeat of the 1987 John Player Special Trophy final by disposing of St. Helens 18-8 at Knowsley Road. Saints led at the break, but tries from winger Des Drummond and full back Brian Johnson sealed Warrington's passage into their second successive Premiership final.

1987 Results

First Round

Castleford	6	Halifax	18
St. Helens	46	Bradford N.	14
Warrington	24	Hull K.R.	12
Wigan	22	Widnes	18

Semi-Finals

St. Helens	8	Warrington	18
Wigan	18	Halifax	10

Final

Wigan	8	Warrington	0

(at Old Trafford, Manchester)

1987 Prizes:

Winners	£9,000
Runners-up	£3,500

History

With the reintroduction of two divisions in 1973-74 there was no longer a need for a play-off to decide the championship.

However, it was decided to continue the tradition of an end-of-season play-off, the winners to receive the newly instituted Premiership Trophy.

In the first season of the Premiership, 1974-75, the top 12 Division One clubs and the top four from Division Two went into a first round draw, the luck of the draw operating through to the final, played on a neutral venue.

The following season the play-off was reduced to the top eight clubs in the First Division, the ties being decided on a merit basis i.e. 1st v. 8th, 2nd v. 7th etc. At the semi-final stage the highest placed clubs had the option of when to play at home in the two-legged tie.

In 1978-79 the two-leg system was suspended because of fixture congestion and the higher placed clubs had home advantage right through to the neutrally staged final.

Two legs returned the following season, but were finally abolished from 1980-81.

A Second Division Premiership tournament was introduced for the first time in 1986-87.

PREMIERSHIP ROLL OF HONOUR

Year	Winners		Runners-up		Venue	Attendance	Receipts
1975	Leeds	26	St. Helens	11	Wigan	14,531	£7,795
1976	St. Helens	15	Salford	2	Swinton	18,082	£13,138
1977	St. Helens	32	Warrington	20	Swinton	11,178	£11,626
1978	Bradford N.	17	Widnes	8	Swinton	16,813	£18,677
1979	Leeds	24	Bradford N.	2	Huddersfield	19,486	£21,291
1980	Widnes	19	Bradford N.	5	Swinton	10,215	£13,665
1981	Hull K.R.	11	Hull	7	Leeds	29,448	£47,529
1982	Widnes	23	Hull	8	Leeds	12,100	£23,749
1983	Widnes	22	Hull	10	Leeds	17,813	£34,145
1984	Hull K.R.	18	Castleford	10	Leeds	12,515	£31,769
1985	St. Helens	36	Hull K.R.	16	Elland Rd, Leeds	15,518	£46,950
1986	Warrington	38	Halifax	10	Elland Rd, Leeds	13,683	£50,879
1987	Wigan	8	Warrington	0	Old Trafford, Man'r	38,756	£165,166

Trophy number four. . . Wigan celebrate the capture of the Stones Bitter Premiership Trophy.

Sole tryscorer and Harry Sunderland Trophy winner Joe Lydon, subjected to the attentions of Mark Forster (above) and Brian Johnson.

PREMIERSHIP FINAL . . . . A REVIEW

1974-75
Leeds 26 Holmes (2g) (Marshall 3g); Alan Smith (1t), Hynes (1t, 1dg) (Eccles), Dyl, Atkinson (2t), Mason (1t), Hepworth; Dickinson, Ward, Pitchford, Cookson, Batten, Haigh
St. Helens 11 G. Pimblett; L. Jones (1t), Wilson, Hull, Mathias (1t); Walsh, Heaton (1t); Warlow (Cunningham), A. Karalius, Mantle (K. Gwilliam), E. Chisnall, Nicholls, Coslett (1g)
Referee: W.H. Thompson (Huddersfield)

1975-76
St. Helens 15 G. Pimblett (3g); L. Jones, Glynn (1t), Noonan, Mathias; Benyon, Heaton (K. Gwilliam); Mantle, A. Karalius (1t), James, Nicholls, E. Chisnall (1t), Coslett
Salford 2 Watkins (2dg); Fielding, Richards, Hesketh, Graham; Butler, Nash; Coulman, Raistrick, Sheffield, Knighton (Turnbull), Dixon, E. Prescott
Referee: M. J. Naughton (Widnes)

1976-77
St. Helens 32 G. Pimblett (7g, 1t); L. Jones, Benyon (1t), Cunningham (1t), Mathias (1t), Glynn (Ashton); K. Gwilliam (1t); D. Chisnall, Liptrot, James (1t), Nicholls (A. Karalius), E. Chisnall, Pinner
Warrington 20 Finnegan; Curling, Bevan (Cunliffe), Hesford (4g), M. Kelly; A. Gwilliam (1t), Gordon (1t); Weavill (1t), Price, Case, Martyn (Peers), Lester, B. Philbin (1t)
Referee: G.F. Lindop (Wakefield)

1977-78
Bradford N. 17 Mumby (2g); Barends (1t), Roe (1t), Austin, D. Redfearn (1t) Wolford (1dg), A. Redfearn; I. Van Bellen (Fox), Raistrick, Thompson, Joyce (Forsyth), Trotter, Haigh (1t)
Widnes 8 Eckersley; Wright, Hughes, Aspey (2t), Woods (1g); Gill, Bowden; Mills, Elwell, Shaw (Ramsey) (George), Adams, Hull, Laughton
Referee: J.E. Jackson (Pudsey)

1978-79
Leeds 24 Hague; Alan Smith (1t), D. Smith (1t), Dyl (Fletcher), Atkinson; Dick (7g, 1dg); J. Sanderson, Harrison, Ward (1t), Pitchford, Joyce, Eccles (Adams), Cookson
Bradford N. 2 Mumby; D. Parker, Okulicz, Gant, Spencer; Ferres (1g), A. Redfearn; Thompson, Bridges, Forsyth (I. Van Bellen), Trotter (Mordue), Grayshon, Casey
Referee: W.H. Thompson (Huddersfield)

1979-80
Widnes 19 Burke (1g); Wright (1t), George, Aspey (1t), Bentley (1t); Eckersley (1dg), Bowden; Shaw, Elwell (1t, 1dg), M. O'Neill, L. Gorley (1t), Hull (Hogan), Adams
Bradford N. 5 Mumby (1g); MacLean (Ferres), D. Redfearn (1t), D. Parker, Gant; Stephenson, A. Redfearn; Thompson, Bridges, Forsyth, Clarkson (G. Van Bellen), Grayshon, Hale
Referee: W.H. Thompson (Huddersfield)

1980-81
Hull K.R. 11 Proctor; Hubbard (1g), M. Smith (1t), Hogan (1t), Muscroft; Hartley (1t), Harkin; Holdstock, Watkinson, Millington, Lowe, Casey, Hall (Burton)
Hull 7 Woods (2g); Peacham, Elliott, Wilby, Prendiville; Banks, Dean; Tindall, Wileman, Stone, Skerrett (Madley), Crane (1t), Norton
Referee: J. Holdsworth (Leeds)

1981-82
Widnes 23 Burke (4g, 1t); Wright (1t), Kieron O'Loughlin, Cunningham (A. Myler), Basnett (1t); Hughes (1t), Gregory; M. O'Neill, Elwell, Lockwood (Whitfield), L. Gorley, E. Prescott, Adams (1t)
Hull 8 Kemble; O'Hara (Day), Leuluai, S. Evans, Prendiville; Topliss, Harkin; Tindall, Wileman (Lloyd), Stone, Skerrett, Crooks (1t, 2g, 1dg), Norton
Referee: S. Wall (Leigh)

1982-83
Widnes 22 Burke; Linton, Hughes, Lydon (5g), Basnett (2t); A. Myler (1t), Gregory (1t) (Hulme); M. O'Neill, Elwell, L. Gorley, Whitfield (S. O'Neill), Prescott, Adams
Hull 10 Kemble; O'Hara (1t), Day (Solal), Leuluai, S. Evans; Topliss (1t), Dean; Skerrett, Bridges, Stone, Rose, Crooks (2g), Norton (Crane)
Referee: F. Lindop (Wakefield)

1983-84
Hull K.R. 18 Fairbairn; Clark, M. Smith (1t), Prohm (1t), Laws (1t); Dorahy (1t, 1g), Harkin; Holdstock, Rudd, Millington (Robinson), Burton (Lydiat), Broadhurst, Hall
Castleford 10 Roockley; Coen, Marchant, Hyde, Kear (1t); Robinson, R. Beardmore (3g); Ward, Horton, Connell, Crampton, Atkins, Joyner
Referee: R. Campbell (Widnes)

1984-85
St. Helens 36 Veivers (1t); Ledger (2t), Peters, Meninga (2t) (Allen), Day (4g); Arkwright, Holding; Burke (Forber), Ainsworth (1t), P. Gorley, Platt, Haggerty, Pinner (1t)
Hull K.R. 16 Fairbairn (1t, 2g); Clark, Robinson (1t), Prohm, Laws (1t); M. Smith, G. Smith (Harkin); Broadhurst, Watkinson, Ema (Lydiat), Kelly, Hogan, Hall
Referee: S. Wall (Leigh)

1985-86
Warrington 38 Paul Ford (Johnson 1t); Forster (1t), Cullen, R. Duane, Carbert; Bishop (1t, 5g), A. Gregory; Boyd (2t), Tamati (1t), Jackson (1t), Sanderson (McGinty), Roberts, M. Gregory
Halifax 10 Whitfield (3g) (Smith); Riddlesden, T. Anderson, C. Anderson (1t), Wilson; Crossley, Stephens; Scott, McCallion, Robinson, Juliff, James (Bond), Dixon
Referee: F. Lindop (Wakefield)

ROUND BY ROUND 1975-1986

( ) indicates position in league
( )² indicates Second Division Club

● Top 12 Division One clubs and top
four Division Two clubs went into a draw.
The luck of the draw operated through to
the final, played on a neutral ground.

1974-75
First round
(1) St. Helens 42 v. (3)² Oldham 5
(8) Castleford 37 v. (10) Wakefield T. 7
(2) Wigan 19 v. (4)² Swinton 17
(7) Bradford N. 22 v. (6) Warrington 14
(12) Dewsbury 8 v. (11) Keighley 9
(4) Featherstone R. 8 v. (3) Leeds 27
(1)² Huddersfield 18 v. (2)² Hull K.R. 35
(5) Widnes 12 v. (9) Salford 20
Second round
Wigan 35 v. Salford 17
Leeds 28 v. Castleford 8
Hull K.R. 29 v. Keighley 10
Bradford N. 5 v. St. Helens 5
Replay
St. Helens 14 v. Bradford N. 5
Semi-finals
Wigan 16 v. St. Helens 22
Leeds 18 v. Hull K.R. 8
Final
Leeds 26 v. St. Helens 11 (at Wigan)

● Format reduced to the top eight Division
One clubs, the ties being decided on a merit
basis of 1st v. 8th, 2nd v. 7th, etc. Two-legged
semi-finals with the higher placed club having
choice of home or away in first match.

1975-76
First round
(1) Salford 21 v. (8) Hull K.R. 6
(2) Featherstone R. 10 v. (7) Wakefield T. 14
(3) Leeds 12 v. (6) Widnes 2
(4) St. Helens 19 v. (5) Wigan 6
Semi-finals
First leg
Leeds 5 v. St. Helens 12
Salford 10 v. Wakefield T. 5
Second leg
St. Helens 21 v. Leeds 4
Wakefield T. 5 v. Salford 14
Final
St. Helens 15 v. Salford 2 (at Swinton)

1976-77
First round
(1) Featherstone R. 13 v. (8) Bradford N. 2
(2) St. Helens 10 v. (7) Wigan 10
(3) Castleford 25 v. (6) Salford 17
*(4) Hull K.R. 18 v. (5) Warrington 13
*Hull K.R. disqualified for playing Phil Lowe
as an ineligible player.
Replay
Wigan 3 v. St. Helens 8
Semi-finals
First leg
Castleford 12 v. St. Helens 36
Featherstone R. 17 v. Warrington 13

Second leg
St. Helens 25 v. Castleford 13
Warrington 11 v. Featherstone R. 1
Final
St. Helens 32 v. Warrington 20 (at Swinton)
1977-78
First round
(1) Widnes 33 v. *(9) Warrington 8
(2) Bradford N. 18 v. (8) Leeds 10
(3) St. Helens 29 v. (6) Salford 11
(4) Hull K.R. 17 v. (5) Wigan 0
*Warrington replaced Featherstone R.
who finished 7th but were expelled when
their players went on strike, demanding
the re-instatement of Gordon Appleyard
as chairman.
Semi-finals
First leg
Hull K.R. 12 v. Widnes 22
St. Helens 14 v. Bradford N. 10
Second leg
Bradford N. 19 v. St. Helens 12
Widnes 13 v. Hull K.R. 19
Final
Bradford N. 17 v. Widnes 8 (at Swinton)

1978-79
First round
(1) Hull K.R. 17 v. (8) Bradford N. 18
(2) Warrington 17 v. (7) Castleford 10
(3) Widnes 8 v. (6) Wigan 12
(4) Leeds 21 v. (5) St. Helens 10
Semi-finals
Leeds 20 v. Wigan 10
Warrington 11 v. Bradford N. 14
Final
Leeds 24 v. Bradford N. 2
  (at Huddersfield)
*The two-leg system was suspended
because of a fixture congestion.

1979-80
First round
(1) Bradford N. 30 v. (8) St. Helens 0
(2) Widnes 20 v. (7) Hull K.R. 10
(3) Hull 0 v. (6) Leigh 8
(4) Salford 13 v. (5) Leeds 27
Semi-finals
First leg
Leeds 14 v. Widnes 4
Leigh 12 v. Bradford N. 14
Second leg
Widnes 14 v. Leeds 3
Bradford N. 17 v. Leigh 4
Final
Widnes 19 v. Bradford N. 5 (at Swinton)

● Format amended to one-legged semi-
finals based on highest placed clubs
having home advantage.

1980-81
First round
(1) Bradford N. 12 v. (8) St. Helens 14
(2) Warrington 7 v. (7) Hull 19
(3) Hull K.R. 14 v. (6) Widnes 12
(4) Wakefield T. 8 v. (5) Castleford 25

Semi-finals
Hull K.R. 30 v. St. Helens 17
Castleford 11 v. Hull 12
Final
Hull K.R. 11 v. Hull 7 (at Leeds)
1981-82
First round
(1) Leigh 1 v. (8) Warrington 1
(2) Hull 23 v. (7) St. Helens 8
(3) Widnes 39 v. (6) Leeds 11
*(4) Hull K.R. 17 v. (5) Bradford N. 8
*Match awarded to Hull K.R. after
Bradford walked off in 56th minute.
Replay
Warrington 10 v. Leigh 9 (at Wigan)
Semi-finals
Widnes 16 v. Hull K.R. 15
Hull 27 v. Warrington 7
Final
Widnes 23 v. Hull 8 (at Leeds)

1982-83
First round
(1) Hull 24 v. (8) Oldham 21
(2) Hull K.R. 35 v. (7) Castleford 14
(3) Wigan 9 v. (6) Leeds 12
(4) St. Helens 7 v. (5) Widnes 11
Semi-finals
Hull 19 v. Leeds 5
Hull K.R. 10 v. Widnes 21
Final
Widnes 22 v. Hull 10 (at Leeds)

1983-84
First round
(1) Hull K.R. 54 v. (8) Leeds 0
(2) Hull 42 v. (7) Bradford N. 12
(3) Warrington 13 v. (6) St. Helens 19
(4) Castleford 36 v. (5) Widnes 4
Semi-finals
Hull 12 v. Castleford 22
Hull K.R. 21 v. St. Helens 16
Final
Hull K.R. 18 v. Castleford 10 (at Leeds)

1984-85
First round
(1) Hull K.R. 42 v. (8) Bradford N. 18
(2) St. Helens 26 v. (7) Widnes 2
(3) Wigan 46 v. (6) Hull 12
(4) Leeds 36 v. (5) Oldham 18
Semi-finals
Hull K.R. 15 v. Leeds 14
St. Helens 37 v. Wigan 14
Final
St. Helens 36 v. Hull K.R. 16
  (at Elland Rd, Leeds)

1985-86
First round
(1) Halifax 32 v. (8) Hull 20
(2) Wigan 47 v. (7) Hull K.R. 0
(3) St. Helens 22 v. (6) Leeds 38
(4) Warrington 10 v. (5) Widnes 8
Semi-finals
Halifax 16 v. Leeds 13
Wigan 12 v. Warrington 23
Final
Warrington 38 v. Halifax 10
  (at Elland Rd, Leeds)

THE HARRY SUNDERLAND TROPHY

The trophy, in memory of the famous Queenslander, a former Australian Tour Manager, broadcaster and journalist, is presented to the Man of the Match in the end of season Championship or Premiership final.

The award is donated and judged by the Rugby League Writers' Association and is now sponsored by Stones Bitter.

The Harry Sunderland Trophy Roll of Honour

Year	Winner	Team	Position
1965	Terry Fogerty	Halifax (v. St. Helens)	Second row
1966	Albert Halsall	St. Helens (v. Halifax)	Prop
1967	Ray Owen	Wakefield T. (v. St. Helens)	Scrum half
1968	Gary Cooper	Wakefield T. (v. Hull K.R.)	Full back
1969	Bev Risman	Leeds (v. Castleford)	Full back
1970	Frank Myler	St. Helens (v. Leeds)	Stand off
1971	Bill Ashurst	Wigan (v. St. Helens)	Second row
1972	Terry Clawson	Leeds (v. St. Helens)	Prop
1973	Mick Stephenson	Dewsbury (v. Leeds)	Hooker
1974	Barry Philbin	Warrington (v. St. Helens)	Loose forward
1975	Mel Mason	Leeds (v. St. Helens)	Stand off
1976	George Nicholls	St. Helens (v. Salford)	Second row
1977	Geoff Pimblett	St. Helens (v. Warrington)	Full back
1978	Bob Haigh	Bradford N. (v. Widnes)	Loose forward
1979	Kevin Dick	Leeds (v. Bradford N.)	Stand off
1980	Mal Aspey	Widnes (v. Bradford N.)	Centre
1981	Len Casey	Hull K.R. (v. Hull)	Second row
1982	Mick Burke	Widnes (v. Hull)	Full back
1983	Tony Myler	Widnes (v. Hull)	Stand off
1984	John Dorahy	Hull K.R. (v. Castleford)	Stand off
1985	Harry Pinner	St. Helens (v. Hull K.R.)	Loose forward
1986	Les Boyd	Warrington (v. Halifax)	Prop
1987	Joe Lydon	Wigan (v. Warrington)	Winger

PREMIERSHIP RECORDS   First staged 1975

ALL ROUNDS

TEAM

Highest score: Hull K.R. 54 v. Leeds 0 1984
(Also widest margin)
Biggest attendance: 38,756 Wigan v. Warrington
.........Final at Old Trafford 1987

INDIVIDUAL

Most goals:
9 by Andy Gregory (Widnes) v. Leeds...Round 1 1982
Most points:
22 (7g, 2t) by John Dorahy (Hull K.R.) v. Leeds
.............Round 1 1984

Most tries:
4 by David Hall (Hull K.R.) v. Castleford
.............Round 1 1983
4 by Phil Ford (Wigan) v. Hull...........Round 1 1985
4 by Ellery Hanley (Wigan) v. Hull K.R.
.............Round 1 1986

PREMIERSHIP FINAL RECORDS

TEAM

Most final appearances: 4 by Widnes, St. Helens
Most wins: 3 by Widnes, St. Helens
Highest score (and widest margin):
Warrington 38 v. Halifax 10 1986
Biggest attendance:
38,756 Wigan v. Warrington
(at Old Trafford, Man'r) 1987

INDIVIDUAL

Most tries: No player has scored 3 or more

Most goals:
8 by Kevin Dick (Leeds) v. Bradford N.............1979
Most points: 17 (7g, 1t) by Geoff Pimblett (St. Helens)
v. Warrington..........1977

SECOND DIVISION
PREMIERSHIP TROPHY

1987 Final

Hunslet hopes of a Second Division double were sent crashing by a powerhouse display from Swinton's front row forwards in the inaugural Second Division final which preceded the major final at Old Trafford.

Champions Hunslet could not hold the Station Road threesome of Joe Grima, Gary Ainsworth and Roby Muller, livewire hooker Ainsworth rounding off an impressive performance with a last minute try and the Man of the Match award.

The extremely mobile number nine had a big hand in four of the title runners-up's five tries, plus winning the scrums 11-4. The all-round display helped him to complete a unique double, having been outstanding in the victorious St. Helens side in the 1985 First Division Premiership final.

Ainsworth was flanked by the two hard-working New Zealanders, Grima grabbing Swinton's third try in the 62nd minute after all three front row men had combined in a 50-yard midfield dash.

To complete a remarkable day for front row men, Hunslet's best player was also a prop, Andy Bateman highlighting his performance by charging through for both the South Leeds side's tries.

The first touchdown saw him at his most formidable as he pounded on to Alan Platt's pass to make light of two attempted tackles and lunge over to level the scores at 4-4 in the 18th minute.

The highly effective Ainsworth had created Swinton's opening score with a blind side break to put winger Derek Bate clear for his 31st try of the season.

Les Holliday regained the lead for Swinton with a 31st minute drop goal, but it was two misses which paved the way for 12 opportunist points gained in the closing minutes of each half.

The Lions' skipper attempted a towering drop kick in the 39th minute, the ball bouncing back off the post into the hands of Alan Derbyshire who was ruled onside as the ball had touched a Hunslet player in flight, the second row man grabbing a soft try. Andy Rippon's goal gave the Manchester side an 11-4 interval lead.

The other freak score came in the 78th minute when the ball rebounded yet again for scrum half Martin Lee to gather and send in Ainsworth, Rippon adding the goal.

Swinton overcame the loss of two players. High-scoring centre Paul Topping was stretchered off in the 25th minute with a broken cheekbone, to be followed in the 66th minute by substitute Alan Ratcliffe with a broken leg, second row man Mike Holliday returning after being led off badly shaken in the 16th minute.

The highly entertaining seven-try encounter proved that the new style Second Division Premiership final was anything but second class fare and the success of the concept of a two-for-one promotion was proved correct by a turn out of more than 22,000 at the kick off to watch two teams who had been attracting a combined attendance of around 3,000 per match during the season.

Swinton received the newly commissioned Stones Bitter Premiership Trophy and a £4,000 prize cheque, while Hunslet added a consolation £1,500 to their title purse.

SECOND DIVISION PREMIERSHIP TROPHY

17th May   **Old Trafford, Manchester**

HUNSLET 10   **SWINTON 27**

Andy Kay	1.	Mark Viller
Phil Tate	2.	Derek Bate
Colin Penola	3.	Paul Topping
Jimmy Irvine	4.	Jeff Brown
Warren Wilson	5.	Andy Rippon
Ged Coates	6.	Steve Snape
Graham King	7.	Martin Lee
Andy Sykes	8.	Joe Grima
Phil Gibson	9.	Gary Ainsworth
Andy Bateman	10.	Roby Muller
Alan Platt	11.	Alan Derbyshire
Chris Bowden	12.	Mike Holliday
Graeme Jennings, Capt.	13.	Les Holliday, Capt.
Gary Senior	14.	John Allen
Keith Mason	15.	Alan Ratcliffe

T: Bateman (2)
G: Platt
Substitutions:
Senior for Gibson (30 min.)
Mason for Platt (64 min.)
Half-time: 4-11
Referee: John McDonald (Wigan)

T: Bate, Derbyshire, Grima, Lee,
Ainsworth
G: Rippon (3), L. Holliday (dg)
Substitutions:
Allen for M. Holliday (16 min.)
Ratcliffe for Topping (25 min.)

Jubilant Swinton, first-ever holders of the Stones Bitter Second Division Premiership Trophy.

169

1987 Round by Round

Champions Hunslet gained crushing revenge on eighth-placed Carlisle — one of only three sides to inflict league defeat — with a 54-0 hammering at Elland Road. The home side ran in nine tries, opening with solo efforts from winger Warren Wilson and full back Andy Kay to launch a 24-point interval lead. A further 30 points were added without reply in a one-sided second half, Hunslet's impressive all-round display being crowned by Alan Platt landing nine goals from 10 attempts.

Swinton centre Paul Topping touched down after only 54 seconds to set the tone for a 59-14 hammering of visitors Bramley. Unbeaten at home for more than 12 months, the Lions tallied 10 tries and rattled up a half century of points for the third time in the season, the second against Bramley.

Third-placed Whitehaven progressed to the semi-finals after a scare from Sheffield Eagles in a 29-24 encounter at the Recreation Ground. The Yorkshire men were the best side for an hour, leading 18-12 into the last quarter before tries from Willie Richardson, Steve Burney and Ralph McConnell, plus two Richardson goals, stretched the Cumbrians into a 28-18 lead with time fast running out.

Doncaster ran out of steam in their bid to round off a highly creditable campaign with Premiership success and went down 30-18 at home to Rochdale Hornets. In front of a crowd of 2,543, the Dons failed to find their league form and were trailing 24-2 at the break. The Tatters Field men rallied in the second period with tries from Andy Timson, Mark Gibbon and Wayne Morrell, while David Noble succeeded in adding three goals to complete his record of playing and scoring in every match during the season.

In the semi-finals, Hunslet overwhelmed an ineffective Rochdale Hornets, 32-8. The home side scored two tries in the first 16 minutes through Graham King and Graeme Jennings, though Rochdale managed to hold the score to 10-4 at half-time. Eight points from Alan Platt within 13 minutes of the restart set the title holders on the way to success, with the Hornets being well served by scrum half Steve Nash at the age of 38.

Runners-up Swinton made it a top-two clash for Old Trafford with a hard earned 12-6 victory over Whitehaven at Station Road. The Lions trailed to a Gary Hetherington try and Willie Richardson goal in injury time of the first half when Jeff Brown scored in the corner, Paul Topping adding a magnificent touchline goal. The winning try came in the 71st minute when Roby Muller crossed near the post for Topping to add a simple goal.

1987 Results

First Round

Doncaster	18	Rochdale H.	30
Hunslet	54	Carlisle	0
Swinton	59	Bramley	14
Whitehaven	29	Sheffield E.	24

Semi-Finals

| Hunslet | 32 | Rochdale H. | 8 |
| Swinton | 12 | Whitehaven | 6 |

Final

| Hunslet | 10 | Swinton | 27 |

(at Old Trafford, Manchester)

1987 Prizes

| Winners | £4,000 |
| Runners-up | £1,500 |

LANCASHIRE CUP

1986 Final

Only two weeks after languishing in the reserves, Wigan scrum half Mike Ford followed up an impressive display against the Australians by earning the Man of the Match award as the Riversiders extended their record haul of the Lancashire Cup to 18.

Big spending Wigan, fielding two New Zealanders, one Australian and a South African, relied on two of the youngest British players on the St. Helens pitch to retain the county trophy and deny Oldham their first knockout cup success for 28 years.

Ford — playing against his hometown club — highlighted a dashing performance by scoring the opening try two minutes before the interval, while the man he replaced in the number seven jersey, Shaun Edwards, revelled in his former regular full back position.

Edwards was an 11th hour switch, forcing Steve Hampson onto the substitutes bench, and he responded with a two-try show.

It was Ford who created Edwards' first touchdown 13 minutes after the break, the scrum half's 50-yard breathtaking run splitting the Oldham defence.

Ford's double burst either side of half-time was the platform for Wigan's four tries to one triumph. Oldham led 6-2 after 29 minutes through a try from Australian centre Gary Bridge, created by fellow countryman, prop Bruce Clark, who lived up to his nickname of 'Bruiser' as he sent three Wigan defenders scattering.

Ford's try, after a 50-yard burst by Kiwi Test centre Dean Bell, plus two Henderson Gill goals, gave Wigan an 8-6 interval lead.

Winger Gill justified his return to the Great Britain ranks by creating both second half tries for Wigan who began to produce the form which had amassed 154 points in the previous three Grunhalle Lager Lancashire Cup-ties.

Gill's electrifying runs set up touchdowns for Edwards and right wingman Joe Lydon, his try in the dying minutes being added to his 70th minute drop goal.

For good measure, Gill hit five goals from six attempts to run Ford and Edwards close for Man of the Match rating.

As it was, all-action Ford thoroughly deserved the individual award to stop a recent trend of overseas stars dominating the final, the last two recipients being Australians Steve Ella and Mal Meninga.

The Knowsley Road clash attracted a crowd of 20,180, only the second 20,000-plus Lancashire Cup final crowd for 22 years.

Oldham's Australian centre Gary Warnecke, tackled by Dean Bell (left) and Ellery Hanley.

GRUNHALLE LAGER LANCASHIRE CUP FINAL

19th October   St. Helens

OLDHAM 6		WIGAN 27
Hussein M'Barki	1.	Shaun Edwards
Paul Sherman	2.	Joe Lydon
Gary Bridge	3.	David Stephenson
Gary Warnecke	4.	Dean Bell
Mike Taylor	5.	Henderson Gill
David Topliss, Capt.	6.	Ellery Hanley
Paddy Kirwan	7.	Mike Ford
Bruce Clark	8.	Graeme West, Capt.
Terry Flanagan	9.	Martin Dermott
David Hobbs	10.	Brian Case
Tom Nadiole	11.	Ian Roberts
Mick Worrall	12.	Ian Potter
Stuart Raper	13.	Andy Goodway
Neil Clawson	14.	Steve Hampson
Colin Hawkyard	15.	Rob Louw

T: Bridge
G: Hobbs
Substitution:
Hawkyard for Raper (Half-time)
Half-time: 6-8
Referee: Jim Smith (Halifax)

T: Edwards (2), Ford, Lydon
G: Gill (5), Lydon (dg)
Substitution:
Louw for Roberts (67 min.)
Attendance: 20,180

1986-87 Round by Round

The eight-tie first round was marked by three high scoring affairs. St. Helens created four new scoring records with the 112-0 rout of Second Division Carlisle at Knowsley Road. As the rampaging Saints ran in 20 tries, it was a personal triumph for centre Paul Loughlin who notched a club record 40 points from two tries and 16 goals from 20 attempts. St. Helens fell seven points short of the record 119 registered by Huddersfield back in 1914. They averaged two points a minute in the second half having led 32-0 at the break, only four players not putting their name on the scoresheet. Whitehaven found themselves trailing 6-0 after two minutes at home to a makeshift Fulham side who were making their first appearance of the season having escaped from yet another threat of extinction. The Cumbrians then produced a club record victory of 72-6, with Norman Lofthouse collecting a try and 10 goals. At Central Park, holders Wigan scored 52 points without reply against Second Division Rochdale Hornets. New Zealander Dean Bell earned the Man of the Match award on his home debut together with two tries, as did Joe Lydon and David Stephenson, plus a hat-trick for Henderson Gill.

In an encounter high in effort but low in quality, Oldham beat visitors Leigh 29-22. The Roughyeds scored 12 points in the opening 11 minutes and led 16-12 at the interval before Leigh went in front two minutes after the restart. Four minutes later Oldham were back in the lead with second row man Mick Worrall a key figure. Warrington scrum half Andy Gregory gave Great Britain coach Maurice Bamford a timely reminder with a five-star performance, laying on the first two tries and adding four goals as the Wire disposed of Salford 28-20 at Wilderspool. The Red Devils were well served by half backs, two-try Darren Bloor and Australian Mark Wakefield. Blackpool Borough failed to find their league form at home to Barrow, going down 30-6 to a Cumbrian side inspired by Australian packman Mark Meskell. Runcorn Highfield celebrated their best attendance at Canal Street — 2,500 — but the joy did not last long with a 48-10 defeat at the hands of neighbours Widnes and the after-match theft of the £5,000-plus gate money. Swinton travelled to Derwent Park to take an early 7-0 lead over Workington Town before the Cumbrians scored the first of their three tries through winger Ian Bower and went on to a 25-16 victory. Town were well led by new Australian duo Errol Hillier and Phil Hurst.

In the second round, Wigan gave Second Division Whitehaven a taste of their own medicine. The Cumbrians, having run in 72 points in the first round over Fulham, were hammered 74-6 at Central Park, South African winger Ray Mordt celebrating his return after injury with a four-try haul, plus contributions from Great Britain duo Ellery Hanley of four tries, and Henderson Gill, two tries and eight goals. St. Helens beat Warrington 19-15 at Knowsley Road with second row man Roy Haggerty outstanding. Bidding to impress the watching Great Britain coach Maurice Bamford, Haggerty scored a vital try 12 minutes after the restart with the score at 8-8. The Saints extended their lead to 10 points before a Mark Roberts try and Paul Bishop goal cut the margin to four points with four minutes left. A 50-yard solo try by New Zealand Test star Kurt Sorensen clinched victory for Widnes in a tense 12-10 encounter at Barrow. Oldham entertained Second Division Workington Town who were unfortunate to be trailing 10-9 at the interval. The Roughyeds then staged a second half scoring burst of 18 points in 10 minutes to secure a 46-13 success, highlighted by two tries each for Australian duo Gary Warnecke and Stuart Raper.

The semi-finals produced thrilling contests. More than 28,000 fans packed Central Park for the Wigan-St. Helens derby clash, the massive crowd maintaining Rugby League's reputation for good behaviour by tolerating a late kick off and a 13-minute stoppage due to floodlight failure. Wigan, who sprung a surprise by fielding the unheralded Australian capture Ian Roberts, ended the Saints' 100 per cent record with a 22-16 victory. Success was not clinched until seven minutes from time when Ellery Hanley claimed his 15th try of the season and Henderson Gill added his fifth goal of the night. Unfancied Oldham bravely fought their way to a first Lancashire Cup final appearance for 18 years with a memorable win over Widnes at the Watersheddings. The Chemics came back from behind to lead 14-8 just 14 minutes before the final whistle. Former Great Britain pack star David Hobbs emerged as the Oldham hero with a try and two goals to record a 16-14 home victory and a personal tally of 12 points.

Wigan's Joe Lydon, five points in 1986 final.

1986 RESULTS

First Round

Blackpool B.	6	Barrow	30
Oldham	29	Leigh	22
Runcorn H.	10	Widnes	48
St. Helens	112	Carlisle	0
Warrington	28	Salford	20
Whitehaven	72	Fulham	6
Wigan	52	Rochdale H.	0
Workington T.	25	Swinton	16

Second Round

Barrow	10	Widnes	12
Oldham	46	Workington T.	13
St. Helens	19	Warrington	15
Wigan	74	Whitehaven	6

Semi-Finals

Oldham	16	Widnes	14
Wigan	22	St. Helens	16

Final

Oldham	6	Wigan	27
(at St. Helens)			

1986 Man of the Match Mike Ford.

LANCASHIRE CUP ROLL OF HONOUR

Season	Winners		Runners-up		Venue	Attendance	Receipts
1905-06	Wigan	0	Leigh	0	Broughton	16,000	£400
(replay)	Wigan	8	Leigh	0	Broughton	10,000	£200
1906-07	Broughton R.	15	Warrington	6	Wigan	14,048	£392
1907-08	Oldham	16	Broughton R.	9	Rochdale	14,000	£340
1908-09	Wigan	10	Oldham	9	Broughton	20,000	£600
1909-10	Wigan	22	Leigh	5	Broughton	14,000	£296
1910-11	Oldham	4	Swinton	3	Broughton	14,000	£418
1911-12	Rochdale H.	12	Oldham	5	Broughton	20,000	£630
1912-13	Wigan	21	Rochdale H.	5	Salford	6,000	£200
1913-14	Oldham	5	Wigan	0	Broughton	18,000	£610
1914-15	Rochdale H.	3	Wigan	2	Salford	4,000	£475
1915-16 to 1917-18 *Competition suspended*							
1918-19	Rochdale H.	22	Oldham	0	Salford	18,617	£1,365
1919-20	Oldham	7	Rochdale H.	0	Salford	19,000	£1,615
1920-21	Broughton R.	6	Leigh	3	Salford	25,000	£1,800
1921-22	Warrington	7	Oldham	5	Broughton	18,000	£1,200
1922-23	Wigan	20	Leigh	2	Salford	15,000	£1,200
1923-24	St. Helens Recs.	17	Swinton	0	Wigan	25,656	£1,450
1924-25	Oldham	10	St. Helens Recs.	0	Salford	15,000	£1,116
1925-26	Swinton	15	Wigan	11	Broughton	17,000	£1,115
1926-27	St. Helens	10	St. Helens Recs.	2	Warrington	19,439	£1,192
1927-28	Swinton	5	Wigan	2	Oldham	22,000	£1,275
1928-29	Wigan	5	Widnes	4	Warrington	19,000	£1,150
1929-30	Warrington	15	Salford	2	Wigan	21,012	£1,250
1930-31	St. Helens Recs.	18	Wigan	3	Swinton	16,710	£1,030

Season	Winners		Runners-up		Venue	Attendance	Receipts
1931-32	Salford	10	Swinton	8	Broughton	26,471	£1,654
1932-33	Warrington	10	St. Helens	9	Wigan	28,500	£1,675
1933-34	Oldham	12	St. Helens Recs.	0	Swinton	9,085	£516
1934-35	Salford	21	Wigan	12	Swinton	33,544	£2,191
1935-36	Salford	15	Wigan	7	Warrington	16,500	£950
1936-37	Salford	5	Wigan	2	Warrington	17,500	£1,160
1937-38	Warrington	8	Barrow	4	Wigan	14,000	£800
1938-39	Wigan	10	Salford	7	Swinton	27,940	£1,708
1939-40*	Swinton	5	Widnes	4	Widnes	5,500	£269
	Swinton	16	Widnes	11	Swinton	9,000	£446
	Swinton won on aggregate 21-15						
1940-41 to 1944-45 *Competition suspended during war-time*							
1945-46	Widnes	7	Wigan	3	Warrington	28,184	£2,600
1946-47	Wigan	9	Belle Vue R.	3	Swinton	21,618	£2,658
1947-48	Wigan	10	Belle Vue R.	7	Warrington	23,110	£3,043
1948-49	Wigan	14	Warrington	8	Swinton	39,015	£5,518
1949-50	Wigan	20	Leigh	7	Warrington	35,000	£4,751
1950-51	Wigan	28	Warrington	5	Swinton	42,541	£6,222
1951-52	Wigan	14	Leigh	6	Swinton	33,230	£5,432
1952-53	Leigh	22	St. Helens	5	Swinton	34,785	£5,793
1953-54	St. Helens	16	Wigan	8	Swinton	42,793	£6,918
1954-55	Barrow	12	Oldham	2	Swinton	25,204	£4,603
1955-56	Leigh	26	Widnes	9	Wigan	26,507	£4,090
1956-57	Oldham	10	St. Helens	3	Wigan	39,544	£6,274
1957-58	Oldham	13	Wigan	8	Swinton	42,497	£6,918
1958-59	Oldham	12	St. Helens	2	Swinton	38,780	£6,933
1959-60	Warrington	5	St. Helens	4	Wigan	39,237	£6,424
1960-61	St. Helens	15	Swinton	9	Wigan	31,755	£5,337
1961-62	St. Helens	25	Swinton	9	Wigan	30,000	£4,850
1962-63	St. Helens	7	Swinton	4	Wigan	23,523	£4,122
1963-64	St. Helens	15	Leigh	4	Swinton	21,231	£3,857
1964-65	St. Helens	12	Swinton	4	Wigan	17,383	£3,393
1965-66	Warrington	16	Rochdale H.	5	St. Helens	21,360	£3,800
1966-67	Wigan	16	Oldham	13	Swinton	14,193	£3,558
1967-68	St. Helens	2	Warrington	2	Wigan	16,897	£3,886
(replay)	St. Helens	13	Warrington	10	Swinton	7,577	£2,485
1968-69	St. Helens	30	Oldham	2	Wigan	17,008	£4,644
1969-70	Swinton	11	Leigh	2	Wigan	13,532	£3,651
1970-71	Leigh	7	St. Helens	4	Swinton	10,776	£3,136
1971-72	Wigan	15	Widnes	8	St. Helens	6,970	£2,204
1972-73	Salford	25	Swinton	11	Warrington	6,865	£3,321
1973-74	Wigan	19	Salford	9	Warrington	8,012	£2,750
1974-75	Widnes	6	Salford	2	Wigan	7,403	£2,833
1975-76	Widnes	16	Salford	7	Wigan	7,566	£3,880
1976-77	Widnes	16	Workington T.	11	Wigan	8,498	£6,414
1977-78	Workington T.	16	Wigan	13	Warrington	9,548	£5,038
1978-79	Widnes	15	Workington T.	13	Wigan	10,020	£6,261
1979-80	Widnes	11	Workington T.	0	Salford	6,887	£7,100
1980-81	Warrington	26	Wigan	10	St. Helens	6,442	£8,629
1981-82	Leigh	8	Widnes	3	Wigan	9,011	£14,029
1982-83	Warrington	16	St. Helens	0	Wigan	6,462	£11,732
1983-84	Barrow	12	Widnes	8	Wigan	7,007	£13,160
1984-85	St. Helens	26	Wigan	18	Wigan	26,074	£62,139
1985-86	Wigan	34	Warrington	8	St. Helens	19,202	£56,030
1986-87	Wigan	27	Oldham	6	St. Helens	20,180	£60,329
	*Emergency War-time competition						

175

LANCASHIRE CUP FINAL .... A REVIEW

1964-65
St. Helens 12 F. Barrow; T. Pimblett, Northey, Benyon (1t), Killeen (3g); Harvey, Murphy; Tembey, Dagnall, Warlow, French, Hicks (1t), Laughton
Swinton 4 Gowers (2g); Harries, Fleet, Buckley, Speed; Parkinson, Williams; Bate, D. Clarke, Halliwell, Rees, Simpson, Hurt
Referee: E. Clay (Leeds)

1965-66
Warrington 16 Bootle (2g); Fisher (1t), Pickavance, Melling (2t), Glover (1t); Aspinall, Smith; Payne, Oakes, Winslade, Robinson, Thomas, Hayes
Rochdale H. 5 Pritchard; Pratt, Starkey (1t, 1g), Chamberlain, Unsworth; Garforth, Fishwick; Birchall, Ashcroft, Owen, Parr (Drui), Toga, Baxter
Referee: E. Clay (Leeds)

1966-67
Wigan 16 Ashby; Boston (1t), Ashton (1t), Holden, Lake; C. Hill, Parr; Gardiner, Clarke, J. Stephens, Lyon, Gilfedder (2g, 1t), Major
Oldham 13 McLeod; Dolly, McCormack, Donovan (1t), Simms; Warburton (5g), Canning; Wilson, Taylor, Fletcher, Smethurst, Irving, Mooney
Referee: P. Geraghty (York)

1967-68
St. Helens 2 F. Barrow; Vollenhoven, Whittle, Benyon, A. Barrow; Douglas, Bishop; Warlow, Sayer, Watson, Hogan, Mantle, Coslett (1g)
Warrington 2 Affleck; Coupe, Melling, Harvey (Pickavance), Glover; Aspinall (1g), Gordon; Ashcroft, Harrison, Brady, Parr, Briggs, Clarke
Referee: G.F. Lindop (Wakefield)
Replay
St. Helens 13 F. Barrow; Vollenhoven, Smith, Benyon, Jones (1t); Douglas (Houghton 2g), Bishop; Warlow (1t), Sayer, Watson, E. Chisnall (1t), Mantle, Coslett (Egan)
Warrington 10 Conroy; Coupe, Melling (1t), Allen (2g), Glover; Scahill, Gordon (1t); Ashcroft, Harrison, Price, Parr, Briggs, Clarke
Referee: G.F. Lindop (Wakefield)

1968-69
St. Helens 30 Rhodes; F. Wilson (2t), Benyon, Myler, Williams (1t); Whittle, Bishop (1t); Warlow, Sayer, Watson, Rees (1t), E. Chisnall (1t) Coslett (6g)
Oldham 2 Murphy; Elliott, Larder, McCormack, Whitehead; Briggs (1g), Canning; K. Wilson, Taylor, Fletcher (Maders), Irving, McCourt, Hughes
Referee: W.H. Thompson (Huddersfield)

1969-70
Swinton 11 Gowers; Gomersall, Fleet, Buckley, Philbin (1t); Davies, Kenny (4g); Bate, D. Clarke, Mackay, Holliday, Smith, Robinson
Leigh 2 Grainey; Tickle, Warburton, Collins, Stringer (Brown); Eckersley, Murphy (1g); D. Chisnall, Ashcroft, Watts, Welding, Lyon, Fiddler
Referee: E. Clay (Leeds)

1970-71
Leigh 7 Ferguson (2g); Tickle (Canning), L. Chisnall, Collins, Walsh; Eckersley (1t), Murphy; D. Chisnall, Ashcroft, Watts, Grimes, Clarkson, Mooney
St. Helens 4 F. Barrow; L. Jones, Benyon, Walsh, Wilson; Myler, Whittle; Halsall, A. Karalius, Rees (Prescott), Mantle, E. Chisnall, Coslett (2g)
Referee: W.H. Thompson (Huddersfield)

1971-72
Wigan 15 Tyrer (3g); Eastham (1t), Francis (1t), Fuller, Wright (Gandy); D. Hill, Ayres (1t); Ashcroft, Clarke, Fletcher, Ashurst, Kevin O'Loughlin, Laughton
Widnes 8 Dutton; Brown, McLoughlin, Aspey (1g), Gaydon (1t); D. O'Neill (1t), Bowden; Warlow, Foran, Doughty, Kirwan, Walsh (Lowe), Nicholls
Referee: W.H. Thompson (Huddersfield)

1972-73
Salford 25 Charlton (1t); Eastham (1t), Watkins (1t, 5g), Hesketh, Richards (1t); Gill, Banner (1t); Mackay, Walker, Ward, Whitehead, Dixon, Prescott
Swinton 11 Jackson; Fleay (1t), Cooke, Buckley, Gomersall; Kenny (1g) (M. Philbin), Gowers (3g); Halsall, Evans, Bate, R. Smith (Holliday), Hoyle, W. Pattinson
Referee: W.H. Thompson (Huddersfield)

1973-74
Wigan 19 Francis; Vigo, D. Hill, Keiron O'Loughlin (2t), Wright (1t); Cassidy, Ayres (1g); Smethurst, Clarke, Gray (4g), Irving, D. Robinson, Cunningham
Salford 9 Charlton; Fielding, Watkins (1t, 3g), Hesketh, Holland; Gill, Banner; Mackay, Walker, Davies (Grice), Dixon, Kear (Knighton), E. Prescott
Referee: W.H. Thompson (Huddersfield)

1974-75
Widnes 6 Dutton (1g); George (1t), D. O'Neill, Aspey, A. Prescott; Hughes (1dg), Bowden; Mills, Elwell, J. Stephens, Adams, Blackwood, Laughton
Salford 2 Charlton; Fielding (1g), Dixon, Graham, Richards; Taylor, Banner; Mackay, Devlin, Grice, Knighton, Coulman, E. Prescott
Referee: G.F. Lindop (Wakefield)

1975-76
Widnes 16 Dutton (3g, 1dg); A. Prescott (1t),
George (1t), Aspey (1t), Jenkins; Hughes,
Bowden; Mills, Elwell, Nelson, Foran,
Fitzpatrick (Sheridan), Adams
Salford 7 Watkins (2g); Fielding, Butler,
Hesketh, Richards (1t); Gill, Nash; Fiddler,
Hawksley, Dixon (Mackay), Turnbull,
Knighton, E. Prescott
Referee: W.H. Thompson (Huddersfield)
1976-77
Widnes 16 Dutton (4g, 1dg); Wright (1t),
Aspey, George (1t), A. Prescott; Eckersley,
Bowden (1dg); Ramsey, Elwell, Nelson,
Dearden, Adams, Laughton
Workington T. 11 Charlton; Collister,
Wilkins (1t), Wright, MacCorquodale (4g);
Lauder, Walker; Mills, Banks, Calvin,
Bowman, L. Gorley, W. Pattinson (P. Gorley)
Referee: W.H. Thompson (Huddersfield)
1977-78
Workington T. 16 Charlton (Atkinson);
Collister, Risman, Wright (1t), MacCorquodale
(4g); Wilkins (1t), Walker (2dg); Watts, Banks,
Bowman, L. Gorley, W. Pattinson, P. Gorley
Wigan 13 Swann; Vigo, Davies (Burke 1g),
Willicombe (1t), Hornby; Taylor, Nulty (1t, 1g);
Hogan, Aspinall, Irving, Ashurst (1t),
Blackwood, Melling (Regan)
Referee: W.H. Thompson (Huddersfield)
1978-79
Widnes 15 Eckersley; Wright (1t), Aspey,
George, Burke (3g); Hughes, Bowden; Mills,
Elwell, Shaw, Adams, Dearden (Hull),
Laughton (2t)
Workington T. 13 Charlton; Collister, Risman,
Wilkins (1t), MacCorquodale (1t, 2g), McMillan,
Walker; Beverley, Banks, Bowman, Blackwood,
P. Gorley, W. Pattinson (L. Gorley 1t)
Referee: W.H. Thompson (Huddersfield)
1979-80
Widnes 11 Eckersley; Wright, Aspey, Hughes
(George), Burke (2g); Moran (1t), Bowden;
Hogan, Elwell (1dg), Shaw, L. Gorley, Dearden,
Adams (1t)
Workington T. 0 Charlton; MacCorquodale,
Maughan, Thompson, Beck; Rudd, Walker
(Roper); Beverley, Banks, Wellbanks (Varty),
W. Pattinson, Lewis, Dobie
Referee: W.H. Thompson (Huddersfield)
1980-81
Warrington 26 Finnegan; Thackray (1t),
I. Duane, Bevan (1t), Hesford (7g, 1t);
K. Kelly, A. Gwilliam; Courtney, Waller, Case,
Martyn (1t), Eccles (Potter), Hunter

Wigan 10 Fairbairn (1t, 2g); Ramsdale (1t),
Willicombe, Davies, Hornby; M. Foy, Bolton
(Coyle); Breheny, Pendlebury (M. Smith),
S. O'Neill, Melling, Clough, Hollingsworth
Referee: D. G. Kershaw (York)
1981-82
Leigh 8 Hogan; Drummond, Bilsbury (1t),
Donlan (1dg), Worgan; Woods (2g), Green;
Wilkinson, Tabern, Cooke, Martyn (Platt),
Clarkson, McTigue
Widnes 3 Burke; George, Hughes,
Cunningham, Bentley (1t); Moran, Gregory;
M. O'Neill, Elwell, Lockwood, L. Gorley,
E. Prescott, Adams
Referee: W.H. Thompson (Huddersfield)
1982-83
Warrington 16 Hesford (2g); Fellows (1t),
R. Duane, Bevan, M. Kelly (1t); Cullen,
K. Kelly (1t); Courtney, Webb, Cooke
(D. Chisnall), Eccles (1t), Fieldhouse, Gregory
St. Helens 0 Parkes (Smith); Ledger,
Arkwright, Haggerty, Litherland; Peters,
Holding; James, Liptrot, Bottell (Mathias),
Moorby, P. Gorley, Pinner
Referee: J. Holdsworth (Leeds)
1983-84
Barrow 12 Tickle (1dg); Moore, Whittle,
Ball (3g, 1dg), Milby; McConnell (1t), Cairns;
Hodkinson, Wall, McJennett, Herbert, Szymala,
Mossop
Widnes 8 Burke; Lydon (1t, 2g), Hughes,
Keiron O'Loughlin, Basnett; A. Myler,
Gregory; S. O'Neill, Elwell, K. Tamati,
Whitfield, E. Prescott, Adams
Referee: K. Allatt (Southport)
1984-85
St. Helens 26 Veivers (Haggerty 1t); Ledger,
Allen, Meninga (2t), Day (1t, 5g); Arkwright,
Holding; Burke, Liptrot, P. Gorley, Platt,
Round, Pinner
Wigan 18 Edwards; Ferguson, Stephenson,
Whitfield (3g), Gill (1t) (Pendlebury); Cannon,
Fairhurst; Courtney, Kiss (1t), Case, West (1t),
Wane, Potter
Referee: R. Campbell (Widnes)
1985-86
Wigan 34 Edwards (1t); Henley-Smith
(Hampson), Stephenson (7g), Hanley (1t),
Whitfield; Ella (2t), Ford; Dowling, Kiss (1t),
Wane (Case), Du Toit, Goodway, Potter
Warrington 8 Johnson (1t); Carbert (2g), Cullen,
Blake (Forster), Thackray; Kelly, A. Gregory;
Eccles, Webb, Jackson, Boyd (Tamati),
M. Gregory, Rathbone
Referee: J. Holdsworth (Kippax)

177

MAN OF THE MATCH AWARDS

An award for the adjudged man of the match in the Lancashire Cup final was first presented in 1974-75. For four years the award was sponsored by the *Rugby Leaguer* newspaper. From 1978-85 the trophy was presented by Burtonwood Brewery, then from 1986 by Greenall Whitley, as part of their sponsorship of the Lancashire Cup. Under the auspices of the *Rugby Leaguer*, the choice was made by the Editor, while the breweries invited a panel of the Press to make the decision.

Season	Winner	Team	Position
1974-75	Mike Coulman	Salford (v. Widnes)	Second row
1975-76	Mick George	Widnes (v. Salford)	Centre
1976-77	David Eckersley	Widnes (v. Workington T.)	Stand off
1977-78	Arnold Walker	Workington T. (v. Wigan)	Scrum half
1978-79	Arnold Walker	Workington T. (v. Widnes)	Scrum half
1979-80	Mick Adams	Widnes (v. Workington T.)	Loose forward
1980-81	Tony Waller	Warrington (v. Wigan)	Hooker
1981-82	Ray Tabern	Leigh (v. Widnes)	Hooker
1982-83	Steve Hesford	Warrington (v. St. Helens)	Full back
1983-84	David Cairns	Barrow (v. Widnes)	Scrum half
1984-85	Mal Meninga	St. Helens (v. Wigan)	Centre
1985-86	Steve Ella	Wigan (v. Warrington)	Stand off
1986-87	Mike Ford	Wigan (v. Oldham)	Scrum half

LANCASHIRE CUP FINAL RECORDS

TEAM

Most appearances: 32 by Wigan

Most wins: 18 by Wigan

Highest score: Wigan 34 v. Warrington 8 1985

Widest margin: St. Helens 30 v. Oldham 2 1968

Biggest attendance:
42,793 St. Helens v. Wigan (at Swinton) 1953

INDIVIDUAL

Most tries:
4 by Brian Nordgren (Wigan) v. Leigh 1949

Most goals:
7 by Jim Ledgard (Leigh) v. Widnes 1955
   Steve Hesford (Warrington) v. Wigan 1980
   David Stephenson (Wigan) v. Warrington .. 1985

Most points:
17 (7g, 1t) by Steve Hesford (Warrington) v. Wigan
   1980

First trophy of the 1986-87 season for Wigan skipper Graeme West.

YORKSHIRE CUP

1986 Final

Underdogs Hull, seeking their fourth Yorkshire Cup haul in five years, found themselves down to 11 men after only four minutes of a pulsating final against Challenge Cup holders Castleford.

The Airlie Birds had prop forward Andy Dannatt sent off in the fourth minute for alleged butting, skipper Lee Crooks joining him on the walk to the dressing room for a 10-minute spell in the sin bin for dissent.

Castleford second row man Martin Ketteridge touched down during their absence to add to his third minute penalty. Whether the two-man dismissal period was the turning point was debatable. Crooks returned to the field to find his charges trailing 6-0 but helped inspire the depleted Hull side to greater heights, as with the shock semi-final victory with 12 men at Bradford.

There is rarely consolation in defeat, but proud Hull played a major part in a spectacular final. The nine tries brought a Yorkshire Cup final record aggregate of 55 points. Hull's contribution of 24 points was the most by a beaten side in a White Rose final, as it was in the Challenge Cup epic at Wembley in 1985.

The second quarter opened at 6-6 and a burst of scoring brought a see-saw scoreline. A 22nd minute try from Australian forward Brett Atkins was goalled by Ketteridge, only for Hull's Kiwi star Dane O'Hara to notch his second try four minutes later to close the gap to 12-10.

Three minutes to half-time and Hull served up one of the competition's most memorable tries, endorsing their pre-planned policy of all-out attack against one of the game's renowned ball playing outfits. The move swept the length and breadth of the field with Phil Windley (twice), Fred Ah Kuoi, Paul Eastwood, Garry Schofield and O'Hara handling. Castleford's defence was equal to the high speed attack and Hull were halted just before the line only for the ball to be passed along to winger Michael Brand for a richly deserved try.

Crooks added the goal and a penalty kick on the stroke of half-time to give the valiant Boulevarders a surprise 18-12 lead.

Hull's hopes were dashed by consecutive touchdowns from Castleford Test aspirant Kevin Beardmore. The hooker's double blow came in the 42nd and 57th minutes, Ketteridge adding both goals.

The twin-try haul was the highlight of the 1984 tourist's hard-working display as he bid to impress the watching Great Britain management, becoming the first hooker to win the White Rose Trophy as Man of the Match.

The last 10 minutes produced another 11 points as Hull refused to lie down. A 63rd minute penalty goal by Crooks had pulled Hull back to 24-20 and the crafty Bob Beardmore dropped a goal to give Castleford more breathing space, victory being virtually assured in the 78th minute with a try from the powerful Kevin Ward. Ketteridge contributed his county final record-equalling fifth goal to bring his personal points tally to 14, a new record for the Yorkshire Cup final.

As time ran out, the Airlie Birds added a 79th minute try from Brand to emphasise their contribution to yet another excellent big match to the recent list of top value occasions in recent seasons.

JOHN SMITHS YORKSHIRE CUP FINAL

11th October		Leeds

CASTLEFORD 31		HULL 24
Colin Scott	1.	Gary Kemble
David Plange	2.	Michael Brand
Tony Marchant	3.	Garry Schofield
Chris Johns	4.	Dane O'Hara
Gary Hyde	5.	Paul Eastwood
John Joyner, Capt.	6.	Fred Ah Kuoi
Bob Beardmore	7.	Phil Windley
Kevin Ward	8.	Dave Brown
Kevin Beardmore	9.	Shaun Patrick
Barry Johnson	10.	Andy Dannatt
Martin Ketteridge	11.	Steve Norton
Brett Atkins	12.	Lee Crooks
Keith England	13.	Jon Sharp
Gary Lord	14.	Neil Puckering
Alan Shillito	15.	Gary Divorty

T: K. Beardmore (2), Ketteridge,
    Atkins, Ward
G: Ketteridge (5), R. Beardmore (dg)
Substitutions:
Lord for Hyde (38 min.)
Shillito for Atkins (79 min.)
Referee: John McDonald (Wigan)

T: O'Hara (2), Brand (2)
G: Crooks (4)
Substitutions:
Puckering for Brown (43 min.)
Divorty for Norton (73 min.)
Half-time: 12-18
Attendance: 11,132

1986 Round by Round

Mansfield Marksman's acceptance into the competition extended the new preliminary round to two ties, Marksman suffering a 56-0 humiliation at Halifax two weeks before the official start to the league season. The Thrum Hallers ran in 10 tries with full back Steve Smith bagging a try and eight goals. Visitors Doncaster led 6-4 at Sheffield before the Eagles pulled well ahead, only for the Dons to rally with winger Neil Turner scoring their fourth try four minutes from the end. David Noble failed to add the goal and Sheffield finished 22-20 ahead.

In the first round, Castleford gained revenge for their Okells Charity Shield defeat by Halifax with a 16-10 home success. New Australian centre Chris Johns marked his Castleford debut with a vital try after fellow countryman Graham Eadie had scored a touchdown to put Halifax in the lead 10-8. Two Martin Ketteridge penalty goals were the only second half scores. Holders Hull K.R. recovered from the shock of two interceptions by veteran Huddersfield Barracudas forward Billy Platt paving the way for tries by winger Mark Campbell and romped to a 52-30 victory, inspired by scrum half Wayne Parker and loose forward Gavin Miller. Lowly Keighley were well served by scrum half Paul Moses and forwards Mick Hawksworth and Fred

Turner but rarely troubled Leeds who ran home 40-4 winners at Headingley, Kevin Dick and David Creasser each registering two tries. Former Great Britain packman Dick Jasiewicz set up two tries and scored one himself under the watchful eye of Test coach Maurice Bamford as Bradford Northern disposed of Hunslet 40-12 at Elland Road. Northern stand off John Woods scored a hat-trick in a game marred by the sending off of Hunslet forward Kelvin Skerrett and the visitors' Mark Fleming in separate incidents.

Featherstone Rovers cast aside the threat of Second Division York leading 13-12 after 49 minutes with a scoring burst of 28 points in the last 25 minutes, Graham Steadman, Alan Banks and Deryck Fox each collecting a brace of tries in the 40-13 win. Unbeaten Sheffield Eagles opened with a try by the strong running Derek Bridgeman before visitors Dewsbury rallied with touchdowns from skipper Paul Shuttleworth and Pat Howley. A drop goal from hooker Dave Cholmondeley was followed by a try from Roy Rafferty as Sheffield fought back, Rafferty failing to add the decisive goal kick to leave Dewsbury 10-9 winners. Lack of forward power cost Second Division Bramley dear at the Boulevard as Hull held on to gain an unconvincing 29-22 success. The Villagers had levelled the score at 22-22 with scrum half Steve Carroll outstanding, creating comeback tries for captain Paul Fletcher and Les Howard. Hull secured victory with a Lee Crooks drop goal and a clinching try from Gary Divorty, their third try of the match directly from an up and under. Two tries in two minutes just before the break provided the platform for Wakefield Trinity's 14-12 triumph at Batley.

In the second round, Castleford justified the bookmakers' rating as favourites by dismissing the challenge of Leeds by 38-16 at Wheldon Road. The Glassblowers ran in

eight tries, with skipper John Joyner the main architect, but Ketteridge could add only one conversion and two penalty goals. Lowly Second Division Dewsbury proved no match for revitalised Bradford Northern at Odsal, going down 42-10. The contest was a formality after the first quarter, Northern running in a total of eight tries despite the absence of Lancashire-based duo John Woods and Phil Ford, caught up in a motorway tailback. Hull's 21-12 victory at home to Wakefield Trinity was marked by a Man of the Match performance by Kiwi wing star Dane O'Hara, playing at centre as the only experienced player in a depleted Hull back division. In a battle of the Rovers at Craven Park, Hull Kingston and Featherstone drew 20-20 after the visitors had led 18-8 three minutes into the second half. In the replay 48 hours later, the Colliers won 23-12 with two brilliant tries from Paul Lyman, Quinn's fourth and last goal taking his career total to 3,000 points.

In the semi-finals, an already weakened Hull were reduced to 12 men when prop forward Steve Crooks was sent off after half an hour. Within three minutes, hosts Bradford Northern opened up a 10-6 lead, captain Steve Donlan claiming two tries. Aided by a 12-4 scrum pull from hooker Shaun Patrick, the Airlie Birds fought back led by the impressive Lee Crooks. Veteran Steve Norton, playing his first match after a close season knee operation, created a try for youngster Jon Sharp before Kiwi Fred Ah Kuoi added a second half touchdown to give Hull a surprise 16-12 win and their fourth county final in five years. As expected, Challenge Cup holders Castleford swept through to the final with a brilliant 30-2 win at Featherstone. The visitors maintained their 100 per cent record with ease. Individual honours went to 17-year-old Shaun Irwin, making his county cup debut in place of the injured John Joyner.

1986 RESULTS

Preliminary Round

Halifax	56	Mansfield M.	0
Sheffield E.	22	Doncaster	20

First Round

Batley	12	Wakefield T.	14
Castleford	16	Halifax	10
Featherstone R.	40	York	13
Hunslet	12	Bradford N.	40
Hull	29	Bramley	22
Hull K.R.	52	Huddersfield B.	30
Leeds	40	Keighley	4
Sheffield E.	9	Dewsbury	10

Second Round

Bradford N.	42	Dewsbury	10
Castleford	38	Leeds	16
Hull	21	Wakefield T.	12
Hull K.R.	20	Featherstone R.	20

Replay

Featherstone R.	23	Hull K.R.	12

Semi-Finals

Bradford N.	12	Hull	16
Featherstone R.	2	Castleford	30

Final

Castleford	31	Hull	24
(at Leeds)			

YORKSHIRE CUP ROLL OF HONOUR

Year	Winners		Runners-up		Venue	Attendance	Receipts
1905-06	Hunslet	13	Halifax	3	Bradford P.A.	18,500	£465
1906-07	Bradford	8	Hull K.R.	5	Wakefield	10,500	£286
1907-08	Hunslet	17	Halifax	0	Leeds	15,000	£397
1908-09	Halifax	9	Hunslet	5	Wakefield	13,000	£356
1909-10	Huddersfield	21	Batley	0	Leeds	22,000	£778
1910-11	Wakefield T.	8	Huddersfield	2	Leeds	19,000	£696
1911-12	Huddersfield	22	Hull K.R.	10	Wakefield	20,000	£700
1912-13	Batley	17	Hull	3	Leeds	16,000	£523
1913-14	Huddersfield	19	Bradford N.	3	Halifax	12,000	£430
1914-15	Huddersfield	31	Hull	0	Leeds	12,000	£422
1918-19	Huddersfield	14	Dewsbury	8	Leeds	21,500	£1,309
1919-20	Huddersfield	24	Leeds	5	Halifax	24,935	£2,096
1920-21	Hull K.R.	2	Hull	0	Leeds	20,000	£1,926
1921-22	Leeds	11	Dewsbury	3	Halifax	20,000	£1,650
1922-23	York	5	Batley	0	Leeds	33,719	£2,414
1923-24	Hull	10	Huddersfield	4	Leeds	23,300	£1,728
1924-25	Wakefield T.	9	Batley	8	Leeds	25,546	£1,912
1925-26	Dewsbury	2	Huddersfield	0	Wakefield	12,616	£718
1926-27	Huddersfield	10	Wakefield T.	3	Leeds	11,300	£853
1927-28	Dewsbury	8	Hull	2	Leeds	21,700	£1,466
1928-29	Leeds	5	Featherstone R.	0	Wakefield	13,000	£838
1929-30	Hull K.R.	13	Hunslet	7	Leeds	11,000	£687
1930-31	Leeds	10	Huddersfield	2	Halifax	17,812	£1,405
1931-32	Huddersfield	4	Hunslet	2	Leeds	27,000	£1,764
1932-33	Leeds	8	Wakefield T.	0	Huddersfield	17,685	£1,183
1933-34	York	10	Hull K.R.	4	Leeds	22,000	£1,480
1934-35	Leeds	5	Wakefield T.	5	Dewsbury	22,598	£1,529
Replay	Leeds	2	Wakefield T.	2	Huddersfield	10,300	£745
Replay	Leeds	13	Wakefield T.	0	Hunslet	19,304	£1,327
1935-36	Leeds	3	York	0	Halifax	14,616	£1,113
1936-37	York	9	Wakefield T.	2	Leeds	19,000	£1,294
1937-38	Leeds	14	Huddersfield	8	Wakefield	22,000	£1,508
1938-39	Huddersfield	18	Hull	10	Bradford	28,714	£1,534
1939-40	Featherstone R.	12	Wakefield T.	9	Bradford	7,077	£403
1940-41	Bradford N.	15	Dewsbury	5	Huddersfield	13,316	£939
1941-42	Bradford N.	24	Halifax	0	Huddersfield	5,989	£635

Year	Winners		Runners-up		Venue	Attendance	Receipts
1942-43	Dewsbury	7	Huddersfield	0	Dewsbury	11,000	£680
	Huddersfield	2	Dewsbury	0	Huddersfield	6,252	£618
	Dewsbury won on aggregate 7-2						
1943-44	Bradford N.	5	Keighley	2	Bradford	10,251	£757
	Keighley	5	Bradford N.	5	Keighley	8,993	£694
	Bradford N. won on aggregate 10-7						
1944-45	Hunslet	3	Halifax	12	Hunslet	11,213	£744
	Halifax	2	Hunslet	0	Halifax	9,800	£745
	Halifax won on aggregate 14-3						
1945-46	Bradford N.	5	Wakefield T.	2	Halifax	24,292	£1,934
1946-47	Wakefield T.	10	Hull	0	Leeds	34,300	£3,718
1947-48	Wakefield T.	7	Leeds	7	Huddersfield	24,344	£3,461
Replay	Wakefield T.	8	Leeds	7	Bradford	32,000	£3,251
1948-49	Bradford N.	18	Castleford	9	Leeds	31,393	£5,053
1949-50	Bradford N.	11	Huddersfield	4	Leeds	36,000	£6,365
1950-51	Huddersfield	16	Castleford	3	Leeds	28,906	£5,152
1951-52	Wakefield T.	17	Keighley	3	Huddersfield	25,495	£3,347
1952-53	Huddersfield	18	Batley	8	Leeds	14,705	£2,471
1953-54	Bradford N.	7	Hull	2	Leeds	22,147	£3,833
1954-55	Halifax	22	Hull	14	Leeds	25,949	£4,638
1955-56	Halifax	10	Hull	10	Leeds	23,520	£4,385
Replay	Halifax	7	Hull	0	Bradford	14,000	£2,439
1956-57	Wakefield T.	23	Hunslet	5	Leeds	30,942	£5,609
1957-58	Huddersfield	15	York	8	Leeds	22,531	£4,123
1958-59	Leeds	24	Wakefield T.	20	Bradford	26,927	£3,833
1959-60	Featherstone R.	15	Hull	14	Leeds	23,983	£4,156
1960-61	Wakefield T.	16	Huddersfield	10	Leeds	17,456	£2,937
1961-62	Wakefield T.	19	Leeds	9	Bradford	16,329	£2,864
1962-63	Hunslet	12	Hull K.R.	2	Leeds	22,742	£4,514
1963-64	Halifax	10	Featherstone R.	0	Wakefield	13,238	£2,471
1964-65	Wakefield T.	18	Leeds	2	Huddersfield	13,527	£2,707
1965-66	Bradford N.	17	Hunslet	8	Leeds	17,522	£4,359
1966-67	Hull K.R.	25	Featherstone R.	12	Leeds	13,241	£3,482
1967-68	Hull K.R.	8	Hull	7	Leeds	16,729	£5,515
1968-69	Leeds	22	Castleford	11	Wakefield	12,573	£3,746
1969-70	Hull	12	Featherstone R.	9	Leeds	11,089	£3,419
1970-71	Leeds	23	Featherstone R.	7	Bradford	6,753	£1,879
1971-72	Hull K.R.	11	Castleford	7	Wakefield	5,536	£1,589
1972-73	Leeds	36	Dewsbury	9	Bradford	7,806	£2,659
1973-74	Leeds	7	Wakefield T.	2	Leeds	7,621	£3,728
1974-75	Hull K.R.	16	Wakefield T.	13	Leeds	5,823	£3,090
1975-76	Leeds	15	Hull K.R.	11	Leeds	5,743	£3,617
1976-77	Leeds	16	Featherstone R.	12	Leeds	7,645	£5,198
1977-78	Castleford	17	Featherstone R.	. 7	Leeds	6,318	£4,528
1978-79	Bradford N.	18	York	8	Leeds	10,429	£9,188
1979-80	Leeds	15	Halifax	6	Leeds	9,137	£9,999
1980-81	Leeds	8	Hull K.R.	7	Huddersfield	9,751	£15,578
1981-82	Castleford	10	Bradford N.	5	Leeds	5,852	£10,359
1982-83	Hull	18	Bradford N.	7	Leeds	11,755	£21,950
1983-84	Hull	13	Castleford	2	Elland Rd, Leeds	14,049	£33,572
1984-85	Hull	29	Hull K.R.	12	Hull C. FC	25,237	£68,639
1985-86	Hull K.R.	22	Castleford	18	Leeds	12,686	£36,327
1986-87	Castleford	31	Hull	24	Leeds	11,132	£31,888

YORKSHIRE CUP FINAL .... A REVIEW

1964-65
Wakefield T. 18 Metcalfe; Jones (2t), Thomas, Fox (2t, 3g), Coetzer; Poynton, Owen; Campbell, Shepherd, Vines, Haigh, Plumstead, Holliday
Leeds 2 Dewhurst (1g); Cowan, Broatch, Gemmell, Wrigglesworth; Shoebottom, Seabourne; W. Drake, Lockwood, Chamberlain, Clark, Neumann, J. Sykes
Referee: D.T.H. Davies (Manchester)

1965-66
Bradford N. 17 Scattergood; Williamson (2t), Brooke (1t), Rhodes, Walker; Stockwell, Smales; Tonkinson, Morgan, Hill, Ashton, Clawson (4g), Rae
Hunslet 8 Langton (1g); Lee (1t), Shelton, Render, Thompson (1t); Preece, Marchant; Hartley, Prior, Baldwinson, Ramsey, Gunney, Ward
Referee: W.E. Lawrinson (Warrington)

1966-67
Hull K.R. 25 C. Kellett (5g); Young (1t), A. Burwell (1t), Moore (1t), Blackmore (1t); Millward, Bunting; F. Fox, Flanagan (1t), Tyson, Holliday, Foster, Major
Featherstone R. 12 D. Kellett; Thomas, Greatorex, Wrigglesworth (1t), Westwood; M. Smith, Dooler; Dixon, Kosanovic, Forsyth (1t), A. Morgan, Lyons, Smales (3g)
Referee: B. Baker (Wigan)

1967-68
Hull K.R. 8 Kellett (1g); Young, Moore, Elliott, A. Burwell (1t); Millward (1t), Cooper; Holliday, Flanagan, Mennell, Lowe, Hickson (Foster), Major
Hull 7 Keegan; Oliver, Doyle-Davidson, Maloney (1g), Stocks; Devonshire, Davidson (1t, 1g); Harrison, McGlone, Broom, Edson, J. Macklin, Sykes
Referee: D.T.H. Davies (Manchester)

1968-69
Leeds 22 Risman (5g); Alan Smith (1t), Hynes, Watson (1t), Atkinson (1t); Shoebottom, Seabourne; Clark, Crosby, K. Eyre, Ramsey (Hick 1t), A. Eyre, Batten
Castleford 11 Edwards; Howe, Hill (1t, 2g), Thomas, Stephens; Hardisty (2g), Hargrave; Hartley, C. Dickinson, Ward, Small, Lockwood (Redfearn), Reilly
Referee: J. Manley (Warrington)

1969-70
Hull 12 Owbridge; Sullivan (1t), Gemmell, Maloney (2g), A. Macklin; Hancock, Davidson; Harrison, McGlone, J. Macklin (1t), Kirchin, Forster, Brown (1g)

Featherstone R. 9 C. Kellett (3g); Newlove, Jordan, M. Smith, Hartley (T. Hudson); D. Kellett, Nash (1t); Tonks, Farrar, Lyons, A. Morgan, Thompson, Smales
Referee: R.L. Thomas (Oldham)

1970-71
Leeds 23 Holmes; Alan Smith (2t), Hynes (4g), Cowan, Atkinson (1t); Wainwright (Langley), Shoebottom; J. Burke, Dunn (1t), Cookson, Ramsey (1t), Haigh, Batten
Featherstone R. 7 C. Kellett (2g); M. Smith, Cotton, Newlove, Hartley (1t); Harding (Coventry), Hudson; Windmill, D. Morgan, Lyons, Rhodes, Thompson, Farrar
Referee: D.S. Brown (Preston)

1971-72
Hull K.R. 11 Markham; Stephenson, Coupland, Kirkpatrick, Longstaff (1t); Millward (4g), Daley; Wiley, Flanagan, Millington, Wallis, Palmer (Cooper), Brown
Castleford 7 Edwards; Foster (1t), S. Norton, Worsley, Lowndes; Hargrave, Stephens; Hartley, Miller, I. Van Bellen (Ackroyd 2g), A. Dickinson, Lockwood, Blakeway
Referee: A. Givvons (Oldham)

1972-73
Leeds 36 Holmes (3t); Alan Smith, Hynes (1g), Dyl (2t), Atkinson (1t); Hardisty (1t), Hepworth (Langley); Clawson (5g) (Fisher), Ward, Ramsey, Cookson, Eccles (1t), Batten
Dewsbury 9 Rushton; Ashcroft (1t), Childe, Day, Yoward; Agar (3g), A. Bates; Bell (Beverley), M. Stephenson, Lowe, Grayshon, J. Bates (Lee), Hankins
Referee: M.J. Naughton (Widnes)

1973-74
Leeds 7 Holmes; Langley (1t) (Marshall 1g), Hynes (1g), Dyl, Atkinson; Hardisty, Hepworth; Jeanes (Ramsey), Ward, Clarkson, Eccles, Cookson, Batten
Wakefield T. 2 Wraith (Sheard); D. Smith, Crook (1g), Hegarty, B. Parker; Topliss, Bonnar; Valentine, Morgan, Bratt, Knowles (Ballantyne), Endersby, Holmes
Referee: M.J. Naughton (Widnes)

1974-75
Hull K.R. 16 Smithies; Sullivan (Dunn 1t), Watson (2t), Coupland, Kirkpatrick (1t); Millward, Stephenson; Millington, Heslop, Rose, Wallis, N. Fox (2g) (Madley), Brown
Wakefield T. 13 Sheard; D. Smith (1t), Crook (2g), Hegarty (1t), Archer; Topliss, Bonnar; Ballantyne, Handscombe, Bratt (1t), Skerrett, A. Tonks (Goodwin), (Holmes), Morgan
Referee: M.J. Naughton (Widnes)

1975-76
Leeds 15 Marshall; Alan Smith, Hague, Dyl (1t), Atkinson; Holmes (4g, 1dg), Hynes; Harrison, Payne, Pitchford, (Dickinson), Eccles, Batten, Cookson (1t)
Hull K.R. 11 Wallace; Dunn, A. Burwell, Watson, Sullivan (1t); Turner, Millward (1dg), Millington, Dickinson, Lyons, Rose, N. Fox (2g, 1t), Hughes (Holdstock)
Referee: J.V. Moss (Manchester)
1976-77
Leeds 16 Marshall (2g); Hague, Hynes, Dyl (2t), D. Smith; Holmes, Banner; Dickinson, Ward, Pitchford, Eccles (1t), Burton, Cookson (1t)
Featherstone R. 12 Box; Bray (1t), Coventry, Quinn (3g), K. Kellett; Newlove, Fennell; Gibbins, Bridges, Farrar, Stone, P. Smith (1t), Bell (Spells)
Referee: M.J. Naughton (Widnes)
1977-78
Castleford 17 Wraith; Richardson, Joyner, P. Johnson, Fenton; Burton (2t, 1dg), Pickerill (Stephens); Fisher (Woodall), Spurr, Weston, Huddlestone, Reilly, Lloyd (5g)
Featherstone R. 7 Marsden; Evans, Gilbert, Quinn (1g) (N. Tuffs), K. Kellett; Newlove, Butler; Townend (1g), Bridges, Farrar, Gibbins, Stone (P. Smith 1t), Bell
Referee: M.J. Naughton (Widnes)
1978-79
Bradford N. 18 Mumby; Barends, Gant (1t), D. Parker (1t), D. Redfearn; Slater (Wolford), A. Redfearn (1t); Thompson, Fisher, Forsyth (Joyce), Fox (3g), Trotter, Haigh (1t)
York 8 G. Smith (1t); T. Morgan, Day (Crossley), Foster, Nicholson; Banks (2g), Harkin; Dunkerley, Wileman, Harris, Rhodes, Hollis (1dg) (Ramshaw), Cooper
Referee: M.J. Naughton (Widnes)
1979-80
Leeds 15 Hague; Alan Smith (2t), D. Smith (1t), Dyl, Atkinson; Holmes (J. Sanderson), Dick (3g); Dickinson, Ward, Pitchford, Eccles, D. Heron (Adams), Cookson
Halifax 6 Birts (3g); Howard (Snee), Garrod, Cholmondeley, Waites; Blacker, Langton; Jarvis (Callon), Raistrick, Wood, Scott, Sharp, Busfield
Referee: M.J. Naughton (Widnes)
1980-81
Leeds 8 Hague; Alan Smith (1t), D. Smith, Atkinson, Oulton; Holmes, Dick (2g, 1dg); Harrison, Ward, Pitchford, Eccles, Cookson (Carroll), D. Heron

Hull K.R. 7 Robinson; McHugh (1t), M. Smith, Hogan (2g), Youngman; Hall, Harkin; Holdstock, Price, Crooks (Rose), Lowe, Casey, Crane
Referee: R. Campbell (Widnes)
1981-82
Castleford 10 Claughton; Richardson, Fenton, Hyde (1t), Morris; Joyner (1t), R. Beardmore; Hardy (P. Norton), Spurr, B. Johnson, Finch (2g), Ward, Timson
Bradford N. 5 Mumby; Barends, Hale, A. Parker (1t), Gant; Hanley (1g), A. Redfearn; Grayshon, Noble, Sanderson (D. Redfearn), G. Van Bellen (Jasiewicz), Idle, Rathbone
Referee: M.R. Whitfield (Widnes)
1982-83
Hull 18 Kemble; Evans (1t), Day, Leuluai, Prendiville (1t); Topliss, Harkin; Skerrett, Bridges, Stone, Rose (2t), Crooks (2g, 2dg), Crane (Norton)
Bradford N. 7 Mumby; Barends, Gant, A. Parker, Pullen (Smith); Whiteman (1t), Carroll (1g, 2dg); Grayshon, Noble, G. Van Bellen (Sanderson), Idle, Jasiewicz, Hale
Referee: S. Wall (Leigh)
1983-84
Hull 13 Kemble; Solal, Schofield, Leuluai, O'Hara (1t); Topliss, Dean; Edmonds, Wileman, Skerrett, Proctor (1t), Crooks, Crane (1t, 1dg)
Castleford 2 Coen; Fenton, Marchant, Hyde (Orum), Kear; Joyner, R. Beardmore (1g); Connell, Horton, Reilly, Timson, James, England
Referee: W.H. Thompson (Huddersfield)
1984-85
Hull 29 Kemble (2t); Leuluai, Schofield (4g, 1dg), Evans (1t), O'Hara; Ah Kuoi, Sterling; Edmonds, Patrick, Crooks (1t), Norton (1t), Proctor, Divorty (Rose)
Hull K.R. 12 Fairbairn (1t); Clark, Robinson (1t), Prohm, Laws; M. Smith, Harkin (Rudd); Broadhurst, Watkinson, Ema (Hartley), Burton, Kelly, Hall (1t)
Referee: G.F. Lindop (Wakefield)
1985-86
Hull K.R. 22 Fairbairn (Lydiat); Clark (1t), Dorahy (5g), Prohm, Laws; G. Smith, Harkin; D. Harrison, Watkinson, Ema, Burton, Hogan (Kelly), Miller (2t)
Castleford 18 Lord; Plange, Marchant (2t), Hyde, Spears; Diamond (1g), R. Beardmore (1t, 2g); Ward, K. Beardmore, Johnson, England, Ketteridge, Joyner
Referee: R. Campbell (Widnes)

THE WHITE ROSE TROPHY

First awarded in 1966, the trophy is presented to the adjudged man of the match in the Yorkshire Cup final.

Donated by the late T.E. Smith, of York, the award is organised by the Yorkshire Federation of Rugby League Supporters' Clubs and judged by a panel of the Press.

The Humberside clubs and Leeds have dominated the trophy, their players winning 16 of 21 awards, including the first 11 in succession.

Season	Winner	Team	Position
1966-67	Cyril Kellett	Hull K.R. (v. Featherstone R.)	Full back
1967-68	Chris Davidson	Hull (v. Hull K.R.)	Scrum half
1968-69	Barry Seabourne	Leeds (v. Castleford)	Scrum half
1969-70	Joe Brown	Hull (v. Featherstone R.)	Loose forward
1970-71	Syd Hynes	Leeds (v. Featherstone R.)	Centre
1971-72	Ian Markham	Hull K.R. (v. Castleford)	Full back
1972-73	John Holmes	Leeds (v. Dewsbury)	Full back
1973-74	Keith Hepworth	Leeds (v. Wakefield T.)	Scrum half
1974-75	Roger Millward	Hull K.R. (v. Wakefield T.)	Stand off
1975-76	Neil Fox	Hull K.R. (v. Leeds)	Second row
1976-77	Les Dyl	Leeds (v. Featherstone R.)	Centre
1977-78	Bruce Burton	Castleford (v. Featherstone R.)	Stand off
1978-79	Bob Haigh	Bradford N. (v. York)	Loose forward
1979-80	Alan Smith	Leeds (v. Halifax)	Winger
1980-81	Kevin Dick	Leeds (v. Hull K.R.)	Scrum half
1981-82	Barry Johnson	Castleford (v. Bradford N.)	Prop
1982-83	Keith Mumby	Bradford N. (v. Hull)	Full back
1983-84	Mick Crane	Hull (v. Castleford)	Loose forward
1984-85	Peter Sterling	Hull (v. Hull K.R.)	Scrum half
1985-86	Gavin Miller	Hull K.R. (v. Castleford)	Loose forward
1986-87	Kevin Beardmore	Castleford (v. Hull)	Hooker

YORKSHIRE CUP FINAL RECORDS

TEAM
Most appearances: 20 Huddersfield, Leeds
Most wins: 16 Leeds
Highest score: Leeds 36 v. Dewsbury 9............ 1972
Widest margin win: Huddersfield 31 v. Hull 0... 1914
Biggest attendance:
36,000 Bradford N. v. Huddersfield (at Leeds).. 1949

INDIVIDUAL
Most tries:
4 by Stan Moorhouse (Huddersfield) v. Leeds.... 1919
Most points:
14 by (5g, 1t) by Martin Ketteridge (Castleford)
v. Hull 1986
Most goals:
No player has scored more than 5.

1986 Man of the Match Kevin Beardmore.

1986 CHARITY SHIELD

Halifax's new recruit, Neil Hague, won them the Okells Charity Shield and a £5,000 prize cheque with a coolly taken drop goal four minutes from time.

The former Leeds utility back — in only his second outing for the Thrum Hall side — produced his one-point clincher three minutes after a superb solo try from Colin Whitfield had pulled Halifax back to 8-8 in the 73rd minute.

Silk Cut Challenge Cup winners Castleford looked set to hold onto their 8-4 lead after surviving a fierce Halifax siege when Whitfield struck. There seemed no danger when the former Wigan star sauntered through from 50 yards out. But a lazy look to the left, then to the right, threw Castleford into disarray as he accelerated smoothly away.

A desperate ankle tap broke Whitfield's composure without stopping him as he stumbled the last few yards to the line. The former Great Britain Under-24 international failed to make it a perfect personal finishing touch by sending the angled goal kick wide.

Three minutes later, up stepped Hague to draw on the experience of a long and distinguished career with Leeds to stay calm under pressure and strike a soaring 35-yard drop goal to secure a hard-earned victory for the Slalom Lager Champions.

Equally cool on a sunny day in Douglas was Halifax stand off and skipper Chris Anderson, who collected both the Okells Charity Shield and the Man of the Match award from Okells Brewery chairman John Cowley.

The Thrum Hall player-coach was expected to start easing himself out of the action, but the Australian once again established himself as the driving force and pivot of the well-organised Halifax outfit.

Full back Steve Smith was making a strong claim for the individual match honour before having to leave the field in the 49th minute with a head injury, Whitfield taking over the full back role to be in a position for the decisive try.

Without producing their Wembley form, Castleford were always formidable opposition and for a long time appeared to have more purpose than Halifax in a hard tackling contest which again belied the charity match title.

The Wheldon Road side went into a 6-0 lead after 23 minutes when centre Gary Lord did well to get David Plange moving and then followed his winger's kick to touch down, second row man Martin Ketteridge adding the goal kick.

Just before the interval, Halifax winger Wilf George completed an impressive first half to pop up for a try that put the League champions back in the contest. The former Huddersfield and Widnes winger's positional play had been a revelation.

For Halifax, loose forward Paul Dixon added smart distribution to his forceful midfield running, while Welshman Brian Juliff marked a rare front row performance with typical aggressive running.

With the scrums 9-8 to Halifax, there was little to choose between the opposing scrum halves, both Bob Beardmore and Gary Stephens displaying a variety of ploys.

Halifax second row man Peter Bell and Castleford centre Shaun Irwin had contrasting debuts, the new packman producing a sound performance while Irwin's first outing ended after only 11 minutes through injury.

The second Okells Charity Shield encounter again proved to be a popular pre-season contest with more than 3,000 fans in the picturesque Douglas Bowl, 25 per cent of the crowd being Manx people according to the official gate returns.

The clubs attended a celebration dinner at their Palace Hotel base before joining the ferry loads of supporters from throughout Rugby League territory at a successful Rugby League cabaret evening.

OKELLS CHARITY SHIELD

24th August   **Douglas Bowl, Isle of Man**

CASTLEFORD 8		**HALIFAX 9**
David Roockley	1.	Steve Smith
David Plange	2.	Eddie Riddlesden
Gary Lord	3.	Colin Whitfield
Shaun Irwin	4.	Neil Hague
Tony Spears	5.	Wilf George
John Joyner, Capt.	6.	Chris Anderson, Capt.
Bob Beardmore	7.	Gary Stephens
Kevin Ward	8.	Roy Dickinson
Kevin Beardmore	9.	Seamus McCallion
Barry Johnson	10.	Brian Juliff
Martin Ketteridge	11.	Mick Scott
Dean Mountain	12.	Peter Bell
Keith England	13.	Paul Dixon
Roy Southernwood	14.	Scott Wilson
Ian Fletcher	15.	Neil James

T: Lord
G: Ketteridge (2)
Substitutions:
Southernwood for Irwin (11 min.)
Fletcher for Joyner (49 min.)
Half-time: 6-4
Referee: Fred Lindop (Wakefield)

T: George, Whitfield
G: Hague (dg)
Substitutions:
Wilson for Smith (49 min.)
James for Scott (Half-time)
Attendance: 3,276

CHARITY SHIELD ROLL OF HONOUR

Year	Winners		Runners-up		Attendance
1985-86	Wigan	34	Hull K.R.	6	4,066
1986-87	Halifax	9	Castleford	8	3,276

CHARITY SHIELD .... A REVIEW
1985-86

Wigan 34 Hampson; P. Ford, Stephenson (7g), Donlan (2t), Gill (2t); Edwards, M. Ford (1t); Courtney (Mayo), Kiss, Campbell, West (Lucas), Du Toit, Wane

Hull K.R. 6 Fairbairn (Lydiat 1g); Clark (1t), Robinson, Prohm, Laws; M. Smith, G. Smith; D. Harrison, Watkinson, Ema, Kelly (Rudd), Burton, Hogan
Referee: R. Campbell (Widnes)

MAN OF THE MATCH AWARDS

Season	Winner	Team	Position
1985-86	Shaun Edwards	Wigan (v. Hull K.R.)	Stand off
1986-87	Chris Anderson	Halifax (v. Castleford)	Stand off

Isle of Man action as Halifax loose forward Paul Dixon is chased by Castleford's Keith England, Seamus McCallion supporting.

BBC-2 FLOODLIT TROPHY

The BBC-2 Floodlit Trophy competition was launched in 1965 for clubs with floodlights. Eight clubs competed in the first year and the total had grown to 22 by 1980 when the competition was abolished as part of the BBC's financial cut-backs.

For 15 years the matches became a regular television feature on Tuesday evenings throughout the early winter months.

Although the format changed slightly over the years, it was basically a knockout competition on the lines of the Challenge Cup.

In 1966 the Floodlit Competition was used to introduce the limited tackle rule, then four tackles, which proved such a great success it was adopted in all other matches before the end of the year.

BBC-2 FLOODLIT TROPHY FINALS

(Only the 1967, at Leeds, and 1972, at Wigan, finals were played on neutral grounds)

Season	Winners		Runners-up		Venue	Attendance	Receipts
1965-66	Castleford	4	St. Helens	0	St. Helens	11,510	£1,548
1966-67	Castleford	7	Swinton	2	Castleford	8,986	£1,692
1967-68	Castleford	8	Leigh	5	Leeds	9,716	£2,099
1968-69	Wigan	7	St. Helens	4	Wigan	13,479	£3,291
1969-70	Leigh	11	Wigan	6	Wigan	12,312	£2,854
1970-71	Leeds	9	St. Helens	5	Leeds	7,612	£2,189
1971-72	St. Helens	8	Rochdale H.	2	St. Helens	9,300	£2,493
1972-73	Leigh	5	Widnes	0	Wigan	4,691	£1,391
1973-74	Bramley	15	Widnes	7	Widnes	4,422	£1,538
1974-75	Salford	0	Warrington	0	Salford	4,473	£1,913
Replay	Salford	10	Warrington	5	Warrington	5,778	£2,434
1975-76	St. Helens	22	Dewsbury	2	St. Helens	3,858	£1,747
1976-77	Castleford	12	Leigh	4	Leigh	5,402	£2,793
1977-78	Hull K.R.	26	St. Helens	11	Hull K.R.	10,099	£6,586
1978-79	Widnes	13	St. Helens	7	St. Helens	10,250	£7,017
1979-80	Hull	13	Hull K.R.	3	Hull	18,500	£16,605

BBC2 FLOODLIT TROPHY . . . . A REVIEW

1965-66
Castleford 4 Edwards; C. Battye, M. Battye, Willett (2g), Briggs; Hardisty, Millward; Terry, J. Ward, C. Dickinson, Bryant, Taylor, Small
St. Helens 0 F. Barrow; Vollenhoven, Wood, Benyon, Killeen; Murphy, Prosser; French, Dagnall, Watson, Hicks, Mantle, Laughton
Referee: L. Gant (Wakefield)
1966-67
Castleford 7 Edwards; Howe, Stenton, Willett (1g), Austin (1t); Hardisty, Hepworth (1g); Hartley, C. Dickinson, McCartney, Bryant, Small, Walker
Swinton 2 Gowers; Whitehead (1g), Gomersall, Buckley, Davies; Fleet, G. Williams; Halliwell, D. Clarke, Scott (Cummings), Rees, Simpson, Robinson
Referee: J. Manley (Warrington)
1967-68
Castleford 8 Edwards; Harris, Thomas, Stenton, Willett (4g); Hardisty, Hepworth; Hartley, J. Ward, Walton, Bryant (C. Dickinson), Redfearn, Reilly

Leigh 5 Grainey; Tickle (1t), Lewis, Collins, Walsh; Entwistle, A. Murphy; Whitworth, Ashcroft, Major, Welding, M. Murphy, Gilfedder (1g)
Referee: G.F. Lindop (Wakefield)
1968-69
Wigan 7 Tyrer (2g); Francis, Ashton, Ashurst, Rowe; C. Hill (1t), Jackson; J. Stephens, Clarke, Mills, Fogerty (Lyon), Kevin O'Loughlin, Laughton
St. Helens 4 Williams; Wilson, Benyon, Myler, Wills; Whittle, Bishop; Warlow, Sayer, Watson, Mantle, Hogan, Coslett (2g)
Referee: E. Clay (Leeds)
1969-70
Leigh 11 Ferguson (3g) (Lewis); Tickle (1t), Dorrington, Collins, Walsh; Eckersley, Murphy (1g); D. Chisnall, Ashcroft, Watts, Welding, Grimes, Lyon
Wigan 6 C. Hill; Wright, Francis (2g), Rowe, Kevin O'Loughlin; D. Hill (1g), Jackson; J. Stephens, Clarke, Ashcroft, Ashurst, Mills, Laughton
Referee: W.H. Thompson (Huddersfield)

1970-71
Leeds 9 Holmes (2g); Alan Smith, Hynes (1t, 1g), Cowan, Atkinson; Wainwright, Shoebottom; J. Burke, Fisher, Barnard, Haigh, Ramsey, Batten
St. Helens 5 F. Barrow; L. Jones (1t), Benyon, Walsh, Wilson; Whittle, Heaton; Rees, A. Karalius, E. Chisnall, Mantle, E. Prescott, Coslett (1g)
Referee: E. Lawrinson (Warrington)
1971-72
St. Helens 8 G. Pimblett; L. Jones, Benyon, Walsh, Wilson; Kelly, Heaton; Rees, A. Karalius, E. Chisnall, E. Prescott, Mantle, Coslett (4g)
Rochdale H. 2 Chamberlain (1g); Brelsford, Crellin, Taylor, Glover; Myler, Gartland; Birchall, P. Clarke, Brown, Welding, Sheffield (Hodkinson), Delooze
Referee: E. Clay (Leeds)
1972-73
Leigh 5 Hogan; Lawson (1t) (Lester), Atkin, Collins, Stacey; A. Barrow, Sayer (Ryding); Grimes, D. Clarke, Fletcher, Fiddler (1g), F. Barrow, Martyn
Widnes 0 Dutton; A. Prescott, Aspey, Blackwood, McDonnell; Lowe, Ashton; Mills, Elwell, Warlow, Foran, Sheridan, Nicholls
Referee: G.F. Lindop (Wakefield)
1973-74
Bramley 15 Keegan; Goodchild (1t), Bollon, Hughes, Austin (1t); T. Briggs, Ward (1g) (Ashman); D. Briggs, Firth, Cheshire, D. Sampson (1t), Idle, Wolford (2g)
Widnes 7 Dutton (2g); D. O'Neill, Hughes, Aspey, Macko (1t); Warburton, Bowden; Hogan, Elwell, Nelson, Sheridan, Blackwood (Foran) Laughton
Referee: D. G. Kershaw (York)
1974-75
Salford 0 Charlton; Fielding, Hesketh, Graham, Richards; Brophy (Taylor), Banner; Coulman, Devlin, Grice, Knighton, Dixon, E. Prescott
Warrington 0 Whitehead; Sutton, Cunliffe (Lowe), Whittle, Bevan; Briggs, Gordon; D. Chisnall, Ashcroft, Wright, Gaskell, Conroy, B. Philbin (Jewitt)
Referee: W.H. Thompson (Huddersfield)
Replay
Salford 10 Stead; Fielding (1t), Watkins (2g), Hesketh, Richards (1t); Gill, Banner; Grice, Walker, Mackay, Dixon, Knighton, E. Prescott

Warrington 5 Cunliffe; Whitehead (1g), Pickup, Whittle, Bevan (1t); Noonan (Briggs), Gordon; D. Chisnall, Ashcroft, Wanbon, Conroy, Nicholas (Brady), B. Philbin
Referee: W.H. Thompson (Huddersfield)
1975-76
St. Helens 22 G. Pimblett (2g); L. Jones, Benyon (1t), Hull (1t), Mathias (2t); Wilson (1t), Heaton (1dg); Mantle, A. Karalius, James, Nicholls, E. Chisnall, Coslett (1g)
Dewsbury 2 Langley; Hegarty, Chalkley, Simpson, Mitchell; N. Stephenson (1g) (Lee), A. Bates; Beverley, Price, Hankins, Halloran (Artis), Bell, Grayshon
Referee: W.H. Thompson (Huddersfield)
1976-77
Castleford 12 Wraith; Fenton, Joyner, P. Johnson, Walsh (1t); Burton (1t), Stephens; Khan, Spurr, A. Dickinson, Reilly, Lloyd (3g), S. Norton
Leigh 4 Hogan; A. Prescott, Stacey, Woods, Walsh (1t); Taylor, Sayer; D. Chisnall, Ashcroft (1dg), Fletcher, Macko, Grimes, Boyd
Referee: J.E. Jackson (Pudsey)
1977-78
Hull K.R. 26 Hall (4g); Dunn (2t), M. Smith (1t), Watson, Sullivan (1t); Hartley (1t), Millward; Millington, Watkinson, Cunningham (Hughes), Lowe, Rose (1t), Casey
St. Helens 11 G. Pimblett (Platt); L. Jones (Courtney), Noonan, Cunningham (1t), Glynn (2t, 1g); Francis, K. Gwilliam; D. Chisnall, Liptrot, James, Hope, A. Karalius, Pinner
Referee: M. J. Naughton (Widnes)
1978-79
Widnes 13 Eckersley; Wright (2t), Hughes, Aspey, P. Shaw; Burke (2g, 1t), Bowden; Hogan, Elwell, Mills, Adams, Dearden, Laughton
St. Helens 7 G. Pimblett (2g), L. Jones, Glynn, Cunningham, Mathias; Francis, Holding; D. Chisnall (1t), Liptrot, James, Nicholls, Knighton (E. Chisnall), Pinner
Referee: J. McDonald (Wigan)
1979-80
Hull 13 Woods; Bray, G. Evans (1t), Coupland, Dennison (1t, 2g); Newlove, Hepworth; Tindall, Wileman, Farrar, Stone, Boxall (Birdsall 1t), Norton
Hull K.R. 3 Robinson; Hubbard (1t), M. Smith, Watson, Sullivan; Hall, Agar; Holdstock, Tyreman, Lockwood, Clarkson (Hartley), Lowe, Hogan (Millington)
Referee: W.H. Thompson (Huddersfield)

CAPTAIN MORGAN TROPHY

This sponsored competition, with a winners' prize of £3,000, lasted only one season. Entry was restricted to the 16 clubs who won their Yorkshire and Lancashire Cup first round ties. The Lancashire contingent was made up to eight by including the side which lost their first round county Cup-tie by the narrowest margin. The first round of the Captain Morgan Trophy was zoned with clubs being drawn against those in their own county. The remainder of the competition was integrated. The final was on a neutral ground as follows:

1973-74   Warrington   4   Featherstone R.   0   Salford   5,259   £2,265

1973-74
Warrington 4 Whitehead (2g); M. Philbin, Noonan, Reynolds (Pickup), Bevan; Whittle, Gordon; D. Chisnall, Ashcroft, Brady, Wanbon (Price), Wright, Mather

Featherstone R. 0 Box; Coventry, M. Smith, Hartley, Bray; Mason, Wood; Tonks, Bridges, Harris, Gibbins (Stone), Rhodes, Bell
Referee: G.F. Lindop (Wakefield)

Second Division title celebrations for Hunslet, with skipper Terry Webb hoisted high.

LEAGUE

1986-87 CHAMPIONSHIP

A huge investment in talent from around the world paid dividends for Wigan with the ultimate return ... their first Championship title for 27 years.

The Riversiders romped to the Stones Bitter title and a record £20,000 cheque with a multi-nation squad consisting of 11 Great Britain players, two New Zealand Test stars, a pair of former South African Rugby Union caps and an English-born Australian. All coached by the newly-imported New Zealander Graham Lowe, mentor of the Kiwi Test side for the past three years.

Wigan clinched the league honours on 5th April, more than two weeks before the end of the campaign, finishing 15 points ahead of their nearest competitors, St. Helens, and smashing a series of First Division records established by the Saints since the reintroduction of two divisions in 1973.

Most tries: 174, beating 156 by St. Helens in 1984-85.

Most points: 941, beating 920 by St. Helens in 1984-85.

Least tries conceded: 29, beating 36 by St. Helens in 1974-75.

Least points conceded: 193, beating 229 by St. Helens in 1974-75.

Most league points: 56, from 28 wins, beating 53, from 26 wins and a draw, by St. Helens in 1974-75.

The Central Park outfit secured title success with a run of 17 successive league victories, their only two defeats of the season being at the hands of Warrington.

Lowe's charges rounded off a memorable league campaign with a burst of high scoring, from the start of March running in 60 points against Bradford Northern, Wakefield Trinity (72), Halifax (42), Featherstone Rovers (62), Oldham (54) and St. Helens (42).

Ellery Hanley, signed by Wigan in a record £150,000 deal in September 1985, revelled in the high scoring run-in to create a First Division record of 44 tries in the season and equalling the First Division record of five tries in a match.

St. Helens — who collected the first-ever Championship runners-up prize of £8,000 — led the table until 11th January, Warrington taking over temporarily until 1st March when Wigan capitalised on their backlog of fixtures to top the pile for the rest of the season.

In the Second Division, new look Hunslet, with David Ward controversially installed as coach alongside team manager Peter Jarvis and fielding a host of new signings including captain Terry Webb, took pole position on 5th October, a superiority they never relinquished.

The South Leeds club celebrated the launch of their new 21-year lease at Elland Road with a second Division Two title, after a 24-year break, and a £10,000 prize cheque from new league sponsors Stones Bitter. Their only defeats in a 28-match campaign came in away fixtures at Swinton, Sheffield Eagles and Carlisle.

Swinton were also promoted, for the second time in three seasons, receiving £4,000 in prize money.

The two-up, four-down promotion and relegation formula was a one-off format to pave the way for the introduction of a new style 14-club Stones Bitter Championship in 1987-88.

The 1986-87 campaign opened with the controversial absence of Fulham. The Londoners, who had finished the previous season in liquidation, folded after the publication of the Second Division fixtures based on a format of the 18 clubs being divided into six groups of three, each group playing four other groups to provide 28 games.

After the League's Management Committee had decided to award four points to those clubs due to meet Fulham, amid protests from the three clubs not scheduled to play in the capital city, Fulham made an 11th hour bid for reinstatement and played their first league fixture three weeks after the opening of the season.

The battle to avoid the drop into the Second Division was a cliffhanger, the fourth relegation place resting on the result of the last Championship fixture of the season!

With Wakefield Trinity, Barrow and Featherstone Rovers already booked for lower grade football, the final position rested between Hull, Salford and Oldham.

Salford pulled off a creditable 23-12 victory at Bradford Northern on the penultimate evening of the campaign — their ninth success in 11 matches in a remarkable survival run.

Thus the final Stones Bitter Championship match saw the once-mighty Hull entertaining Widnes, needing victory to avoid relegation only four years after celebrating title success. Urged on by more than 7,000 fans, the Airlie Birds gained a 21-4 victory over a much weakened Widnes side to send Oldham back into the Second Division after five seasons in the top ranks.

The Roughyeds had plummeted into the relegation zone with six successive end of season defeats and went down with 26 league points, the most by a relegated club in the present two-division era. It was also a disappointing finale to Frank Myler's time as coach at Watersheddings.

Leigh also figured in the most thrilling relegation struggle for years, securing First Division safety in their last match, a late victory at third-placed Warrington. Inspired by the appointment of coach Billy Benyon in December, replacing Tommy Dickens, the Hilton Park side won eight of their last 10 league fixtures while reaching the semi-finals of the Silk Cut Challenge Cup.

The innovation of a Second Division Premiership on the same top-eight basis as in the premier league was hailed as a success, the final place in the play-off not being determined until the last Second Division fixture of the season, Carlisle winning at Blackpool Borough.

Great Britain prop Brian Case, voted the Wigan Player of the Year.

Hunslet prop Andy Bateman, a Greenalls Second Division Player of the Year nominee and called up for Great Britain summer training.

Hunslet's Jimmy Irvine with Jed Coates in support.

FINAL TABLES 1986-87

STONES BITTER CHAMPIONSHIP

	P.	W.	D.	L.	Dr.	FOR Gls.	Trs.	Pts.	Dr.	AGAINST Gls.	Trs.	Pts.	Pts.
Wigan	30	28	0	2	3	121	174	941	3	37	29	193	56
St. Helens	30	20	1	9	7	130	142	835	5	78	76	465	41
Warrington	30	20	1	9	10	101	129	728	8	80	74	464	41
Castleford	30	20	0	10	3	110	102	631	7	65	73	429	40
Halifax	30	17	1	12	5	80	97	553	3	78	82	487	35
Hull K.R.	30	16	0	14	10	74	72	446	5	77	93	531	32
Bradford N.	30	15	1	14	11	92	90	555	4	89	92	550	31
Widnes	30	14	0	16	6	86	105	598	7	89	107	613	28
Salford	30	14	0	16	3	79	87	509	2	101	113	656	28
Leigh	30	13	1	16	3	87	93	549	8	83	109	610	27
Hull	30	13	1	16	6	72	97	538	4	99	112	650	27
Leeds	30	13	0	17	3	75	103	565	9	79	101	571	26
Oldham	30	13	0	17	4	85	95	554	3	106	116	679	26
Featherstone R.	30	8	1	21	8	89	78	498	10	107	138	776	17
Barrow	30	7	2	21	4	70	78	456	9	110	124	725	16
Wakefield T.	30	4	1	25	4	61	65	386	3	134	168	943	9

SECOND DIVISION

	P.	W.	D.	L.	Dr.	FOR Gls.	Trs.	Pts.	Dr.	AGAINST Gls.	Trs.	Pts.	Pts.
Hunslet	28	25	0	3	0	91	135	722	4	39	34	218	50
Swinton	28	23	1	4	13	104	123	713	3	52	54	323	47
Whitehaven	28	21	0	6	1	80	104	577	6	45	52	304	43
Doncaster	28	20	1	7	2	100	96	586	6	67	62	388	41
Rochdale H.	28	19	1	8	7	86	85	519	11	49	65	369	39
Sheffield E.	28	17	0	11	3	93	109	625	10	76	66	426	34
Bramley	28	16	0	12	3	62	70	407	12	62	76	440	32
Carlisle	28	15	1	12	7	66	81	463	6	72	74	446	31
Blackpool B.	28	14	0	14	4	71	96	530	7	77	79	477	28
York	28	11	0	17	12	72	84	492	3	75	96	537	22
Runcorn H.	28	10	1	17	3	54	70	391	5	82	91	533	21
Fulham	28	8	2	18	9	76	75	461	6	95	109	632	18
Batley	28	9	0	19	5	49	58	335	10	81	89	528	18
Workington T.	28	9	0	19	7	69	65	405	8	92	115	652	18
Huddersfield B.	28	8	0	20	10	69	77	456	5	98	118	673	16
Mansfield M.	28	8	0	20	16	69	53	366	2	81	107	592	16
Dewsbury	28	8	0	20	4	56	53	328	3	86	97	563	16
Keighley	28	7	0	21	6	54	63	366	5	92	113	641	14

TWO DIVISION CHAMPIONSHIP ROLL OF HONOUR

	FIRST DIVISION	SECOND DIVISION
1902-03	Halifax	Keighley
1903-04	Bradford	Wakefield Trinity
1904-05	Oldham	Dewsbury
1962-63	Swinton	Hunslet
1963-64	Swinton	Oldham
1973-74	Salford	Bradford Northern
1974-75	St. Helens	Huddersfield
1975-76	Salford	Barrow
1976-77	Featherstone Rovers	Hull
1977-78	Widnes	Leigh
1978-79	Hull Kingston Rovers	Hull
1979-80	Bradford Northern	Featherstone Rovers
1980-81	Bradford Northern	York
1981-82	Leigh	Oldham
1982-83	Hull	Fulham
1983-84	Hull Kingston Rovers	Barrow
1984-85	Hull Kingston Rovers	Swinton
1985-86	Halifax	Leigh
1986-87	Wigan	Hunslet

THE UPS AND DOWNS OF TWO DIVISION FOOTBALL

● Figure in brackets indicates position in division.

	RELEGATED	PROMOTED
1902-03	St. Helens (17)	Keighley (1)
	Brighouse (18)	Leeds (2)
1903-04	Keighley (17)	Wakefield Trinity (1)
	Huddersfield (18)	St. Helens (2)
*1904-05	St. Helens (17)	Dewsbury (1)
	Runcorn (18)	Barrow (2)
1962-63	Oldham (15)	Hunslet (1)
	Bramley (16)	Keighley (2)
*1963-64	Keighley (15)	Oldham (1)
	Hull (16)	Leigh (2)
1973-74	Oldham (13)	Bradford Northern (1)
	Hull K.R. (14)	York (2)
	Leigh (15)	Keighley (3)
	Whitehaven (16)	Halifax (4)
1974-75	York (13)	Huddersfield (1)
	Bramley (14)	Hull K.R. (2)
	Rochdale Hornets (15)	Oldham (3)
	Halifax (16)	Swinton (4)

1975-76	Dewsbury (13) Keighley (14) Huddersfield (15) Swinton (16)	Barrow (1) Rochdale Hornets (2) Workington T. (3) Leigh (4)
1976-77	Rochdale Hornets (13) Leigh (14) Barrow (15) Oldham (16)	Hull (1) Dewsbury (2) Bramley (3) New Hunslet (4)
1977-78	Hull (13) New Hunslet (14) Bramley (15) Dewsbury (16)	Leigh (1) Barrow (2) Rochdale Hornets (3) Huddersfield (4)
1978-79	Barrow (13) Featherstone Rovers (14) Rochdale Hornets (15) Huddersfield (16)	Hull (1) New Hunslet (2) York (3) Blackpool Borough (4)
1979-80	Wigan (13) Hunslet (14) York (15) Blackpool Borough (16)	Featherstone Rovers (1) Halifax (2) Oldham (3) Barrow (4)
1980-81	Halifax (13) Salford (14) Workington T. (15) Oldham (16)	York (1) Wigan (2) Fulham (3) Whitehaven (4)
1981-82	Fulham (13) Wakefield T. (14) York (15) Whitehaven (16)	Oldham (1) Carlisle (2) Workington T. (3) Halifax (4)
1982-83	Barrow (13) Workington T. (14) Halifax (15) Carlisle (16)	Fulham (1) Wakefield T. (2) Salford (3) Whitehaven (14)
1983-84	Fulham (13) Wakefield T. (14) Salford (15) Whitehaven (16)	Barrow (1) Workington T. (2) Hunslet (3) Halifax (4)
1984-85	Barrow (13) Leigh (14) Hunslet (15) Workington T. (16)	Swinton (1) Salford (2) York (3) Dewsbury (4)
1985-86	York (14) Swinton (15) Dewsbury (16)	Leigh (1) Barrow (2) Wakefield T. (3)
1986-87	Oldham (13) Featherstone R. (14) Barrow (15) Wakefield T. (16)	Hunslet (1) Swinton (2)

*Two divisions scrapped following season.

FIRST DIVISION RECORDS
Since reintroduction in 1973

INDIVIDUAL

Match records

Most tries:
5 Roy Mathias (St. Helens) v. Rochdale H.   Feb 17, 1974
Roy Mathias (St. Helens) v. Workington T.
  Dec 23, 1979
Parry Gordon (Warrington) v. Dewsbury Mar 3, 1974
Peter Glynn (St. Helens) v. Hull Oct 16, 1977
Steve Fenton (Castleford) v. Dewsbury Jan 27, 1978
Steve Hartley (Hull K.R.) v. Huddersfield Apr 13, 1979
Kevin Meadows (Oldham) at Salford Apr 20, 1984
John Woods (Bradford N.) v. Swinton Oct 13, 1985
John Basnett (Widnes) v. Hull K.R. Nov 2, 1986
Ellery Hanley (Wigan) v. Bradford N. Mar 1, 1987

Most goals: 13 Geoff Pimblett (St. Helens) v. Bramley
Mar 5, 1978

Most points: 38 (11g, 4t) Bob Beardmore (Castleford) v.
Barrow Mar 22, 1987

Season records

Most tries: 44 Ellery Hanley (Wigan) 1986-87
Most goals: 130 Steve Hesford (Warrington) 1978-79
Most points: 295 (101g, 1dg, 23t) John Woods (Leigh)
1983-84

TEAM

Highest score: Bradford N. 72 v. Hunslet 12 Oct 7, 1984
  Wakefield T. 6 v. Wigan 72 Mar 29, 1987
  (Also biggest away win and widest margin)

Most points by losing team: Hunslet 40 v. Barrow 41
Sep 9, 1984

Scoreless draw: Wigan 0 v. Castleford 0 Jan 26, 1974

Highest score draw: Widnes 28 v. St. Helens 28
Apr 23, 1984

Best opening sequence: 13 wins then a draw by Widnes
1981-82

Longest winning run: 25 by St. Helens
Won last 13 of 1985-86 and first 12 of 1986-87.
(Also longest unbeaten run.)

Longest losing run: 20 by Whitehaven 1983-84

Longest run without a win: 23, including 3 draws, by
Whitehaven 1981-82 (Also worst opening sequence)

Biggest attendance: 21,813 Wigan v. St. Helens
Dec 26, 1985

100 Division One tries
165 Keith Fielding (Salford)
144 David Smith (Wakefield T., Leeds, Bradford N.)
139 Stuart Wright (Wigan, Widnes)
138 Ellery Hanley (Bradford N., Wigan)
136 Roy Mathias (St. Helens)
130 John Bevan (Warrington)
126 Steve Hartley (Hull K.R.)
     David Topliss (Wakefield T., Hull, Oldham)
122 Maurice Richards (Salford)
     Steve Evans (Featherstone R., Hull, Wakefield T.,
       Bradford N.)
     John Joyner (Castleford)
113 David Redfearn (Bradford N.)
111 John Woods (Leigh, Bradford N.)

500 Division One goals
845 Steve Hesford (Warrington)
803 Steve Quinn (Featherstone R.)
786 George Fairbairn (Wigan, Hull K.R.)
695 John Woods (Leigh, Bradford N.)
586 Sammy Lloyd (Castleford, Hull)

1,000 Division One points
1,760 John Woods (Leigh, Bradford N.)
1,756 Steve Hesford (Warrington)
1,738 Steve Quinn (Featherstone R.)
1,720 George Fairbairn (Wigan, Hull K.R.)
1,264 Sammy Lloyd (Castleford, Hull)
1,109 Mick Burke (Widnes, Oldham)
1,057 Keith Mumby (Bradford N.)

*Sammy Lloyd, top Division One goalkicker in 1975
and 1976.*

20 Division One tries in a season

1973-74	36	Keith Fielding (Salford)
	29	Roy Mathias (St. Helens)
	21	David Smith (Wakefield T.)
1974-75	21	Maurice Richards (Salford)
	21	Roy Mathias (St. Helens)
1975-76	26	Maurice Richards (Salford)
	20	David Smith (Wakefield T.)
1976-77	22	David Topliss (Wakefield T.)
	21	Keith Fielding (Salford)
	21	Ged Dunn (Hull K.R.)
	20	David Smith (Leeds)
	20	Stuart Wright (Widnes)
1977-78	26	Keith Fielding (Salford)
	25	Steve Fenton (Castleford)
	24	Stuart Wright (Widnes)
	20	David Smith (Leeds)
	20	Bruce Burton (Castleford)
	20	John Bevan (Warrington)
1978-79	28	Steve Hartley (Hull K.R.)
1979-80	24	Keith Fielding (Salford)
	21	Roy Mathias (St. Helens)
	21	Steve Hubbard (Hull K.R.)
	20	David Smith (Leeds)
1980-81	20	Steve Hubbard (Hull K.R.)
1981-82		David Hobbs (Featherstone R.) was top scorer with 19 tries.
1982-83	22	Bob Eccles (Warrington)
	20	Steve Evans (Hull)
1983-84	28	Garry Schofield (Hull)
	23	John Woods (Leigh)
	20	James Leuluai (Hull)
1984-85	40	Ellery Hanley (Bradford N.)
	34	Gary Prohm (Hull K.R.)
	23	Henderson Gill (Wigan)
	22	Barry Ledger (St. Helens)
	22	Mal Meninga (St. Helens)
1985-86	22	Ellery Hanley (Wigan)
1986-87	44	Ellery Hanley (Wigan)
	24	Phil Ford (Bradford N.)
	24	Henderson Gill (Wigan)
	23	Garry Schofield (Hull)
	21	John Henderson (Leigh)

Top Division One goalscorers

1973-74	126	David Watkins (Salford)
1974-75	96	Sammy Lloyd (Castleford)
1975-76	118	Sammy Lloyd (Castleford)
1976-77	113	Steve Quinn (Featherstone R.)
1977-78	116	Steve Hesford (Warrington)
1978-79	130	Steve Hesford (Warrington)
1979-80	104	Steve Hubbard (Hull K.R.)
1980-81	96	Steve Diamond (Wakefield T.)
1981-82	110	Steve Quinn (Featherstone R.)
		John Woods (Leigh)
1982-83	105	Bob Beardmore (Castleford)
1983-84	106	Steve Hesford (Warrington)
1984-85	114	Sean Day (St. Helens)
1985-86	85	David Stephenson (Wigan)
1986-87	120	Paul Loughlin (St. Helens)

Top Division One pointscorer 1986-87
252 (120g, 3t) Paul Loughlin (St. Helens)

SECOND DIVISION RECORDS
Since reintroduction in 1973

INDIVIDUAL

Match records

Most tries: 6 Ged Dunn (Hull K.R.) v. New Hunslet Feb 2, 1975

Most goals: 15 Mick Stacey (Leigh) v. Doncaster Mar 28, 1976

Most points: 38 (13g, 4t) John Woods (Leigh) v. Blackpool B. Sep 11, 1977

Season records

Most tries: 48 Steve Halliwell (Leigh) 1985-86

Most goals: 166 Lynn Hopkins (Workington T.) 1981-82

Most points: 395 (163g, 3dg, 22t) Lynn Hopkins (Workington T.) 1981-82

TEAM

Highest score: Leigh 92 v. Keighley 2 Apr 30, 1986 (Also widest margin)

Highest away: Kent Invicta 8 v. Barrow 80 Apr 8, 1984

Most points by losing team:
Hunslet 38 v. Blackpool B. 32 Sep 22, 1985
Carlisle 32 v. Blackpool B. 33 Oct 27, 1985

Highest score draw: Huddersfield B. 32 v. Keighley 32 Apr 17, 1986

Scoreless draw: Dewsbury 0 v. Rochdale H. 0. Jan 30, 1983

Longest winning run: 30 by Leigh in 1985-86. Hull won all 26 matches in 1978-79

Longest losing run: 40 by Doncaster (16 in 1975-76 and 24 in 1976-77)

Biggest attendance: 12,424 Hull v. New Hunslet May 18, 1979

1986-87 Top Division Two scorers

Most tries: 25 Derek Bate (Swinton)

Most goals: 100 David Noble (Doncaster)

Most points: 222 (98g, 2dg, 6t) David Noble (Doncaster)

NB. Division One and Two records do not include scores in abandoned matches that were replayed.

TWO DIVISION SCORING

A record total of 1,607 tries were scored in Division One last season, reflecting the modern era of high-speed spectacular rugby.

It beat the previous best of 1,595 in 1984-85 to maintain the steady rise in the tryscoring rate since the first season of the reintroduction of two divisions in 1973-74.

The total dropped to a modern low of 1,261 the following season, but has since risen with a number of rule changes which have made the game faster and more open. Increasing the value of a try from three to four points in 1983 obviously also pushed the points totals to record figures.

Previous two-division eras compare poorly with the present tryscoring rate. In 1962-63 only 1,144 tries were scored in a similar 30-match programme, with just 100 more the following season.

Over 80 years ago, three seasons of Divison One rugby produced an average of 768 tries over three seasons despite each club having a 34-match programme.

Wigan led last season's scoring bonanza with a Division One record total of 174 tries, beating the 156 by St. Helens in 1984-85, while conceding a record low of only 29.

Despite the big increase in tries scored, the number of placed goals, although more than the previous season, remains comparatively low.

From a record high of 1,508 in 1973-74 they dropped to a record low of 1,296 in 1985-86. The introduction in 1976-77 of the differential penalty rule which prevented kicks at goal for scrum offences had some effect but the goals total remained high until the last two seasons.

The number of drop goals per season has varied with a succession of rule changes since they were reduced from two to one point in 1974.

Only 48 were scored in Division One during that first season of devaluation but they grew to a peak of 147 in 1980-81.

There was an unaccountable fall to 64 in 1982-83 before the hand-over rule pushed the total up to 108, but it has dropped below a century in each of the last three seasons.

The fluctuating number of matches in Division Two over the years make comparisons for the lower league difficult.

The following tables show the scoring totals for each two-division season:

DIVISION ONE

Season	Matches each club played	Goals	1-Point drop goals	Tries	Pts
1902-03	34	541	—	692	3,158
1903-04	34	568	—	796	3,524
1904-05	34	659	—	817	3,769
1962-63	30	1,269	—	1,144	5,970
1963-64	30	1,234	—	1,244	6,200
1973-74	30	1,508	—	1,295	6,901
1974-75	30	1,334	48	1,261	6,499
1975-76	30	1,498	53	1,331	7,042
1976-77	30[1]	1,435	91	1,423	7,230
1977-78	30[2]	1,402	99	1,443	7,232
1978-79	30	1,367	119	1,448	7,197
1979-80	30	1,389	131	1,349	6,956
1980-81	30	1,439	147	1,342	7,051
1981-82	30	1,486	132	1,354	7,166
1982-83	30	1,369	64	1,386	6,960
1983-84	30	1,472	108	1,479	8,968
1984-85	30	1,464	84	1,595	9,392
1985-86	30	1,296	80	1,435	8,412
1986-87	30	1,412	90	1,607	9,342

[1] Salford & Leeds played 29 matches — their final match was abandoned and not replayed. This match was expunged from league records.
[2] Featherstone R. & Bradford N. played 29 matches — their final match was cancelled following Featherstone's strike.

DIVISION TWO

Season	Matches each club played	Goals	1-Point drop goals	Tries	Pts
1902-03	34	542	—	723	3,253
1903-04	32	510	—	786	3,378
1904-05	26[1]	369	—	516	2,286
1962-63	26	907	—	856	4,382
1963-64	24[2]	739	—	701	3,581
1973-74	26	1,054	—	955	4,973
1974-75	26	992	36	919	4,777
1975-76	26	1,034	49	963	5,006
1976-77	26	942	78	1,046	5,100
1977-78	26	976	86	1,020	5,098
1978-79	26	971	114	972	4,972
1979-80	26	1,046	106	1,069	5,405
1980-81	28	1,133	123	1,220	6,049
1981-82	32	1,636	150	1,589	8,189
1982-83	32	1,510	103	1,648	8,067
1983-84	34	1,782	254	1,897	11,406
1984-85	28[3]	1,542	226	1,666	9,974
1985-86	34	1,722	130	2,021	11,658
1986-87	28	1,323	112	1,496	8,742

[1] Birkenhead withdrew after 4 matches. These matches were expunged from league records.
[2] Bradford N. withdrew after 13 matches. These matches were expunged from league records.
[3] The 20 clubs played only 28 matches each.

FOURTEEN-SEASON TABLE

St. Helens confirmed their position as the most successful Division One side since the reintroduction of two divisions in 1973 in terms of most points gained. They retained the lead with 20 victories and a draw taking their 14-season total to 558 points from 420 matches.

The Saints are the only club to have finished in the top eight in each season although their only championship success was in 1974-75. In addition to St. Helens only Widnes, Castleford, Leeds and Warrington have remained in Division One.

Three clubs have spent the entire 14 seasons in Division Two ... Batley, Doncaster and Runcorn Highfield.

Bradford Northern, Hull and Leigh were all Division Two champions who went on to win the Division One title only a few seasons after promotion, while Hull Kingston Rovers, Halifax and Wigan are other former lower grade clubs who have won the trophy.

Halifax achieved the quickest Division One championship win when they took the title in 1985-86 in only their second campaign after being promoted.

The highest place gained by a newly-promoted club is third by Hull in 1979-80 after winning the Division Two championship with a 100 per cent record the previous season.

Division One champions who were relegated a few seasons after winning the major title were Salford, Featherstone Rovers and Leigh.

The records of the five clubs who have appeared in Division One throughout the 14 seasons are as follows:

Scrum half Neil Holding, a St. Helens' regular for the past decade.

	P	W	D	L	F	A	Pts
1. St. Helens	420	270	18	132	8,463	5,488	558
2. Widnes	420	262	17	141	7,170	5,323	541
3. Leeds	419	239 ·	16	164	7,534	6,098	494
4. Warrington	420	236	15	169	7,035	5,863	487
5. Castleford	420	211	23	186	7,548	6,505	445

● Although Bradford Northern and Hull Kingston Rovers have had only 13 seasons in Division One their records compare more favourably with some of the above. Three times champions Rovers have gained 490 points and twice champions Northern 449.

TWO DIVISION FINAL TABLES

Three eras
1902-05, 1962-64, 1973-86

1902-03:

FIRST DIVISION

	P.	W.	D.	L.	F.	A.	Pts.
Halifax	34	23	3	8	199	85	49
Salford	34	20	5	9	244	130	45
Swinton	34	18	7	9	254	119	43
Runcorn	34	19	4	11	239	139	42
Broughton R.	34	17	7	10	222	97	41
Oldham	34	20	0	14	200	128	40
Bradford	34	16	5	13	220	161	37
Warrington	34	14	7	13	148	164	35
Hunslet	34	16	3	15	185	220	35
Hull	34	16	2	16	204	192	34
Batley	34	15	4	15	176	214	34
Leigh	34	12	5	17	136	178	29
Widnes	34	13	2	19	131	167	28
Hull K.R.	34	13	2	19	155	215	28
Huddersfield	34	13	2	19	116	196	28
Wigan	34	10	6	18	125	174	26
St. Helens	34	9	2	23	125	309	20
Brighouse R.	34	7	4	23	79	270	18

SECOND DIVISION

	P.	W.	D.	L.	F.	A.	Pts.
Keighley	34	27	2	5	270	92	56
Leeds	34	26	1	7	334	98	53
Millom	34	22	3	9	238	118	47
Rochdale H.	34	20	6	8	323	88	46
Holbeck	34	20	5	9	213	83	45
Barrow	34	22	0	12	230	140	44
Wakefield T.	34	18	2	14	263	196	38
Bramley	34	16	4	14	179	151	36
Birkenhead	34	14	6	14	125	140	34
Manningham	34	14	5	15	141	170	33
Lancaster	34	13	4	17	123	214	30
Normanton	34	12	4	18	160	228	28
York	34	11	4	19	111	190	26
South Shields	34	10	2	22	158	264	22
Castleford	34	9	4	21	105	268	22
Dewsbury	34	8	5	21	123	245	21
Morecambe	34	9	2	23	88	220	20
Stockport	34	5	1	28	69	348	11

1903-04:

FIRST DIVISION

	P.	W.	D.	L.	F.	A.	Pts.
Bradford	34	25	2	7	303	96	52
Salford	34	25	2	7	366	108	52
Broughton R.	34	21	4	9	306	142	46
Hunslet	34	22	1	11	250	157	45
Oldham	34	20	3	11	215	110	43
Leeds	34	19	5	10	211	145	43
Warrington	34	17	3	14	214	153	37
Hull K.R.	34	17	2	15	191	167	36
Halifax	34	14	3	17	125	148	31
Wigan	34	11	6	17	177	174	28
Swinton	34	12	4	18	139	215	28
Batley	34	12	3	19	139	241	27
Hull	34	12	3	19	148	258	27
Widnes	34	11	5	18	126	243	27
Leigh	34	10	5	19	174	250	25
Runcorn	34	11	2	21	151	245	24
Keighley	34	8	5	21	129	319	21
Huddersfield	34	10	0	24	160	353	20

CHAMPIONSHIP PLAY-OFF
at Hanson Lane, Halifax

BRADFORD	1	1	5
SALFORD	0	0	0

SECOND DIVISION

	P.	W.	D.	L.	F.	A.	Pts.
Wakefield T.	32	27	1	4	389	57	55
St. Helens	32	23	3	6	328	105	49
Holbeck	32	24	1	7	256	120	49
Rochdale H.	32	22	2	8	319	104	46
York	32	20	1	11	244	97	41
Brighouse R.	32	19	3	10	192	136	41
Castleford	32	18	3	11	185	194	39
Bramley	32	16	4	12	181	180	36
Barrow	32	16	3	13	219	162	35
Pontefract	32	14	6	12	174	150	34
Dewsbury	32	12	3	17	185	205	27
Millom	32	12	2	18	185	209	26
Lancaster	32	8	2	22	129	291	18
Birkenhead	32	7	0	25	75	334	14
South Shields	32	6	1	25	140	336	13
Morecambe	32	5	3	24	72	287	13
Normanton	32	4	0	28	105	411	8

PROMOTION PLAY-OFF
at Huddersfield

ST. HELENS	1	2	7
HOLBECK	0	0	0

1904-05:

FIRST DIVISION

	P.	W.	D.	L.	F.	A.	Pts.
Oldham	34	25	1	8	291	158	51
Bradford	34	23	2	9	294	156	48
Broughton R.	34	22	2	10	295	175	46
Leeds	34	20	4	10	232	150	44
Warrington	34	20	2	12	220	150	42
Salford	34	19	2	13	276	204	40
Wigan	34	18	1	15	230	195	37
Hull	34	15	4	15	224	214	34
Hunslet	34	16	1	17	240	216	33
Halifax	34	15	2	17	204	155	32
Leigh	34	14	3	17	165	209	31
Hull K.R.	34	15	0	19	200	220	30
Swinton	34	13	2	19	155	196	28
Wakefield T.	34	13	2	19	154	211	28
Batley	34	12	3	19	160	228	27
Widnes	34	13	1	20	128	280	27
St. Helens	34	9	1	24	168	351	19
Runcorn	34	7	1	26	133	301	15

SECOND DIVISION

	P.	W.	D.	L.	F.	A.	Pts.
Dewsbury	26	22	2	2	247	48	46
Barrow	26	22	0	4	286	68	44
York	26	18	3	5	205	76	39
Keighley	26	15	2	9	259	94	32
Huddersfield	26	14	2	10	231	143	30
Rochdale H.	26	11	4	11	154	145	26
Millom	26	12	0	14	139	173	24
Pontefract	26	10	1	15	156	175	21
Castleford	26	9	3	14	104	199	21
Normanton	26	9	1	16	105	228	19
Brighouse R.	26	8	1	17	111	169	17
Lancaster	26	8	1	17	106	257	17
Morecambe	26	7	2	17	88	272	16
Bramley	26	5	2	19	95	239	12

1962-63:

FIRST DIVISION

	P.	W.	D.	L.	F.	A.	Pts.
Swinton	30	22	1	7	372	231	45
St. Helens	30	19	1	10	525	260	39
Widnes	30	19	1	10	325	301	39
Castleford	30	16	3	11	370	321	35
Wakefield T.	30	16	1	13	432	359	33
Warrington	30	15	2	13	391	337	32
Leeds	30	16	0	14	333	364	32
Wigan	30	14	2	14	476	393	30
Huddersfield	30	14	0	16	298	278	28
Hull K.R.	30	13	1	16	389	387	27
Featherstone R.	30	12	3	15	389	407	27
Workington T.	30	12	3	15	410	441	27
Halifax	30	13	1	16	354	417	27
Hull	30	10	2	18	352	462	22
Oldham	30	9	1	20	288	432	19
Bramley	30	9	0	21	266	580	18

SECOND DIVISION

	P.	W.	D.	L.	F.	A.	Pts.
Hunslet	26	22	0	4	508	214	44
Keighley	26	21	0	5	450	187	42
York	26	16	1	9	418	243	33
Blackpool B.	26	15	0	11	281	247	30
Rochdale H.	26	14	1	11	282	243	29
Barrow	26	14	0	12	413	280	28
Leigh	26	14	0	12	361	264	28
Batley	26	13	1	12	275	322	27
Whitehaven	26	12	2	12	318	306	26
Doncaster	26	10	0	16	283	329	20
Liverpool C.	26	9	1	16	159	328	19
Salford	26	8	1	17	271	442	17
Dewsbury	26	8	0	18	200	345	16
Bradford N.	26	2	1	23	163	632	5

● Birkenhead resigned from the League after four games. These are not included in the league table. Birkenhead lost all four matches, conceding 93 points, with none scored.

1963-64:

FIRST DIVISION

	P.	W.	D.	L.	F.	A.	Pts.
Swinton	30	25	0	5	401	202	50
Wigan	30	21	2	7	530	294	44
St. Helens	30	20	1	9	418	266	41
Featherstone R.	30	18	1	11	485	364	37
Workington T.	30	18	1	11	436	332	37
Castleford	30	18	0	12	436	338	36
Wakefield T.	30	16	0	14	488	339	32
Halifax	30	15	1	14	368	388	31
Hull K.R.	30	15	0	15	448	368	30
Warrington	30	15	0	15	374	380	30
Hunslet	30	14	0	16	371	487	28
Widnes	30	13	0	17	338	386	26
Leeds	30	10	0	20	323	493	20
Huddersfield	30	10	0	20	264	413	20
Keighley	30	5	0	25	253	599	10
Hull	30	4	0	26	267	551	8

SECOND DIVISION

	P.	W.	D.	L.	F.	A.	Pts.
Oldham	24	21	1	2	508	168	43
Leigh	24	16	2	6	411	224	34
Dewsbury	24	15	2	7	239	220	32
Barrow	24	14	1	9	351	280	29
Bramley	24	14	0	10	300	256	28
Blackpool B.	24	12	1	11	299	303	25
York	24	12	0	12	317	250	24
Rochdale H.	24	8	1	15	209	271	17
Liverpool C.	24	8	1	15	200	261	17
Batley	24	8	0	16	174	304	16
Whitehaven	24	8	0	16	173	341	16
Salford	24	8	0	16	218	392	16
Doncaster	24	7	1	16	182	311	15

● Bradford Northern disbanded after playing 13 matches. They won one and lost 12. For 109, Against 284. These matches were declared null and void.

1973-74:

FIRST DIVISION

	P.	W.	D.	L.	F.	A.	Pts.
Salford	30	23	1	6	632	299	47
St. Helens	30	22	2	6	595	263	46
Leeds	30	20	1	9	554	378	41
Widnes	30	18	1	11	431	329	37
Warrington	30	16	1	13	414	368	33
Dewsbury	30	16	1	13	389	474	33
Wakefield T.	30	16	0	14	470	411	32
Featherstone R.	30	14	2	14	443	397	30
Castleford	30	12	4	14	420	411	28
Rochdale H.	30	13	2	15	379	415	28
Wigan	30	12	3	15	427	364	27
Bramley	30	11	3	16	344	457	25
Oldham	30	12	1	17	341	494	25
Hull K.R.	30	9	2	19	428	552	20
Leigh	30	7	0	23	326	655	14
Whitehaven	30	7	0	23	308	634	14

SECOND DIVISION

	P.	W.	D.	L.	F.	A.	Pts.
Bradford N.	26	24	0	2	607	221	48
York	26	21	0	5	429	219	42
Keighley	26	20	0	6	439	250	40
Halifax	26	18	0	8	460	298	36
Workington T.	26	17	0	9	421	310	34
Hull	26	16	0	10	465	256	32
Swinton	26	15	0	11	405	276	30
Batley	26	12	0	14	286	311	24
Barrow	26	11	0	15	214	291	22
Huddersfield	26	9	0	17	363	394	18
N. Hunslet	26	7	0	19	272	418	14
Blackpool B.	26	7	0	19	272	585	14
Doncaster	26	3	0	23	158	684	6
Huyton	26	2	0	24	182	460	4

1974-75

FIRST DIVISION

	P.	W.	D.	L.	F.	A.	Pts.
St. Helens	30	26	1	3	561	229	53
Wigan	30	21	0	9	517	341	42
Leeds	30	19	1	10	581	359	39
Featherstone R.	30	19	1	10	431	339	39
Widnes	30	18	1	11	382	305	37
Warrington	30	17	1	12	428	356	35
Bradford N.	30	16	1	13	393	376	33
Castleford	30	14	3	13	480	427	31
Salford	30	14	1	15	451	351	29
Wakefield T.	30	12	5	13	440	419	29
Keighley	30	13	0	17	300	424	26
Dewsbury	30	11	0	19	350	506	22
York	30	10	0	20	359	498	20
Bramley	30	9	0	21	338	493	18
Rochdale H.	30	8	0	22	219	400	16
Halifax	30	5	1	24	269	676	11

SECOND DIVISION

	P.	W.	D.	L.	F.	A.	Pts.
Huddersfield	26	21	0	5	489	213	42
Hull K.R.	26	20	1	5	628	249	41
Oldham	26	19	0	7	406	223	38
Swinton	26	17	1	8	399	254	35
Workington T.	26	16	0	10	371	275	32
Whitehaven	26	14	1	11	285	234	29
Huyton	26	12	2	12	301	291	26
Hull	26	12	1	13	344	309	25
Barrow	26	12	2	13	338	315	24
Leigh	26	11	1	14	302	348	23
New Hunslet	26	10	2	14	309	384	22
Blackpool B.	26	7	1	18	261	417	15
Batley	26	4	1	21	197	520	9
Doncaster	26	1	1	24	147	745	3

1975-76

FIRST DIVISION

	P.	W.	D.	L.	F.	A.	Pts.
Salford	30	22	1	7	555	350	45
Featherstone R.	30	21	2	7	526	348	44
Leeds	30	21	0	9	571	395	42
St. Helens	30	19	1	10	513	315	39
Wigan	30	18	3	9	514	399	39
Widnes	30	18	1	11	448	369	37
Wakefield T.	30	17	0	13	496	410	34
Hull K.R.	30	17	0	13	446	472	34
Castleford	30	16	1	13	589	398	33
Warrington	30	15	2	13	381	456	32
Bradford N.	30	13	1	16	454	450	27
Oldham	30	11	1	18	380	490	23
Dewsbury	30	10	1	19	287	484	21
Keighley	30	7	0	23	274	468	14
Huddersfield	30	5	0	25	370	657	10
Swinton	30	3	0	27	238	581	6

SECOND DIVISION

	P.	W.	D.	L.	F.	A.	Pts.
Barrow	26	20	3	3	366	213	43
Rochdale H.	26	19	3	4	347	200	41
Workington T.	26	18	4	4	519	228	40
Leigh	26	19	1	6	571	217	39
Hull	26	19	1	6	577	278	39
New Hunslet	26	15	1	10	371	308	31
York	26	12	1	13	447	394	25
Bramley	26	11	1	14	344	370	23
Huyton	26	10	0	16	242	373	20
Whitehaven	26	8	2	16	253	347	18
Halifax	26	7	1	18	322	460	15
Batley	26	6	1	19	228	432	13
Blackpool B.	26	6	1	19	224	460	13
Doncaster	26	2	0	24	195	726	4

1976-77

FIRST DIVISION

	P.	W.	D.	L.	F.	A.	Pts.
Featherstone R.	30	21	2	7	568	334	44
St. Helens	30	19	1	10	547	345	39
Castleford	30	19	1	10	519	350	39
Hull K.R.	30	18	1	11	496	415	37
Warrington	30	18	0	12	532	406	36
Salford	*29	17	1	11	560	402	35
Wigan	30	15	2	13	463	416	32
Bradford N.	30	15	2	13	488	470	32
Leeds	*29	14	2	13	467	439	30
Widnes	30	15	0	15	403	393	30
Wakefield T.	30	13	2	15	487	480	28
Workington T.	30	13	1	16	352	403	27
Rochdale H.	30	11	0	19	367	449	22
Leigh	30	8	1	21	314	634	17
Barrow	30	8	0	22	345	628	16
Oldham	30	7	0	23	322	666	14

*The Salford v. Leeds match was abandoned after a fatal injury to Chris Sanderson (Leeds) and not replayed. Leeds were winning 5-2 after 38 mins. but the match was declared null and void.

SECOND DIVISION

	P.	W.	D.	L.	F.	A.	Pts.
Hull	26	22	1	3	599	238	45
Dewsbury	26	19	2	5	429	199	40
Bramley	26	19	0	7	464	377	38
New Hunslet	26	17	3	6	411	231	37
York	26	17	0	9	422	279	34
Keighley	26	16	1	9	486	235	33
Huddersfield	26	13	0	13	397	329	26
Whitehaven	26	11	1	14	290	346	23
Huyton	26	11	0	15	302	402	22
Halifax	26	10	0	16	301	429	20
Swinton	26	8	2	16	261	406	18
Batley	26	7	1	18	262	461	15
Blackpool B.	26	5	1	20	233	464	11
Doncaster	26	1	0	25	243	704	2

1977-78

FIRST DIVISION

	P.	W.	D.	L.	F.	A.	Pts.
Widnes	30	24	2	4	613	241	50
**Bradford N.	29	21	2	6	500	291	44
St. Helens	30	22	1	7	678	384	45
Hull K.R.	30	16	3	11	495	419	35
Wigan	30	17	1	12	482	435	35
Salford	30	16	0	14	470	446	32
Featherstone R.	29	15	2	12	443	452	32
Leeds	30	15	1	14	512	460	31
Warrington	30	15	0	15	561	367	30
Castleford	30	13	2	15	515	583	28
Workington T.	30	11	4	15	406	519	26
Wakefield T.	30	12	1	17	393	450	25
Hull	30	10	3	17	358	480	23
New Hunslet	30	11	0	19	318	518	22
Bramley	30	5	4	21	281	608	14
Dewsbury	30	2	2	26	207	579	6

**Bradford N. second on percentage as last game was cancelled following Featherstone's strike.

SECOND DIVISION

	P.	W.	D.	L.	F.	A.	Pts.
Leigh	26	21	0	5	538	231	42
Barrow	26	21	0	5	521	234	42
Rochdale H.	26	21	0	5	437	200	42
Huddersfield	26	18	0	8	502	324	36
York	26	16	2	8	447	286	34
Oldham	26	17	0	9	419	325	34
Keighley	26	11	3	12	357	337	25
Swinton	26	11	1	14	369	385	23
Whitehaven	26	10	2	14	277	326	22
Huyton	26	9	2	15	250	352	20
Doncaster	26	9	0	17	304	528	18
Batley	26	5	1	20	233	496	11
Blackpool B.	26	5	1	20	262	543	11
Halifax	26	2	0	24	182	531	4

1978-79

FIRST DIVISION

	P.	W.	D.	L.	F.	A.	Pts.
Hull K.R.	30	23	0	7	616	344	46
Warrington	30	22	0	8	521	340	44
Widnes	30	21	2	7	480	322	44
Leeds	30	19	1	10	555	370	39
St. Helens	30	16	2	12	485	379	34
Wigan	30	16	1	13	484	411	33
Castleford	30	16	1	13	498	469	33
Bradford N.	30	16	0	14	523	416	32
Workington T.	30	13	3	14	378	345	29
Wakefield T.	30	13	1	16	382	456	27
Leigh	30	13	1	16	406	535	27
Salford	30	11	2	17	389	435	24
Barrow	30	9	2	19	368	536	20
Featherstone R.	30	8	1	21	501	549	17
Rochdale H.	30	8	0	22	297	565	16
Huddersfield	30	7	1	22	314	725	15

SECOND DIVISION

	P.	W.	D.	L.	F.	A.	Pts.
Hull	26	26	0	0	702	175	52
New Hunslet	26	21	1	4	454	218	43
York	26	17	1	8	426	343	35
Blackpool B.	26	15	3	8	321	272	33
Halifax	26	15	2	9	312	198	32
Dewsbury	26	15	0	11	368	292	30
Keighley	26	12	2	12	357	298	26
Bramley	26	12	1	13	375	342	25
Oldham	26	10	1	15	297	435	21
Whitehaven	26	8	3	15	297	408	19
Swinton	26	7	2	17	349	452	16
Doncaster	26	7	0	19	259	547	14
Huyton	26	3	3	20	261	513	9
Batley	26	4	1	21	194	479	9

1979-80

FIRST DIVISION

	P.	W.	D.	L.	F.	A.	Pts.
Bradford N.	30	23	0	7	448	272	46
Widnes	30	22	1	7	546	293	45
Hull	30	18	3	9	454	326	39
Salford	30	19	1	10	495	374	39
Leeds	30	19	0	11	590	390	38
Leigh	30	16	1	13	451	354	33
Hull K.R.	30	16	1	13	539	445	33
St. Helens	30	15	2	13	505	410	32
Warrington	30	15	2	13	362	357	32
Wakefield T.	30	14	2	14	435	466	30
Castleford	30	13	2	15	466	475	28
Workington T.	30	12	2	16	348	483	26
Wigan	30	9	3	18	366	523	21
Hunslet	30	7	1	22	346	528	15
York	30	6	1	23	375	647	13
Blackpool B.	30	5	0	25	230	613	10

SECOND DIVISION

	P.	W.	D.	L.	F.	A.	Pts.
Featherstone R.	26	21	2	3	724	280	44
Halifax	26	19	3	4	463	213	41
Oldham	26	19	3	4	513	276	41
Barrow	26	18	1	7	582	280	37
Whitehaven	26	15	1	10	397	276	31
Dewsbury	26	13	2	11	408	343	28
Rochdale H.	26	9	5	12	315	373	23
Swinton	26	11	1	14	331	436	23
Batley	26	10	2	14	232	370	22
Bramley	26	10	1	15	330	451	21
Keighley	26	10	0	16	342	396	20
Huddersfield	26	10	0	16	363	423	20
Huyton	26	5	0	21	209	555	10
Doncaster	26	1	1	24	196	733	3

1980-81

SLALOM LAGER CHAMPIONSHIP

	P.	W.	D.	L.	F.	A.	Pts.
Bradford N.	30	20	1	9	447	345	41
Warrington	30	19	1	10	459	330	39
Hull K.R.	30	18	2	10	509	408	38
Wakefield T.	30	18	2	10	544	454	38
Castleford	30	18	2	10	526	459	38
Widnes	30	16	2	12	428	356	34
Hull	30	17	0	13	442	450	34
St. Helens	30	15	1	14	465	370	31
Leigh	30	14	1	15	416	414	29
Leeds	30	14	0	16	388	468	28
Barrow	30	13	0	17	405	498	26
Featherstone R.	30	12	0	18	467	446	24
Halifax	30	11	0	19	385	450	22
Salford	30	10	1	19	473	583	21
Workington T.	30	9	3	18	335	457	21
Oldham	30	7	2	21	362	563	16

1981-82

SLALOM LAGER CHAMPIONSHIP

	P.	W.	D.	L.	F.	A.	Pts.
Leigh	30	24	1	5	572	343	49
Hull	30	23	1	6	611	273	47
Widnes	30	23	1	6	551	317	47
Hull K.R.	30	22	1	7	565	319	45
Bradford N.	30	20	1	9	425	332	41
Leeds	30	17	1	12	514	418	35
St. Helens	30	17	1	12	465	415	35
Warrington	30	14	2	14	403	468	30
Barrow	30	13	0	17	408	445	26
Featherstone R.	30	12	1	17	482	493	25
Wigan	30	12	0	18	424	435	24
Castleford	30	10	1	19	486	505	21
Fulham	30	9	1	20	365	539	19
Wakefield T.	30	9	1	20	341	526	19
York	30	4	2	24	330	773	10
Whitehaven	30	2	3	25	224	565	7

SECOND DIVISION

	P.	W.	D.	L.	F.	A.	Pts.
York	28	23	0	5	649	331	46
Wigan	28	20	3	5	597	293	43
Fulham	28	20	0	8	447	237	40
Whitehaven	28	19	1	8	409	250	39
Huddersfield	28	18	1	9	429	310	37
Swinton	28	17	2	9	440	302	36
Keighley	28	14	1	13	445	501	29
Hunslet	28	13	1	14	447	430	27
Bramley	28	13	1	14	433	431	27
Rochdale H.	28	13	0	15	406	418	26
Batley	28	12	0	16	328	405	24
Dewsbury	28	11	1	16	346	364	23
Doncaster	28	5	0	23	250	562	10
Blackpool B.	28	4	1	23	212	419	9
Huyton	28	2	0	26	211	796	4

SECOND DIVISION

	P.	W.	D.	L.	F.	A.	Pts.
Oldham	32	30	0	2	734	276	60
Carlisle	32	28	0	4	649	296	56
Workington T.	32	24	0	8	777	311	48
Halifax	32	22	0	10	516	340	44
Salford	32	20	1	11	656	433	41
Hunslet	32	18	1	13	481	452	37
Keighley	32	18	0	14	514	426	36
Cardiff C.	32	17	1	14	566	549	35
Dewsbury	32	16	0	16	357	464	32
Swinton	32	15	0	17	514	418	30
Huddersfield	32	13	1	18	370	523	27
Bramley	32	13	0	19	381	513	26
Rochdale H.	32	10	1	21	361	484	21
Batley	32	8	0	24	357	596	16
Blackpool B.	32	7	0	25	341	608	14
Doncaster	32	5	1	26	319	793	11
Huyton	32	5	0	27	296	707	10

1982-83

SLALOM LAGER CHAMPIONSHIP

	P.	W.	D.	L.	F.	A.	Pts.
Hull	30	23	1	6	572	293	47
Hull K.R.	30	21	1	8	496	276	43
Wigan	30	20	3	7	482	270	43
St. Helens	30	19	1	10	516	395	39
Widnes	30	18	2	10	534	357	38
Leeds	30	18	2	10	480	443	38
Castleford	30	18	1	11	629	458	37
Oldham	30	15	2	13	346	320	32
Bradford N.	30	14	2	14	381	314	30
Leigh	30	13	3	14	488	374	29
Warrington	30	13	2	15	423	410	28
Featherstone R.	30	10	4	16	350	447	24
Barrow	30	11	1	18	472	505	23
Workington T.	30	6	2	22	318	696	14
Halifax	30	5	1	24	221	651	11
Carlisle	30	2	0	28	252	751	4

SECOND DIVISION

	P.	W.	D.	L.	F.	A.	Pts.
Fulham	32	27	1	4	699	294	55
Wakefield T.	32	25	2	5	672	381	52
Salford	32	24	0	8	686	363	48
Whitehaven	32	20	3	9	464	298	43
Bramley	32	20	1	11	560	369	41
Hunslet	32	17	5	10	553	448	39
Swinton	32	19	1	12	549	454	39
Cardiff C.	32	17	2	13	572	444	36
Keighley	32	15	5	12	470	423	35
York	32	15	0	17	516	455	30
Blackpool B.	32	13	1	18	381	433	27
Huddersfield	32	13	1	18	397	524	27
Rochdale H.	32	10	5	17	361	469	25
Dewsbury	32	8	1	23	325	507	17
Batley	32	6	1	25	305	719	13
Huyton	32	6	0	26	250	687	12
Doncaster	32	2	1	29	307	799	5

1983-84

SLALOM LAGER CHAMPIONSHIP

	P.	W.	D.	L.	F.	A.	Pts.
Hull K.R.	30	22	2	6	795	421	46
Hull	30	22	1	7	831	401	45
Warrington	30	19	2	9	622	528	40
Castleford	30	18	3	9	686	438	39
Widnes	30	19	1	10	656	457	39
St. Helens	30	18	1	11	649	507	37
Bradford N.	30	17	2	11	519	379	36
Leeds	30	15	3	12	553	514	33
Wigan	30	16	0	14	533	465	32
Oldham	30	15	2	13	544	480	32
Leigh	30	14	0	16	623	599	28
Featherstone R.	30	11	2	17	464	562	24
Fulham	30	9	1	20	401	694	19
Wakefield T.	30	7	0	23	415	780	14
Salford	30	5	0	25	352	787	10
Whitehaven	30	3	0	27	325	956	6

SECOND DIVISION

	P.	W.	D.	L.	F.	A.	Pts.
Barrow	34	32	0	2	1126	332	64
Workington T.	34	24	2	8	714	504	50
Hunslet	34	24	0	10	900	597	48
Halifax	34	23	2	9	722	539	48
Blackpool B.	34	20	3	11	615	466	43
Swinton	34	21	0	13	764	437	42
York	34	19	2	13	743	570	40
Bramley	34	16	2	16	584	545	34
Kent Invicta	34	17	0	17	595	700	34
Huddersfield	34	15	3	16	600	545	33
Cardiff C.	34	15	1	18	710	717	31
Rochdale H.	34	13	3	18	551	667	29
Batley	34	13	0	21	477	738	26
Dewsbury	34	12	0	22	526	698	24
Carlisle	34	12	0	22	539	780	24
Huyton	34	9	2	23	431	760	20
Keighley	34	7	3	24	425	728	17
Doncaster	34	2	1	31	384	1083	5

1984-85

SLALOM LAGER CHAMPIONSHIP

	P.	W.	D.	L.	F.	A.	Pts.
Hull K.R.	30	24	0	6	778	391	48
St. Helens	30	22	1	7	920	508	45
Wigan	30	21	1	8	720	459	43
Leeds	30	20	1	9	650	377	41
Oldham	30	18	1	11	563	439	37
Hull	30	17	1	12	733	550	35
Widnes	30	17	0	13	580	517	34
Bradford N.	30	16	1	13	600	500	33
Featherstone R.	30	15	0	15	461	475	30
Halifax	30	12	2	16	513	565	26
Warrington	30	13	0	17	530	620	26
Castleford	30	12	1	17	552	518	25
Barrow	30	9	1	20	483	843	19
Leigh	30	8	2	20	549	743	18
Hunslet	30	7	1	22	463	952	15
Workington T.	30	2	1	27	297	935	5

SECOND DIVISION

	P.	W.	D.	L.	F.	A.	Pts.
Swinton	28	24	1	3	727	343	49
Salford	28	20	3	5	787	333	43
York	28	21	1	6	717	430	43
Dewsbury	28	21	1	6	539	320	43
Carlisle	28	19	0	9	547	437	38
Whitehaven	28	16	3	9	496	385	35
Batley	28	17	0	11	489	402	34
Fulham	28	16	1	11	521	526	33
Mansfield M.	28	15	0	13	525	398	30
Blackpool B.	28	15	0	13	486	434	30
Wakefield T.	28	12	2	14	450	459	26
Rochdale H.	28	12	2	14	436	466	26
Huddersfield B.	28	12	1	15	476	476	25
Runcorn H.	28	11	1	16	462	538	23
Keighley	28	11	0	17	495	567	22
Bramley	28	9	2	17	439	492	20
Sheffield E.	28	8	0	20	424	582	16
Doncaster	28	6	2	20	353	730	14
Southend I.	28	4	0	24	347	690	8
Brigend	28	1	0	27	258	966	2

1985-86

SLALOM LAGER CHAMPIONSHIP

	P.	W.	D.	L.	F.	A.	Pts.
Halifax	30	19	6	5	499	365	44
Wigan	30	20	3	7	776	300	43
St. Helens	30	20	2	8	729	503	42
Warrington	30	20	1	9	665	393	41
Widnes	30	19	3	8	520	454	41
Leeds	30	15	3	12	554	518	33
Hull K.R.	30	16	1	13	507	500	33
Hull	30	15	2	13	616	508	32
Oldham	30	13	4	13	524	549	30
Salford	30	14	0	16	508	561	28
Castleford	30	12	1	17	551	585	25
Bradford N.	30	11	1	18	447	473	23
Featherstone R.	30	9	3	18	419	616	21
York	30	9	0	21	413	592	18
Swinton	30	8	0	22	371	648	16
Dewsbury	30	5	0	25	313	847	10

SECOND DIVISION

	P.	W.	D.	L.	F.	A.	Pts.
Leigh	34	33	0	1	1156	373	66
Barrow	34	27	0	7	1012	398	54
Wakefield T.	34	24	1	9	680	435	49
Whitehaven	34	22	0	12	619	479	44
Rochdale H.	34	21	0	13	763	485	42
Blackpool B.	34	20	0	14	769	570	40
Batley	34	18	3	13	567	450	39
Bramley	34	17	1	16	608	663	35
Fulham	34	16	1	17	679	709	33
Doncaster	34	16	1	17	611	650	33
Carlisle	34	15	2	17	585	682	32
Sheffield E.	34	14	1	19	516	617	29
Workington T.	34	13	0	21	684	723	26
Hunslet	34	11	3	20	594	795	25
Huddersfield B.	34	8	4	22	542	841	20
Runcorn H.	34	9	2	23	489	790	20
Keighley	34	9	2	23	401	918	20
Mansfield M.	34	2	1	31	383	1080	5

CHAMPIONSHIP PLAY-OFFS

Following the breakaway from the English Rugby Union, 22 clubs formed the Northern Rugby Football League. Each club played 42 matches and Manningham won the first Championship as league leaders in 1895-96.

This format was then abandoned and replaced by the Yorkshire Senior and Lancashire Senior Combination leagues until 1901-02 when 14 clubs broke away to form the Northern Rugby League with Broughton Rangers winning the first Championship.

The following season two divisions were formed with the Division One title going to Halifax (1902-03), Bradford (1903-04), who won a play-off against Salford 5-0 at Halifax after both teams tied with 52 points, and Oldham (1904-05).

In 1905-06 the two divisions were merged with Leigh taking the Championship as league leaders. They won the title on a percentage basis as the 31 clubs did not play the same number of matches. The following season the top four play-off was introduced as a fairer means of deciding the title.

The top club played the fourth-placed, the second meeting the third, with the higher club having home advantage. The final was staged at a neutral venue.

It was not until 1930-31 that all clubs played the same number of league matches, but not all against each other, the top four play-off being a necessity until the reintroduction of two divisions in 1962-63.

This spell of two division football lasted only two seasons and the restoration of the Championship table brought about the introduction of a top-16 play-off, this format continuing until the reappearance of two divisions in 1973-74.

Since then the Championship Trophy has been awarded to the leaders of the First Division, with the Second Division champions receiving a silver bowl.

Slalom Lager launched a three-year sponsorship deal of the Championship and the Premiership in 1980-81 in a £215,000 package, extending the deal for another three years from 1983-84 for £270,000. From 1986-87, the sponsorship was taken over by brewers Bass, under the Stones Bitter banner, in a new £400,000 three-year deal.

CHAMPIONSHIP PLAY-OFF FINALS

Season	Winners		Runners-up		Venue	Attendance	Receipts
Top Four Play-Offs							
1906-07	Halifax	18	Oldham	3	Huddersfield	13,200	£722
1907-08	Hunslet	7	Oldham	7	Salford	14,000	£690
Replay	Hunslet	12	Oldham	2	Wakefield	14,054	£800
1908-09	Wigan	7	Oldham	3	Salford	12,000	£630
1909-10	Oldham	13	Wigan	7	Broughton	10,850	£520
1910-11	Oldham	20	Wigan	7	Broughton	15,543	£717
1911-12	Huddersfield	13	Wigan	5	Halifax	15,000	£591
1912-13	Huddersfield	29	Wigan	2	Wakefield	17,000	£914
1913-14	Salford	5	Huddersfield	3	Leeds	8,091	£474
1914-15	Huddersfield	35	Leeds	2	Wakefield	14,000	£750
COMPETITION SUSPENDED DURING WAR TIME							
1919-20	Hull	3	Huddersfield	2	Leeds	12,900	£1,615
1920-21	Hull	16	Hull K.R.	14	Leeds	10,000	£1,320
1921-22	Wigan	13	Oldham	2	Broughton	26,000	£1,825
1922-23	Hull K.R.	15	Huddersfield	5	Leeds	14,000	£1,370
1923-24	Batley	13	Wigan	7	Broughton	13,729	£968
1924-25	Hull K.R.	9	Swinton	5	Rochdale	21,580	£1,504
1925-26	Wigan	22	Warrington	10	St. Helens	20,000	£1,100
1926-27	Swinton	13	St. Helens Recs.	8	Warrington	24,432	£1,803
1927-28	Swinton	11	Featherstone R.	0	Oldham	15,451	£1,136
1928-29	Huddersfield	2	Leeds	0	Halifax	25,604	£2,028
1929-30	Huddersfield	2	Leeds	2	Wakefield	32,095	£2,111
Replay	Huddersfield	10	Leeds	0	Halifax	18,563	£1,319
1930-31	Swinton	14	Leeds	7	Wigan	31,000	£2,100
1931-32	St. Helens	9	Huddersfield	5	Wakefield	19,386	£943
1932-33	Salford	15	Swinton	5	Wigan	18,000	£1,053
1933-34	Wigan	15	Salford	3	Warrington	31,564	£2,114
1934-35	Swinton	14	Warrington	3	Wigan	27,700	£1,710
1935-36	Hull	21	Widnes	2	Huddersfield	17,276	£1,208

Season	Winners		Runners-up		Venue	Attendance	Receipts
1936-37	Salford	13	Warrington	11	Wigan	31,500	£2,000
1937-38	Hunslet	8	Leeds	2	Elland Rd., Leeds	54,112	£3,572
1938-39	Salford	8	Castleford	6	Man. City FC	69,504	£4,301

WAR-TIME EMERGENCY PLAY-OFFS
For the first two seasons the Yorkshire League and Lancashire League champions met in a two-leg final as follows:

1939-40	Swinton	13	Bradford N.	21	Swinton	4,800	£237
	Bradford N.	16	Swinton	9	Bradford	11,721	£570
	Bradford N. won 37-22 on aggregate						
1940-41	Wigan	6	Bradford N.	17	Wigan	11,245	£640
	Bradford N.	28	Wigan	9	Bradford	20,205	£1,148
	Bradford N. won 45-15 on aggregate						

For the remainder of the War the top four in the War League played-off as follows:

1941-42	Dewsbury	13	Bradford N.	0	Leeds	18,000	£1,121
1942-43	Dewsbury	11	Halifax	3	Dewsbury	7,000	£400
	Halifax	13	Dewsbury	22	Halifax	9,700	£683

Dewsbury won 33-16 on aggregate but the Championship was declared null and void because they had played an ineligible player

1943-44	Wigan	13	Dewsbury	9	Wigan	14,000	£915
	Dewsbury	5	Wigan	12	Dewsbury	9,000	£700
	Wigan won 25-14 on aggregate						
1944-45	Halifax	9	Bradford N.	2	Halifax	9,426	£955
	Bradford N.	24	Halifax	11	Bradford	16,000	£1,850
	Bradford N. won 26-20 on aggregate						
1945-46	Wigan	13	Huddersfield	4	Man. C. FC	67,136	£8,387
1946-47	Wigan	13	Dewsbury	4	Man. C. FC	40,599	£5,895
1947-48	Warrington	15	Bradford N.	5	Man. C. FC	69,143	£9,792
1948-49	Huddersfield	13	Warrington	12	Man. C. FC	75,194	£11,073
1949-50	Wigan	20	Huddersfield	2	Man. C. FC	65,065	£11,500
1950-51	Workington T.	26	Warrington	11	Man. C. FC	61,618	£10,993
1951-52	Wigan	13	Bradford N.	6	Huddersfield Town FC	48,684	£8,215
1952-53	St. Helens	24	Halifax	14	Man. C. FC	51,083	£11,503
1953-54	Warrington	8	Halifax	7	Man. C. FC	36,519	£9,076
1954-55	Warrington	7	Oldham	3	Man. C. FC	49,434	£11,516
1955-56	Hull	10	Halifax	9	Man. C. FC	36,675	£9,179
1956-57	Oldham	15	Hull	14	Bradford	62,199	£12,054
1957-58	Hull	20	Workington T.	3	Bradford	57,699	£11,149
1958-59	St. Helens	44	Hunslet	22	Bradford	52,560	£10,146
1959-60	Wigan	27	Wakefield T.	3	Bradford	83,190	£14,482
1960-61	Leeds	25	Warrington	10	Bradford	52,177	£10,475
1961-62	Huddersfield	14	Wakefield T.	5	Bradford	37,451	£7,979

TWO DIVISIONS 1962-63 and 1963-64

Top Sixteen Play-Offs

1964-65	Halifax	15	St. Helens	7	Swinton	20,786	£6,141
1965-66	St. Helens	35	Halifax	12	Swinton	30,634	£8,750
1966-67	Wakefield T.	7	St. Helens	7	Leeds	20,161	£6,702
Replay	Wakefield T.	21	St. Helens	9	Swinton	33,537	£9,800
1967-68	Wakefield T.	17	Hull K.R.	10	Leeds	22,586	£7,697
1968-69	Leeds	16	Castleford	14	Bradford	28,442	£10,130
1969-70	St. Helens	24	Leeds	12	Bradford	26,358	£9,791
1970-71	St. Helens	16	Wigan	12	Swinton	21,745	£10,200
1971-72	Leeds	9	St. Helens	5	Swinton	24,055	£9,513
1972-73	Dewsbury	22	Leeds	13	Bradford	18,889	£9,479

CHAMPIONSHIP FINAL . . . . A 10-YEAR REVIEW

1961-62   HUDDERSFIELD 14   Dyson (4g); Breen, Deighton, Booth, Wicks (1t); Davies, Smales (1t); Slevin, Close, Noble, Kilroy, Bowman, Ramsden
WAKEFIELD T. 5   Round; F. Smith, Skene, N. Fox (1t, 1g), Hirst; Poynton, Holliday; Wilkinson, Kosanovic, Firth, Briggs, Vines, Turner
Referee: N. T. Railton (Wigan)

TWO DIVISIONS — NO PLAY-OFFS 1963 and 1964

1964-65   HALIFAX 15   James (3g); Jackson (1t), Burnett (2t), Kellett, Freeman; Robinson, Daley; Roberts, Harrison, Scroby, Fogerty, Dixon, Renilson
ST. HELENS 7   F. Barrow; Harvey, Vollenhoven, Northey, Killeen (1t, 2g); Murphy, Smith; Tembey (Warlow), Dagnall, Watson, French, Mantle, Laughton
Referee: D. S. Brown (Dewsbury)

1965-66   ST. HELENS 35   F. Barrow; A. Barrow (1t), Murphy (1g), Benyon, Killeen (3t, 6g); Harvey, Bishop; Halsall (3t), Sayer, Watson, French, Warlow (Hitchen), Mantle
HALIFAX 12   Cooper (3g); Jones, Burnett, Dixon, Freeman; Robinson, Baker (1t); Roberts, Harrison, Scroby, Ramshaw (Duffy), Fogerty (1t), Renilson
Referee: J. Manley (Warrington)

1966-67   WAKEFIELD T. 7   Cooper; Hirst, Brooke, N. Fox (2g), Coetzer; Poynton, Owen (1t); Bath, Prior, Campbell, Clarkson, Haigh, D. Fox
ST. HELENS 7   F. Barrow; Vollenhoven, A. Barrow, Smith, Killeen (2g); Douglas, Bishop; Warlow, Sayer, Watson (1t), French, Hogan (Robinson), Mantle
Referee: G. Philpott (Leeds)

Replay: WAKEFIELD T. 21   Cooper; Hirst (1t), Brooke (2t), N. Fox (3g), Coetzer; Poynton (1t), Owen (1t); Bath, Prior, Campbell, Clarkson, Haigh, D. Fox
ST. HELENS 9   F. Barrow; Vollenhoven (1t), A. Barrow, Smith, Killeen (2g); Douglas, Bishop (1g); Warlow, Sayer, Watson, French, Hogan, Mantle
Referee: J. Manley (Warrington)

1967-68   WAKEFIELD T. 17   G. Cooper; Coetzer, Brooke, N. Fox (1t, 2g), Batty; Poynton (1g), Owen (1t); Jeanes (1t), Shepherd, D. Fox (1g), Haigh, McLeod, Hawley
HULL K.R. 10   Wainwright; C. Young, Moore (1t), A. Burwell, Longstaff (1t); Millward (2g), C. Cooper; L. Foster, Flanagan, Mennell, Lowe, Major, F. Foster
Referee: D. S. Brown (Preston)

1968-69   LEEDS 16   Risman (4g); Cowan (1t), Hynes, Watson, Atkinson (1t); Shoebottom, Seabourne (Langley); Clark (Hick), Crosby, K. Eyre, Joyce, Ramsey (1g), Batten
CASTLEFORD 14   Edwards; Briggs, Howe, Thomas, Lowndes; Hardisty (1t, 1g), Hepworth, Hartley, C. Dickinson (1t), J. Ward, Redfearn (3g), Lockwood, Reilly (Fox)
Referee: W. H. Thompson (Huddersfield)

1969-70   ST. HELENS 24   F. Barrow; L. Jones, Benyon, Walsh (1t, 2g), E. Prescott (2t), Myler, Heaton; Halsall, Sayer (1t), Watson, Mantle, E. Chisnall, Coslett (4g)
LEEDS 12   Holmes (3g); Alan Smith (1t), Hynes, Cowan (1t), Atkinson; Shoebottom, Seabourne; J. Burke, Crosby, A. Eyre, Ramsey (Hick), Eccles, Batten
Referee: W. H. Thompson (Huddersfield)

1970-71   ST. HELENS 16   Pimblett; L. Jones, Benyon (1t), Walsh, Blackwood (1t); Whittle, Heaton; J. Stephens, A. Karalius, Rees (Wanbon), Mantle, E. Chisnall, Coslett (5g)
WIGAN 12   Tyrer (1g); Kevin O'Loughlin; Francis, Rowe, Wright; D. Hill, Ayres, Hogan, Clarke, Fletcher, Ashurst (1t, 2g), Robinson (1t) (Cunningham), Laughton
Referee: E. Lawrinson (Warrington)

1971-72   LEEDS 9   Holmes (Hick); Alan Smith, Langley, Dyl, Atkinson (1t); Hardisty, Barham; Clawson (3g), Ward, Fisher (Pickup), Cookson, Eccles, Batten
ST. HELENS 5   Pimblett; L. Jones (Whittle), Benyon, Walsh (1g), Wilson; Kelly, Heaton; Rees, Greenall (1t), J. Stephens, Mantle, E. Chisnall, Coslett
Referee: S. Shepherd (Oldham)

1972-73   DEWSBURY 22   Rushton; Ashcroft, Clark, N. Stephenson (5g, 1t), Day; Agar (1t), A. Bates; Beverley (Taylor), M. Stephenson (2t), Lowe, Grayshon, J. Bates, Whittington
LEEDS 13   Holmes; Alan Smith, Hynes (1g), Dyl (1t), Atkinson; Hardisty, Hepworth; Clawson (1g), Fisher (Ward), Clarkson (Langley), Cookson (1t), Eccles (1t), Haigh
Referee: H. G. Hunt (Prestbury)

LEAGUE LEADERS TROPHY

While the top 16 play-off decided the Championship between 1964 and 1973 it was decided to honour the top club in the league table with a League Leaders Trophy. The winners were:

1964-65 St. Helens
1965-66 St. Helens
1966-67 Leeds
1967-68 Leeds
1968-69 Leeds
1969-70 Leeds
1970-71 Wigan
1971-72 Leeds
1972-73 Warrington

CLUB CHAMPIONSHIP (Merit Table)

With the reintroduction of two divisions, a complicated merit table and Division Two preliminary rounds system produced a 16 club play-off with the Club Championship finalists as follows:

Season	Winners		Runners-up		Venue	Attendance	Receipts
1973-74	Warrington	13	St. Helens	12	Wigan	18,040	£10,032

This format lasted just one season and was replaced by the Premiership.

CLUB CHAMPIONSHIP FINAL . . . . A REVIEW

1973-74 WARRINGTON 13 Whitehead (2g); M. Philbin (1t), Noonan (1t), Pickup (Lowe), Bevan; Whittle, A. Murphy; D. Chisnall, Ashcroft, Brady (1t), Wanbon (Gaskell), Mather, B. Philbin

ST. HELENS 12 Pimblett; Brown, Wills, Wilson (2t), Mathias; Eckersley, Heaton; Mantle, Liptrot, M. Murphy, E. Chisnall (Warlow), Nicholls, Coslett (3g)

Referee: P. Geraghty (York)

PREMIERSHIP

With the further reintroduction of two divisions in 1973-74, it was declared that the title of Champions would be awarded to the leaders of the First Division.

However, it was also decided to continue the tradition of an end-of-season play-off, the winners to receive the newly instituted Premiership Trophy.

*For full details of the Premiership Trophy see the CUPS section.

Barry Philbin, loose forward for 1974 Club Championship winners Warrington.

COUNTY LEAGUE

In the early seasons of the code the Lancashire Senior and Yorkshire Senior Competitions, not to be confused with the later reserve leagues, were major leagues. The winners were:

	Lancashire SC	Yorkshire SC
1895-96	Runcorn	Manningham
1896-97	Broughton Rangers	Brighouse Rangers
1897-98	Oldham	Hunslet
1898-99	Broughton Rangers	Batley
1899-00	Runcorn	Bradford
1900-01	Oldham	Bradford
1901-02	Wigan	Leeds

With the introduction of two divisions in 1902-03, the county league competitions were scrapped until they reappeared as the Lancashire League and Yorkshire League in 1907-08. Clubs from the same county played each other home and away to decide the titles. These games were included in the main championship table along with inter-county fixtures. The county leagues continued until 1970, with the exception of war-time interruptions and two seasons when regional leagues with play-offs operated during the 1960s two division era. They were then abolished when a more integrated fixture formula meant clubs did not play all others from the same county, this system later being replaced by the present two division structure.

LANCASHIRE LEAGUE CHAMPIONS

Season	Winners
1907-08	Oldham
1908-09	Wigan
1909-10	Oldham
1910-11	Wigan
1911-12	Wigan
1912-13	Wigan
1913-14	Wigan
1914-15	Wigan
1915-18	Competition Suspended during war-time
1918-19	Rochdale H.
1919-20	Widnes
1920-21	Wigan
1921-22	Oldham
1922-23	Wigan
1923-24	Wigan
1924-25	Swinton
1925-26	Wigan
1926-27	St. Helens R.
1927-28	Swinton
1928-29	Swinton
1929-30	St. Helens
1930-31	Swinton
1931-32	St. Helens
1932-33	Salford
1933-34	Salford
1934-35	Salford
1935-36	Liverpool S.
1936-37	Salford
1937-38	Warrington
1938-39	Salford
1939-40	Swinton War Emergency
1940-41	Wigan Leagues
1941-45	Competition Suspended during war-time
1945-46	Wigan
1946-47	Wigan
1947-48	Warrington
1948-49	Warrington
1949-50	Wigan
1950-51	Warrington
1951-52	Wigan
1952-53	St. Helens
1953-54	Warrington
1954-55	Warrington
1955-56	Warrington
1956-57	Oldham
1957-58	Oldham
1958-59	Wigan
1959-60	St. Helens
1960-61	Swinton
1961-62	Wigan
1962-64	See Regional

YORKSHIRE LEAGUE CHAMPIONS

Season	Winners
1907-08	Hunslet
1908-09	Halifax
1909-10	Wakefield T.
1910-11	Wakefield T.
1911-12	Huddersfield
1912-13	Huddersfield
1913-14	Huddersfield
1914-15	Huddersfield
1915-18	Competition Suspended during war-time
1918-19	Hull
1919-20	Huddersfield
1920-21	Halifax
1921-22	Huddersfield
1922-23	Hull
1923-24	Batley
1924-25	Hull K.R.
1925-26	Hull K.R.
1926-27	Hull
1927-28	Leeds
1928-29	Huddersfield
1929-30	Huddersfield
1930-31	Leeds
1931-32	Hunslet
1932-33	Castleford
1933-34	Leeds
1934-35	Leeds
1935-36	Hull
1936-37	Leeds
1937-38	Leeds
1938-39	Castleford
1939-40	Bradford N. War Emergency
1940-41	Bradford N. Leagues
1941-45	Competition Suspended during war-time
1945-46	Wakefield T.
1946-47	Dewsbury
1947-48	Bradford N.
1948-49	Huddersfield
1949-50	Huddersfield
1950-51	Leeds
1951-52	Huddersfield
1952-53	Halifax
1953-54	Halifax
1954-55	Leeds
1955-56	Halifax
1956-57	Leeds
1957-58	Halifax
1958-59	Wakefield T.
1959-60	Wakefield T.
1960-61	Leeds
1961-62	Wakefield T.
1962-64	See Regional

LANCASHIRE LEAGUE CHAMPIONS

Season	Winners
1964-65	St. Helens
1965-66	St. Helens
1966-67	St. Helens
1967-68	Warrington
1968-69	St. Helens
1969-70	Wigan

YORKSHIRE LEAGUE CHAMPIONS

Season	Winners
1964-65	Castleford
1965-66	Wakefield T.
1966-67	Leeds
1967-68	Leeds
1968-69	Leeds
1969-70	Leeds

REGIONAL LEAGUES

DURING the 1962-63 and 1963-64 two divisions campaigns the county leagues were replaced by the Eastern and Western Divisions. Each club played four other clubs home and away. There was then a top four play-off to decide the regional championship. The finals were played at neutral venues as follows:

Eastern Division

1962-63	Hull K.R.	13	Huddersfield	10	Leeds	6,751	£1,342
1963-64	Halifax	20	Castleford	12	Huddersfield	10,798	£1,791

Western Division

1962-63	Workington T.	9	Widnes	9	Wigan	13,588	£2,287
Replay	Workington T.	10	Widnes	0	Wigan	7,584	£1,094
1963-64	St. Helens	10	Swinton	7	Wigan	17,363	£3,053

EASTERN DIVISION FINAL . . . . A REVIEW

1962-63 HULL K.R. 13 Kellett (2g); Paul (2t), Major, B. Burwell, Harris (1t); A. Burwell, Bunting; Coverdale, Flanagan, J. Drake, Tyson, Murphy, Bonner
HUDDERSFIELD 10 Dyson (2g); Senior, Booth, Haywood (1t), Stocks; Deighton, Smales (1t); Rowe, Close, Noble, Kilroy, Bowman, Redfearn
Referee: T. W. Watkinson (Manchester)

1963-64 HALIFAX 20 James (4g); Jackson (2t), Burnett, Kellett, Freeman; Robinson (1t), Marchant; Roberts, Shaw, Scott, Dixon (1t), Fogerty, Renilson
CASTLEFORD 12 Edwards; Howe (1t), G. Ward, Small, Gamble; Hardisty, Hepworth: Hirst, C. Dickinson (1t), Clark (3g), Bryant, Walker, Walton
Referee: R. L. Thomas (Oldham)

WESTERN DIVISION FINAL . . . . A REVIEW

1962-63 WORKINGTON T. 9 Lowden (3g); Glastonbury, O'Neil, Brennan, Pretorious (1t); Archer, Roper; Herbert, Ackerley, W. Martin, Edgar, McLeod, Foster
WIDNES 9 Randall (3g); R. Chisnall, Lowe, Thompson (1t), Heyes; F. Myler, Owen; Hurtsfield, Kemel, E. Bate, R. Bate, Measures, V. Karalius
Referee: M. Coates (Pudsey)

Replay WORKINGTON T. 10 Lowden (2g); Glastonbury (1t), O'Neil, Brennan, Pretorious (1t); Archer, Roper; Herbert, Ackerley, W. Martin, Edgar, McLeod, Foster
WIDNES 0 Randall; A. Hughes, Lowe, Thompson, Heyes; F. Myler, Owen; Hurstfield, Kemel, E. Bate, R. Bate, Measures, V. Karalius
Referee: M. Coates (Pudsey)

1963-64 ST. HELENS 10 Coslett (2g); Vollenhoven, Williams, Northey (1t), Killeen; Harvey, Murphy; Tembey, Burdell, Owen, French (1t), Warlow, Laughton
SWINTON 7 Gowers; Speed, Fleet, Parkinson, Stopford (1t); Williams, Cartwright; Bate, D. Clarke, Halliwell, Morgan, Rees, Blan (2g)
Referee: E. Clay (Leeds)

LEAGUE LEADERS .... A REVIEW

The following is a list of the League leaders since the formation of the Northern Union, with the exception of the three eras of two-division football — 1902-05, 1962-64 and 1973-85 — which are comprehensively featured earlier in this section. From 1896 to 1901, the League was divided into a Lancashire Senior Competition and a Yorkshire Senior Competition, winners of both leagues being listed for those seasons. From 1905 to 1930 not all the clubs played each other, the League being determined on a percentage basis.

LSC — Lancashire Senior Competition
LL — Lancashire League
YSC — Yorkshire Senior Competition
YL — Yorkshire League
WEL — War Emergency League
★ Two points deducted for breach of professional rules
† Decided on a percentage basis after Belle Vue Rangers withdrew shortly before the start of the season.

		P.	W.	D.	L.	F.	A.	Pts.	
1895-96	Manningham	42	33	0	9	367	158	66	
1896-97	Broughton R.	26	19	5	2	201	52	43	LSC
	Brighouse R.	30	22	4	4	213	68	48	YSC
1897-98	Oldham	26	23	1	2	295	94	47	LSC
	Hunslet	30	22	4	4	327	117	48	YSC
1898-99	Broughton R.	26	21	0	5	277	74	42	LSC
	Batley	30	23	2	5	279	75	48	YSC
1899-00	Runcorn	26	22	2	2	232	33	46	LSC
	Bradford	30	24	2	4	324	98	50	YSC
1900-01	Oldham	26	22	1	3	301	67	45	LSC
	Bradford	30	26	1	3	387	100	51★	YSC
1901-02	Broughton R.	26	21	1	4	285	112	43	
1902-05	Two Divisions								
1905-06	Leigh	30	23	2	5	245	130	48	80.00%
1906-07	Halifax	34	27	2	5	649	229	56	82.35%
1907-08	Oldham	32	28	2	2	396	121	58	90.62%
1908-09	Wigan	32	28	0	4	706	207	56	87.50%
1909-10	Oldham	34	29	2	3	604	184	60	88.23%
1910-11	Wigan	34	28	1	5	650	205	57	83.82%
1911-12	Huddersfield	36	31	1	4	996	238	63	87.50%
1912-13	Huddersfield	32	28	0	4	732	217	56	87.50%
1913-14	Huddersfield	34	28	2	4	830	258	58	85.29%
1914-15	Huddersfield	34	28	4	2	888	235	60	88.24%
1915-18	Competitive matches suspended during First World War								
1918-19	Rochdale H.	12	9	0	3	92	52	18	75.00% LL
	Hull	16	13	0	3	392	131	26	81.25% YL
1919-20	Huddersfield	34	29	0	5	759	215	58	85.29%
1920-21	Hull K.R.	32	24	1	7	432	233	49	76.56%
1921-22	Oldham	36	29	1	6	521	201	59	81.94%
1922-23	Hull	36	30	0	6	587	304	60	83.33%
1923-24	Wigan	38	31	0	7	824	228	62	81.57%
1924-25	Swinton	36	30	0	6	499	224	60	83.33%
1925-26	Wigan	38	29	3	6	641	310	61	80.26%
1926-27	St. Helens R.	38	29	3	6	544	235	61	80.26%
1927-28	Swinton	36	27	3	6	439	189	57	79.16%

		P.	W.	D.	L.	F.	A.	Pts.	
1928-29	Huddersfield	38	26	4	8	476	291	56	73.68%
1929-30	St. Helens	40	27	1	12	549	295	55	68.75%
1930-31	Swinton	38	31	2	5	504	156	64	
1931-32	Huddersfield	38	30	1	7	636	368	61	
1932-33	Salford	38	31	2	5	751	165	64	
1933-34	Salford	38	31	1	6	715	281	63	
1934-35	Swinton	38	30	1	7	468	175	61	
1935-36	Hull	38	30	1	7	607	306	61	
1936-37	Salford	38	29	3	6	529	196	61	
1937-38	Hunslet	36	25	3	8	459	301	53	
1938-39	Salford	40	30	3	7	551	191	63	
1939-40	Swinton	22	17	0	5	378	158	34	WEL LL
	Bradford N.	28	21	0	7	574	302	42	WEL YL
1940-41	Wigan	16	15	1	0	297	71	31	WEL LL
	Bradford N.	25	23	1	1	469	126	47	WEL YL
1941-42	Dewsbury	24	19	1	4	431	172	39	81.25% WEL
1942-43	Wigan	16	13	0	3	301	142	26	81.25% WEL
1943-44	Wakefield T.	22	19	0	3	359	97	38	86.36% WEL
1944-45	Bradford N.	20	17	0	3	337	69	34	85.00% WEL
1945-46	Wigan	36	29	2	5	783	219	60	
1946-47	Wigan	36	29	1	6	567	196	59	
1947-48	Wigan	36	31	1	4	776	258	63	
1948-49	Warrington	36	31	0	5	728	247	62	
1949-50	Wigan	36	31	1	4	853	320	63	
1950-51	Warrington	36	30	0	6	738	250	60	
1951-52	Bradford N.	36	28	1	7	758	326	57	
1952-53	St. Helens	36	32	2	2	769	273	66	
1953-54	Halifax	36	30	2	4	538	219	62	
1954-55	Warrington	36	29	2	5	718	321	60	
1955-56	Warrington	34	27	1	6	712	349	55	80.88% †
1956-57	Oldham	38	33	0	5	893	365	66	
1957-58	Oldham	38	33	1	4	803	415	67	
1958-59	St. Helens	38	31	1	6	1005	450	63	
1959-60	St. Helens	38	34	1	3	947	343	69	
1960-61	Leeds	36	30	0	6	620	258	60	
1961-62	Wigan	36	32	1	3	885	283	65	
1962-64	Two Divisions								
1964-65	St. Helens	34	28	0	6	621	226	56	
1965-66	St. Helens	34	28	1	5	521	275	57	
1966-67	Leeds	34	29	0	5	704	373	58	
1967-68	Leeds	34	28	0	6	720	271	56	
1968-69	Leeds	34	29	2	3	775	358	60	
1969-70	Leeds	34	30	0	4	674	314	60	
1970-71	Wigan	34	30	0	4	662	308	60	
1971-72	Leeds	34	28	2	4	750	325	58	
1972-73	Warrington	34	27	2	5	816	400	56	

Malcolm Reilly, appointed coach of Great Britain in January 1987.

COACHES

Between June 1986 and June 1987 a total of 22 clubs made first team coaching changes, some more than once. Seventeen new coaches had their first senior appointments bringing the total of coaches since the start of the 1974-75 season to 185.

This chapter is a compilation of those appointments, featuring a club-by-club coaches register, an index, plus a detailed dossier of the 1986-87 coaches.

CLUB-BY-CLUB REGISTER

The following is a list of coaches each club has had since the start of the 1974-75 season.

BARROW

Frank Foster	May 73 - Apr. 83
Tommy Dawes	May 83 - Feb. 85
Tommy Bishop	Feb. 85 - Apr. 85
Ivor Kelland	May 85 - Feb. 87
Dennis Jackson	Feb. 87 -

BATLEY

Don Fox	Nov. 72 - Oct. 74
Alan Hepworth	Nov. 74 - Apr. 75
Dave Cox	May 75 - June 75
Trevor Walker	June 75 - June 77
Albert Fearnley	June 77 - Oct. 77
Dave Stockwell	Oct. 77 - June 79
★Tommy Smales	June 79 - Oct. 81
Trevor Lowe	Oct. 81 - May 82
Terry Crook	June 82 - Nov. 84
George Pieniazek	Nov. 84 - Nov. 85
Brian Lockwood	Nov. 85 -

★Ex-forward

Albert Fearnley, coach at Batley, then Blackpool Borough, between 1977-79.

BLACKPOOL BOROUGH

Tommy Blakeley	Aug. 74 - Apr. 76
Jim Crellin	May 76 - Mar. 77
Joe Egan Jnr.	Mar. 77 - Oct. 77
Albert Fearnley (Mgr)	Nov. 77 - Apr. 79
Bakary Diabira	Nov. 78 - June 79
Graham Rees	June 79 - Mar. 80
Geoff Lyon	July 80 - Aug. 81
Bob Irving	Aug. 81 - Feb. 82
John Mantle	Feb. 82 - Mar. 82
Tommy Dickens	Mar. 82 - Nov. 85
Stan Gittins	Nov. 85 -

BRADFORD NORTHERN

Ian Brooke	Jan. 73 - Sept. 75
Roy Francis	Oct. 75 - Apr. 77
Peter Fox	Apr. 77 - May 85
Barry Seabourne	May 85 -

BRAMLEY

Arthur Keegan	May 73 - Sept. 76
Peter Fox	Sept. 76 - Apr. 77
★Tommy Smales	May 77 - Dec. 77
Les Pearce	Jan. 78 - Oct. 78
Don Robinson	Oct. 78 - May 79
Dave Stockwell	June 79 - June 80
Keith Hepworth	June 80 - May 82
Maurice Bamford	May 82 - Oct. 83
Peter Jarvis	Oct. 83 - Apr. 85
Ken Loxton	Apr. 85 - Dec. 85
Allan Agar	Dec. 85 - Apr. 87

★Ex-forward

CARLISLE

Allan Agar	May 81 - June 82
Mick Morgan	July 82 - Feb. 83
John Atkinson	Feb. 83 - Feb. 86
Alan Kellett	Feb. 86 - May 86
Roy Lester	June 86 -

CASTLEFORD

Dave Cox	Apr. 74 - Nov. 74
★Malcolm Reilly	Dec. 74 - May 87
Dave Sampson	May 87 -

★Shortly after his appointment Reilly returned to Australia to fulfil his contract before resuming at Castleford early the next season.

222

DEWSBURY

Maurice Bamford	June 74 - Oct. 74
Alan Hardisty	Oct. 74 - June 75
Dave Cox	June 75 - July 77
Ron Hill	July 77 - Dec. 77
Lewis Jones	Dec. 77 - Apr. 78
Jeff Grayshon	May 78 - Oct. 78
Alan Lockwood	Oct. 78 - Oct. 80
Bernard Watson	Oct. 80 - Oct. 82
Ray Abbey	Nov. 82 - Apr. 83
*Tommy Smales	May 83 - Feb. 84
Jack Addy	Feb. 84 - Jan. 87
Dave Busfield	Jan. 87 - Apr. 87
Terry Crook	Apr. 87 -

*Ex-forward

DONCASTER

Ted Strawbridge	Feb. 73 - Apr. 75
Derek Edwards	July 75 - Nov. 76
Don Robson	Nov. 76 - Sept. 77
Trevor Lowe	Sept. 77 - Apr. 79
*Tommy Smales	Feb. 78 - Apr. 79
Billy Yates	Apr. 79 - May 80
Don Vines	Sept. 79 - Jan. 80
Bill Kenny	June 80 - May 81
Alan Rhodes	Aug. 81 - Mar. 83
Clive Sullivan M.B.E.	Mar. 83 - May 84
John Sheridan	June 84 -

*Ex-forward, who shared the coaching post with
Trevor Lowe for just over a year.

FEATHERSTONE ROVERS

*Tommy Smales	July 74 - Sept. 74
Keith Goulding	Sept. 74 - Jan. 76
†Tommy Smales	Feb. 76 - May 76
Keith Cotton	June 76 - Dec. 77
Keith Goulding	Dec. 77 - May 78
Terry Clawson	July 78 - Nov. 78
†Tommy Smales	Nov. 78 - Apr. 79
Paul Daley	May 79 - Jan. 81
Vince Farrar	Feb. 81 - Nov. 82
Allan Agar	Dec. 82 - Oct. 85
George Pieniazek	Nov. 85 - Nov. 86
Paul Daley	Nov. 86 - Apr. 87
Peter Fox	May 87 -

*Ex-forward
†Ex-scrum half

FULHAM

Reg Bowden	July 80 - June 84
Roy Lester	June 84 - Apr. 86
Bill Goodwin	Apr. 86 -

HALIFAX

Derek Hallas	Aug. 74 - Oct. 74
Les Pearce	Oct. 74 - Apr. 76
Alan Kellett	May 76 - Apr. 77
Jim Crellin	June 77 - Oct. 77
Harry Fox	Oct. 77 - Feb. 78
Maurice Bamford	Feb. 78 - May 80
Mick Blacker	June 80 - June 82
Ken Roberts	June 82 - Sept. 82
Colin Dixon	Sept. 82 - Nov. 84
Chris Anderson	Nov. 84 -

HUDDERSFIELD BARRACUDAS

Brian Smith	Jan. 73 - Mar. 76
Keith Goulding	Mar. 76 - Dec. 76
Bob Tomlinson	Jan. 77 - May 77
Neil Fox	June 77 - Feb. 78
*Roy Francis	-
Keith Goulding	May 78 - July 79
Ian Brooke	July 79 - Mar. 80
Maurice Bamford	May 80 - May 81
Les Sheard	June 81 - Nov. 82
Dave Mortimer	Nov. 82 - Aug. 83
Mel Bedford	Aug. 83 - Nov. 83
Brian Lockwood	Nov. 83 - Feb. 85
Chris Forster	Feb. 85 - Dec. 86
Jack Addy	Jan. 87 -

*Although Roy Francis was appointed he was
unable to take over and Dave Heppleston stood
in until the next appointment.

HULL

David Doyle-Davidson	May 74 - Dec. 77
Arthur Bunting	Jan. 78 - Dec. 85
Kenny Foulkes	Dec. 85 - May 86
Len Casey	June 86 -

HULL KINGSTON ROVERS

Arthur Bunting	Feb. 72 - Nov. 75
Harry Poole	Dec. 75 - Mar. 77
Roger Millward M.B.E.	Mar. 77 -

HUNSLET

Paul Daley	Apr. 74 - Aug. 78
Bill Ramsey	Aug. 78 - Dec. 79
Drew Broatch	Dec. 79 - Apr. 81
Paul Daley	Apr. 81 - Nov. 85
*Peter Jarvis	Nov. 85 -
*David Ward	July 86 -

Joint coaches from July 1986.

KEIGHLEY

Alan Kellett	Jan. 73 - May 75
Roy Sabine	Aug. 75 - Oct. 77
Barry Seabourne	Nov. 77 - Mar. 79
Albert Fearnley (Mgr)	Apr. 79 - Aug. 79
Alan Kellett	Apr. 79 - Apr. 80
Albert Fearnley	May 80 - Feb. 81
Bakary Diabira	Feb. 81 - Sept. 82
Lee Greenwood	Sept. 82 - Oct. 83
Geoff Peggs	Nov. 83 - Sept. 85
Peter Roe	Sept. 85 - July 86
Colin Dixon ⎱ Les Coulter ⎰	July 86 -

LEEDS

Roy Francis	June 74 - May 75
Syd Hynes	June 75 - Apr. 81
Robin Dewhurst	June 81 - Oct. 83
Maurice Bamford	Nov. 83 - Feb. 85
Malcolm Clift	Feb. 85 - May 85
Peter Fox	May 85 - Dec. 86
Maurice Bamford	Dec. 86 -

Bill Francis, coach at Oldham for an 18-month stint.

LEIGH

Eddie Cheetham	May 74 - Mar. 75
Kevin Ashcroft	June 75 - Jan. 77
Bill Kindon	Jan. 77 - Apr. 77
John Mantle	Apr. 77 - Nov. 78
Tom Grainey	Nov. 78 - Dec. 80
*Alex Murphy	Nov. 80 - June 82
*Colin Clarke	June 82 - Dec. 82
Peter Smethurst	Dec. 82 - Apr. 83
Tommy Bishop	June 83 - June 84
John Woods	June 84 - May 85
Alex Murphy	Feb. 85 - Nov. 85
Tommy Dickens	Nov. 85 - Dec. 86
Billy Benyon	Dec. 86 -

From Dec. 80 to June 82 Clarke was officially appointed coach and Murphy manager

MANSFIELD MARKSMAN

Mick Blacker	May 84 - Oct. 85
Bill Kirkbride	Nov. 85 - Mar. 86
Steve Dennison	Apr. 86 - Dec. 86
Jim Crellin	Dec. 86 -

OLDHAM

Jim Challinor	Aug. 74 - Dec. 76
Terry Ramshaw	Jan. 77 - Feb. 77
Dave Cox	July 77 - Dec. 78
Graham Starkey (Mngr)	Jan. 79 - May 81
Bill Francis	June 79 - Dec. 80
Frank Myler	May 81 - Apr. 83
Peter Smethurst	Apr. 83 - Feb. 84
Frank Barrow	Feb. 84 - Feb. 84
Brian Gartland	Mar. 84 - June 84
Frank Myler	June 84 - Apr. 87

ROCHDALE HORNETS

Frank Myler	May 71 - Oct. 74
Graham Starkey	Oct. 74 - Nov. 75
Henry Delooze	Nov. 75 - Nov. 76
Kel Coslett	Nov. 76 - Aug. 79
Paul Longstaff	Sept. 79 - May 81
Terry Fogerty	May 81 - Jan. 82
Dick Bonser	Jan. 82 - May 82
Bill Kirkbride	June 82 - Sept. 84
Charlie Birdsall	Sept. 84 - Apr. 86
Eric Fitzsimons	June 86 -

RUNCORN HIGHFIELD

Terry Gorman	Aug. 74 - May 77
Geoff Fletcher	Aug. 77 - June 86
Frank Wilson	July 86 - Nov. 86
Arthur Daley } Paul Woods }	Nov. 86 - Apr. 87
Bill Ashurst	Apr. 87 -

ST. HELENS

Eric Ashton M.B.E.	May 74 - May 80
Kel Coslett	June 80 - May 82
Billy Benyon	May 82 - Nov. 85
Alex Murphy	Nov. 85 -

SALFORD

Les Bettinson	Dec. 73 - Mar. 77
Colin Dixon	Mar. 77 - Jan. 78
Stan McCormick	Feb. 78 - Mar. 78
Alex Murphy	May 78 - Nov. 80
Kevin Ashcroft	Nov. 80 - Mar. 82
Alan McInnes	Mar. 82 - May 82
Malcolm Aspey	May 82 - Oct. 83
Mike Coulman	Oct. 83 - May 84
Kevin Ashcroft	May 84 -

SHEFFIELD EAGLES

Alan Rhodes	Apr. 84 - May 86
Gary Hetherington	July 86 -

Arnie Walker, coach of Whitehaven for only four months.

SWINTON

Austin Rhodes	June 74 - Nov. 75
Bob Fleet	Nov. 75 - Nov. 76
John Stopford	Nov. 76 - Apr. 77
Terry Gorman	June 77 - Nov. 78
Ken Halliwell	Nov. 78 - Dec. 79
Frank Myler	Jan. 80 - May 81
Tom Grainey	May 81 - Oct. 83
Jim Crellin	Nov. 83 - May 86
Bill Holliday } Mike Peers }	June 86 -

WAKEFIELD TRINITY

Peter Fox	June 74 - May 76
Geoff Gunney	June 76 - Nov. 76
Brian Lockwood	Nov. 76 - Jan. 78
Ian Brooke	Jan. 78 - Jan. 79
Bill Kirkbride	Jan. 79 - Apr. 80
Ray Batten	Apr. 80 - May 81
Bill Ashurst	June 81 - Apr. 82
Ray Batten	May 82 - July 83
Derek Turner	July 83 - Feb. 84
Bob Haigh	Feb. 84 - May 84
Geoff Wraith	May 84 - Oct. 84
David Lamming	Oct. 84 - Apr. 85
Len Casey	Apr. 85 - June 86
Tony Dean	June 86 - Dec. 86
Trevor Bailey	Dec. 86 - Apr. 87
David Topliss	May 87 -

WARRINGTON

Alex Murphy	May 71 - May 78
Billy Benyon	June 78 - Mar. 82
Kevin Ashcroft	Mar. 82 - May 84
Reg Bowden	June 84 - Mar. 86
Tony Barrow	Mar. 86 -

WHITEHAVEN

Jeff Bawden	May 72 - May 75
Ike Southward	Aug. 75 - June 76
Bill Smith	Aug. 76 - Oct. 78
Ray Dutton	Oct. 78 - Oct. 79
Phil Kitchin	Oct. 79 - Jan. 82
Arnold Walker	Jan. 82 - May 82
Tommy Dawes	June 82 - May 83
Frank Foster	June 83 - June 85
Phil Kitchin	June 85 -

225

WIDNES

Vince Karalius	Jan. 72 - May 75
Frank Myler	May 75 - May 78
Doug Laughton	May 78 - Mar. 83
Harry Dawson ⎫ Colin Tyrer ⎭	Mar. 83 - May 83
*Vince Karalius ⎫ Harry Dawson ⎭	May 83 - May 84
Eric Hughes	June 84 - Jan. 86
Doug Laughton	Jan. 86 -

Dawson quit as coach in March 1984 with Karalius continuing as team manager.

WIGAN

Ted Toohey	May 74 - Jan. 75
Joe Coan	Jan. 75 - Sept. 76
Vince Karalius	Sept. 76 - Sept. 79
Kel Coslett	Oct. 79 - Apr. 80
George Fairbairn	Apr. 80 - May 81
Maurice Bamford	May 81 - May 82
Alex Murphy	June 82 - Aug. 84
Colin Clarke ⎫ Alan McInnes ⎭	Aug. 84 - May 86
Graham Lowe	Aug. 86 -

REPRESENTATIVE REGISTER

The following is a list of international and county coaches since 1974-75.

GREAT BRITAIN

Jim Challinor	Dec. 71 - Aug. 74 (Inc. tour)
David Watkins	1977 World Championship
Peter Fox	1978
Eric Ashton	1979 tour
Johnny Whiteley	Aug. 80 - Nov. 82
Frank Myler	Dec. 82 - Aug. 84 (Inc. tour)
Maurice Bamford	Oct. 84 - Dec. 86
Malcolm Reilly	Jan. 87 -

WORKINGTON TOWN

Ike Southward	Aug. 73 - June 75
Paul Charlton	June 75 - June 76
Ike Southward	June 76 - Feb. 78
Sol Roper	Feb. 78 - Apr. 80
Keith Irving	Aug. 80 - Oct. 80
Tommy Bishop	Nov. 80 - June 82
Paul Charlton	July 82 - Dec. 82
Dave Cox	Mar. 83 - Mar. 83
Harry Archer/Bill Smith	May 83 - June 84
Bill Smith	June 84 - Apr. 85
Jackie Davidson	Apr. 85 - Jan. 86
Keith Davies	Feb. 86 - Mar. 87
Norman Turley	Mar. 87 -

YORK

Keith Goulding	Nov. 73 - Sept. 74
Gary Cooper	Dec. 74 - Sept. 76
Mal Dixon	Sept. 76 - Dec. 78
Paul Daley	Jan. 79 - May 79
David Doyle-Davidson	July 79 - July 80
Bill Kirkbride	Aug. 80 - Apr. 82
Alan Hardisty	May 82 - Jan. 83
Phil Lowe	Mar. 83 - Mar. 87
Danny Sheehan	Mar. 87 -

ENGLAND

Alex Murphy	Jan. 75 - Nov. 75 (Inc. World Championship tour)
Peter Fox	1976-77
Frank Myler	1977-78
Eric Ashton	1978-79 & 1979-80
Johnny Whiteley	1980-81 & 1981-82
Reg Parker (Mngr)	1984-85

WALES

Les Pearce	Jan. 75 - Nov. 75 (Inc. World Championship tour)
David Watkins ⎫ Bill Francis ⎭	1976-77
Kel Coslett ⎫ Bill Francis ⎭	1977-78
Kel Coslett	1978-79 to 1981-82
David Watkins	1982-83, 1984-85

GREAT BRITAIN UNDER-24s
Johnny Whiteley 1976-82
Frank Myler   1983-84

GREAT BRITAIN UNDER-21s
Maurice Bamford Oct. 84 - Dec. 86
Malcolm Reilly   Jan. 87 -

CUMBRIA
Ike Southward   1975-76
Frank Foster   1976-77 & 1977-78
Sol Roper   1978-79
Frank Foster   1979-80
Phil Kitchin   1980-81 to 1981-82
Frank Foster   1982-83
Jackie Davidson 1985-86
Phil Kitchin   1986-87

LANCASHIRE
Alex Murphy   1973-74 to 1977-78
Eric Ashton M.B.E.   1978-79 to 1979-80
Tom Grainey   1980-81 to 1981-82
Doug Laughton   1982-83
Alex Murphy   1985-86 to 1986-87

YORKSHIRE
Johnny Whiteley 1970-71 to 1979-80
Arthur Keegan   1980-81
Johnny Whiteley 1981-82 to 1982-83
Peter Fox   1985-86 to 1986-87

OTHER NATIONALITIES
Dave Cox   1974-75 to 1975-76

INDEX OF COACHES

The following is an index of the 185 coaches who have held first team coaching posts since the start of the 1974-75 season with the alphabetical listing of clubs they coached in this period.

Ray Abbey (Dewsbury)
Jack Addy (Dewsbury, Huddersfield B.)
Allan Agar (Bramley, Carlisle, Featherstone R.)
Dave Alred (Bridgend)
Chris Anderson (Halifax)
Harry Archer (Workington T.)
Kevin Ashcroft (Leigh, Salford, Warrington)
Eric Ashton M.B.E. (St. Helens)
Bill Ashurst (Runcorn H., Wakefield T.)
Mal Aspey (Salford)
John Atkinson (Carlisle)

Trevor Bailey (Wakefield T.)
Maurice Bamford (Bramley, Dewsbury, Halifax, Huddersfield, Leeds, Wigan)
Frank Barrow (Oldham)
Tony Barrow (Warrington)
Ray Batten (Wakefield T.)
Jeff Bawden (Whitehaven)
Mel Bedford (Huddersfield)
Billy Benyon (Leigh, St. Helens, Warrington)
Les Bettinson (Salford)

Charlie Birdsall (Rochdale H.)
Tommy Bishop (Barrow, Leigh, Workington T.)
Mick Blacker (Halifax, Mansfield M.)
Tommy Blakeley (Blackpool B.)
Dick Bonser (Rochdale H.)
Reg Bowden (Fulham, Warrington)
Drew Broatch (Hunslet)
Ian Brooke (Bradford N., Huddersfield, Wakefield T.)
Arthur Bunting (Hull, Hull K.R.)
Dave Busfield (Dewsbury)

Len Casey (Hull, Wakefield T.)
Jim Challinor (Oldham)
Paul Charlton (Workington T.)
Eddie Cheetham (Leigh)
Colin Clarke (Leigh, Wigan)
Terry Clawson (Featherstone R.)
Malcolm Clift (Leeds)
Joe Coan (Wigan)
Gary Cooper (York)
Kel Coslett (Rochdale H., St. Helens, Wigan)
Keith Cotton (Featherstone R.)
Mike Coulman (Salford)
Les Coulter (Keighley)
Dave Cox (Batley, Castleford, Dewsbury, Huyton, Oldham, Workington T.)
Jim Crellin (Blackpool B., Halifax, Mansfield M., Swinton)
Terry Crook (Batley, Dewsbury)

Arthur Daley (Runcorn H.)
Paul Daley (Featherstone R., Hunslet, York)
Jackie Davidson (Workington T.)
Keith Davies (Workington T.)
Tommy Dawes (Barrow, Whitehaven)
Harry Dawson (Widnes)
Tony Dean (Wakefield T.)
Henry Delooze (Rochdale H.)
Steve Dennison (Mansfield M.)
Robin Dewhurst (Leeds)
Bakary Diabira (Blackpool B., Keighley)
Tommy Dickens (Blackpool B., Leigh)
Colin Dixon (Halifax, Keighley, Salford)
Mal Dixon (York)
David Doyle-Davidson (Hull, York)
Ray Dutton (Whitehaven)

Derek Edwards (Doncaster)
Joe Egan Jnr. (Blackpool B.)

George Fairbairn (Wigan)
Vince Farrar (Featherstone R.)
Albert Fearnley (Batley, Blackpool B., Keighley)
Eric Fitzsimons (Rochdale H.)
Bob Fleet (Swinton)
Geoff Fletcher (Huyton)
Terry Fogerty (Rochdale H.)
Chris Forster (Huddersfield B.)
Frank Foster (Barrow, Whitehaven)
Kenny Foulkes (Hull)
Don Fox (Batley)
Harry Fox (Halifax)
Neil Fox (Huddersfield)
Peter Fox (Bradford N., Bramley, Featherstone R., Leeds, Wakefield T.)
Bill Francis (Oldham)
Roy Francis (Bradford N., Huddersfield, Leeds)

Brian Gartland (Oldham)
Stan Gittins (Blackpool B.)
Bill Goodwin (Fulham, Kent Invicta)
Terry Gorman (Huyton, Swinton)
Keith Goulding (Featherstone R., Huddersfield, York)
Tom Grainey (Leigh, Swinton)
Jeff Grayshon (Dewsbury)
Lee Greenwood (Keighley)
Geoff Gunney (Wakefield T.)

Bob Haigh (Wakefield T.)
Derek Hallas (Halifax)
Ken Halliwell (Swinton)
Alan Hardisty (Dewsbury, York)

Alan Hepworth (Batley)
Keith Hepworth (Bramley)
Gary Hetherington (Sheffield E.)
Ron Hill (Dewsbury)
Bill Holliday (Swinton)
Eric Hughes (Widnes)
Syd Hynes (Leeds)

Bob Irving (Blackpool B.)
Keith Irving (Workington T.)

Dennis Jackson (Barrow)
Peter Jarvis (Bramley, Hunslet)
Lewis Jones (Dewsbury)

Vince Karalius (Widnes, Wigan)
Arthur Keegan (Bramley)
Ivor Kelland (Barrow)
Alan Kellett (Carlisle, Halifax, Keighley)
Bill Kenny (Doncaster)
Bill Kindon (Leigh)
Bill Kirkbride (Mansfield M., Rochdale H., Wakefield T., York)
Phil Kitchin (Whitehaven)

Dave Lamming (Wakefield T.)
Steve Lane (Kent Invicta)
Doug Laughton (Widnes)
Roy Lester (Carlisle, Fulham)
Alan Lockwood (Dewsbury)
Brian Lockwood (Batley, Huddersfield, Wakefield T.)
Paul Longstaff (Rochdale H.)
Graham Lowe (Wigan)
Phil Lowe (York)
Trevor Lowe (Batley, Doncaster)
Ken Loxton (Bramley)
Geoff Lyon (Blackpool B.)

John Mantle (Blackpool B., Cardiff C., Leigh)
Stan McCormick (Salford)
Alan McInnes (Salford, Wigan)
Roger Millward M.B.E. (Hull K.R.)
Mick Morgan (Carlisle)
David Mortimer (Huddersfield)
Alex Murphy (Leigh, St. Helens, Salford, Warrington, Wigan)
Frank Myler (Oldham, Rochdale H., Swinton, Widnes)
Les Pearce (Bramley, Halifax)
Mike Peers (Swinton)
Geoff Peggs (Keighley)
George Pieniazek (Batley, Featherstone R.)
Harry Poole (Hull K.R.)

Bill Ramsey (Hunslet)
Terry Ramshaw (Oldham)
Graham Rees (Blackpool B.)
Malcolm Reilly (Castleford)
Alan Rhodes (Doncaster, Sheffield E.)
Austin Rhodes (Swinton)
Ken Roberts (Halifax)
Don Robinson (Bramley)
Don Robson (Doncaster)
Peter Roe (Keighley)
Sol Roper (Workington T.)

Roy Sabine (Keighley)
Dave Sampson (Castleford)
Barry Seabourne (Bradford N., Keighley)
Les Sheard (Huddersfield)
Danny Sheehan (York)
John Sheridan (Doncaster)
Tommy Smales [*Scrum-half*] (Featherstone R.)
Tommy Smales [*Forward*] (Batley, Bramley,
    Dewsbury, Doncaster, Featherstone R.)
Peter Smethurst (Leigh, Oldham)
Bill Smith (Whitehaven, Workington T.)
Brian Smith (Huddersfield)
Ike Southward (Whitehaven, Workington T.)
Graham Starkey (Oldham, Rochdale H.)
Dave Stockwell (Bramley, Batley)
John Stopford (Swinton)
Ted Strawbridge (Doncaster)
Clive Sullivan M.B.E. (Doncaster, Hull)

Bob Tomlinson (Huddersfield)
Ted Toohey (Wigan)
David Topliss (Wakefield T.)
Norman Turley (Workington T.)
Derek Turner (Wakefield T.)
Colin Tyrer (Widnes)

Don Vines (Doncaster)

Arnold Walker (Whitehaven)
Trevor Walker (Batley)
David Ward (Hunslet)
John Warlow (Bridgend)
David Watkins (Cardiff C.)
Bernard Watson (Dewsbury)
Frank Wilson (Runcorn H.)
Jeff Woods (Bridgend)
John Woods (Leigh)
Paul Woods (Runcorn H.)
Geoff Wraith (Wakefield T.)

Billy Yates (Doncaster)

DOSSIER OF 1986-87 COACHES

The following is a dossier of the coaching and playing careers of coaches holding first team posts from June 1986 to the end of May 1987. BF — beaten finalist.

JACK ADDY
Dewsbury: Feb. 84 - Jan. 87 (Promotion)
Huddersfield B.: Jan. 87 -
Played for: Dewsbury

ALLAN AGAR
Carlisle: May 81 - June 82 (Promotion)
Featherstone R.: Dec. 82 - Oct. 85
          (RL Cup winners)
Bramley: Dec. 85 - Apr. 87
Played for: Featherstone R., Dewsbury, New Hunslet, Hull K.R., Wakefield T., Carlisle, Bramley

CHRIS ANDERSON
Halifax   Nov. 84 - (Div. 1 champs, RL
           Cup winners, Premier BF,
           Charity Shield winners)
Played for: Canterbury-Bankstown (Aus.), Widnes, Hull K.R., Halifax

KEVIN ASHCROFT
Leigh: June 75 - Jan. 77 (Promotion,
           Floodlit Trophy BF)
Salford: Nov. 80 - Mar. 82
Warrington: Mar. 82 - May 84
           (Lancs. Cup winners)
Salford: May 84 - (Promotion)
Played for: Dewsbury, Rochdale H., Leigh, Warrington, Salford

BILL ASHURST
Wakefield T.: June 81 - Apr. 82
Runcorn H.:   Apr. 87 -
Played for: Wigan, Penrith (Aus.), Wakefield T.

TREVOR BAILEY
Wakefield T.: Dec. 86 -
Non-professional player

MAURICE BAMFORD
Dewsbury: Aug. - Oct. 74
Halifax: Feb. 78 - May 80
           (Yorks. Cup BF., Promotion)
Huddersfield: May 80 - May 81
Wigan: May 81 - May 82

Bramley: May 82 - Oct. 83
Leeds: Nov. 83 - Feb. 85
                       (John Player winners)
Leeds: Dec. 86 -
Great Britain &
  Under-21s: Oct. 84 - Dec. 86
Played for: Dewsbury, Hull, Batley

TONY BARROW
Warrington: Mar. 86 - (Premier winners and
                       BF, John Player BF)
Played for: St. Helens, Leigh

BILLY BENYON
Warrington: June 78 - Mar. 82
                       (Lancs. Cup winners,
                       John Player winners and BF)
St. Helens: May 82 - Nov. 85
                       (Lancs. Cup winners and BF,
                       Premier winners)
Leigh: Dec. 86 -
Played for: St. Helens, Warrington

DAVE BUSFIELD
Dewsbury: Jan. - Apr. 87
Played for: Featherstone R., Halifax, Hull,
Dewsbury

LEN CASEY
Wakefield T.:   Apr. 85 - (Promotion)
Hull: June 86 - (Yorks. Cup BF)
Played for: Hull, Hull K.R., Bradford N.,
Wakefield T.

LES COULTER
Keighley: July 86 -
Non-professional player

JIM CRELLIN
Blackpool B.:   May 76 - Mar. 77
                       (John Player BF)
Halifax: June 77 - Oct. 77
Swinton: Nov. 83 - May 86 (Div. 2
                       champs)
Mansfield M.:   Dec. 86 -
Played for: Workington T., Oldham, Rochdale H.

TERRY CROOK
Batley: June 82 - Nov. 84
Dewsbury: Apr. 87 -
Played for: Wakefield T., Bramley, Batley

ARTHUR DALEY
Runcorn H.:   Nov. 86 - Apr. 87
Played for: Leigh, Cardiff C.,/Bridgend, Runcorn H.

PAUL DALEY
New Hunslet: Apr. 74 - Aug. 78 (Promotion)
York: Jan. 79 - May 79 (Promotion)
Featherstone R.:   May 79 - Jan. 81 (Div. 2
                       champs)
Hunslet: Apr. 81 - Nov. 85 (Promotion)
Featherstone R.:   Nov. 86 - Apr. 87
Played for: Halifax, Bradford N., Hull K.R.,
Hunslet

KEITH DAVIES
Workington T.:   Feb. 86 - Mar. 87
Played for: Workington T.

TONY DEAN
Wakefield T.:   June - Dec. 86
Played for: Batley, Barrow, Hunslet, Hull,
Rochdale H.

STEVE DENNISON
Mansfield M.:   Apr. - Dec. 86
Played for: Hull, Mansfield M.

TOMMY DICKENS
Blackpool B.:   Mar. 82 - Nov. 85
Leigh: Nov. 85 - Dec. 86
                       (Div. 2 champs)
Played for: Leigh, Warrington, Widnes

COLIN DIXON
Salford: Mar. 77 - Jan. 78
Halifax: Sept. 82 - Nov. 84 (Promotion)
Keighley: July 86 -
Played for: Halifax, Salford, Hull KR

ERIC FITZSIMONS
Rochdale H.:   June 86 -
Played for: Oldham, Hunslet, Rochdale H.

GEOFF FLETCHER
Runcorn H.:   Aug. 77 - June 86
Played for: Leigh, Oldham, Wigan, Workington T.,
Runcorn H.

CHRIS FORSTER
Huddersfield B.:   Feb. 85 - Dec. 86
Played for: Huddersfield, Hull, Bramley

PETER FOX

Featherstone R.:	Jan. 71 - May 74
	(RL Cup winners & BF)
Wakefield T.:	June 74 - May 76
	(Yorks. Cup BF)
Bramley:	Sept. 76 - Apr. 77 (Promotion)
Bradford N.:	Apr. 77 - May 85 (Div. 1
	champs (2), Yorks. Cup winners
	and BF (2), Premier winners
	and BF (2), John Player winners)
Leeds:	May 85 - Dec. 86
Featherstone R.:	May 87 -
England:	1977 (2 matches)
Great Britain:	1978 (3 Tests v. Australia)
Yorkshire:	1985-86, 1986-87

Played for: Featherstone R., Batley, Hull K.R., Wakefield T.

STAN GITTINS

Blackpool B.:	Nov. 85 -

Played for: Batley, Swinton

BILL GOODWIN

Kent Invicta:	Apr. 83 - Nov. 83
Kent Invicta:	Aug. 84 - May 85
Fulham:	Apr. 86 -

Played for: Doncaster, Featherstone R., Batley

GARY HETHERINGTON

Sheffield E.:	July 86 -

Played for: York, Leeds, Kent I., Sheffield E.

BILL HOLLIDAY

Swinton:	June 86 - (Promotion, Div. 2
	Premier winners)

Played for: Whitehaven, Hull K.R., Swinton, Rochdale H.

DENNIS JACKSON

Barrow:	Feb. 87 -

Played for: Barrow, Blackpool B., Whitehaven, Workington T.

PETER JARVIS

Bramley:	Oct. 83 - Apr. 85
Hunslet:	Nov. 85 - (Div. 2 champs, Div. 2 Premier BF)

Played for: Hunslet, Bramley, Halifax, Huddersfield

IVOR KELLAND

Barrow:	May 85 - Feb. 87 (Promotion)

Played for: Barrow

PHIL KITCHIN

Whitehaven:	Oct. 79 - Jan. 82 (Promotion)
Whitehaven:	June 85 -
Cumbria:	1980-81, 1981-82, 1986-87

Played for: Whitehaven, Workington T.

DOUG LAUGHTON

Widnes:	May 78 - Mar. 83
	(RL Cup winners (2) and BF,
	Lancs. Cup winners (2) and BF,
	John Player winners and BF,
	Premier winners (2))
Widnes:	Jan. 86 -

Played for: Wigan, St. Helens, Widnes

ROY LESTER

Fulham:	June 84 - Apr. 86
Carlisle:	June 86 -

Played for: Warrington, Leigh, Fulham

BRIAN LOCKWOOD

Wakefield T.:	Nov. 76 - Jan. 78
Huddersfield:	Nov. 84 - Feb. 85
Batley:	Nov. 85 -

Played for: Castleford, Balmain (Aus.), Canterbury-Bankstown (Aus.), Wakefield T., Hull K.R., Widnes, Oldham

GRAHAM LOWE

Othuhu (NZ):	Mar. 77 - Sept. 78
	(Champions (2), Cup winners)
Brisbane Norths (Aus.):	Mar. 79 - Sept. 82
	(Premier winners)
New Zealand:	1983-86
Wigan:	Aug. 86 - (Lancs. Cup winners,
	John Player winners,
	Div. 1 champs, Premier
	winners)

Played for: Othuhu (NZ)

PHIL LOWE

York:	Mar. 83 - Mar. 87 (Promotion)

Played for: Hull K.R., Manly (Aus.)

ROGER MILLWARD M.B.E.

Hull K.R.:	Mar. 77 - (Div. 1 champs (3),
	RL Cup winners and BF (2),
	John Player winners and BF (2),
	Premier winners (2) and BF,
	Yorks. Cup winners and BF (2),
	Floodlit Trophy winners and BF,
	Charity Shield BF)

Played for: Castleford, Hull K.R., Cronulla (Aus.)

ALEX MURPHY

Leigh:	Nov. 66 - May 71 (RL Cup winners, Lancs. Cup winners and BF, Floodlit Trophy winners and BF)
Warrington:	May 71 - May 78 (League Leaders, Club Merit winners, RL Cup winners and BF, John Player winners (2), Floodlit Trophy BF, Capt. Morgan winners, Premier BF)
Salford:	May 78 - Nov. 80
Leigh:	Nov. 80 - June 82 (Div. 1 champs, Lancs. Cup winners)
Wigan:	June 82 - Aug. 84 (John Player winners, RL Cup BF)
Leigh:	Feb. 85 - Nov. 85
St. Helens:	Nov. 85 - (RL Cup BF)
Lancashire:	1973-74 to 1977-78; 1985-86 Champions (2)
England:	1975 (including World Championship (European Champions))

Played for: St. Helens, Leigh, Warrington

FRANK MYLER

Rochdale H.:	May 71 - Oct. 74 (John Player BF, Floodlit Trophy BF)
Widnes:	May 75 - May 78 (Div. 1 champs, RL Cup BF (2), Lancs. Cup winners (2), John Player winners and BF, Premier BF)
Swinton:	Jan. 80 - May 81
Oldham:	May 81 - May 83 (Div. 2 champs)
Oldham:	June 84 - Apr. 87 (Lancs. Cup BF)
GB Under-24s:	1983
England:	1978 — (European Champions)
Great Britain:	1983-84 and 1984 tour

Played for: Widnes, St. Helens, Rochdale H.

MIKE PEERS

Swinton:	June 86 - (Promotion, Div. 2 Premier winners)

Played for: Warrington, Swinton

GEORGE PIENIAZEK

Batley:	Nov. 84 - Nov. 85
Featherstone R.:	Nov. 85 - Nov. 86

Played for: Bramley, Keighley, Wakefield T., Batley

MALCOLM REILLY

Castleford:	Dec. 74 - Apr. 87 (Yorks. Cup winners (3) and BF (2), Floodlit Trophy winners, John Player winners, Premier BF, RL Cup winners, Charity Shield BF)
Great Britain & Under-21s:	Jan 87

Played for: Castleford, Manly (Aus.)

PETER ROE

Keighley:	Sept. 85 - July 86

Played for: Keighley, Bradford N., York, Hunslet, Queanbeyan (Aus.)

DAVE SAMPSON

Castleford:	Apr. 87 -

Played for: Wakefield T., Bramley, Castleford

BARRY SEABOURNE

Keighley:	Nov. 77 - Mar. 79
Bradford N.:	May 85 -

Played for: Leeds, Bradford N., Keighley

DANNY SHEEHAN

York:	Mar. 87 -

Played for: York

JOHN SHERIDAN

Doncaster:	June 84 -

Played for: Castleford

DAVID TOPLISS

Wakefield T.:	May 87 -

Played for: Wakefield T., Hull, Oldham

NORMAN TURLEY

Workington T.:	Mar. 87 -

Played for: Warrington, Blackpool B., Rochdale H., Swinton, Runcorn H., Barrow, Workington T.

DAVID WARD

Hunslet:	July 86 — (Div. 2 champs, Div. 2 Premier BF)

Played for: Leeds

FRANK WILSON

Runcorn H.:	July 86 - Nov. 86

Played for: St. Helens, Workington T., Warrington, Salford, Runcorn H.

PAUL WOODS

Runcorn H.:	Nov. 86 - Apr. 87

Played for: Widnes, Hull, Cardiff C., Runcorn H.

Wally Lewis, the 1986 Australian tour skipper.

1986 KANGAROOS

In line with the modern entertainment trend, Australia followed up their all-conquering 1982 Kangaroos with ... Invincibles II.

The 1986 green-and-golds performed another clean sweep to win all 13 fixtures in Britain — their shortest-ever tour itinerary. The Australians have not lost on British soil since Great Britain won the second Test at Bradford in 1978, a remarkable winning run of 32 matches.

The 28-man squad amassed 452 points, including an 85-try haul, and passed the 30-point mark in nine of their 13 matches, their lowest score being 20.

Australia won the Ashes for the seventh successive series with convincing scorelines of 38-16 and 34-4 before Britain regained their pride by holding the rampant visitors to 24-15 in the third Test at Wigan.

The Kangaroos' on-field success was mirrored at the box office. This 16th round-the-world visit attracted a total attendance of 212,068. The average gate of 16,313 was second only to the 16,732 in 1948 and 33 per cent up on the last tour.

Two attendance records were created. The bold move to hire Manchester United's Old Trafford soccer stadium paid off handsomely with a record gate for any tour fixture in Britain of 50,583, producing the biggest receipts outside of Wembley — £251,061. The opening attendance of 30,622 for the clash with Wigan was the biggest for any tour game against a club side.

The aggregate turnout for the three Whitbread Trophy Bitter Tests was 101,560, only the second time a three-match series in Britain had passed the 100,000 mark, the record 114,883 being established in 1948.

The tourists' half share of the tour receipts was £345,634 to give a record windfall after meeting their total tour costs of £230,000. Thus, the Kangaroos set off for their seven-match visit to France with a profit of more than £115,000 with the Gallic takings still to come. Britain's cash bonanza amounted to around £150,000.

Inevitably, from the day the 1986 Kangaroos landed in Manchester, there were comparisons with their 1982 counterparts, the first tourists to Britain to return home unbeaten and, in doing so, achieve a whitewash Test result.

The 1986 Australians scored more points due to the intervening increase of the try to four points. Their try tally in 13 games was 85, compared with the 97 in 15 matches scored four years earlier. Significantly, 14 tries were conceded in 1986, double the total of 1982.

Five of the Invincible squad of 1982 made the 1986 trip ... skipper Wally Lewis, Brett Kenny, Gene Miles, Mal Meninga and Peter Sterling.

Lewis was an outstanding tourist, compensating for the disappointment of his visit four years earlier when, as vice-captain, he failed to establish himself in the Test side. Sterling confirmed his status as number one scrum half in the world, Kenny showing why he had been voted International Player of the Year, while the four-year gap had seen Miles promoted from the second string to Test rating in a direct swap with Meninga.

The Kangaroo forwards were all tour debutants. From a nervous start at Wigan, the packmen gained in maturity and while not receiving the individual acclaim of the 1982 forwards, they moulded into an effective unit which provided a springboard for the powerful, star-studded back division. Prop forward Greg Dowling and second row giant Noel Cleal drew on their experience of British club football, with Wigan and Widnes respectively, to gain top marks.

Cleal broke his arm in the 11th tour match, at Hull, missing the third Test and the French visit. Injuries also curtailed the activities of Des Hasler and Steve Folkes to three games, and first Test men Les Kiss and Steve Roach to four matches.

As always, the tour developed a number of players' reputations on the international scene. Loose forward Bob Lindner established himself as successor to Ray Price's number 13 jersey, while newcomers Paul Dunn and Les Davidson made rapid progress to Test status. Conversely, Balmain's tall second row man Paul Sironen, a Test candidate at the start of the tour, failed to realise his potential.

An indication of the in-depth strength of the Kangaroos was the quality of their accepted second string side — the Emus. Full back Gary Belcher, centre Mal Meninga, stand off Terry Lamb and hooker Ben Elias would have walked into any other Test side in the world.

Lamb emerged as one of the most popular tourists, featuring in all 13 matches, topping the try tally with 15, and adding 13 goals to become second top points scorer with 86.

The honour of leading the points chart went to Michael O'Connor, the St. George centre-cum-Test winger. Arguably the success of the full European tour, O'Connor kicked 31 goals and ran in seven tries in nine British appearances. His first Test in Britain was marked by amassing an Anglo-Aussie Test record haul of 22 points. The previous record of 20 points had been jointly held by Great Britain's Roger Millward (1970) and Lewis Jones (1954), plus fellow countrymen Mick Cronin (1979) and Graeme Langlands (1963).

His first Test hat-trick of tries, emulated by centre partner Miles, equalled the

Winger Michael O'Connor, top points scorer on the tour and new Test points record holder.

Australian record against Britain set by Jim Devereux (1908), Reg Gasnier (1959 and 1963), and Ken Irvine (1963 and 1966).

Despite the Test whitewash, Britain's 21-year-old centre Garry Schofield rewrote the record books with a world class display of try poaching. His total of five tries — from a British tally of six — was the most by a Great Britain player in a home series against Australia, although Jim Leytham, of Wigan, tallied six in Australia in 1910.

Schofield also added a drop goal for a 21-point haul to beat Neil Fox's 20, from seven goals and two tries in 1959, as the most by a British player in a home series. The threequarter also became the fifth British player to score at least one try in each Test of a series and the first since Workington Town's Ike Southward in Australia in 1958.

The tryscoring prodigy now lies third in the all-time list of Great Britain try scorers in Tests against Australia. His seven tries in six Tests puts him behind Billy Boston with nine touchdowns, and Mick Sullivan's eight.

The three-match Test series was sponsored by Whitbread Trophy Bitter as part of their £170,000 two-year deal. Man of the Match awards were presented to both sides in each Test, the roll of honour being:

First Test: Deryck Fox (Britain) and Wally Lewis (Australia).

Second Test: Kevin Ward (Britain) and Noel Cleal (Australia).

Third Test: Garry Schofield (Britain) and Paul Dunn (Australia).

The coveted Man of the Series awards went to Castleford prop Ward, capped only once prior to the Kangaroo Tests, and Australian skipper Lewis, a dominant, match-winning leader.

Second row giant Noel Cleal, second Test Man of the Match and broken arm victim at Hull.

TOUR RESULTS

Date		Result	Score	Opposition	Venue	Attendance
Oct.	12th	W	26-18	Wigan	Wigan	30,622
	15th	W	46-10	Hull K.R.	Hull K.R.	6,868
	19th	W	40-0	Leeds	Leeds	11,389
	21st	W	48-12	Cumbria	Barrow	4,233
	25th	W	38-16	GREAT BRITAIN	Old Trafford, Manchester	50,583
	29th	W	36-2	Halifax	Halifax	7,193
Nov.	2nd	W	32-8	St. Helens	St. Helens	15,381
	4th	W	22-16	Oldham	Oldham	5,678
	8th	W	34-4	GREAT BRITAIN	Elland Road, Leeds	30,808
	12th	W	20-4	Widnes	Widnes	10,268
	16th	W	48-0	Hull	Hull	8,213
	18th	W	38-0	Bradford N.	Bradford	10,663
	22nd	W	24-15	GREAT BRITAIN	Wigan	20,169

TOUR SUMMARY

					FOR			AGAINST			
P.	W.	D.	L.	T.	G.	Dr.	Pts.	T.	G.	Dr.	Pts.
13	13	0	0	85	56	0	452	14	24	1	105

TEST SUMMARY

					FOR			AGAINST			
P.	W.	D.	L.	T.	G.	Dr.	Pts.	T.	G.	Dr.	Pts.
3	3	0	0	17	14	0	96	6	5	1	35

TOUR RECORDS

Biggest attendance: 50,583, first Test at Old Trafford, Manchester

Highest score: 48-12 v. Cumbria; 48-0 v. Hull

Widest margin: 48-0 v. Hull

Narrowest margin victory: Beat Oldham 22-16

Highest score against: Beat Wigan 26-18

Most tries in a match: 5 by Terry Lamb v. Hull K.R.

Most goals in a match: 6 by Michael O'Connor v. Hull

Most points in a match: 26 by Terry Lamb (5 tries and 3 goals) v. Hull K.R.

Most tries on tour: 15 by Terry Lamb

Most goals on tour: 31 by Michael O'Connor

Most points on tour: 90 (31 goals and 7 tries) by Michael O'Connor

Most appearances: All 13 (including 7 as substitute) by Terry Lamb

Most full appearances: 9 by Dale Shearer

Sin bin: Garry Jack v. Wigan; Terry Lamb v. Cumbria; Steve Roach v. Great Britain, first Test; Paul Dunn v. Halifax; Garry Jack v. St. Helens; Martin Bella and Steve Folkes v. Oldham; Brett Kenny v. Widnes; Greg Dowling v. Hull; Martin Bella v. Bradford N.

Opponents' sin bin: Kevin Pape (Cumbria); Lee Crooks and Joe Lydon (Great Britain, first Test); Brian Juliff (Halifax); Chris Arkwright and Paul Round (St. Helens); Mick Worrall and Paul Sherman (Oldham); Steve Crooks and Andy Dannatt (Hull); Ian Howcroft (Bradford N.); Chris Burton (Great Britain, third Test)

TOUR PARTY

Managers: John Fleming and Gordon Treichel

Coach: Don Furner

Physiotherapist: Larry Brittan

Doctor: Bill Monaghan

PLAYER	CLUB	App	Sub	T	G	Pts
ALEXANDER, Greg	Penrith (NSW)	5	1	8	5	42
BELCHER, Gary	Canberra (NSW)	6	—	2	—	8
BELLA, Martin	North Sydney (NSW)	6	—	1	—	4
CLEAL, Noel	Manly-Warringah (NSW)	7	—	3	—	12
DALEY, Phil	Manly-Warringah (NSW)	3	1	—	—	—
DAVIDSON, Les	South Sydney (NSW)	5	4	—	—	—
DOWLING, Greg	Wynnum-Manly (Qld)	6	1	1	—	4
DUNN, Paul	Canterbury-Bankstown (NSW)	6	1	—	—	—
ELIAS, Ben	Balmain (NSW)	6	—	3	—	12
FOLKES, Steven	Canterbury-Bankstown (NSW)	3	—	—	—	—
HASLER, Des	Manly-Warringah (NSW)	2	1	2	—	8
JACK, Garry	Balmain (NSW)	7	—	5	—	20
KENNY, Brett	Parramatta (NSW)	8	1	4	—	16
KISS, Les	North Sydney (NSW)	4	—	1	—	4
LAMB, Terry	Canterbury-Bankstown (NSW)	6	7	15	13	86
LANGMACK, Paul	Canterbury-Bankstown (NSW)	6	—	1	—	4
LEWIS, Wally	Wynnum-Manly (Qld)	7	—	6	—	24
LINDNER, Bob	Wynnum-Manly (Qld)	7	—	3	—	12
MENINGA, Mal	Canberra (NSW)	8	3	5	7	34
MILES, Gene	Wynnum-Manly (Qld)	8	—	6	—	24
MORTIMER, Chris	Canterbury-Bankstown (NSW)	6	—	3	—	12
NIEBLING, Bryan	Redcliffe (Qld)	7	—	1	—	4
O'CONNOR, Michael	St. George (NSW)	8	1	7	31	90
ROACH, Steve	Balmain (NSW)	4	—	—	—	—
SHEARER, Dale	Manly-Warringah (NSW)	9	—	6	—	24
SIMMONS, Royce	Penrith (NSW)	7	—	—	—	—
SIRONEN, Paul	Balmain (NSW)	5	2	—	—	—
STERLING, Peter	Parramatta (NSW)	7	—	2	—	8

(Qld): Queensland   (NSW): New South Wales

Left to right: Back row: Meninga, Hasler, Jack, Kiss, Shearer, Bella, Langmack, Mortimer, Alexander, Folkes, Kenny, Miles. Middle row: Monaghan, Davidson, Niebling, Cleal, Dunn, Furner, Lindner, Roach, Dowling, Daley, Sironen, Brittan. Front row: Lamb, O'Connor, Sterling, Treichel, Lewis, Fleming, Simmons, Belcher, Elias.

MATCH BY MATCH

12th October

WIGAN 18
AUSTRALIA 26

1. Jack
2. Kiss
3. Miles
4. Kenny
5. O'Connor
6. Lewis
7. Sterling
8. Roach
9. Simmons
10. Niebling
11. Sironen (Lamb)
12. Cleal
13. Lindner (Davidson)

T: O'Connor, Kiss, Lewis, Sterling, Cleal
G: O'Connor (3)

Wigan:
Hampson; Bell, Stephenson, Lydon, Gill; Edwards (Du Toit), Ford; West, Dermott (Louw), Case, Roberts, Potter, Goodway

T: Bell, Lydon, Edwards
G: Gill (3)

Half-time: 2-16

Referee: John Holdsworth (Kippax)
Attendance: 30,622

A massive crowd of 30,622 — the biggest for a club match against any tourists — witnessed an epic thriller. With the contest billed as the 'fourth Test,' Australia paid Wigan the compliment of fielding a virtual Test side.

The 16th Kangaroos made a blistering start which resembled a replay of the invincible 1982 tourists, holding a handsome 20-2 lead after 47 minutes with tries from O'Connor — after only three minutes — Sterling, Cleal and captain Lewis.

Scrum half Ford, a late inclusion due to Hanley being forced out with injury, earned the Man of the Match rating as Wigan staged a thrilling revival, starting with a 53rd minute try by Bell. Seven minutes later Edwards shot to the line and Australia were stung into producing top class threequarter play for Kiss to cross.

Wigan refused to lie down and Bell's angled run paved the way for a spectacular Lydon touchdown and a frenzied Wigan assault on the Kangaroos' line. Even considering the tourists' limited four-day stay and the fielding of 10 debutants on British soil, the watching Great Britain management left Central Park with renewed hope of a Test upset.

15th October

HULL K.R. 10
AUSTRALIA 46

1. Belcher
2. Mortimer
3. Miles
4. Meninga
5. Shearer
6. Lamb
7. Hasler (Alexander)
8. Dowling
9. Elias
10. Bella
11. Folkes (Davidson)
12. Dunn
13. Langmack

T: Lamb (5), Elias (2), Mortimer, Langmack
G: Lamb (3), Meninga (2)

Hull K.R.:
Fairbairn; Clark, Dorahy (Stead), Boustead, Laws; M. Smith; W. Parker; Broadhurst, Rudd, Ema, Kelly, D. Harrison (Busby), Speckman

T: Boustead
G: Dorahy (3)

Half-time: 10-20

Referee: Gerry Kershaw (Easingwold)
Attendance: 6,868

Stand off Lamb led the slaughter with five tries and three goals as the Kangaroos revealed their immense powers of reserve at Craven Park.

The Australian second string swept aside a limited Hull K.R. challenge, scoring nine tries to one. Lamb, the smallest tourist at 5ft 5in, was head and shoulders above the rest, his five touchdowns coming from intelligent support play, brilliant handling and a turn of speed.

It was another tourist of small stature — acting captain Elias — who also stood out in the powerful Australian side. Playing more like an extra half back than a hooker, Elias punished Rovers' attempts at head high tackles by twice ducking and weaving for tries.

Scrum half Hasler was taken to hospital with a dislocated thumb as the only setback in a show of reserve strength. The overseas dominance of the game was emphasised by the Hull K.R. points coming from try-scoring Australian Boustead and Dorahy, on target with three goal kicks. New Zealander Broadhurst was the home Man of the Match!

19th October

LEEDS	0
AUSTRALIA	40

1. Jack
2. Kiss
3. Kenny
4. Miles
5. O'Connor
6. Lewis
7. Sterling (Lamb)
8. Roach
9. Simmons
10. Niebling (Dowling)
11. Sironen
12. Cleal
13. Lindner

T: O'Connor (2), Lewis (2), Jack, Cleal, Dowling, Kenny
G: O'Connor (4)

Leeds:
Gill (Medley); Creasser, Ettingshausen, McGaw, Francis; Holmes, Gascoigne; Grayshon, Morris, Smith (Skerrett), Owen, Price, Heron

Half-time: 0-22

Referee: Robin Whitfield (Widnes)
Attendance: 11,389

The rampant Kangaroos continued to attract the inevitable comparisons with their 1982 all-conquering counterparts by demolishing a token Leeds challenge, running in eight tries without reply.

The Headingley walkover took the current scoring tally to 112 points for and 28 against, compared with the three-match figures of four years earlier of 74-23.

After only eight days of fixtures, coach Furner was already aware of the danger which arose towards the end of the 1982 tour . . . bored indifference with the weakness of the opposition.

It crept in as the green-and-golds strolled to a 22-0 interval lead and added four further touchdowns without extending themselves. Over elaboration was a criticism but that tendency led to a series of spectacular tries, with Man of the Match Sterling a key figure in the sweeping movements until his substitution in the 73rd minute.

21st October

Barrow

CUMBRIA	12
AUSTRALIA	48

1. Belcher
2. Shearer
3. Mortimer
4. Meninga
5. O'Connor
6. Lamb
7. Alexander
8. Daley (Sironen)
9. Elias
10. Bella
11. Dunn
12. Davidson
13. Langmack

T: Lamb (3), Alexander (3), Shearer (2), Belcher, Meninga G: Lamb (3), O'Connor

Cumbria:
Smith (Workington T.); James (Barrow), Pape (Carlisle), Kay (Barrow), Beck (Workington T.); Cameron (Whitehaven), Cairns (Barrow); Kendall (Barrow), Falcon (Workington T.), Simpson (Whitehaven), Mossop (Barrow), L. Holliday (Swinton), Huddart (Leigh). Substitutions: Lofthouse (Whitehaven) for Holliday, W. Pattinson (Workington T.) for Beck.

T: Cameron, Holliday
G: Cameron (2)

Half-time: 6-28

Referee: John McDonald (Wigan)
Attendance: 4,233

Australia's second choice half backs Lamb and Alexander grabbed a hat-trick apiece as the Kangaroos hit the 160-point mark in only their fourth outing.

In cold, blustery conditions at Barrow's Craven Park ground, the visitors ran in a total of 10 tries but could only add four goals, one from Test marksman O'Connor and three from Lamb to bring his contribution to 18 points.

Australia opened their account after only two minutes with Lamb's first touchdown and it was always apparent that the visitors had too much speed and strength for a Cumbrian side consisting mainly of Second Division players.

Davidson collected the Kangaroos' Man of the Match award, while the Cumbrian choice was scrum half Cairns who formed an effective half back combination with Whitehaven's Cameron — the scorer of a try and two goals — while the only forward to stand out was tryscorer Les Holliday.

FIRST TEST

A British record Test crowd of 50,583 braved relentless rain for the first-ever Rugby League international at Manchester United's Old Trafford ground, spurred on by the pre-match promise of a closing of the gap between Great Britain and all-conquering Australia.

Seven Kangaroo tries and a 22-point deficit proved the optimistic build-up to the history-making 97th Anglo-Aussie Test to be a little hollow.

Great Britain coach Maurice Bamford, having taken his charges into the magnificent Old Trafford arena on a wave of confidence after the most intensive preparation for a British squad, walked into the shell-shocked home dressing room seconds after the 38-16 blitz and bid to boost the shattered morale of the downhearted players with the controversial announcement of the same line-up for the second Test.

Despite the atrocious weather, the near-capacity crowd paid a British Test record £251,061, enticed by the growing belief that Australia's run of 10 successive victories over Britain — stretching back to 1978 — could be halted. The 50,000-plus hopefuls and millions of television viewers around the world saw that the gap was as wide as ever.

Ironically, the British camp again found some consolation in the continuing sequence of Australian trouncings. They justifiably pointed to Joe Lydon's great 65-yard try as superior to any of the Kangaroos' seven touchdowns, just as the Lions had scored the outstanding try in each of the three defeats of 1984. It was the first try by a British full back in a Test against Australia and the perfect answer to the criticism of Bamford's shock selection of the Wigan utility star in the number one jersey.

Britain's three touchdowns was their highest tally against the green-and-golds for 12 years, the other two being superbly carved out for ace poacher Garry Schofield by clubmate Lee Crooks. The Hull packman was by far Britain's most progressive forward, being as constructive and effective as any of the opposition six despite the blot on his copybook of yet another trip to the sin bin.

That misdemeanour probably cost Crooks the British Man of the Match award, the vote going to Featherstone Rovers scrum half Deryck Fox. The number seven's performance was symptomatic of the entire home side ... full of honest endeavour and spirit, but just not good enough.

The Australian individual award went to skipper Wally Lewis, the stand off acting as the perfect pivot between a world class set of backs and a pack of forwards who were capable without being as awe-inspiring as their forerunners.

The visitors could be excused for kicking off with some trepidation, facing a highly motivated British side boasting new found confidence, a record partisan crowd and the worst of the adverse elements in driving wind and rain. Instead the Australians turned round with a 16-0 lead, aided to a great extent by an opening 40 minutes of British tactical ineptitude littered with never-ending handling errors, accentuated by lack of operation of a kicking game, a much vaunted part of their pre-match planning.

On the credit side, Bamford's men mounted a 10-minute revival at the start of the second half, pulling back to 16-10. The true potential of the side was shown with tries from Schofield and Lydon before Wigan winger Henderson Gill made a casual hash of fielding Lewis's kick off after Lydon's spectacular touchdown. Instead of mounting a further pressure attack, Britain had to drop out, and the tourists scored almost immediately to signal the end of the home cause.

FIRST WHITBREAD TROPHY BITTER TEST

25th October   **Old Trafford, Manchester**

GREAT BRITAIN 16		AUSTRALIA 38
Joe Lydon (Wigan)	1.	Gary Jack
Tony Marchant (Castleford)	2.	Les Kiss
Garry Schofield (Hull)	3.	Brett Kenny
Ellery Hanley (Wigan)	4.	Gene Miles
Henderson Gill (Wigan)	5.	Michael O'Connor
Tony Myler (Widnes)	6.	Wally Lewis, Capt.
Deryck Fox (Featherstone R.)	7.	Peter Sterling
Kevin Ward (Castleford)	8.	Greg Dowling
David Watkinson (Hull K.R.), Capt	9.	Royce Simmons
John Fieldhouse (Widnes)	10.	Steve Roach
Lee Crooks (Hull)	11.	Noel Cleal
Ian Potter (Wigan)	12.	Bryan Niebling
Andy Goodway (Wigan)	13.	Bob Lindner
Shaun Edwards (Wigan)	14.	Terry Lamb
Andy Platt (St. Helens)	15.	Mal Meninga

T: Schofield (2), Lydon
G: Crooks, Gill
Half-time: 0-16
Referee: Julien Rascagneres (France)
Attendance: 50,583

T: O'Connor (3), Miles (3), Jack
G: O'Connor (5)
Substitutions:
Meninga for Kiss (51 min.)
Lamb for Lindner (77 min.)

Scorechart		Scoreline	
Minute	*Score*	*GB*	*Aus*
9:	Miles (T)	0	4
21:	O'Connor (T)	·0	8
25:	O'Connor (PG)	0	10
32:	O'Connor (T)	0	14
36:	O'Connor (PG)	0	16
46:	Crooks (PG)	2	16
50:	Schofield (T)	6	16
54:	Lydon (T)	10	16
56:	Miles (T)		
	O'Connor (G)	10	22
64:	O'Connor (T)	10	26
73:	Miles (T)		
	O'Connor (G)	10	32
76:	Jack (T)		
	O'Connor (G)	10	38
79:	Schofield (T)		
	Gill (G)	16	38
	Scrums	7	5
	Penalties	15	13

Try scorer Gary Jack.

29th October

HALIFAX	2
AUSTRALIA	36

1. Belcher
2. Kenny
3. Meninga
4. Mortimer
5. Cleal
6. Lamb
7. Alexander (O'Connor)
8. Dunn
9. Elias
10. Bella
11. Sironen
12. Davidson
13. Langmack

T: Alexander (2), Lamb (2), Belcher, Kenny, Meninga
G: Lamb (4)

Halifax:
Eadie; Wilson, Whitfield, C. Anderson (Beevers), Smith; Hague, Stephens; Neller, Preece, Juliff, Bell (Fairbank), Dixon, Rix

G: Whitfield

Half-time: 2-14

Referee: Mick Beaumont (Huddersfield)
Attendance: 7,193

Champions Halifax, although understrength, provided a spirited display before being overwhelmed by Australia's reserve side, inspired by powerhouse centre Meninga who scored a try and had a hand in four others.

The Kangaroos fielded only two current Test stars with centre Kenny and second row forward Cleal having a run out on the wings.

Halifax were subjected to a seven-try tanning as Australia took their points tally to a massive 234 in just six matches. While Meninga took on the star role as try-maker, his colleague on the Test substitutes bench, stand off Lamb, notched another two touchdowns to take his total to 10 in only three full appearances.

The Thrum Hall side were well served by scrum half Stephens with a performance reminiscent of his Great Britain days, back row forward Dixon, and, in the early stages, Australian player-coach Anderson.

Visiting coach Don Furner criticised referee Beaumont for the heavy penalty deficit and the disallowing of two Australian touchdowns.

2nd November

ST. HELENS	8
AUSTRALIA	32

1. Jack
2. Shearer
3. Kenny
4. Miles
5. Meninga
6. Lewis
7. Sterling
8. Dowling (Lamb)
9. Simmons
10. Roach (Dunn)
11. Cleal
12. Niebling
13. Lindner

T: Shearer (2), Niebling, Miles, Meninga, Cleal
G: Meninga (3), Lamb

St. Helens:
Veivers; Ledger, Loughlin, Halliwell, McCormack; Clark, Holding; Burke, Liptrot (Allen), Forber (Round), Haggerty, Platt, Arkwright

G: Loughlin (4)

Half-time: 6-14

Referee: Fred Lindop (Wakefield)
Attendance: 15,381

Championship leaders St. Helens, with 21 consecutive league wins to their credit, were earmarked to provide the tourists with their stiffest test.

But the Kangaroos soaked up all the Saints had to offer and replied with six touchdowns to take their try tally past the 50-mark and their points average to 37 a match.

Australia paid Alex Murphy's men the compliment of fielding a Test side, with the exception of the injured wingmen O'Connor and Kiss, which allowed Meninga to make a hero's return to Knowsley Road. In his wing role, Meninga hit only three goals from seven attempts, but added a last-minute try.

Saints trailed 14-6 at the break and put the tourists under intense pressure at the restart with a 15-minute onslaught. Australia held out and sealed victory with an outstanding try in the 66th minute, skipper Lewis taking out at least four home players with one of his trademark passes for Cleal to touch down.

Centre Loughlin scored Saints' points with four penalty goals, while three players were sent to the sin bin, Arkwright in the first half, then fellow Saint Round and visiting full back Jack after a 50th minute flare up. Test prop Roach was taken off with a dislocated elbow after only three minutes.

4th November

OLDHAM 16
AUSTRALIA 22

1. Belcher
2. Shearer
3. Meninga
4. Mortimer
5. O'Connor
6. Lamb
7. Alexander
8. Daley
9. Elias
10. Bella (Sironen)
11. Folkes
12. Davidson
13. Langmack

T: Lamb (2), Elias, Alexander
G: O'Connor (3)

Oldham:
Edwards; Sherman, Foy, Warnecke, M'Barki; Topliss, Ashton; Clark, Flanagan, Clawson (Nadiole), Hobbs (Hawkyard), Worrall, Raper

T: Hawkyard, Foy
G: Worrall (3), Hobbs

Half-time: 8-14

Referee: Kevin Allatt (Southport)
Attendance: 5,678

Battling Oldham earned one distinction in their first meeting with the tourists since 1973. The Roughyeds' six-point defeat was to become Australia's lowest winning margin.

A 60-second penalty goal by Hobbs put Oldham into the lead and it was another 17 minutes before a harassed Australian second string could draw level. Then a two-try burst from stand off Lamb helped to put them 14-2 ahead after 26 minutes. A glorious try from substitute Hawkyard — a 12th minute replacement for the injured Hobbs — with Worrall adding the goal, gave an interval scoreline of 14-8 to Australia.

Two Worrall penalty goals made it 14-12 on the hour as Oldham mounted intense pressure. But captain Elias inspired a worried-looking Kangaroo side, touching down in the 61st minute and creating the position for a try for Alexander 12 minutes later to edge the tourists to safety. Oldham crowned a praiseworthy display with a consolation try from former Test centre Foy in the dying seconds, created by loose forward Raper, son of former Kangaroo star, Johnny.

Referee Allatt — subject of Australian criticism for his interpretation of the obstruction rule — reacted to a flare-up at the first scrum by sending four players to the sin bin — Oldham's Sherman and Worrall, plus tourists Bella and Folkes.

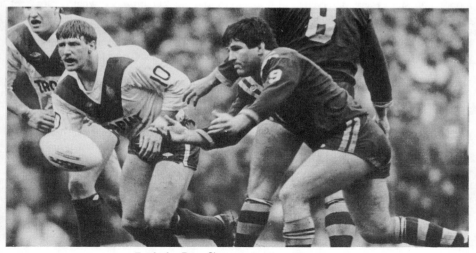

Test hooker Royce Simmons, seven tour appearances.

SECOND TEST

For the opening 28 minutes, Great Britain responded to coach Maurice Bamford's vote of confidence and dared to threaten Australia's eight-year unbeaten run against them.

Despite the absence of the injured Ellery Hanley, presenting ace goalkicker Michael O'Connor with a third minute penalty goal for obstruction, the loss of skipper David Watkinson with a shin injury after 20 minutes, and a remarkable decision to take a hurried tap penalty rather than kick at goal, Britain rattled the Kangaroos with old-fashioned Test resistance.

As Britain strove to take the lead for the first time in the series, stand off Tony Myler — having been denied a try by a Wally Lewis ankle tap — broke clear from deep in his own territory. His majestic run brought him face-to-face with Australian full back Gary Jack, support now at hand from ace try poacher Garry Schofield, Tony Marchant and Henderson Gill.

One pass was needed to reward the Lions for their early endeavour and give them the morale booster they deserved. Instead, Myler brought cries of anguish from every corner of the packed Elland Road stadium by kicking over Jack's head, the ball flying over the dead ball line.

The error of judgement sentenced Britain to re-open the catalogue of errors which led to their downfall at Old Trafford two weeks earlier. This time the mistake rate rose, from 14 lost balls on a rain sodden Manchester pitch to 18 in perfect conditions, Lee Crooks being the main culprit with seven.

A typical handling foul-up brought about the first of Australia's six tries in the 28th minute. Deryck Fox and Kevin Ward messed up a planned move and Man of the Match Noel Cleal brushed aside substitute Andy Platt to send loose forward Bob Lindner dashing to the posts, O'Connor adding the goal. The free-scoring winger added a try five minutes later by exposing Joe Lydon's inexperience at full back to give the tourists a 12-0 half-time lead.

There was to be no repeat of Britain's superb second half rally of a fortnight earlier. Rather, they started to go downhill rapidly. There was no lack of effort from the likes of Gill, Ward, Fox, Ian Potter and Andy Goodway, but hard work was no answer to the world class skills of Lewis, half back partner Peter Sterling, the rampaging Cleal and company.

Sterling's pass sent Lewis sidestepping with ease past Schofield, Goodway and Lydon after 47 minutes. A powerful break by Cleal gave full back Jack a clear run to the line three minutes later. And when Myler had the ball stolen, Greg Dowling and Sterling carved a huge channel for Jack to score his third try of the series in the 57th minute.

Wigan's Shaun Edwards came on for the luckless Myler but Australia continued to serve up their now traditional brand of entertaining rugby which brought both appreciative applause from the 30,000-plus crowd, plus chants of 'what a load of rubbish' aimed at Britain.

Centre Brett Kenny started and finished their final try in the 70th minute, the classic movement also featuring Dale Shearer and Jack, with O'Connor adding his fifth goal to give him a tally of 14 points.

As Australia waited patiently for the final whistle and the Ashes celebrations, O'Connor blotted his copybook by missing a pass and the ever-eager Schofield nipped in to collect a 77th minute touchdown, his 12th in 10 Tests.

British coach Bamford was clearly drained by the 30-point defeat, having pinned his hopes on the first Test squad. This time there was a brief, emotional Press conference and an acceptance that team changes would be inevitable.

SECOND WHITBREAD TROPHY BITTER TEST

8th November   **Elland Road, Leeds**

GREAT BRITAIN 4		AUSTRALIA 34
Joe Lydon (Wigan)	1.	Gary Jack
Barry Ledger (St. Helens)	2.	Dale Shearer
Garry Schofield (Hull)	3.	Brett Kenny
Tony Marchant (Castleford)	4.	Gene Miles
Henderson Gill (Wigan)	5.	Michael O'Connor
Tony Myler (Widnes)	6.	Wally Lewis, Capt.
Deryck Fox (Featherstone R.)	7.	Peter Sterling
Kevin Ward (Castleford)	8.	Greg Dowling
David Watkinson (Hull K.R.), Capt.	9.	Royce Simmons
John Fieldhouse (St. Helens)	10.	Paul Dunn
Lee Crooks (Hull)	11.	Noel Cleal
Ian Potter (Wigan)	12.	Bryan Niebling
Andy Goodway (Wigan)	13.	Bob Lindner
Shaun Edwards (Wigan)	14.	Terry Lamb
Andy Platt (St. Helens)	15.	Mal Meninga

T: Schofield

Substitutions:
Platt for Watkinson (20 min.)
Edwards for Myler (58 min.)
Half-time: 0-12
Referee: Julien Rascagneres (France)
Attendance: 30,808

T: Jack (2), Lindner, Lewis,
O'Connor, Kenny
G: O'Connor (5)
Substitutions:
Lamb for Sterling (78 min.)
Meninga for Niebling (78 min.)

Scorechart		*Scoreline*	
Minute	*Score*	*GB*	*Aus*
3:	O'Connor (PG)	0	2
28:	Lindner (T)		
	O'Connor (G)	0	8
33:	O'Connor (T)	0	12
47:	Lewis (T)		
	O'Connor (G)	0	18
50:	Jack (T)		
	O'Connor (G)	0	24
57:	Jack (T)	0	28
70:	Kenny (T)		
	O'Connor (G)	0	34
77:	Schofield (T)	4	34
	Scrums	4	8
	Penalties	11	8

Try scorer Bob Lindner.

12th November

WIDNES	4
AUSTRALIA	**20**

1. Belcher
2. Shearer
3. Meninga
4. Mortimer
5. Kiss (Kenny)
6. Lamb
7. Alexander
8. Davidson
9. Elias
10. Bella
11. Sironen
12. Folkes (Daley)
13. Langmack

T: Alexander, Mortimer, Bella
G: Lamb (2), Meninga (2)

Widnes:
Burke; Moran, D. Wright, Dowd, Basnett; A. Myler, D. Hulme; S. O'Neill, McKenzie, M. O'Neill, Eyres, P. Hulme, Pinner

G: Burke (2)

Half-time: 2-8

Referee: Geoff Berry (Batley)
Attendance: 10,268

The Kangaroos took their winning run of matches into double figures but paid dearly with injury prone Test candidates Kiss and Folkes receiving serious setbacks. Kiss came off with knee ligament damage while the second row man sustained a fractured cheekbone.

The tourists produced the only try of the first half to lead 8-2 at the break, former Great Britain full back Burke having opened the scoring with an 11th minute penalty goal, Lamb replying with two successful shots at goal. A fine individual try from scrum half Alexander after 38 minutes gave Australia the edge in a close-run half.

Substitute Kenny was sent to the sin bin 13 minutes into the second half, Burke hitting the penalty award to narrow the gap to four points, both sides producing some excellent play matched only by top class defence.

The visitors took control in the final quarter, Langmack creating a try for Canterbury Bankstown teammate Mortimer, prop Bella rounding off an outstanding match with a powerhouse touchdown, Meninga adding two goals.

16th November

HULL	0
AUSTRALIA	**48**

1. Jack
2. Shearer
3. Miles
4. Meninga
5. O'Connor
6. Lamb
7. Sterling
8. Dowling
9. Simmons
10. Daley
11. Cleal (Hasler)
12. Niebling (Davidson)
13. Langmack

T: Lamb (2), Hasler (2), Sterling, Meninga, Shearer, Miles, Jack
G: O'Connor (6)

Hull:
Kemble; Eastwood, O'Hara, Vass, McCoid; Ah Kuoi, Windley (Pearce); Brown, S. Crooks, Dannatt (Sharp), Norton, L. Crooks, Lazenby

Half-time: 0-22

Referee: Jim Smith (Halifax)
Attendance: 8,213

Australia, falling only two points short of the half century, were in the wars at the Boulevard. The first of four brawls broke out after only two minutes.

Within 15 minutes, the tourists had suffered a major blow with Test star Cleal breaking an arm and second row colleague Niebling retiring with a thigh injury. A third casualty in a bruising encounter was Langmack with a broken nose.

Hull hooker Steve Crooks was sent to the sin bin for an eighth minute foul, while rival props Dowling and Dannatt were sin-binned early in the second half after a stand-up fight, the Hull forward having to be helped off, not to return though, ironically, to win the home Man of the Match award!

The injuries and brawling marred the Kangaroos' widest margin win of the tour in a typical performance of pace, power and top speed handling. All their backs except O'Connor shared in the nine-try romp, the winger adding six goals as his contribution.

18th November

| BRADFORD N. | 0 |
| AUSTRALIA | 38 |

1. Belcher
2. Shearer
3. Kenny
4. Mortimer
5. Alexander
6. Lewis
7. Hasler
8. Dunn
9. Elias
10. Bella (Meninga)
11. Davidson
12. Sironen
13. Lindner (Lamb)

T: Lindner, Mortimer, Lewis, Kenny, Alexander, Meninga, Lamb
G: Alexander (5)

Bradford N.:
Mumby; Ford, Donlan, Hellewell, Simpson; Woods, Holmes; Howcroft, Brentley (Noble), Fenech, Jasiewicz, Fairbank (Sherratt), Graham

Half-time: 0-16

Referee: Derek Fox (Wakefield)
Attendance: 10,663

Ever-present tourist Terry Lamb, second top points scorer.

Even relentless rain and dense fog could not hide the Kangaroos' brilliance as they swept aside the challenge of Championship title contenders Northern, who became the third top Yorkshire side to be nilled by the tourists.

Australia ran in seven tries as they raced past the 400-point mark, skipper Lewis showing record Rugby Union recruit Holmes the full array of League skills in a commanding performance.

Lewis set up a try for Lindner with a pass and one for Mortimer with a kick before using his strength to scramble over for his own touchdown. He regularly drew appreciative applause from the five-figure crowd and delighted his drenched audience with an audacious back flip to his half back partner Hasler.

The tourists led 16-0 at the break, heavy fog descending at the start of the second half. When it lifted, the visitors had extended their lead to 32-0 on the hour with Meninga and Lamb having slipped on, the latter maintaining his record of playing in every tour match and extending his try tally to 15.

THIRD TEST

After being threatened with extinction, the British Lion came roaring back. With the inclusion of five fresh faces, renewed determination and re-found application, Great Britain took the seemingly invincible Australians to the brink of defeat.

Three controversial decisions by Perpignan referee Julien Rascagneres undermined Britain's transformation from no-hopers who had conceded a total of 72 points in the previous two Tests to potential conquerors of the best side in world Rugby League.

As early as the opening minutes, the Gallic man-in-the-middle overlooked a suspiciously forward pass from prop Greg Dowling to centre Gene Miles who touched down behind an incredulous British defence, Michael O'Connor adding the goal.

When recalled second row man Chris Burton was sent to the sin bin in the 52nd minute, the home crowd were stunned as the retaliating Kangaroo skipper Wally Lewis was not ordered to join him.

Five minutes later, Mr Rascagneres made a momentous decision as Britain had spectacularly fought their way back into contention at 12-12, the pendulum swinging markedly in favour of the home side.

Australian winger Dale Shearer, following up a kick within the British 25-yard zone, was hauled down by opposite number John Basnett. The immediate and post-match inquests produced a verdict from both camps that the kick was too long and British defenders were in a cover position. Controversially, the referee awarded a penalty try, O'Connor adding the goal to put Australia 18-12 ahead.

Again Britain rallied in a bid to gain two World Cup points, Joe Lydon contributing a penalty goal and Garry Schofield a drop goal. But British hopes crashed as Lewis played a captain's role by coolly jinking through ample cover for O'Connor to add

his fourth goal.

Emerging from the despair of Old Trafford and Elland Road, coach Maurice Bamford rebuilt his British side with the introduction of five new players and two positional changes. In came winger Basnett, centre David Stephenson, scrum half Andy Gregory, and fit-again back row men Chris Burton and Harry Pinner.

Gregory and Pinner dominated proceedings from the base of the scrum, while Basnett was rampant on the left flank. The sheer commitment of Warrington number seven Gregory inspired the British outfit, while opponent Peter Sterling had a torrid afternoon under the constant pressure.

Pinner, skipper for the New Zealand Tests 12 months earlier, marked his return to the Test arena after a lengthy lay off with an ankle injury with a typical display of ball handling and prompting.

Once again, Britain produced the most memorable tries. Trailing 12-0 after 26 minutes, Pinner found Widnes teammate Tony Myler who tore upfield with the inevitable Schofield in support, Gill adding the goal.

Six minutes into the second half, Pinner combined with Lee Crooks to put Stephenson away and that man Schofield again charged up to score his fifth try of the series out of Britain's total of six.

Schofield received the home Man of the Match award, edging out the aggressive Gregory and full back Lydon. A kicking game had always been a key part of Britain's pre-series planning. Lydon produced the goods at the third attempt, a barrage of strategic, diagonal, long-range kicks continually driving the Australians into rear-guard action.

The Australian hierarchy warmly welcomed Britain's re-emergence from the doldrums and expressed delight at the World Cup-rated encounter restoring the dignity and tradition of Test football.

THIRD WHITBREAD TROPHY BITTER TEST

22nd November   **Wigan**

GREAT BRITAIN 15   AUSTRALIA 24

Joe Lydon (Wigan)	1.	Gary Jack
Henderson Gill (Wigan)	2.	Dale Shearer
Garry Schofield (Hull)	3.	Brett Kenny
David Stephenson (Wigan)	4.	Gene Miles
John Basnett (Widnes)	5.	Michael O'Connor
Tony Myler (Widnes)	6.	Wally Lewis, Capt.
Andy Gregory (Warrington)	7.	Peter Sterling
Kevin Ward (Castleford)	8.	Greg Dowling
David Watkinson (Hull K.R.), Capt.	9.	Royce Simmons
Lee Crooks (Hull)	10.	Paul Dunn
Chris Burton (Hull K.R.)	11.	Mal Meninga
Andy Goodway (Wigan)	12.	Bryan Niebling
Harry Pinner (Widnes)	13.	Bob Lindner
Shaun Edwards (Wigan)	14.	Terry Lamb
Ian Potter (Wigan)	15.	Les Davidson

T: Schofield (2)

G: Lydon (2), Gill, Schofield (dg)

Substitution:

Potter for Burton (63 min.)

Half-time: 6-12

Referee: Julien Rascagneres (France)

Attendance: 20,169

T: Lindner, Shearer, Lewis, Miles

G: O'Connor (4)

Substitutions:

Davidson for Dunn (73 min.)

Lamb for Meninga (78 min.)

Try scorer Dale Shearer.

Scorechart

Minute	Score	*Scoreline* GB	Aus
2:	Miles (T)		
	O'Connor (G)	0	6
21:	Lindner (T)		
	O'Connor (G)	0	12
28:	Schofield (T)		
	Gill (G)	6	12
46:	Schofield (T)		
	Lydon (G)	12	12
57:	Shearer (T)		
	O'Connor (G)	12	18
62:	Lydon (PG)	14	18
69:	Schofield (DG)	15	18
73:	Lewis (T)		
	O'Connor (G)	15	24
	Scrums	9	7
	Penalties	9	7

Centre Gene Miles, scorer of a record-equalling first Test hat-trick of tries.

Papua New Guinea in action on their 1979 tour of the British amateur game.

KUMULS

THE KUMULS

Autumn 1987 stages the first-ever Papua New Guinea tour of the British professional circuit, an eight-match itinerary being highlighted by a World Cup-rated Whitbread Trophy Bitter Test against Great Britain at Wigan.

The Kumuls — named after the islands' Birds of Paradise — will also meet Cumbria, Lancashire and Yorkshire, three club sides and the Great Britain amateur side.

Papua have previously visited Britain in 1979 when they played three amateur clubs after a seven-match tour of France, featuring two Tests.

Their only other major tour was of New Zealand in 1983, playing seven games including a Test. Squads have made brief visits to Australia and New Zealand, including three matches in Australia in 1971.

Since being installed as full members of the International Board on 26 November 1978, Papua New Guinea have won only one Test match, a shock 24-22 defeat of New Zealand in a 1986 World Cup-rated encounter at Port Moresby. The Kumuls also secured a 13-13 draw against France in 1981.

Their acceptance by the International Board came a year after the 37-6 defeat of a France World Cup tour team. In 1975 the Papuans lost 40-12 to an England side on their way home from the World Championship in Australia and New Zealand.

Rugby League is believed to have been first played in Papua New Guinea during the 1930s in the Wau-Bulolo goldfields area. Australian servicemen also played on the islands during the Second World War, though official competition was not launched until 1949 with the formation of a league in Port Moresby.

The 13-a-side code's popularity has rapidly grown, Rugby League now being the country's national sport. The Papua New Guinea Rugby Football League was officially founded in 1974 with a four-zone structure for administration and representative purposes.

Because of the physical nature of the country and the large distances separating townships, competitions are organised on a local basis, only representative sides undertaking the extensive travel, usually by air.

There are 27 leagues affiliated to the national governing body, the largest being centred in Port Moresby, the nation's capital with a population of 150,000. The Port Moresby structure is a 10-club competition with three senior and two junior grades, under-19 and under-17. Two full rounds of competition over 18 weeks determine the minor premierships in each grade, the top five teams taking part in a grand final to determine the ultimate premiership winners.

This type of tournament reflects the Australian influence in the rapid development of the 13-a-side code in Papua New Guinea.

A feature of the Papuan promotion of the game is the staging of up to six matches on one ground in a day. In Port Moresby, admission charges are equivalent to £1 for matches from 10am to nearly 6pm in temperatures of around 90°F. Average gates for the traditional Sunday programme in the capital city are around 6,000, while Test matches attract 15,000 capacity gates, with many more non-paying customers perched in trees around the ground.

Enthusiasm is equally evident in the smaller Rugby League centres outside Port Moresby. A grand final in the town of Kimbe attracted 9,000 spectators from a total population of only 13,000, while the attendance at Mount Hagen for the Test with Great Britain in 1984 was officially returned at 7,510, though inadequate stadium fencing allowed over 10,000 to view the match.

For representative contests, the country is divided into four zones to take part in the National Championships.

TEST MATCHES

The following is a list of Test Matches involving Papua New Guinea since they became full members of the International Board in November 1978.

14 Oct. 1979 v. France	Lost	9-16	Albi
28 Oct. 1979 v. France	Lost	2-15	Carcassonne
23 Aug. 1981 v. France	Drew	13-13	Port Moresby
25 July 1982 v. New Zealand	Lost	5-56	Port Moresby
2 Oct. 1982 v. Australia	Lost	2-38	Port Moresby
2 Oct. 1983 v. New Zealand	Lost	20-60	Auckland
5 Aug. 1984 v. Great Britain	Lost	20-38	Mount Hagen
10 Aug. 1986 v. New Zealand	Lost	26-36	Goroka
17 Aug. 1986 v. New Zealand	Won	24-22	Port Moresby
4 Oct. 1986 v. Australia	Lost	12-62	Port Moresby

	P	W	D	L	F	A
TOTALS	10	1	1	8	133	356

RECORDS

For Papua New Guinea
Highest score: Lost 26-36 v. New Zealand, at Goroka, 10 August 1986
Most tries in a match: No player has scored 3 or more
Most goals in a match: 5 by D. Kovae v. New Zealand, At Goroka, 10 August 1986
Most points in a match: 10 (5g) by D. Kovae v. New Zealand, at Goroka, 10 August 1986
Biggest attendance: 15,000 v. New Zealand, at Port Moresby, 17 August 1986
15,000 v. Australia, at Port Moresby, 4 October 1986

Against Papua New Guinea
Highest Score: 62-12 v. Australia, at Port Moresby, 4 October 1986
Widest margin: 56-5 v. New Zealand, at Port Moresby, 25 July 1982
Most tries in a match: 6 by H. McGahan (New Zealand), at Auckland, 2 October 1983
Most goals in a match: 9 by G. Smith (New Zealand), at Port Moresby, 25 July 1982
Most points in a match: 24 (6t) by H. McGahan (New Zealand), at Auckland, 2 October 1983

Other International matches

6 July 1975 v. England	Lost	12-40	Port Moresby
1977 v. France	Won	37-6	Port Moresby
30 July 1978 v. New Zealand	Lost	20-31	Port Moresby

Papua New Guinea on defence against the 1982 BARLA tourists.

PAPUA NEW GUINEA TEAMS

The following is a compendium of Papua New Guinea Test and World Cup teams since being granted full International Board status in November 1978.
Key: ★, Captain; t, try; g, goal; dg, drop goal; (WC), World Cup

1979 France
Albi: 14 Oct.
Lost 9-16
Kuveu
★Sapu
Kombinari 3g
Tinemau
Kapani 1t
Joseph
Kila
Gau
Geni
Koki
Bangkoma
Monama
Waninara
Subs: Sirosi
        Giheno

1979 France
Carcassonne: 28 Oct.
Lost 2-15
Kuveu
Kapani
Akis
Aope
Tinemau
Joseph
Kila 1g
Gomia
Gau
Koki
★Sapu
Waninara
Karava

1981 France
Port Moresby: 23 Aug.
Drew 13-13
Kuveu 1t
Kapani 1t
Tinemau 1t
Limi
Akis
★Wagambie
Haili 2g
Koki
Paiyesi
Gau
Waketsi
Bangkoma
Aope
Subs: Ralda
        Yip

1982 New Zealand
Port Moresby: 25 July
Lost 5-56
Kuveu
Rero 1t
Pilokos
Peter
Sasama
Joseph
Kila 1g
Gau
Tenakanai
Ralda
Taumaku
Waninara
★Wagambie
Subs: Tep
        Katsir

1982 Australia
Port Moresby: 2 Oct.
Lost 2-38
Kuveu 1g
Rero
Segeyaro
Yip
Timi
★Joseph
Kabavas
Gau
Asotau
Tep
Taumaku
Tete
Loitive
Subs: Matmillo
        Togili

1983 New Zealand
Auckland: 2 Oct.
Lost 20-60
Kitimun 1t
Nil
Noifa
Katsir
Waluka
Segeyaro 1t
Kila 1t
Tep
Ario 1t
Koki
Gua
★Loitive
Togili
Subs: Taumaku 1g
        Heni

1984 Great Britain
Mount Hagen: 5 Aug.
Lost 20-38
Kitimun
Karai
Noifa 1t
Numapo 2g
Tolik 1t
Gabob
Kila
★Tep
Asarufa
Jekis 1t
Kubak
Loitive
Taumuka 1t
Subs: Peter
        Wek

1986 New Zealand
Goroka: 10 Aug.
Lost 26-36
Kuveu
Katsir
Atoi 1t
Numapo
Tivelit
Haili 1t
Gebob
Tep 1t
Heni
Ako
Loitive
Waketsi 1t
Taumaku
Subs: Peng, Kovae 5g

1986 New Zealand (Also WC)
Port Moresby: 17 Aug.
Won 24-22
Kovae 4g
Katsir
Atoi 1t
Numapo
Kerekere
Haili 2t
*Kila
Tep
Heni
Lomutopa
Ako 1t
Waketsi
Taumaku
Subs: Saea
     Andy

1986 Australia (Also WC)
Port Moresby: 4 Oct.
Lost 12-62
Kovae 2g
Katsir
Atoi
Numapo 2t
Kerekere
Haili
*Kila
Tep
Heni
Lomutopa
Ako
Waketsi
Taumaku
Subs: Saea
     Andy

Papua New Guinea Test stars David Tinemau (left) and Dekot Koki in traditional tribal dance attire.

PAPUA NEW GUINEA REGISTER

The following is an index of players who have appeared for Papua New Guinea or toured since the country became full members of the International Board in November 1978.

Appearances refer to Test matches only. Substitute appearances are in lower case letters and are included even when a player may not have played as official information does not differentiate.

Key: B, Britain; A, Australia; F, France; NZ, New Zealand.

AIYA, O.
Tours: NZ 1983
AKIS, P.
Appearances: 1979 F; 1981 F
Tours: Britain 1979
AKO, R.
Appearances: 1986 NZ2, A
ANDY, N.
Appearances: 1986 nz, a
AOPE, H.
Appearances: 1979 F; 1981 F
Tours: Britain 1979
ARIO, K.
Appearances: 1983 NZ
Tours: NZ 1983
ASORIFA, F.
Appearances: 1984 B
ASOTAU, O.
Appearances: 1982 A
ATOI, Lauta
Appearances: 1986 NZ2, A
BANGKOMA, N.
Appearances: 1979 f; 1981 F
Tours: 1979 Britain
GAU, T.
Appearances: 1979 F2; 1981 F; 1982 NZ,A; 1983 NZ
Tours: NZ 1983
GEBOB, G.
Appearances: 1984 B; 1986 NZ
GENI, L.
Appearances: 1979 F
Tours: Britain 1979
GIHENO, F.
Appearances: 1979 f
Tours: Britain 1979

GOMIA, J.
Appearances: 1979 F
Tours: Britain 1979
HAILI, D.
Appearances: 1981 F; 1986 NZ2, A
HENI, R.
Appearances: 1983 nz; 1986 NZ2, A
Tours: NZ 1983
JAKIS, R.
Appearances: 1984 B
JOSEPH, J.
Appearances: 1979 F2; 1982 NZ,A
Tours: Britain 1979; NZ 1983
KABAVAS, A.
Appearance: 1982 A
KAPANI, V.
Appearances: 1979 F2; 1981 F
Tours: Britain 1979
KARAI, N.
Appearances: 1984 B
KARAVA, V.
Appearances: 1979 F
Tours: Britain 1979
KATSIR, J.
Appearances: 1982 nz; 1983 NZ; 1986 NZ2,A
Tours: NZ 1983
KELLY, J.
Tours: NZ 1983
KEREKERE, M.
Appearances: 1986 NZ,A
KILA, P.
Appearances: 1979 F2; 1982 NZ; 1983 NZ; 1984 B
Tours: Britain 1979; NZ 1983
KILA, T.
Appearances: 1986 NZ,A
KIMIA, S.
Tours: NZ 1983
KITIMUN, M.
Appearances: 1983 NZ, 1984 B
Tours: NZ 1983
KOKI, D.
Appearances: 1979 F2; 1981 F; 1983 NZ
Tours: Britain 1979; NZ 1983
KOMBINARI, P.
Appearances: 1979 F
Tours: Britain 1979
KOVAE, D.
Appearances: 1986 nz,NZ,A
KUBAK, R.
Appearances: 1984 B
KUVEU, K.
Appearances: 1979 F2; 1981 F; 1982 NZ2,A; 1986 NZ
Tours: Britain 1979

LAIWA, D.
Tours: Britain 1979
LIMI, A.
Appearances: 1981 F
Tours: Britain 1979
LOITIVE, R.
Appearances: 1982 A; 1983 NZ; 1984 B; 1986 NZ
Tours: NZ 1983
LOMUTOPA, A.
Appearances: 1986 A, NZ
MATMILLO, F.
Appearances: 1982 a
Tours: NZ 1983
MINADI, L.
Tours: NZ 1983
MONAMA, P.
Appearances: 1979 F
Tours: Britain 1979
NGALA, L.
Tours: NZ 1983
NIL, K.
Appearances: 1983 NZ
Tours: NZ 1983
NOIFA, D.
Appearances: 1983 NZ; 1984 B
Tours: NZ 1983
NUMAPO, B.
Appearances: 1984 B; 1986 NZ2,A
PAIYESI, H.
Appearances: 1981 F
PENG, P.
Appearances: 1986 nz
PETER, J.
Appearances: 1982 NZ; 1984 b
PILOKOS, Y.
Appearances: 1982 NZ
POSU, K.
Tours: Britain 1979
RALDA, P.
Appearances: 1981 f; 1982 NZ
RERO, A.
Appearances: 1982 NZ,A
SAEA, K.
Appearances; 1986 nz,a
SAPU, S.
Appearances: 1979 F2
Tours: 1979
SASAMA, S.
Appearances: 1982 NZ

SEGEYARO, I.
Appearances: 1982 A; 1983 NZ
Tours: NZ 1983
SIROSI, C.
Appearances: 1979 f
Tours: Britain 1979
SOM, R.
Tours: Britain 1979
TAMTU, D.
Tours: Britain 1979
TAUMAKU, A.
Appearances: 1982 NZ,A; 1983 nz; 1984 B; 1986 NZ
Tours: NZ 1983
TENAKANAI, J.
Appearances: 1982 NZ
TEP. J.
Appearances: 1982 nz,A; 1983 NZ; 1984 B;
1986 NZ2,A
Tours: NZ 1983
TETE, L.
Appearances: 1982 A
TIMI, D.
Appearances: 1982 A
TINEMAU, D.
Appearances: 1979 F2; 1981 F
Tours: Britain 1979
TIVELIT, A.
Appearances: 1986 NZ
TOGILI, E.
Appearances: 1982 a; 1983 NZ
Tours: NZ 1983
TOLIK, B.
Appearances: 1984 B
TORE, M.
Tours: Britain 1979
WAGAMBI, J.
Appearances: 1981 F; 1982 NZ
Tours: NZ 1983
WAKETSI, B.
Appearances: 1981 F; 1986 NZ,A
WALUKA, W.
Appearances: 1983 NZ
Tours: NZ 1983
WANIMARA, J.
Appearances: 1979 F2; 1982 NZ
Tours: Britain 1979
WARTABAR, J.
Tours; Britain 1979
WEK, P.
Appearances: 1984 b
WEMAS, S.
Tours: NZ 1983
YIP, J.
Appearances: 1981 f: 1982 A

PAPUA NEW GUINEA TOURS

1979 to Britain and France

Managers R. Cutmore and T. Lavutul
Coach: U. Sabumei
Captain S. Sapu
P. Akis
H. Aope
N. Bangkoma
L. Geni
F. Giheno
Z. Gomia
J. Joseph
V. Kapani
V. Karava
P. Kila
D. Koki
P. Kombinari
K. Kuveu
D. Laiwa
A. Limi
P. Monama
K. Posu
C. Sirosi
R. Som
D. Tamtu
D. Tinemau
M. Tore
J. Wanimara
J. Wartabar

SUMMARY	P	W	D	L	F	A
In France	7	2	0	5	81	89

Lost Test Series 2-0

In Britain	3	1	0	2	52	56

The matches in Britain were against amateur teams as follows:

St. Helens	lost	17 - 19
Britain (at Hull)	lost	12 - 28
Cumbria (at Barrow)	won	23 - 9

MEMO

The Kumuls made a good impression in France, but disappointed when they visited Britain. They were well beaten by Great Britain amateurs 28-12 at the Boulevard, Hull, before a crowd of 2,651.

1983 to New Zealand

Managers: J. Keviame and H. Arek
Coach: U. Sabumei
Captain: L. Ngala
O. Aiya
K. Ario
T. Gau
R. Heni
J. Joseph
J. Katsir
J. Kelly
P. Kila
S. Kimia
M. Kitimun
D. Koki
R. Loitive
F. Matmillo
L. Minadi
K. Nil
D. Noifa
I. Segeyaro
A. Taumaku
J. Tep
E. Togili
J. Wagambi
W. Waluka
S. Wemas

SUMMARY	P	W	D	L	F	A
	7	4	0	3	234	213

Lost Test Series 1-0

MEMO

Despite a 60-20 hammering in the Test against New Zealand and a 56-32 defeat against the Maoris, the Kumuls regarded this as a very successful tour.

Their victories included a 62-16 win over Wellington.

Poka Kila was top scorer on tour with 16 goals, two tries and 40 points.

Hugh McGahan of New Zealand scored a Test record six tries in the match at Carlaw Park, Auckland.

Australian centre Harry Wells, a hat-trick of World Cups.

WORLD CUP

1954   Played in France   WON BY GREAT BRITAIN
(Decided on league places, but a play-off was necessary when Britain and France finished level top with five points.)

Great Britain	Australia	France	New Zealand
Manager: G. Shaw	Managers: J. McMahon	Manager: A. Blain	Manager: T. McKenzie
	S. O'Neill	Coaches: J. Duhau	Coach: J. Amos
	Coach: V. Hey	R. Duffort	
D. Valentine (Huddersfield), Capt.	C. Churchill, Capt.	Puig-Aubert, Capt.	C. Eastlake, Capt.
W. Banks (Huddersfield)	R. Banks	J. Audobert	H. Anderson
H. Bradshaw (Huddersfield)	R. Bull	G. Benausse	A. Atkinson
G. Brown (Leeds)	H. Crocker	V. Cantoni	J. Austin
R. Coverdale (Hull)	B. Davies	A. Carrere	D. Blanchard
G. Helme (Warrington)	P. Diversi	R. Contrastin	J. Bond
F. Kitchen (Leigh)	D. Flannery	J. Crespo	J. Butterfield
P. Jackson (Barrow)	D. Hall	J. Delaye	N. Denton
J. Ledgard (Leigh)	G. Hawick	R. Guilhem	J. Edwards
A. Naughton (Warrington)	K. Holman	A. Jiminez	L. Erikson
D. Robinson (Wakefield T.)	K. Kearney	J. Krawzyk	I. Grey
D. Rose (Leeds)	K. McCaffery	J. Merquey	C. Johnson
R. Rylance (Huddersfield)	I. Moir	J. Pambrun	G. McDonald
S. Smith (Hunslet)	K. O'Shea	F. Rinaldi	R. McKay
M. Sullivan (Huddersfield)	N. Pidding	A. Save	W. McLennan
J. Thorley (Halifax)	N. Provan	C. Teisseire	G. Menzies
B. Watts (York)	A. Watson	G. Verdier	W. Sorensen
J. Whiteley (Hull)	H. Wells	M. Voron	J. Yates

FRANCE 22   NEW ZEALAND 13
Paris: 30 October   13,240
France: Puig-Aubert (5g); Contrastin (1t), Merquey, Jiminez, Cantoni; Benausse, Teisseire; Krawzyk, Audobert (1t), Rinaldi, Pambrun, Delaye (1t), Crespo (1t)
New Zealand: Anderson; Edwards (1t), Eastlake (1t), McKay (1t), Menzies; Sorensen, Erikson; McLennan, Blanchard, Johnson, Yates, Bond (2g), Atkinson
Referee: C. F. Appleton (England)

GREAT BRITAIN 28   AUSTRALIA 13
Lyon: 31 October   10,250
Britain: Ledgard (5g); Rose (1t), Jackson (2t), Sullivan, Kitchen (1t); Brown (2t), Helme; Thorley, Smith, Coverdale, Watts, Robinson, Valentine
Australia: Churchill; Pidding (2g), Wells (2t), Watson, Moir; McCaffery, Holman; Bull, Kearney (1t), Hall, Provan, Davies, Diversi
Referee: R. Guidicelli (France)

AUSTRALIA 34   NEW ZEALAND 15
Marseilles: 7 November   20,000
Australia: Churchill; Flannery, Watson (3t), Wells, Pidding (5g); Banks, Hawick (1t); Davies, Kearney (1t), Bull (1t), O'Shea (1t), Crocker, Diversi (1t)

New Zealand: Denton; Edwards, McKay (6g), Eastlake, Menzies; Sorensen, Erikson (1t); McLennan, Blanchard, Johnson, Butterfield, Yates, Atkinson
Referee: R. Guidicelli (France)

GREAT BRITAIN 13   FRANCE 13
Toulouse: 7 November   37,471
Britain: Ledgard (2g); Rose (1t), Jackson, Naughton, Sullivan; Brown (1t), Helme (1t); Thorley, Smith, Coverdale, Watts, Robinson, Valentine
France: Puig-Aubert (2g); Contrastin (2t), Merquey, Jiminez, Cantoni; Benausse, Crespo; Krawzyk (1t), Audobert, Rinaldi, Delaye, Pambrun, Guilhem
Referee: C. F. Appleton (England)

GREAT BRITAIN 26   NEW ZEALAND 6
Bordeaux: 11 November   14,000
Britain: Ledgard (1t,4g); Rose (1t), Jackson (1t), Sullivan, Kitchen (2t); Brown (1t), Helme; Thorley, Smith, Coverdale, Watts, Robinson, Valentine
New Zealand: Gray; Edwards, McKay (3g), Eastlake, Austin, Sorensen, Erikson; McLennan, Blanchard, Bond, Butterfield, McDonald, Atkinson
Referee: R. Guidicelli (France)

FRANCE 15   AUSTRALIA 5

Nantes: 11 November   13,000

France: Puig-Aubert (3g); Contrastin (1t),
Merquey (1t), Teisseire, Cantoni (1t); Jiminez,
Crespo; Rinaldi, Audobert, Krawzyk, Save,
Pambrun, Verdier
Australia: Churchill; Flannery, Hawick,
Watson, Pidding (1g); Banks, Holman; Davies,
Kearney, Bull, O'Shea (1t), Crocker, Diversi
Referee: C. F. Appleton (England)

Final Table

	P	W	D	L	F	A	Pts
Great Britain	3	2	1	0	67	32	5
France	3	2	1	0	50	31	5
Australia	3	1	0	2	52	58	2
New Zealand	3	0	0	3	34	82	0

PLAY OFF
GREAT BRITAIN 16   FRANCE 12

Paris: 13 November   30,368

Britain: Ledgard (2g); Rose (1t), Jackson,
Naughton, Sullivan; Brown (2t), Helme (1t);
Thorley, Smith, Coverdale, Watts, Robinson,
Valentine
France: Puig-Aubert (3g); Contrastin (1t),
Merquey, Teisseire, Cantoni (1t); Jiminez,
Crespo; Krawzyk, Audobert, Rinaldi,
Pambrun, Save, Verdier
Referee: C. F. Appleton (England)

1957   Played in Australia   WON BY AUSTRALIA
(Decided on league places)

Great Britain	Australia	France	New Zealand
Managers: W. Fallowfield	Manager: N. C. Robinson	Manager: A. Blain	Manager: K. Blow
H. Rawson	Coach: R. Poole	Coach: J. Duhau	Coach: W. Telford
A. Prescott (St. Helens), Capt.	R. Poole, Capt.	J. Merquey, Capt.	C. Johnson, Capt.
E. Ashton (Wigan)	K. Barnes	A. Appelian	R. Ackland
W. Boston (Wigan)	B. Carlson	G. Benausse	V. Bakalich
A. Davies (Oldham)	B. Clay	G. Berthomieu	K. Bell
J. Grundy (Barrow)	B. Davies	H. Delhoste	S. Belsham
G. Gunney (Hunslet)	G. Hawick	F. Ferrero	J. Butterfield
T. Harris (Hull)	K. Holman	J. Foussat	P. Creedy
P. Jackson (Barrow)	K. Kearney	G. Husson	R. Griffiths
L. Jones (Leeds)	K. McCaffery	R. Jean	B. Hadfield
S. Little (Oldham)	W. Marsh	A. Jiminez	W. McLennan
T. McKinney (St. Helens)	I. Moir	F. Levy	H. Maxwell
G. Moses (St. Helens)	K. O'Shea	R. Medus	G. Menzies
R. Price (Warrington)	N. Provan	A. Parent	K. Pearce
A. Rhodes (St. Helens)	R. Ritchie	A. Rives	R. Percy
J. Stevenson (Leeds)	D. Schofield	J. Rouqueyrol	J. Riddell
M. Sullivan (Huddersfield)	T. Tyquin	A. Save	W. Sorensen
D. Turner (Oldham)	A. Watson	G. Verdier	G. Turner
J. Whiteley (Hull)	H. Wells	M. Voron	J. Yates

GREAT BRITAIN 23   FRANCE 5

Sydney: 15 June   50,007

Britain: Moses; Boston (1t), Jackson (1t),
Davies, Sullivan (2t); Jones (4g),
Stevenson (1t); Prescott, Harris, Little,
Grundy, Gunney, Turner
France: Rives; Husson, Jiminez, Merquey (1t),
Voron; Benausse (1g), Jean; Ferrero, Appelian,
Berthomieu, Save, Parent, Rouqueyrol
Referee: D. Lawler (Australia)

AUSTRALIA 25   NEW ZEALAND 5

Brisbane: 15 June   29,636

Australia: Barnes (5g); Moir (1t), Wells (1t),
Poole, Carlson (1t); Hawick, Holman; Marsh,
Kearney, Davies, O'Shea (1t), Provan (1t), Clay
New Zealand: Creedy; Bakalich, Sorensen (1g),
Ackland, Hadfield; Menzies, Belsham;
McLennan, Butterfield, Maxwell, Johnson (1t),
Yates, Percy
Referee: V. Belsham (New Zealand)

263

AUSTRALIA 31 GREAT BRITAIN 6
Sydney: 17 June 57,955
Australia: Carlson (4g); Watson, Wells (1t), Poole, Moir (2t); Clay (1t), McCaffery (2t); Marsh, Kearney, Davies (1g), O'Shea (1t), Provan, Schofield
Britain: Moses; Boston, Ashton, Davies, Sullivan; Jones (3g), Stevenson; Prescott, Harris, Little, Whiteley, Grundy, Turner
Referee: V. Belsham (New Zealand)

FRANCE 14 NEW ZEALAND 10
Brisbane: 17 June 28,000
France: Rives; Husson, Merquey, Voron, Foussat (2t); Benausse (4g), Jean; Delhoste, Appelian, Medus, Berthomieu, Parent, Rouqueyrol
New Zealand: Creedy (1g); Bakalich, Sorensen (1t 1g), Ackland, Hadfield (1t); Menzies, Belsham; McLellan, Butterfield, Maxwell, Johnson, Yates, Percy
Referee: D. Lawler (Australia)

AUSTRALIA 26 FRANCE 9
Sydney: 22 June 35,158
Australia: Carlson (1t, 7g); Watson, Poole (1t), Wells, Moir; Clay, McCaffery; Marsh (1t), Kearney, Davies, O'Shea (1t), Provan, Schofield

France: Rives; Husson, Jiminez, Foussat, Voron; Benausse (1t, 3g), Jean; Ferrero, Appelian, Delhoste, Medus, Parent, Levy
Referee: V. Belsham (New Zealand)

GREAT BRITAIN 21 NEW ZEALAND 29
Sydney: 25 June 14,263
Britain: Moses; Ashton, Jackson (1t), Jones (1t, 3g), Sullivan (1t); Rhodes, Stevenson; Prescott, McKinney, Little (1t), Grundy (1t), Gunney, Turner
New Zealand: Creedy; Hadfield (1t), Sorensen (7g), Turner (1t), Griffiths; Menzies (1t), Belsham; McLennan (1t), Butterfield, Yates, Maxwell, Johnson, Riddell (1t)
Referee: D. Lawler (Australia)

Final Table
	P	W	D	L	F	A	Pts
Australia	3	3	0	0	82	20	6
Great Britain	3	1	0	2	50	65	2
New Zealand	3	1	0	2	44	60	2
France	3	1	0	2	28	59	2

1960 Played in England WON BY GREAT BRITAIN
(Decided on league places)

Great Britain	Australia	France	New Zealand
Manager: W. Fallowfield	Managers: P. Duggan	Manager: A. Blain	Managers: G. Plant
	J. O'Toole	Coaches: R. Duffort	T. Skinner
	Coach: K. Barnes	D. Duhau	Coach: T. Hardwick
E. Ashton (Wigan), Capt.	K. Barnes, Capt.	J. Barthe, Capt.	C. Johnson, Capt.
W. Boston (Wigan)	D. Beattie	A. Boldini	R. Ackland
J. Challinor (Warrington)	R. Boden	A. Casas	J. Butterfield
A. Davies (Oldham)	A. Brown	J. Dubon	M. Cooke
E. Fraser (Warrington)	R. Bugden	R. Erramouspe	R. Cooke
R. Greenhough (Warrington)	B. Carlson	G. Fages	N. Denton
T. Harris (Hull)	R. Gasnier	Y. Gourbal	C. Eastlake
V. Karalius (St. Helens)	B. Hambly	R. Gruppi	R. Griffiths
B. McTigue (Wigan)	K. Irvine	J. Guiraud	B. Hadfield
A. Murphy (St. Helens)	N. Kelly	A. Lacaze	T. Kilkelly
F. Myler (Widnes)	L. Morgan	C. Mantoulan	H. Maxwell
A. Rhodes (St. Helens)	R. Mossop	A. Marty	G. Menzies
B. Shaw (Hunslet)	B. Muir	J. Merquey	L. Oliff
J. Shaw (Halifax)	G. Parcell	Y. Mezard	G. Phillips
M. Sullivan (Wigan)	J. Raper	L. Poletti	T. Reid
D. Turner (Wakefield T.)	E. Rasmussen	A. Quaglio	N. Roberts
J. Whiteley (Hull)	W. Rayner	R. Rey	W. Sorensen
J. Wilkinson (Wakefield T.)	H. Wells	A. Vadon	G. Turner

New Zealand skipper Cyril Eastlake is too late to prevent Great Britain stand off Gordon Brown scoring in the 1954 World Cup encounter at Bordeaux.

New Zealand wingman Neville Denton evades Great Britain's Bobby Greenhough in the 1960 World Cup encounter at Bradford, with Alex Murphy in the background.

GREAT BRITAIN 23   NEW ZEALAND 8
Bradford: 24 September   20,577
Britain: Fraser (4g); Greenhough, Ashton (1t),
Davies (1t), Sullivan; Myler (1t), Murphy (1t);
Wilkinson, Harris, McTigue (1t), Karalius,
Whiteley, Turner
New Zealand: Eastlake; Hadfield (1t), Turner,
Sorensen (1g), Denton; Menzies, Roberts;
Maxwell, Butterfield, Johnson, Ackland,
Kilkelly, M. Cooke (1t)
Referee: E. Martung (France)

AUSTRALIA 13   FRANCE 12
Wigan: 24 September   20,278
Australia: Carlson (2g); Morgan, Gasnier (1t),
Wells, Irvine; Brown, Muir; Beattie, Kelly (1t),
Mossop, Hambly, Rasmussen, Raper (1t)
France: Poletti; Dubon, Rey, Mantoulan,
Gruppi (2t); Merquey, Fages; Quaglio, Casas,
Boldini, Barthe, Erramouspe, Lacaze (3g)
Referee: E. Clay (England)

GREAT BRITAIN 33   FRANCE 7
Swinton: 1 October   22,923
Britain: Fraser (6g); Challinor, Rhodes (2t),
Davies (2t), Sullivan (1t); Myler (1t), Murphy;
Wilkinson (1t), J. Shaw, McTigue, B. Shaw,
Karalius, Whiteley
France: Poletti; Dubon (1t), Rey, Mantoulan,
Gruppi; Merquey, Guiraud; Quaglio, Casas,
Erramouspe, Barthe, Mezard, Lacaze (2g)
Referee: E. Martung (France)

AUSTRALIA 21   NEW ZEALAND 15
Leeds: 1 October   10,773
Australia: Barnes; Carlson (3t,3g), Wells (1t),
Gasnier (1t), Irvine; Brown, Muir; Beattie,
Kelly, Parcell, Hambly, Mossop, Raper

New Zealand: Phillips; Hadfield (1t),
Turner (1t), Eastlake (3g), Denton;
Menzies (1t), Roberts; Maxwell, Butterfield,
Johnson, Ackland, Oliff, M. Cooke
Referee: E. Clay (England)

GREAT BRITAIN 10   AUSTRALIA 3
Bradford: 8 October   32,773
Britain: Rhodes (2g); Boston (1t), Ashton,
Davies, Sullivan (1t); Myler, Murphy;
Wilkinson, J. Shaw, McTigue, B. Shaw,
Turner, Karalius
Australia: Barnes; Boden, Gasnier, Wells,
Carlson (1t); Brown, Muir; Beattie, Kelly,
Parcell, Mossop, Rasmussen, Hambly
Referee: E. Martung (France)

NEW ZEALAND 9   FRANCE 0
Wigan: 8 October   2,876
New Zealand: Phillips; Hadfield, Turner,
Griffiths, Eastlake (3g); Menzies, Roberts;
Reid (1t), Butterfield, Johnson, Ackland, Oliff,
M. Cooke
France: Poletti; Dubon, Rey, Mantoulan,
Gruppi; Merquey, Fages; Boldini, Vadon,
Quaglio, Barthe, Erramouspe, Lacaze
Referee: E. Clay (England)

Final Table

	P	W	D	L	F	A	Pts
Great Britain	3	3	0	0	66	18	6
Australia	3	2	0	1	37	37	4
New Zealand	3	1	0	2	32	44	2
France	3	0	0	3	19	55	0

1968   Played in Australia and New Zealand   WON BY AUSTRALIA
(Decided by top two in league table meeting in play-off final.)

Great Britain	Australia	France	New Zealand
Manager: W. Fallowfield	Manager: A. Kingston	Managers: J. Guiraud	Manager: D. Wilson
Coach: C. Hutton	Coach: H. Bath	F. Soubie	Coach: B. Barchard
		Coach: R. Lacoste	
B. Risman (Leeds), Capt.	J. Raper, Capt.	G. Ailleres, Capt.	J. Bond, Capt.
K. Ashcroft (Leigh)	A. Beetson	A. Alesina	E. Carson
J. Atkinson (Leeds)	A. Branson	Y. Begou	J. Clarke
T. Bishop (St. Helens)	R. Coote	J. Capdouze	O. Danielson
I. Brooke (Wakefield T.)	B. Fitzsimmons	J. Clar	J. Dixon
A. Burwell (Hull KR)	R. Fulton	J. Cros	S. Dunn
M. Clark (Leeds)	J. Greaves	A. Ferren	J. Ellwood
D. Edwards (Castleford)	B. James	M. Frattini	A. Kriletich
P. Flanagan (Hull KR)	F. Jones	R. Garrigues	B. Lee

R. French (Widnes)
R. Haig (Wakefield T.)
R. Millward (Hull KR)
A. Morgan (Featherstone R.)
C. Renilson (Halifax)
M. Shoebottom (Leeds)
C. Sullivan (Hull)
J. Warlow (St. Helens)
C. Watson (St. Helens)
C. Young (Hull KR)

J. King
G. Langlands
D. Manteit
E. Rasmussen
J. Rhodes
E. Simms
W. Smith
R. Thornett
L. Williamson
J. Wittenberg

J. Gruppi
J. Lecompte
J. Ledru
H. Marracq
H. Mazard
M. Molinier
F. De Nadai
D. Pelerin
C. Sabatie
V. Serrano

C. McMaster
R. Mincham
C. O'Neil
D. Parkinson
P. Schultz
H. Sinel
G. Smith
R. Tait
H. Tatana
E. Wiggs

AUSTRALIA 25   GREAT BRITAIN 10
Sydney: 25 May   62,256
Australia: Simms (8g); Rhodes, Greaves, Langlands, King; Branson, Smith (1t); Beetson, Jones, Wittenberg, Coote (1t), Thornett, Raper (1t)
Britain: Risman (2g); Brooke (1t), Shoebottom, Burwell, Sullivan (1t); Millward, Bishop; Clark, Ashcroft, Watson, French, Haigh, Renilson
Referee: J. Percival (New Zealand)

FRANCE 15   NEW ZEALAND 10
Auckland: 25 May   18,000
France: Cros; Pellerin, Molinier, Lecompte, Ferren; Capdouze (1t,5g), Garrigues (1g); Aillieres, Begou, Sabatie, De Nadai, Marracq, Clar
New Zealand: Tait; Mincham, Sinel, Schultz, Wiggs (5g); Bond, Clarke; Danielson, O'Neil, Smith, Lee, Dixon, Kriletich. Sub: Tatana
Referee: C. Pearce (Australia)

AUSTRALIA 31   NEW ZEALAND 12
Brisbane: 1 June   23,608
Australia: Simms (8g); Rhodes (1t), Greaves, Langlands, King (2t); Branson, Smith; Wittenberg, Jones (1t), Rasmussen, Coote (1t), Thornett, Raper. Sub: Fulton
New Zealand: Mincham, Dunn (1t), Schultz (1t), Wiggs (3g); Bond, Clarke; Smith, O'Neil, Tatana, Lee, Dixon, Kriletich. Sub: Tait
Referee: J. Percival (New Zealand)

FRANCE 7   GREAT BRITAIN 2
Auckland: 2 June   15,760
France: Cros; Pelerin, Molinier, Lecompte, Ledru (1t); Capdouze (1g), Garrigues (1g); Aillieres, Begou, Sabatie, Marracq, Mazard, Clar
Britain: Risman (1g); Sullivan, Brooke, Burwell, Atkinson; Millward, Bishop; Clark, Flanagan, Watson, Morgan, Haigh, Renilson. Sub: Warlow
Referee: C. Pearce (Australia)

AUSTRALIA 37   FRANCE 4
Brisbane: 8 June   32,662
Australia: Simms (5g); James, Rhodes, Greaves (1t), Williamson (2t); Fulton (2t), Smith (1t,3g); Wittenberg, Fitzsimmons, Beetson, Coote (1t), Manteit, Raper
France: Cros; Ferren, Molinier, Gruppi, Ledru; Capdouze (2g), Frattini; Sabatie, Begou, Serrano, Alesina, Mazard, Clar.
Sub: De Nadai
Referee: J. Percival (New Zealand)

GREAT BRITAIN 38   NEW ZEALAND 14
Sydney: 8 June   14,105
Britain: Risman (7g); Sullivan (3t), Brooke (1t), Burwell (2t), Atkinson; Millward, Bishop; Clark, Flanagan, Warlow, French, Morgan (1t), Renilson. Subs: Shoebottom (1t), Watson
New Zealand: Ellwood; Mincham, Dunn, Schultz (2t), Wiggs (4g); Tait, Carson; McMaster, O'Neil, Smith, Sinel, Lee, Kriletich. Sub: Dixon
Referee: C. Pearce (Australia)

Final Table

	P	W	D	L	F	A	Pts
Australia	3	3	0	0	93	26	6
France	3	2	0	1	26	49	4
Great Britain	3	1	0	2	50	46	2
New Zealand	3	0	0	3	36	84	0

FINAL
AUSTRALIA 20   FRANCE 2
Sydney: 10 June   54,290
Australia: Simms (4g); Williamson (2t), Langlands, Greaves (1t), Rhodes; Fulton, Smith; Wittenberg, Jones, Beetson, Thornett, Raper, Coote (1t). Sub: Rasmussen
France: Cros; Pelerin, Gruppi, Lecompte, Ledru; Capdouze (1g), Garrigues; Sabatie, Begou, Ailleres, De Nadai, Marracq, Clar
Referee: J. Percival (New Zealand)

1970 Played in England WON BY AUSTRALIA
(Decided by top two in table meeting in play-off final.)

Great Britain	Australia	France	New Zealand
Manager: J. Harding	Managers: K. Arthurson	Manager: R. Forges	Manager: C. Mountford
Coach: J. Whiteley	J. Quinn		Coach: L. Blanchard
	Coach: H. Bath		
F. Myler (St. Helens), Capt.	R. Coote, Capt.	J. Clar, Capt.	F. Christian, Capt.
K. Ashcroft (Leigh)	R. Branighan	R. Biffi	M. Brereton
J. Atkinson (Leeds)	J. Brown	E. Bonal	W. Burgoyne
P. Charlton (Salford)	J. Cootes	F. Bonet	E. Carson
D. Chisnall (Leigh)	R. Costello	J. Cabero	G. Cooksley
R. Dutton (Widnes)	R. Fulton	J. Capdouze	W. Deacon
A. Fisher (Bradford N./Leeds)	M. Harris	R. Coquand	D. Gailey
R. Haigh (Leeds)	R. McCarthy	G. Cremoux	L. Graham
D. Hartley (Castleford)	B. McTaggart	J. Cros	J. Greengrass
K. Hepworth (Castleford)	J. O'Neill	R. Garrigues	E. Heatley
C. Hesketh (Salford)	R. O'Reilly	J. Gruppi	E. Kereopa
S. Hynes (Leeds)	D. Pittard	G. Guiraud	A. Kriletich
K. Jones (Wigan)	P. Sait	S. Marsolan	D. Ladner
D. Laughton (Wigan)	E. Simms	H. Mazard	B. Lowther
M. Reilly (Castleford)	W. Smith	M. Molinier	R. McGuinn
M. Shoebottom (Leeds)	G. Sullivan	F. de Nadai	C. O'Neil
A. Smith (Leeds)	R. Turner	D. Pelerin	G. Smith
J. Thompson (Featherstone R.)	E. Walters	A. Ruiz	J. Whittaker
C. Watson (St. Helens)	L. Williamson	C. Sabatie	G. Woollard

AUSTRALIA 47 NEW ZEALAND 11
Wigan: 21 October 9,586
Australia: Simms (10g,1t);Williamson, Cootes (2t), Fulton (1t), Branighan (1t); Pittard, Smith (1t); O'Neill, Walters, O'Reilly, McCarthy (1t), Sait, Coote (1t).
Sub: Turner (1t)
New Zealand: Ladner (4g); McGuinn, Christian, Lowther, Brereton; Woollard, Cooksley; Smith (1t), O'Neil, Gailey, Deacon, Heatley, Kriletich. Subs: Greengrass, Graham
Referee: W. H. Thompson (England)

GREAT BRITAIN 11 AUSTRALIA 4
Leeds: 24 October 15,084
Britain: Dutton (3g); Smith, Hynes (1t,1g), Myler, Atkinson; Shoebottom, Hepworth; Hartley, Fisher, Watson, Thompson, Laughton, Reilly
Australia: Simms (1g); Harris, Branighan, Fulton (1g); Williamson; Pittard, Smith; O'Neill, Walters, O'Reilly, McCarthy, Sait, Sullivan
Referee: G. F. Lindop (England)

NEW ZEALAND 16 FRANCE 15
Hull: 25 October 3,824
New Zealand: Ladner (5g); Whittaker, Christian, Lowther, Brereton (1t); Woollard, Cooksley (1t); Greengrass, O'Neil, Gailey, Smith, Kereopa, Kriletich. Subs: Graham, Deacon
France: Cros; Marsolan (2t), Molinier, Ruiz, Bonal (1t); Capdouze (3g), Garrigues; Sabatie, Cabero, Bonet, Mazard, Biffi, Clar.
Sub: de Nadai
Referee: W. H. Thompson (England)

GREAT BRITAIN 6 FRANCE 0
Castleford: 28 October 8,958
Britain: Dutton (3g); Jones, Hynes, Myler, Atkinson; Shoebottom, Hepworth; Hartley, Ashcroft, Watson, Thompson, Laughton, Reilly
France: Cros; Marsolan, Molinier, Ruiz, Bonal; Capdouze, Guiraud; Sabatie, Cabero, de Nadai, Mazard, Cremoux, Clar. Subs: Pelerin, Bonet
Referee: G. F. Lindop (England)

GREAT BRITAIN 27 NEW ZEALAND 17
Swinton: 31 October 5,609

Britain: Dutton (6g); Jones, Hynes (1t),
Hesketh (1t), Atkinson (1t); Shoebottom,
Hepworth; Chisnall, Ashcroft, Watson (1t),
Thompson, Haigh, Laughton (1t).
Sub: Charlton
New Zealand: Ladner (4g); Whittaker,
Christian (1t), Lowther, Brereton; Woollard,
Cooksley; Greengrass, O'Neil, Kereopa,
Smith (1t), Heatley, Kriletich (1t).
Sub: Graham
Referee: G. F. Lindop (England)

FRANCE 17 AUSTRALIA 15
Bradford: 1 November 6,215

France: Cros; Marsolan (2t), Molinier, Gruppi,
Pelerin; Capdouze (1t,3g), Garrigues (1g);
Sabatie, Cabero, Bonet, de Nadai, Biffi, Clar
Australia: Simms (3g); Branighan, Cootes (2t),
Fulton (1t), Williamson; Pittard, Smith;
McTaggart, Walters, O'Reilly, McCarthy, Sait,
Coote. Subs: Turner, Sullivan
Referee: W. H. Thompson (England)

Final Table

	P	W	D	L	F	A	Pts
Great Britain	3	3	0	0	44	21	6
Australia	3	1	0	2	66	39	2
France	3	1	0	2	32	37	2
New Zealand	3	1	0	2	44	89	2

FINAL

GREAT BRITAIN 7 AUSTRALIA 12
Leeds: 7 November 18,776

Britain: Dutton (1g); Smith, Hynes (1g),
Myler, Atkinson (1t); Shoebottom, Hepworth;
Hartley, Fisher, Watson, Thompson,
Laughton, Reilly. Subs: Hesketh, Haigh
Australia: Simms (3g); Williamson (1t),
Cootes (1t), Sait, Harris; Fulton, Smith;
O'Neill, Turner, O'Reilly, McCarthy, Costello,
Coote. Subs: Branighan, Walters
Referee: G. F. Lindop (England)

1972 Played in France WON BY GREAT BRITAIN
(Decided by top two in table meeting in play-off final.)

Great Britain	Australia	France	New Zealand
Manager: W. Spaven	Managers: A. Kingston	Manager:	Manager: T. Wellsmore
Coach: J. Challinor	J. Clark	Coach:	Coach: D. Barchard
	Coach: H. Bath		
C. Sullivan (Hull), Capt.	G. Langlands, Capt.	F. de Nadai, Capt.	F. Christian, Capt.
J. Atkinson (Leeds)	A. Beetson	M. Anglade	M. Brereton
P. Charlton (Salford)	R. Branighan	E. Bonal	W. Burgoyne
T. Clawson (Leeds)	J. Elford	J. Bonal	A. Coll
C. Dixon (Salford)	R. Fulton	J. Franc	W. Collicoat
C. Hesketh (Salford)	J. Grant	M. Frattini	G. Cooksley
J. Holmes (Leeds)	M. Harris	J. Garzino	M. Eade
D. Jeanes (Leeds)	F. Jones	S. Gleyzes	D. Gailey
R. Irving (Oldham)	S. Knight	B. Guilhem	P. Gurnick
A. Karalius (St. Helens)	R. McCarthy	J. M. Imbert	D. Mann
B. Lockwood (Castleford)	J. O'Neill	S. Marsolan	M. Mohi
P. Lowe (Hull KR)	R. O'Reilly	M. Mazare	P. Orchard
S. Nash (Featherstone R.)	T. Raudonikis	M. Molinier	J. O'Sullivan
G. Nicholls (Widnes)	P. Sait	A. Rodriguez	R. Paul
D. O'Neill (Widnes)	G. Starling	A. Ruiz	B. Tracey
D. Redfearn (Bradford N.)	G. Stevens	J. Sauret	R. Walker
M. Stephenson (Dewsbury)	G. Sullivan	V. Serrano	J. Whittaker
D. Topliss (Wakefield T.)	E. Walters	R. Toujas	D. Williams
J. Walsh (St. Helens)	D. Ward	C. Zalduendo	J. Wilson

The 1972 World Cup Great Britain squad, left to right.

Back row: W. Spaven (Manager), T. Clawson, P. Lowe, D. Jeanes, C. Dixon, G. Nicholls, K. Kelly, A. Karalius, M. Stephenson, B. Lockwood, R. Irving, D. Redfearn, J. Challinor (Coach).

Front row: J. Holmes, J. Walsh, C. Hesketh, C. Sullivan, P. Charlton, S. Nash, J. Atkinson, D. O'Neill.

FRANCE 20   NEW ZEALAND 9
Marseilles: 28 October   20,748
France: Toujas; Marsolan, Molinier, Ruiz (1t),
J. Bonal (2t,1g); Guilhem (4g), Frattini (1dg);
de Nadai, Franc, Garzino, Serrano, Gleyzes,
Anglade. Sub: Zalduendo
New Zealand: Whittaker; Orchard (2t),
O'Sullivan, Christian, Brereton (1t); Williams,
Tracey; Mohi, Burgoyne, Paul, Gailey,
Gurnick, Eade. Subs: Cooksley, Coll
Referee: G. Jameau (France)

GREAT BRITAIN 27   AUSTRALIA 21
Perpignan: 29 October   6,324
Britain: Charlton; Sullivan (1t), Hesketh,
Walsh, Atkinson (1t); O'Neill (1t), Nash;
Clawson (6g); Stephenson (1t), Jeanes,
Lowe (1t), Lockwood, Nicholls. Sub: Holmes
Australia: Langlands (4g); Harris, Branighan,
Starling, Knight; Fulton (3t), Raudonikis (1t);
O'Neill, Walters, Beetson, McCarthy (1dg),
Elford, Sullivan. Subs: Ward, Sait
Referee: M. Teisseire (France)

AUSTRALIA 9   NEW ZEALAND 5
Paris: 1 November   8,000
Australia: Langlands; Grant, Branighan (1g),
Starling, Knight; Fulton (1t,1dg), Ward (1t);
O'Neill, Walters, O'Reilly, Sullivan, Elford,
Sait. Sub: Stevens
New Zealand: Wilson (1g); Orchard, Brereton,
Christian, Whittaker (1t); Williams, Tracey;
Mann, Burgoyne, Gailey, Eade, Paul, Gurnick.
Sub: Walker
Referee: M. J. Naughton (England)

GREAT BRITAIN 13   FRANCE 4
Grenoble: 1 November   5,321
Britain: Charlton; Sullivan (1t), Hesketh,
Walsh, Atkinson; O'Neill, Nash; Clawson (2g),
Stephenson, Lockwood, Lowe (2t), Dixon,
Nicholls
France: Toujas; Marsolan, Molinier, Ruiz,
J. Bonal (1g); Guilhem, Imbert; de Nadai,
Franc, Sauret, Serrano (1g), Gleyzes,
Rodriguez. Sub: Zalduendo
Referee: F. Gril (France)

GREAT BRITAIN 53   NEW ZEALAND 19
Pau: 4 November   7,500
Britain: Charlton (1t); Sullivan (1t),
Hesketh (1t), Walsh, Atkinson (2t);
Holmes (2t,10g), Nash (1t); Jeanes (1t),
Stephenson (1t), Lockwood, Lowe, Irving,
Nicholls (1t). Subs: Redfearn, Karalius
New Zealand: Wilson (2g); Orchard, Brereton,
Christian, Whittaker (1t); Williams (1t), Tracey;
Mann, Burgoyne, Gailey, Eade (1t),
Coll (1t), Gurnick. Subs: Collicoat, Walker
Referee: G. Jameau (France)

AUSTRALIA 31   FRANCE 9
Toulouse: 5 November   10,332
Australia: Langlands; Grant, Harris (2t),
Starling, Branighan (5g); Fulton (1t), Ward;
O'Neill (1t), Walters (1t), O'Reilly, Beetson,
Stevens, Sait (2t)
France: Toujas; Marsolan, Molinier, Ruiz (1t),
E. Bonal (3g); Mazare, Frattini; Zalduendo,
Franc, Garzino, Serrano, Gleyzes, de Nadai.
Subs: Guilhem, Anglade
Referee: M. J. Naughton (England)

Final Table

	P	W	D	L	F	A	Pts
Great Britain	3	3	0	0	93	44	6
Australia	3	2	0	1	61	41	4
France	3	1	0	2	33	53	2
New Zealand	3	0	0	3	33	82	0

FINAL

GREAT BRITAIN 10   AUSTRALIA 10
Lyons: 11 November   4,231
10-10 after 80 minutes. Extra time of 20
minutes produced no further score. Britain
awarded trophy because of higher position in
league table.

Britain: Charlton; Sullivan (1t), Hesketh,
Walsh, Atkinson; Holmes, Nash; Clawson (2g),
Stephenson (1t), Jeanes, Lowe, Lockwood,
Nicholls. Sub: Irving
Australia: Langlands; Grant, Harris, Starling,
Branighan (2g); Fulton, Ward; O'Neill (1t),
Walters, O'Reilly, Beetson (1t), Stevens,
Sullivan
Referee: G. Jameau (France)

1975 Played in all five countries WON BY AUSTRALIA
(Decided on league places)

England
In Australia and New Zealand
Manager: W. Oxley
Coach: A. Murphy
R. Millward (Hull KR), Capt.
J. Atkinson (Leeds)
J. Bridges (Featherstone R.)
D. Chisnall (Warrington)
E. Chisnall (St. Helens)
P. Cookson (Leeds)
M. Coulman (Salford)
G. Dunn (Hull KR)
L. Dyl (Leeds)
G. Fairbairn (Wigan)
K. Fielding (Salford)
K. Gill (Salford)
P. Gordon (Warrington)
T. Martyn (Warrington)
M. Morgan (Wakefield T.)
S. Nash (Featherstone R.)
G. Nicholls (St. Helens)
D. Noonan (Warrington)
S. Norton (Castleford)
J. Walsh (St. Helens)

*The following players also appeared
in the World Cup but did not tour*
Down Under:
M. Adams (Widnes), P. Charlton (Salford),
D. Eckersley (St. Helens), C. Forsyth (Bradford N.)
J. Gray (Wigan), J. Grayshon (Dewsbury),
B. Hogan (Wigan), J. Holmes (Leeds),
E. Hughes (Widnes), R. Irving (Wigan),
P. Jackson (Bradford N.), B. Philbin (Warrington),
D. Redfearn (Bradford N.),
J. Thompson (Featherstone R.), S. Wright (Wigan)

Wales
In Australia and New Zealand
Manager: R. Simpson
Coach: L. Pearce
D. Watkins (Salford), Capt.
P. Banner (Salford)
B. Butler (Swinton)
K. Coslett (St. Helens)
E. Cunningham (St. Helens)
C. Dixon (Salford)
R. Evans (Swinton)
A. Fisher (Leeds)
W. Francis (Wigan)
J. Mantle (St. Helens)
R. Mathias (St. Helens)
J. Mills (Widnes)
M. Nicholas (Warrington)
P. Rowe (Blackpool B.)
C. Sullivan (Hull KR)
D. Treasure (Oldham)
G. Turner (Hull KR)
R. Wanbon (Warrington)
D. Willicombe (Wigan)
F. Wilson (St. Helens)

*The following players also appeared
in the World Cup but did not tour*
Down Under:
J. Bevan (Warrington), S. Gallacher (Keighley),
B. Gregory (Wigan), M. James (St. Helens),
C. Jones (Leigh), M. Murphy (Bradford N.),
M. Richards (Salford), R. Wallace (York)

Australia
**In England, Wales
and France**
Managers: R. Abbott,
      J. Cairns
Coach: G. Langlands
A. Beetson, Capt.
J. Brass
M. Cronin
G. Eadie
D. Fitzgerald
R. Higgs
J. Lang
I. Mackay
A. McMahon
J. Mayes
J. Peard
G. Pierce
G. Piggins　　*(cont.)*

France
**In Australia
and New Zealand**
Manager: R. Forges
Coach: Puig Aubert
J. Calle, Capt.
M. Anglade
E. Bonal
M. Cassins
B. Curt
F. de Nadia
A. Dumas
Z. Gleyzes
A. Gonzales
D. Hermet
J. M. Imbert
V. Kaminski
M. Maique　　*(cont.)*

New Zealand
**In England, Wales
and France**
Manager: B. Watson
Coach: G. Menzies
K. Stirling, Capt.
F. Ah Kuoi
R. Baxendale
L. Beehre
A. Coll
W. Collicoat
T. Conroy
B. Dickison
M. Eade
A. Gordon
J. Greengrass
P. Gurnick
R. Jarvis　　*(cont.)*

L. Platz
J. Porter
J. Quayle
T. Randall
T. Raudonikis
J. Rhodes
S. Rogers
I. Schubert
G. Veivers
*The following players also
appeared in the World Cup
but did not tour Europe:*
C. Anderson, R. Branighan,
R. Coote, J. Donnelly, T. Fahey,
R. Fulton, M. Harris,
G. Langlands, J. O'Neill,
T. Pickup, R. Sait, G. Stevens,
R. Strudwick, D. Wright
Non-playing substitute:
J. Payne

M. Mayorgas
A. Ruiz
R. Terrats
F. Tranier
C. Zalduendo
*The following players also
appeared in the World Cup
but did not tour Down Under:*
Y. Alvernhe, J. Bosc, G. Buchi,
P. Chauvet, P. Clergeau, M. De
Matos, F. Duthill, G. Garcia,
J. Grechi, B. Guilhem, M. Laffargue,
J. Lacoste, M. Molinier,
M. Moussad, M. Pillan,
J. Sauret, V. Serrano
C. Thenegal, J. Tremoulille,
G. Vigouroux,
Non-playing substitutes:
J. Castel, G. Laskawieck

P. Orchard
L. Proctor
J. Smith
D. Sorensen
K. Sorensen
D. Williams
*The following players also
appeared in the World Cup
but did not tour Europe:*
M. Brereton, J. Hibbs, P. Matete,
D. Munro, J. O'Sullivan,
G. West, J. Whittaker

FRANCE 14 WALES 7
Toulouse: 2 March 7,563
France: Tranier; E. Bonal, Molinier,
Terrats (1t), Curt (1t); Lacoste (1dg),
Imbert (1dg); De Nadai, Kaminski,
Serrano (3g), Gleyzes, Hermet, Anglade.
Sub: Castel
Wales: Francis; Mathias, Willicombe,
Wilson (1t), Richards; Watkins, Banner;
Murphy, Evans, Butler, Mantle, Dixon,
Coslett (2g). Sub: Wallace
Referee: G. F. Lindop (England)

ENGLAND 20 FRANCE 2
Leeds: 16 March 10,842
England: Charlton; Fielding (2t), Noonan, Dyl,
Atkinson; Gill, Millward (1t); D. Chisnall,
Gray (4g), Jackson, Martyn, Nicholls, Philbin.
Sub: Morgan (1t)
France: Tranier; E. Bonal, Molinier, Terrats,
Curt; Lacoste, Imbert; De Nadai, Kamininski,
Serrano (1g), Gleyzes, Hermet, Anglade
Referee: K. Page (Australia).
Replaced by H. G. Hunt (England) after 25
minutes because of illness.

AUSTRALIA 36 NEW ZEALAND 8
Brisbane: 1 June 10,000
Australia: Langlands (2t); Anderson,
Fulton (1t), Cronin (2t,6g), Fahey; Pickup,
Strudwick; Randall (1t), Lang, Wright,
Stevens, Platz (1t), Coote. Sub: Branighan (1t),
Sait

New Zealand: Collicoat (1g), Brereton,
O'Sullivan, Whittaker (1t), Orchard; Williams,
Stirling (1t); West, Conroy, Hibbs, Coll,
Baxendale, Eade
Referee: F. Escande (France)

WALES 12 ENGLAND 7
Brisbane: 10 June 6,000
Wales: Francis; Sullivan (1t), Willicombe,
Watkins (3g), Mathias; Treasure (1t), Banner;
Mills, Fisher, Wanbon, Cunningham, Dixon,
Coslett. Subs: Wilson, Mantle
England: Fairbairn (2g); Fielding, Noonan,
Dyl, Atkinson, Millward, Nash; D. Chisnall,
Morgan, Coulman, E. Chisnall, Nicholls,
Norton. Subs: Gill, Martyn (1t)
Referee: D. Lancashire (Australia)

AUSTRALIA 30 WALES 13
Sydney: 14 June 25,386
Australia: Langlands (1t); Harris (1t),
Fulton (1t), Cronin (9g), Rhodes; Pickup,
Raudonikis (1t); Randall, Lang, O'Neill, Platz,
Stevens, Sait. Sub: Donnelly
Wales: Francis; Sullivan, Watkins (5g),
Willicombe, Mathias; Turner, Treasure; Mills,
Fisher (1t), Wanbon, Cunningham, Mantle,
Coslett. Subs: Wilson, Rowe
Referee: F. Escande (France)

NEW ZEALAND 27 FRANCE 0
Christchurch: 15 June 2,500
New Zealand: Whittaker; Orchard, O'Sullivan,
Williams, Munro; Jarvis (2t), Stirling (1t);
Greengrass, Conroy (1t), D. Sorensen (6g),
Coll, Baxendale, Eade (1t). Subs: Collicoat,
Proctor

France: Tranier; Dumas, Terrats, Ruiz,
E. Bonal; Calle, Imbert; Zalduendo, Gonzales,
Cassins, Gleyzes, De Nadai, Mayorgas
Referee: L. Bruyeres (Australia)

NEW ZEALAND 17   ENGLAND 17
Auckland: 21 June   12,000
New Zealand: Whittaker; Orchard (1t),
O'Sullivan, Williams (2t), Munro; Jarvis,
Stirling; Greengrass, Conroy, D. Sorensen (4g),
Coll, Baxendale, Eade. Subs: Collicoat, Proctor
England: Fairbairn (2t,4g); Fielding, Walsh,
Dyl, Atkinson (1t); Gill, Nash; D. Chisnall,
Bridges, E. Chisnall, Nicholls, Cookson,
Norton. Sub: Morgan
Referee: L. Bruyeres (Australia)

AUSTRALIA 26   FRANCE 6
Brisbane: 22 June   9,000
Australia: Langlands; Harris (2t), Fulton (2t),
Cronin (1t,4g), Rhodes; Pickup (1t),
Raudonikis; Beetson, Lang, Donnelly, Platz,
Randall, Coote
France: Tranier; Dumas, Ruiz, Terrats, Curt;
Calle (3g), Imbert; De Nadai, Kaminski,
Cassins, Maique, Gleyzes, Anglade.
Sub: Zalduendo
Referee: J. Percival (New Zealand)

AUSTRALIA 10   ENGLAND 10
Sydney: 28 June   33,858
Australia: Langlands; Rhodes, Fulton,
Cronin (2g), Harris; Pickup, Raudonikis;
Beetson, Lang, Randall, Stevens, Platz,
Coote (1t). Subs: Anderson (1t), Donnelly
England: Fairbairn (2g); Fielding, Walsh, Dyl,
Dunn (1t); Millward, Nash; Coulman, Bridges,
Morgan, Nicholls, Cookson, Norton.
Subs: Gill (1t), E. Chisnall
Referee: J. Percival (New Zealand)

NEW ZEALAND 13   WALES 8
Auckland: 28 June   9,368
New Zealand: Collicoat (5g); Orchard (1t),
O'Sullivan, Williams, Munro; Jarvis, Stirling;
Proctor, Conroy, D. Sorensen, Coll, Baxendale,
Eade
Wales: Francis (1t); Mathias, Willicombe,
Watkins (1g), Sullivan; Treasure, Banner;
Mills (1t), Fisher, Wanbon, Mantle, Dixon,
Coslett. Sub: Butler
Referee: L. Bruyeres (Australia)

WALES 16   ENGLAND 22
Warrington: 20 September   5,034
Wales: Francis; Sullivan, Watkins (5g),
Wilson, Bevan; Treasure, Banner (1t); Mantle,
Fisher, James, Gregory, Cunningham,
Coslett (1t). Subs: Turner, Rowe
England: Fairbairn (6g); Fielding (1t),
Hughes (1t), Holmes (1t), Atkinson; Gill,
Millward; Hogan, Bridges (1dg), Forsyth,
Irving, Grayshon, Norton. Subs: Eckersley,
Nicholls
Referee: M. Cailol (France)

NEW ZEALAND 8   AUSTRALIA 24
Auckland: 27 September   20,000
New Zealand: Collicoat (4g); Orchard, Matete,
Williams, Ah Kuoi; Jarvis, Stirling;
Greengrass, Conroy, D. Sorensen, Coll,
Baxendale, Eade. Subs: Smith, K. Sorensen
Australia: Eadie; Rhodes, Cronin (1t,6g),
Brass, Schubert (1t); Peard, Mayes; Veivers,
Piggins, Mackay, Platz, Higgs (1t), Quayle (1t).
Subs: Raudonikis, Fitzgerald
Referee: G. F. Lindop (England)

FRANCE 2   ENGLAND 48
Bordeaux: 11 October   1,581
France: De Matos; Grechi, Ruiz, Terrats,
Laffargue, Calle (1g), Imbert; Garcia, Duthil,
Gonzales, Bosc, Tremouille, Buchi.
Subs: Thenegal, Vigouroux
England: Fairbairn (4g); Fielding (4t),
Hughes (1t), Holmes (2t), Dunn (2t); Gill (1t),
Millward (2g); Hogan (1t), Bridges,
Forsyth (1t), Grayshon, Irving, Norton. Subs:
Nicholls, Eckersley
Referee: J. Percival (New Zealand)

FRANCE 12   NEW ZEALAND 12
Marseilles: 17 October   10,000
France: Pillon; Grechi, Ruiz, Guilhem (3g),
Chauvet (2t); Calle, Imbert; Thenegal,
Gonzales, Zalduendo, Sauret, Tremouille,
Terrats. Sub: Moussard
New Zealand: Collicoat (3g); Orchard,
Williams, Smith, Dickison; Jarvis (1t), Stirling;
Greengrass, Conroy, Proctor (1t), Coll,
Baxendale, Gurnick. Sub: Gordon
Referee: W. H. Thompson (England)

WALES 6   AUSTRALIA 18
Swansea: 19 October   11,112
Wales: Watkins (3g); Mathias, Francis,
Wilson, Bevan; Turner, Banner; Mills, Fisher,
Mantle, Cunningham, Dixon, Coslett.
Sub: Rowe
Australia: Eadie; McMahon, Cronin (3g),
Rogers, Schubert (3t); Peard (1t), Mayes;
Beetson, Piggins, Veivers, Randall, Higgs,
Quayle. Subs: Mackay, Porter
Referee: J. Percival (New Zealand)

ENGLAND 27   NEW ZEALAND 12
Bradford: 25 October   5,937
England: Fairbairn (3g); Wright (1t),
Hughes (1t), Holmes, Dunn (1t); Gill (3t),
Millward; Hogan, Bridges, Forsyth, Grayshon,
Adams, Norton (1t). Subs: Dyl, Nicholls
New Zealand: Collicoat (2g); Orchard,
Smith (1t), Williams, Dickison; Jarvis, Stirling;
Proctor, Conroy, Greengrass, Baxendale, Coll,
Eade. Subs: Gordon (1t,1g), Gurnick
Referee: A. Lacaze (France)

FRANCE 2   AUSTRALIA 41
Perpignan: 26 October   10,440
France: Pillon; Grechi, Ruiz, Guilhem (1g),
Chauvet; Calle, Imbert; Zalduendo, Gonzales,
Thenegal, Sauret, Tremouille, Terrats.
Subs: Clergeau, Moussard
Australia: Eadie (1t,7g); Rhodes (1t),
Rogers (2t), Brass, Porter; Peard (1t),
Raudonikis (1t); Beetson, Lang, Randall (1t),
Higgs (1t), Platz (1t), Pierce. Sub: Schubert
Referee: W. H. Thompson (England)

ENGLAND 16   AUSTRALIA 13
Wigan: 1 November   9,393
England: Fairbairn (5g); Dunn, Holmes (1t),
Dyl, Redfearn; Gill, Millward; Hogan, Bridges,
Thompson, Grayshon (1t), Irving, Norton.
Subs: Hughes, Adams
Australia: Eadie; Schubert (3t), Brass,
Cronin (2g), Rhodes; Peard, Mayes; Beetson,
Piggins, Mackay, Higgs, Randall, Pierce.
Sub: Rogers
Referee: J. Percival (New Zealand)

WALES 25   NEW ZEALAND 24
Swansea: 2 November   2,645
Wales: Watkins (5g); Mathias, Wilson,
Willicombe (1t), Bevan (1t); Francis (2t),
Banner; Mills, Fisher, Murphy, Mantle (1t),
Gallacher, Gregory. Sub: Jones
New Zealand: Collicoat (1g); Orchard (1t),
Ah Kuoi, Williams, Gordon (1t,5g); Jarvis,
Smith; D. Sorensen, Conroy, Greengrass (1t),
K. Sorensen, Coll (1t), Gurnick. Subs: Proctor,
Dickison
Referee: G. Jameau (France)

WALES 23   FRANCE 2
Salford: 6 November   2,247
Wales: Watkins (4g); Mathias, Wilson,
Willicombe (1t), Bevan (1t); Francis (1t),
Banner (1t); Mantle, Evans, Murphy,
Gregory (1t), Gallagher, Jones. Subs: Turner,
Butler
France: Calle; Grechi, Terrats, Guilhem (1g),
Curt; Lacoste, Imbert; Alvernhe, Gonzales,
Moossard, Tremouille, Sauret, Mayorgas.
Sub: Maique
Referee: G. F. Lindop (England)

Final Table

	P	W	D	L	F	A	Pts
Australia	8	6	1	1	198	69	13
England	8	5	2	1	167	84	12
Wales	8	3	0	5	110	130	6
New Zealand	8	2	2	4	121	149	6
France	8	1	1	6	40	204	3

1977   Played in Australia and New Zealand   WON BY AUSTRALIA
(Decided by top two in league table meeting in play-off final.)

Great Britain	Australia	France	New Zealand
Manager: R. Parker	Managers: D. Hall	Manager: P. De Jean	Manager: D. Barchard
Coach: D. Watkins	C. Brown	Coach: Y. Begou	Coach: R. Ackland
	Coach: T. Fearnley		

Great Britain	Australia	France	New Zealand
R. Millward (Hull KR) Capt.	A. Beetson, Capt.	J. Calle, Capt.	T. Coll, Capt.
E. Bowman (Workington T.)	S. Crear	G. Alard	F. Ah Kuoi
L. Casey (Hull KR)	M. Cronin	C. Baile	R. Baxendale
L. Dyl (Leeds)	G. Eadie	H. Bonnet	W. Collicoat
K. Elwell (Widnes)	T. Fahey	J. Bourret	O. Filipaina
G. Fairbairn (Wigan)	D. Fitzgerald	J. Brial	K. Fisher
K. Fielding (Salford)	R. Gartner	M. Caravaca	M. Graham
W. Francis (Wigan)	N. Geiger	M. Cassin	Whetu Henry
K. Gill (Salford)	M. Harris	M. Chantal	Whare Henry
A. Hodkinson (Rochdale H.)	R. Higgs	P. Chauvet	C. Jordan
P. Hogan (Barrow)	J. Kolc	J. Cologni	M. O'Donnell
J. Holmes (Leeds)	A. McMahon	H. Daniel	D. O'Hara
S. Lloyd (Castleford)	J. Peard	J. Garcia	L. Proctor
S. Nash (Salford)	G. Pierce	J. Guigue	A. Rushton
G. Nicholls (St. Helens)	T. Randall	J. Imbert	J. Smith
S. Pitchford (Leeds)	T. Raudonikis	J. M. Imbert	D. Sorensen
P. Smith (Featherstone R.)	R. Reddy	C. Laskaweic	K. Sorensen
J. Thompson (Featherstone R.)	M. Thomas	G. Lepine	J. Whittaker
D. Ward (Leeds)	G. Veivers	J. Mayorgas	D. Williams
S. Wright (Widnes)		M. Moussard	
		J. Moya	
		G. Rodriguez	
		J. Roosebrouck	
		A. Ruiz	
		P. Saboureau	
		J. Sauret	
		R. Terrats	

NEW ZEALAND 12   AUSTRALIA 27
Auckland: 29 May   18,000

New Zealand: Collicoat (3g); O'Hara, Filipaina, Jordan, Fisher; Williams, Smith (1t); Whetu Henry, Rushton (1t), D. Sorensen, K. Sorensen, Coll, Whare Henry
Australia: Eadie; Harris (1t), Cronin (6g), Thomas (1t), McMahon (2t); Peard (1t), Raudonikis; Veivers, Geiger, Fitzgerald, Randall, Higgs, Pierce
Referee: W. H. Thompson (England)

GREAT BRITAIN 23   FRANCE 4
Auckland: 5 June   10,000

Britain: Fairbairn (7g); Fielding, Holmes, Dyl (1t), Wright (1t); Millward (1t), Nash; Thompson, Ward, Pitchford, Nicholls, Bowman, Hogan. Subs: Casey, Gill
France: Guigue; Moya, Laskawiec, Ruiz, Chauvet; Calle (2g), Alard; Cassin, Bonnet, Daniel, Sauret, Cologni, Roosebrouck.
Sub: Rodriguez
Referee: R. Cooper (New Zealand)

AUSTRALIA 21   FRANCE 9
Sydney: 11 June   13,321

Australia: Eadie (2t); McMahon (1t), Cronin (3g), Thomas, Fahey; Peard, Raudonikis; Veivers (1t), Geiger, Fitzgerald (1t), Randall, Beetson, Reddy.
Subs: Gartner, Higgs
France: Guigue; Moya, Bourrett, Terrats, Laskawiec (1t); Calle (3g), Allard; Cassin, Garcia, Chantal, Sauret, Caravaca, Roosebrouck. Subs: J. M. Imbert, Rodriguez
Referee: W. H. Thompson (England)

NEW ZEALAND 12   GREAT BRITAIN 30
Christchurch: 12 June   9,000

New Zealand: Collicoat (3g); Fisher (1t), Ah Kuoi, Filipaina, Whittaker (1t); Williams, Smith; Proctor, Rushton, Whetu Henry, K. Sorensen, Coll, Whare Henry. Sub: Graham
Britain: Fairbairn (6g); Wright (2t), Holmes, Dyl, Francis; Millward (1t), Nash; Thompson, Ward, Pitchford, Nicholls (1t), Bowman (1t), Hogan (1t). Sub: Casey
Referee: M. Caillol (France)

AUSTRALIA 19   GREAT BRITAIN 5

Brisbane: 18 June   27,000

Australia: Eadie (2t); McMahon, Cronin (5g), Thomas, Fahey; Peard, Raudonikis; Fitzgerald, Geiger, Veivers, Beetson, Randall (1t), Pierce. Sub: Higgs
Britain: Fairbairn (1g); Wright, Francis, Dyl, Fielding; Millward (1t), Nash; Thompson, Ward, Pitchford, Nicholls, Bowman, Hogan. Subs: Smith, Holmes
Referee: M. Caillol (France)

NEW ZEALAND 28   FRANCE 20

Auckland: 19 June   8,000

New Zealand: O'Donnell; Fisher (1t), Ah Kuoi, Williams, Whittaker; Jordan (1t,8g), Smith (1t); Proctor, Rushton, Whetu Henry, Coll, K. Sorensen, Graham (1t)
France: Calle; Moya (4g), Ruiz, Terrats, Guigue (1t); Alard, J. M. Imbert; Cassin, Garcia, Sauret, Caravaca, Cologni (2t), Roosebrouck (1t). Subs: J. Imbert, Moussard
Referee: D. Lancashire (Australia)

Final Table

	P	W	D	L	F	A	Pts
Australia	3	3	0	0	67	26	6
Great Britain	3	2	0	1	58	35	4
New Zealand	3	1	0	2	52	77	2
France	3	0	0	3	33	72	0

FINAL

AUSTRALIA 13   GREAT BRITAIN 12

Sydney: 25 June   24,457

Australia: Eadie; McMahon (1t), Cronin (2g), Gartner (1t), Harris; Peard, Kolc (1t); Veivers, Geiger, Randall, Beetson, Higgs, Pierce. Sub: Fitzgerald
Britain: Fairbairn (3g); Wright, Holmes, Dyl, Francis; Millward, Nash; Thompson, Elwell, Pitchford (1t), Casey, Bowman, Hogan. Subs: Gill (1t), Smith
Referee: W. H. Thompson (England)

1985-88

Details to the end of May 1987. One match in each Test series between the countries has been also designated as a World Cup match. The top two teams in the league table at the end of the home-away series will contest the final in 1988.

NEW ZEALAND 18   AUSTRALIA 0

Auckland: 7 July 1985   19,000

New Zealand: Kemble; Bell, Prohm, Leuluai (1t), O'Hara; Filipaina (3g), Friend (2t); Wright, H. Tamati, K. Tamati, Graham, K. Sorensen, McGahan. Subs: Ropati, Cowan
Australia: Jack; Ribot, Meninga, Ella, Ferguson; Lewis, Hasler; Tunks, Elias, Roach, Vautin, Wynn, Pearce. Subs: Close, Dowling
Referee: J. Rascagneres (France)

GREAT BRITAIN 6   NEW ZEALAND 6

Elland Road, Leeds: 9 November 1985
22,209

Britain: Burke (Widnes); Drummond (Leigh), Schofield (Hull), Edwards (Wigan), Lydon (Widnes); Hanley (Wigan), Fox (Featherstone R.); Grayshon (Leeds), Watkinson (Hull KR), Fieldhouse (Widnes), Goodway (Wigan), Potter (Wigan), Pinner (St. Helens). Subs: L. Crooks (Hull, 3g), Arkwright (St. Helens)
New Zealand: Kemble; Williams, Bell, Leuluai, O'Hara; Ah Kuoi, Friend; K. Tamati, Wallace, D. Sorensen (1g), Graham (1t), K. Sorensen, Prohm. Subs: Filipaina, McGahan
Referee: B. Gomersall (Australia)

FRANCE 0   NEW ZEALAND 22

Perpignan: 7 December 1985   5,000

France: Pallares; Ratier, Berge, Palisses, Couston; Espugna, Guasch; Chantal, Bernabe, Titeux, Montgaillard, Palanque, G. Laforgue. Subs: Perez, Rabot
New Zealand: Kemble (1t); Bell, Ah Kuoi, Leuluai, O'Hara; Filipaina (3g), Friend; K. Sorensen (1t), Wallace, D. Sorensen, McGahan (2t), Wright, O'Regan. Subs: Elia, Todd
Referee: R. Campbell (England)

FRANCE 10   GREAT BRITAIN 10

Avignon: 16 February 1986   4,000

France: Dumas (1t,3g); Couston, Maury, Fourquet, Laroche; Espugna, Entat; Chantal, Baco, Titeux, G. Laforgue, Palanque, Bernabe. Subs: Rabot, Berge
Britain: Burke (Widnes); Drummond (Leigh), Schofield (Hull), Hanley (Wigan, 1t), Gill (Wigan); A. Myler (Widnes), Fox (Featherstone R.); L. Crooks (Hull, 3g), Watkinson (Hull KR), Wane (Wigan), Potter (Wigan), Fieldhouse (Widnes), Pinner (St. Helens)
Referee: K. Roberts (Australia)

AUSTRALIA 32 NEW ZEALAND 12
Brisbane: 29 July 1986 22,811
Australia: Jack; O'Connor (1t,4g), Miles (1t), Kenny (2t), Kiss; Lewis (1t), Sterling (1t); Roach, Simmons, Tunks, Cleal, Folkes, Pearce. Subs: Lamb, Niebling
New Zealand: Kemble; Williams (2t), Ropati, Prohm, O'Hara; Filipaina (2g), Freeman; Todd, Harvey, K. Sorensen, Graham, McGahan, O'Regan. Subs: Cooper, Wright
Referee: R. Whitfield (England)

PAPUA NEW GUINEA 24
NEW ZEALAND 22
Port Moresby: 17 August 1986 15,000
Papua New Guinea: Kovae (4g); Katsir, Atoi (1t), Numapo, Kerekere; Haili (2t), Kila; Tep, Heni, Lomutopa, Ako (1t), Waketsi, Taumaku. Subs: Saea, Andy
New Zealand: Kemble; Leuluai, O'Hara, Crequer, Ropati (1t); Elia, Cooper; Shelford, Wallace (1t), Wright, Steward, McGahan (1t). Sub: Brown (1t,3dg)
Referee: K. Roberts (Australia)

PAPUA NEW GUINEA 12 AUSTRALIA 62
Port Moresby: 4 October 1986 17,000
Papua New Guinea: Kovae (2g); Katsir, Atoi, Numapo (2t), Kerekere; Haili, Kila; Tep, Heni, Lomutopa, Ako, Waketsi, Taumaku. Subs: Saea
Australia: Jack (1t); O'Connor (2t,7g), Miles, C. Mortimer (1t), Kiss (2t); Lewis (1t), Hasler (1t); Roach (1t), Simmons, Niebling, Dunn, Cleal (2t), Lindner (1t). Subs: Meninga, Sironen
Referee: N. Kesha (New Zealand)

GREAT BRITAIN 15 AUSTRALIA 24
Wigan: 22 November 1986 20,169
Britain: Lydon (Wigan, 2g); Gill (Wigan, 1g), Schofield (Hull, 2t,dg), Stephenson (Wigan), Basnett (Widnes); A. Myler (Widnes), A. Gregory (Warrington); Ward (Castleford), Watkinson (Hull KR), Crooks (Hull), Burton (Hull KR), Goodway (Wigan), Pinner (Widnes). Sub: Potter (Wigan)
Australia: Jack; Shearer (1t), Kenny, Miles (1t), O'Connor (4g); Lewis (1t), Sterling; Dowling, Simmons, Dunn, Meninga, Niebling, Lindner (1t). Subs: Davidson, Lamb
Referee: J. Rascagneres (France)

FRANCE 0 AUSTRALIA 52
Carcassonne: 13 December 1986 3,000
France: Wozniack; Rodriguez, Fourquet, F. Laforgue, Ratier; Palisses, Scicchitano; Chantal, Bernabe, Titeux, G. Laforgue, Verdes, Gestas. Subs: Dumas, Storer
Australia: Jack (3t); Shearer (4t), Kenny, Miles, O'Connor (1t,6g); Lewis, Sterling; Dowling, Simmons, Dunn, Folkes (1t), Niebling (1t), Lindner. Subs: Lamb, Davidson
Referee: G. F. Lindop (Wakefield)

GREAT BRITAIN 52 FRANCE 4
Leeds: 24 January 1987 6,567
Britain: Lydon (Wigan, 1t,8g); Forster (Warrington, 1t), Schofield (Hull), Stephenson (Wigan), Gill (Wigan); Hanley (Wigan, 2t), Edwards (Wigan, 2t); Hobbs (Oldham), K. Beardmore (Castleford), L. Crooks (Hull), Goodway (Wigan, 1t), Haggerty (St. Helens), M. Gregory (Warrington, 2t). Subs: Creasser (Leeds), England (Castleford)
France: Perez (2g); Couston, Palisses, Ratier, Pons; Espugna, Dumas; Storer, Mantese, Rabot, Verdes, Palanque, Bernabe. Subs: Rocci, Titeux
Referee: M. Stone (Australia)

Table (at end of May 1987)

	P	W	D	L	F	A	Pts
Australia	5	4	0	1	170	57	8
New Zealand	5	2	1	2	80	62	5
Great Britain	4	1	2	1	83	44	4
Papua New Guinea	2	1	0	1	36	84	2
France	4	0	1	3	14	136	1

Tony Myler, Great Britain's stand-off in the three Tests against Australia.

GREAT BRITAIN

TEST REVIEW

The 1986-87 campaign opened with the long-awaited visit of the Kangaroos, bidding to extend their run of 10 consecutive victories against Britain and emulate their 1982 predecessors by completing a Test whitewash.

Down to earth came Britain's sky-high hopes as Australia ran in seven tries in the opening Whitbread Trophy Bitter Test at Manchester United's Old Trafford stadium in front of a British record Test crowd of 50,583. Loyal British coach Maurice Bamford gambled by immediately naming the same side for the second Test at Elland Road.

Further down went British spirits as the rampant Antipodeans cruised to a 34-4 success which heralded the introduction of five new faces for the third Test at Wigan, doubling as a World Cup qualifier.

Up came Britain ... at last. The recalled Andy Gregory and Harry Pinner spearheaded a home revival, highlighted by the record-breaking feats of Garry Schofield, as recharged Great Britain were defeated 24-15. Amid restored pride were claims of a controversial penalty try awarded to the visitors by French referee Julien Rascagneres, the clinching Wally Lewis touchdown and an opening try for Gene Miles from a suspected forward pass.

The three Whitbread Trophy Bitter Tests are fully chronicled in the 1986 KANGAROOS section.

Just a month after the Kangaroos' farewell, British coach Maurice Bamford made the shock announcement that he would not be seeking to renew his contract at the end of the season as his wife has multiple sclerosis.

The League decided that Bamford should continue in charge of the national side for the forthcoming Tests against France in January and February, with a new appointment being made for the two Under-21 internationals in March.

However, after consultation with Great Britain manager Les Bettinson, a meeting of 7 January invited Castleford's Malcolm Reilly to take the post and the former Test loose forward was the subject of a Press conference less than 24 hours later.

Reilly, shortlisted for the top post twice previously, was contracted until the end of the 1988 tour Down Under, being allowed to remain with Castleford to the end of the 1986-87 season.

Currently the longest serving coach with one club, Reilly immediately took over control, he and Bettinson making seven changes from the side which faced Australia in the Third Test at Central Park.

In came debutant winger Mark Forster (Warrington), a new half back pairing in Wigan's Ellery Hanley and Shaun Edwards, front row men David Hobbs (Oldham) and Kevin Beardmore (Castleford), plus back row forwards Roy Haggerty (St. Helens) and Warrington's Mike Gregory, both gaining their first caps.

The changes were partly enforced by Reilly's non-consideration of players who had not figured regularly in the previous month. Injury ruled out third Kangaroo Test performers John Basnett, Tony Myler and Kevin Ward, while Andy Gregory had been in dispute with Warrington before moving to Wigan.

Reilly's new look line-up swept to a record-breaking 52-4 victory in the World Cup-rated encounter at Headingley, Leeds. The nine-try slaughter was Britain's highest score and widest margin against the French.

Even allowing for the amateurish opposition, Reilly's new charges could not be faulted for exposing every weakness in matching Australia's 52-point tally of a month earlier, while keeping their line intact.

Despite Wigan paying a world record £130,000 for Andy Gregory, Reilly plumped for the in-form Central Park colleague

Shaun Edwards in the number seven jersey. On the ground where he became the youngest-ever Great Britain player only two years earlier, Edwards showed just how quickly he had matured.

Still only 20, he dictated play like a veteran while retaining the dash of his youth. The scrum half scored two tries, both solo efforts, one a superb break from a scrum in the 73rd minute to confirm his Man of the Match rating.

New boy Haggerty challenged strongly for the individual match honour with a powerful second row running display, while loose forward Mike Gregory gained confidence with every passing minute, reflected by his two-try haul in the final quarter.

Wingman Forster, winner of the autumn Whitbread Trophy Bitter Test invitation sprint, again displayed his speed with a 70-yard run for his first British touchdown, while hooker Beardmore marked his first full Test appearance with a lively show in the loose in addition to a 13-10 scrum pull.

Of the established Test men, prop forward Lee Crooks again blotted his copybook. The Hull skipper gave another excellent distributive display on attack and was Britain's top defender with 32 tackles, though his reckless tendency earned him yet another trip to the sin bin.

Joe Lydon was in faultless form at full back, opening the try account with a superb weaving run and adding eight goals for a 20-point haul which left him only one short of the individual British record against France.

Downtrodden France never gave up, despite being outclassed. There were glimpses of the traditional Gallic flair with Thierry Bernabe outstanding at loose forward. One praiseworthy feature was their discipline, conceding only four penalties — none for foul play — compared with 10 by Britain. What a difference a fortnight makes!

The eve of the return Test at Carcassonne became Rugby League's version of the French Revolution. An emergency meeting of the French League sacked national coach, Australian Tas Baitieri, and suspended the powers of their president Jacques Soppelsa amid the declaration of a £90,000 debt.

Up to four hours before kick off, the French players were refusing to turn out. Baitieri insisted they took to the field and the fired-up Tricolours did so with ferocity.

Reilly, returning to France 17 years after his only cross-Channel Test appearance, branded the French 'animals'. A display of fiery passion was marred by outbursts of punching and kicking.

Castleford prop Kevin Ward, Great Britain's Man of the Series against the Australians.

In the 52nd minute loose forward Gregory suffered a broken nose and fractured cheekbone after being flattened by a vicious right hook from prop forward Jean-Luc Rabot. Australian referee Mick Stone sent both players to the sin bin for 10 minutes, Gregory being substituted by debutant forward Paul Dixon, of Halifax.

In the 62nd minute French prop Pierre Allieres was sent off for kneeing centre Garry Schofield in the back as the French players' passion turned to frustration.

In contrast to the Headingley Test two weeks earlier, the French tackling was a revelation, yet they gave away two soft tries. Beardmore scampered through for a fourth minute touchdown after dummying at the play-the-ball, Lydon adding the easy goal. Then on the hour skipper Ellery Hanley picked up a loose ball near the French line to saunter over for a simple try, Lydon adding his fourth goal.

Thirteen minutes earlier, Britain had produced a rare piece of good football fanning the ball from a scrum on the right touchline across field for left winger Henderson Gill to take Schofield's long pass, slip a tackle and race in for a classic try from 25 yards.

France had taken a surprise 8-6 lead after 31 minutes when Britain continued to complain about a disallowed Schofield try while French stand off Dominique Espugna raced 65 yards to touch down, Perez adding his second goal. Lydon and Perez each added a penalty goal to give France a fully deserved 10-8 half-time shock lead, Britain keeping their composure to seal victory with 12-points in the opening 20 minutes of the second half.

New half back duo, clubmates Gregory and Edwards, failed to jell, while captain Hanley was closely marked. Britain looked best when Lydon joined the attack, the full back also kicking well tactically and scoring from all four goal attempts.

Beardmore crowned an impressive all-round performance by winning the scrums 8-7 and taking the Whitbread Trophy Bitter Man of the Match award.

New Great Britain cap Keith England in action in Carcassonne.

Great Britain in October 1986, left to right. Back row: Lyman, Ward, Goodway, Fieldhouse, Myler, Platt. Centre row: Stabler (Physio), Gill, Crooks, Hanley, Larder (Asst. Coach), Lydon, Marchant, Potter, McKenzie (Conditioner). Front row: Fox, Edwards, Bettinson (Manager), Watkinson (Captain), Bamford (Coach), Mason, Schofield.

A much changed Great Britain only four months later in February 1987, left to right. Back row: Forster, Lydon, M. Gregory, Hobbs, Gill, Burton, Haggerty. Front row: Edwards, Schofield, K. Beardmore, Hanley (Captain), England, A. Gregory.

FIRST WHITBREAD TROPHY BITTER TEST

24th January   Leeds

GREAT BRITAIN 52		**FRANCE 4**
Joe Lydon (Wigan)	1.	Andre Perez (Toulouse)
Mark Forster (Warrington)	2.	Didier Couston (Le Pontet)
Garry Schofield (Hull)	3.	Roger Palisses (St. Esteve)
David Stephenson (Wigan)	4.	Hugues Ratier (Lezignan)
Henderson Gill (Wigan)	5.	Cyril Pons (St. Gaudens)
Ellery Hanley (Wigan) Capt.	6.	Dominique Espugna (Lezignan)
Shaun Edwards (Wigan)	7.	Gilles Dumas (St. Gaudens)
David Hobbs (Oldham)	8.	Yves Storer (St. Gaudens)
Kevin Beardmore (Castleford)	9.	Yannick Mantese (Albi)
Lee Crooks (Hull)	10.	Jean-Luc Rabot (Villeneuve)
Andy Goodway (Wigan)	11.	Daniel Verdes (Villeneuve)
Roy Haggerty (St. Helens)	12.	Marc Palanque (Le Pontet) Capt.
Mike Gregory (Warrington)	13.	Thierry Bernabe (Le Pontet)
David Creasser (Leeds)	14.	Patrick Rocci (Albi)
Keith England (Castleford)	15.	Serge Titeux (Le Pontet)

T: Edwards (2), Gregory (2),
Hanley (2), Goodway, Lydon
Forster
G: Lydon (8)
Substitutions:
Creasser for Stephenson (27 min.)
England for Hobbs (62 min.)
Manager: Les Bettinson
Coach: Malcolm Reilly

G: Perez (2)
Substitutions:
Rocci for Palisses (16 min.)
Titeux for Dumas (73 min.)
Half-time: 24-4
Referee: Mick Stone (Sydney)
Attendance: 6,567

Scorechart

Minute	Score	GB	France
5:	Lydon (T)	4	0
15:	Lydon (P)	6	0
22:	Goodway (T)		
	Lydon (G)	12	0
26:	Forster (T)		
	Lydon (G)	18	0
32:	Edwards (T)		
	Lydon (G)	24	0
35:	Perez (P)	24	2
40:	Perez (P)	24	4
45:	Lydon (P)	26	4
48:	Hanley (T)		
	Lydon (G)	32	4
61:	Gregory (T)	36	4
72:	Edwards (T)		
	Lydon (G)	42	4
78:	Hanley (T)		
	Lydon (G)	48	4
79:	Gregory (T)	52	4
	Scrums	13	10
	Penalties	4	10

SECOND WHITBREAD TROPHY BITTER TEST

8th February   **Carcassonne**

GREAT BRITAIN 20   FRANCE 10

Great Britain	No.	France
Joe Lydon (Wigan)	1.	Andre Perez (Toulouse)
Mark Forster (Warrington)	2.	Gaston Berteloitte (Toulouse)
Garry Schofield (Hull)	3.	Denis Bienes (St. Gaudens)
Ellery Hanley (Wigan) Capt.	4.	Jacques Moliner (Lezignan)
Henderson Gill (Wigan)	5.	Hugues Ratier (Lezignan)
Shaun Edwards (Wigan)	6.	Dominique Espugna (Lezignan)
Andy Gregory (Wigan)	7.	Christian Scicchitanno (Carpentras)
David Hobbs (Oldham)	8.	Jean-Luc Rabot (Villeneuve)
Kevin Beardmore (Castleford)	9.	Patrick Trinque (Carcassonne)
Keith England (Castleford)	10.	Pierre Allieres (Toulouse)
Chris Burton (Hull K.R.)	11.	Daniel Verdes (Villeneuve)
Roy Haggerty (St. Helens)	12.	Marc Palanque (Le Pontet) Capt.
Mike Gregory (Warrington)	13.	Thierry Bernabe (Le Pontet)
David Stephenson (Wigan)	14.	Gilles Dumas (St. Gaudens)
Paul Dixon (Halifax)	15.	Yves Storer (St. Gaudens)

T: Beardmore, Gill, Hanley
G: Lydon (4)
Substitution:
Dixon for M. Gregory (63 min.)
Half-time: 8-10
Manager: Les Bettinson
Coach: Malcolm Reilly

T: Espugna
G: Perez (3)
Substitution:
Storer for Palanque (71 min.)
Referee: Mick Stone (Sydney)
Attendance: 2,000

Try Scorer Henderson Gill.

Scorechart

Minute	Score	GB	France
			Scoreline
4:	Beardmore (T)		
	Lydon (G)	6	0
6:	Perez (P)	6	2
31:	Espugna (T)		
	Perez (G)	6	8
36:	Lydon (P)	8	8
39:	Perez (P)	8	10
47:	Gill (T)		
	Lydon (G)	14	10
60:	Hanley (T)		
	Lydon (G)	20	10
	Scrums	8	7
	Penalties	13	11

TESTS

● Although early Tests were played under the titles of Northern Union or England, it is acceptable to regard them as Great Britain.
W-Win, D-Drawn, L-Lost refer to Great Britain.

GREAT BRITAIN v. AUSTRALIA

Date	Result	Score	Venue	Attendance
12 Dec. 1908	D	22-22	QPR, London	2,000
23 Jan. 1909	W	15-5	Newcastle	22,000
15 Feb. 1909	W	6-5	Birmingham	9,000
18 Jun. 1910	W	27-20	Sydney	42,000
†2 Jul. 1910	W	22-17	Brisbane	18,000
8 Nov. 1911	L	10-19	Newcastle	6,500
16 Dec. 1911	D	11-11	Edinburgh	6,000
1 Jan. 1912	L	8-33	Birmingham	4,000
27 Jun. 1914	W	23-5	Sydney	40,000
29 Jun. 1914	L	7-12	Sydney	55,000
4 Jul. 1914	W	14-6	Sydney	34,420
26 Jun. 1920	L	4-8	Brisbane	28,000
3 Jul. 1920	L	8-21	Sydney	40,000
10 Jul. 1920	W	23-13	Sydney	32,000
1 Oct. 1921	W	6-5	Leeds	32,000
5 Nov. 1921	L	2-16	Hull	21,504
14 Jan. 1922	W	6-0	Salford	21,000
23 Jun. 1924	W	22-3	Sydney	50,000
28 Jun. 1924	W	5-3	Sydney	33,842
12 Jul. 1924	L	11-21	Brisbane	36,000
23 Jun. 1928	W	15-12	Brisbane	39,200
14 Jul. 1928	W	8-0	Sydney	44,548
21 Jul. 1928	L	14-21	Sydney	37,000
5 Oct. 1929	L	8-31	Hull K.R.	20,000
9 Nov. 1929	W	9-3	Leeds	31,402
4 Jan. 1930	D	0-0	Swinton	34,709
15 Jan. 1930	W	3-0	Rochdale	16,743
6 Jun. 1932	W	8-6	Sydney	70,204
18 Jun. 1932	L	6-15	Brisbane	26,500
16 Jul. 1932	W	18-13	Sydney	50,053
7 Oct. 1933	W	4-0	Belle Vue, Manchester	34,000
11 Nov. 1933	W	7-5	Leeds	29,618
16 Dec. 1933	W	19-16	Swinton	10,990
29 Jun. 1936	L	8-24	Sydney	63,920
4 Jul. 1936	W	12-7	Brisbane	29,486
18 Jul. 1936	W	12-7	Sydney	53,546
16 Oct. 1937	W	5-4	Leeds	31,949
13 Nov. 1937	W	13-3	Swinton	31,724
18 Dec. 1937	L	3-13	Huddersfield	9,093
17 Jun. 1946	D	8-8	Sydney	64,527
6 Jul. 1946	W	14-5	Brisbane	40,500
20 Jul. 1946	W	20-7	Sydney	35,294
9 Oct. 1948	W	23-21	Leeds	36,529
6 Nov. 1948	W	16-7	Swinton	36,354
29 Jan. 1949	W	23-9	Bradford	42,000
12 Jun. 1950	W	6-4	Sydney	47,215
1 Jul. 1950	L	3-15	Brisbane	35,000
22 Jul. 1950	L	2-5	Sydney	47,178
4 Oct. 1952	W	19-6	Leeds	34,505
8 Nov. 1952	W	21-5	Swinton	32,421
13 Dec. 1952	L	7-27	Bradford	30,509
12 Jun. 1954	L	12-37	Sydney	65,884
3 Jul. 1954	W	38-21	Brisbane	46,355
17 Jul. 1954	L	16-20	Sydney	67,577
17 Nov. 1956	W	21-10	Wigan	22,473
1 Dec. 1956	L	9-22	Bradford	23,634
15 Dec. 1956	W	19-0	Swinton	17,542
14 Jun. 1958	L	8-25	Sydney	68,777
5 Jul. 1958	W	25-18	Brisbane	32,965
19 Jul. 1958	W	40-17	Sydney	68,720
17 Oct. 1959	L	14-22	Swinton	35,224
21 Nov. 1959	W	11-10	Leeds	30,184
12 Dec. 1959	W	18-12	Wigan	26,089
9 Jun. 1962	W	31-12	Sydney	70,174
30 Jun. 1962	W	17-10	Brisbane	34,766
14 Jul. 1962	L	17-18	Sydney	42,104
16 Oct. 1963	L	2-28	Wembley	13,946
9 Nov. 1963	L	12-50	Swinton	30,833
30 Nov. 1963	W	16-5	Leeds	20,497
25 Jun. 1966	W	17-13	Sydney	57,962
16 Jul. 1966	L	4-6	Brisbane	45,057
23 Jul. 1966	L	14-19	Sydney	63,503
21 Oct. 1967	W	16-11	Leeds	22,293
3 Nov. 1967	L	11-17	White City, London	17,445
9 Dec. 1967	L	3-11	Swinton	13,615
6 Jun. 1970	L	15-37	Brisbane	42,807
20 Jun. 1970	W	28-7	Sydney	60,962
4 Jul. 1970	W	21-17	Sydney	61,258
3 Nov. 1973	W	21-12	Wembley	9,874
24 Nov. 1973	L	6-14	Leeds	16,674
1 Dec. 1973	L	5-15	Warrington	10,019
15 Jun. 1974	L	6-12	Brisbane	30,280
6 Jul. 1974	W	16-11	Sydney	48,006
20 Jul. 1974	L	18-22	Sydney	55,505
21 Oct. 1978	L	9-15	Wigan	17,644
5 Nov. 1978	W	18-14	Bradford	26,447
18 Nov. 1978	L	6-23	Leeds	29,627
16 Jun. 1979	L	0-35	Brisbane	23,051
30 Jun. 1979	L	16-24	Sydney	26,837
14 Jul. 1979	L	2-28	Sydney	16,844
30 Oct. 1982	L	4-40	Hull C. AFC	26,771
20 Nov. 1982	L	6-27	Wigan	23,216
28 Nov. 1982	L	8-32	Leeds	17,318
9 Jun. 1984	L	8-25	Sydney	30,190
26 Jun. 1984	L	6-18	Brisbane	26,534
7 Jul. 1984	L	7-20	Sydney	18,756
25 Oct. 1986	L	16-38	Man U. AFC	50,583
8 Nov. 1986	L	4-34	Elland Rd, Leeds	30,808
22 Nov. 1986	L	15-24	Wigan	20,169

	Played	Won	Drawn	Lost	Tries	Goals	Dr	Pts for
Great Britain	99	49	4	46	242	249	5	1238
Australia	99	46	4	49	282	312	5	1502

† 1910 Tour:
   Australian records do not recognise this as a Test match, while most British sources claim this second Test win clinched the series and there was no need for a third Test.
   Britain played two matches against Australasian sides which included New Zealanders. These are accepted as Tests by Australia. Both were played at Sydney, the first on July 9 was drawn 13-13, the second on July 13 was won by Australasia 32-15.

GREAT BRITAIN-AUSTRALIA TEST MATCH RECORDS

Britain
Highest score: 40-17 Third Test at Sydney July 19, 1958 (Also widest margin win)
Most tries in a match: 4 by J. Leytham (Wigan) Second Test at Brisbane July 2, 1910
Most goals in a match: 10 by B. L. Jones (Leeds) Second Test at Brisbane July 3, 1954
Most points in a match: 20 by B. L. Jones (as above)
20 (7g,2t) by R. Millward (Hull KR) Second Test at Sydney June 20, 1970.
Biggest attendance: 50,583 First Test at Old Trafford, Manchester, Oct 25, 1986

Australia
Highest score: 50-12 Second Test at Swinton, Nov 9, 1963 (Also widest margin win)
Most tries in a match: 3 by J. Devereux, First Test at QPR, London, Dec 12, 1908
3 by R. Gasnier, First Test at Swinton, Oct 17, 1959
3 by R. Gasnier, First Test at Wembley, Oct 16, 1963
3 by K. Irvine, Second Test at Swinton, Nov 9, 1963
3 by K. Irvine, Third Test at Sydney, July 23, 1966
3 by G. Miles, First Test at Old Trafford, Manchester, Oct 25, 1986
3 by M. O'Connor, First Test at Old Trafford, Manchester, Oct 25, 1986
Most goals in a match: 10 by M. Cronin, First Test at Brisbane, June 16, 1979
Most points in a match: 22 (5g,3t) by M. O'Connor at Old Trafford, Manchester, Oct 25, 1986
Biggest attendance: 70,204 First Test at Sydney, June 6, 1932
● In a World Cup match at Perpignan, France, on October 29, 1972, R. Fulton scored three tries.

Garry Schofield touching down in the first Test at Old Trafford, Manchester.

GREAT BRITAIN v. NEW ZEALAND

Date	Result		Venue	Attendance
25 Jan. 1908	W	14-6	Leeds	8,182
8 Feb. 1908	L	6-18	Chelsea	14,000
15 Feb. 1908	L	5-8	Cheltenham	4,000
30 Jul. 1910	W	52-20	Auckland	16,000
1 Aug. 1914	W	16-13	Auckland	15,000
31 Jul. 1920	W	31-7	Auckland	34,000
7 Aug. 1920	W	19-3	Christchurch	10,000
14 Aug. 1920	W	11-10	Wellington	4,000
2 Aug. 1924	L	8-16	Auckland	22,000
6 Aug. 1924	L	11-13	Wellington	6,000
9 Aug. 1924	W	31-18	Dunedin	14,000
2 Oct. 1926	W	28-20	Wigan	14,500
13 Nov. 1926	W	21-11	Hull	7,000
15 Jan. 1927	W	32-17	Leeds	6,000
4 Aug. 1928	L	13-17	Auckland	28,000
18 Aug. 1928	W	13-5	Dunedin	12,000
25 Aug. 1928	W	6-5	Christchurch	21,000
30 Jul. 1932	W	24-9	Auckland	25,000
13 Aug. 1932	W	25-14	Christchurch	5,000
20 Aug. 1932	W	20-18	Auckland	6,500
8 Aug. 1936	W	10-8	Auckland	6,500
15 Aug. 1936	W	23-11	Auckland	17,000
10 Aug. 1946	L	8-13	Auckland	10,000
4 Oct. 1947	W	11-10	Leeds	28,445
8 Nov. 1947	L	7-10	Swinton	29,031
20 Dec. 1947	W	25-9	Bradford	42,680
29 Jul. 1950	L	10-16	Christchurch	10,000
12 Aug. 1950	L	13-20	Auckland	20,000
6 Oct. 1951	W	21-15	Bradford	37,475
10 Nov. 1951	W	20-19	Swinton	29,938
15 Dec. 1951	W	16-12	Leeds	18,649
24 Jul. 1954	W	27-7	Auckland	22,097
31 Jul. 1954	L	14-20	Greymouth	4,240
14 Aug. 1954	W	12-6	Auckland	6,186
8 Oct. 1955	W	25-6	Swinton	21,937
12 Nov. 1955	W	27-12	Bradford	24,443
17 Dec. 1955	L	13-28	Leeds	10,438
26 Jul. 1958	L	10-15	Auckland	25,000
9 Aug. 1958	W	32-15	Auckland	25,000
30 Sept. 1961	L	11-29	Leeds	16,540
21 Oct. 1961	W	23-10	Bradford	19,980
4 Nov. 1961	W	35-19	Swinton	22,536
28 Jul. 1962	L	0-19	Auckland	14,976
11 Aug. 1962	L	8-27	Auckland	16,411
25 Sept. 1965	W	7-2	Swinton	8,541
23 Oct. 1965	W	15-9	Bradford	15,740
6 Nov. 1965	D	9-9	Wigan	7,919
6 Aug. 1966	W	25-8	Auckland	14,494
20 Aug. 1966	W	22-14	Auckland	10,657
11 Jul. 1970	W	19-15	Auckland	15,948
19 Jul. 1970	W	23-9	Christchurch	8,600
25 Jul. 1970	W	33-16	Auckland	13,137
25 Sept. 1971	L	13-18	Salford	3,764
16 Oct. 1971	L	14-17	Castleford	4,108
6 Nov. 1971	W	12-3	Leeds	5,479
27 Jul. 1974	L	8-13	Auckland	10,466
4 Aug. 1974	W	17-8	Christchurch	6,316
10 Aug. 1974	W	20-0	Auckland	11,574
21 Jul. 1979	W	16-8	Auckland	9,000
5 Aug. 1979	W	22-7	Christchurch	8,500
11 Aug. 1979	L	11-18	Auckland	7,000
18 Oct. 1980	D	14-14	Wigan	7,031
2 Nov. 1980	L	8-12	Bradford	10,946
15 Nov. 1980	W	10-2	Leeds	8,210
14 Jul. 1984	L	0-12	Auckland	10,238
22 Jul. 1984	L	12-28	Christchurch	3,824
28 Jul. 1984	L	16-32	Auckland	7,967
19 Oct. 1985	L	22-24	Leeds	12,591
2 Nov. 1985	W	25-8	Wigan	15,506
9 Nov. 1985	D	6-6	Elland Rd, Leeds	22,209

	Played	Won	Lost	Drawn	Tries	Goals	Dr	Pts for
Great Britain	70	43	24	3	254	205	3	1186
New Zealand	70	24	43	3	163	204	0	916

GREAT BRITAIN-NEW ZEALAND TEST MATCH RECORDS

Britain

Highest score: 52-20 First Test at Auckland, July 30, 1910 (Also widest margin win)

Most tries in a match: 4 by W. Boston (Wigan) First Test at Auckland, July 24, 1954
4 by G. Schofield (Hull) Second Test at Wigan, Nov 2, 1985

Most goals in a match: 7 by N. Fox (Wakefield T.) Third Test at Swinton, Nov 4, 1961
7 by E. Fraser (Warrington) Second Test at Auckland, Aug 9, 1958

Most points in a match: 16 (4t) by G. Schofield (Hull) Second Test at Wigan, Nov 2, 1985
Biggest attendance: 42,680 Third Test at Bradford, Dec 20, 1947

● In a World Cup match at Pau, France, on November 4, 1972, Britain won 53-19 with J. Holmes (Leeds) scoring 26 points from 10 goals and two tries.
In a World Cup match at Sydney on June 8, 1968, Bev Risman scored 7 goals.

New Zealand
Highest score: 32-16 Third Test at Auckland, July 28, 1984
Widest margin win: 19-0 First Test at Auckland, July 28, 1962
                        27-8 Second Test at Auckland, Aug 11, 1962
No player has scored three tries or more in a Test.
Most goals and points: 7g-14pts by D. White Second Test at Greymouth, July 31, 1954
                        J. Fagan, First Test at Headingley, Sep 30, 1961
                        E. Wiggs, Second Test at Auckland, Aug 20, 1966
Biggest attendance: 34,000 First Test at Auckland, July 31, 1920
● In a World Cup match at Sydney, Australia, on June 25, 1957, W. Sorenson also scored 7 goals, 14 points.

GREAT BRITAIN v. FRANCE
● **Results since France were given Test match status.**

26 Jan. 1957	W 45-12	Leeds	20,221	4 Mar. 1967	L 13-23	Wigan	7,448
3 Mar. 1957	D 19-19	Toulouse	16,000	11 Feb. 1968	W 22-13	Paris	8,000
10 Apr. 1957	W 29-14	St. Helens	23,250	2 Mar. 1968	W 19-8	Bradford	14,196
3 Nov. 1957	W 25-14	Toulouse	15,000	30 Nov. 1968	W 34-10	St. Helens	6,080
23 Nov. 1957	W 44-15	Wigan	19,152	2 Feb. 1969	L 9-13	Toulouse	10,000
2 Mar. 1958	W 23-9	Grenoble	20,000	7 Feb. 1971	L 8-16	Toulouse	14,960
14 Mar. 1959	W 50-15	Leeds	22,000	17 Mar. 1971	W 24-2	St. Helens	7,783
5 Apr. 1959	L 15-24	Grenoble	8,500	6 Feb. 1972	W 10-9	Toulouse	11,508
6 Mar. 1960	L 18-20	Toulouse	15,308	12 Mar. 1972	W 45-10	Bradford	7,313
26 Mar. 1960	D 17-17	St. Helens	14,000	20 Jan. 1974	W 24-5	Grenoble	5,500
11 Dec. 1960	W 21-10	Bordeaux	8,000	17 Feb. 1974	W 29-0	Wigan	10,105
28 Jan. 1961	W 27-8	St Helens	18,000	6 Dec. 1981	W 37-0	Hull	13,173
17 Feb. 1962	L 15-20	Wigan	17,277	20 Dec. 1981	L 2-19	Marseilles	6,500
11 Mar. 1962	L 13-23	Perpignan	14,000	20 Feb. 1983	W 20-5	Carcassonne	3,826
2 Dec. 1962	L 12-17	Perpignan	5,000	6 Mar. 1983	W 17-5	Hull	6,055
3 Apr. 1963	W 42-4	Wigan	19,487	29 Jan. 1984	W 12-0	Avignon	4,000
8 Mar. 1964	W 11-5	Perpignan	4,326	17 Feb. 1984	W 10-0	Leeds	7,646
18 Mar. 1964	W 39-0	Leigh	4,750	1 Mar. 1985	W 50-4	Leeds	6,491
6 Dec. 1964	L 8-18	Perpignan	15,000	17 Mar. 1985	L 16-24	Perpignan	5,000
23 Jan. 1965	W 17-7	Swinton	9,959	16 Feb. 1986	D 10-10	Avignon	4,000
16 Jan. 1966	L 13-18	Perpignan	6,000	1 Mar. 1986	W 24-10	Wigan	8,112
5 Mar. 1966	L 4-8	Wigan	14,004	24 Jan. 1987	W 52-4	Leeds	6,567
22 Jan. 1967	W 16-13	Carcassonne	10,650	8 Feb. 1987	W 20-10	Carcassonne	2,000

	Played	Won	Drawn	Lost	Tries	Goals	Dr	Pts for
Great Britain	46	30	3	13	202	197	0	1030
France	46	13	3	30	86	120	3	510

GREAT BRITAIN-FRANCE TEST MATCH RECORDS

Britain

Highest score:	52-4 at Leeds, January 24, 1987
	(Also widest margin win)
Most tries in a match:	4 by A. Murphy (St. Helens) at Leeds, March 14, 1959
Most goals in a match:	10 by B. Ganley (Oldham) at Wigan, November 23, 1957
Most points in a match:	21 (9g, 1t) by B.L. Jones (Leeds) at Leeds, January 26, 1957
	21 (9g,1t) by N. Fox (Wakefield T.) at Wigan, April 3, 1963
	21 (9g,1t) by N. Fox (Wakefield T.) at Leigh, March 18, 1964
Biggest attendance:	23,250 at St. Helens, April 10, 1957

France

Highest score:	24-15 at Grenoble, April 5, 1959
	24-16 at Perpignan, March 17, 1985
Widest margin win:	19-2 at Marseilles, December 20, 1981
Most tries in a match:	3 by D. Couston at Perpignan, March 17, 1985
Most goals in a match:	7 by P. Lacaze at Wigan, March 4, 1967
Most points in a match:	14 by P. Lacaze (as above).
	14 (4g,2t) by G. Benausse at Wigan, February 17, 1962
Biggest attendance:	20,000 at Grenoble, March 2, 1958

●In a World Cup match at Toulouse on November 7, 1954, there were 37,471

Additional Great Britain v. France

Pre-Test status

22 May 1952	L	12-22	Paris	16,466
24 May 1953	L	17-28	Lyons	
27 Apr. 1954	W	17-8	Bradford	14,153
11 Dec. 1955	L	5-17	Paris	18,000
11 Apr. 1956	W	18-10	Bradford	10,453

Other match

31 July 1982	L	7-8	Venice	1,500

GREAT BRITAIN v PAPUA NEW GUINEA

5 Aug. 1984	W	38-20	Mt. Hagen	7,510

Shaun Edwards, two-try Man of the Match in Great Britain's record 52-4 victory over France in January 1987.

GREAT BRITAIN REPRESENTATION CLUB-BY-CLUB

Only six of last season's clubs have not had a player selected for Great Britain in Test or World Cup matches — Blackpool Borough, Bramley and Doncaster, plus newcomers Carlisle, Mansfield Marksman and Sheffield Eagles. Of the extinct clubs only Broughton Rangers (later Belle Vue Rangers), Merthyr Tydfil, St. Helens Recs and the old Runcorn had players selected for Britain.

Wigan hold the record for most players selected with a remarkable number of 71. Of those players, seven once lined up in a Test together — another record. They were backs Martin Ryan, Gordon Ratcliffe, Ernie Ashcroft, Jack Hilton and Tommy Bradshaw; plus forwards Ken Gee and Joe Egan. Hilton scored both Britain's tries in the 6-4 victory over Australia at Sydney on 12 June, 1950.

Mick Sullivan gained Test honours with four clubs — Huddersfield (16), Wigan (19), St. Helens (10) and York (1). Billy Boston gained the most Test honours with a single club, making all 31 of his appearances for Britain while with Wigan.

The following is a club-by-club register of Great Britain players. The figure in brackets after a player's name is the number of Great Britain appearances he made while serving the club under whose entry he is listed, and the number after the + sign indicates playing substitute. This is followed by the time span between his first and last British cap while at that club.

BARROW (19 players)
W. Burgess (16) 1924-29
W. Burgess (13) 1962-68
D. Cairns (2) 1984
C. Camilleri (2) 1980
C. Carr (7) 1924-26
F. Castle (4) 1952-54
R. Francis (1) 1947
H. Gifford (2) 1908
D. Goodwin (5) 1957-58
J. Grundy (12) 1955-57
P. Hogan (4+1) 1977-78
W. Horne (8) 1946-52
P. Jackson (27) 1954-58
J. Jones (1) 1946
B. Knowelden (1) 1946
E. Szymala (1+1) 1981
E. Toohey (3) 1952
L. A. Troup (2) 1936
J. Woods (1) 1933

BATLEY (4 players)
N. Field (1) 1963
F. Gallagher (8) 1924-26
C. Gibson (+1) 1985
J. Oliver (4) 1928

BRADFORD NORTHERN (26 players)
D. Barends (2) 1979
E. Batten (4) 1946-47
I. Brooke (5) 1966
L. Casey (5) 1979
W. T. H. Davies (3) 1946-47
A. Fisher (8) 1970-78
T. Foster (3) 1946-48
J. Grayshon (11) 1979-82
E. Hanley (10+1) 1984-85
R. Jasiewicz (1) 1984
J. Kitching (1) 1946
A. Mann (2) 1908
K. Mumby (11) 1982-84
B. Noble (11) 1982-84
T. Price (1) 1970
J. Rae (1) 1965
W. Ramsey (+1) 1974
A. Rathbone (4+1) 1982-85
A. Redfearn (1) 1979
D. Redfearn (6+1) 1972-74
T. Smales (3) 1965
H. Smith (2) 1926
J. Thompson (1) 1978
K. Traill (8) 1950-54
E. Ward (20) 1946-52
F. Whitcombe (2) 1946

BROUGHTON/BELLE VUE RANGERS (8 players)
W. Bentham (2) 1924
L. Clampitt (3) 1907-14
E. Gwyther (6) 1947-51
A. Hogg (1) 1907
S. McCormick (2) 1948
D. Phillips (1) 1950
J. Price (2) 1921
J. Ruddick (3) 1907-10

CASTLEFORD (22 players)
A. Atkinson (11) 1929-36
K. Beardmore (2+1) 1984-87
W. Bryant (4+1) 1964-67
A. Croston (1) 1937
B. Cunniffe (1) 1937
W. J. Davies (1) 1933
D. Edwards (3+2) 1968-71
K. England (1+1) 1987
A. Hardisty (12) 1964-70
D. Hartley (9) 1968-70
K. Hepworth (11) 1967-70
J. Joyner (14+2) 1978-84
B. Lockwood (7) 1972-74
A. Marchant (3) 1986
R. Millward (1) 1966
S. Norton (2+1) 1974
M. Reilly (9) 1970
P. Small (1) 1962

G. Stephens (5) 1979
D. Walton (1) 1965
J. Ward (3) 1963-64
K. Ward (4) 1984-86

DEWSBURY (6 players)
A. Bates (2 + 2) 1974
F. Gallagher (4) 1920-21
J. Ledgard (2) 1947
R. Pollard (1) 1950
M. Stephenson (5 + 1) 1971-72
H. Street (4) 1950

**FEATHERSTONE ROVERS
(13 players)**
T. Askin (6) 1928
K. Bridges (3) 1974
T. Clawson (2) 1962
M. Dixon (2) 1962-64
S. Evans (5 + 3) 1979-80
Deryck Fox (9) 1985-86
Don Fox (1) 1963
D. Hobbs (7 + 1) 1984
G. Jordan (2) 1964-67
A. Morgan (4) 1968
S. Nash (16) 1971-74
P. Smith (1 + 5) 1977-84
J. Thompson (19 + 1) 1970-77

FULHAM (1 player)
J. Dalgreen (1) 1982

HALIFAX (29 players)
A. Ackerley (2) 1952-58
A. Bassett (2) 1946
J. Beames (2) 1921
N. Bentham (2) 1929
H. Beverley (2) 1937
O. Burgham (1) 1911
A. Daniels (2) 1952-55
W. T. Davies (1) 1911
C. Dixon (1) 1968
P. Dixon (+ 1) 1987
P. Eccles (1) 1907
T. Fogerty (+ 1) 1966
A. Halmshaw (1) 1971
N. James (1) 1986
R. Lloyd (1) 1920
A. Milnes (2) 1920
S. Prosser (1) 1914
D. Rees (1) 1926
C. Renilson (7 + 1) 1965-68
J. Riley (1) 1910
K. Roberts (10) 1963-66
A. Robinson (3) 1907-08
D. Schofield (1) 1955
J. Shaw (5) 1960-62
J. C. Stacey (1) 1920
J. Thorley (4) 1954
J. Wilkinson (6) 1954-55
F. Williams (2) 1914
D. Willicombe (1) 1974

HUDDERSFIELD (24 players)
J. Bowden (3) 1954
K. Bowman (3) 1962-63
B. Briggs (1) 1954
S. Brogden (9) 1929-33
J. Chilcott (3) 1914
D. Clark (11) 1911-20
D. Close (1) 1967
R. Cracknell (2) 1951
J. Davies (2) 1911
F. Dyson (1) 1959
B. Gronow (7) 1911-20
F. Longstaff (2) 1914
K. Loxton (1) 1971
S. Moorhouse (2) 1914
R. Nicholson (3) 1946-48
J. Rogers (7) 1914-21
K. Senior (2) 1965-67
T. Smales (5) 1962-64
M. Sullivan (16) 1954-57
G. Thomas (8) 1920-21
D. Valentine (15) 1948-54
R. Valentine (1) 1967
H. Wagstaff (12) 1911-21
H. Young (1) 1929

HULL (30 players)
W. Batten (1) 1921
H. Bowman (8) 1924-29
F. Boylen (1) 1908
R. Coverdale (4) 1954
M. Crane (1) 1982
L. Crooks (11 + 2) 1982-87
A. Dannatt (2) 1985
G. Divorty (2) 1985
J. Drake (1) 1960
W. Drake (1) 1962
S. Evans (2) 1982
V. Farrar (1) 1978
R. Gemmell (2) 1968-69
T. E. Gwynne (3) 1928-29
T. Harris (25) 1954-60
M. Harrison (7) 1967-73
W. Holder (1) 1907
A. Keegan (9) 1966-69
E. Morgan (2) 1921
S. Norton (9) 1978-82
W. Proctor (+ 1) 1984
P. Rose (1) 1982
G. Schofield (15) 1984-87
T. Skerrett (6) 1980-82
W. Stone (8) 1920-21
C. Sullivan (17) 1967-73
H. Taylor (3) 1907
R. Taylor (2) 1921-26
D. Topliss (1) 1982
J. Whiteley (15) 1957-62

**HULL KINGSTON ROVERS
(25 players)**
C. Burton (8 + 1) 1982-87
A. Burwell (7 + 1) 1967-69
L. Casey (7 + 2) 1977-83
G. Clark (3) 1984-85
A. Dockar (1) 1947
G. Fairbairn (3) 1981-82
J. Feetham (1) 1929
P. Flanagan (14) 1962-70
F. Foster (1) 1967
D. Hall (2) 1984
P. Harkin (+ 1) 1985
S. Hartley (3) 1980-81
P. Hogan (2 + 2) 1979
R. Holdstock (2) 1980
W. Holliday (8 + 1) 1964-67
D. Laws (1) 1986
B. Lockwood (1 + 1) 1978-79
P. Lowe (12) 1970-78
R. Millward (27 + 1) 1967-78
H. Poole (1) 1964
P. Rose (1 + 3) 1974-78
M. Smith (10 + 1) 1979-84
B. Tyson (3) 1963-67
D. Watkinson (12 + 1) 1979-86
C. Young (5) 1967-68

HUNSLET (23 players)
W. Batten (9) 1907-11
H. Beverley (4) 1936-37
A. Burnell (3) 1951-54
H. Crowther (1) 1929
J. Evans (4) 1951-52
K. Eyre (1) 1965
B. Gabbitas (1) 1959
G. Gunney (11) 1954-65
D. Hartley (1) 1964
J. Higson (2) 1908
D. Jenkins (1) 1929
A. Jenkinson (2) 1911
W. Jukes (6) 1908-10
B. Prior (1) 1966
W. Ramsey (7) 1965-66
B. Shaw (5) 1956-60
G. Shelton (7) 1964-66
F. Smith (9) 1910-14
S. Smith (4) 1954
C. Thompson (2) 1951
L. White (7) 1932-33
R. Williams (3) 1954
H. Wilson (3) 1907

KEIGHLEY (1 player)
T. Hollindrake (1) 1955

LEEDS (60 players)
L. Adams (1) 1932
J. Atkinson (26) 1968-80
J. Bacon (11) 1920-26
R. Batten (3) 1969-73
J. Birch (1) 1907
S. Brogden (7) 1936-37
J. Brough (5) 1928-36
G. Brown (6) 1954-55
M. Clark (5) 1968
T. Clawson (3) 1972
D. Creasser (2 + 1) 1985-87
W. A. Davies (2) 1914
K. Dick (2) 1980
R. Dickinson (2) 1985
L. Dyl (11) 1974-82
A. Fisher (3) 1970-71
R. Gemmell (1) 1964
J. Grayshon (2) 1985
R. Haigh (3 + 1) 1970-71
D. Hallas (2) 1961
F. Harrison (3) 1911
D. Heron (1 + 1) 1982
J. Holmes (14 + 6) 1971-82
S. Hynes (12 + 1) 1970-73
J. W. Jarman (2) 1914
D. Jeanes (3) 1972
D. Jenkins (1) 1947
B. L. Jones (15) 1954-57
K. Jubb (2) 1937
J. Lowe (1) 1932
I. Owens (4) 1946
S. Pitchford (4) 1977
H. Poole (2) 1966
R. Powell (+ 1) 1985
D. Prosser (1) 1937
Keith Rayne (4) 1984
Kevin Rayne (1) 1986
B. Risman (5) 1968
D. Robinson (5) 1956-60
D. Rose (4) 1954
B. Seabourne (1) 1970
B. Shaw (1) 1961
M. Shoebottom (10 + 2) 1968-71
B. Simms (1) 1962
A. Smith (10) 1970-73
S. Smith (10) 1929-33
J. Stevenson (15) 1955-58
S. Stockwell (3) 1920-21
A. Terry (1) 1962
A. Thomas (4) 1926-29
P. Thomas (1) 1907
J. Thompson (12) 1924-32
A. Turnbull (1) 1951
D. Ward (12) 1977-82
W. Ward (1) 1910
F. Webster (3) 1910
R. Williams (9) 1948-51
H. Woods (1) 1937
G. Wriglesworth (5) 1965-66
F. Young (1) 1908

Leigh full back Chris Johnson, one cap in 1985.

LEIGH (19 players)
K. Ashcroft (5) 1968-70
J. Cartwright (7) 1920-21
D. Chisnall (2) 1970
J. Darwell (5) 1924
S. Donlan (+ 2) 1984
D. Drummond (22) 1980-86
P. Foster (3) 1955
C. Johnson (1) 1985
F. Kitchen (2) 1954
J. Ledgard (9) 1948-54
G. Lewis (1) 1965
M. Martyn (2) 1958-59
W. Mooney (2) 1924
S. Owen (1) 1958
C. Pawsey (7) 1952-54
W. Robinson (2) 1963
Joe Walsh (1) 1971
W. Winstanley (2) 1910
J. Woods (7 + 3) 1979-83

MERTHYR TYDFIL (1 player)
D. Jones (2) 1907

OLDHAM (39 players)
A. Avery (4) 1910-11
C. Bott (1) 1966
A. Brough (2) 1924
T. Clawson (9) 1973-74
A. Davies (20) 1955-60
E. Davies (3) 1920
T. Flanagan (4) 1983-84
D. Foy (3) 1984-85
B. Ganley (3) 1957-58
A. Goodway (11) 1983-85
W. Hall (4) 1914
H. Hilton (7) 1920-21
D. Hobbs (5) 1987
D. Holland (4) 1914
R. Irving (8 + 3) 1967-72
K. Jackson (2) 1957
E. Knapman (1) 1924
S. Little (10) 1956-58
T. Llewellyn (2) 1907
J. Lomas (2) 1911
W. Longworth (3) 1908
L. McIntyre (1) 1963
T. O'Grady (5) 1954
J. Oster (1) 1929
D. Parker (2) 1964
D. Phillips (3) 1946
F. Pitchford (2) 1958-62
T. Rees (1) 1929
S. Rix (9) 1924-26
R. Sloman (5) 1928
A. Smith (6) 1907-08
I. Southward (7) 1959-62
L. Thomas (1) 1947
D. Turner (11) 1956-58
G. Tyson (4) 1907-08
T. White (1) 1907
C. Winsdale (1) 1959
A. Wood (4) 1911-14
M. Worrall (3) 1984

ROCHDALE HORNETS (8 players)
J. Baxter (1) 1907
J. Bennett (6) 1924
J. Bowers (1) 1920
T. Fogerty (1) 1974
E. Jones (4) 1920
M. Price (2) 1967
J. Robinson (2) 1914
T. Woods (2) 1911

RUNCORN (2 players)
J. Jolley (3) 1907
R. Padbury (1) 1908

RUNCORN HIGHFIELD/ HUYTON/LIVERPOOL/WIGAN HIGHFIELD (4 players)
R. Ashby (1) 1964
W. Belshaw (6) 1936-37
N. Bentham (6) 1928
H. Woods (5) 1936

ST. HELENS (44 players)
C. Arkwright (+2) 1985
L. Aston (3) 1947
W. Benyon (5+1) 1971-72
T. Bishop (15) 1966-69
F. Carlton (1) 1958
E. Chisnall (4) 1974
E. Cunningham (1) 1978
R. Dagnall (4) 1961-65
D. Eckersley (2+2) 1973-74
A. Ellaby (13) 1928-33
L. Fairclough (6) 1926-29
J. Fieldhouse (1) 1986
A. Fildes (4) 1932
A. Frodsham (3) 1928-29
P. Gorley (2+1) 1980-81
D. Greenall (6) 1951-54
R. Haggerty (2) 1987
M. Hicks (1) 1965
N. Holding (4) 1984
R. Huddart (12) 1959-63
L. Jones (1) 1971
A. Karalius (4+1) 1971-72
V. Karalius (10) 1958-61
K. Kelly (2) 1972
B. Ledger (2) 1985-86
J. Mantle (13) 1966-73
S. McCormick (1) 1948
T. McKinney (1) 1957
R. Mathias (1) 1979
G. Moses (9) 1955-57
A. Murphy (26) 1958-66
F. Myler (9) 1970
G. Nicholls (22) 1973-79
H. Pinner (5+1) 1980-86
A. Platt (+3) 1985-86
A. Prescott (28) 1951-58
A. Rhodes (4) 1957-61
J. Stott (1) 1947
M. Sullivan (10) 1961-62
J. Tembey (1) 1963-64
A. Terry (10) 1958-61
John Walsh (4+1) 1972
J. Warlow (3+1) 1964-68
C. Watson (29+1) 1963-71

ST. HELENS RECS (5 players)
F. Bowen (3) 1928
A. Fildes (11) 1926-29
J. Greenall (1) 1921
J. Owen (1) 1921
J. Wallace (1) 1926

SALFORD (27 players)
W. Burgess (1) 1969
P. Charlton (17+1) 1970-74
M. Coulman (2+1) 1971
G. Curran (6) 1946-48
E. Curzon (1) 1910
T. Danby (3) 1950
C. Dixon (11+2) 1969-74
A. Edwards (7) 1936-37
J. Feetham (7) 1932-33
K. Fielding (3) 1974-77
K. Gill (5+2) 1974-77
J. Gore (1) 1926
C. Hesketh (21+2) 1970-74
B. Hudson (8) 1932-37
E. Jenkins (9) 1933-37
J. Lomas (5) 1908-10
T. McKinney (7) 1951-54
A. Middleton (1) 1929
S. Nash (8) 1977-82
M. Richards (2) 1974
A. Risman (17) 1932-46
J. Spencer (1) 1907
J. Ward (1) 1970
S. Warwick (2) 1907
D. Watkins (2+4) 1971-74
W. Watkins (7) 1933-37
W. Williams (2) 1929-32

SWINTON (15 players)
T. Armitt (8) 1933-37
A. Buckley (7) 1963-66
F. Butters (2) 1929
W. Davies (1) 1968
B. Evans (10) 1926-33
F. Evans (4) 1924
J. Evans (3) 1926
K. Gowers (14) 1962-66
H. Halsall (1) 1929
M. Hodgson (16) 1929-37
R. Morgan (2) 1963
W. Rees (11) 1926-29
D. Robinson (12) 1965-67
J. Stopford (12) 1961-66
J. Wright (1) 1932

WAKEFIELD TRINITY (22 players)
I. Brooke (8) 1967-68
N. Fox (29) 1959-69
R. Haigh (2) 1968-70
W. Horton (14) 1928-33
D. Jeanes (5) 1971-72
B. Jones (3) 1964-66
H. Kershaw (2) 1910
F. Mortimer (2) 1956
H. Murphy (1) 1950
H. Newbould (1) 1910
J. Parkin (17) 1920-29
C. Pollard (1) 1924
E. Pollard (2) 1932

H. Poynton (3) 1962
D. Robinson (5) 1954-55
G. Round (8) 1959-62
T. Skerrett (4) 1979
S. Smith (1) 1929
D. Topliss (3) 1973-79
D. Turner (13) 1959-62
D. Vines (3) 1959
J. Wilkinson (7) 1959-62

WARRINGTON (41 players)
J. Arkwright (6) 1936-37
K. Ashcroft (+1) 1974
W. Aspinall (1) 1966
W. Belshaw (2) 1937
N. Bentham (2) 1929
J. Bevan (6) 1974-78
T. Blinkhorn (1) 1929
E. Brooks (3) 1908
J. Challinor (3) 1958-60
N. Courtney (+1) 1982
W. Cunliffe (11) 1920-26
G. Dickenson (1) 1908
W. Dingsdale (3) 1929-33
R. Duane (3) 1983-84
R. Eccles (1) 1982
J. Featherstone (6) 1948-52
M. Forster (2) 1987
E. Fraser (16) 1958-61
L. Gilfedder (5) 1962-63
R. Greenough (1) 1960
A. Gregory (1) 1986
M. Gregory (2) 1987
G. Helme (12) 1948-54
K. Holden (1) 1963
A. Johnson (6) 1946-47
K. Kelly (2) 1980-82
T. McKinney (3) 1955
J. Miller (6) 1933-36
A. Murphy (1) 1971
A. Naughton (2) 1954
T. O'Grady (1) 1961
H. Palin (2) 1947
K. Parr (1) 1968
A. Pimblett (3) 1948
R. Price (9) 1954-57
R. Ryan (5) 1950-52
R. Ryder (1) 1952
F. Shugars (1) 1910
G. Skelhorne (7) 1920-21
G. Thomas (1) 1907
D. Whitehead (3) 1971

WHITEHAVEN (5 players)
V. Gribbin (1) 1985
W. Holliday (1) 1964
R. Huddart (4) 1958
P. Kitchin (1) 1965
A. Walker (1) 1980

WIDNES (33 players)
M. Adams (11 + 2) 1979-84
J. Basnett (2) 1984-86
K. Bentley (1) 1980
M. Burke (14 + 1) 1980-86
F. Collier (1) 1964
R. Dutton (6) 1970
K. Elwell (3) 1977-80
J. Fieldhouse (6) 1985-86
R. French (4) 1968
L. Gorley (4 + 1) 1980-82
A. Gregory (8 + 1) 1981-84
I. Hare (1) 1967
F. Higgins (6) 1950-51
H. Higgins (2) 1937
E. Hughes (8) 1978-82
A. Johnson (4) 1914-20
G. Kemel (2) 1965
V. Karalius (2) 1963
D. Laughton (4) 1973-79
J. Lydon (9 + 1) 1983-85
T. McCue (6) 1936-46
J. Measures (2) 1963
J. Mills (6) 1974-79
A. Myler (14) 1983-86
F. Myler (14 + 1) 1960-67
G. Nicholls (7) 1971-72
D. O'Neill (2 + 1) 1971-72
M. O'Neill (3) 1982-83
H. Pinner (1) 1986
G. Shaw (1) 1980
N. Silcock (12) 1932-37
J. Warlow (3) 1971
S. Wright (7) 1977-78

WIGAN (71 players)
R. Ashby (1) 1965
E. Ashcroft (11) 1947-54
E. Ashton (26) 1957-63
W. Ashurst (3) 1971-72
F. Barton (1) 1951
J. Barton (2) 1960-61
J. Bennett (1) 1926
D. Bevan (1) 1952
W. Blan (3) 1951
D. Bolton (23) 1957-63
W. Boston (31) 1954-63
T. Bradshaw (6) 1947-50
F. Carlton (1) 1962
B. Case (4) 1984
W. Cherrington (1) 1960
C. Clarke (7) 1965-73
A. Coldrick (4) 1914
F. Collier (1) 1963
J. Cunliffe (4) 1950-54
S. Edwards (4 + 2) 1985-87
J. Egan (14) 1946-50
R. Evans (4) 1961-62
G. Fairbairn (14) 1977-80
T. Fogerty (1) 1967
P. Ford (1) 1985
W. Francis (4) 1967-77
D. Gardiner (1) 1965
K. Gee (17) 1946-51
H. Gill (10) 1981-87
A. Goodway (7) 1985-87
J. Gray (5 + 3) 1974
A. Gregory (1) 1987
E. Hanley (7) 1985-87
C. Hill (1) 1966
D. Hill (1) 1971
J. Hilton (4) 1950
T. Howley (6) 1924
W. Hudson (1) 1948
D. Hurcombe (8) 1920-24
B. Jenkins (12) 1907-14
K. Jones (2) 1970
R. Kinnear (1) 1929
N. Kiss (1) 1985
D. Laughton (11) 1970-71
J. Lawrenson (3) 1948
J. Leytham (5) 1907-10
J. Lydon (6) 1986-87

B. McTigue (25) 1958-63
J. Miller (1) 1911
J. Morley (2) 1936-37
I. Potter (7 + 1) 1985-86
J. Price (4) 1924
R. Ramsdale (8) 1910-14
G. Ratcliffe (3) 1947-50
J. Ring (2) 1924-26
D. Robinson (1) 1970
M. Ryan (4) 1947-50
W. Sayer (7) 1961-63
J. Sharrock (4) 1910-11
N. Silcock (3) 1954
R. Silcock (1) 1908
D. Stephenson (4) 1982-87
J. Sullivan (25) 1924-33
M. Sullivan (19) 1957-60
G. Thomas (1) 1914
J. Thomas (8) 1907-11
S. Wane (2) 1985-86
E. Ward (3) 1946-47
L. White (2) 1947
D. Willicombe (2) 1974
W. Winstanley (3) 1911

WORKINGTON TOWN (9 players)
E. Bowman (4) 1977
P. Charlton (1) 1965
B. Edgar (11) 1958-66
N. Herbert (6) 1961-62
W. Martin (1) 1962
V. McKeating (2) 1951
A. Pepperell (2) 1950-51
I. Southward (4) 1958
G. Wilson (3) 1951

YORK (7 players)
E. Dawson (1) 1956
H. Field (3) 1936
G. Smith (3) 1963-64
J. Stevenson (4) 1959-60
M. Sullivan (1) 1963
B. Watts (5) 1954-55
L. White (4) 1946

Widnes Test forward John Fieldhouse who was transferred to St. Helens after the first 1986 clash with Australia.

GREAT BRITAIN TEAMS
. . . A 20-year review

The following is a compendium of Great Britain Test and World Cup teams since the 1967-68 season.

Initials are included where more than one celebrated player shared a surname in the same era. Only playing substitutes are included on the teamsheet.

(WC): World Cup   t: try   g: goal
dg: drop goal   * captain

1967 Australia
Leeds: 21 Oct
Won 16-11
Keegan (Hull)
Young, C (Hull KR) 1t
Brooke (Wakefield)
Price, M (Rochdale)
Burgess (Barrow)
Millward (Hull KR) 3g, 1t
Bishop (St. Helens) 1g
*Holliday (Hull KR) 1g
Flanagan (Hull KR)
Watson (St. Helens)
Irving (Oldham)
Mantle (St. Helens)
Robinson, D (Swinton)

1967 Australia
White City (London): 3 Nov
Lost 11-17
Keegan (Hull)
Young, C (Hull KR)
Brooke (Wakefield)
Fox, N (Wakefield) 3g
Francis, W (Wigan)
Millward (Hull KR)
Bishop (St. Helens) 1t,1g
*Holliday (Hull KR)
Flanagan (Hull KR)
Watson (St. Helens)
Irving (Oldham)
Mantle (St. Helens)
Foster, F (Hull KR)

1967 Australia
Swinton: 9 Dec
Lost 3-11
Keegan (Hull)
Young, C (Hull KR)
Brooke (Wakefield)
Price, M (Rochdale) 1t
Jordan (Featherstone)
Millward (Hull KR)
Bishop (St. Helens)
*Holliday (Hull KR)
Flanagan (Hull KR)
Watson (St. Helens)
Irving (Oldham)
Valentine, R (Huddersfield)
Robinson, D (Swinton)
Sub: Burwell (Hull KR)
Renilson (Halifax)

1968 France
Paris: 11 Feb
Won 22-13
Risman, B (Leeds) 5g,2t
Young, C (Hull KR)
Brooke (Wakefield)
*Fox, N (Wakefield) 1t
Burwell (Hull KR) 1t
Millward (Hull KR) 1t
Bishop (St. Helens)
Clark, M (Leeds)
Flanagan (Hull KR)
Watson (St. Helens)
French (Widnes)
Morgan, A (Featherstone)
Renilson (Halifax)
Sub: Edwards, D (Castleford)

1968 France
Bradford: 2 March
Won 19-8
Risman, B (Leeds) 2g
Young, C (Hull KR) 1t
Brooke (Wakefield)
*Fox, N (Wakefield) 2t
Burwell (Hull KR) 2t
Millward (Hull KR) 1t
Bishop (St. Helens)
Clark, M (Leeds)
Flanagan (Hull KR)
Watson (St. Helens)
French (Widnes)
Morgan, A (Featherstone) 1t
Renilson (Halifax)

1968 Australia (WC)
Sydney: 25 May
Lost 10-25
*Risman, B (Leeds) 2g
Brooke (Wakefield) 1t
Burwell (Hull KR)
Shoebottom (Leeds)
Sullivan, C (Hull) 1t
Millward (Hull KR)
Bishop (St. Helens)
Clark, M (Leeds)
Ashcroft, K (Leigh)
Watson (St. Helens)
French (Widnes)
Haigh (Wakefield)
Renilson (Halifax)

1968 France (WC)
Auckland: 2 June
Lost 2-7
*Risman, B (Leeds) 1g
Sullivan, C (Hull)
Brooke (Wakefield)
Burwell (Hull KR)
Atkinson, J (Leeds)
Millward (Hull KR)
Bishop (St. Helens)
Clark, M (Leeds)
Flanagan (Hull KR)
Watson (St. Helens)
Morgan, A (Featherstone)
Haigh (Wakefield)
Renilson (Halifax)
Sub: Warlow (St. Helens)

1968 New Zealand (WC)
Sydney: 8 June
Won 38-14

*Risman, B (Leeds) 7g
Sullivan, C (Hull) 3t
Brooke (Wakefield) 1t
Burwell (Hull KR) 2t
Atkinson, J (Leeds)
Millward (Hull KR)
Bishop (St. Helens)
Clark, M (Leeds)
Flanagan (Hull KR)
Warlow (St. Helens)
French (Widnes)
Morgan, A (Featherstone) 1t
Renilson (Halifax)
Sub: Shoebottom (Leeds) 1t
    Watson (St. Helens)

1968 France
St. Helens: 30 Nov
Won 34-10

Keegan (Hull)
Burgess, W (Barrow) 3t
Fox, N (Wakefield) 5g
Gemmell (Hull) 2t
Burwell (Hull KR) 1t
Davies, W (Swinton)
*Bishop (St. Helens)
Hartley, D (Castleford)
Ashcroft, K (Leigh) 1t
Warlow (St. Helens)
Dixon, C (Halifax) 1t
Parr (Warrington)
Renilson (Halifax)

1969 France
Toulouse: 2 Feb
Lost 9-13

Keegan (Hull)
Burgess, W (Salford)
Fox, N (Wakefield) 3g
Gemmell (Hull)
Burwell (Hull KR)
Shoebottom (Leeds)
*Bishop (St. Helens)
Hartley, D (Castleford)
Ashcroft, K (Leigh)
Watson (St. Helens)
Dixon, C (Salford) 1t
Mantle (St. Helens)
Batten, R (Leeds)

1970 Australia
Brisbane: 6 June
Lost 15-37

Price, T (Bradford) 3g
Sullivan, C (Hull)
*Myler (St. Helens)
Shoebottom (Leeds)
Atkinson, J (Leeds)
Hardisty (Castleford)
Hepworth (Castleford)
Chisnall, D (Leigh)
Flanagan (Hull KR) 1t
Watson (St. Helens) 1t
Laughton (Wigan) 1t
Robinson, D (Wigan)
Reilly (Castleford)
Sub: Irving (Oldham)

1970 Australia
Sydney: 20 June
Won 28-7

Edwards, D (Castleford)
Smith, A (Leeds)
Hynes (Leeds) 1g
*Myler (St. Helens)
Atkinson, J (Leeds) 1t
Millward (Hull KR) 7g,2t
Hepworth (Castleford)
Hartley, D (Castleford)
Fisher (Bradford) 1t
Watson (St. Helens)
Laughton (Wigan)
Thompson, J (Featherstone)
Reilly (Castleford)
Sub: Shoebottom (Leeds)

1970 Australia
Sydney: 4 July
Won 21-17

Shoebottom (Leeds)
Smith, A (Leeds)
Hynes (Leeds) 1t
*Myler (St. Helens)
Atkinson, J (Leeds) 2t
Millward (Hull KR) 3g,1t
Hepworth (Castleford)
Hartley, D (Castleford) 1t
Fisher (Bradford)
Watson (St. Helens)
Laughton (Wigan)
Thompson, J (Featherstone)
Reilly (Castleford)

1970 New Zealand
Auckland: 11 July
Won 19-15

Shoebottom (Leeds)
Smith, A (Leeds)
Hynes (Leeds) 2g,1t
*Myler (St. Helens)
Atkinson, J (Leeds) 1t
Millward (Hull KR) 1t
Seabourne (Leeds)
Hartley, D (Castleford)
Fisher (Bradford)
Watson (St. Helens)
Laughton (Wigan) 2t
Thompson, J (Featherstone)
Reilly (Castleford)

1970 New Zealand
Christchurch: 19 July
Won 23-9

Dutton (Widnes) 4g
Smith, A (Leeds)
Hynes (Leeds)
*Myler (St. Helens) 1t
Atkinson, J (Leeds)
Millward (Hull KR) 2t
Hepworth (Castleford)
Hartley, D (Castleford)
Fisher (Bradford)
Watson (St. Helens)
Laughton (Wigan) 1t
Thompson, J (Featherstone)
Reilly (Castleford) 1t

1970 New Zealand
Auckland: 25 July
Won 33-16

Dutton (Widnes) 5g
Smith, A (Leeds) 1t
Hesketh (Salford) 1t
*Myler (St. Helens)
Atkinson, J (Leeds)
Millward (Hull KR) 1g
Hepworth (Castleford) 1t
Watson (St. Helens) 1t
Fisher (Bradford)
Ward, J (Salford)
Irving (Oldham)
Lowe, P (Hull KR) 2t
Reilly (Castleford)
Sub: Hynes (Leeds) 1t

1970 Australia (WC)
Leeds: 24 Oct
Won 11-4
Dutton (Widnes) 3g
Smith, A (Leeds)
Hynes (Leeds) 1t,1g
*Myler (St. Helens)
Atkinson, J (Leeds)
Shoebottom (Leeds)
Hepworth (Castleford)
Hartley, D (Castleford)
Fisher (Bradford)
Watson (St. Helens)
Laughton (Wigan)
Thompson, J (Featherstone)
Reilly (Castleford)

1970 France (WC)
Castleford: 28 Oct
Won 6-0
Dutton (Widnes) 3g
Jones, K (Wigan)
Hynes (Leeds)
*Myler (St. Helens)
Atkinson, J (Leeds)
Shoebottom (Leeds)
Hepworth (Castleford)
Hartley, D (Castleford)
Ashcroft, K (Leigh)
Watson (St. Helens)
Laughton (Wigan)
Thompson, J (Featherstone)
Reilly (Castleford)

1970 New Zealand (WC)
Swinton: 31 Oct
Won 27-17
Dutton (Widnes) 6g
Jones, K (Wigan)
Hynes (Leeds) 1t
Hesketh (Salford) 1t
Atkinson, J (Leeds) 1t
Shoebottom (Leeds)
Hepworth (Castleford)
Chisnall, D (Leigh)
Ashcroft, K (Leigh)
Watson (St. Helens) 1t
Haigh (Leeds)
Thompson, J (Featherstone)
*Laughton (Wigan) 1t
Sub: Charlton (Salford)

1970 Australia (WC)
Leeds: 7 Nov
Lost 7-12
Dutton (Widnes) 1g
Smith, A (Leeds)
Hynes (Leeds) 1g
*Myler (St. Helens)
Atkinson, J (Leeds) 1t
Shoebottom (Leeds)
Hepworth (Castleford)
Hartley, D (Castleford)
Fisher (Leeds)
Watson (St. Helens)
Laughton (Wigan)
Thompson, J (Featherstone)
Reilly (Castleford)
Sub: Hesketh (Salford)
     Haigh (Leeds)

1971 France
Toulouse: 7 Feb
Lost 8-16
Whitehead (Warrington) 1g
Smith, A (Leeds) 1t
*Hynes (Leeds)
Benyon (St. Helens)
Atkinson, J (Leeds)
Hill, D (Wigan)
Shoebottom (Leeds)
Jeanes (Wakefield) 1t
Fisher (Leeds)
Warlow (Widnes)
Mantle (St. Helens)
Haigh (Leeds)
Laughton (Wigan)
Sub: Hesketh (Salford)
     Thompson, J (Featherstone)

1971 France
St. Helens: 17 March
Won 24-2
Whitehead (Warrington) 1t,3g
Smith, A (Leeds) 1t
Hesketh (Salford)
Benyon (St. Helens) 1t
Atkinson, J (Leeds)
Millward (Hull KR) 2t
Nash (Featherstone)
Warlow (Widnes)
Fisher (Leeds)
Watson (St. Helens)
Mantle (St. Helens)
Thompson, J (Featherstone) 1t
*Laughton (Wigan)
Sub: Watkins, D (Salford)
     Coulman (Salford)

1971 New Zealand
Salford: 25 Sep
Lost 13-18
Whitehead (Warrington) 2g
Jones, L (St. Helens)
Benyon (St. Helens) 1t
Hesketh (Salford) 1t
Sullivan, C (Hull)
*Millward (Hull KR)
Nash (Featherstone)
Warlow (Widnes)
Karalius, A (St. Helens)
Jeanes (Wakefield)
Ashurst (Wigan) 1t
Coulman (Salford)
Mantle (St. Helens)
Sub: Edwards, D (Castleford)

1971 New Zealand
Castleford: 16 Oct
Lost 14-17
Edwards, D (Castleford)
Sullivan, C (Hull) 1t
Watkins, D (Salford) 1g
Hesketh (Salford)
Walsh, Joe (Leigh) 1t
*Millward (Hull KR) 1t
Murphy, A (Warrington)
Harrison, M (Hull)
Karalius, A (St. Helens)
Coulman (Salford) 1t
Dixon, C (Salford)
Mantle (St. Helens)
Haigh (Leeds)
Sub: Benyon (St. Helens)
     Stephenson, M (Dewsbury)

1971 New Zealand
Leeds: 6 Nov
Won 12-3
Edwards, D (Castleford)
Sullivan, C (Hull)
Hesketh (Salford)
Holmes (Leeds) 2g,2dg
Atkinson, J (Leeds) 2t
*Millward (Hull KR)
Loxton (Huddersfield)
Harrison, M (Hull)
Karalius, A (St. Helens)
Jeanes (Wakefield)
Irving (Oldham)
Nicholls (Widnes)
Halmshaw (Halifax)
Sub: O'Neill, D (Widnes)

1972 France
Toulouse: 6 Feb
Won 10-9
Charlton (Salford)
*Sullivan, C (Hull) 1t
Holmes (Leeds) 2g
Benyon (St. Helens) 1t
Atkinson, J (Leeds)
Kelly (St. Helens)
Nash (Featherstone)
Harrison, M (Hull)
Karalius, A (St. Helens)
Jeanes (Wakefield)
Ashurst (Wigan)
Lowe, P (Hull KR)
Nicholls (Widnes)

1972 France
Bradford: 12 March
Won 45-10
Charlton (Salford) 1t
*Sullivan, C (Hull) 1t
Holmes (Leeds) 1t,6g
Benyon (St. Helens) 1t
Atkinson, J (Leeds) 1t
Kelly (St. Helens)
Nash (Featherstone)
Harrison, M (Hull)
Stephenson, M (Dewsbury) 1t
Jeanes (Wakefield) 1t
Ashurst (Wigan) 2t
Lowe, P (Hull KR) 1t
Nicholls (Widnes)
Sub: Walsh, John (St. Helens) 1t
    Irving (Oldham)

1972 Australia (WC)
Perpignan: 29 Oct
Won 27-21
Charlton (Salford)
*Sullivan, C (Hull) 1t
Hesketh (Salford)
Walsh, John (St. Helens)
Atkinson, J (Leeds) 1t
O'Neill, D (Widnes) 1t
Nash (Featherstone)
Clawson (Leeds) 6g
Stephenson, M (Dewsbury) 1t
Jeanes (Leeds)
Lockwood (Castleford)
Lowe, P (Hull KR) 1t
Nicholls (Widnes)
Sub: Holmes (Leeds)

1972 France (WC)
Grenoble: 1 Nov
Won 13-4
Charlton (Salford)
*Sullivan, C (Hull) 1t
Hesketh (Salford)
Walsh, John (St. Helens)
Atkinson, J (Leeds)
O'Neill, D (Widnes)
Nash (Featherstone)
Clawson (Leeds) 2g
Stephenson, M (Dewsbury)
Lockwood, B (Castleford)
Dixon, C (Salford)
Lowe, P (Hull KR) 2t
Nicholls (Widnes)

1972 New Zealand (WC)
Pau: 4 Nov
Won 53-19
Charlton (Salford) 1t
*Sullivan, C (Hull) 1t
Hesketh (Salford) 1t
Walsh, John (St. Helens)
Atkinson, J (Leeds) 2t
Holmes (Leeds) 10g,2t
Nash (Featherstone) 1t
Jeanes (Leeds) 1t
Stephenson, M (Dewsbury) 1t
Lockwood (Castleford)
Irving (Oldham)
Lowe, P (Hull KR)
Nicholls (Widnes) 1t
Sub: Redfearn, D (Bradford)
    Karalius, A (St. Helens)

1972 Australia (WC)
Lyon: 11 Nov
Drew 10-10
Charlton (Salford)
*Sullivan, C (Hull) 1t
Hesketh (Salford)
Walsh, John (St. Helens)
Atkinson, J (Leeds)
Holmes (Leeds)
Nash (Featherstone)
Clawson (Leeds) 2g
Stephenson, M (Dewsbury) 1t
Jeanes (Leeds)
Lockwood, B (Castleford)
Lowe, P (Hull KR)
Nicholls (Widnes)
Sub: Irving (Oldham)

1973 Australia
Wembley: 3 Nov
Won 21-12
Charlton (Salford)
*Sullivan (Hull)
Hynes (Leeds)
Hesketh (Salford)
Atkinson, J (Leeds)
Topliss (Wakefield)
Nash (Featherstone) 1dg
Clawson (Oldham) 4g
Clarke (Wigan) 1t
Lockwood (Castleford) 1t
Nicholls (St. Helens)
Lowe, P (Hull KR) 2t
Batten (Leeds)

1973 Australia
Leeds: 24 Nov
Lost 6-14
Charlton (Salford)
*Sullivan (Hull)
Hynes (Leeds)
Hesketh (Salford)
Atkinson, J (Leeds)
Topliss (Wakefield)
Nash (Featherstone)
Clawson (Oldham) 3g
Clarke (Wigan)
Lockwood (Castleford)
Mantle (St. Helens)
Lowe, P (Hull KR)
Batten, R (Leeds)
Sub: Eckersley (St. Helens)
    Dixon, C (Salford)

1973 Australia
Warrington: 1 Dec
Lost 5-15
Charlton (Salford)
Smith, A (Leeds)
Hynes (Leeds)
Hesketh (Salford)
*Sullivan, C (Hull)
Eckersley (St. Helens)
Millward (Hull KR) 1t,1g
Clawson (Oldham)
Clarke (Wigan)
Harrison, M (Hull)
Nicholls (St. Helens)
Lowe, P (Hull KR)
Laughton (Widnes)
Sub: Watkins, D (Salford)
    Dixon, C (Salford)

1974 France
Grenoble: 20 Jan
Won 24-5

Charlton (Salford)
Fielding (Salford) 3t
Willicombe (Halifax) 1t
Hesketh (Salford)
Redfearn, D (Bradford)
Gill, K (Salford) 1t
Bates, A (Dewsbury)
Clawson (Oldham) 3g
Bridges (Featherstone)
Lockwood (Castleford)
Dixon, C (Salford)
Nicholls (St. Helens)
*Laughton (Widnes) 1t
Sub: Watkins, D (Salford)
     Gray (Wigan)

1974 France
Wigan: 17 Feb
Won 29-0

Charlton (Salford) 2t
Fielding (Salford)
Willicombe (Wigan) 1t
Hesketh (Salford)
Redfearn, D (Bradford) 2t
Gill, K (Salford)
Bates, A (Dewsbury)
Clawson (Oldham) 2g
Bridges (Featherstone)
Fogerty (Rochdale)
Dixon, C (Salford)
Nicholls (St. Helens)
*Laughton (Widnes) 1t
Sub: Watkins, D (Salford) 1g
     Gray (Wigan) 1t,1g

1974 Australia
Brisbane: 15 June
Lost 6-12

Charlton (Salford)
Redfearn, D (Bradford)
Watkins, D (Salford) 1g
*Hesketh (Salford)
Bevan, J (Warrington)
Millward (Hull KR)
Nash (Featherstone)
Clawson (Oldham) 2g
Bridges (Featherstone)
Mills (Widnes)
Dixon, C (Salford)
Thompson, J (Featherstone)
Nicholls (St. Helens)
Sub: Eckersley (St. Helens)
     Gray (Wigan)

1974 Australia
Sydney: 6 July
Won 16-11

Charlton (Salford)
Dyl (Leeds)
Eckersley (St. Helens)
*Hesketh (Salford)
Millward (Hull KR)
Gill, K (Salford) 1t
Nash (Featherstone)
Mills (Widnes)
Gray (Wigan) 3g,1dg
Thompson, J (Featherstone)
Dixon, C (Salford) 1t
Chisnall, E (St. Helens) 1t
Nicholls (St. Helens)
Sub: Norton (Castleford)

1974 Australia
Sydney: 20 July
Lost 18-22

Charlton (Salford)
Richards (Salford) 1t
Dyl (Leeds) 1t
*Hesketh (Salford)
Bevan, J (Warrington)
Gill, K (Salford)
Nash (Featherstone)
Clawson (Oldham)
Gray (Wigan) 6g
Thompson, J (Featherstone)
Dixon, C (Salford)
Chisnall, E (St. Helens)
Nicholls (St. Helens)
Sub: Millward (Hull KR)
     Rose, P (Hull KR)

1974 New Zealand
Auckland: 27 July
Lost 8-13

Charlton (Salford)
Redfearn, D (Bradford)
Dyl (Leeds)
*Hesketh (Salford)
Bevan, J (Warrington) 1t
Gill, K (Salford)
Nash (Featherstone) 1t
Clawson (Oldham) 1g
Gray (Wigan)
Thompson, J (Featherstone)
Dixon, C (Salford)
Norton (Castleford)
Nicholls (St. Helens)
Sub: Ashcroft (Warrington)

1974 New Zealand
Christchurch: 4 Aug
Won 17-8

Charlton (Salford)
Redfearn, D (Bradford) 1t
Dyl (Leeds) 1t
Dixon, C (Salford)
Richards (Salford)
*Hesketh (Salford) 1t
Nash (Featherstone)
Mills (Widnes)
Gray (Wigan) 4g
Thompson, J (Featherstone)
Chisnall, E (St. Helens)
Norton (Castleford)
Nicholls (St. Helens)
Sub: Bates, A (Dewsbury)

1974 New Zealand
Auckland: 10 Aug
Won 20-0

Charlton (Salford)
Redfearn, D (Bradford)
Willicombe (Wigan)
Dyl (Leeds) 1t
Bevan, J (Warrington) 2t
*Hesketh (Salford) 1t
Nash (Featherstone)
Clawson (Oldham)
Gray (Wigan) 4g
Thompson, J (Featherstone)
Chisnall, E (St. Helens)
Dixon, C (Salford)
Nicholls (St. Helens)
Sub: Bates, A (Dewsbury)
     Ramsey (Bradford)

1977 France (WC)
Auckland: 5 June
Won 23-4

Fairbairn (Wigan) 7g
Fielding (Salford)
Holmes (Leeds)
Dyl (Leeds) 1t
Wright, S (Widnes) 1t
*Millward (Hull KR) 1t
Nash (Salford)
Thompson, J (Featherstone)
Ward, D (Leeds)
Pitchford, S (Leeds)
Bowman, E (Workington)
Nicholls (St. Helens)
Hogan (Barrow)
Sub: Gill, K (Salford)
     Casey (Hull KR)

1977 New Zealand (WC)
Christchurch: 12 June
Won 30-12
Fairbairn (Wigan) 6g
Wright, S (Widnes) 2t
Holmes (Leeds)
Dyl (Leeds)
Francis, W (Wigan)
*Millward (Hull KR) 1t
Nash (Salford)
Thompson, J (Featherstone)
Ward, D (Leeds)
Pitchford, S (Leeds)
Bowman, E (Workington) 1t
Nicholls (St. Helens) 1t
Hogan (Barrow) 1t
Sub: Casey (Hull KR)

1977 Australia (WC)
Brisbane: 18 June
Lost 5-19
Fairbairn (Wigan) 1g
Wright, S (Widnes)
Francis, W (Wigan)
Dyl (Leeds)
Fielding (Salford)
*Millward (Hull KR) 1t
Nash (Salford)
Thompson, J (Featherstone)
Ward, D (Leeds)
Pitchford, S (Leeds)
Bowman, E (Workington)
Nicholls (St. Helens)
Hogan (Barrow)
Sub: Holmes (Leeds)
     Smith, P (Featherstone)

1977 Australia (WC)
Sydney: 25 June
Lost 12-13
Fairbairn (Wigan) 3g
Wright, S (Widnes)
Holmes (Leeds)
Dyl (Leeds)
Francis, W (Wigan)
*Millward (Hull KR)
Nash (Salford)
Thompson, J (Featherstone)
Elwell (Widnes)
Pitchford, S (Leeds) 1t
Bowman, E (Workington)
Casey (Hull KR)
Hogan (Barrow)
Sub: Gill, K (Salford) 1t
     Smith, P (Featherstone)

1978 Australia
Wigan: 21 Oct
Lost 9-15
Fairbairn (Wigan) 3g
Wright, S (Widnes)
Hughes (Widnes)
Cunningham (St. Helens)
Bevan, J (Warrington) 1t
*Millward (Hull KR)
Nash (Salford)
Thompson, J (Bradford)
Ward, D (Leeds)
Rose, P (Hull KR)
Nicholls (St. Helens)
Casey (Hull KR)
Norton (Hull)
Sub: Holmes (Leeds)
     Hogan (Barrow)

1978 Australia
Bradford: 5 Nov
Won 18-14
Fairbairn (Wigan) 6g
Wright, S (Widnes) 2t
Joyner (Castleford)
Dyl (Leeds)
Atkinson, J (Leeds)
*Millward (Hull KR)
Nash (Salford)
Mills (Widnes)
Fisher (Bradford)
Lockwood (Hull KR)
Nicholls (St. Helens)
Lowe, P (Hull KR)
Norton (Hull)
Sub: Holmes (Leeds)
     Rose, P (Hull KR)

1978 Australia
Leeds: 18 Nov
Lost 6-23
Fairbairn (Wigan)
Wright, S (Widnes)
Joyner (Castleford)
Bevan, J (Warrington) 1t
Atkinson, J (Leeds)
*Millward (Hull KR) 1t
Nash (Salford)
Mills (Widnes)
Fisher (Bradford)
Farrar (Hull)
Nicholls (St. Helens)
Lowe, P (Hull KR)
Norton (Hull)
Sub: Holmes (Leeds)
     Rose, P (Hull KR)

1979 Australia
Brisbane: 16 June
Lost 0-35
Woods, J (Leigh)
Barends (Bradford)
Joyner (Castleford)
Hughes (Widnes)
Mathias (St. Helens)
Holmes (Leeds)
Stephens (Castleford)
Mills (Widnes)
Ward, D (Leeds)
Skerrett (Wakefield)
Nicholls (St. Helens)
*Laughton (Widnes)
Norton (Hull)
Sub: Evans, S (Featherstone)
     Hogan (Hull KR)

1979 Australia
Sydney: 30 June
Lost 16-24
Fairbairn (Wigan)
Barends (Bradford)
Joyner (Castleford) 1t
Woods, J (Leigh) 5g
Hughes (Widnes) 1t
Holmes (Leeds)
Stephens (Castleford)
*Nicholls (St. Helens)
Ward, D (Leeds)
Skerrett (Wakefield)
Casey (Bradford)
Grayshon (Bradford)
Adams, M (Widnes)
Sub: Evans, S (Featherstone)
     Watkinson (Hull KR)

1979 Australia
Sydney: 14 July
Lost 2-28
Fairbairn (Wigan) 1g
Evans, S (Featherstone)
Joyner (Castleford)
Woods, J (Leigh)
Hughes (Widnes)
Topliss (Wakefield)
Redfearn, A (Bradford)
*Nicholls (St. Helens)
Ward, D (Leeds)
Casey (Bradford)
Hogan (Hull KR)
Grayshon (Bradford)
Norton (Hull)
Sub: Holmes (Leeds)
     Adams, M (Widnes)

301

1979 New Zealand
Auckland: 21 July
Won 16-8
Fairbairn (Wigan) 1t,2g
Evans, S (Featherstone) 1t
Joyner (Castleford)
Smith, M (Hull KR) 1t
Hughes (Widnes) 1t
Holmes (Leeds)
Stephens (Castleford)
Casey (Bradford)
Ward, D (Leeds)
*Nicholls (St. Helens)
Hogan (Hull KR)
Grayshon (Bradford)
Adams, M (Widnes)
Sub: Lockwood (Hull KR)

1980 New Zealand
Wigan: 18 Oct
Drew 14-14
*Fairbairn (Wigan) 4g
Camilleri (Barrow) 1t
Joyner (Castleford)
Smith, M (Hull KR) 1t
Bentley (Widnes)
Hartley, S (Hull KR)
Dick (Leeds)
Holdstock (Hull KR)
Watkinson (Hull KR)
Skerrett (Hull)
Gorley, L (Widnes)
Grayshon (Bradford)
Casey (Hull KR)
Sub: Pinner (St. Helens)

1981 France
Hull: 6 Dec
Won 37-0
Fairbairn (Hull KR) 1g
Drummond (Leigh) 2t
Smith, M (Hull KR)
Woods, J (Leigh) 1t, 7g
Gill (Wigan) 3t
Hartley (Hull KR) 1t
Gregory (Widnes)
Grayshon (Bradford)
*Ward, D (Leeds)
Skerrett (Hull)
Gorley, L (Widnes)
Gorley, P (St. Helens)
Norton (Hull)
Sub: Burke (Widnes)
　　Szymala (Barrow)

1979 New Zealand
Christchurch: 5 Aug
Won 22-7
Fairbairn (Wigan) 5g
Evans, S (Featherstone) 1t
Joyner (Castleford)
Smith, M (Hull KR)
Hughes (Widnes) 1t
Holmes (Leeds)
Stephens (Castleford)
*Nicholls (St. Helens)
Ward, D (Leeds)
Skerrett (Wakefield)
Casey (Bradford) 1t
Grayshon (Bradford) 1t
Adams, M (Widnes)

1980 New Zealand
Bradford: 2 Nov
Lost 8-12
*Fairbairn (Wigan) 4g
Drummond (Leigh)
Joyner (Castleford)
Smith, M (Hull KR)
Camilleri (Barrow)
Kelly (Warrington)
Dick (Leeds)
Holdstock (Hull KR)
Elwell (Widnes)
Shaw, G (Widnes)
Casey (Hull KR)
Grayshon (Bradford)
Pinner (St. Helens)
Sub: Evans, S (Featherstone)
　　Gorley, L (Widnes)

1981 France
Marseilles: 20 Dec
Lost 2-19
Burke (Widnes)
Drummond (Leigh)
Smith, M (Hull KR)
Woods, J (Leigh) 1g
Gill (Wigan)
Hartley (Hull KR)
Gregory (Widnes)
*Grayshon (Bradford)
Watkinson (Hull KR)
Skerrett (Hull)
Gorley, L (Widnes)
Szymala (Barrow)
Norton (Hull)
Sub: Gorley, P (St. Helens)

1979 New Zealand
Auckland: 11 Aug
Lost 11-18
Fairbairn (Wigan) 1g
Evans, S (Featherstone)
Joyner (Castleford)
Smith, M (Hull KR) 1t
Hughes (Widnes) 1t
Holmes (Leeds)
Stephens (Castleford) 1t
Skerrett (Wakefield)
Ward, D (Leeds)
*Nicholls (St. Helens)
Casey (Bradford)
Grayshon (Bradford)
Adams, M (Widnes)
Sub: Woods, J (Leigh)
　　Hogan (Hull KR)

1980 New Zealand
Leeds: 15 Nov
Won 10-2
Burke (Widnes) 2g
Drummond (Leigh) 2t
Joyner (Castleford)
Evans, S (Featherstone)
Atkinson, J (Leeds)
Woods, J (Leigh)
Walker (Whitehaven)
Skerrett (Hull)
Elwell (Widnes)
*Casey (Hull KR)
Gorley, P (St. Helens)
Adams, M (Widnes)
Norton (Hull)

1982 Australia
Hull City FC: 30 Oct
Lost 4-40
Fairbairn (Hull KR)
Drummond (Leigh)
Hughes (Widnes)
Dyl (Leeds)
Evans, S (Hull)
Woods, J (Leigh)
*Nash (Salford)
Grayshon (Bradford)
Ward, D (Leeds)
Skerrett (Hull)
Gorley, L (Widnes)
Crooks, L (Hull) 2g
Norton (Hull)
Sub: D. Heron (Leeds)

1982 Australia

Wigan: 20 Nov

Lost 6-27

Mumby (Bradford) 3g
Drummond (Leigh)
Smith, M (Hull KR)
Stephenson, D (Wigan)
Gill (Wigan)
Holmes (Leeds)
Kelly, K (Warrington)
*Grayshon (Bradford)
Dalgreen (Fulham)
Skerrett (Hull)
Eccles (Warrington)
Burton (Hull KR)
Heron, D (Leeds)
Sub: Woods, J (Leigh)
    Rathbone (Bradford)

1983 France

Hull: 6 March

Won 17-5

Mumby (Bradford) 4g
Drummond (Leigh)
Joyner (Castleford)
Duane, R (Warrington) 1t
Lydon (Widnes)
Myler, A (Widnes)
Gregory (Widnes) 1t
O'Neill, M (Widnes)
Noble (Bradford)
Goodway (Oldham)
*Casey (Hull KR)
Rathbone (Bradford)
Flanagan (Oldham)
Sub: Smith, P (Featherstone) 1t

1984 Australia

Sydney: 9 June

Lost 8-25

Burke (Widnes) 2g
Drummond (Leigh)
Schofield (Hull) 1t
Mumby (Bradford)
Hanley (Bradford)
Foy, D (Oldham)
Holding (St. Helens)
Crooks, L (Hull)
*Noble (Bradford)
Goodway (Oldham)
Burton (Hull KR)
Worrall, M (Oldham)
Adams (Widnes)
Sub: Lydon (Widnes)
    Hobbs, D (Featherstone)

1982 Australia

Leeds: 28 Nov

Lost 8-32

Fairbairn (Hull KR)
Drummond (Leigh)
Stephenson, D. (Wigan)
Smith, M (Hull KR)
Evans (Hull) 1t
*Topliss (Hull)
Gregory (Widnes)
O'Neill, M (Widnes)
Noble (Bradford)
Rose (Hull)
Smith, P (Featherstone)
Crooks, L (Hull) 2g, 1dg
Crane (Hull)
Sub: Courtney (Warrington)

1984 France

Avignon: 29 Jan

Won 12-0

*Mumby (Bradford)
Drummond (Leigh)
Duane, R (Warrington)
Foy, D (Oldham) 1t
Clark (Hull KR)
Lydon (Widnes)
Cairns (Barrow)
Rayne, Keith (Leeds)
Watkinson (Hull KR)
Goodway (Oldham) 1t
Worrall, M (Oldham)
Hobbs, D (Featherstone)
Hall (Hull KR)
Sub: Hanley (Bradford)
    Crooks, L (Hull) 2g

1984 Australia

Brisbane: 26 June

Lost 6-18

Burke (Widnes) 1g
Drummond (Leigh)
Schofield (Hull) 1t
Mumby (Bradford)
Hanley (Bradford)
Myler, A (Widnes)
Holding (St. Helens)
Rayne, Keith (Leeds)
*Noble (Bradford)
Crooks, L (Hull)
Burton (Hull KR)
Worrall (Oldham)
Sub: Gregory (Widnes)
    Adams (Widnes)

1983 France

Carcassonne: 20 Feb

Won 20-5

Burke (Widnes) 1g
Drummond (Leigh)
Joyner (Castleford) 1t
Duane, R (Warrington)
Lydon (Widnes) 1t, 3g
Myler, A (Widnes)
Gregory (Widnes)
O'Neill, M (Widnes)
Noble (Bradford) 1t
Goodway (Oldham) 1t
*Casey (Hull KR)
Rathbone (Bradford)
Flanagan (Oldham)
Sub: Woods, J (Leigh)
    Smith, P (Featherstone)

1984 France

Leeds: 17 Feb

Won 10-0

Mumby (Bradford)
Clark (Hull KR)
Joyner (Castleford)
Schofield (Hull)
Basnett (Widnes)
Hanley (Bradford)
Cairns (Barrow)
Rayne, Keith (Leeds)
*Noble (Bradford)
Ward, K (Castleford)
Jasiewicz (Bradford)
Hobbs, D (Featherstone) 5g
Hall (Hull KR)
Sub: Smith, M (Hull KR)
    Smith, P (Featherstone)

1984 Australia

Sydney: 7 July

Lost 7-20

Burke (Widnes) 1g
Drummond (Leigh)
Schofield (Hull)
Mumby (Bradford)
Hanley (Bradford) 1t
Myler, A (Widnes)
Holding (St. Helens) 1dg
Hobbs, D (Featherstone)
*Noble (Bradford)
Case (Wigan)
Burton (Hull KR)
Goodway (Oldham)
Adams (Widnes)

303

1984 New Zealand
Auckland: 14 July
Lost 0-12
Burke (Widnes)
Drummond (Leigh)
Schofield (Hull)
Mumby (Bradford)
Hanley (Bradford)
Smith, M (Hull KR)
Holding (St. Helens)
Hobbs, D (Featherstone)
*Noble (Bradford)
Case (Wigan)
Burton (Hull KR)
Goodway (Oldham)
Adams (Widnes)

1984 New Zealand
Christchurch: 22 July
Lost 12-28
Burke (Widnes) 2g
Drummond (Leigh)
Hanley (Bradford) 1t
Mumby (Bradford)
Lydon (Widnes)
Myler, A (Widnes) 1t
Gregory (Widnes)
Hobbs, D (Featherstone)
*Noble (Bradford)
Case (Wigan)
Burton (Hull KR)
Goodway (Oldham)
Adams (Widnes)
Sub: Joyner (Castleford)
    Beardmore, K (Castleford)

1984 New Zealand
Auckland: 28 July
Lost 16-32
Burke (Widnes) 4g
Drummond (Leigh)
Hanley (Bradford) 1t
Mumby (Bradford) 1t
Lydon (Widnes)
Myler, A (Widnes)
Gregory (Widnes)
Hobbs, D (Featherstone)
*Noble (Bradford)
Case (Wigan)
Adams (Widnes)
Goodway (Oldham)
Flanagan (Oldham)
Sub: Donlan (Leigh)
    Joyner (Castleford)

1984 Papua New Guinea
Mount Hagen: 5 Aug
Won 38-20
Burke (Widnes) 1t, 5g
Drummond (Leigh) 2t
Hanley (Bradford) 1t
Mumby (Bradford) 1t
Lydon (Widnes)
Myler, A (Widnes)
Gregory (Widnes)
Rayne, Keith (Leeds) 1t
*Noble (Bradford)
Goodway (Oldham)
Flanagan (Oldham)
Hobbs, D (Featherstone) 1t
Adams (Widnes)
Sub: Donlan (Leigh)
    Proctor (Hull)

1985 France
Leeds: 1 March
Won 50-4
Edwards (Wigan)
Ledger (St. Helens)
Creasser (Leeds) 8g
Gribbin (Whitehaven) 1t
Gill (Wigan) 1t
Hanley (Bradford) 2t
Fox (Featherstone) 2t, 1g
Dickinson (Leeds)
Watkinson (Hull KR) 1t
Dannatt (Hull)
*Goodway (Oldham)
Rathbone (Bradford)
Divorty (Hull) 1t
Sub: Gibson (Batley)
    Platt (St. Helens)

1985 France
Perpignan: 17 March
Lost 16-24
Johnson, C (Leigh)
Clark (Hull KR)
Creasser (Leeds) 1g
Foy, D (Oldham) 1t
Ford, P (Wigan) 2t
*Hanley (Bradford)
Fox (Featherstone)
Dickinson (Leeds)
Kiss (Wigan)
Wane (Wigan)
Dannatt (Hull)
Rathbone (Bradford)
Divorty (Hull) 1g
Sub: Harkin (Hull KR)
    Powell (Leeds)

1985 New Zealand
Leeds: 19 Oct
Lost 22-24
Burke (Widnes) 3g
Drummond (Leigh)
Schofield (Hull)
Hanley (Wigan) 1t
Lydon (Widnes) 1t,2g
Myler, A (Widnes)
Fox (Featherstone)
Crooks, L (Hull)
Watkinson (Hull KR)
Fieldhouse (Widnes)
Goodway (Wigan) 1t
Potter (Wigan)
*Pinner (St. Helens)
Sub: Arkwright (St. Helens)

1985 New Zealand
Wigan: 2 Nov
Won 25-8
Burke (Widnes)
Drummond (Leigh)
Schofield (Hull) 4t
Hanley (Wigan)
Lydon (Widnes) 4g
Myler, A (Widnes)
Fox (Featherstone)
Grayshon (Leeds)
Watkinson (Hull KR)
Fieldhouse (Widnes)
Goodway (Wigan)
Potter (Wigan)
*Pinner (St. Helens) 1dg
Sub: Edwards (Wigan)
    Burton (Hull KR)

1985 New Zealand (Also WC)
Elland Rd, Leeds: 9 Nov
Drew 6-6
Burke (Widnes)
Drummond (Leigh)
Schofield (Hull)
Edwards (Wigan)
Lydon (Widnes)
Hanley (Wigan)
Fox (Featherstone)
Grayshon (Leeds)
Watkinson (Hull KR)
Fieldhouse (Widnes)
Goodway (Wigan)
Potter (Wigan)
*Pinner (St. Helens)
Sub: Arkwright (St. Helens)
Sub: Crooks, L (Hull) 3g

1986 France (Also WC)
Avignon: 16 Feb
Drew 10-10
Burke (Widnes)
Drummond (Leigh)
Schofield (Hull)
Hanley (Wigan) 1t
Gill (Wigan)
Myler, A (Widnes)
Fox (Featherstone)
Crooks, L (Hull) 3g
Watkinson (Hull KR)
Wane (Wigan)
Potter (Wigan)
Fieldhouse (Widnes)
*Pinner (St. Helens)
Sub: Platt (St. Helens)

1986 France
Wigan: 1 Mar
Won 24-10
Lydon (Wigan)
Drummond (Leigh) 1t
Schofield (Hull) 1t,2g
Marchant (Castleford) 1t
Laws (Hull KR)
Myler, A (Widnes)
Fox (Featherstone)
Crooks, L (Hull) 2g
*Watkinson (Hull KR)
Fieldhouse (Widnes)
Rayne, Kevin (Leeds)
James (Halifax) 1t
Potter (Wigan)
Sub: Platt (St. Helens)

1986 Australia
Manch. U. FC: 25 Oct
Lost 16-38
Lydon (Wigan) 1t
Marchant (Castleford)
Schofield (Hull) 2t
Hanley (Wigan)
Gill (Wigan) 1g
Myler, A (Widnes)
Fox (Featherstone)
Ward (Castleford)
*Watkinson (Hull KR)
Fieldhouse (Widnes)
Crooks, L (Hull) 1g
Potter (Wigan)
Goodway (Wigan)

1986 Australia
Elland Rd, Leeds: 8 Nov
Lost 4-34
Lydon (Wigan)
Ledger (St. Helens)
Schofield (Hull) 1t
Marchant (Castleford)
Gill (Wigan)
Myler, A (Widnes)
Fox (Featherstone)
Ward (Castleford)
*Watkinson (Hull KR)
Fieldhouse (St. Helens)
Crooks, L (Hull)
Potter (Wigan)
Goodway (Wigan)
Sub: Edwards (Wigan)
      Platt (St. Helens)

1986 Australia (Also WC)
Wigan: 22 Nov
Lost 15-24
Lydon (Wigan) 2g
Gill (Wigan) 1g
Schofield (Hull) 2t, 1dg
Stephenson (Wigan)
Basnett (Widnes)
Myler, A (Widnes)
Gregory, A (Warrington)
Ward (Castleford)
*Watkinson (Hull KR)
Crooks, L (Hull)
Burton (Hull KR)
Goodway (Wigan)
Pinner (Widnes)
Sub: Potter (Wigan)

1987 France (Also WC)
Leeds: 24 Jan
Won 52-4
Lydon (Wigan) 1t, 8g
Forster (Warrington) 1t
Schofield (Hull)
Stephenson (Wigan)
Gill (Wigan)
*Hanley (Wigan) 2t
Edwards (Wigan) 2t
Hobbs (Oldham)
Beardmore, K (Castleford)
Crooks, L (Hull)
Goodway (Wigan) 1t
Haggerty (St. Helens)
Gregory, M (Warrington) 2t
Sub: Creasser (Leeds)
      England (Castleford)

1987 France
Carcassonne: 8 Feb
Won 20-10
Lydon (Wigan) 4g
Forster (Warrington)
Schofield (Hull)
*Hanley (Wigan) 1t
Gill (Wigan) 1t
Edwards (Wigan)
Gregory, A (Wigan)
Hobbs (Oldham)
Beardmore, K (Castleford) 1t
England (Castleford)
Burton (Hull KR)
Haggerty (St. Helens)
Gregory, M (Warrington)
Sub: Dixon (Halifax)

Featherstone Rovers scrum half Deryck Fox, capped nine times between 1985-86.

GREAT BRITAIN RECORDS

Most appearances

46	Mick Sullivan*
31	Billy Boston
29 + 1	Cliff Watson
29	George Nicholls
29	Neil Fox
28 + 1	Roger Millward
28	Alan Prescott
27	Phil Jackson
27	Alex Murphy
26	Eric Ashton
26	John Atkinson
25	Brian McTigue
25	Jim Sullivan
25	Tommy Harris

*Mick Sullivan's record number of appearances include a record run of 36 successive matches. In addition he played in two matches against France before they were given Test status.

Most tries

40, Mick Sullivan, also scoring two against France before they were given Test status.

Most goals and points

93 goals, (14 tries), 228 points, Neil Fox.

Longest Test careers

14 years	—	Gus Risman
1932 to 1946 (17 appearances)		
13 years 9 months	—	Billy Batten
1908 to 1921 (10 appearances)		
13 years 6 months	—	Alex Murphy
1958 to 1971 (27 appearances)		
12 years 9 months	—	Roger Millward
1966 to 1978 (28 + 1 appearances)		
12 years 6 months	—	John Atkinson
1968 to 1980 (26 appearances)		
12 years 6 months	—	Terry Clawson
1962 to 1974 (14 appearances)		

Youngest Test player

Shaun Edwards was 18 years 135 days old when he made his Great Britain Test debut against France at Leeds on 1 March, 1985. Born on 17 October, 1966, he beat the previous record held by Roger Millward (born 16 September, 1947) who was not quite 18 years 6 months old when he made his debut for Britain against France at Wigan on 5 March, 1966. Five months earlier Millward was a non-playing substitute for the second Test against New Zealand.

Oldest Test player

Jeff Grayshon (born 4 March, 1949), was 36 years 8 months when he played in his last Test for Britain, against New Zealand at Elland Road, Leeds, on 9 November, 1985.

Record team changes

The record number of team changes made by the Great Britain selectors is 10. This has happened on three occasions — all against Australia — and in the first two cases resulted in unexpected victories.

In 1929, Britian crashed 31-8 to Australia in the first Test at Hull KR and retained only three players for the second Test at Leeds where they won 9-3.

After their biggest ever defeat of 50-12 in the 1963 second Test at Swinton, Britain dropped nine players and were forced to make another change when Vince Karalius was injured and replaced by Don Fox. Britain stopped Australia making a clean sweep of the series by winning 16-5 at Leeds in the last Test.

Following the 40-4 first Test defeat at Hull City's soccer ground in 1982, the selectors again made 10 changes, not including subsitutes. The changes made little difference this time as Britain went down 27-6 in the second Test at Wigan.

Britain have never fielded the same team for three or more successive Tests.

GREAT BRITAIN REGISTER

The following is a record of the 556 players who have appeared for Great Britain in 241 Test and World Cup matches.

It does not include matches against France before 1957, the year they were given official Test match status.

Figures in brackets are the total of appearances, with the plus sign indicating substitute appearances, e.g. (7+3).

For matches against touring teams, the year given is for the first half of the season.

World Cup matches are in bold letters except when also classified as Test matches. Substitute appearances are in lower case letters.

A - Australia, F - France, NZ - New Zealand, P - Papua New Guinea.

ACKERLEY, A (2) Halifax: 1952 A; 1958 NZ
ADAMS, L (1) Leeds: 1932 A
ADAMS, M (11+2) Widnes: 1979 Aa, NZ3; 1980 NZ; 1984 A2a, NZ3, P
ARKWRIGHT, C (+2) St. Helens: 1985 nz2
ARKWRIGHT, J (6) Warrington: 1936 A2, NZ; 1937 A3
ARMITT, T (8) Swinton: 1933 A; 1936 A2, NZ2; 1937 A3
ASHBY, R (2) Liverpool: 1964 F; Wigan: 1965 F
ASHCROFT, E (11) Wigan: 1947 NZ2; 1950 A3, NZ; 1954 A3, NZ2
ASHCROFT, K (5+1) Leigh: **1968 A**; 1968 F; 1969 F; **1970 F,NZ**; Warrington: 1974 nz
ASHTON, E (26) Wigan: **1957 A,NZ**; 1958 A2,NZ2; 1959 F, A3; 1960 F2; **1960 NZ,A**; 1961 NZ3; 1962 F3,A3; 1963 F,A2
ASHURST, W (3) Wigan: 1971 NZ; 1972 F2
ASKIN, T (6) Featherstone R: 1928 A3,NZ3
ASPINALL, W (1) Warrington: 1966 NZ
ASTON, L (3) St. Helens: 1947 NZ3
ATKINSON, A (11) Castleford: 1929 A3; 1932 A3,NZ3; 1933 A; 1936 A
ATKINSON, J (26) Leeds: **1968 F,NZ**; 1970 A3,NZ3; **1970 A2,F,NZ**; 1971 F2,NZ; 1972 F2; **1972 A2,F,NZ**; 1973 A2; 1978 A2; 1980 NZ
AVERY, A (4) Oldham: 1910 A,NZ; 1911 A2

BACON, J (11) Leeds: 1920 A3,NZ3; 1921 A3; 1924 A; 1926 NZ
BARENDS, D (2) Bradford N: 1979 A2
BARTON, F (1) Wigan: 1951 NZ
BARTON, J. (2) Wigan: 1960 F; 1961 NZ
BASNETT, J. (2) Widnes: 1984 F; 1986 A
BASSETT, A (2) Halifax: 1946 A2
BATES, A (2+2) Dewsbury: 1974 F2,nz2
BATTEN, E (4) Bradford N: 1946 A2,NZ; 1947 NZ
BATTEN, R. (3) Leeds: 1969 F; 1973 A2
BATTEN, W (10) Hunslet: 1907 NZ; 1908 A3; 1910 A2,NZ; 1911 A2; Hull: 1921 A
BAXTER, J (1) Rochdale H: 1907 NZ
BEAMES, J (2) Halifax: 1921 A2

BEARDMORE, K (2+1) Castleford: 1984 nz; 1987 F2:
BELSHAW, W (8) Liverpool S: 1936 A3,NZ2; 1937 A; Warrington: A2
BENNETT, J (7) Rochdale H: 1924 A3,NZ3; Wigan: 1926 NZ
BENTHAM, N (10) Wigan H: 1928 A3,NZ3; Halifax: 1929 A2; Warrington: 1929(cont) A2
BENTHAM, W (2) Broughton R: 1924 NZ2
BENTLEY, K (1) Widnes: 1980 NZ
BENYON, W (5+1) St. Helens: 1971 F2,NZ,nz; 1972 F2
BEVAN, D (1) Wigan: 1952 A
BEVAN, J (6) Warrington: 1974 A2,NZ2; 1978 A2
BEVERLEY, H (6) Hunslet: 1936 A3; 1937 A; Halifax: A2
BIRCH, J (1) Leeds: 1907 NZ
BISHOP, T (15) St. Helens: 1966 A3,NZ2; 1967 A3; 1968 F3; **1968 A,F,NZ**; 1969 F
BLAN, W (3) Wigan: 1951 NZ3
BLINKHORN, T (1) Warrington: 1929 A
BOLTON, D (23) Wigan: 1957 F3; 1958 F,A2; 1959 F,A3; 1960 F2; 1961 NZ3; 1962 F2,A,NZ2; 1963 F,A2
BOSTON, W (31) Wigan: 1954 A2,NZ3; 1955 NZ; 1956 A3; 1957 F5; **1957 F,A**; 1958 F; 1959 A; 1960 F; **1960 A**; 1961 F,NZ3; 1962 F2,A3,NZ; 1963 F
BOTT, C (1) Oldham: 1966 F
BOWDEN, J (3) Huddersfield: 1954 A2,NZ
BOWEN, F (3) St. Helens Rec: 1928 NZ3
BOWERS, J (1) Rochdale H: 1920 NZ
BOWMAN, E (4) Workington T: **1977 F, NZ, A2**
BOWMAN, H (8) Hull: 1924 NZ2; 1926 NZ2; 1928 A2,NZ; 1929 A
BOWMAN, M (3) Huddersfield: 1962 F; 1963 F,A
BOYLEN, F (1) Hull: 1908 A
BRADSHAW, T (6) Wigan: 1947 NZ2; 1950 A3,NZ
BRIDGES, K (3) Featherstone R: 1974 F2,A
BRIGGS, B (1) Huddersfield: 1954 NZ
BROGDEN, S (16) Huddersfield: 1929 A; 1932 A3, NZ3; 1933 A2; Leeds: 1936 A3,NZ2; 1937 A2

BROOKE, I (13) Bradford N: 1966 A3,NZ2;
Wakefield: 1967 A3; 1968 F2; **1968 A,F,NZ**
BROOKS, E (3) Warrington: 1908 A3
BROUGH, A (2) Oldham: 1924 A,NZ
BROUGH, J (5) Leeds: 1928 A2,NZ2; 1936A
BROWN, G (6) Leeds: **1954 F2,NZ,A**; 1955 NZ2
BRYANT, W (4+1) Castleford: 1964 F2; 1966 Aa;
1967 F
BUCKLEY, A (7) Swinton: 1963 A; 1964 F; 1965
NZ; 1966 F,A2,NZ
BURGESS, W (16) Barrow: 1924 A3,NZ3; 1926 NZ3;
1928 A3,NZ2; 1929 A2
BURGESS, W (14) Barrow: 1962 F; 1963 A; 1965 NZ2;
1966 F,A3,NZ2; 1967 F,A; 1968 F; Salford: 1969 F
BURGHAM, O (1) Halifax: 1911 A
BURKE, M (14+1) Widnes: 1980 NZ; 1981 fF; 1983 F;
1984 A3, NZ3, P; 1985 NZ3; 1986 F
BURNELL, A (3) Hunslet: 1951 NZ2; 1954 NZ
BURTON, C (8+1) Hull KR: 1982 A; 1984 A3, NZ2;
1985 nz; 1986 A; 1987 F
BURWELL, A (7+1) Hull KR: 1967 a; 1968 F3; **1968
A,F,NZ**; 1969 F
BUTTERS, F (2) Swinton: 1929 A2

CAIRNS, D (2) Barrow: 1984 F2
CAMILLERI, C (2) Barrow: 1980 NZ2
CARLTON, F (5) St. Helens: 1958 NZ; Wigan:
1962 NZ
CARR, C (7) Barrow: 1924 A2,NZ2; 1926 NZ3
CARTWRIGHT, J (7) Leigh: 1920 A,NZ3; 1921 A3
CASE, B (4) Wigan: 1984 A, NZ3
CASEY, L (12+2) Hull KR: **1977 f,nz,A**; 1978 A;
Bradford N: 1979 A2,NZ3; Hull KR: 1980 NZ3;
1983 F2
CASTLE, F (4) Barrow: 1952 A3; 1954 A
CHALLINOR, J (3) Warrington: 1958 A,NZ; **1960 F**
CHARLTON, P (18+1) Workington T: 1965 NZ;
Salford: **1970 nz**; 1972 F2; **1972 A2,F,NZ**; 1973 A3;
1974 F2,A3,NZ3
CHERRINGTON, N (1) Wigan: 1960 F
CHILCOTT, J (3) Huddersfield: 1914 A3
CHISNALL, D (2) Leigh: 1970 A; **1970 NZ**
CHISNALL, E (4) St. Helens: 1974 A2,NZ2
CLAMPITT, L (3) Broughton R: 1907 NZ; 1911 A;
1914 NZ
CLARK, D (11) Huddersfield: 1911 A2; 1914 A3; 1920
A3,NZ3
CLARK, G (3) Hull KR: 1984 F2; 1985 F
CLARK, M (5) Leeds: 1968 F2; **1968 A,F,NZ**
CLARKE, C (7) Wigan: 1965 NZ; 1966 F,NZ; 1967 F;
1973 A3
CLAWSON, T (14) Featherstone R: 1962 F2; Leeds:
1972 A2,F; Oldham: 1973 A3; 1974 F2,A2,NZ2
CLOSE, D (1) Huddersfield: 1967 F
COLDRICK, A (4) Wigan: 1914 A3,NZ
COLLIER, F (2) Wigan: 1963 A; Widnes: 1964 F
COULMAN, M (2+1) Salford: 1971 f,NZ2

COURTNEY, N (+1) Warrington: 1982 a
COVERDALE, R (4) Hull: **1954 F2,NZ,A**
CRACKNELL, R (2) Huddersfield: 1951 NZ2
CRANE, M (1) Hull: 1982 A
CREASSER, D (2+1) Leeds: 1985 F2; 1987 f
CROOKS, L (11+2) Hull: 1982 A2; 1984 f, A2; 1985
NZ nz; 1986 F2, A3; 1987 F
CROSTON, A (1) Castleford: 1937 A
CROWTHER, H (1) Hunslet: 1929 A
CUNNIFFE, B (1) Castleford: 1937 A
CUNNINGHAM, E (1) St. Helens: 1978 A
CUNLIFFE, J (4) Wigan: 1950 A,NZ; 1951 NZ; 1954 A
CUNLIFFE, W (11) Warrington: 1920 A,NZ2; 1921
A3; 1924 A3,NZ; 1926 NZ
CURRAN, G (6) Salford: 1946 A,NZ; 1947 NZ;
1948 A3
CURZON, E (1) Salford: 1910 A

DAGNALL, R (4) St.Helens: 1961 NZ2; 1964 F;
1965 F
DALGREEN, J (1) Fulham: 1982 A
DANBY, T (3) Salford: 1950 A2,NZ
DANIELS, A (3) Halifax: 1952 A2; 1955 NZ
DANNATT, A (2) Hull: 1985 F2
DARWELL, J (5) Leigh: 1924 A3,NZ2
DAVIES, A (20) Oldham: 1955 NZ; 1956 A3; **1957
F,A**; 1957 F2; 1958 F,A2,NZ2; 1959 F2,A; **1960
NZ,F,A**; 1960 F
DAVIES, B (3) Oldham: 1920 NZ3
DAVIES, J (2) Huddersfield: 1911 A2
DAVIES, W.A (2) Leeds: 1914 A,NZ
DAVIES, W.J (1) Castleford: 1933 A
DAVIES, W.T (1) Halifax: 1911 A
DAVIES, W.T.H (3) Bradford N: 1946 NZ;
1947 NZ2
DAVIES, W (1) Swinton: 1968 F
DAWSON, E (1) York: 1956 A
DICK, K (2) Leeds: 1980 NZ2
DICKENSON, G (1) Warrington: 1908 A
DICKINSON, R (2) Leeds: 1985 F2
DINGSDALE, W (3) Warrington: 1929 A2; 1933 A
DIVORTY, G (2) Hull: 1985 F2
DIXON, C (12+2) Halifax: 1968 F; Salford: 1969 F;
1971 NZ; **1972 F**; 1973 a2; 1974 F2,A3,NZ3
DIXON, M (2) Featherstone R: 1962 F; 1964 F
DIXON, P (+1) Halifax: 1987 f
DOCKAR, A (1) Hull KR: 1947 NZ
DONLAN, S (+2) Leigh: 1984 nz, p
DRAKE, J (1) Hull: 1960 F
DRAKE, W (1) Hull: 1962 F
DRUMMOND, D (22) Leigh: 1980 NZ2; 1981 F2;
1982 A3; 1983 F2; 1984 F, A3, NZ3, P; 1985
NZ3; 1986 F2
DUANE, R (3) Warrington: 1983 F2; 1984 F
DUTTON, R (6) Widnes: 1970 NZ2; **1970 A2,F,NZ**
DYSON, F (1) Huddersfield: 1959 A

DYL, L (11) Leeds: 1974 A2,NZ3; **1977 F,NZ,A2**; 1978 A; 1982 A

ECCLES, P (1) Halifax: 1907 NZ
ECCLES, R (1) Warrington: 1982 A
ECKERSLEY, D (2+2) St.Helens: 1973 Aa; 1974 Aa
EDGAR, B (11) Workington T: 1958 A,NZ; 1961 NZ; 1962 A3,NZ; 1965 NZ; 1966 A3
EDWARDS, A (7) Salford: 1936 A3,NZ2; 1937 A2
EDWARDS, D (3+2) Castleford: 1968 f; 1970 A; 1971 NZ2nz
EDWARDS, S (4+2) Wigan: 1985 F,nzNZ; 1986a; 1987 F2
EGAN, J (14) Wigan: 1946 A3; 1947 NZ3; 1948 A3; 1950 A3,NZ2
ELLABY, A (13) St.Helens: 1928 A3,NZ2; 1929 A2; 1932 A3,NZ2; 1933 A
ELWELL, K (3) Widnes: **1977 A;** 1980 NZ2
ENGLAND, K (1+1) Castleford: 1987 fF
EVANS, B (10) Swinton: 1926 NZ; 1928 NZ; 1929 A; 1932 A2,NZ3; 1933 A2
EVANS, F (4) Swinton: 1924 A2,NZ2
EVANS, J (4) Hunslet: 1951 NZ; 1952 A3
EVANS, J (3) Swinton: 1926 NZ3
EVANS, R (4) Wigan: 1961 NZ2; 1962 F,NZ
EVANS, S (7+3) Featherstone R: 1979 Aa2,NZ3, 1980 NZnz; Hull: 1982 A2
EYRE, K (1) Hunslet: 1965 NZ

FAIRBAIRN, G (17) Wigan: **1977 F,NZ,A2**; 1978 A3; 1979 A2,NZ3; 1980 NZ2; Hull KR: 1981 F; 1982 A2
FAIRCLOUGH, L (6) St.Helens: 1926 NZ; 1928 A2,NZ2; 1929 A
FARRAR, V (1) Hull: 1978 A
FEATHERSTONE, J (6) Warrington: 1948 A; 1950 NZ2; 1952 A3
FEETHAM, J (8) Hull KR: 1929 A; Salford: 1932 A2,NZ2; 1933 A3
FIELD, H (3) York: 1936 A,NZ2
FIELD, N (1) Batley: 1963 A
FIELDHOUSE, J (7) Widnes: 1985 NZ3; 1986 F2, A; St. Helens: 1986 A
FIELDING, K (3) Salford: 1974 F2; **1977 F**
FILDES, A (15) St.Helens Recs: 1926 NZ2; 1928 A3,NZ3; 1929 A3; St.Helens: 1932 A,NZ3
FISHER, A (11) Bradford N: 1970 A2,NZ3; **1970 A;** Leeds: **A;** 1971 F2; Bradford N: 1978 A2
FLANAGAN, P (14) Hull KR: 1962 F; 1963 F; 1966 A3,NZ; 1967 A3; 1968 F2; **1968 F,NZ;** 1970 A
FLANAGAN, T (4) Oldham: 1983 F2; 1984 NZ, P
FOGERTY, T (2+1) Halifax: 1966 nz; Wigan: 1967 F; Rochdale H: 1974 F
FORD, P (1) Wigan: 1985 F
FORSTER, M (2) Warrington: 1987 F2
FOSTER, F (1) Hull KR: 1967 A

FOSTER, P (3) Leigh: 1955 NZ3
FOSTER, T (3) Bradford N: 1946 NZ; 1948 A2
FOX, Deryck (9) Featherstone R: 1985 F2, NZ3; 1986 F2, A2
FOX, Don (1) Featherstone R: 1963 A
.FOX, N (29) Wakefield T: 1959 F,A2; 1960 F3; 1961 NZ2; 1962 F3,A3,NZ2; 1963 A2,F; 1964 F; 1965 F; 1966 F; 1967 F2,A; 1968 F3; 1969 F
FOY, D (3) Oldham: 1984 F, A; 1985 F
FRANCIS, R (1) Barrow: 1947 NZ
FRANCIS, W (4) Wigan: 1967 A; **1977 NZ,A2**
FRASER, E (16) Warrington: 1958 A3,NZ2; 1959 F2,A; 1960 F3; **1960 F,NZ;** 1961 F,NZ2
FRENCH, R (4) Widnes: 1968 F2; **1968 A,NZ**
FRODSHAM, A (3) St.Helens: 1928 NZ2; 1929 A

GABBITAS, B (1) Hunslet: 1959 F
GALLAGHER, F (12) Dewsbury: 1920 A3; 1921 A; Batley: 1924 A3,NZ3; 1926 NZ2
GANLEY, B (3) Oldham: 1957 F2; 1958 F
GARDINER, D (1) Wigan: 1965 NZ
GEE, K (17) Wigan: 1946 A3,NZ; 1947 NZ3; 1948 A3; 1950 A3,NZ2; 1951 NZ2
GEMMELL, R (3) Leeds: 1964 F; Hull: 1968 F; 1969 F
GIBSON, C (+1) Batley: 1985 f
GIFFORD, H (2) Barrow: 1908 A2
GILFEDDER, L (5) Warrington: 1962 A,NZ2,F; 1963 F
GILL, H (10) Wigan: 1981 F2; 1982 A; 1985 F; 1986 F, A3; 1987 F2
GILL, K (5+2) Salford: 1974 F2,A2,NZ; **1977 f,a**
GOODWAY, A (18) Oldham: 1983 F2; 1984 F, A3, NZ3, P; 1985 F; Wigan: 1985 NZ3; 1986 A3; 1987 F
GOODWIN, D (5) Barrow: 1957 F2; 1958 F,NZ2
GORE, J (1) Salford: 1926 NZ
GORLEY, L (4+1) Widnes: 1980 NZnz; 1981 F2; 1982 A
GORLEY, P (2+1) St.Helens: 1980 NZ; 1981 Ff
GOWERS, K (14) Swinton: 1962 F; 1963 F,A3; 1964 F2; 1965 NZ2; 1966 F2,A,NZ2
GRAY, J (5+3) Wigan: 1974 f2,A2a,NZ3
GRAYSHON, J (13) Bradford N: 1979 A2,NZ3; 1980 NZ2; 1981 F2; 1982 A2; Leeds: 1985 NZ2
GREENALL, D (6) St.Helens: 1951 NZ3; 1952 A2; 1954 NZ
GREENALL, J (1) St.Helens Rec: 1921 A
GREENOUGH, R (1) Warrington: **1960 NZ**
GREGORY, A (10+1) Widnes: 1981 F2; 1982 A; 1983 F2; 1984 a, NZ2, P; Warrington: 1986 A; Wigan: 1987 F
GREGORY, M (2) Warrington: 1987 F2
GRIBBIN, V (1) Whitehaven: 1985 F
GRONOW, B (7) Huddersfield: 1911 A2, 1920 A2, NZ3

GRUNDY, J (12) Barrow: 1955 NZ3; 1956 A3; 1957 F3; **1957 F,A,NZ**
GUNNEY, G (11) Hunslet: 1954 NZ3; 1956 A; 1957 F3; **1957 F,NZ**; 1964 F; 1965 F
GWYNNE, T. E (3) Hull: 1928 A,NZ; 1929 A
GWYTHER, E (6) Belle Vue R: 1947 NZ2; 1950 A3; 1951 NZ

HAGGERTY, R (2) St Helens: 1987 F2
HAIGH, R (5+1) Wakefield T: **1968 A,F**; Leeds: **1970 NZ,a**; 1971 F,NZ
HALL, D (2) Hull KR: 1984 F2
HALL, W (4) Oldham: 1914 A3,NZ
HALLAS, D (2) Leeds: 1961 F,NZ
HALMSHAW, A (1) Halifax: 1971 NZ
HALSALL, H (1) Swinton: 1929 A
HANLEY, E (17+1) Bradford N: 1984 fF, A3, NZ3, P; 1985 F2; Wigan: 1985 NZ3; 1986 F, A; 1987 F2
HARDISTY, A (12) Castleford: 1964 F3; 1965 F,NZ; 1966 A3,NZ; 1967 F2; 1970 A
HARE, I (1) Widnes: 1967 F
HARKIN, P (+1) Hull KR: 1985 f
HARRIS, T (25) Hull: 1954 NZ2; 1956 A3; 1957 F5; **1957 F,A**; 1958 A3,NZ,F; 1959 F2,A3; 1960 F2; **1960 NZ**
HARRISON, F (3) Leeds: 1911 A3
HARRISON, M (7) Hull: 1967 F2; 1971 NZ2; 1972 F2; 1973 A
HARTLEY, D (11) Hunslet: 1964 F2; Castleford: 1968 F; 1969 F; 1970 A2,NZ2; **1970 A2,F**
HARTLEY, S (3) Hull KR: 1980 NZ; 1981 F2
HELME, G (12) Warrington: 1948 A3; 1954 A3,NZ2; **1954 F2,A,NZ**
HEPWORTH, K (11) Castleford: 1967 F2; 1970 A3,NZ2; **1970 A2,F,NZ**
HERBERT, N (6) Workington T: 1961 NZ; 1962 F,A3,NZ
HERON, D (1+1) Leeds: 1982 aA
HESKETH, C (21+2) Salford: 1970 NZ; **1970 NZ,a**; 1971 Ff,NZ3; **1972 A2,F,NZ**; 1973 A3; 1974 F2,A3,NZ3
HICKS, M (1) St.Helens: 1965 NZ
HIGGINS, F (6) Widnes: 1950 A3,NZ2; 1951 NZ
HIGGINS, H (2) Widnes: 1937 A2
HIGSON, J (2) Hunslet: 1908 A2
HILL, C (1) Wigan: 1966 F
HILL, D (1) Wigan: 1971 F
HILTON, H (7) Oldham: 1920 A3,NZ3; 1921 A
HILTON, J (4) Wigan: 1950 A2,NZ2
HOBBS, D (9+1) Featherstone R: 1984 F2, Aa, NZ3, P; Oldham: 1987 F2
HODGSON, M (16) Swinton: 1929 A2; 1932 A3,NZ3; 1933 A3; 1936 A3,NZ; 1937 A
HOGAN, P (6+3) Barrow: **1977 F,NZ,A2**; 1978 a; Hull KR: 1979 Aa,NZ,nz
HOGG, A (1) Broughton R: 1907 NZ

HOLDEN, K (1) Warrington: 1963 A
HOLDER, W (1) Hull: 1907 NZ
HOLDING, N (4) St. Helens: 1984 A3, NZ
HOLDSTOCK, R (2) Hull KR: 1980 NZ2
HOLLAND, D (4) Oldham: 1914 A3,NZ
HOLLIDAY, W (9+1) Whitehaven: 1964 F; Hull KR: 1965 F,NZ3; 1966 Ff; 1967 A3
HOLLINDRAKE, T (1) Keighley: 1955 NZ
HOLMES, J (14+6) Leeds: 1971 NZ; 1972 F2; **1972 Aa,NZ**; **1977 F,NZ,Aa**; 1978 a3; 1979 A2a,NZ3; 1982 A
HORNE, W (8) Barrow: 1946 A3; 1947 NZ; 1948 A; 1952 A3
HORTON, W (14) Wakefield T: 1928 A3,NZ3; 1929 A; 1932 A3,NZ; 1933 A3
HOWLEY, T (6) Wigan: 1924 A3,NZ3
HUDDART, R (16) Whitehaven: 1958 A2,NZ2; St.Helens: 1959 A; 1961 NZ3; 1962 F2,A3,NZ2; 1963 A
HUDSON, B (8) Salford: 1932 NZ; 1933 A2; 1936 A,NZ2; 1937 A2
HUDSON, W (1) Wigan: 1948 A
HUGHES, E (8) Widnes: 1978 A; 1979 A3,NZ3; 1982 A
HURCOMBE, D (8) Wigan: 1920 A2,NZ; 1921 A; 1924 A2,NZ2
HYNES, S (12+1) Leeds: 1970 A2,NZ2nz; **1970 A2,F,NZ**; 1971 F; 1973 A3

IRVING, R (8+3) Oldham: 1967 F2,A3; 1970 a,NZ; 1971 NZ; 1972 f; **1972 NZ,a**

JACKSON, K (2) Oldham: 1957 F2
JACKSON, P (27) Barrow: 1954 A3,NZ3; **1954 F2,A,NZ**; 1955 NZ3; 1956 A3; **1957 F,NZ**; 1957 F5; 1958 F,A2,NZ
JAMES, N (1) Halifax: 1986 F
JARMAN, J.W. (2) Leeds: 1914 A2
JASIEWICZ, R (1) Bradford N: 1984 F
JEANES, D (8) Wakefield T: 1971 F,NZ2; 1972 F2; Leeds: **1972 A2,NZ**
JENKINS, B (12) Wigan: 1907 NZ3; 1908 A3; 1910 A,NZ; 1911 A2, 1914 A,NZ
JENKINS, D (1) Hunslet: 1929 A
JENKINS, D (1) Leeds: 1947 A
JENKINS, E (9) Salford: 1933 A; 1936 A3,NZ2; 1937 A3
JENKINSON, A (2) Hunslet: 1911 A2
JOHNSON, A (4) Widnes: 1914 A,NZ; 1920 A2
JOHNSON, A (6) Warrington: 1946 A2,NZ; 1947 NZ3
JOHNSON, C (1) Leigh: 1985 F
JOLLEY, J (3) Runcorn: 1907 NZ3
JONES, B (3) Wakefield T: 1964 F; 1965 F; 1966 F
JONES, B.L (15) Leeds: 1954 A3,NZ3; 1955 NZ3; 1957 F3; **1957 F,A,NZ**
JONES, D (2) Merthyr: 1907 NZ2

JONES, E (4) Rochdale H: 1920 A,NZ3
JONES, J (1) Barrow: 1946 NZ
JONES, K (2) Wigan: **1970 F,NZ**
JONES, L (1) St.Helens: 1971 NZ
JORDAN, G (2) Featherstone R: 1964 F; 1967 A
JOYNER, J (14+2) Castleford: 1978 A2; 1979
    A3,NZ3; 1980 NZ3; 1983 F2; 1984 F, nz2
JUBB, K (2) Leeds: 1937 A2
JUKES, W (6) Hunslet: 1908 A3; 1910 A2,NZ

KARALIUS, A (4+1) St.Helens: 1971 NZ3; 1972 F;
    1972 nz
KARALIUS, V (12) St.Helens: 1958 A2,NZ2; 1959
    F; **1960 NZ,F,A**; 1960 F; 1961 F; Widnes:
    1963 A2
KEEGAN, A (9) Hull: 1966 A2; 1967 F2,A3; 1968 F;
    1969 F
KELLY, K (4) St.Helens: 1972 F2; Warrington: 1980
    NZ; 1982 A
KEMEL, G (2) Widnes: 1965 NZ2
KERSHAW, H (2) Wakefield T: 1910 A,NZ
KINNEAR, R (1) Wigan: 1929 A
KISS, N (1) Wigan: 1985 F
KITCHEN, F (2) Leigh: **1954 A,NZ**
KITCHIN, P (1) Whitehaven: 1965 NZ
KITCHING, J (1) Bradford N: 1946 A
KNAPMAN, E (1) Oldham: 1924 NZ
KNOWELDEN, B (1) Barrow: 1946 NZ

LAUGHTON, D (15) Wigan: 1970 A3,NZ2; **1970
    A2,F,NZ**; 1971 F2; Widnes: 1973 A; 1974 F2;
    1979 A
LAWRENSON, J (3) Wigan: 1948 A3
LAWS, D (1) Hull K.R: 1986 F
LEDGARD, J (11) Dewsbury: 1947 NZ2; Leigh:
    1948 A; 1950 A2,NZ; 1951 NZ; **1954 F2,A,NZ**
LEDGER, B (2) St. Helens: 1985 F; 1986 A
LEWIS, G (1) Leigh: 1965 NZ
LEYTHAM, J (5) Wigan: 1907 NZ2; 1910 A2,NZ
LITTLE, S (10) Oldham: 1956 A; 1957 F5; **1957
    F,A,NZ**; 1958 F
LLEWELLYN, T (2) Oldham: 1907 NZ2
LLOYD, R (1) Halifax: 1920 A
LOCKWOOD, B (8+1) Castleford: **1972 A2,F,NZ**;
    1973 A2; 1974 F; Hull KR: 1978 A; 1979 nz
LOMAS, J (7) Salford: 1908 A2; 1910 A2,NZ;
    Oldham: 1911 A2
LONGSTAFF, F (2) Huddersfield: 1914 A,NZ
LONGWORTH, W (3) Oldham: 1908 A3
LOWE, J (1) Leeds: 1932 NZ
LOWE, P (12) Hull KR: 1970 NZ; 1972 F2; **1972
    A2,F,NZ**; 1973 A3, 1978 A2
LOXTON, K (1) Huddersfield: 1971 NZ
LYDON, J (15+1) Widnes: 1983 F2; 1984 F, a,
    NZ2, P; 1985 NZ3; Wigan: 1986 F, A3; 1987 F2

MANN, A (2) Bradford N: 1908 A2

MANTLE, J (13) St.Helens: 1966 F2,A3; 1967 A2;
    1969 F; 1971 F2,NZ2; 1973 A
MARCHANT, A (3) Castleford: 1986 F, A2
MARTIN, W (1) Workington T: 1962 F
MARTYN, M (2) Leigh: 1958 A; 1959 A
McCORMICK, S (3) Belle Vue R: 1948 A2;
    St.Helens: A
McCUE, T (6) Widnes: 1936 A; 1937 A; 1946 A3,NZ
McINTYRE, L (1) Oldham: 1963 A
McKEATING, V (2) Workington T: 1951 NZ2
McKINNEY, R (11) Salford: 1951 NZ; 1952 A2;
    1954 A3,NZ; Warrington: 1955 NZ3; St.Helens:
    1957 NZ
McTIGUE, B (25) Wigan: 1958 A2,NZ2; 1959 F2,A3;
    1960 F2; **1960 NZ,F,A**; 1961 F,NZ3; 1962
    F,A3,NZ2; 1963 F
MATHIAS, R (1) St.Helens: 1979 A
MEASURES, J (2) Widnes: 1963 A2
MIDDLETON, A (1) Salford: 1929 A
MILLER, J (1) Wigan: 1911 A
MILLER, J (6) Warrington: 1933 A3; 1936 A,NZ2
MILLS, J (6) Widnes: 1974 A2,NZ; 1978 A2; 1979 A
MILLWARD, R (28+1) Castleford: 1966 F; Hull
    KR: 1967 A3; 1968 F2; **1968 A,F,NZ**; 1970
    A2,NZ3; 1971 F,NZ3; 1973 A; 1974 A2a; **1977
    F,NZ,A2**; 1978 A3
MILNES, A (2) Halifax: 1920 A2
MOONEY, W (2) Leigh: 1924 NZ2
MOORHOUSE, S (2) Huddersfield: 1914 A,NZ
MORGAN, A (4) Featherstone R: 1968 F2;
    1968 F,NZ
MORGAN, E (2) Hull: 1921 A2
MORGAN, R (2) Swinton: 1963 F,A
MORLEY, J (2) Wigan: 1936 A; 1937 A
MORTIMER, F (2) Wakefield T: 1956 A2
MOSES, G (9) St.Helens: 1955 NZ2; 1956 A; 1957
    F3; **1957 F,A,NZ**
MUMBY, K (11) Bradford N: 1982 A; 1983 F; 1984
    F2, A3, NZ3, P
MURPHY, A (27) St.Helens: 1958 A3,NZ; 1959
    F2,A; **1960 NZ,F,A**; 1960 F; 1961 F,NZ3; 1962
    F,A3; 1963 A2; 1964 F; 1965 F,NZ; 1966 F2;
    Warrington: 1971 NZ
MURPHY, H (1) Wakefield T: 1950 A
MYLER, A (14) Widnes: 1983 F2; 1984 A2, NZ2, P;
    1985 NZ2; 1986 F2, A3
MYLER, F (23+1) Widnes: **1960 NZ,F,A**; 1960 F;
    1961 F; 1962 F; 1963 A; 1964 F; 1965 F,NZ;
    1966 A,NZnz; 1967 F2; St.Helens: 1970
    A3,NZ3; **1970 A2,F**

NASH, S (24) Featherstone R: 1971 F,NZ; 1972 F2;
    1972 A2,F,NZ; 1973 A2; 1974 A3,NZ3; Salford:
    1977 F,NZ,A2; 1978 A3; 1982 A
NAUGHTON, A (2) Warrington: **1954 F2**
NEWBOULD, H (1) Wakefield T: 1910 A

NICHOLLS, G (29) Widnes: 1971 NZ; 1972 F2; **1972 A2,F,NZ**; St.Helens: 1973 A2; 1974 F2,A3,NZ3; **1977 F,NZ,A**; 1978 A3; 1979 A3,NZ3

NICHOLSON, R (3) Huddersfield: 1946 NZ; 1948 A2

NOBLE, B (11) Bradford N: 1982 A; 1983 F2; 1984 F, A3, NZ3, P

NORTON, S (11+1) Castleford: 1974 a,NZ2; Hull: 1978 A3; 1979 A2; 1980 NZ; 1981 F2; 1982 A

O'GRADY, T (6) Oldham: 1954 A2,NZ3; Warrington: 1961 NZ

OLIVER, J (4) Batley: 1928 A3,NZ

O'NEILL, D (2+1) Widnes: 1971 nz; **1972 A,F**

O'NEILL, M (3) Widnes: 1982 A; 1983 F2

OSTER, J (1) Oldham: 1929 A

OWEN, J (1) St.Helens Recs: 1921 A

OWEN, S (1) Leigh: 1958 F

OWENS, I (4) Leeds: 1946 A3,NZ

PADBURY, R (1) Runcorn: 1908 A

PALIN, H (2) Warrington: 1947 NZ2

PARKER, D (2) Oldham: 1964 F2

PARKIN, J (17) Wakefield T: 1920 A2,NZ3; 1921 A2;1924 A3,NZ; 1926 NZ2; 1928 A,NZ; 1929 A2

PARR, K (1) Warrington: 1968 F

PAWSEY, C (7) Leigh: 1952 A3; 1954 A2,NZ2

PEPPERELL, A (2) Workington T: 1950 NZ; 1951 NZ

PHILLIPS, D (4) Oldham: 1946 A3, Belle Vue R: 1950 A

PIMBLETT, A (3) Warrington: 1948 A3

PINNER, H (6+1) St.Helens: 1980 nzNZ; 1985 NZ3; 1986 F; Widnes: 1986 A

PITCHFORD, F (2) Oldham: 1958 NZ; 1962 F

PITCHFORD, S (4) Leeds: **1977 F,NZ,A2**

PLATT, A (+3) St. Helens: 1985 f; 1986 fa

POLLARD, C (1) Wakefield T: 1924 NZ

POLLARD, E (2) Wakefield T: 1932 A2

POLLARD, R (1) Dewsbury: 1950 NZ

POOLE, H (3) Hull KR: 1964 F; Leeds: 1966 NZ2

POTTER, I (7+1) Wigan: 1985 NZ3; 1986 F2, A2a

POWELL, R (+1) Leeds: 1985 f

POYNTON, H (3) Wakefield T: 1962 A2,NZ

PRESCOTT, A (28) St.Helens: 1951 NZ2; 1952 A3; 1954 A3,NZ3; 1955 NZ3; 1956 A3; 1957 F5; **1957 F,A,NZ**; 1958 F,A2

PRICE, J (6) Broughton R: 1921 A2; Wigan: 1924 A2,NZ2

PRICE, M (2) Rochdale H: 1967 A2

PRICE, R (9) Warrington: 1954 A,NZ2; 1955 NZ; 1956 A3; 1957 F2

PRICE, T (1) Bradford N: 1970 A

PRIOR, B (1) Hunslet: 1966 F

PROCTOR, W (+1) Hull: 1984 p

PROSSER, D (1) Leeds: 1937 A

PROSSER, S (1) Halifax: 1914 A

RAE, J (1) Bradford N: 1965 NZ

RAMSDALE, R (8) Wigan: 1910 A2; 1911 A2; 1914 A3,NZ

RAMSEY, W (7+1) Hunslet: 1965 NZ2; 1966 F,A2,NZ2; Bradford N; 1974 nz

RATCLIFFE, G (3) Wigan: 1947 NZ; 1950 A2

RATHBONE, A (4+1) Bradford N: 1982 a; 1983 F2; 1985 F2

RAYNE, KEITH (4) Leeds: 1984 F2, A, P

RAYNE, KEVIN (1) Leeds: 1986 F

REDFEARN, A (1) Bradford N: 1979 A

REDFEARN, D (6+1) Bradford N: **1972 nz**; 1974 F2,A,NZ3

REES, D (1) Halifax: 1926 NZ

REES, T (1) Oldham: 1929 A

REES, W (11) Swinton: 1926 NZ2; 1928 A3,NZ3; 1929 A3

REILLY, M (9) Castleford: 1970 A3,NZ3; **1970 A2,F**

RENILSON, C (7+1) Halifax: 1965 NZ; 1967 a; 1968 F3; **1968 A,F,NZ**

RHODES, A (4) St.Helens: **1957 NZ; 1960 F,A**; 1961 NZ

RICHARDS, M (2) Salford: 1974 A,NZ

RILEY, J (1) Halifax: 1910 A

RING, J (2) Wigan: 1924 A; 1926 NZ

RISMAN, A (17) Salford: 1932 A,NZ3; 1933 A3; 1936 A2,NZ2; 1937 A3; 1946 A3

RISMAN, B (5) Leeds: 1968 F2; **1968 A,F,NZ**

RIX, S (9) Oldham: 1924 A3,NZ3; 1926 NZ3

ROBERTS, K (10) Halifax: 1963 A; 1964 F2; 1965 F,NZ3; 1966 F,NZ2

ROBINSON, A (3) Halifax: 1907 NZ; 1908 A2

ROBINSON, Dave (13) Swinton: 1965 NZ; 1966 F2,A3,NZ2; 1967 F2,A2; Wigan: 1970 A

ROBINSON, Don (10) Wakefield T: **1954 F2,NZ,A**; 1955 NZ; Leeds: 1956 A2; 1959 A2; 1960 F

ROBINSON, J (2) Rochdale H: 1914 A2

ROBINSON, W (2) Leigh: 1963 F,A

ROGERS, J (7) Huddersfield: 1914 A; 1920 A3; 1921 A3

ROSE, D (4) Leeds: **1954 F2,A,NZ**

ROSE, P (2+3) Hull KR: 1974 a; 1978 Aa2; Hull: 1982 A

ROUND, G (8) Wakefield T: 1959 A; 1962 F2,A3,NZ2

RUDDICK, J (3) Broughton R: 1907 NZ2; 1910 A

RYAN, M (4) Wigan: 1947 NZ; 1948 A2; 1950 A

RYAN, R (5) Warrington: 1950 A,NZ2; 1951 NZ; 1952 A

RYDER, R (1) Warrington: 1952 A

SAYER, W (7) Wigan: 1961 NZ; 1962 F,A3,NZ; 1963 A
SCHOFIELD, D (1) Halifax: 1955 NZ
SCHOFIELD, G (15) Hull: 1984 F, A3, NZ; 1985 NZ3; 1986 F2, A3; 1987 F2
SEABOURNE, B (1) Leeds: 1970 NZ
SENIOR, K (2) Huddersfield: 1965 NZ; 1967 F
SHARROCK, J (4) Wigan: 1910 A2,NZ; 1911 A
SHAW, B (6) Hunslet: 1956 A2; **1960 F,A**; 1960 F; Leeds: 1961 F
SHAW, G (1) Widnes: 1980 NZ
SHAW, J (5) Halifax: **1960 F,A**; 1960 F; 1961 F; 1962 NZ
SHELTON, G (7) Hunslet: 1964 F2; 1965 NZ3; 1966 F2
SHOEBOTTOM, M (10+2) Leeds: **1968 A,nz**; 1969 F; 1970 A2a,NZ; **1970 A2,F,NZ**; 1971 F
SHUGARS, F (1) Warrington: 1910 NZ
SILCOCK, N (12) Widnes: 1932 A2,NZ2; 1933 A3; 1936 A3; 1937 A2
SILCOCK, N (3) Wigan: 1954 A3
SILCOCK, R (1) Wigan: 1908 A
SIMMS, B (1) Leeds: 1962 F
SKELHORNE, G (7) Warrington: 1920 A,NZ3; 1921 A3
SKERRETT, T (10) Wakefield T: 1979 A2,NZ2; Hull: 1980 NZ2; 1981 F2; 1982 A2
SLOMAN, R (5) Oldham: 1928 A3,NZ2
SMALES, T (8) Huddersfield: 1962 F; 1963 F,A; 1964 F2; Bradford N: 1965 NZ3
SMALL, P (1) Castleford: 1962 NZ
SMITH, A (6) Oldham: 1907 NZ3; 1908 A3
SMITH, A (10) Leeds: 1970 A2,NZ3; **1970 A2**; 1971 F2; 1973 A
SMITH, F (9) Hunslet: 1910 A,NZ; 1911 A3; 1914 A3,NZ
SMITH, G (3) York: 1963 A; 1964 F2
SMITH, H (2) Bradford N: 1926 NZ2
SMITH, M (10+1) Hull KR: 1979 NZ3; 1980 NZ2; 1981 F2; 1982 A2; 1984 f,NZ
SMITH, P (1+5) Featherstone R: **1977 a2;**1982 A; 1983 f2; 1984 f
SMITH, S (11) Wakefield T: 1929 A; Leeds: A2; 1932 A3,NZ3; 1933 A2
SMITH, S (4) Hunslet: **1954 A,NZ,F2**
SOUTHWARD, I (11) Workington T: 1958 A3,NZ; Oldham: 1959 F2,A2; 1960 F2; 1962 NZ
SPENCER, J (1) Salford: 1907 NZ
STACEY, J.C (1) Halifax: 1920 NZ
STEPHENS, G (5) Castleford: 1979 A2,NZ3
STEPHENSON, D (4) Wigan: 1982 A2; 1986 A; 1987 F
STEPHENSON, M (5+1) Dewsbury: 1971 nz; 1972 F; **1972 A2.F.NZ**
STEVENSON, J (19) Leeds: 1955 NZ3; 1956 A3; 1957 F5; **1957 F,A,NZ**; 1958 F; York: 1959 A2; 1960 F2

STOCKWELL, S (3) Leeds: 1920 A; 1921 A2
STONE, W (8) Hull: 1920 A3,NZ3; 1921 A2
STOPFORD, J (12) Swinton: 1961 F; 1963 F,A2; 1964 F2; 1965 F,NZ2; 1966 F2,A
STOTT, J (1) St.Helens: 1947 NZ
STREET, H (4) Dewsbury: 1950 A3,NZ
SULLIVAN, C (17) Hull: 1967 F; **1968 A,F,NZ**; 1970 A; 1971 NZ3; 1972 F2; **1972 A2,F,NZ**; 1973 A3
SULLIVAN, J (25) Wigan: 1924 A3,NZ; 1926 NZ3; 1928 A3,NZ3; 1929 A3; 1932 A3,NZ3; 1933 A3
SULLIVAN, M (46) Huddersfield: **1954 F2,NZ,A**; 1955 NZ3; 1956 A3; 1957 F3; **1957 F,A,NZ**; Wigan: 1957 F2; 1958 F,A3,NZ2; 1959 F2,A3; 1960 F3; **1960 F,NZ,A**; St.Helens: 1961 F,NZ2; 1962 F3,A3,NZ; York: 1963 A
SZYMALA, E (1+1) Barrow: 1981 fF

TAYLOR, H (3) Hull: 1907 NZ3
TAYLOR, R (2) Hull: 1921 A; 1926 NZ
TEMBEY, J (2) St.Helens: 1963 A; 1964 F
TERRY, A (11) St.Helens: 1958 A2; 1959 F2,A3; 1960 F; 1961 F,NZ; Leeds: 1962 F
THOMAS, A (4) Leeds: 1926 NZ2; 1929 A2
THOMAS, G (1) Warrington: 1907 NZ
THOMAS, G (9) Wigan: 1914 A; Huddersfield: 1920 A3,NZ2; 1921 A3
THOMAS, J (8) Wigan: 1907 NZ; 1908 A3; 1910 A2,NZ; 1911 A
THOMAS, L (1) Oldham: 1947 NZ
THOMAS, P (1) Leeds: 1907 NZ
THOMPSON, C (2) Hunslet: 1951 NZ2
THOMPSON, J (12) Leeds: 1924 A,NZ2; 1928 A,NZ; 1929 A; 1932 A3,NZ3
THOMPSON, J (20+1) Featherstone R: 1970 A2,NZ2; **1970 A2,F,NZ**; 1971 Ff; 1974 A3,NZ3; **1977 F,NZ,A2**; Bradford N: 1978 A
THORLEY, J (4) Halifax: **1954 F2,NZ,A**
TOOHEY, E (3) Barrow: 1952 A3
TOPLISS, D (4) Wakefield T: 1973 A2; 1979 A; Hull: 1982 A
TRAILL, K (8) Bradford N: 1950 NZ2; 1951 NZ; 1952 A3; 1954 A,NZ
TROUP, L A (2) Barrow: 1936 NZ2
TURNBULL, A (1) Leeds: 1951 NZ
TURNER, D (24) Oldham: 1956 A2; 1957 F5; **1957 F,A,NZ**; 1958 F; Wakefield: 1959 A; 1960 F3; **1960 NZ,A**; 1961 F,NZ; 1962 A2,NZ2,F
TYSON, B (3) Hull KR: 1963 A; 1965 F; 1967 F
TYSON, G (4) Oldham: 1907 NZ; 1908 A3

VALENTINE, D (15) Huddersfield: 1948 A3; 1951 NZ; 1952 A2; 1954 A3,NZ2; **1954 F2,NZ,A**
VALENTINE, R (1) Huddersfield: 1967 A
VINES, D (3) Wakefield T: 1959 F2,A

WAGSTAFF, H (12) Huddersfield: 1911 A2; 1914 A3,NZ; 1920 A2,NZ2; 1921 A2

WALKER, A (1) Whitehaven: 1980 NZ

WALLACE, J (1) St.Helens Recs: 1926 NZ

WALSH, Joe (1) Leigh: 1971 NZ

WALSH, John (4 + 1) St.Helens: 1972 f; **1972 A2,F,NZ**

WALTON, D (1) Castleford: 1965 F

WANE, S (2) Wigan: 1985 F; 1986 F

WARD, D (12) Leeds: **1977 F,NZ,A**; 1978 A; 1979 A3,NZ3;1981 F; 1982 A

WARD, Edward (3) Wigan: 1946 A2; 1947 NZ

WARD, Ernest (20) Bradford N: 1946 A3,NZ; 1947 NZ2; 1948 A3; 1950 A3,NZ2; 1951 NZ3; 1952 A3

WARD, J (4) Castleford: 1963 A; 1964 F2; Salford: 1970 NZ

WARD, K (4) Castleford: 1984 F; 1986 A3

WARD, W (1) Leeds: 1910 A

WARLOW, J (6 + 1) St.Helens: 1964 F; **1968 f,NZ**; 1968 F; Widnes: 1971 F2,NZ

WARWICK, S (2) Salford: 1907 NZ2

WATKINS, D (2 + 4) Salford: 1971 f,NZ; 1973 a; 1974 f2,A

WATKINS, W (7) Salford: 1933 A; 1936 A2,NZ2; 1937 A2

WATKINSON, D (12 + 1) Hull KR: 1979 a; 1980 NZ; 1981 F; 1984 F; 1985 F, NZ3; 1986 F2, A3

WATSON, C (29 + 1) St.Helens: 1963 A2; 1966 F2,A3,NZ2; 1967 F,A3; 1968 F2; **1968 A,F,nz**; 1969 F; 1970 A3,NZ3; **1970 A2,F,NZ**; 1971 F

WATTS, B (5) York: **1954 F2,NZ,A**; 1955 NZ

WEBSTER, F (3) Leeds: 1910 A2,NZ

WHITCOMBE, F (2) Bradford N: 1946 A2

WHITE, L (7) Hunslet: 1932 A3,NZ2; 1933 A2

WHITE, L (6) York: 1946 A3,NZ; Wigan: 1947 NZ2

WHITE, T (1) Oldham: 1907 NZ

WHITEHEAD, D (3) Warrington: 1971 F2,NZ

WHITELEY, J (15) Hull: **1957 A**; 1958 A3,NZ; 1959 F2,A2; 1960 F; **1960 NZ,F**; 1961 NZ2; 1962 F

WILKINSON, J (13) Halifax: 1954 A,NZ2; 1955 NZ3; Wakefield T: 1959 A; 1960 F2; **1960 NZ,F,A**; 1962 NZ

WILLIAMS, F (2) Halifax: 1914 A2

WILLIAMS, R (12) Leeds: 1948 A2; 1950 A2,NZ2; 1951 NZ3; Hunslet: 1954 A2,NZ

WILLIAMS, W (2) Salford: 1929 A; 1932 A

WILLICOMBE, D (3) Halifax: 1974 F; Wigan: F,NZ

WILSON, G (3) Workington T: 1951 NZ3

WILSON, H (3) Hunslet: 1907 NZ3

WINSLADE, C (1) Oldham: 1959 F

WINSTANLEY, W (5) Leigh: 1910 A,NZ; Wigan: 1911 A3

WOOD, A (4) Oldham: 1911 A2; 1914 A,NZ

WOODS, H (6) Liverpool S: 1936 A3,NZ2; Leeds: 1937 A

WOODS, J (1) Barrow: 1933 A

WOODS, J (7 + 3) Leigh: 1979 A3,nz; 1980 NZ; 1981 F2; 1982 Aa; 1983 f

WOODS, T (2) Rochdale H: 1911 A2

WORRALL, M (3) Oldham: 1984 F, A2

WRIGHT, J (1) Swinton: 1932 NZ

WRIGHT, S (7) Widnes: **1977 F,NZ,A2**; 1978 A3

WRIGLESWORTH, G (5) Leeds: 1965 NZ; 1966 A2,NZ2

YOUNG, C (5) Hull KR: 1967 A3; 1968 F2

YOUNG, F (1) Leeds: 1908 A

YOUNG, H (1) Huddersfield: 1929 A

Great Britain Under-21s skipper Shaun Edwards.

UNDER-21s

Great Britain's young Lions savaged their French counterparts, running up a total of 94 points in a double record breaker.

The 40-7 victory in St. Jean de Luz was the highest score by a British junior side in France. Two weeks later, at St. Helens, the Under-21s ran in 54 points to top the previous best tally of 48 points set by the Under-24s in December 1983.

High-ranking police chief Graham Ainui made Rugby League history by becoming the first Papua New Guinea referee to take charge of international matches. Otherwise there was little to enthuse about.

With the French code in turmoil, trapped in a web of political manoeuvres, the Gallic youngsters provided only token opposition.

In the opening encounter in St. Jean de Luz — the debut of international Rugby League in the Basque region — Britain coasted home despite having their rhythm disrupted by the loss of three key forwards after the opening half hour.

Fielding 11 new caps in the 15-man squad, Britain swept into a 18-0 lead after only 17 minutes, the first touchdown coming after five minutes from Widnes centre Darren Wright, Warrington half back Paul Bishop adding the goal. St. Helens centre Paul Loughlin kicked ahead for teammate Kevin McCormack to score in the 10th minute. Leeds' barnstorming second row man Paul Medley sidestepped his way under the posts for Loughlin to add the goal.

France rallied briefly with seven points in a three-minute spell before Hull winger Paul Eastwood scored an unconverted try three minutes before the interval.

Either side of the break, Britain lost powerhouse forwards Medley and Hull's Neil Puckering who, along with clubmate Andy Dannatt, had been punching holes in the dispirited French defence.

In the 47th minute winger McCormack crowned an impressive international debut with his second touchdown, Loughlin tacking on the goal to take the scoreline to 28-7. With substitute back Mike Ford already operating in the back row of the pack, Britain were further hampered by Dannatt having to leave the field with a leg injury.

France had also used both substitutes and lost second row man Charles Frizon after the break, the 12-a-side contest being dominated by Britain despite their lack of fluid approach work.

Hull loose forward Gary Divorty, only recently returned from a knee injury, rounded off a classy display by claiming the final two tries in the 74th and 80th minutes, both goaled by Loughlin. Divorty, capped twice for Britain in the 1985 French Tests, won the Man of the Match award.

Divorty started the Knowsley Road encounter as he had left off in France, scoring the opening try after only eight minutes. Loughlin added the goal, the first of seven, his two second half tries bringing a points tally of 22, a record for an Under-21 or Under-24 international.

Tries from Puckering, McCormack and Ford, plus a Loughlin goal, took Britain to 20-0 after 18 minutes and signalled the end of the match as a contest. Once again France rallied on the half hour with a Frederick Bourrel try and a goal from Claude Gibert.

But the young Gauls could not hold the blockbusting Puckering, who completed his hat-trick with tries in the 34th and 38th minutes for Britain to turn round with a 32-6 lead.

With skipper and Man of the Match Shaun Edwards dictating play, Britain cantered through the second period with Loughlin notching a brace of tries on his home patch and Eastwood touching down before the try of the match in the 76th minute from hooker Martin Dermott, who rounded off a magnificent long-range break from Divorty.

8th March

St. Jean de Luz

GREAT BRITAIN 40

Chris Bibb (Featherstone R.)	1.	
Paul Eastwood (Hull)	2.	
Darren Wright (Widnes)	3.	
Paul Loughlin (St. Helens)	4.	
Kevin McCormack (St. Helens)	5.	
Paul Bishop (Warrington)	6.	
Shaun Edwards (Wigan), Capt.	7.	
Andy Dannatt (Hull)	8.	
Martin Dermott (Wigan)	9.	
Neil Puckering (Hull)	10.	
Gary Sanderson (Warrington)	11.	
Paul Medley (Leeds)	12.	
Gary Divorty (Hull)	13.	
Mike Ford (Leigh)	14.	
Dean Mountain (Castleford)	15.	

T: McCormack (2), Divorty (2),
   Wright, Medley, Eastwood
G: Loughlin (5), Bishop
Substitutions:
Mountain for Medley (36 min.)
Ford for Puckering (46 min.)
Manager: Les Bettinson
Coach: Malcolm Reilly

FRANCE 7

Olivier Molitor (Le Pontet)
Patrick Marginet (St. Esteve)
Eric Vergniol (Villeneuve)
David Fraysse (Entraygues)
Jerome Ferret (Lezignan)
Didier Lacourt (Avignon)
Patrick Entat (Avignon), Capt.
Franck Romano (Carpentras)
Eric Gouaze (Toulouse)
Andre Parpagiola (Toulouse)
Charles Frizon (Toulouse)
Daniel Divet (Limoux)
Patrick Alberola (Carcassonne)
Claude Gibert (Perpignan)
Marc Tisseyre (Pamiers)
T: Fraysse
G: Gibert (1, 1dg)
Substitutions:
Gibert for Lacourt (18 min.)
Tisseyre for Romano (18 min.)
Half-time: 22-7
Referee: Graham Ainui (Papua New Guinea)
Attendance: 250

The Great Britain Under-21 squad on duty at St. Helens in March 1987, from left to right:
Back row: Divorty, Sanderson, Dannatt, Loughlin, Medley, Disley, McCormack.
Middle row: Phil Larder (Asst. Coach), Russell, Eastwood, Puckering, Lidbury, Mike Stabler (Physio).
Front row: Bishop, Bibb, Les Bettinson (Manager), Edwards (Captain), Malcolm Reilly (Coach), Dermott, Ford.

21st March   **St. Helens**

GREAT BRITAIN 54   **FRANCE 6**

Chris Bibb (Featherstone R.)	1.	Olivier Molitor (Le Pontet)
Paul Eastwood (Hull)	2.	Patrick Marginet (St. Esteve)
Richard Russell (Wigan)	3.	Didier Buttignol (Avignon)
Paul Loughlin (St. Helens)	4.	Philippe Bourrel (Lezignan)
Kevin McCormack (St. Helens)	5.	Frederick Bourrel (Limoux)
Mike Ford (Leigh)	6.	Claude Gibert (Perpignan)
Shaun Edwards (Wigan), Capt.	7.	Jean Frizon (Toulouse)
Andy Dannatt (Hull)	8.	Marc Tisseyre (Pamiers)
Martin Dermott (Wigan)	9.	Mathieu Khedimi (St. Esteve)
Neil Puckering (Hull)	10.	Andre Parpagiola (Toulouse)
Gary Sanderson (Warrington)	11.	Gilbert Ailleres (Toulouse), Capt.
Paul Medley (Leeds)	12.	Daniel Divet (Limoux)
Gary Divorty (Hull)	13.	Stephan Laurent (Villefranche)
Paul Bishop (Warrington)	14.	Toniol Laurent (Toulouse)
Gary Disley (Salford)	15.	Nicolas Fabry (Lezignan)

T: Puckering (3), Loughlin (2), Divorty, Ford, McCormack, Eastwood, Dermott
G: Loughlin (7)
Substitutions:
Bishop for Ford (56 min.)
Disley for Puckering (56 min.)
Manager: Les Bettinson
Coach: Malcolm Reilly

T: F. Bourrell
G: Gibert
Half-time: 32-6
Referee: Graham Ainui (Papua New Guinea)
Attendance: 1,403
Substitutions:
Fabry for Buttignol (56 min.)
Laurent for Marginet (64 min.)

GREAT BRITAIN UNDER-21s RESULTS

25 Nov. 1984	W	24-8	v.	F	Castleford
16 Dec. 1984	W	8-2	v.	F	Albi
9 Oct. 1985	L	12-16	v.	NZ	Bradford
19 Jan. 1986	L	6-19	v.	F	St. Esteve
2 Feb. 1986	W	6-2	v.	F	Whitehaven
8 Mar. 1987	W	40-7	v.	F	St. Jean de Luz
21 Mar. 1987	W	54-6	v.	F	St. Helens

Key: A - Australia, F - France, NZ - New Zealand

GREAT BRITAIN UNDER-21s REGISTER

The following is a register of appearances for Great Britain Under-21s since this classification of match was introduced in 1984.

Figures in brackets are the total appearances, with the plus sign indicating substitute appearances, e.g. (3 + 1).

Away matches are in bold letters. Substitute appearances are in lower case letters.

ALLEN, S. (1) St. Helens: 1984 F

BECKWITH, M. (1+1) Whitehaven: 1986 f, F
BIBB, C. (2) Featherstone R.: 1987 **F**, F
BISHOP, P. (1+1) Warrington: 1987 **F**, f

CARBERT, B. (3) Warrington: 1985 NZ; 1986 **F**, F
CLARK, G. (2) Hull K.R.: 1984 F, **F**
CONWAY, M. (1) Leeds: 1984 F
CREASSER, D. (5) Leeds: 1984 F, **F**; 1985 NZ;
  1986 **F**, F
CROOKS, L. (2) Hull: 1984 F, **F**
CURRIER, A. (2) Widnes: 1984 F, **F**

DALTON, J. (3) Whitehaven: 1985 NZ; 1986 **F**, F
DANNATT, A. (6) Hull: 1984 F, **F**; 1985 NZ;
  1986 **F**; 1987 **F**, F
DERMOTT, M. (2) Wigan: 1987 **F**, F
DISLEY, G. (+1) Salford: 1987 f
DIVORTY, G. (6) Hull: 1984 F; 1985 NZ;
  1986 **F**, F; 1987 **F**, F

EASTWOOD, P. (2) Hull: 1987 **F**, F
EDWARDS, S. (4) Wigan: 1984 F; 1985 NZ;
  1987 **F**, F

FORD, M. (3+1) Wigan: 1985 NZ; 1986 **F**;
  Leigh: 1987 f, F
FORSTER, M. (3) Warrington: 1985 NZ; 1986 **F**, F
FOX, D. (1) Featherstone R.: 1984 **F**

GREGORY, M. (1) Warrington: 1984 **F**
GRIBBIN, V. (1+1) Whitehaven: 1984 f, **F**;
GROVES, P. (3) Salford: 1984 F, **F**; 1985 NZ

HARCOMBE, K. (1) Rochdale H.: 1986 F
HILL, B. (+1) Leeds: 1986 f
HUGHES, G. (1) Leigh: 1986 F
HULME, D. (2+1) Widnes: 1985 nz; 1986 **F**, F

LOUGHLIN, P. (2) St. Helens: 1987 **F**, F
LYMAN, P. (3) Featherstone R.: 1985 NZ; 1986 **F**, F
LYON, D. (2) Widnes: 1985 NZ; 1986 **F**

McCORMACK, K. (2) St. Helens: 1987 **F**, F
MEDLEY, P. (2) Leeds: 1987 **F**, F
MOUNTAIN. D. (+1) Castleford: 1987 f

POWELL, R. (5) Leeds: 1984 F, **F**; 1985 NZ;
  1986 **F**, F
PROCTOR, W. (+1) Hull: 1984 f
PUCKERING, N. (4) Hull: 1986 **F**, F; 1987 **F**, F

RIPPON, A. (1) Swinton: 1984 **F**
ROUND, P. (1+1) St. Helens: 1984 F, f
RUSSELL, R. (1) Wigan: 1987 F

SANDERSON, G. (2) Warrington: 1987 **F**, F
SCHOFIELD, G. (2) Hull: 1984 **F**, F

WANE, S. (3) Wigan: 1984 **F**; 1985 NZ; 1986 **F**
WESTHEAD, J. (1+2) Leigh: 1985 nz; 1986 f, **F**
WRIGHT, D. (1) Widnes: 1987 F

GREAT BRITAIN UNDER-24s RESULTS

3 Apr. 1965	W	17-9	v. F	Toulouse
20 Oct. 1965	W	12-5	v. F	Oldham
26 Nov. 1966	L	4-7	v. F	Bayonne
17 Apr. 1969	W	42-2	v. F	Castleford
14 Nov. 1976	W	19-2	v. F	Hull K.R.
5 Dec. 1976	W	11-9	v. F	Albi
12 Nov. 1977	W	27-9	v. F	Hull
18 Dec. 1977	W	8-4	v. F	Tonneins
4 Oct. 1978	L	8-30	v. A	Hull K.R.
14 Jan. 1979	W	15-3	v. F	Limoux
24 Nov. 1979	W	14-2	v. F	Leigh
13 Jan. 1980	W	11-7	v. F	Carcassonne
5 Nov. 1980	L	14-18	v. NZ	Fulham
10 Jan. 1981	W	9-2	v. F	Villeneuve
16 Jan. 1982	W	19-16	v. F	Leeds
21 Feb. 1982	W	24-12	v. F	Tonneins
16 Jan. 1983	W	19-5	v. F	Carpentras
11 Nov. 1983	W	28-23	v. F	Villeneuve
4 Dec. 1983	W	48-1	v. F	Oldham

GREAT BRITAIN UNDER-24s REGISTER
Since reintroduction in 1976

The following is a register of appearances for Great Britain Under-24s since this classification of match was reintroduced in 1976, until it was replaced by the new Under-21 level in 1984.

Figures in brackets are the total appearances, with the plus sign indicating substitute appearances, e.g. (7+3).

Away matches are in bold letters. Substitute appearances are in lower case letters.

ARKWRIGHT, C. (1) St. Helens: 1982 F
ASHTON, R. (3) Oldham: 1983 **F**, **F**, F

BANKS, B. (1) York: 1979 **F**
BELL, K. (2) Featherstone R.: 1977 F, **F**
BENTLEY, K. (+1) Widnes: 1980 nz
BURKE, M. (5) Widnes: 1979 F; 1980 **F**, NZ;
  1982 F; 1983 **F**
BURTON, B. (2) Castleford: 1976 F, **F**

319

CAIRNS, D. (2) Barrow: 1979 F; 1982 **F**
CASE, B. (3+1) Warrington: 1979 **F**; 1980 NZ: 1981 **F**; 1982 f
CLARK, G. (3) Hull K.R.: 1983 **F, F,** F
CRAMPTON, J. (4) Hull: 1976 F, **F**; 1977 F, **F**
CROOKS, L. (1) Hull: 1983 F

DICKINSON, R. (5) Leeds: 1976 F, **F**; 1977 F, **F**; 1978 A
DRUMMOND, D. (5) Leigh: 1979 F; 1980 **F**; 1981 **F**; 1982 F, **F**
DUANE, R. (2) Warrington: 1983 **F, F**
DUNN, B. (2) Wigan: 1983 **F,** F

ECCLES, R. (2) Warrington: 1978 A; 1979 F
ENGLAND, K. (+1) Castleford: 1983 f
EVANS, S. (3) Featherstone R.: 1980 NZ; 1981 **F**; Hull: 1982 **F**

FENNELL, D. (1) Featherstone R.: 1978 A
FENTON, S. (6) Castleford: 1977 F, **F**; 1979 F; 1980 **F,** NZ; 1981 **F**
FIELDHOUSE, J. (1+1) Warrington: 1983 **F,** f
FLANAGAN, T. (5) Oldham: 1980 NZ; 1981 **F**; 1983 **F, F,** F
FORD, Phil (1) Warrington: 1982 **F**
FOX, V. (1) Whitehaven: 1980 NZ
FOY, D. (2) Oldham: 1983 **F,** F

GIBBINS, M. (2) Featherstone R.: 1977 F, **F**
GILBERT, J. (2+1) Featherstone R.: 1977 F; 1977 f; 1981 **F**
GILL, H. (1) Wigan: 1982 F
GOODWAY, A. (2) Oldham: 1983 **F,** F
GREGORY, A. (1) Widnes: 1982 F

HALL, D. (+1) Hull K.R.: 1976 f
HANLEY, E. (2) Bradford N.: 1982 F; 1983 F
HARKIN, P. (1) Hull K.R.: 1981 **F**
HARTLEY, I. (1) Workington T.: 1979 **F**
HOBBS, D. (2) Featherstone R.: 1982 F, **F**
HOGAN, P. (2) Barrow: 1978 A; Hull K.R.: 1979 **F**
HOLDING, N. (4) St. Helens: 1979 **F**; 1980 F, NZ; 1983 **F**
HOLDSTOCK, R. (3) Hull K.R.: 1978 A; 1979 F; 1980 **F**
HORNBY, J. (2) Wigan: 1978 A; 1979 **F**
HYDE, G. (1+1) Castleford: 1980 NZ; 1982 f

JAMES, K. (1) Bramley: 1980 **F**
JOHNSON, B. (2) Castleford: 1982 F, **F**
JOYNER, J. (4+1) Castleford: 1976 f; 1977 F, **F**; 1978 A; 1979 **F**

LEDGER, B. (2) St. Helens: 1983 **F,** F
LIPTROT, G. (4) St. Helens: 1977 F, **F**; 1978 A; 1979 **F**
LYDON, J. (3) Widnes: 1983 **F, F,** F

MASKILL, C. (1) Wakefield T.: 1983 **F**
MOLL, D. (1) Keighley: 1983 **F**
MUMBY, K. (6) Bradford N.: 1976 F, **F**; 1977 F, **F**; 1978 A; 1981 **F**
MUSCROFT, P. (3) New Hunslet: 1976 F, **F**; 1978 A
MYLER, A. (3) Widnes: 1982 **F**; 1983 **F,** F
MYLER, J. (1+1) Widnes: 1982 f; **F**

NOBLE, B. (4) Bradford N.: 1982 F, **F**; 1983 **F,** F
NULTY, J. (2) Wigan: 1976 F, **F**

O'NEILL, M. (3+2) Widnes: 1980 nz; 1982 F, f; 1983 **F, F**
O'NEILL, P. (3) Salford: 1980 **F,** NZ; 1981 **F**
O'NEILL, S. (2) Wigan: 1979 **F**; 1981 **F**

PINNER, H. (4+4) St. Helens: 1976 F, **F**; 1977 f, f; 1978 a; 1979 f, **F**; 1980 **F**
POTTER, I. (4) Warrington: 1979 **F**; 1981 **F**; Leigh: 1982 F, **F**
PROCTOR, W. (1) Hull: 1983 **F**

RATHBONE, A. (+1) Leigh: 1979 f
RAYNE, Keith (2) Wakefield T.: 1979 F; 1980 **F**
RICHARDSON, T. (1) Castleford: 1979 **F**
ROE, P. (4) Bradford N.: 1976 F, **F**; 1977 F, **F**
RUDD, I. (1+1) Workington T.: 1979 f; 1980 **F**

SCHOFIELD, G. (+2) Hull: 1983 f, f
SHEPHERD, M. (2) Huddersfield: 1977 F, **F**
SKERRETT, T. (1) Wakefield T.: 1977 F
SMITH, D. (2) Leeds: 1976 F, **F**
SMITH, Malcolm (1) Wigan: 1979 F
SMITH, Mike (7) Hull K.R.: 1976 F, **F**; 1977 **F**; 1978 A; 1979 **F,** F; 1980 **F**
SMITH, P. (1) Featherstone R.: 1978 A
SMITH, R. (+1) Salford: 1983 f
STEPHENSON, D. (5) Salford: 1979 F; 1980 **F,** NZ; 1982 F; Wigan: 1982 **F**
SWANN, M. (1) Leigh: 1979 F
SYZMALA, E. (2) Barrow: 1976 F, **F**

THACKRAY, R. (1) Warrington: 1980 NZ
TIMSON, A. (2) Castleford: 1982 F, **F**
TURNBULL, S. (2) Salford: 1976 F, **F**

VAN BELLEN, G. (2) Bradford N.: 1980 NZ; 1982 **F**

WARD, D. (+2) Leeds: 1976 f, f
WARD, K. (3) Castleford: 1980 **F,** NZ; 1981 **F**
WHITFIELD, C. (1) Salford: 1981 **F**
WILKINSON, A. (1) Leigh: 1977 **F**
WOOD, J. (2) Widnes: 1977 F, **F**
WOODS, J. (5) Leigh: 1977 F, **F**; 1978 A; 1979 **F,** F
WORRALL, M. (3) Oldham: 1983 **F, F,** F

ENGLAND & WALES

The following is a register of England and Wales appearances since their reintroduction in 1975, but does not include England's challenge match against Australia played after the 1975 World Championship.

Figures in brackets are the total appearances since 1975, with the plus sign indicating substitute appearances, e.g. (7 + 3).

A few players also played in the 1969-70 European Championship and this is shown as an additional total outside bracket, e.g. (11)2.

World Championship matches are in bold letters. Substitute appearances are in lower case letters.

A - Australia, E - England, F - France, NZ - New Zealand, W - Wales.

ENGLAND REGISTER
Since reintroduction in 1975

ADAMS, M. (3 + 2) Widnes: 1975 **NZ, a**; 1978 F;
  1979 W; 1981 w
ARKWRIGHT, C. (+ 1) St. Helens: 1984 w
ATKINSON, J. (7) 4 Leeds: 1975 W, **F, W, NZ, W**;
  1978 F, W

BANKS, B. (+ 1) York: 1979 f
BEARDMORE, K. (1) Castleford: 1984 W
BEVERLEY, H. (1) Workington T: 1979 W
BRIDGES, K. (7) Featherstone R: 1975 **NZ, A, W, F,
  NZ, A**; 1977 W
BURKE, M. (1) Widnes: 1984 W

CAIRNS, D. (1) Barrow: 1984 W
CASE, B. (1) Warrington: 1981 F
CASEY, L. (5) Hull K.R.: 1978 F, W; 1980 W; 1981
  F, W
CHARLTON, P. (1) Salford: 1975 **F**
CHISNALL, D. (3 +1) Warrington: 1975 w, **F, W, NZ**
CHISNALL, E. (3 +1) St. Helens: 1975 F, **W, NZ, a**
CLARK, G. (1) Hull K.R.: 1984 W
COOKSON, P. (2) Leeds: 1975 **NZ, A**
COULMAN, M. (5) Salford: 1975 F, W, **W, A**; 1977 F
CUNNINGHAM, J. (2) Barrow: 1975 F, W

DONLAN, S. (1) Leigh: 1984 W
DRUMMOND, D. (5) Leigh: 1980 W, F; 1981 F, W;
  1984 W
DUNN, G. (6) Hull K.R.: 1975 W, **A, F, NZ, A**; 1977 F
DYL, L. (12 +1) Leeds: 1975 F, W, **F, W, NZ, A,
  nz, A**; 1977 W, F; 1978 F, W; 1981 W

ECKERSLEY, D. (+ 5) St. Helens: 1975 f, **w**, f;
  Widnes: 1977 w; 1978 w
ELWELL, K. (2) Widnes: 1978 F, W
EVANS, S. (3) Featherstone R: 1979 F; 1980 W, F

FAIRBAIRN, G. (15) Wigan: 1975 **W, NZ, A, W, F,
  NZ, A**; 1977 W, F; 1978 F; 1980 W, F; 1981 F,
  W; Hull K.R.: 1981 W

FARRAR, V. (1) Featherstone R: 1977 F
FENTON, S. (2) Castleford: 1981 F, W
FIELDING, K. (7) Salford: 1975 F, **F, W, NZ, A,
  W, F**
FORSYTH, C. (3) Bradford N: 1975 **W, F, NZ**

GILL, H. (1) Wigan: 1981 W
GILL, K. (9 + 2) Salford: 1975 W, **F, w, NZ, a, W, F,
  NZ, A**; 1977 W, F
GLYNN, P. (2) St. Helens: 1979 W, F
GOODWAY, A. (1) Oldham: 1984 W
GORLEY, L. (1 + 1) Workington T: 1977 W.
  Widnes: 1981 w
GORLEY, P. (2 + 1) St. Helens: 1980 W, f; 1981 W
GRAY, J. (3) Wigan: 1975 F, W, **F**
GRAYSHON, J. (9 +1) Dewsbury: 1975 **W, F, NZ, A**;
  1977 W. Bradford N: 1979 W, F; 1980 w, F;
  1981 W

HANLEY, E. (1) Bradford N.: 1984 W
HARRISON, M. (2) Leeds: 1978 F, W
HOBBS, D. (1) Featherstone R.: 1984 W
HOGAN, B. (5) Wigan: 1975 **W, F, NZ, A**; 1977 W
HOGAN, P. (1) Hull K.R.: 1979 F
HOLDING, N. (1) St. Helens: 1980 W
HOLDSTOCK, R. (3) Hull K.R.: 1980 W, F; 1981 W
HOLMES, J. (5 + 2) Leeds: 1975 **W, F, NZ, A**;
  1977 W, f; 1978 f
HUDDART, M. (1) Whitehaven: 1984 W
HUGHES, E. (8 +1) Widnes: 1975 **W, F, NZ, a**;
  1977 F; 1978 F, W; 1979 W, F
IRVING, R. (3) Wigan: 1975 **W, F, A**

JACKSON, P. (2) Bradford N.: 1975 W, **F**
JONES, L. (1) St. Helens: 1977 W
JOYNER, J. (4) Castleford: 1980 W, F; 1981 F, W
KELLY, A. (1) Hull K.R.: 1984 W
KELLY, K. (3) Warrington: 1979 W; 1981 F, W
LAUGHTON, D. (1) Widnes: 1977 W
LEDGER, B. (+ 1) St. Helens: 1984 w

LIPTROT, G. (2) St. Helens: 1979 W, F
LOCKWOOD, B. (2)+1 Hull K.R.: 1979 W, F
LOWE, P. (3)2 Hull K.R.: 1977 F; 1978 F; 1981 W

MARTYN, T. (4+1) Warrington: 1975 W, **F, w**;
  1979 W, F
MILLINGTON, J. (2) Hull K.R.: 1975 F; 1981 W
MILLWARD, R. (13)3+1 Hull K.R.: 1975 F, W,
  F, W, A, W, F, NZ, A; 1977 W, F; 1978 F, W
MORGAN, M. (3+3) Wakefield T: 1975 f, W, f, **W,
  nz, A**
MUMBY, K. (2) Bradford N: 1979 W, F
MURPHY, M. (1) Oldham: 1975 F

NASH, S. (7) Featherstone R: 1975 **W, NZ, A**.
  Salford: 1978 F, W; 1981 W, W
NICHOLLS, G. (7+4) St. Helens: 1975 F, **F, W, NZ,
  A, w, nz, f**; 1977 f; 1978 F, W
NOONAN, D. (3) Warrington: 1975 W, **F, W**
NORTON, S. (11) Castleford: 1975 **W, NZ, A, W, F,
  NZ, A**; 1977 F. Hull: 1978 W; 1981 W, W

O'NEILL, S. (1) Wigan: 1981 F

PATTINSON, W. (1+1) Workington T: 1981 f, W
PHILBIN, B. (1) Warrington: 1975 **F**
PIMBLETT, G. (1) St. Helens: 1978 W
PINNER, H. (3) St. Helens: 1980 W, F; 1981 F
POTTER, I. (2) Warrington: 1981 F, W

RAYNE, Keith (2) Wakefield T: 1980 W, F

REDFEARN, A. (2) Bradford N: 1979 F; 1980 F
REDFEARN, D. (2) Bradford N: 1975 F, **A**
REILLY, M. (+1)2 Castleford: 1977 w
RICHARDSON, T. (1) Castleford: 1981 W
ROSE, P. (2) Hull K.R.: 1977 F; 1978 W

SCHOFIELD, G. (1) Hull: 1984 W
SHEARD, L. (1) Wakefield T: 1975 W
SMITH, D. (1) Leeds: 1977 F
SMITH, K. (1) Wakefield T: 1979 W
SMITH, M. (5) Hull K.R.: 1980 W, F; 1981 F, W, W
SMITH, P. (1) Featherstone R: 1980 F
STEPHENS, G. (1) Castleford: 1979 W
SZYMALA, E. (+1) Barrow: 1979 f

THOMPSON, J. (2+1)1 Featherstone R: 1975 **A**;
  1977 W. Bradford N: 1978 w
TINDALL, K. (1) Hull: 1979 F
TOPLISS, D. (1) Wakefield T: 1975 F

WADDELL, H. (1) Blackpool B.: 1984 W
WALKER, A. (1) Whitehaven: 1981 W
WALSH, J. (3) St. Helens: 1975 F, **NZ, A**
WARD, D. (6) Leeds: 1977 F; 1980 W, F;
  1981 F, W, W
WATKINSON, D. (+1) Hull K.R.: 1977 w
WOODS, J. (3+4) Leigh: 1979 w, F; 1980 w, F;
  1981 f, w, W
WRIGHT, S. (7) Wigan: 1975 **NZ**. Widnes: 1977 W;
  1978 F, W; 1979 W, F; 1980 W

WALES REGISTER
Since reintroduction in 1975

BANNER, P. (9) Salford: 1975 F, E, **F, E, NZ**.
  Featherstone R: 1975 (cont.) **E, A, NZ, F**
BAYLISS, S. (1) St. Helens: 1981 E
BEVAN, J. (17) Warrington: 1975 F, E, **E, A, NZ, F**;
  1977 E, F; 1978 A; 1979 F, E; 1980 F, E;
  1981 F, E, E; 1982 A
BOX, H. (5) Featherstone R: 1979 F, E; 1980 F, E.
  Wakefield T: 1981 F
BUTLER, B. (2+2) Swinton: 1975 **F, nz**. Warrington:
  1975 (cont.) f; 1977 F

CAMBRIANI, A. (3) Fulham: 1981 F, E, E
CAMILLERI, C. (3) Barrow: 1980 F. Widnes:
  1982 A. Bridgend: 1984 E
COSLETT, K. (8)2 St. Helens: 1975 F, E, **F, E, A,
  NZ, E, A**
CUNNINGHAM, E (8) St. Helens: 1975 **E, A, E, A**;
  1977 E; 1978 F, E, A
CUNNINGHAM, T. (2) Warrington: 1979 F, E
CURLING, D. (+1) Warrington: 1977 f

DAVID, T. (2) Cardiff C: 1981 E; 1982 A

DAVIES, F. (1) New Hunslet: 1978 E
DAVIES, M. (1) Bridgend: 1984 E
DIAMOND, S. (2+1) Wakefield T: 1980 F, e; 1981 F
DIXON, C. (10)3 Salford: 1975 F, E, **F, E, NZ, A**;
  1977 E, F; 1978 F. Hull K.R.: 1981 E

EVANS, R. (5) Swinton: 1975 E, **F, F**; 1978 F;
  Salford: 1978 E

FENWICK, S. (2) Cardiff C: 1981 E; 1982 A
FISHER, A. (10)4 Leeds: 1975 F, **E, A, NZ**.
  Castleford: 1975 (cont.) **E, A, NZ**; 1977 E, F.
  Bradford N: 1978 A
FLOWERS, N. (4) Wigan: 1980 F, E; 1981 E.
  Bridgend: 1984 E
FORD, Phil (1) Warrington: 1984 E
FRANCIS, R. (19) Wigan: 1975 F, E, **F, E, A, NZ,
  E, A, NZ, F**; 1977 E, F. St. Helens: 1978 F, E,
  A; 1979 F, E. Oldham: 1980 F, E

GALLACHER, S. (3+1) Keighley: 1975 f, E, **NZ, F**
GREGORY, B. (3) Wigan: 1975 **E, NZ, F**

The England side which lost 2-6 to Wales at Leeds in January 1977, left to right. Back row: Doug Laughton, Les Dyl, Mal Reilly, Jimmy Thompson, Stuart Wright, John Holmes, Brian Hogan, Les Gorley, Jeff Grayshon. Front row: Peter Fox (Coach), Keith Bridges, Ken Gill, Roger Millward (Captain), Harry Womersley (Manager), David Eckersley, George Fairbairn, Les Jones, Dennis Wright (Physio).

The Welsh team which beat France 29-7 at Widnes in January 1978, left to right. Back row: Mike Nicholas, Roy Mathias, Peter Rowe, Jim Mills, Ron Simpson (Manager), Glyn Shaw, Mel James, Colin Dixon, David Willicombe, Kel Coslett (Coach). Front row: Gordon Pritchard, Clive Jones, Paul Woods, Bill Francis (Captain), Eddie Cunningham, Clive Sullivan, John Risman, Dick Evans.

GRIFFITHS, C. (+2) St. Helens: 1980 f; 1981 f

HALLETT, L. (2) Cardiff C: 1982 A. Bridgend: 1984 E
HERDMAN, M. (2+1) Fulham: 1981 e, E; 1982 A
HOPKINS, L. (1) Workington T: 1982 A

JAMES, M. (11) St. Helens: 1975 E; 1978 F, E, A; 1979 F, E; 1980 F, E; 1981 F, E, E
JOHNS, G. (+2) Salford: 1979 f. Blackpool B: 1984 e
JONES, C. (1+3) Leigh: 1975 nz, F; 1978 f, e
JULIFF, B. (8) Wakefield T: 1979 F, E; 1980 F, E; 1981 F, E: Wigan: 1982 A; 1984 E

McJENNETT, M. (2+1) Barrow: 1980 F; 1982 a; 1984 E
MANTLE, J. (11+1)3 St. Helens: 1975 F, E, F, e, A, NZ, E, A, NZ, F; 1977 E; 1978 E
MATHIAS, R. (20) St. Helens: 1975 F, E, F, E, A, NZ, A, NZ, F; 1977 E, F; 1978 F, E, A; 1979 F, E; 1980 F, E; 1981 F, E
MILLS, J. (13)4 Widnes: 1975 F, E, E, A, NZ, A, NZ; 1977 E, F; 1978 F, E, A; 1979 E
MURPHY, M. (4+1) Bradford N: 1975 F, NZ, F; 1977 f. St. Jacques, France: 1979 F

NICHOLAS, M. (4+2) Warrington: 1975 F, e; 1977 E, F; 1978 F; 1979 e

O'BRIEN, C. (1) Bridgend: 1984 E
OWEN, G. (2) Oldham: 1981 E, F
OWEN, R. (+2) St. Helens: 1981 f, e

PARRY, D. (6) Blackpool B: 1980 F, E; 1981 F, E, E; 1982 A
PREECE, C. (1) Bradford N: 1984 E
PRENDIVILLE, P. (4+2) Hull: 1979 e; 1980 E; 1981 F, e; 1982 A; 1984 E

PRITCHARD, G. (1+2) Barrow: 1978 f, e; Cardiff C.: 1981 E

RICHARDS, M. (2)1 Salford: 1975 F; 1977 E
RINGER, P. (2) Cardiff C: 1981 E; 1982 A
RISMAN, J. (2+1) Workington T: 1978 F; 1979 f, E
ROWE, P. (4+3)2 Blackpool B: 1975 a, e, a. Huddersfield: 1977 E, F; 1979 F, E
RULE, S. (1) Salford: 1981 E

SELDON, C. (1+1) St. Helens: 1980 f, E
SHAW, G. (7) Widnes: 1978 F, A; 1980 F, E; 1981 E. Wigan: 1982 A; 1984 E
SKERRETT, T. (7) Wakefield T: 1978 A; 1979 F, E; 1980 F. Hull: 1981 F, E; 1984 E
SULLIVAN, C. (10)4 Hull K.R.: 1975 E, A, NZ, E; 1977 F; 1978 F, E, A; 1979 F, E

TREASURE, D. (5) Oldham: 1975 E, A, NZ, E; 1977 F
TURNER, G. (3+3) Hull K.R.: 1975 e, A, e, A, f. Hull: 1978 E

WALLACE, R. (+1) York: 1975 f
WALTERS, G. (2+1) Hull: 1980 E. 1981 E. Bridgend 1984 e
WANBON, R. (3)3+1 Warrington: 1975 E, A, NZ
WATKINS, D. (14) Salford: 1975 F, E, F, E, A, NZ, E, A, NZ, F; 1977 E; 1978 E, A; 1979 F
WILKINS, R. (1+1) Workington T: 1977 e, F
WILLIAMS, B. (1) Cardiff C: 1982 A
WILLICOMBE, D. (11)+2 Wigan: 1975 F, E, F, E, A, NZ, NZ, F; 1978 F, E, A
WILSON, D. (4) Swinton: 1981 F, E, E; 1984 E
WILSON, F. (7+2)4 St. Helens: 1975 F, E, F, e, a, E, A, NZ, F
WOODS, P. (10) Widnes: 1977 E, F; 1978 F, E, A. Rochdale H: 1979 F, E. Hull: 1980 E; 1981 F, E

Capped eight times for England RU, Tom Brophy signed professional for Barrow in 1966-67.

RU to RL

RU to RL

A REVIEW OF INTERNATIONAL RUGBY UNION SIGNINGS

Since the historic breakaway movement of 1895 when the Northern Union — later to become the Rugby Football League — divorced itself from the Rugby Union, 212 home international players have changed codes.

This tally of converts does not include the 24 internationals who made the switch when their clubs joined the Northern Union.

The total of 212 capped players is made up on the following national basis:

Wales	144
England	48
Scotland	13
Ireland	7

RUGBY LEAGUE CAPS

Of those 212 Rugby Union international players, only 41 have gone on to gain Rugby League honours with Great Britain in Test or World Cup matches.

Wales has provided 28 dual caps, England 10, Scotland three and Ireland none.

The former Rugby Union international to have made most appearances for Great Britain in the 13-a-side code was Lewis Jones. Having left Wales to join Leeds in 1952, he featured in 15 Test and World Cup games, gaining the distinction of touring Australia and New Zealand in both codes.

RUGBY UNION CAPS

The most capped Rugby Union international to switch codes was Steve Fenwick, who played 30 times for Wales and on four occasions for the British Lions before signing professional forms for Cardiff City on their formation in 1981. He is one of six players who made 20 or more Rugby Union international appearances, as follows:

Steve Fenwick	30 Wales	+ 4 Lions
Terry Holmes	25 Wales	+ 1 Lions
Rob Ackerman	22 Wales	+ 2 Lions
David Watkins	21 Wales	+ 6 Lions
William Welsh	21 Scotland	+ 1 Lions
James Webb	20 Wales	+ 3 Lions

The most capped England Rugby Union international to turn to League was Richard Lockwood, holder of 14 caps when he became one of the first players to sign for a Northern Union club, Wakefield Trinity, after the split of 1895.

RUGBY UNION CAPTAINS

The only Rugby League players to have captained their country at Rugby Union are David Watkins, Steve Fenwick, Terry Holmes (Wales), Richard Lockwood (England) and Robin Thompson (Ireland). Thompson also skippered the 1955 British Lions.

DOUBLE TOURISTS

Only six players have been British Lions in both Rugby League and Union. The half dozen — all Welsh backs — toured Australia and New Zealand with Great Britain Rugby League after making a major tour of the same countries with the British Isles Rugby Union, with the exception of Maurice Richards whose 15-a-side tour was to South Africa.

	RU Tour	RL Tour
John Bevan	1971	1974
Lewis Jones	1950*	1954
Jack Morley	1930	1936
Terry Price	1966*	1970
Maurice Richards	1968 (SA)	1974*
David Watkins	1966	1974

*Replaced injured player

● Bev Risman toured New Zealand and Australia with the 1959 British Lions Rugby Union party and captained the Great Britain Rugby League World Cup squad Down Under in 1968. In addition to his 1954 tour of Australasia, Lewis Jones also visited Down Under with the 1957 Great Britain World Cup squad.

THE RECRUITING CLUBS

Leeds have made the most Rugby Union home international captures with a total of 30, including a record 25 from Wales. Oldham have signed the most England Rugby Union players, nine.

A breakdown of the Rugby Union signings, club by club, is:

Key: E, England; I, Ireland; S, Scotland; W, Wales

Leeds (3E, 2S, 25W)	30
Oldham (9E, 1S, 9W)	19
Wigan (1E, 2S, 14W)	17
Salford (4E, 1S, 11W)	16
Huddersfield (1E, 3I, 3S, 9W)	16
St. Helens (1E, 12W)	13
Hull (2E, 1I, 8W)	11
Bradford N. (3E, 1S, 4W)	8
Rochdale H. (3E, 5W)	8
Warrington (1E, 1I, 6W)	8
Halifax (7W)	7
Swinton (7W)	7
Wakefield T. (6E)	6
Hunslet (2E, 3W)	5
Hull K.R. (4W)	4
Barrow (2E, 1W)	3
Batley (1S, 2W)	3
Leigh (2E, 1W)	3
Dewsbury (1E, 1W)	2
Runcorn H. (1E, 1S)	2
Whitehaven (1S, 1W)	2
York (2W)	2
Castleford (1S)	1
Sheffield E. (1E)	1
Widnes (1W)	1
Workington T. (1I)	1

In addition, 16 other international players signed for now defunct clubs, including one each at the old Castleford and Runcorn clubs.

Only six present day clubs have never signed a Rugby Union international: Blackpool Borough, Bramley, Carlisle, Doncaster, Featherstone Rovers and Mansfield Marksman.

THE RUGBY UNION CLUBS

Cardiff have lost the most Rugby Union internationals to Rugby League with 22. They are one of six Welsh clubs who have had 10 or more internationals switch codes, as follows:

Cardiff	22
Llanelli	20
Newport	18
Neath	16
Swansea	13
Pontypool	10

THE POSITIONS

Of the 212 home international Rugby Union players who have switched codes, 114 have been forwards, only 11 of those being hookers. The back position to produce most international converts has been the wing, with 29.

The following is a list of each position and the total of Rugby Union internationals who have signed professional:

Full back	21
Wing	29
Centre	23
Stand off	16
Scrum half	15
Forward	114

● Some players were capped in more than one position.

Of the 41 former Rugby Union internationals who have played for Great Britain Rugby League, 18 were forwards, 10 wingers, four full backs, three centres, three stand offs and only one scrum half, namely Robert Lloyd, of Halifax, capped in 1920. Two utility backs also went on to play for Great Britain.

RECORD FEES

Terry Holmes received a record £80,000 contract when he signed for Bradford Northern on 3 December 1985 after playing 25 times for Wales Rugby Union at scrum half.

One of the first record fees for a Rugby Union international recruit was the £300 Hull Kingston Rovers paid to Daniel Rees, the Swansea centre, in 1905.

The fees grew steadily from hundreds to thousands of pounds until there was a big leap when Leeds captured Lewis Jones, the Llanelli 'Golden Boy', in 1952 for £6,000.

Accurate figures for signing fees are rarely disclosed, but the following list of reported sums give an indication of how the amounts have escalated since Jones switched codes, the players being mostly Welsh and all backs.

Lewis Jones, a big money recruit from the 15-a-side code.

Fee	Player	Position	From	To	Signed
£6,000	Lewis Jones	Back	(Llanelli & Wales)	Leeds	1952-53
£6,500	Bev Risman	Centre/ stand off	(Loughborough Coll. & England)	Leigh	1960-61
£7,500	Malcolm Price	Centre	(Pontypool & Wales)	Oldham	1961-62
£9,000	Terry Price	Full back	(Llanelli & Wales)	Bradford N.	1967-68
£15,000	David Watkins	Stand off	(Newport & Wales)	Salford	1967-68
£27,500	Clive Griffiths	Full back	(Llanelli & Wales)	St. Helens	1979-80
£80,000	Terry Holmes	Scrum half	(Cardiff & Wales)	Bradford N.	1985-86

Former England and Moseley RU winger Keith Fielding touches down for Great Britain, one of a hat-trick in France at Grenoble in 1974.

Dual-code cap Tommy Woods, a 1909-10 capture by Rochdale Hornets.

Dewsbury's Edward Jackett, former 13-cap England RU full back.

Ex-Harlequin winger Tom Danby, a 1949-50 recruit for Salford, capped three times for Great Britain.

Bev Risman, capped eight times for England RU, plus four appearances for the British Lions, before joining Leigh.

REGISTER

The following is a list of the home international Rugby Union players who switched codes after the Northern Union breakaway of 1895.
Key: E, England; I, Ireland; S, Scotland; W, Wales.
FB, Full back; WG, Wing; C, Centre;
SO, Stand off; SH, Scrum half; H, Hooker; F, Forward, other than hooker.
In bold: British Isles Rugby Union tourist.
★ Played for Great Britain Rugby League in a Test or World Cup match.
+ British Isles Rugby Union appearances.

ENGLAND	RU Club	Position	RU Caps	RL Club	Signed
ASHWORTH, Abel	Oldham	F	1	Rochdale H.	1895-96
BELL, Frederick	Northern	F	3	Hunslet	1899-00
★BOYLEN, Francis	Hartlepool R.	F	4	Hull	1908-09
BRADSHAW, Harry	Bramley	F	7	Leeds	1895-96
BROADLEY, Thomas	Bingley	F	6	Bradford	1896-97
BROPHY, Tom	Liverpool	SO	8	Barrow	1966-67
★BROUGH, Jim	Silloth	FB	2	Leeds	1925-26
COCKERHAM, Arthur	Bradford Olicana	F	1	Manningham	1900-01
★**COULMAN, Mike**	Moseley	F	9+1	Salford	1968-69
★DANBY, Thomas	Harlequins	WG	1	Salford	1949-50
FAIRBROTHER, Keith	Coventry	F	12	Leigh	1974-75
★FIELDING, Keith	Moseley	WG	10	Salford	1973-74
★FRENCH, Ray	St. Helens	F	4	St. Helens	1961-62
GRAY, Arthur	Otley	FB	3	Wakefield T.	1946-47
HANCOCK, John	Newport	F	2	Salford	1955-56
HAVELOCK, Harold	Hartlepool R.	F	3	Hull	1908-09
★HOLLAND, David	Devonport Albion	F	3	Oldham	1913-14
HOLLIDAY, Thomas	Aspatria	FB	7	Oldham	1926-27
HOUGHTON, Samuel	Birkenhead W.	FB	2	Runcorn	1895-96
IRVIN, Samuel	Devonport Albion	FB	1	Oldham	1905-06
JACKETT, Edward	Leicester	FB	13	Dewsbury	1911-12
JEWITT, J.H.	Hartlepool R.	F	1	Broughton R.	1902-03
LAMPKOWSKI, Mike	Headingley	SH	4	Wakefield T.	1976-77
LEADBETTER, Michael	Broughton Park	F	1	Rochdale H.	1974-75
LOCKWOOD, Richard	Heckmondwike	WG	14	Wakefield T.	1895-96
MARSDEN, George	Morley	SO	3	Bradford	1900-01
MORDELL, Bob	Rosslyn Park	F	1	Oldham	1979-80
NANSON, William	Carlisle	F	2	Oldham	1908-09
PETERS, James	Plymouth	SO	5	Barrow	1913-14
POOLE, Robert	Hartlepool R.	FB	1	Broughton R.	1903-04
QUINN, Pat	New Brighton	C	5	Leeds	1956-57

ENGLAND	RU Club	Position	RU Caps	RL Club	Signed
REDFERN, Steve	Leicester	F	1	Sheffield R.	1984-85
REGAN, Martin	Liverpool	SO	12	Warrington	1956-57
RICHARDS, Ernest	Plymouth Albion	SH	2	London H.	1933-34
*RISMAN, Bev	Loughborough Coll.	C/SO	8+4	Leigh	1960-61
ROBERTS, Reginald	Coventry	H	1	Huddersfield	1933-34
SADLER, Edward	Royal Signals	F	2	Oldham	1933-34
SHOOTER, John (Jack)	Morley	F	4	Hunslet	1900-01
SMITH, Keith	Roundhay	C	4	Wakefield T.	1977-78
VARLEY, Harry	Liversedge	SH	1	Oldham	1895-96
WALTON, William	Castleford	F	1	Wakefield T.	1895-96
WARD, Herbert	Bradford	FB	1	Bradford	1899-00
WARD, John	Castleford	F	1	Castleford	1896-97
WEST, Bryan	Northampton	F	8	Wakefield T.	1970-71
WILSON, Ken	Gloucester	F	1	Oldham	1963-64
*WOOD, Alfred	Gloucester	FB	3	Oldham	1908-09
*WOODS, Thomas	Bridgewater Albion	F	1	Rochdale H.	1909-10
WOODS, Thomas	Pontypool	F	5	Wigan	1921-22

● G.W.M. Bonner, the Bradford Rugby Union full back, toured Australia and New Zealand with the 1930 British Lions Rugby Union squad but never played for England. He signed for Wakefield Trinity in 1932-33.

  Tom Fletcher switched codes with Seaton in 1898-99. Seaton were not a senior club and he signed for Oldham later in the season. He played once for England Rugby Union.

● In addition, the following England Rugby Union internationals switched codes when their club joined the Northern Union in 1895 or soon after:

	Club	Position	RU Caps		Club	Position	RU caps
Berry, John	Tyldesley	SH	3	Lowrie, Frederick	Batley	F	2
Coop, Thomas	Leigh	FB	1	Morfitt, Samuel	Hull K.R.	WG	6
Dobson, Thomas	Bradford	C	1	Myers, Harry	Keighley	SH	1
Duckett, Horace	Bradford	SH	2	Nichol, William	Brighouse R.	F	2
Dyson, John (Jack)	Huddersfield	WG	4	Northmore, Samuel	Millom	SO	1
Firth, Frederick	Halifax	WG	3	Rhodes, John	Hull K.R.	F	3
Fletcher, Thomas	Seaton	WG	1	Speed, Harry	Castleford	F	4
Holmes, Edgar	Manningham	F	2	Starks, Anthony	Hull K.R.	F	2
Hughes, George	Barrow	F	1	Toothill, Jack	Bradford	F	12
Jackson, Walter	Halifax	C	1	Valentine, James	Swinton	WG	4
Jowett, Donald	Heckmondwike	F	6	Whiteley, W.	Bramley	F	1
Knowles, Edward	Millom	F	2	Wood, Robert	Liversedge	SH	1

Cumbrian Jim Brough, capped in both codes and a Leeds signing from Silloth RU club in 1925-26.

Ray French, capped four times for both England RU and Great Britain.

Mike Coulman, a Salford recruit in 1968-69 after RU honours with Moseley, England and the British Lions.

Centre Keith Smith, capped four times for England RU before switching codes with Wakefield Trinity.

IRELAND	RU Club	Position	RU Caps	RL Club	Signed
COLLOPY, Richard	Bective R.	F	13	Huddersfield	1925-26
DALY, John	London Irish	F	7	Huddersfield	1948-49
FREEAR, Albert	Lansdowne	WG	3	Hull	1904-05
GOODALL, Ken	Derry	F	19	Workington T.	1970-71
QUINLAN, Sean	Blackrock & Highfield	WG	4	Oldham	1958-59
REID, Patrick	Garryowen	C	4	Huddersfield	1947-48
THOMPSON, Robin	Instonians	F	11 + 3	Warrington	1956-57

● Alfred Patrick Atkins (Bective R., wing, 1 cap 1924) was suspended sine die by the Irish Rugby Union after signing amateur forms for Huddersfield although he never played for them.

Five-cap Scottish RU winger Ron Cowan, a 1962-63 capture by Leeds. The ex-Selkirk British Lion is pictured scoring Leeds' first try in the 19-8 victory over Castleford in the 1971 Challenge Cup semi-final at Odsal Stadium, Bradford.

SCOTLAND	RU Club	Position	RU Caps	RL Club	Signed
COTTINGTON, Gordon S.	Kelso, Headingley	H	5	Castleford	1936-37
COWAN, Ron	Selkirk	WG	5 + 1	Leeds	1962-63
DOUGLAS, George	Jedforest	F	1	Batley	1921-22
DUFFY, Hugh	Jedforest	F	1	Salford	1954-55
GRAY, Gordon	Gala	H	4	Huddersfield	1937-38
*KINNEAR, Roy**	Heriots F.P.	C	3 + 4	Wigan	1926-27
LAIDLAW, Alex	Hawick	F	1	Bradford	1898-99
LITTLE, Anthony	Hawick	F	1	Wigan	1905-06
*ROSE, David	Jedforest	WG	7	Huddersfield	1953-54
SHILLINGLAW, Brian	Gala & Army	SH	5	Whitehaven	1961-62
*VALENTINE, David	Hawick	F	2	Huddersfield	1947-48
WELSH, William	Hawick	F	21 + 1	London H.	1933-34
WRIGHT, Thomas	Hawick	C	1	Leeds	1948-49

Scottish scrum half Brian Shillinglaw, a 1961-62 signing by Whitehaven after gaining five RU caps.

Huddersfield's Scottish forward Dave Valentine, capped 15 times for Great Britain after an RU career with Scotland and Hawick.

WALES	RU Club	Position	RU Caps	RL Club	Signed
ACKERMAN, Rob	Cardiff	WG/C	22 + 2	Whitehaven	1985-86
ANDREWS, Frank	Pontypool	F	4	Hunslet	1913-14
ANDREWS, George	Newport	WG	5	Leeds	1926-27
ANTHONY, Leslie	Neath	F	3	Oldham	1948-49
BADGER, Owen	Llanelli	C	4	Swinton	1897-98
BAKER, Ambrose	Neath	F	5	Oldham	1923-24
*BASSETT, Arthur	Cardiff	WG	6	Halifax	1938-39
BENNETT, Ivor	Aberavon	F	1	Warrington	1937-38
BEVAN, John	Cardiff	WG	10 + 1	Warrington	1973-74
BEYNON, Benjamin	Swansea	SO	2	Oldham	1922-23
BLACKMORE, Jacob	Abertillery	F	1	Hull K.R.	1910-11
BLAKEMORE, Reg	Newport	F	1	St. Helens	1947-48
BOWEN, William	Swansea	SO	6	Leeds	1922-23
BROWN, Archie	Newport	SH	1	Leeds	1921-22
CALE, W. Ray	Pontypool	F	7	St. Helens	1950-51
*COLDRICK, Percy	Newport	F	6	Wigan	1912-13
COLLINS, Tom	Mountain Ash	C	1	Hull	1923-24
COOK, Terence	Cardiff	WG	2	Halifax	1950-51
CORNISH, Frederick	Cardiff	F	4	Hull	1899-00
COSLETT, Kel	Aberavon	FB	3	St. Helens	1962-63
DAVID, Richard	Cardiff	SO	1	Wigan	1907-08
DAVID, Tommy	Pontypridd	F	4	Cardiff City	1981-82
*DAVIES, Avon	Aberavon	C	2	Leeds	1912-13
DAVIES, D. John	Neath	F	1	Leeds	1962-63
DAVIES, Gwynne	Cardiff	WG	3	Wigan	1930-31
DAVIES, Howell	Neath	FB	2	Huddersfield	1912-13
DAVIES, Idwal	Swansea	C	1	Leeds	1938-39
*DAVIES, William T. H.	Swansea	SO	6	Bradford N.	1939-40
DAY, Hubert	Newport	H	5	Salford	1931-32
DEVEREUX, Don	Neath	P	3	Huddersfield	1957-58
DOWELL, William	Pontypool	F	7	Warrington	1908-09
EDWARDS, David	Glyneath	F	1	Rochdale H.	1921-22
EVANS, Arthur	Pontypool	F	3	Halifax	1924-25
EVANS, Colin	Pontypool	SH	1	Leeds	1959-60
EVANS, Elwyn	Llanelli	C	1	Broughton R.	1925-26
EVANS, Emrys	Llanelli	F	3	Salford	1939-40
*EVANS, Frank	Llanelli	WG	1	Swinton	1921-22
EVANS, Jack	Llanelli	F	3	Swinton	1897-98
EVANS, William	Brynmawr	F	1	Leeds	1911-12
FENDER, Norman	Cardiff	F	6	York	1931-32
FENWICK, Steve	Bridgend	C	30 + 4	Cardiff City	1981-82
FOWLER, Isaac	Llanelli	SH	1	Batley	1919-20
GALLACHER, Stuart	Llanelli	F	1	Bradford N.	1970-71

WALES	RU Club	Position	RU Caps	RL Club	Signed
*GORE, Jack	Blaina	F	4	Salford	1924-25
GORE, William	Newbridge	H	3	Warrington	1947-48
GRIFFITHS, Clive	Llanelli	FB	1	St. Helens	1979-80
*GRONOW, Ben	Bridgend	F	4	Huddersfield	1910-11
HARRIS, Daniel	Cardiff	F	8	Leigh	1961-62
HAYWARD, Donald	Newbridge	F	15+3	Wigan	1954-55
HAYWARD, George	Swansea	F	5	Wigan	1913-14
HICKMAN, Arthur	Neath	WG	2	Swinton	1934-35
HINAM, Sidney	Cardiff	F	5	Rochdale H.	1926-27
HODDER, Wilfred	Pontypool	F	3	Wigan	1921-22
HOLMES, Terry	Cardiff	SH	25+1	Bradford N.	1985-86
HOPKIN, William	Newport	WG	1	Swinton	1938-39
HOPKINS, Ray	Maesteg	SH	1+1	Swinton	1972-73
HOWELLS, Brynmor	Llanelli	FB	1	Broughton R.	1934-35
HUGHES, Gomer	Penarth	F	3	Swinton	1934-35
HUZZEY, Viv	Cardiff	WG	5	Oldham	1900-01
ISAACS, Iorweth	Cardiff	F	2	Leeds	1933-34
†JAMES, David	Swansea	SO/SH	4	Broughton R.	1898-99
JAMES, David R.	Treorchy	H	2	Leeds	1931-32
†JAMES, Evan	Swansea	SO/SH	5	Broughton R.	1898-99
JAMES, William	Aberavon	WG	2	Leeds	1925-26
JARRETT, Keith	Newport	C/FB	10	Barrow	1969-70
*JENKINS, David Morgan	Treorchy	F	4	Hunslet	1926-27
JENKINS, David Rees	Swansea	H	2	Leeds	1928-29
JENKINS, Ernest	Newport	F	2	Rochdale H.	1910-11
JONES, Bedwellty	Abertillery	F	4	Oldham	1913-14
*JONES, David	Treherbert	F	13	Merthyr Tydfil	1907-08
JONES, David L.	Newport	F	5	Wigan	1926-27
JONES, Edgar	Llanelli	F	5	Leeds	1935-36
JONES, Harold	Neath	F	2	Wigan	1929-30
JONES, Iorwerth	Llanelli	F	5	Leeds	1931-32
JONES, Joseph	Swansea	C	1	Leeds	1924-25
★JONES, Keri	Cardiff	WG	5	Wigan	1968-69
★JONES, Lewis	Llanelli	FB/C/WG	10+3	Leeds	1952-53
JONES, William	Llanelli	SH	2	St. Helens	1934-35
JOWETT, Frederick	Swansea	WG	1	Hull K.R.	1905-06
LEMON, Arthur	Neath	F	13	St. Helens	1933-34
*LLOYD, Robert	Pontypool	SH	7	Halifax	1914-15
*MANTLE, John	Newport	F	2	St. Helens	1964-65
*MATHIAS, Roy	Llanelli	WG	1	St. Helens	1972-73
MERRY, Augustus	Pill Harriers	H	2	Hull	1912-13
MILLER, Fred	Mountain Ash	F	7	Hull	1901-02
MOORE, William	Bridgend	F	1	Rochdale H.	1933-34
*MORGAN, Edgar	Llanelli	F	4	Hull	1921-22
★MORLEY, Jack	Newport	WG	14+3	Wigan	1932-33
MURPHY, Cornelius	Cross Keys	H	3	Acton & Willesden	1935-36

336

*Ambrose Baker
(Oldham) 1923-24*

*Arthur Bassett
(Halifax) 1938-39*

*Emrys Evans
(Salford) 1939-40*

*Frank Evans
(Swinton) 1921-22*

*Jack Evans
(Swinton) 1897-98*

*Jack Gore
(Salford) 1924-25*

*Edgar Morgan
(Hull) 1921-22*

*Tommy Rees
(Oldham) 1928-29*

*Brian Sparks
(Halifax) 1957-58*

337

Welsh winger John Bevan, capped by Wales and the British Lions at RU before gaining RL caps with Great Britain and Wales.

Ten-cap Wales RU sensation Keith Jarrett who launched a controversial League career with Barrow in 1969-70.

Glyn Shaw, the ex-Neath and Wales forward who earned Great Britain and Wales honours in the 13-a-side code.

Welsh duo John Mantle (left) and John Warlow flank St. Helens teammate Bill Sayer.

WALES	RU Club	Position	RU Caps	RL Club	Signed
OLIVER, George	Pontypool	F	4	Hull	1921-22
O'NEILL, William	Cardiff	F	11	Warrington	1908-09
OSBORNE, William	Mountain Ash	F	6	Huddersfield	1903-04
OWEN, Garfield	Newport	FB	6	Halifax	1956-57
PARSONS, George	Newport	F	1	St. Helens	1947-48
PASCOE, Daniel	Bridgend	F	2	Leeds	1926-27
PEARCE, Gary	Llanelli	SO	3	Hull	1986-87
PERRETT, Frederick	Neath	H	5	Leeds	1913-14
PHILLIPS, Bryn	Aberavon	F	5	Huddersfield	1925-26
POOK, Thomas	Newport	F	1	Holbeck	1898-99
POWELL, Wickham	Cardiff	WG	4	Rochdale H.	1920-21
*PRICE, Malcolm	Pontypool	C	9+5	Oldham	1961-62
*PRICE, Terry	Llanelli	FB	8	Bradford N.	1967-68
PROSSER, David	Neath	F	2	York	1934-35
*PROSSER, Glyn	Neath	F	4	Huddersfield	1935-36
PUGSLEY, Joseph	Cardiff	H	7	Salford	1911-12
RALPH, Ray (Dickie)	Newport	SO	7	Leeds	1933-34
REES, Alan	Maesteg	SO	3	Leeds	1962-63
REES, Daniel	Swansea	C	5	Hull K.R.	1905-06
REES, Evan	Swansea	C	1	Dewsbury	1919-20
REES, Lewis	Cardiff	F	1	Oldham	1934-35
*REES, Thomas	London Welsh	FB	4	Oldham	1928-29
RHAPPS, Jack	Penygraig	F	1	Salford	1897-98
RICHARDS, Gwyn	Cardiff	SO	1	Huddersfield	1931-32
RICHARDS, Kenneth	Bridgend	SO	5	Salford	1961-62
*RICHARDS, Maurice	Cardiff	WG	9+3	Salford	1969-70
RICHARDS, Rees	Aberavon	F	3	Wigan	1913-14
*RING, Johnny	Aberavon	WG	1	Wigan	1922-23
RINGER, Paul	Llanelli	F	8	Cardiff City	1981-82
ROBINS, Russell	Pontypridd	F	13+4	Leeds	1958-59
ROSSER, Melville	Penarth	C/FB	2	Leeds	1924-25
SAMUEL, Frederick	Mountain Ash	FB	3	Hull	1922-23
SCOURFIELD, Thomas	Torquay Athletic	FB	1	Huddersfield	1932-33
*SHAW, Glyn	Neath	F	12	Widnes	1977-78
SHEA, Jerry	Newport	C	4	Wigan	1921-22
SPARKS, Brian	Neath	F	7	Halifax	1957-58
THOMAS, Harold	Neath	F	6	Salford	1937-38
THOMAS, Rhys	Pontypool	F	8	Warrington	1912-13
THOMAS, Trevor	Abertillery	F	1	Oldham	1931-32
*THOMPSON, Joseph	Cross Keys	F	1	Leeds	1922-23
TRUMP, Leonard	Newport	F	4	Hull K.R.	1912-13
WANBON, Bobby	Aberavon	F	1	St. Helens	1967-68
*WARLOW, John	Llanelli	F	1	St. Helens	1963-64
*WATKINS, David	Newport	SO	21+6	Salford	1967-68
WATKINS, Edward	Neath	SH	4	Halifax	1924-25

WALES	RU Club	Position	RU Caps	RL Club	Signed
WATKINS, Edward	Cardiff	F	8	Wigan	1938-39
WATKINS, Emlyn	Blaina	F	3	Leeds	1926-27
WEBB, James	Abertillery	F	20+3	St. Helens	1912-13
WILLIAMS, Brinley	Llanelli	WG	3	Batley	1920-21
WILLIAMS, Brynmor	Swansea	SH	3+3	Cardiff City	1982-83
WILLIAMS, Eddie	Neath	SH	2	Huddersfield	1925-26
WILLIAMS, Evan	Aberavon	C	2	Leeds	1925-26
WILLIAMS, Leslie	Cardiff	WG/C	7	Hunslet	1948-49
WILLIAMS, Sydney	Aberavon	WG	3	Salford	1939-40
*WILLIAMS, William	Crumlin	F	4	Salford	1927-28

† David and Evan James played openly for Broughton Rangers in 1897-98 but had been reinstated as amateurs by the Welsh Rugby Union. They returned to the Northern Union after appearing in the Wales v. England match on 7 January 1899.

● In addition, the following Wales Rugby Union internationals switched codes when their club joined the Northern Union in 1895. Both left Wales before the 1895 breakaway.

Name	Wales Club	Position	Caps	NU Club
Fitzgerald, G. David	Cardiff	C	2	Leigh
McCutcheon, William A.	Swansea	C	7	Oldham
Stadden, William	Cardiff	SH	8	Huddersfield

Jubilant Yorkshire, 1986 War of the Roses Trophy holders.

WAR OF THE ROSES

WAR OF THE ROSES

Yorkshire established a 2-0 lead in the Rodstock War of the Roses series with another convincing victory, this time on home soil.

Having pulled off a surprise 26-10 success in the inaugural county of origin encounter at Wigan a year earlier, the White Rose side repeated the performance at Headingley.

Peter Fox's charges provided all the outstanding individuals, with their teamwork being far superior to a strangely lethargic Lancashire outfit.

Billed as a credible Test trial with selection for the first Whitbread Trophy Bitter Test against Australia only weeks away, the two county line-ups contained a total of 20 capped players.

Yorkshire centre Ellery Hanley was awarded Man of the Match rating by Great Britain manager Les Bettinson, his strong running display being marked by a try, and the setting up of another.

But it was an uncapped performer who took the opportunity to impress the British management. Featherstone Rovers loose forward Paul Lyman pressed his mounting claim for a Test place by running superbly for the opening try and working hard throughout before being substituted in the final minutes.

His club teammate Deryck Fox once again outplayed his opposite number and Test rival Andy Gregory in a battle of the scrum halves.

A third Featherstone Rovers player, second row man Peter Smith, also caught the eye with a non-stop tackling stint in his first representative outing for well over two years. Yorkshire hooker Brian Noble was another industrious packman, returning to the representative arena for the first time since captaining the 1984 Great Britain touring team.

In a lack-lustre Lancashire side, only threequarter partners David Stephenson and John Basnett enhanced their repu-

tations, collecting all the Red Rose points.

Anxious to break Fox's stranglehold on the Great Britain number seven jersey, Gregory toiled behind a beaten pack, Test candidates John Fieldhouse, Chris Arkwright and Andy Platt failing to rise above subdued mediocrity.

Wigan utility star Joe Lydon, being groomed for the Test full back role, was given the job for Lancashire by coach Alex Murphy and caused consternation in the British camp with an unsteady performance, both on defence and fielding high balls.

Yorkshire opened the scoring after only three minutes with a planned move by Featherstone Rovers duo Fox and Lyman. The scrum half took a tap penalty just inside the Lancashire half and ran across field, dummying before bringing Lyman charging straight up field. The speedy forward displayed his trademark — a devastating

Lancashire scrum half Andy Gregory.

sidestep — to leave Lydon stranded.

Skipper John Joyner fed Hanley for the Wigan star to pull out of one tackle and step away from another in a 25-yard dash to the posts, while centre partner Tony Marchant added a third touchdown after snatching up a David Hobbs pass which had gone to ground.

Oldham front row man Hobbs added three goals in contrast to a solitary successful kick by Stephenson to give Yorkshire an 18-2 lead after 35 minutes.

The strong-running Basnett hit back with a try just before half-time, Stephenson adding the goal to take the interval scoreline to 18-8.

The home side did not enjoy the same freedom after the break and were restricted to two penalty goals from Hobbs before Gill

rounded off their scoring with the best touchdown of the night. Joyner again put Hanley free near halfway and Gill took over to round off the move in spectacular wingman fashion.

Lancashire, who had failed to capitalise on a 10-5 scrum and 12-9 penalty advantage, had some pride salvaged when Stephenson contributed a fine individual try in the 77th minute, to which he added the goal.

A crowd of 5,983 again confirmed the growing potential of the Rodstock War of the Roses venture, the only withdrawals from the original selections being Yorkshire forward duo Lee Crooks and Andy Goodway — both injured — paving the way for the county debuts of Hull K.R.'s Andy Kelly and York's Gary Price.

RODSTOCK WAR OF THE ROSES

17th September		Leeds

YORKSHIRE 26		LANCASHIRE 14
Ian Wilkinson (Leeds)	1.	Joe Lydon (Wigan)
Carl Gibson (Leeds)	2.	Mark Forster (Warrington)
Tony Marchant (Castleford)	3.	Ronnie Duane (Warrington)
Ellery Hanley (Wigan)	4.	David Stephenson (Wigan)
Henderson Gill (Wigan)	5.	John Basnett (Widnes)
John Joyner (Castleford) Capt.	6.	Shaun Edwards (Wigan)
Deryck Fox (Featherstone R.)	7.	Andy Gregory (Warrington) Capt.
Andy Kelly (Hull K.R.)	8.	Derek Pyke (Leigh)
Brian Noble (Bradford N.)	9.	Graham Liptrot (St. Helens)
David Hobbs (Oldham)	10.	John Fieldhouse (Widnes)
Peter Smith (Featherstone R.)	11.	Chris Arkwright (St. Helens)
Gary Price (York)	12.	Andy Platt (St. Helens)
Paul Lyman (Featherstone R.)	13.	Mike Gregory (Warrington)
Andy Mason (Bramley)	14.	John Henderson (Leigh)
Paul Medley (Leeds)	15.	Roy Haggerty (St. Helens)

T: Gill, Hanley, Lyman, Marchant
G: Hobbs (5)
Substitutes:
Mason for Gibson (64 min.)
Medley for Lyman (73 min.)
Coach: Peter Fox
Half-time: 18-8
Referee: John McDonald (Wigan)
Attendance: 5,983

T: Basnett, Stephenson
G: Stephenson (3)
Substitutes:
Haggerty for Pyke (Half-time)
Henderson for Duane (45 min.)
Coach: Alex Murphy

LANCASHIRE v. YORKSHIRE RESULTS
All county championship matches except where stated.

Date	Result		Score	Venue	Attendance
7 Dec. 1895	Yorkshire	won	8 - 0	Oldham	9,059
29 Feb. 1896	Lancashire	won	8 - 3	Huddersfield	5,300
21 Nov. 1896	Lancashire	won	7 - 3	Oldham	15,000
20 Nov. 1897	Yorkshire	won	7 - 6	Bradford P.A.	11,000
5 Nov. 1898	Yorkshire	won	20 - 9	Salford	8,000
4 Nov. 1899	Lancashire	won	16 - 13	Halifax	9,000
3 Nov. 1900	Lancashire	won	24 - 5	Rochdale	18,000
15 Feb. 1902	Yorkshire	won	13 - 8	Hull	15,000
15 Nov. 1902	Lancashire	won	13 - 0	Salford	14,000
14 Nov. 1903	Lancashire	won	8 - 0	Leeds	11,000
12 Nov. 1904	Yorkshire	won	14 - 5	Oldham	8,500
4 Nov. 1905	Lancashire	won	8 - 0	Hull	8,000
3 Nov. 1906	Lancashire	won	19 - 0	Salford	5,000
2 Nov. 1907	Yorkshire	won	15 - 11	Halifax	7,000
31 Oct. 1908	Lancashire	won	13 - 0	Salford	5,000
4 Nov. 1909	Yorkshire	won	27 - 14	Hull	6,000
7 Nov. 1910	Lancashire	won	17 - 3	Wigan	2,000
25 Jan. 1912	Lancashire	won	13 - 12	Halifax	3,199
16 Dec. 1912	Yorkshire	won	20 - 8	Oldham	4,000
10 Dec. 1913	Yorkshire	won	19 - 11	Huddersfield	3,500
24 Sept. 1919	Lancashire	won	15 - 5	Broughton	5,000
21 Oct. 1920	Yorkshire	won	18 - 3	Hull	7,000
4 Oct. 1921	Yorkshire	won	5 - 2	Rochdale	4,000
7 Dec. 1922	Match drawn	—	11 - 11	Hull K.R.	8,000
8 Dec. 1923	Lancashire	won	6 - 5	Oldham	8,000
29 Nov. 1924	Lancashire	won	28 - 9	Halifax	6,000
12 Dec. 1925	Lancashire	won	26 - 10	St. Helens	13,000
30 Oct. 1926	Lancashire	won	18 - 13	Wakefield	9,000
29 Oct. 1927	Lancashire	won	35 - 19	Warrington	12,000
3 Nov. 1928	Lancashire	won	33 - 10	Halifax	6,520
22 Mar. 1930	Lancashire	won	18 - 3	Rochdale	4,000
18 Oct. 1930	Yorkshire	won	25 - 15	Wakefield	9,000
17 Oct. 1931	Lancashire	won	11 - 8	Warrington	10,049
29 Oct. 1932	Yorkshire	won	30 - 3	Wakefield	4,000
25 Sept. 1933	Yorkshire	won	15 - 12	Oldham	2,000
*9 Jan. 1935	Match drawn	—	5 - 5	Leeds	1,500
12 Oct. 1935	Lancashire	won	16 - 5	Widnes	6,700
21 Oct. 1936	Lancashire	won	28 - 6	Castleford	7,648
12 Feb. 1938	Lancashire	won	10 - 9	Rochdale	3,653
*26 Oct. 1938	Match drawn	—	10 - 10	Leeds	3,000
10 Nov. 1945	Lancashire	won	17 - 16	Swinton	11,059
9 Nov. 1946	Yorkshire	won	13 - 10	Hunslet	5,000
12 Nov. 1947	Lancashire	won	22 - 10	Wigan	6,270
3 May 1949	Lancashire	won	12 - 3	Halifax	7,000

344

Date	Result		Score	Venue	Attendance
5 Oct. 1949	Lancashire	won	22 - 13	Warrington	15,000
18 Oct. 1950	Yorkshire	won	23 - 15	Huddersfield	6,547
10 Oct. 1951	Yorkshire	won	15 - 5	Leigh	11,573
28 Apr. 1953	Yorkshire	won	16 - 8	Hull	8,400
14 Oct. 1953	Lancashire	won	18 - 10	Leigh	12,870
6 Oct. 1954	Yorkshire	won	20 - 10	Bradford	8,500
26 Sept. 1955	Lancashire	won	26 - 10	Oldham	8,000
26 Sept. 1956	Lancashire	won	35 - 21	Hull	8,500
23 Sept. 1957	Yorkshire	won	25 - 11	Widnes	6,200
24 Sept. 1958	Yorkshire	won	35 - 19	Hull K.R.	5,000
29 Oct. 1958	Yorkshire	won	16 - 15	Leigh	8,500
11 Nov. 1959	Yorkshire	won	38 - 28	Leigh	6,417
31 Aug. 1960	Lancashire	won	21 - 20	Wakefield	15,045
9 Oct. 1961	Lancashire	won	14 - 12	Leigh	4,970
26 Sept. 1962	Yorkshire	won	22 - 8	Wakefield	7,956
11 Sept. 1963	Lancashire	won	45 - 20	St. Helens	11,200
23 Sept. 1964	Yorkshire	won	33 - 10	Hull	7,100
10 Nov. 1965	Yorkshire	won	16 - 13	Swinton	5,847
21 Sept. 1966	Lancashire	won	22 - 17	Leeds	10,528
24 Jan. 1968	Lancashire	won	23 - 17	Widnes	8,322
25 Sept. 1968	Yorkshire	won	10 - 5	Hull K.R.	6,656
3 Sept. 1969	Lancashire	won	14 - 12	Salford	4,652
13 Jan. 1971	Yorkshire	won	32 - 12	Castleford	2,000
24 Feb. 1971	Yorkshire	won	34 - 8	Castleford	4,400
29 Sept. 1971	Yorkshire	won	42 - 22	Leigh	4,987
11 Oct. 1972	Yorkshire	won	32 - 18	Castleford	2,474
19 Sept. 1973	Lancashire	won	17 - 15	Widnes	3,357
25 Sept. 1974	Yorkshire	won	20 - 14	Keighley	1,219
16 Oct. 1974	Lancashire	won	29 - 11	Widnes	3,114
20 Dec. 1975	Yorkshire	won	17 - 7	Wigan	700
1 Mar. 1977	Yorkshire	won	18 - 13	Castleford	2,730
†19 Oct. 1977	Lancashire	won	33 - 8	Widnes	5,056
27 Sept. 1978	Lancashire	won	23 - 7	Widnes	4,283
12 Sept. 1979	Yorkshire	won	19 - 16	Castleford	2,738
24 Sept. 1980	Lancashire	won	17 - 9	Widnes	1,593
9 Sept. 1981	Yorkshire	won	21 - 15	Castleford	1,222
23 May 1982	Yorkshire	won	22 - 21	Leigh	1,738
WR11 Sept. 1985	Yorkshire	won	26 - 10	Wigan	6,743
WR17 Sept. 1986	Yorkshire	won	26 - 14	Leeds	5,983

* Match abandoned but result stands   †Queen's Jubilee match   WR War of the Roses
● There were also a few Lancashire-Yorkshire matches played during the First World War but not of a competitive nature.

SUMMARY
Lancashire won 41   Yorkshire won 39   Drawn 3

Tryscoring elation for Yorkshire centre Tony Marchant.

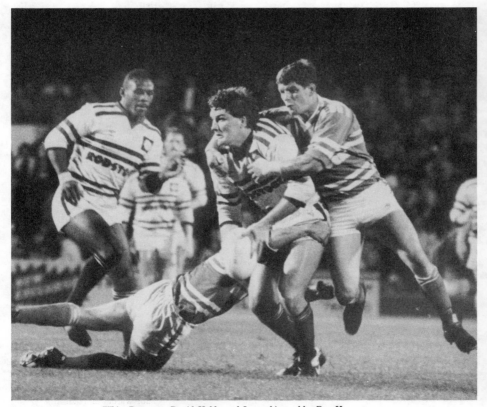

White Rose prop David Hobbs and Lancashire tackler Roy Haggerty.

LANCASHIRE v. YORKSHIRE RECORDS

LANCASHIRE

Highest score:	45-20 at St. Helens, 11 Sept. 1963
Widest margin win:	As above and 33-8 at Widnes, 19 Oct. 1977
Most tries in a match:	No player has scored more than 3
Most goals in a match:	9 by L. Gilfedder (Wigan) at St. Helens, 11 Sept. 1963
Most points in a match:	18 by L. Gilfedder (Wigan) as above
Biggest home attendance:	18,000 at Rochdale, 3 Nov. 1900

OTHER RECORDS (not involving Yorkshire)

Highest score:	60-12 v. Cumberland at Wigan, 10 Sept. 1958
Most tries in a match:	4 by T. O'Grady (Oldham) v. Cumberland at Wigan, 6 Sept. 1956
	4 by W. Burgess (Barrow) v. Cumberland at Widnes, 12 Sept. 1962
Most goals in a match:	12 by E. Fraser (Warrington) v. Cumberland at Wigan, 10 Sept. 1958
Most points in a match:	24 by E. Fraser (Warrington) as above
Biggest home attendance:	24,000 v. Australia at Warrington, 26 Sept. 1929

YORKSHIRE

Highest score:	42-22 at Leigh, 29 Sept. 1971
Widest margin win:	30-3 at Wakefield, 29 Oct. 1932
Most tries in a match:	No player has scored more than 3
Most goals in a match:	10 by V. Yorke (York) at Hull K.R., 24 Sept. 1958
Most points in a match:	20 by V. Yorke (York) as above
Biggest home attendance:	15,045 at Wakefield, 31 Aug. 1960

OTHER RECORDS (not involving Lancashire)

Highest score:	51-12 v. Cumberland at Hunslet, 17 Oct. 1923
Highest against:	55-11 v. Australia at Huddersfield, 26 Nov. 1952
Most tries in a match:	5 by J. Parkin (Wakefield T.) v. Cumberland at Halifax, 14 Nov. 1921
Most goals in a match:	10 also by N. Fox (Wakefield T.) v. Australia at York, 28 Sept. 1959
Most points in a match:	23 by N. Fox (Wakefield T.) as above
Biggest home attendance:	19,376 v. Australia at Wakefield, 4 Oct. 1967

LANCASHIRE TEAMS

. . . A 20-year review. Initials are included where more than one celebrated player shared a surname in the same era. Only playing substitutes are listed.

1967 Cumberland
Workington: 12 Sept.
Won 19-6

F. Barrow (St. Helens)
Burgess (Barrow) 2t
Hesketh (Salford)
F. Myler (St. Helens) 1t
Glover (Warrington)
Aspinall (Warrington) 1t, 2g
Bishop (St. Helens) 1t
Halsall (St. Helens)
Burdell (Salford)
Brady (Warrington)
Sanderson (Barrow)
Parr (Warrington)
Clarke (Warrington)
Sub: Laughton (Wigan)

1967 Australia
Salford: 11 Oct.
Lost 2-14

F. Barrow (St. Helens)
Burgess (Barrow)
Hesketh (Salford)
F. Myler (St. Helens)
Glover (Warrington)
Aspinall (Warrington)
Bishop (St. Helens)
Halliwell (Barrow) 1g
Burdell (Salford)
Brady (Warrington)
Sanderson (Barrow)
Parr (Warrington)
Clarke (Warrington)
Subs: Tees (Barrow)
    S. Whitehead (Salford)

1968 Yorkshire
Widnes: 24 Jan.
Won 23-17

Tyrer (Wigan) 4g
Burgess (Barrow)
Buckley (Swinton)
F. Myler (St. Helens)
Glover (Warrington) 1t
D. O'Neill (Widnes) 2t
Bishop (St. Helens)
Halliwell (Barrow) 1t
Burdell (Salford)
Fletcher (Oldham) 1t
Fogerty (Wigan)
French (Widnes)
Laughton (Wigan)
Sub: Warburton (Oldham)

1968 Yorkshire

Hull K.R.: 25 Sept.

Lost 5-10

Dutton (Widnes) 1g
D. Whitehead (Oldham)
Benyon (St. Helens)
Glover (Warrington)
Jones (St. Helens)
D. O'Neill (Widnes)
Williams (Swinton)
Halliwell (Salford)
Taylor (Oldham)
Fletcher (Oldham)
French (Widnes)
S. Whitehead (Salford)
Lyon (Wigan)
Subs: Hesketh (Salford) 1t
    J. Stephens (Wigan)

1968 Cumberland

St. Helens: 6 Nov.

Won 24-19

Dutton (Widnes) 3g
Burgess (Barrow) 2t
Hesketh (Salford)
Gemmell (Hull) 2t
Tickle (Leigh)
Brophy (Barrow)
Bishop (St. Helens)
J. Stephens (Wigan)
Sayer (St. Helens)
Brown (Rochdale)
E. Chisnall (St. Helens) 2t
Welding (Leigh)
Robinson (Swinton)
Sub: D. O'Neill (Widnes)

1969 Yorkshire

Salford: 3 Sept.

Won 14-12

Dutton (Widnes) 4g
Jones (St. Helens)
Hesketh (Salford)
Benyon (St. Helens)
Murray (Barrow) 1t
W. Davies (Swinton)
Gordon (Warrington)
J. Stephens (Wigan)
Taylor (Oldham)
Fletcher (Wigan)
Nicholls (Widnes)
Welding (Leigh)
Laughton (Wigan) 1t
Subs: Tees (Rochdale)
    B. Hogan (Wigan)

1969 Cumberland

Workington: 24 Sept.

Won 30-10

Dutton (Widnes) 6g
Burgess (Salford)
Hesketh (Salford)
F. Myler (St. Helens)
Murray (Barrow)
A. Murphy (Leigh) 3t
Gordon (Warrington) 1t
J. Stephens (Wigan)
Ashcroft (Leigh)
Sanderson (Barrow)
Robinson (Swinton) 1t
Welding (Leigh)
Laughton (Wigan) 1t
Sub: D. Hill (Wigan)

1970 Cumberland

Barrow: 11 Nov.

Won 28-5

John Walsh (St. Helens) 5g
S. Wright (Wigan) 1t
Benyon (St. Helens)
Hesketh (Salford) 1t
Joe Walsh (Leigh)
F. Myler (St. Helens) 2t
Boylan (Widnes)
D. Chisnall (Leigh)
Ashcroft (Leigh) 1t
Brown (Rochdale)
E. Prescott (St. Helens) 1t
E. Chisnall (St. Helens)
Laughton (Wigan)
Subs: Martin Murphy (Oldham)
    Nicholls (Widnes)

1971 Yorkshire

Castleford: 13 Jan.

Lost 12-32

Dutton (Widnes) 3g
S. Wright (Wigan)
Benyon (St. Helens)
D. O'Neill (Widnes)
Joe Walsh (Leigh)
W. Davies (Swinton) 1t
A. Murphy (Leigh)
Mick Murphy (Barrow)
Clarke (Wigan)
Brown (Rochdale)
E. Chisnall (St. Helens)
E. Prescott (St. Helens)
Laughton (Wigan) 1t
Subs: Boylan (Widnes)
    Nicholls (Widnes)

1971 Yorkshire (Play-off)

Castleford: 24 Feb.

Lost 8-34

Tyrer (Wigan) 1g
Joe Walsh (Leigh)
Buckley (Swinton)
Hesketh (Salford)
Jones (St. Helens) 1t
D. O'Neill (Widnes)
Boylan (Widnes)
J. Stephens (St. Helens)
Ashcroft (Leigh)
B. Hogan (Wigan)
Nicholls (Widnes) 1t
Cramant (Swinton)
Robinson (Wigan)
Subs: Eckersley (Leigh)
    Clarke (Wigan)

1971 Cumberland

Workington: 15 Sept.

Lost 7-17

Dutton (Widnes) 2g
Keiron O'Loughlin (Wigan)
Benyon (St. Helens) 1t
Eckersley (Leigh)
Fuller (Wigan)
D. O'Neill (Widnes)
Boylan (Leigh)
D. Chisnall (Warrington)
A. Karalius (St. Helens)
Brown (Rochdale)
Cunningham (Wigan)
Wills (Huyton)
Nicholls (Widnes)
Subs: Whittle (St. Helens)
    Welding (Rochdale)

1971 Yorkshire

Leigh: 29 Sept.

Lost 22-42

Dutton (Widnes) 5g
Jones (St. Helens)
Benyon (St. Helens)
Hesketh (Salford)
Joe Walsh (Leigh)
D. O'Neill (Widnes)
Kenny (Swinton) 1t
J. Stephens (St. Helens) 1t
A. Karalius (St. Helens)
Mick Murphy (Barrow)
Lester (Leigh)
Ashurst (Wigan)
Clark (Oldham) 1t
Subs: Eckersley (Leigh)
    Welding (Rochdale) 1t

1972 Cumberland
Warrington: 27 Sept.
Won: 26-16
Martin Murphy (Oldham)
Hodgkinson (Oldham)
Benyon (St. Helens)
John Walsh (St. Helens) 1t, 4g
E. Hughes (Widnes)
K. Kelly (St. Helens) 1t
Banner (Salford)
Halsall (Swinton)
A. Karalius (St. Helens) 2t
J. Stephens (St. Helens)
E. Prescott (Salford)
B. Gregory (Warrington) 1t
Nicholls (Widnes) 1t
Subs: Hesketh (Salford)
      Birchall (Rochdale)

1973 Yorkshire
Widnes: 19 Sept.
Won 17-15
D. Whitehead (Warrington) 3g
Brelsford (Rochdale)
Benyon (St. Helens) 1t
Hesketh (Salford)
E. Hughes (Widnes)
Eckersley (St. Helens)
Gordon (Warrington)
Fiddler (Leigh) 1g
Evans (Swinton)
Brady (Warrington)
Nicholls (St. Helens) 1t
Welding (Rochdale)
E. Prescott (Salford) 1t
Subs: Noonan (Warrington)
      Briggs (Warrington)

1974 Yorkshire
Keighley: 25 Sept.
Lost 14-20
D. Whitehead (Warrington) 4g
S. Wright (Wigan)
John Walsh (St. Helens)
Hesketh (Salford) 1t
E. Hughes (Widnes)
Whittle (Warrington)
Gordon (Warrington)
D. Chisnall (Warrington)
Evans (Swinton)
Fiddler (Leigh)
T. Martyn (Leigh) 1t
B. Gregory (Oldham)
B. Philbin (Warrington)
Sub: Robinson (Wigan)

1972 Yorkshire
Castleford: 11 Oct.
Lost 18-32
Dutton (Widnes) 2g
Hodgkinson (Oldham) 1t
Benyon (St. Helens)
John Walsh (St. Helens) 1g
E. Hughes (Widnes) 1t
D. O'Neill (Widnes) 1t
Banner (Salford)
Halsall (Swinton)
A. Karalius (St. Helens)
J. Stephens (St. Helens) 1t
E. Chisnall (St. Helens)
B. Gregory (Warrington)
Ashurst (Wigan)

1974 Other Nationalities
Salford: 11 Sept.
Won 14-13
D. Whitehead (Warrington) 1g
S. Wright (Wigan)
John Walsh (St. Helens)
Noonan (Warrington)
Jones (St. Helens)
Whittle (Warrington) 1t
Gordon (Warrington)
D. Chisnall (Warrington)
Evans (Swinton)
Fiddler (Leigh) 3g
Nicholls (St. Helens)
E. Prescott (Salford)
B. Philbin (Warrington)
Sub: B. Gregory (Oldham) 1t

1974 Yorkshire (Play-off)
Widnes: 16 Oct.
Won 29-11
Dutton (Widnes) 7g
S. Wright (Wigan) 1t
Hesketh (Salford) 1t
Noonan (Warrington) 2t
E. Hughes (Widnes)
Gill (Salford) 1t
Gordon (Warrington)
D. Chisnall (Warrington)
Ashcroft (Warrington)
Brady (Warrington)
Nicholls (St. Helens)
E. Prescott (Salford)
B. Philbin (Warrington)
Subs: Aspey (Widnes)
      T. Martyn (Leigh)

1973 Cumbria
Barrow: 5 Sept.
Won 18-6
D. Whitehead (Warrington) 3g
Brelsford (Rochdale)
Benyon (St. Helens) 1t
Hesketh (Salford)
E. Hughes (Widnes) 1t
Eckersley (St. Helens)
Gordon (Warrington)
Fiddler (Leigh) 1t
Evans (Swinton)
Brady (Warrington)
Nicholls (St. Helens)
Welding (Rochdale)
Laughton (Widnes)
Sub: Noonan (Warrington) 1t

1974 Cumbria
Warrington: 18 Sept.
Won 29-4
D. Whitehead (Warrington) 4g, 1t
S. Wright (Wigan) 1t
Noonan (Warrington) 2t
Hesketh (Salford)
E. Hughes (Widnes) 1t
Whittle (Warrington)
Nulty (Wigan)
D. Chisnall (Warrington) 1t
Evans (Swinton)
Fiddler (Leigh)
Robinson (Wigan)
B. Gregory (Oldham)
T. Martyn (Leigh) 1t

1975 Other Nationalities
St. Helens: 25 Nov.
Won 36-7
Dutton (Widnes) 6g
J. Davies (Leigh)
Pimblett (St. Helens)
Butler (Salford)
George (Widnes)
Gill (Salford) 1t
Bowden (Widnes) 1t
B. Hogan (Wigan)
Elwell (Widnes) 1t
Nelson (Widnes)
Nicholls (St. Helens) 1t
T. Martyn (Warrington) 2t
Adams (Widnes) 1t
Subs: Eckersley (St. Helens)
      Hodkinson (Rochdale) 1t

1975 Cumbria
Workington: 6 Dec.
Won 22-17
Dutton (Widnes) 5g
Davies (Leigh) 1t
Butler (Salford) 1t
George (Widnes)
Jones (St. Helens)
Gill (Salford)
Bowden (Widnes) 2t
B. Hogan (Wigan)
Elwell (Widnes)
Hodkinson (Rochdale)
Nicholls (St. Helens)
T. Martyn (Warrington)
Adams (Widnes)
Subs: Eckersley (St. Helens)
     Turnbull (Salford)

1977 Yorkshire
Widnes: 1 March
Lost 13-18
Fairbairn (Wigan) 3g
Fielding (Salford)
Hughes (Widnes) 1t
Hesford (Warrington)
S. Wright (Widnes)
Gill (Salford)
Bowden (Widnes)
Hodkinson (Rochdale)
Elwell (Widnes) 1dg
J. Wood (Widnes)
T. Martyn (Warrington) 1t
Adams (Widnes)
Boyd (Leigh)
Subs: Aspey (Widnes)
     Pinner (St. Helens)

1978 Cumbria
Whitehaven: 11 Oct.
Lost 15-16
Glynn (St. Helens) 3g
S. Wright (Widnes) 2t
Aspey (Widnes)
E. Hughes (Widnes)
Jones (St. Helens)
K. Kelly (Warrington)
Bowden (Widnes)
D. Chisnall (St. Helens)
Liptrot (St. Helens)
Hodkinson (Rochdale)
Adams (Widnes)
Nicholls (Widnes)
E. Prescott (Salford)
Subs: Keiron O'Loughlin (Wigan) 1t
     Pinner (St. Helens)

1975 Yorkshire
Wigan: 20 Dec.
Lost 7-17
Dutton (Widnes) 2g
Jones (St. Helens)
Butler (Salford)
George (Widnes)
E. Hughes (Widnes)
Gill (Salford)
Bowden (Widnes)
B. Hogan (Wigan)
Evans (Swinton)
Hodkinson (Rochdale)
Turnbull (Salford) 1t
T. Martyn (Warrington)
Adams (Widnes)
Subs: Benyon (St. Helens)
     Nelson (Widnes)

1977 Yorkshire (Jubilee)
Widnes: 19 Oct.
Won 33-8
Pimblett (St. Helens) 5g
Jones (St. Helens)
Aspey (Widnes) 1t
Woods (Leigh) 2t, 2g
S. Wright (Widnes) 1t
Gill (Salford)
Bowden (Widnes)
Wilkinson (Leigh) 1t
Elwell (Widnes) 1t
Gourley (Rochdale)
Adams (Widnes) 1dg
Nicholls (St. Helens)
E. Prescott (Salford)
Sub: Macko (Leigh)

1979 Cumbria
St. Helens: 5 Sept.
Won 23-15
Eckersley (Widnes) 2g
Arkwright (St. Helens) 1t
Woods (Leigh) 1t, 3g
E. Hughes (Widnes) 2t
Hornby (Wigan)
K. Kelly (Warrington)
Bowden (Widnes)
B. Hogan (Wigan)
Elwell (Widnes)
S. O'Neill (Wigan)
W. Melling (Wigan)
Nicholls (St. Helens)
Pinner (St. Helens) 1dg
Subs: Glynn (St. Helens)
     E. Prescott (Salford)

1977 Cumbria
Leigh: 2 Feb.
Won 18-14
M. Hogan (Leigh)
Fielding (Salford) 1t
Stacey (Leigh)
Butler (Salford)
S. Wright (Widnes) 1t
Gill (Salford)
Bowden (Widnes)
Coulman (Salford) 1t
Elwell (Widnes)
Wilkinson (Leigh)
T. Martyn (Warrington)
Adams (Widnes)
Boyd (Leigh)
Sub: Hesford (Warrington) 1t, 3g

1978 Yorkshire
Widnes: 27 Sept.
Won 23-7
Fairbairn (Wigan) 4g
Fielding (Salford) 2t
Aspey (Widnes)
Cunningham (St. Helens) 1t
Bevan (Warrington) 1t
K. Kelly (Warrington) 1t
Bowden (Widnes)
D. Chisnall (St. Helens)
Elwell (Widnes)
Hodkinson (Rochdale)
Adams (Widnes)
Nicholls (St. Helens)
E. Prescott (Salford)
Subs: Glynn (St. Helens)
     Pinner (St. Helens)

1979 Yorkshire
Castleford: 12 Sept.
Lost 16-19
Eckersley (Widnes) 1t
Arkwright (St. Helens)
Keiron O'Loughlin (Wigan)
E. Hughes (Widnes)
Glynn (St. Helens)
Burke (Widnes) 3g
Bowden (Widnes)
S. O'Neill (Wigan)
Elwell (Widnes)
Gourley (Salford)
Adams (Widnes)
W. Melling (Wigan)
Pinner (St. Helens) 2t, 1dg
Subs: Hull (Widnes)
     E. Prescott (Salford)

1980 Cumbria
Barrow: 3 Sept.
Lost 16-19
Burke (Widnes) 2g
Bilsbury (Leigh) 1t
Stephenson (Salford)
Glynn (St. Helens)
Bentley (Widnes)
Woods (Leigh) 2t
Holding (St. Helens)
M. O'Neill (Widnes)
Elwell (Widnes)
Eccles (Warrington) 1t
Dearden (Widnes)
Gittins (Leigh)
Adams (Widnes)
Sub: Flanagan (Oldham)

1980 Yorkshire
Widnes: 24 Sept.
Won 17-9
C. Whitfield (Salford) 4g
Bentley (Widnes)
Bilsbury (Leigh) 1t
M. Foy (Wigan)
Hornby (Wigan) 1t
Woods (Leigh)
Holding (St. Helens) 1t
M. O'Neill (Widnes)
Liptrot (St. Helens)
Eccles (Warrington)
S. O'Neill (Wigan)
Dearden (Widnes)
Adams (Widnes)
Subs: A. Fairhurst (Leigh)
Gittins (Leigh)

1981 Yorkshire
Castleford: 9 Sept.
Lost 15-21
C. Whitfield (Salford) 3g
Drummond (Leigh) 2t
Stephenson (Salford)
M. Foy (Wigan)
Bentley (Widnes) 1t
K. Kelly (Warrington)
A. Gregory (Widnes)
M. O'Neill (Widnes)
Kiss (Wigan)
Case (Warrington)
Potter (Warrington)
Adams (Widnes)
Pinner (St. Helens)
Sub: Donlan (Leigh)

1981 Cumbria
Wigan: 16 Sept.
Lost 15-27
C. Whitfield (Salford) 3g
Drummond (Leigh) 1t
George (Widnes)
Glynn (St. Helens) 1t
Bentley (Widnes)
K. Kelly (Warrington) 1t
Peters (St. Helens)
Hodkinson (Wigan)
Kiss (Wigan)
M. O'Neill (Widnes)
Potter (Warrington)
Case (Warrington)
Pinner (St. Helens)
Subs: Kirwan (Oldham)
Yates (Salford)

1982 Yorkshire
Leigh: 26 May
Lost 21-22
Burke (Widnes) 1t, 6g
Drummond (Leigh)
Stephenson (Wigan) 1t
Woods (Leigh)
Basnett (Widnes)
A. Myler (Widnes) 1t
A. Gregory (Widnes)
M. O'Neill (Widnes)
Kiss (Wigan)
Wilkinson (Leigh)
Potter (Leigh)
F. Whitfield (Widnes)
Flanagan (Oldham)
Sub: Fieldhouse (Warrington)

1982 Cumbria
Workington: 30 May
Won 46-8
Burke (Widnes) 8g
Meadows (St. Helens) 3t
Stephenson (Wigan) 2t
Donlan (Leigh) 3t
Basnett (Widnes)
Keiron O'Loughlin (Widnes)
A. Gregory (Widnes)
M. O'Neill (Widnes) 1t
Kiss (Wigan)
Wilkinson (Leigh)
Potter (Leigh)
Tabern (Leigh) 1t
Flanagan (Oldham)
Subs: C. Whitfield (Wigan)
Fieldhouse (Warrington)

1985 Yorkshire
Wigan: 11 Sept.
Lost 10-26
Burke (Widnes) 1g
Ledger (St. Helens)
Stephenson (Wigan)
Keiron O'Loughlin (Salford)
Lydon (Widnes)
A. Myler (Widnes)
A. Gregory (Warrington) 1t
M. O'Neill (Widnes)
Webb (Warrington)
Forber (St. Helens)
Eccles (Warrington) 1t
Fieldhouse (Widnes)
Pendlebury (Salford)
Subs: Edwards (Wigan)
Wane (Wigan)

1986 Yorkshire
Leeds: 17 Sept.
Lost 14-26
Lydon (Wigan)
Forster (Warrington)
R. Duane (Warrington)
Stephenson (Wigan) 1t, 3g
Basnett (Widnes) 1t
Edwards (Wigan)
A. Gregory (Warrington)
Pyke (Leigh)
Liptrot (St. Helens)
Fieldhouse (Widnes)
Arkwright (St. Helens)
Platt (St. Helens)
M. Gregory (Warrington)
Subs: Henderson (Leigh)
Haggerty (St. Helens)

Two-cap Tony Myler.

351

LANCASHIRE REGISTER

The following is a register of current players who have appeared for Lancashire. Each played at least one first team game last season.

ARKWRIGHT, C. (3) St. Helens

BASNETT, J. (3) Widnes
BENTLEY, K. (4) Widnes
BURKE, M. (5) Widnes

CASE, B. (2) Warrington

DONLAN, S. (1+1) Leigh
DRUMMOND, D. (3) Leigh
DUANE, R. (1) Warrington

ECCLES, R. (3) Warrington
EDWARDS, S. (1+1) Wigan

FAIRBAIRN, G. (2) Wigan
FAIRHURST, A. (+1) Leigh
FIELDHOUSE, J. (2+2) Warrington +2, Widnes 2
FLANAGAN, T. (2+1) Oldham
FORBER, P. (1) St. Helens
FORSTER, M. (1) Warrington
FOY, M. (2) Wigan

GITTINS, T. (1+1) Leigh
GLYNN, P. (4+2) St. Helens
GREGORY, A. (5) Widnes 3, Warrington 2
GREGORY, M. (1) Warrington

HAGGERTY, R. (+1) St. Helens
HENDERSON, J. (+1) Leigh
HESFORD, S. (1+1) Warrington
HOLDING, N. (2) St. Helens
HUGHES, E. (12) Widnes

KELLY, K. (6) St. Helens, Warrington 5
KIRWAN, P. (+1) Oldham
KISS, N. (4) Wigan

LEDGER, B. (1) St. Helens
LIPTROT, G. (3) St. Helens
LYDON, J. (2) Widnes, Wigan

MEADOWS, K. (1) St. Helens
MYLER, A. (2) Widnes

O'LOUGHLIN, Keiron (4+1) Wigan 2+1, Widnes, Salford
O'NEILL, M. (7) Widnes
O'NEILL, S. (3) Wigan

PENDLEBURY, J. (1) Salford
PETERS, S. (1) St. Helens
PINNER, H. (4+3) St. Helens
PLATT, A. (1) St. Helens
POTTER, I. (4) Warrington 2, Leigh 2
PRESCOTT, E. (9+2) Salford 7+2, St. Helens 2
PYKE, D. (1) Leigh

STEPHENSON, D. (6) Salford 2, Wigan 4

TABERN, R. (1) Leigh

WANE, S. (+1) Wigan
WEBB, C. (1) Warrington
WHITFIELD, C. (3+1) Salford 3, Wigan +1
WOODS, J. (5) Leigh
WRIGHT, S. (10) Wigan 6, Widnes 4

YORKSHIRE TEAMS

. . . A 20-year review. Initials are included where more than one celebrated player shared a surname in the same era. Only playing substitutes are listed.

1967 Australia	1967 Cumberland	1968 Lancashire
Wakefield: 4 Oct.	Castleford: 25 Oct.	Widnes: 24 Jan.
Won 15-14	Won 34-23	Lost 17-23
Keegan (Hull)	Keegan (Hull) 2g	Keegan (Hull)
Young (Hull KR)	Goodchild (Halifax) 2t	Young (Hull KR)
Wriglesworth (Bradford)	Stockwell (Bradford)	A. Burwell (Hull KR)
N. Fox (Wakefield) 3g,1t	Longstaff (Huddersfield)	N. Fox (Wakefield) 4g
Francis (Wigan)	Francis (Wigan) 4t	Atkinson (Leeds) 1t
Millward (Hull KR) 1t	Millward (Hull KR) 1t,3g	Millward (Hull KR) 1t
Dooler (Featherstone) 1t	K. Hepworth (Castleford) 1t	Seabourne (Leeds)
Harrison (Hull)	Clark (Leeds)	Clark (Leeds)
Close (Huddersfield)	Close (Huddersfield)	Close (Huddersfield)
Hill (Bradford)	Scroby (Halifax)	Walton (Castleford)
Clarkson (Wakefield)	Bryant (Castleford)	Ramshaw (Bradford) 1t
Small (Castleford)	Clarkson (Wakefield)	Ramsey (Leeds)
Major (Hull KR)	Major (Hull KR)	Major (Hull KR)
Sub: A. Morgan (Featherstone)	Sub: Ramsey (Hunslet)	Sub: A. Hepworth (Bradford)

1968 Cumberland

Whitehaven: 11 Sept.

Won 23-10

Keegan (Hull)
Hurl (Hunslet)
A. Burwell (Hull KR) 1t
Wriglesworth (Bradford) 2t
Atkinson (Leeds) 1t
Millward (Hull KR) 4g,1t
Seabourne (Leeds)
Clark (Leeds)
C. Dickinson (Castleford)
Scroby (Halifax)
Ramsey (Leeds)
A. Morgan (Featherstone)
Reilly (Castleford)

1968 Lancashire

Hull KR: 25 Sept.

Won 10-5

Keegan (Hull) 1t
Francis (Wigan)
Hynes (Leeds)
Wriglesworth (Bradford)
Atkinson (Leeds)
Millward (Hull KR) 2g
Seabourne (Leeds) 1t
Denis Hartley (Castleford)
C. Dickinson (Castleford)
J. Ward (Castleford)
P. Lowe (Hull KR)
A. Morgan (Featherstone)
Reilly (Castleford)

1969 Lancashire

Salford: 3 Sept.

Lost 12-14

Keegan (Hull)
A. Smith (Leeds)
Hynes (Leeds)
A. Burwell (Hull KR)
Francis (Wigan)
Millward (Hull KR) 2g
K.Hepworth (Castleford) 1t
Denis Hartley (Castleford)
C. Dickinson (Castleford)
Macklin (Hull) 1g
P. Lowe (Hull KR) 1t
Lockwood (Castleford)
Batten (Leeds)
Subs: Edwards (Castleford)
      A. Morgan (Featherstone)

1969 Cumberland

Hull KR: 1 Oct.

Won 42-3

Keegan (Hull) 1t
Lowndes (Castleford) 1t
Moore (Hull KR) 3t
A. Burwell (Hull KR)
T. Thompson (Hunslet) 1t
Millward (Hull KR) 6g, 2t
Davidson (Hull) 1t
Harrison (Hull)
M. Stephenson (Dewsbury)
J. Ward (Castleford)
Haigh (Wakefield) 1t
J. Thompson (Featherstone)
Doyle (Batley)

1970 Cumberland

Whitehaven: 14 Sept.

Lost 15-21

Edwards (Castleford)
Slater (Wakefield)
Shoebottom (Leeds)
Watson (Leeds)
Lamb (Bradford) 1t
Wolford (Bramley)
Davidson (Hull)
Denis Hartley (Castleford)
M. Stephenson (Dewsbury) 1t
Clawson (Hull KR) 3g
Lockwood (Castleford)
J. Thompson (Featherstone) 1t
Batten (Leeds)
Sub: Firth (Hull)

1971 Lancashire

Castleford: 13 Jan.

Won 32-12

Jefferson (Keighley) 6g
A. Smith (Leeds) 2t
Hynes (Leeds) 1t
N. Stephenson (Dewsbury) 2t
Atkinson (Leeds)
Topliss (Wakefield)
Shoebottom (Leeds) 1g
Clawson (Hull KR)
C. Dickinson (Castleford)
Jeanes (Wakefield)
Haigh (Leeds)
J. Thompson (Featherstone)
Batten (Leeds) 1t

1971 Lancashire (Play-off)

Castleford: 24 Feb.

Won 34-8

Jefferson (Keighley) 1t,1g
Slater (Wakefield) 2t
Stenton (Castleford)
N. Stephenson (Dewsbury) 3g, 2t
Young (York)
Hardisty (Castleford) 1g
K. Hepworth (Castleford)
Clawson (Hull KR)
C. Dickinson (Castleford)
Jeanes (Wakefield) 1t
Lockwood (Castleford)
Irving (Oldham) 1t
Halmshaw (Halifax)
Subs: Topliss (Wakefield) 1t
      M. Stephenson (Dewsbury)

1971 Lancashire

Leigh: 29 Sept.

Won 42-22

Edwards (Castleford)
Slater (Wakefield)
Watson (Bradford) 1t
N. Stephenson (Dewsbury) 5g,1t
Lamb (Bradford) 1t
Millward (Hull KR) 4g,1t
Nash (Featherstone) 1t
Harrison (Hull)
M. Stephenson (Dewsbury)
Jeanes (Wakefield)
Boxall (Hull)
Irving (Oldham)
Halmshaw (Halifax) 1t
Subs: Topliss (Wakefield) 1t
      Farrar (Featherstone) 1t

1971 Cumberland

Wakefield: 20 Oct.

Won 17-12

Edwards (Castleford)
Slater (Wakefield)
Watson (Bradford) 2t
N. Stephenson (Dewsbury) 2t
Lamb (Bradford)
Millward (Hull KR) 1g
A. Bates (Dewsbury)
Harrison (Hull)
M. Stephenson (Dewsbury)
Farrar (Featherstone)
Boxall (Hull) 1t
Irving (Oldham)
Halmshaw (Halifax)

1972 Cumberland
Whitehaven: 13 Sept.
Lost: 14-23
Rushton (Dewsbury)
A. Smith (Leeds)
Dyl (Leeds)
N. Stephenson (Dewsbury) 4g
D. Redfearn (Bradford)
Millward (Hull KR)
Nash (Featherstone) 2t
Clawson (Leeds)
M. Stephenson (Dewsbury)
Jeanes (Wakefield)
Cookson (Leeds)
J. Bates (Dewsbury)
Halmshaw (Halifax)
Subs: Wraith (Wakefield)
        Irving (Oldham)

1973 Cumbria
Bramley: 12 Sept.
Won 37-12
Jefferson (Keighley) 7g, 1t
A. Smith (Leeds) 3t
Newlove (Featherstone)
Dyl (Leeds)
Atkinson (Leeds)
Topliss (Wakefield) 1t
Nash (Featherstone) 1g
Ballantyne (Wakefield)
M. Morgan (Wakefield) 1t
Davies (Huddersfield)
Irving (Wigan)
J. Thompson (Featherstone) 1t
Stone (Featherstone)
Sub: Idle (Bramley)

1974 Other Nationalities
Hull KR: 18 Sept.
Won 22-15
Marshall (Leeds) 5g
D. Redfearn (Bradford)
Hughes (Bramley)
M. Smith (Featherstone) 1t
Atkinson (Leeds)
Burton (Halifax) 1t
A. Bates (Dewsbury)
Harrison (Leeds)
Farrar (Featherstone)
Ramsey (Bradford) 1t
Grayshon (Dewsbury)
J. Thompson (Featherstone)
Norton (Castleford)
Subs: Langley (Leeds)
        J. Bates (Dewsbury)

1972 Lancashire
Castleford: 11 Oct.
Won 32-18
Jefferson (Keighley) 7g
Lamb (Bradford) 2t
Worsley (Castleford) 1t
Pickup (Huddersfield) 1t
D. Redfearn (Bradford) 1t
Blacker (Bradford)
A. Bates (Dewsbury)
Naylor (Batley)
M. Stephenson (Dewsbury)
T. Lowe (Dewsbury)
Irving (Oldham) 1t
Lockwood (Castleford)
Norton (Castleford)
Subs: Wraith (Wakefield)
        C. Dickinson (Castleford)

1973 Lancashire
Widnes: 19 Sept.
Lost 15-17
Jefferson (Keighley) 3g
A. Smith (Leeds) 1t
Hynes (Leeds)
Holmes (Leeds)
Atkinson (Leeds) 1t
Topliss (Wakefield)
Nash (Featherstone)
Harrison (Hull)
M. Morgan (Wakefield)
Davies (Huddersfield) 1t
Grayshon (Dewsbury)
J. Thompson (Featherstone)
Stone (Featherstone)
Sub: J. Bates (Dewsbury)

1974 Lancashire
Keighley: 25 Sept.
Won 20-14
Marshall (Leeds) 4g
D. Redfearn (Bradford)
Hughes (Bramley)
Roe (Keighley)
Atkinson (Leeds) 1t
Millward (Hull KR) 1t
A. Bates (Dewsbury) 1t
Dixon (York)
Raistrick (Keighley)
Irving (Wigan) 1t
Grayshon (Dewsbury)
Idle (Bramley)
Norton (Castleford)
Subs: Clark (N. Hunslet)
        J. Bates (Dewsbury)

1973 Cumberland (Play-off)
Leeds: 17 Jan.
Won 20-7
Jefferson (Keighley) 4g
Lamb (Bradford)
Worsley (Castleford)
Dyl (Leeds)
D. Redfearn (Bradford) 1t
Topliss (Wakefield) 1t
Hudson (Hull KR)
Dixon (York) 1t
M. Stephenson (Dewsbury)
Lyons (Wakefield) 1t
Irving (Oldham)
Lockwood (Castleford)
Batten (Leeds)
Subs: N. Stephenson (Dewsbury)
        B. Kear (Featherstone)

1974 Cumbria
Workington: 10 Sept.
Lost 7-10
Jefferson (Keighley) 2g
Lamb (Bradford)
Dave Hartley (Featherstone) 1t
M. Smith (Featherstone)
D. Redfearn (Bradford)
Topliss (Wakefield)
Nash (Featherstone)
Harrison (Leeds)
Spurr (Castleford)
Farrar (Featherstone)
Grayshon (Dewsbury)
J. Bates (Dewsbury)
Norton (Castleford)
Subs: Burton (Halifax)
        Ramsey (Bradford)

1974 Lancashire (Play-off)
Widnes: 16 Oct.
Lost 11-29
Sheard (Wakefield)
Lamb (Bradford)
Roe (Keighley) 1t
Burton (Halifax) 1g
Atkinson (Leeds) 1t
Topliss (Wakefield)
A. Bates (Dewsbury)
Dixon (York)
Raistrick (Keighley)
Millington (Hull KR)
Grayshon (Dewsbury)
Irving (Wigan)
Norton (Castleford) 1t

1975 Cumbria

Dewsbury: 19 Nov.

Won 10-7

Wraith (Castleford)
D. Smith (Wakefield) 1t
Holmes (Leeds) 1t, 2g
Dyl (Leeds)
Dunn (Hull KR)
Newlove (Featherstone)
Millward (Hull KR)
Beverley (Dewsbury)
Bridges (Featherstone)
J. Thompson (Featherstone)
Grayshon (Dewsbury)
Irving (Wigan)
Norton (Castleford)
Subs: N. Stephenson (Dewsbury)
   M. Morgan (Wakefield)

1977 Cumbria

Whitehaven: 15 Feb.

Drew 12-12

Wraith (Castleford)
Muscroft (N. Hunslet)
Joyner (Castleford) 1t
Roe (Bradford)
Atkinson (Leeds)
Topliss (Wakefield) 1t
Stephens (Castleford)
J. Thompson (Featherstone)
D. Ward (Leeds)
A. Dickinson (Castleford)
Grayshon (Dewsbury)
Lloyd (Castleford) 3g
M. Morgan (Wakefield)

1977 Lancashire (Jubilee)

Widnes: 19 Oct.

Lost 8-33

Mumby (Bradford)
D. Smith (Leeds)
Hague (Leeds)
Quinn (Featherstone) 1g
Atkinson (Leeds) 1t
Francis (Wigan)
Nash (Salford)
J. Thompson (Bradford)
Bridges (Featherstone)
Farrar (Featherstone)
M. Morgan (York) 1t
Branch (Huddersfield)
Bell (Featherstone)
Subs: Hancock (Hull)
   Griffiths (N. Hunslet)

1975 Other Nationalities

Bradford: 6 Dec.

Drew 16-16

Wraith (Castleford)
D. Smith (Wakefield) 1t
Holmes (Leeds) 2g
N. Stephenson (Dewsbury)
Dunn (Hull KR)
Newlove (Featherstone)
Nash (Salford)
Beverley (Dewsbury)
Bridges (Featherstone) 1t
J. Thompson (Featherstone) 2t
Grayshon (Dewsbury)
Irving (Wigan)
Norton (Castleford)
Subs: Topliss (Wakefield)
   M. Morgan (Wakefield)

1977 Lancashire

Castleford: 1 Mar.

Won 18-13

Mumby (Bradford) 1g
Muscroft (N. Hunslet) 1t
Crook (Wakefield)
Francis (Wigan)
Atkinson (Leeds)
Topliss (Wakefield)
Stephens (Castleford)
J. Thompson (Featherstone)
D. Ward (Leeds) 1t
Farrar (Featherstone)
Rose (Hull KR) 1t
P. Lowe (Hull KR)
Norton (Castleford)
Subs: N. Stephenson (Dewsbury) 1t
   Lloyd (Castleford) 2g

1978 Cumbria

Hull: 20 Sept.

Won 37-9

Mumby (Bradford) 4g
T. Morgan (York)
Joyner (Castleford) 1t
N. Stephenson (Dewsbury) 1t, 1g
Atkinson (Leeds)
Francis (St. Helens) 2t
Nash (Salford)
Harrison (Leeds)
Dalgreen (Warrington) 1t
Pitchford (Leeds) 1t
Casey (Hull KR) 1t
P. Lowe (Hull KR) 1t
Crane (Leeds) 1t
Subs: Topliss (Wakefield)
   Farrar (Hull)

1975 Lancashire

Wigan: 20 Dec.

Won 17-7

Langley (Dewsbury)
D. Smith (Wakefield)
Holmes (Leeds) 4g
Dyl (Leeds)
Atkinson (Leeds) 1t
Topliss (Wakefield)
Stephens (Castleford)
Millington (Hull KR)
Bridges (Featherstone)
Farrar (Featherstone)
Grayshon (Dewsbury)
M. Morgan (Wakefield) 2t
Norton (Castleford)
Subs: Hancock (Hull)
   J. Thompson (Featherstone)

1977 Cumbria (Jubilee)

York: 5 Oct.

Won 28-10

Banks (York)
D. Smith (Leeds) 2t
Marston (York) 1t
Quinn (Featherstone) 5g
Atkinson (Leeds) 2t
Hancock (Hull)
Shepherd (Huddersfield)
Beverley (Dewsbury)
Bridges (Featherstone)
Farrar (Featherstone)
M. Morgan (York)
Boxall (Hull) 1t
Bell (Featherstone)
Subs: Hague (Leeds)
   Branch (Huddersfield)

1978 Lancashire

Widnes: 27 Sept.

Lost 7-23

Mumby (Bradford)
Muscroft (N. Hunslet)
Joyner (Castleford)
M. Smith (Hull KR) 1t
D. Redfearn (Bradford)
Francis (St. Helens)
Stephens (Castleford)
Ballantyne (Castleford)
Wileman (York)
Pitchford (Leeds)
Lloyd (Hull) 2g
P. Smith (Featherstone)
Branch (Huddersfield)
Subs: Topliss (Wakefield)
   Farrar (Hull)

1979 Cumbria

Workington: 29 Aug.

Lost 13-17

Box (Featherstone)
Fletcher (Wakefield) 1t
M. Parrish (Hunslet) 3g
Banks (York) 1t
Fenton (Castleford)
Evans (Featherstone)
Dean (Hunslet) 1dg
Tindall (Hull)
Wileman (Hull)
Gibbins (Featherstone)
Grayshon (Bradford)
Hankins (Dewsbury)
Bell (Featherstone)
Sub: G. Smith (York)

1980 Lancashire

Widnes: 24 Sept.

Lost 9-17

Wraith (Castleford)
Fletcher (Wakefield) 1t
Joyner (Castleford)
Quinn (Featherstone) 3g
Fenton (Castleford)
Topliss (Wakefield)
Stephens (Castleford)
Holdstock (Hull KR)
Watkinson (Hull KR)
Skerrett (Hull)
Grayshon (Bradford)
Kevin Rayne (Wakefield)
Norton (Hull)
Subs: Wilby (Hull)
D. Heron (Leeds)

1982 Cumbria

Castleford: 23 May

Won 22-7

Mumby (Bradford)
Richardson (Castleford) 3t
Joyner (Castleford) 2t
Day (Hull)
Gant (Bradford)
Holmes (Leeds)
Dick (Leeds) 1t, 2g
Tindall (Hull)
D. Ward (Leeds)
R. Dickinson (Leeds)
G. Van Bellen (Bradford)
Casey (Hull KR)
Norton (Hull)
Subs: Dyl (Leeds)
D. Hobbs (Featherstone)

1979 Lancashire

Castleford: 12 Sept.

Won 19-16

Box (Featherstone) 3g
Fletcher (Wakefield)
Joyner (Castleford)
Evans (Featherstone)
Fenton (Castleford)
Burton (Castleford) 1t
Stephens (Castleford)
Beverley (Workington)
Raistrick (Halifax) 1t, 1dg
Gibbins (Featherstone)
Branch (Huddersfield) 1t
Hankins (Dewsbury)
Adams (Leeds) 1t
Subs: Johnson (Castleford)
R. Dickinson (Leeds)

1981 Lancashire

Castleford: 9 Sept.

Won 21-15

Mumby (Bradford) 1t
Richardson (Castleford)
Joyner (Castleford) 2t
Dyl (Leeds) 1t
Fenton (Castleford)
Holmes (Leeds)
Nash (Salford)
Grayshon (Bradford)
D. Ward (Leeds) 1t
Millington (Hull KR)
Finch (Castleford) 3g
P. Smith (Featherstone)
Norton (Hull)

1982 Lancashire

Leigh: 26 May

Won 22-21

Mumby (Bradford)
Pryce (York) 3t
Joyner (Castleford)
Day (Hull)
Gant (Bradford)
Holmes (Leeds)
Dick (Leeds) 1t, 3g, 1dg
Tindall (Hull)
D. Ward (Leeds)
R. Dickinson (Leeds)
G. Van Bellen (Bradford)
P. Smith (Featherstone)
K. Ward (Castleford) 1t
Subs: Dyl (Leeds)
Keith Rayne (Leeds)

1980 Cumbria

Hull KR: 17 Sept.

Lost 16-17

Wraith (Castleford)
Fletcher (Wakefield) 1t
Joyner (Castleford)
Quinn (Featherstone) 4g
Fenton (Castleford)
Hague (Leeds)
Dick (Leeds) 1t, 2dg
Holdstock (Hull KR)
Spurr (Castleford)
Skerrett (Hull)
Grayshon (Bradford)
Kevin Rayne (Wakefield)
Norton (Hull)
Sub: D. Heron (Leeds)

1981 Cumbria

Whitehaven: 23 Sept.

Lost 10-20

Box (Wakefield)
Richardson (Castleford)
Hague (Leeds)
Quinn (Featherstone) 1g
A. Parker (Bradford) 1t
Holmes (Leeds)
Nash (Salford)
R. Dickinson (Leeds)
D. Ward (Leeds)
Standidge (Halifax)
Finch (Castleford) 1t, 1g
Idle (Bradford)
Bell (Featherstone)
Subs: Evans (Featherstone)
White (York)

1985 Lancashire

Wigan: 11 Sept.

Won 26-10

Kay (Hunslet)
Gibson (Batley)
Hyde (Castleford) 1t
Mason (Bramley) 2t
Laws (Hull KR)
Joyner (Castleford)
Fox (Featherstone) 3g
Hill (Leeds)
Watkinson (Hull KR)
M. Morgan (Oldham)
D. Hobbs (Oldham) 1t
Burton (Hull KR)
D. Heron (Leeds) 1t
Subs: Lyman (Featherstone)
Dannatt (Hull)

1985 New Zealand
Bradford: 23 Oct.
Won 18-8

Mumby (Bradford)
Gibson (Batley) 1t
Creasser (Leeds)
Schofield (Hull) 1dg
Mason (Bramley)
Hanley (Wigan) 1t, 1dg
Fox (Featherstone) 2g
Grayshon (Bradford)
Noble (Bradford)
Skerrett (Hull)
Crooks (Hull)
Goodway (Wigan) 1t
D. Heron (Leeds)
Subs: Steadman (York)
Lyman (Featherstone)

1986 Lancashire
Leeds: 17 Sept.
Won 26-14

Wilkinson (Leeds)
Gibson (Leeds)
Marchant (Castleford) 1t
Hanley (Wigan) 1t
Gill (Wigan) 1t
Joyner (Castleford)
Fox (Featherstone)
Kelly (Hull KR)
Noble (Bradford)
Hobbs (Oldham) 5g
P. Smith (Featherstone)
Price (York)
Lyman (Featherstone) 1t
Subs: Mason (Bramley)
Medley (Leeds)

Two-cap David Watkinson.

YORKSHIRE REGISTER

The following is a register of current players who have appeared for Yorkshire. Each played at least one first team game last season.

BELL, K. (4) Featherstone R.
BURTON, C. (1) Hull K.R.

CRANE, M. (1) Leeds
CREASSER, D. (1) Leeds
CROOKS, L. (1) Hull

DANNATT, A (+1) Hull
DICK, K. (3) Leeds
DICKINSON, R. (3+1) Leeds

EVANS, S. (2+1) Featherstone R.

FENTON, S. (5) Castleford
FLETCHER, A. (4) Wakefield T.
FOX, D. (3) Featherstone R.

GIBBINS, M. (2) Featherstone R.
GIBSON, C. (3) Batley 2, Leeds
GILL, H. (1) Wigan
GOODWAY, A. (1) Wigan
GRAYSHON, J. (14) Dewsbury 9, Bradford N. 5

HAGUE, N. (3+1) Leeds
HANLEY, E. (2) Wigan
HERON, D. (2+2) Leeds
HILL, B. (1) Leeds
HOBBS, D. (2+1) Featherstone R. +1, Oldham 2
HOLMES, J. (8) Leeds
HYDE, G. (1) Castleford

IDLE, G. (1+1) Bramley +1, Bradford N.

JOHNSON, Phil. (+1) Castleford
JOYNER, J. (11) Castleford

KAY, A. (1) Hunslet
KELLY, A. (1) Hull K.R.

LAWS, D. (1) Hull K.R.
LYMAN, P. (1+2) Featherstone R.

MARCHANT, A, (1) Castleford
MASON, A. (2+1) Bramley
MEDLEY, P. (+1) Leeds
MUMBY, K. (8) Bradford N.

NOBLE, B. (2) Bradford N.
NORTON, S. (13) Castleford 9, Hull 4

PARRISH, M. (1) Hunslet
PRICE, G. (1) York
PRYCE, G. (1) York

QUINN, S. (5) Featherstone R.

RAYNE, Keith (+1) Leeds
RAYNE, Kevin (2) Wakefield T.
REDFEARN, D. (7) Bradford N.
ROE, P. (3) Keighley 2, Bradford N.

SCHOFIELD, G. (1) Hull
SKERRETT, T. (3) Hull
SMITH, G. (+1) York
SMITH, M. (1) Hull K.R.
SMITH, P. (4) Featherstone R.
SPURR, R. (2) Castleford
STEADMAN, G. (+1) York
STEPHENS, G. (6) Castleford
STEPHENSON, N. (7+3) Dewsbury

TOPLISS, D. (10+5) Wakefield T.

VAN BELLEN, G. (2) Bradford N.

WARD, K. (1) Castleford
WATKINSON, D. (2) Hull K.R.
WHITE, B. (+1) York
WILKINSON, I. (1) Leeds

COUNTY CHAMPIONSHIP TITLES
(including joint titles)

Lancashire	34
Yorkshire	24
Cumbria	16
Cheshire	1

1895-96	Lancashire	1937-38	Lancashire
1896-97	Lancashire	1938-39	Lancashire
1897-98	Yorkshire	1945-46	Lancashire
1898-99	Yorkshire	1946-47	Yorkshire
1899-1900	Lancashire	1947-48	Lancashire
1900-01	Lancashire	1948-49	Cumberland
1901-02	Cheshire	1949-50	Undecided
1902-03	Lancashire	1950-51	Undecided
1903-04	Lancashire	1951-52	Yorkshire
1904-05	Yorkshire	1952-53	Lancashire
1905-06	Lancashire / Cumberland	1953-54	Yorkshire
		1954-55	Yorkshire
1906-07	Lancashire	1955-56	Lancashire
1907-08	Cumberland	1956-57	Lancashire
1908-09	Lancashire	1957-58	Yorkshire
1909-10	Cumberland / Yorkshire	1958-59	Yorkshire
		1959-60	Cumberland
1910-11	Lancashire	1960-61	Lancashire
1911-12	Cumberland	1961-62	Cumberland
1912-13	Yorkshire	1962-63	Yorkshire
1913-14	Undecided	1963-64	Cumberland
1919-20	Undecided	1964-65	Yorkshire
1920-21	Yorkshire	1965-66	Cumberland
1921-22	Yorkshire	1966-67	Cumberland
1922-23	Lancashire / Yorkshire	1967-68	Lancashire
		1968-69	Yorkshire
1923-24	Lancashire	1969-70	Lancashire
1924-25	Lancashire	1970-71	Yorkshire
1925-26	Lancashire	1971-72	Yorkshire
1926-27	Lancashire	1972-73	Yorkshire
1927-28	Cumberland	1973-74	Lancashire
1928-29	Lancashire	1974-75	Lancashire
1929-30	Lancashire	1975-76	Yorkshire
1930-31	Yorkshire	1976-77	Yorkshire
1931-32	Lancashire	1977-78	Not Held
1932-33	Cumberland	1978-79	Lancashire
1933-34	Cumberland	1979-80	Lancashire
1934-35	Cumberland	1980-81	Cumbria
1935-36	Lancashire	1981-82	Cumbria
1936-37	Lancashire	1982-83	Yorkshire

Wigan scrum half Andy Gregory, a world record £130,000 purchase from Warrington in January 1987.

TRANSFERS

TRANSFER REVIEW
1 June 1986 to 31 May 1987

Wigan smashed the world record transfer fee again when they paid £130,000 to Warrington for Test scrum half Andy Gregory on 11 January.

Gregory had originally been listed at £150,000 — another record — a month earlier but this was reduced by the League's Board of Appeal to £130,000. He had asked for a transfer after being suspended and fined by the club for missing training.

The signing came a year after Wigan had paid the previous cash record of £100,000 for Joe Lydon from Widnes. Wigan also hold the record for a cash-plus-player deal of £150,000 with the capture of Ellery Hanley from Bradford Northern in September 1985. They handed over £85,000 — then the cash record — plus Test backs Steve Donlan and Phil Ford.

Gregory had once before been listed at £150,000 when he was with Widnes. Then it was halved on appeal and he moved to Warrington in an exchange deal with Test forward John Fieldhouse in January 1985.

Another £150,000 listing was that of Garry Schofield as a disciplinary measure by Hull in November 1986 after the Test centre missed a club match against Australia. They took him off the list within a week when he apologised.

Fieldhouse, listed at £75,000, again moved in a big exchange deal when he joined St. Helens in November with Harry Pinner, listed at £95,000, going to Widnes.

There were other substantial exchange deals with the straight cash transfers of £30,000 or more limited to eight, the same as in the previous season. The eight were:

Andy Gregory (Warrington)
 to Wigan £130,000
Andy Mason (Bramley) to Leeds.. £48,000
Paul Harkin (Hull K.R.)
 to Bradford N £40,000
Gary Price (York) to Leeds......... £40,000
Ray Ashton (Oldham)
 to Leeds............................... £40,000
Des Drummond (Leigh)
 to Warrington £40,000
Mick Burke (Widnes)
 to Oldham............................ £40,000
Brendan Hill (Leeds)
 to Bradford N. £30,000

From June 1986 to the end of May 1987 the total of transfers between clubs was 211 against 185 the previous year.

There were an additional 63 moves on loan — including players returning to their original clubs. The previous year there had been 123.

There was another major Rugby Union capture with Hull signing Llanelli's Welsh international stand off Gary Pearce for an estimated £65,000 on 19 September. It was easily the most they have paid to a player but short of the world record £80,000 Bradford Northern paid Welsh RU international scrum half Terry Holmes the previous season.

Pearce was one of 13 Rugby Union players to turn professional compared with 10 in the previous 12 months. The most notable of the others were Fulham's signing of half backs Huw Rees, the Penarth and Wales B international, and Keiron Murphy, Richmond's former England Colt. Barrow signed Syd Lowden, who had a long RU career with Sale and Egremont, gaining county honours, before following in his father's footsteps to Rugby League.

Another record deal involved the most ever offered to an amateur Rugby League player. Simon Longstaff, a 17-year-old Wakefield schoolboy, was given a contract worth more than £40,000 by Halifax.

Longstaff, a promising javelin thrower, wished to retain his amateur status a little longer but was promised £28,000 in trust over the next 12 months with incentives that would take his fee past £40,000.

He played loose forward for Normanton Under-17 RL side and centre for Queen Elizabeth Grammar School RU. His father, Paul, is a former Huddersfield, Hull K.R., Castleford and Rochdale Hornets player.

The previous record deal for a junior player was the £35,000 contract Shaun Edwards received when he signed for Wigan on his 17th birthday in 1983. It included payments for representative honours which he soon received as the youngest-ever player to appear for Great Britain.

Wakefield Trinity gave a club record £30,000 contract to another top amateur last season, loose forward Gary Price joining them from Sharlston Under-17s.

All told, 159 left the amateur RL ranks to turn professional compared with 139 in the previous year.

There was another big influx of overseas players with five Australian Test players having their first experience of English club rugby — Kerry Boustead (Hull K.R.), Graham Eadie (Halifax), Bob Lindner (Castleford), Pat Jarvis (St. Helens) and Ian Schubert (Leigh).

Eadie made the biggest impact, with a remarkable comeback after being persuaded to come out of a three-year retirement. The veteran full back, who first toured Britain with the 1973 Kangaroos, crowned his return by scoring a vital try and winning the Lance Todd Trophy as the man of the match in the Wembley victory over St. Helens. He finished his return with a total of 20 tries.

Boustead had a less happy experience, failing to regain the form which made him one of the best wingers of the last decade. He joined Rovers soon after recovery from a broken leg suffered in Australia, but made little impression when given a run in the centre.

Although several of the 1986 Kangaroos were approached by English clubs only Bob Lindner returned, the Test loose forward having agreed terms with Castleford before the tour began. He played only nine matches before returning to Australia.

Wally Lewis, the Australian tour captain, did make a much publicised signing for Wigan for a reported £1,000 per match, but later told them he would not be coming because of an injury problem.

New signings from Australia increased from 68 the previous season to 80. With those already here it brought the total of Australians registered with English clubs to a record 95. The recruiting of New Zealand players dropped from 27 to 16 for a total registration of 35.

With three South Africans and a Moroccan, the total registered overseas players was another record at 134.

The 1987-88 season is the first in which the overseas quota is restricted to three per club. It was five in 1985-86 and four in 1986-87.

Exemptions from the new restrictions include overseas players who have been resident in Britain for more than five years. At least eight players come into this category. Other exemptions agreed with the Department of Employment are players who hold an EEC or British passport without the need for a work permit.

Since the ban on overseas signings was eased in 1983 the season-by-season registration of Australians and New Zealanders has been as follows, Test players in brackets:

	Aus.	NZ	Total
1983-84	34(4)	34(15)	68(19)
1984-85	85(9)	35(10)	120(19)
1985-86	82(11)	42(10)	124(21)
1986-87	95(9)	35(11)	130(19)

The following is a list of all overseas players registered with English clubs during 1986-87.

OVERSEAS REGISTER 1986-87
*Test players as at 1 June 1987
AUSTRALIA (95)

*Anderson, Chris	(Halifax)
Anderson, Tony	(Halifax, Keighley)
Arnold, Bob	(Hunslet)
Ashe, Jeff	(Huddersfield B.)
Atkins, Brett	(Castleford)
Austin, Greg	(Salford)
*Boustead, Kerry	(Hull K.R.)
*Boyd, Les	(Warrington)
Brennan, Rowan	(Wakefield T.)
Bridge, Gary	(Oldham)
*Brown, David	(Hull)
Byron, Gerry	(Rochdale H.)
Carter, Steve	(Barrow)
Clark, Brett	(St. Helens)
Clark, Bruce	(Oldham)
Cleal, Les	(Widnes)
Cogger, John	(Runcorn H.)
Coleman, Craig	(Widnes)
Colwell, Tim	(Blackpool B., Bramley)
Cowie, Robert	(Wakefield T.)
Crossingham, Mark	(Mansfield M., Whitehaven)
Davis, Mike	(Leigh)
*Dorahy, John	(Hull K.R.)
*Eadie, Graham	(Halifax)
Ettingshausen, Andrew	(Leeds)
Fenech, Mario	(Bradford N.)
Finekifoleu, Tisi	(Huddersfield B.)
Gadaskie, Allan	(Blackpool B.)
Gentle, Peter	(Mansfield M.)
Graham, Mal	(Bradford N.)
Haggath, Bob	(Fulham)
Halliwell, Steve	(St. Helens, Wakefield T.)
Harrigan, Ken	(Rochdale H.)
Hastings, Kevin	(Barrow)
Hillier, Errol	(Workington T.)
Howcroft, Ian	(Bradford N.)
Howell, Gary	(Leigh)
Hurst, Phil	(Workington T.)
Jackson, Bob	(Warrington)
*Jarvis, Pat	(St. Helens)
Jennings, Graeme	(Hunslet)
Johns, Chris	(Castleford)
Johnson, Brian	(Warrington)
Kelly, Michael	(Keighley)
Keniff, Damien	(Huddersfield B.)

Kuhnemann, Paul	(Sheffield E.)
King, Craig	(Mansfield M.)
Kirkwood, John	(Hull, York)
Klein, Russell	(Wakefield T.)
Knight, Bob	(Fulham)
*Lindner, Bob	(Castleford)
Long, Mark	(York)
Lyons, Cliff	(Sheffield E.)
McCaffrey, David	(Keighley)
McFarlane, Gary	(Whitehaven)
McGaw, Mark	(Leeds)
McInerney, Mark	(Keighley)
McKenzie, Phil	(Widnes)
McLaren, Guy	(Keighley)
Meskell, Mark	(Barrow)
Miller, Gavin	(Hull K.R.)
Morris, Bob	(Leeds)
Muir, Nick	(Barrow)
Neller, Keith	(Halifax)
O'Connell, Seamus	(Runcorn H.)
O'Doherty, Pat	(Fulham)
Penola, Colin	(Hunslet)
Pratt, George	(Fulham)
Purcell, Craig	(Rochdale H.)
Raiteri, Robert	(Keighley)
Raper, Stuart	(Oldham)
Rix, Grant	(Halifax)
Roberts, Ian	(Wigan)
Schmidt, Darrel	(Widnes)
Schubert, Garry	(Salford, Carlisle)
*Schubert, Ian	(Leigh)
Scott, Colin	(Castleford)
Selby, Geoff	(Salford)
Sheridan, Greg	(Sheffield E.)
Shuttleworth, Greg	(Whitehaven)
Smith, Peter	(Leeds)
Stanton, Glen	(Wakefield T.)
Stevens, Darren	(Mansfield M.)
Strutt, Darren	(York)
Taylor, Craig	(Fulham)
Thompson, Darren	(Rochdale H.)
Veivers, Phil	(St. Helens)
Wakefield, Mark	(Salford)
Warnecke, Gary	(Oldham)
Webb, Terry	(Hunslet)
White, Peter	(Fulham)
White, Steve	(Keighley)
Wilkes, Mark	(Leeds, Workington T.)
Willey, Sean	(York)
Woods, David	(Barrow, Workington T.)

NEW ZEALAND (35)

*Ah Kuoi, Fred	(Hull)
*Bell, Dean	(Wigan)
Blazey, John	(Sheffield E.)
Bourneville, Mark	(Swinton)
*Broadhurst, Mark	(Hull K.R.)
Burgoyne, Pat	(Bramley)
Campbell, Danny	(Runcorn H.)
Clark, Trevor	(Leeds, York)
*Elia, Mark	(St. Helens)
Fisoh, John	(Fulham)
Gillan, Dave	(Fulham)
Grima, Joe	(Swinton)
Jackson, Alan	(Doncaster)
*Kemble, Gary	(Hull)
Kemp, Tony	(Doncaster)
Kilkelly, Boyd	(Doncaster)
Kupe, Darren	(Doncaster)
Leck, Gary	(Carlisle)
*Leuluai, James	(Leigh)
Lonergan, Dean	(Bramley)
Miller, Craig	(Fulham, Sheffield E.)
Moore, Brent	(Blackpool B.)
Muller, Roby	(Swinton)
Murray, Trevor	(Blackpool B.)
*O'Hara, Dane	(Hull)
O'Shea, Terry	(Salford)
Riddell, Mark	(Blackpool B.)
Schaumkell, Kevin	(Bramley)
*Smith, Gordon	(Hull K.R.)
*Sorensen, Kurt	(Widnes)
Subritzky, Peter	(Blackpool B., Carlisle)
*Tamati, Kevin	(Warrington)
Tupaea, Shane	(Mansfield M.)
*West, Graeme	(Wigan)
Wihongi, Hemi	(Carlisle)

SOUTH AFRICA (3)

Du Toit, Nick	(Barrow, Wigan)
Louw, Rob	(Wigan)
Mordt, Ray	(Wigan)

MOROCCO (1)

M'Barki, Hussein	(Oldham)

BRITONS DOWN UNDER

The number of British players given clearance to play Down Under during the summer of 1987 was 19, the same as the previous year.

The short-term exports included Hull skipper Lee Crooks, undertaking his third successive summer contract, and Great Britain teammates Kevin Ward, Mike Gregory and Joe Lydon, all experiencing their first taste of Sydney football.

The following is a list of players granted a clearance before 1 June to play in Australia and New Zealand with the names of the clubs they were due to join. In some cases no advance notice of prospective club was given. At the end of May both Garry Schofield (Hull) and Paul Bishop (Warrington) were involved in clearance disputes in their bid to join Sydney clubs Balmain and Cronulla respectively.

TO AUSTRALIA (18)

Armstrong, Colin	(Carlisle)	Norths, Brisbane
Casey, Leo	(Oldham)	Narellan
Crooks, Lee	(Hull)	Balmain, Sydney
Gregory, Mike	(Warrington)	Cronulla, Sydney
Hetherington, Gary	(Whitehaven)	Corowa
Lightfoot, David	(Whitehaven)	Corowa
Lydon, Joe	(Wigan)	Easts, Sydney
Moses, Paul	(Keighley)	Lifesavers
Newall, John	(Workington T.)	—
Parrish, Steve	(Bradford N.)	Stanthorpe
Rees, Huw	(Fulham)	Wests, Sydney
Rigby, Colin	(Widnes)	Baven
Rowbottom, Mark	(Swinton)	Stanthorpe
Ruane, David	(Widnes)	Baven
Sherratt, Ian	(Oldham)	—
Vass, Stuart	(Hull)	Norths, Brisbane
Walters, Graham	(Runcorn H.)	Norths, Brisbane
Ward, Kevin	(Castleford)	Manly, Sydney

TO NEW ZEALAND (1)

Gray, Neil	(Hunslet)	Huntley

RECORD TRANSFERS

The first £1,000 transfer came in 1921 when Harold Buck joined Leeds from Hunslet, although there were reports at the time that another player was involved in the deal to make up the four-figure transfer. Other claims for the first £1,000 transfer are attached to Stan Brogden's move from Bradford Northern to Huddersfield in 1929.

The following list gives an indication of how transfer fees have grown this century in straight cash deals only:

Season	Player	Position	From	To	Fee
1901-02	Jim Lomas	Centre	Bramley	Salford	£100
1910-11	Jim Lomas	Centre	Salford	Oldham	£300
1912-13	Billy Batten	Centre	Hunslet	Hull	£600
1921-22	Harold Buck	Wing	Hunslet	Leeds	£1,000
1929-30	Stanley Smith	Wing	Wakefield T.	Leeds	£1,075
1933-34	Stanley Brogden	Wing/centre	Huddersfield	Leeds	£1,200
1937-38	Billy Belshaw	Full back	Liverpool S.	Warrington	£1,450
1946-47	Bill Davies	Full back/centre	Huddersfield	Dewsbury	£1,650
1947-48	Bill Hudson	Forward	Batley	Wigan	£2,000
1947-48	Jim Ledgard	Full back	Dewsbury	Leigh	£2,650
1948-49	Ike Owens	Forward	Leeds	Castleford	£2,750
1948-49	Ike Owens	Forward	Castleford	Huddersfield	£2,750
1948-49	Stan McCormick	Wing	Belle Vue R.	St. Helens	£4,000
1949-50	Albert Naughton	Centre	Widnes	Warrington	£4,600
1950-51	Bruce Ryan	Wing	Hull	Leeds	£4,750
1950-51	Joe Egan	Hooker	Wigan	Leigh	£5,000
1950-51	Harry Street	Forward	Dewsbury	Wigan	£5,000
1957-58	Mick Sullivan	Wing	Huddersfield	Wigan	£9,500
1958-59	Ike Southward	Wing	Workington T.	Oldham	£10,650
1960-61	Mick Sullivan	Wing	Wigan	St. Helens	£11,000
1960-61	Ike Southward	Wing	Oldham	Workington T.	£11,002 10s
1968-69	Colin Dixon	Forward	Halifax	Salford	£12,000
1969-70	Paul Charlton	Full back	Workington T.	Salford	£12,500
1972-73	Eric Prescott	Forward	St. Helens	Salford	£13,500
1975-76	Steve Nash	Scrum half	Featherstone R.	Salford	£15,000
1977-78	Bill Ashurst	Forward	Wigan	Wakefield T.	£18,000
1978-79	Clive Pickerill	Scrum half	Castleford	Hull	£20,000
1978-79	Phil Hogan	Forward	Barrow	Hull K.R.	£35,000
1979-80	Len Casey	Forward	Bradford N.	Hull K.R.	£38,000
1980-81	Trevor Skerrett	Forward	Wakefield T.	Hull	£40,000
1980-81	George Fairbairn	Full back	Wigan	Hull K.R.	£72,500
1985-86	Ellery Hanley	Centre/stand off	Bradford N.	Wigan	£85,000
1985-86	Joe Lydon	Centre	Widnes	Wigan	£100,000
1986-87	Andy Gregory	Scrum half	Warrington	Wigan	£130,000

MOST MOVES

Geoff Clarkson extended his record number of transfers to 12 when he left Leigh for Featherstone Rovers on 27 October 1983. He played for 10 different English clubs and had a brief spell in Australia.

Clarkson, born on 12 August 1943 was 40-years-old when he finished playing regular first team rugby in 1983-84. He turned professional with Wakefield Trinity in 1966 after gaining Yorkshire County forward honours with Wakefield Rugby Union Club.

Clarkson's club career in England is as follows:

1966 — Wakefield T.
1968 — Bradford N.
1970 — Leigh
1971 — Warrington
1972 — Leeds
1975 — York
1976 — Bramley
1978 — Wakefield T. and Hull K.R.
1980 — Bradford N. and Oldham
1981 — Leigh
1983 — Featherstone R.

1986-87 SIGNINGS

The following is a register of signings by clubs from 1 June 1986 to 31 May 1987. The right-hand column lists the club from which the player was recruited (ARL Amateur Rugby League, RU — Rugby Union).

In some instances a player who wishes to retain his amateur status is not registered although he may be named in the club's list of appearances.

Although this is a register of signings, it is possible to trace a club's transfers by scrutinising the right hand column.

Indicates where clubs have agreed to a player being signed 'on loan', a temporary transfer, the Rugby Football League prohibiting a subsequent transfer within 28 days. Where a player on loan has not been retained his return to his original club is also marked.

Widnes loose forward Harry Pinner (left) and St. Helens' packman John Fieldhouse (right) in their new club strips after a November 1986 exchange deal.

BARROW

Signed	Player	Club From
2.9.86	*Flynn, Malcolm	Whitehaven
4.9.86	Meskell, Mark	Brisbane Souths, Aus.
4.9.86	Hastings, Kevin	Eastern Suburbs, Aus.
4.9.86	Burns, Paul	Barrow Island ARL
30.9.86	Carey, Paul	Dalton ARL
30.9.86	Muir, Nick	Eastern Suburbs, Aus.
30.9.86	Woods, David	Parramatta, Aus.
1.11.86	Du Toit, Nick	Wigan
7.11.86	Carter, Steve	Brothers, Aus.
9.1.87	*Wilkinson, Chris	Fulham
12.1.87	Gittins, Tommy	Wakefield T.
3.3.87	*Naidole, Tom	Oldham
11.3.87	*Maguire, Steve	Workington T.
13.3.87	Lowden, Syd	Egremont RU

BATLEY

Signed	Player	Club From
17.6.86	McGowan, John	Dewsbury Celtic ARL
2.11.86	Fitzpatrick, Dennis	Huddersfield B.
16.11.86	Spendler, Mark	Dewsbury Moor ARL
11.12.86	Hartley, Neil	Oulton ARL
1.1.87	McGrath, Damian	Dudley Hill ARL
30.1.87	Fenwick, Richard	Crown Inn ARL
10.2.87	Snell, Graham	Crown Inn ARL
29.3.87	Harris, George	Sheffield E.

BLACKPOOL BOROUGH

Signed	Player	Club From
28.6.86	*Lowe, Kevin	Rochdale H.
11.9.86	Moore, Brent	NZ
2.10.86	Riddell, Mark	Mt. Albert, NZ
2.10.86	Murray, Trevor	Mt. Albert, NZ
5.10.86	Gadaskie, Allan	Western Suburbs, Aus.
21.10.86	Ganley, Chris	Fulham
8.11.86	Muir, Nick	Barrow
10.11.86	Colwell, Tim	South Townsville, Aus.
24.12.86	Scott, Alan	Warrington
29.12.86	Crawshaw, Carl	Swinton
31.12.86	Tabern, Ray	Leigh
19.2.87	Green, Jimmy	Wakefield T.
24.2.87	Glover, Michael	Fulham
4.3.87	Roberts, Paul	Salford
10.3.87	Hoare, Sean	Fulham
26.3.87	Walkden, Garry	Leigh
20.5.87	Bamber, Simon	Woolston R. ARL
20.5.87	Stewart, Michael	Woolston R. ARL

BRADFORD NORTHERN

Signed	Player	Club From
1.6.86	Graham, Mal	Oldham
23.7.86	Hellewell, Phil	Dudley Hill ARL
23.7.86	Fairbank, Karl	Elland ARL
7.8.86	Croft, David	Hunslet Parkside ARL
1.10.86	Howcroft, Ian	Kaima, Aus.
4.10.86	Spurr, Bob	Featherstone R.
4.10.86	Bond, Steve	Halifax
22.10.86	Fenech, Mario	South Sydney, Aus.
27.10.86	Jackson, Robert	Mansfield M.
12.11.86	*Sheldon, Ian	Bramley
2.1.87	Hill, Brendan	Leeds
22.1.87	Evans, Steve	Wakefield T.
22.1.87	Hamilton, David	Bradford N. Colts
23.3.87	Grayshon, Jeff	Leeds
26.3.87	Harkin, Paul	Hull K.R.
1.4.87	Hobbs, David	Oldham

BRAMLEY

Signed	Player	Club From
1.8.86	Hobbs, Gary	Bramley Colts
29.8.86	Patterson, John	Huddersfield B.
6.9.86	*Sheldon, Ian	Bradford N.
19.9.86	Sutcliffe, Shaun	Hunslet Junction ARL
19.9.86	Loynes, Dean	Carlisle
3.10.86	Schaumkell, Kevin	Glenora, NZ
3.10.86	Burgoyne, Pat	Glenora, NZ
24.10.86	Booth, Simon	—
24.10.86	Longergan, Dean	City Newton, Aus.
25.10.86	Binder, Tony	Carlisle
16.11.86	Carty, Paul	Bramley Colts
27.11.86	Ingham, Gary	Leeds
28.11.86	Potapi, Vic	Thornbury ARL
29.11.86	Tucker, Neil	Knottingley ARL
12.12.86	Colwell, Tim	Blackpool B.
16.12.86	Gibson, Mark	Pontefract Labour ARL
17.12.86	Rhodes, Chris	York
19.12.86	Duckworth, Ken	Sheepscar WMC ARL
1.1.87	Edmondson, Steve	B.R.K. ARL
26.2.87	Idle, Graham	Rochdale H.
14.3.87	*Payne, Philip	Castleford
14.3.87	*Marsh, Richard	Featherstone R.

CARLISLE

Signed	Player	Club From
24.9.86	Subritzky, Peter	Blackpool B.
3.10.86	Green, Ken	Fulham
21.10.86	Schubert, Garry	Salford
25.10.86	*Wilkinson, Chris	Fulham
28.11.86	Duncanson, Mark	St. Nicholas Arms ARL
5.12.86	Thompson, Ian	Workington T.
10.12.86	MacLagan, Allan	Dalston ARL
30.12.86	Stafford, Peter	Workington T.
14.2.87	Brierley, Steve	Dalston ARL
12.3.87	McCullough, Craig	St. Nicholas Arms ARL
23.3.87	Green, Jimmy	Blackpool B.
1.4.87	Crabtree, Paul	Stanley Rangers ARL

CASTLEFORD

Signed	Player	Club From
21.7.86	Morgan, Mick	Oldham
28.8.86	Scott, Colin	Wynnum-Manly, Aus.
29.8.86	Sampson, Dean	Stanley Rangers ARL
2.9.86	Atkins, Brett	Canberra Raiders, Aus.
5.9.86	Johns, Chris	St. George, Aus.
23.9.86	Lindner, Bob	Wynnum-Manly, Aus.
29.12.86	*Hartley, Iain	Doncaster
19.2.87	Anderson, Grant	Castleford Colts
4.4.87	Boothroyd, Giles	Lock Lane ARL
6.5.87	Hart, Alan	Lock Lane ARL
6.5.87	Hetherington, Simon	Castleford Colts
8.5.87	*Hartley, Iain	Doncaster
8.5.87	*Payne, Phil	Bramley

DEWSBURY

Signed	Player	Club From
28.8.86	Clarke, Philip	—
29.8.86	Jones, Alan	Shaw Cross ARL
29.8.86	Francis, Ian	Dewsbury Colts
29.8.86	Schofield, Darren	Peacock ARL
29.8.86	Wadforth, Ian	Hull K.R.
29.8.86	Riding, David	Batley
4.9.86	Maligranda, Richard	Siddal ARL
26.9.86	Westbury, Mark	Mansfield M.
4.10.86	Whitehead, Paul	Leeds
5.10.86	Burgess, Mark	Rochdale H.
24.10.86	Charlton, Mark	Huddersfield B.
5.12.86	Booth, Dean	Hunslet
5.12.86	Sampson, Roy	Hunslet
14.12.86	*Dickens, Steve	Salford
24.2.87	Hawksworth, Mick	Keighley
5.3.87	Caincross, Chris	Salford

DONCASTER

Signed	Player	Club From
15.8.86	Birkby, Ian	Oldham
19.8.86	Crooks, Martin	Leeds
27.8.86	Jones, Kevin	Castleford
12.9.86	*Chapman, Tony	Featherstone R.
1.10.86	Lane, Garry	—
14.10.86	Kemp, Tony	Randwick, NZ
16.10.86	*Hartley, Iain	Castleford
30.10.86	Kupe, Darren	Waitara, NZ
6.11.86	Ellis, Kevin	Keighley
12.11.86	Jackson, Alan	Waitara, NZ
16.12.86	Martin, David	Ferrybridge Magnet ARL
9.1.87	Ellis, David	Keighley
20.2.87	Smith, Stuart	Wakefield T.
5.3.87	Kilkelly, Boyd	South Island, NZ
10.3.87	*Hartley, Iain	Castleford
30.3.87	Morrell, Wayne	York

Castleford full back Colin Scott, an August 1986 import from Australia.

FEATHERSTONE ROVERS

Signed	Player	Club From
5.9.86	Sykes, Andy	Barrow
25.9.86	Leary, Simon	Mansfield M.
22.10.86	Slater, Martin	Castleford
28.10.86	*Wilkinson, Andrew	Wakefield T.
29.10.86	Hall, Gary	Lock Lane ARL
12.11.86	Kellett, Lee	Leeds Colts
16.11.86	Crossley, John	Halifax
18.11.86	Waites, Brian	York
19.11.86	Geary, Paul	Wakefield T.
11.12.86	Spedding, Paul	Mansfield M.
15.12.86	Beach, Danny	Normanton U-17s ARL
27.12.86	Jones, David	Wakefield T.
7.2.87	*Chapman, Tony	Doncaster
8.3.87	Bradford, Patrick	York All Blacks ARL
8.3.87	Hinchcliffe, Mark	York All Blacks ARL
8.3.87	Bugg, David	Knottingley Welfare ARL
2.4.87	Smales, Ian	Lock Lane ARL
1.5.87	*Marsh, Richard	Bramley

FULHAM

Signed	Player	Club From
11.9.86	Cooper, Dominic	Dewsbury
13.9.86	Render, Andrew	Dewsbury Celtic ARL
13.9.86	Mitchell, Simon	Ealing ARL
13.9.86	Fenn, Colin	South London ARL
28.9.86	Haggath, Bob	Ipswich, Aus.
28.9.86	O'Doherty, Pat	Ipswich, Aus.
28.9.86	O'Brien, Gary	South London ARL
28.9.86	Gillan, David	Southend Invicta
28.9.86	Bridge, Russell	West London Institute ARL
28.9.86	Pratt, George	Western Suburbs, Aus.
23.10.86	Garner, Steve	Blackpool B.
30.10.86	Bowen, Karl	Fulham Travellers ARL
30.10.86	Knight, Bob	Fortitude Valleys, Aus.
2.11.86	Lawrie, Geordie	Ealing ARL
2.11.86	Taylor, Craig	Fortitude Valleys, Aus.
16.11.86	Rampling, Darren	Mayfield ARL
16.11.86	Murphy, Keiron	Richmond RU
30.11.86	Rees, Huw	Penarth RU
30.11.86	White, Peter	Ealing ARL
10.12.86	Rendell, Brian	Ealing ARL
21.12.86	*Wilkinson, Chris	Carlisle
6.2.87	Gibson, Russell	Streatham Celtic ARL
12.2.87	*Garner, Steve	Oldham
21.3.87	Miller, Craig	Sheffield E.
29.3.87	Mayo, John	Wigan

HALIFAX

Signed	Player	Club From
28.6.86	Dickinson, Roy	Leeds
7.7.86	Rix, Grant	Valleys, Aus.
16.7.86	Eadie, Graham	Aus.
17.7.86	Neller, Keith	Valleys, Aus.
5.8.86	Hague, Neil	Leeds
6.10.86	*Smith, Keith	Mansfield M.
7.10.86	Preece, Chris	Bradford N.
30.11.86	Pendlebury, John	Salford
6.1.87	Kemp, Martin	Halifax Colts
8.1.87	Parkinson, Andrew	Shaw Cross ARL
13.2.87	Keyworth, Mark	Dewsbury
26.3.87	Ramsden, Andrew	Dewsbury
26.3.87	Longstaff, Simon	Normanton U-17s ARL

HUDDERSFIELD BARRACUDAS

Signed	Player	Club From
20.8.86	Hesford, Steve	Warrington
2.9.86	Sedgwick, Peter	—
13.9.86	Kinsey, Tony	Fulham
4.10.86	Huck, Philip	Halifax
9.10.86	Ashe, Jeff	Eastern Suburbs, Aus.
18.10.86	*Johnson, William	Swinton
13.11.86	Howard, Andrew	Stanthorpe ARL
15.11.86	Johnson, Dean	Albion ARL
9.1.87	Finekifoleu, Tisi	Hill Hawks, Aus.
9.1.87	Keniff, Damien	Hill Hawks, Aus.

HULL

Signed	Player	Club From
1.8.86	Casey, Len	Wakefield T.
21.8.86	Brown, David	Eastern Suburbs, Aus.
3.9.86	Crooks, Steve	York
6.9.86	Elgar, Nick	West Hull ARL
16.9.86	Dick, Kevin	Leeds
19.9.86	Pearce, Gary	Llanelli RU
19.9.86	Gibbons, Mick	Featherstone R.
25.10.86	Kirkwood, John	Townsville Univ, ARL
4.11.86	Kerman, Richard	Stelrad ARL
6.11.86	Khan, Patrick	Hull Colts
12.11.86	Lazenby, Tracy	Wakefield T.
16.12.86	*Dennison, Steve	Mansfield M.
5.1.87	*Sanderson, Carl	Mansfield M.

HULL KINGSTON ROVERS

Signed	Player	Club From
17.7.86	Boustead, Kerry	Manly, Aus.
5.9.86	Busby, David	Jesmond ARL
12.9.86	Broadhurst, Mark	Papanui, NZ

HUNSLET

Signed	Player	Club From
8.7.86	Coates, Jed	Yew Tree ARL
10.7.86	Webb, Terry	Leeds
11.7.86	Mason, Keith	Dewsbury
28.8.86	Bell, Michael	Hanging Heaton ARL
29.8.86	Leathley, Trevor	Huddersfield B.
29.8.86	Senior, Gary	Huddersfield B.
5.9.86	Jennings, Graeme	Western Suburbs, Aus.
19.9.86	Arnold, Bob	Valleys, Aus.
30.10.86	Lowes, James	Hunslet Parkside ARL
4.11.86	Wilkinson, Shaun	Dewsbury Moor ARL
7.1.87	Sykes, Andy	Featherstone R.
9.2.87	Raw, Andrew	Yew Tree ARL
17.2.87	*Sampson, Roy	Dewsbury
26.2.87	Lumb, Timothy	Shaw Cross ARL
5.3.87	Lay, Steve	Dewsbury Moor ARL

KEIGHLEY

Signed	Player	Club From
7.8.86	*Cerchione, Mario	Halifax
7.8.86	Perrett, Hadyn	Elland ARL
7.8.86	Coulter, David	Elland ARL
7.8.86	Gudor, Mark	Illingworth ARL
7.8.86	Gregorie, Don	Idle Oddfellows ARL
11.8.86	Stockhill, Ian	Bradford N. Colts
12.8.86	Richardson, Peter	Elland ARL
26.8.86	McInerney, Mark	North Sydney, Aus.
28.8.86	Fairbanks, Andy	Elland ARL
28.8.86	Gaukroger, Michael	Elland ARL
30.8.86	Kelly, Michael	Hills District, Aus.
30.8.86	White, Stephen	Penrith, Aus.

4.9.86	Greenwood, Brett	Halifax
28.9.86	Fairbank, Mark	Elland ARL
1.10.86	McCaffrey, David	North Sydney, Aus.
3.10.86	McLaren, Guy	Cronulla, Aus.
9.10.86	Robinson, Kevan	Carlisle
9.10.86	Barrett, David	Swinton
30.10.86	Raiteri, Robert	Wynnum Manly, Aus.
30.10.86	Roe, Peter	Keighley
31.10.86	Caswell, Peter	Mixender ARL
1.1.87	McCaffrey, Michael	—
8.1.87	Hicks, Paul	—
27.1.87	Round, Michael	Spring View ARL
5.3.87	Townsley, Andrew	—
2.4.87	Waller, Vincent	Clowne ARL
2.4.87	Tyers, Andrew	Rotherham Rangers ARL

LEEDS

Signed	Player	Club From
25.7.86	Amann, David	Sandal RU
12.8.86	Morris, Bob	Taree United, Aus.
13.8.86	Smith, Peter	Illawara, Aus.
18.9.86	Gascoigne, Andy	Hull
18.9.86	Skerrett, Trevor	Hull
2.10.86	Price, Gary	York
3.10.86	Ettingshausen, Andrew	Cronulla, Aus.
16.10.86	McGaw, Mark	Cronulla, Aus.
28.10.86	Worthy, John	Leeds Colts
30.10.86	Butt, Ikram	Apperley Bridge ARL
31.10.86	Mason, Andy	Bramley
23.11.86	Fox, Phil	Leigh
5.12.86	Whitehead, Paul	Dewsbury
17.12.86	*Clark, Trevor	York
10.1.87	Ashton, Ray	Oldham
11.1.87	*Ingham, Gareth	Bramley
20.1.87	Sturgess, Andrew	Wyther ARL
25.3.87	Wilkes, Mark	Workington T.
30.4.87	Lord, Mark	St. Annes ARL

LEIGH

Signed	Player	Club From
10.8.86	Owen, Ivor	Leigh Miners Welfare ARL
5.9.86	Howell, Gary	Penrith, Aus.
5.9.86	Schubert, Ian	Western Suburbs, Aus.
20.10.86	Huddart, Milton	Carlisle
25.10.86	*Leului, James	Hull
24.11.86	Standish, Wayne	Culcheth Pack Horse ARL
13.12.86	Jeffrey, Ian	Liverpool RU
23.12.86	*Bentley, Keith	Salford
27.12.86	Miller, Steve	Leigh Miners Welfare ARL
27.1.87	Round, Michael	Spring View ARL
6.2.87	Ford, Mike	Wigan
30.3.87	Robinson, Nigel	Tyldsley RU
30.3.87	Evans, David	Rochdale H.
31.3.87	*Naidole, Tom	Oldham

MANSFIELD MARKSMAN

Signed	Player	Club From
23.7.86	Barrett, Mark	Sowerby Spartans ARL
11.8.86	Leary, Simon	Featherstone R.
12.8.86	Humphreys, Lee	Huddersfield B.
5.9.86	Jackson, Robert	Bradford N.
11.9.86	*Dennison, Steve	Hull
16.9.86	Westbury, Mark	Dewsbury
19.9.86	*Smith, Keith	Halifax
27.9.86	Thompson, Courtney	Old Brodlieans RU
28.9.86	Gentle, Peter	Western Suburbs, Aus.
12.10.86	Stevens, Darren	Western Suburbs, Aus.
12.10.86	Crossingham, Mark	South Sydney, Aus.
12.10.86	Tupaea, Shane	Blackwater Central, NZ
12.11.86	*Deakin, Chris	Rochdale H.
5.12.86	Loynes, Dean	Brighouse Rangers ARL
5.12.86	Portz, Karl	Carlisle
12.12.86	Langton, Terry	Featherstone R.
24.12.86	*Topping, Paul	Swinton
27.12.86	Hough, Michael	Waterhead ARL
9.1.87	King, Craig	Sydney Schools, Aus.
9.1.87	Simpson, Colin	St. Annes ARL
9.1.87	Hull, Andrew	Folly Lane ARL
9.1.87	Whithead, Craig	Rochdale H.
8.2.87	Platt, Billy	Huddersfield B.
15.3.87	Sealey, Camrul	Waterhead ARL
25.3.87	*Ogburn, John	Oldham
25.3.87	Chadwick, Les	Oldham
28.3.87	Lord, Mark	St. Annes ARL

Paul Topping, a seven-week loan signing by Mansfield Marksman from Swinton.

OLDHAM

Signed	Player	Club From
29.8.86	Clark, Bruce	Western Suburbs, Aus
11.9.86	Myler, Chris	Ring O'Bells ARL
11.9.86	Raper, Stuart	Cronulla, Aus.
25.9.86	Bridge, Gary	Balmain, Aus.
30.12.86	*Garner, Steve	Fulham
4.1.87	Wright, Steve	Feltham RU
9.1.87	Fairbank, Mark	Elland ARL
10.1.87	Waddell, Hugh	Blackpool B.
11.1.87	Burke, Mick	Widnes
20.2.87	*Parrish, Michael	Wakefield T.
27.3.87	Grix, Wayne	Mansfield M.
1.4.87	Sherratt, Ian	Bradford N.
29.4.87	*Ogburn, John	Mansfield M.

ROCHDALE HORNETS

Signed	Player	Club From
5.9.86	*Lowe, Kevin	Warrington
5.9.86	Byron, Gerry	Western Suburbs, Aus.
5.9.86	Harrigan, Ken	Western Suburbs, Aus.
6.9.86	Jones, Glen	Wigan
19.9.86	Purcell, Craig	Collegians, Aus.
19.9.86	Thompson, Darren	Collegians, Aus.
26.9.86	Caffrey, Brian	Oldham
4.10.86	*Lowe, Kevin	Blackpool B.
28.10.86	Williams, Dean	Wakefield T.
30.10.86	Hughes, Eric	St. Helens
3.11.86	*Cartwright, Phil	Wakefield T.
8.1.87	Johnson, Willie	Swinton
9.1.87	Causey, Mark	Orrell St. James ARL
9.1.87	Turner, Stephen	Mayfield ARL
9.1.87	Munro, Geoff	Huddersfield B.

RUNCORN HIGHFIELD

Signed	Player	Club From
19.8.86	Campbell, Danny	Leigh
28.8.86	Connors, Sean	Swinton
28.8.86	*Blythin, Kevin	Whitehaven
10.9.86	O'Connell, Seamus	Illawara, Aus.
28.9.86	Cogger, John	Western Suburbs, Aus.
16.10.86	Fraser, Paul	Wigan

ST. HELENS

Signed	Player	Club From
6.7.86	Halliwell, Steve	Leigh
8.7.86	*Parkes, Brian	Wakefield T.
8.7.86	Southward, Philip	St. Helens Colts
8.7.86	Earner, Andrew	St. Helens Colts
2.9.86	Clark, Brett	Western Suburbs, Aus.
12.9.86	Daintith, Ian	Widnes Tigers ARL
29.9.86	Jarvis, Pat	St. George, Aus.
2.11.86	Fieldhouse, John	Widnes
19.12.86	Bayliss, Steve	—
26.12.86	Hopkin, Paul	St. Annes ARL
27.1.87	Devine, Shaun	Leigh Rangers ARL
2.2.87	*Gorley, Peter	Whitehaven

SALFORD

Signed	Player	Club From
22.7.86	Schubert, Garry	Taree United, Aus.
26.7.86	Selby, Geoff	St. George, Aus.
30.7.86	Austin, Greg	Aus.
24.8.86	Whiteley, Chris	Wigan St. Patricks ARL
24.8.86	Mercer, Andrew	West Park RU
5.9.86	Wakefield, Mark	Cronulla, Aus.
23.9.86	Hewitt, David	Manchester RU
9.10.86	Morris, Steve	Warrington
24.10.86	O'Shea, Terry	Te Atatu, NZ
23.11.86	Moran, Mark	Simms Cross ARL
5.1.87	*Dickens, Steve	Dewsbury
10.2.87	Needham, David	St. Annes ARL
2.3.87	Roberts, Paul	Blackpool B.
5.3.87	*Bentley, Keith	Leigh
5.3.87	Regan, Peter	Wigan St. Patricks ARL
9.3.87	Bullough, David	Fulham
1.4.87	Burgess, Andrew	Irlam Hornets ARL

Australian stand off Brett Clark, flown back by St. Helens for the Silk Cut Challenge Cup Final at Wembley.

SHEFFIELD EAGLES

Signed	Player	Club From
21.8.86	Miller, Graig	–
5.9.86	Parkes, Steve	Moorends ARL
5.9.86	Lidbury, Steve	Lock Lane ARL
24.9.86	Blazey, John	Papanui, NZ
10.10.86	Sheridan, Greg	Ryde Eastwood, Aus.
24.10.86	Lyons, Cliff	Manly-Warringah, Aus.
2.11.86	Crowther, Ian	Carlisle
9.11.86	Aston, Mark	Gaffers ARL
19.12.86	Wilson, Andrew	Queens Park ARL
8.1.87	Close, David	Pontefract Labour ARL
8.1.87	Brennan, Peter	–
21.2.87	Kellett, Neil	Mansfield M.

SWINTON

Signed	Player	Club From
3.9.86	Barrett, David	Mansfield M.
24.10.86	Bourneville, Mark	Mount Albert, NZ
27.11.86	Grima, Joe	Ponsonby, NZ
9.12.86	Percival, John	Simms Cross ARL
8.1.87	*Johnson, William	Huddersfield B.
13.2.87	*Topping, Paul	Mansfield M.

WAKEFIELD TRINITY

Signed	Player	Club From
1.6.86	Abrahams, Steve	Sharlston ARL
1.6.86	Diamond, Steve	Castleford
4.7.86	Gittins, Tommy	Warrington
8.7.86	Lingard, Glynn	Sharlston ARL
29.7.86	Evans, Steve	Hull
10.9.86	Brennan, Rowan	Canberra, Aus.
28.9.86	Stanton, Glenn	Balmain, Aus.
28.9.86	Klein, Russell	Brothers, Aus.
9.10.86	Cowie, Robert	Parramatta, Aus.
28.10.86	Price, Gary	Sharlston ARL
30.10.86	*Cartwright, Phil	Rochdale H.
18.12.86	*Wilkinson, Andrew	Featherstone R.
1.1.87	Kelly, Neil	Featherstone R.
2.1.87	*Parrish, Mick	Oldham
23.1.87	Douglas, Ian	Batley
23.1.87	Crooks, Martin	Leeds
23.1.87	Sheldon, Ian	Bradford N.
23.1.87	Jasiewicz, Dick	Bradford N.
24.1.87	Armitage, Des	Leeds
24.1.87	Haggerty, Gary	Pilkington Recs ARL
26.1.87	Van Bellen, Gary	Bradford N.
6.2.87	McDermott, Paul	Whitehaven
25.2.87	Harcombe, Kevin	Rochdale H.
25.2.87	Halliwell, Steve	St. Helens
28.2.87	Walton, Dean	Sharlston ARL
5.3.87	*Dobson, Steve	York
24.3.87	Mallinder, Paul	Bradford N.
31.3.87	*Moll, David	Keighley
31.3.87	*Gilbert, John	Widnes

WARRINGTON

Signed	Player	Club From
20.7.86	Gleaves, Mark	Barrow
9.8.86	Humphries, Tony	Crossfields ARL
14.8.86	*Shaw, Glyn	Rochdale H.
28.8.86	Turner, Robert	Blackbrook ARL
5.2.87	Drummond, Des	Leigh
26.2.87	*Lowndes, Paul	Oldham
26.2.87	Gregory, Damion	Wigan St. Patricks ARL
7.3.87	Mossop, Andrew	Millom ARL
10.3.87	Roskell, Mark	Millom ARL
19.3.87	Percival, Ian	Ring O'Bells ARL
20.3.87	Holden, Keith	Wigan

WHITEHAVEN

Signed	Player	Club From
29.7.86	Lofthouse, Norman	Mirehouse ARL
29.7.86	Fryer, Mark	Bluebell ARL
8.8.86	Richardson, Bill	Egremont ARL
18.8.86	Shuttleworth, Greg	Aus.
28.8.86	McCurrie, Alan	Wakefield T.
2.9.86	Gaffney, John	Whitehaven
5.9.86	McConnell, Ralph	Barrow
28.11.86	McFarlane, Gary	Western Suburbs, Aus.
12.12.86	Bond, Gary	Carlisle
16.12.86	Crossingham, Mark	Mansfield M.
30.1.87	Telford, Robert	Mirehouse ARL
11.5.87	Oglenby, Martin	Glasson Rangers ARL

WIDNES

Signed	Player	Club From
25.9.86	Coleman, Craig	South Sydney, Aus.
3.10.86	Cleal, Les	Tumbarumba, Aus.
2.11.86	Pinner, Harry	St. Helens
1.1.87	Schmidt, Darrel	Tumbarumba, Aus.
11.1.87	Thackray, Rick	Warrington
25.2.87	Worgan, Graham	Leigh
24.3.87	Rutter, Phillip	Prestwich ARL
20.4.87	McMannion, Phil	Widnes Stanley ARL

WIGAN

Signed	Player	Club From
28.8.86	Beswick, David	West Bank ARL
2.9.86	Rodgers, Craig	Wigan St. Patricks ARL
5.9.86	Bell, Dean	Eastern Suburbs, Aus.
14.9.86	Betts, Dennis	Leigh Rangers ARL
1.10.86	Roberts, Ian	South Sydney, Aus.
15.12.86	Reid, Wayne	Wigan St. Patricks ARL
5.1.87	Forshaw, Michael	Wigan St. Patricks ARL
11.1.87	Gregory, Andy	Warrington
17.2.87	Moran, Peter	Wigan St. Patricks ARL

WORKINGTON TOWN

Signed	Player	Club From
28.6.86	Key, Andrew	Great Clifton ARL
15.8.86	Rooney, Neil	Netherall RU
17.8.86	Mawson, Mark	Millom ARL
26.8.86	Law, Michael	Broughton Red Rose ARL
26.8.86	Tubman, Keith	Great Clifton ARL
8.9.86	Lynch, Keith	Netherall RU
8.9.86	Hillier, Errol	Cronulla, Aus.
8.9.86	Hurst, Phil	Cronulla, Aus.
19.9.86	Newall, John	Glasson Rangers ARL
3.10.86	Wilkes, Mark	Eastern Suburbs, Aus.
25.10.86	Johnson, Bob	—
28.10.86	Mounsey, Gary	Glasson Rangers ARL
27.11.86	Woods, David	Barrow
9.12.86	Walker, Cliff	Aspatria ARL
30.12.86	Bond, Garry	Carlisle
28.1.87	Law, Andrew	Broughton Red Rose ARL
3.3.87	Turley, Norman	Barrow

YORK

Signed	Player	Club From
1.7.86	Wigglesworth, Iain	Leeds Colts
31.8.86	Sutton, Mick	Carlisle
3.9.86	Prendiville, Paul	Hull
3.9.86	Long, Mark	North Sydney, Aus.
3.9.86	Willey, Sean	Manly-Warringah, Aus
3.9.86	Strutt, Darren	North Sydney, Aus.
6.9.86	Arnett, Carl	Hull
18.9.86	Waites, Brian	Featherstone R.
3.10.86	Stephenson, Nigel	Dewsbury
17.10.86	*Clark, Trevor	Leeds
4.11.86	Turner, Paul	Knottingley ARL
4.11.86	Maxwell, Paul	Rose and Crown ARL
4.11.86	White, Paul	Queensbury ARL
14.12.86	Ellis, St. John	Southlands ARL
9.1.87	Bell, Steve	York Colts
9.1.87	Grogan, Steve	—
9.1.87	Kerr, Michael	Cess Nock ARL
9.1.87	Kirkwood, John	Hull
9.1.87	Olsen, Steve	Hull K.R. Colts
9.1.87	Carlyle, Brendan	York All Blacks ARL
11.1.87	*Hooper, Trevor	Huddersfield B.
11.1.87	Wilson, Ian	Hull K.R.
23.4.87	Rhodes, Darren	York Colts

New Zealander Trevor Clark, a short term recruit by York from Leeds.

Greenalls Man of Steel for a record second time, Ellery Hanley.

AWARDS

THE 1987 MAN OF STEEL AWARDS

Launched in the 1976-77 season, the Rugby Football League's official awards are presented to the Man of Steel, the personality judged to have made the most impact on the season; the First and Second Division Players of the Year, decided by a ballot of the players; the Young Player of the Year, under-21 at the start of the season; the Coach of the Year and Referee of the Year all chosen by a panel of judges.

Having been sponsored by Trumanns Steel for the first seven years, the awards were taken over by Greenall Whitley in 1983-84. Last season they presented a record £6,000 in prizes at the Variety Centre, Salford.

Greenalls Man of Steel

Wigan's Ellery Hanley became the first person to be awarded the Man of Steel title twice, having taken the top individual prize in 1985.

The Great Britain captain received a record £1,750 and a £300 silver champagne goblet as the personality judged to have made the most impact on the 1986-87 season.

The former Bradford Northern star marked the season by topping the try chart with 63 touchdowns, the most-ever by a non-winger, bringing his tally for the past three seasons to a phenomenal 156.

Hanley set a new First Division record with 44 tries, featuring a record-equalling five in a match. His total included 59 for Wigan, three short of equalling a 61-year-old club record set by winger Johnny Ring.

Of those 59 Wigan touchdowns, 30 came in 17 matches at loose forward, 25 in 19 games at stand off, one in two appearances at centre and a hat-trick as a substitute. The Leeds-born star also scored three tries for Great Britain and one for Yorkshire, his Test cap tally rising to 18.

Greenalls First Division Player of the Year

Record cash transfer scrum half Andy Gregory topped the poll of fellow Stones Bitter Championship players, votes being cast in January and April.

Recruited by Wigan from Warrington at the turn of the year, Gregory made 14 appearances for the Wire, scoring three tries and four goals, before his move to Central Park.

On the run-in to Wigan's league title success, he added another four tries. On the representative front, the former Widnes half back featured in the third Test against Australia and the meeting with France in Carcassonne, bringing his Test cap tally to 11. He captained Lancashire for the second successive season in the Rodstock War of the Roses encounter.

Another Ellery Hanley success . . . this time a 1987 Premiership winners medal.

374

Greenalls Second Division Player of the Year

For the first time, the Second Division Player of the Year title was awarded to an overseas player, Australian utility man John Cogger.

Recruited by Runcorn Highfield from Sydney club Western Suburbs, Cogger made 23 appearances for the Canal Street outfit covering loose forward, second row, scrum half and stand off and contributing 18 tries.

Greenalls Young Player of the Year

Wigan prodigy Shaun Edwards lifted the junior title for the second successive season.

The local product finished seventh in the top try chart with 26 touchdowns, 24 for Wigan and two for Great Britain. His 41 appearances for the Central Park club were divided between 23 at stand off, 15 at scrum half and three at full back.

Edwards was named as substitute for all three Tests against Australia, coming on once. He played in both matches against France, gaining Man of the Match rating in the record-breaking performance at Leeds. He skippered the Under-21s in the encounters with France, being chosen as Man of the Match in the return fixture at St. Helens.

Greenalls Coach of the Year

Former New Zealand national coach Graham Lowe celebrated his first season in British club football with the title of top coach.

After title-winning success in Auckland and Brisbane, he moulded big spending Wigan into a unit which lifted their first Championship title for 27 years, the John Player Special Trophy by a record margin, the Lancashire Cup for a record 18th time and the club's first-ever Premiership Trophy success.

That elusive Championship success broke five records with most tries and points scored, least tries and points conceded and most league points gained with only two defeats.

Greenalls Referee of the Year

Kippax referee John Holdsworth lifted the title to add to his 1981 success, marking a season highlighted by his debut at Wembley.

The Silk Cut Challenge Cup appointment followed taking charge of the 1987 John Player Special Trophy final between Wigan and Warrington at Bolton Wanderers soccer ground.

His seventh campaign as a senior referee also included taking control of the Anglo-French Colts international in Toulouse.

● Each of the five category winners received a cheque for £650 and an inscribed silver wine goblet worth £200.

Greenalls Referee of the Year John Holdsworth, in charge of the 1987 Silk Cut Challenge Cup and John Player Special Trophy Finals.

THE MAN OF STEEL AWARDS ROLL OF HONOUR

	Man of Steel	1st Division Player	2nd Division Player	Young Player	Coach	Referee
1977	David Ward (Leeds)	Mal Reilly (Castleford)	Ged Marsh (Blackpool B.)	David Ward (Leeds)	Eric Ashton MBE (St. Helens)	Billy Thompson (Huddersfield)
1978	George Nicholls (St. Helens)	George Nicholls (St. Helens)	John Woods (Leigh)	John Woods (Leigh)	Frank Myler (Widnes)	Billy Thompson (Huddersfield)
1979	Doug Laughton (Widnes)	Mick Adams (Widnes)	Steve Norton (Hull)	Steve Evans (Featherstone R.)	Doug Laughton (Widnes)	Mick Naughton (Widnes)
1980	George Fairbairn (Wigan)	Mick Adams (Widnes)	Steve Quinn (Featherstone R.)	Roy Holdstock (Hull K.R.)	Peter Fox (Bradford N.)	Fred Lindop (Wakefield)
1981	Ken Kelly (Warrington)	Ken Kelly (Warrington)	John Crossley (York)	Des Drummond (Leigh)	Billy Benyon (Warrington)	John Holdsworth (Kippax)
1982	Mick Morgan (Carlisle)	Steve Norton (Hull)	Mick Morgan (Carlisle)	Des Drummond (Leigh)	Arthur Bunting (Hull)	Fred Lindop (Wakefield)
1983	Allan Agar (Featherstone R.)	Keith Mumby (Bradford N.)	Steve Nash (Salford)	Brian Noble (Bradford N.)	Arthur Bunting (Hull)	Robin Whitfield (Widnes)
1984	Joe Lydon (Widnes)	Joe Lydon (Widnes)	David Cairns (Barrow)	Joe Lydon (Widnes)	Tommy Dawes (Barrow)	Billy Thompson (Huddersfield)
1985	Ellery Hanley (Bradford N.)	Ellery Hanley (Bradford N.)	Graham Steadman (York)	Lee Crooks (Hull)	Roger Millward MBE (Hull K.R.)	Ron Campbell (Widnes)
1986	Gavin Miller (Hull K.R.)	Gavin Miller (Hull K.R.)	Derek Pyke (Leigh)	Shaun Edwards (Wigan)	Chris Anderson (Halifax)	Fred Lindop (Wakefield)
1987	Ellery Hanley (Wigan)	Andy Gregory (Wigan)	John Cogger (Runcorn H.)	Shaun Edwards (Wigan)	Graham Lowe (Wigan)	John Holdsworth (Kippax)

NOMINEES:

1977 1st Division Player: Bruce Burton (Castleford), Vince Farrar (Featherstone R.). 2nd Division Player: Jeff Grayshon (Dewsbury), Keith Hepworth (Hull). Young Player: Jimmy Crampton (Hull), Harry Pinner (St. Helens). Coach: Keith Cotton (Featherstone R.), Mal Reilly (Castleford). Referee: Joe Jackson (Pudsey), Mick Naughton (Widnes).

1978 1st Division Player: Roger Millward (Hull K.R.), Harry Pinner (St. Helens). 2nd Division Player: Phil Hogan (Barrow), Mick Morgan (York). Young Player: Neil Hague (Leeds), Keith Mumby (Bradford N.). Coach: Eric Ashton MBE (St. Helens), John Mantle (Leigh). Referee: Ron Campbell (Widnes), Fred Lindop (Wakefield).

1979 1st Division Player: Brian Lockwood (Hull K.R.), Tommy Martyn (Warrington). 2nd Division Player: Barry Banks (York), John Wolford (Dewsbury). Young Player: Mick Burke (Widnes), John Woods (Leigh). Coach: Billy Benyon (Warrington), Arthur Bunting (Hull). Referee: Fred Lindop (Wakefield), Billy Thompson (Huddersfield).

1980 1st Division Player: Len Casey (Hull K.R.), George Fairbairn (Wigan). 2nd Division Player: Mick Blacker (Halifax), John Wolford (Dewsbury). Young Player: Steve Hubbard (Hull K.R.), Harry Pinner (St. Helens). Coach: Maurice Bamford (Halifax), Arthur Bunting (Hull). Referee: Ron Campbell (Widnes), Billy Thompson (Huddersfield).

1981 1st Division Player: Mick Adams (Widnes), Tommy Martyn (Warrington). 2nd Division Player: Arnie Walker (Whitehaven), Danny Wilson (Swinton). Young Player: Paul Harkin (Hull K.R.), Keith Mumby (Bradford N.). Coach: Reg Bowden (Fulham), Peter Fox (Bradford N.). Referee: Ron Campbell (Widnes), Fred Lindop (Wakefield).

1982 1st Division Player: Jeff Grayshon (Bradford N.), Andy Gregory (Widnes). 2nd Division Player: Denis Boyd (Carlisle), Alan Fairhurst (Swinton). Young Player: Lee Crooks (Hull), Andy Gregory (Widnes). Coach: Doug Laughton (Widnes), Alex Murphy/Colin Clarke (Leigh). Referee: Gerry Kershaw (York), Billy Thompson (Huddersfield).

1983 1st Division Player: Bob Eccles (Warrington), David Topliss (Hull). 2nd Division Player: Tommy David (Cardiff C.), Mike Lampkowski (Wakefield T.). Young Player: Ronnie Duane (Warrington), Andy Goodway (Oldham). Coach: Alex Murphy (Wigan), Frank Myler (Oldham). Referee: John Holdsworth (Leeds), Fred Lindop (Wakefield).

1984 1st Division Player: Garry Schofield (Hull), John Woods (Leigh). 2nd Division Player: Lynn Hopkins (Workington T.), John Wolford (Hunslet). Young Player: Gary Divorty (Hull), Garry Schofield (Hull). Coach: Arthur Bunting (Hull), Roger Millward MBE (Hull K.R.). Referee: Derek Fox (Wakefield), Fred Lindop (Wakefield).

1985 1st Division Player: Harry Pinner (St. Helens), Gary Prohm (Hull K.R.). 2nd Division Player: Terry Langton (Mansfield M.), Peter Wood (Runcorn H.). Young Player: Deryck Fox (Featherstone R.), Andy Platt (St. Helens). Coach: Arthur Bunting (Hull), Colin Clarke/Alan McInnes (Wigan). Referee: Fred Lindop (Wakefield), Stan Wall (Leigh).

1986 1st Division Player: Steve Ella (Wigan), John Fieldhouse (Widnes). 2nd Division Player: John Henderson (Leigh), Graham King (Hunslet). Young Player: Paul Lyman (Featherstone R.), Roy Powell (Leeds). Coach: Roger Millward MBE (Hull K.R.), John Sheridan (Doncaster). Referee: John Holdsworth (Kippax), Robin Whitfield (Widnes).

1987 1st Division Player: Lee Crooks (Hull), Ellery Hanley (Wigan). 2nd Division Player: Andy Bateman (Hunslet), Les Holliday (Swinton). Young Player: Paul Loughlin (St. Helens), Kevin McCormack (St. Helens). Coach: Chris Anderson (Halifax), Alex Murphy (St. Helens). Referee: Kevin Allatt (Southport), Fred Lindop (Wakefield).

GREENALL WHITLEY-SUNDAY PEOPLE SUPREME AWARDS

After nine years of promoting Man of the Month and Personality of the Year awards, Greenall Whitley and the *Sunday People* launched a new Supreme Awards scheme in 1986-87.

Cheques for £250 were presented to the adjudged top player in each position based on form ratings throughout the campaign. The £2,250 scheme rated players in the positions of full back, wing, centre, stand off, scrum half, prop, hooker, second row and loose forward.

1986-87 Supreme Awards

Full back:
1. **Graham Eadie** (Halifax)
2. Phil Veivers (St. Helens)
3. Brian Johnson (Warrington)

Wing:
1. **Phil Ford** (Bradford N.)
2. Henderson Gill (Wigan)
3. Kevin McCormack (St. Helens)

Centre:
1. **Dean Bell** (Wigan)
2. Garry Schofield (Hull)
3. David Stephenson (Wigan)

Stand off:
1. **Shaun Edwards** (Wigan)
2. Chris Anderson (Halifax)
3. Tony Myler (Widnes)

Scrum half:
1. **Andy Gregory** (Wigan)
2. Deryck Fox (Featherstone R.)
3. Bob Beardmore (Castleford)

Prop:
1. **Kurt Sorensen** (Widnes)
2. Kevin Ward (Castleford)
3. Brian Case (Wigan)

Hooker:
1. **Phil McKenzie** (Widnes)
2. Kevin Beardmore (Castleford)
3. Paul Groves (Salford)

Second row:
1. **Lee Crooks** (Hull)
2. Paul Dixon (Halifax)
3. Andy Platt (St. Helens)

Loose forward:
1. **Ellery Hanley** (Wigan)
2. Chris Arkwright (St. Helens)
3. Mike Gregory (Warrington)

Greenall Whitley — Sunday People Supreme Award winner in the second row, Test packman Lee Crooks.

GREENALL WHITLEY TOP SCORERS AWARDS

Launched in the 1976-77 season, the scheme was designed to reward the top try and goal scorers. Sponsored by brewers Greenall Whitley, the 1986-87 awards were worth £25 a try and £5 a goal.

For the second time in three seasons, Ellery Hanley topped the try chart with a massive total of 63 touchdowns, the most by a non-winger. His tally included 59 for Wigan, three for Great Britain and one for Yorkshire. His Greenall Whitley prize amounted to £1,575.

In his first full season in the senior ranks, St. Helens centre Paul Loughlin kicked 190 goals, featuring 12 for Great Britain Under-21s to earn a prize cheque of £950 for his top marksmanship.

Greenall Whitley Top Scorers Awards Roll of Honour

Top Tries		Top Goals	
1976-77	**1981-82**	**1976-77**	**1982-83**
Stuart Wright (Widnes): 31	John Jones (Work'ton T.): 31	Sammy Lloyd (Castle'd): 163	Steve Diamond (Fulham): 136
1977-78	**1982-83**	**1977-78**	**1983-84**
Stuart Wright (Widnes): 33	Bob Eccles (Warrington): 37	Geoff Pimblett (St. Helens): 178	Bob Beardmore (Castleford): 142
			Steve Hesford (Warrington): 142
1978-79	**1983-84**	**1978-79**	
Steve Hartley (Hull K.R.): 35	Garry Schofield (Hull): 38	Sammy Lloyd (Hull): 172	**1984-85**
			Sean Day (St. Helens): 157
1979-80	**1984-85**	**1979-80**	
Keith Fielding (Salford): 30	Ellery Hanley (Bradford N.): 55	Steve Quinn (F'stone R.): 163	**1985-86**
Steve Hubbard (Hull K.R.): 30	**1985-86**		Chris Johnson (Leigh): 173
	Steve Halliwell (Leigh): 49	**1980-81**	
1980-81		Steve Hesford (Warrington): 147	**1986-87**
John Crossley (York): 35	**1986-87**		Paul Loughlin (St. Helens): 190
	Ellery Hanley (Wigan): 63	**1981-82**	
		Lynn Hopkins (Work'ton T.): 190	

DAILY MIRROR-LADA CARS AWARDS

Introduced in the 1979-80 season, the scheme acknowledges the adjudged Team of the Month in both Division One and Two.

A panel of judges representing the Daily Mirror, Lada Cars and the Rugby League selected the two monthly winners who each received a cheque for £250 and a framed citation.

Promoted by the Daily Mirror, the awards were sponsored for the first four seasons by Shopacheck before Lada Cars took over in the 1983-84 season. Lada Cars introduced the first-ever £1,000 Team of the Year title in 1983-84, the 1987 winners being Wigan, holders of the Stones Bitter Championship, the John Player Special Trophy, the Lancashire Cup and the Stones Bitter Premiership Trophy.

The Daily Mirror-Lada Cars Awards Roll of Honour

	1979-80 First Division	1980-81 First Division	1981-82 First Division	1982-83 First Division
Aug./ Sept.	Salford	Hull K.R.	Leigh	Leeds
Oct.	Leigh	Castleford	Widnes	Hull
Nov.	Leeds	Featherstone R.	Hull K.R.	Castleford
Dec.	Hull	Warrington	Hull*	Wigan
Jan.	Bradford N.	Halifax		Wigan
Feb.	Widnes	Wakefield T.	Leigh	Castleford
Mar.	Hull	Widnes	Bradford N.	Hull
Apr./ May	Leigh	Bradford N.	Hull	Widnes

	Second Division	Second Division	Second Division	Second Division
Aug./ Sept.	Halifax	Huddersfield	Oldham	Fulham
Oct.	Batley	Fulham	Swinton	Huyton
Nov.	Featherstone R.	Wigan	Carlisle	Wakefield T.
Dec.	Oldham	Blackpool B.	Carlisle*	Salford
Jan.	Whitehaven	Keighley		Whitehaven
Feb.	Halifax	York	Huyton	Hunslet
Mar.	Barrow	Whitehaven	Oldham	Fulham
Apr./ May	Swinton	Batley	Oldham	Cardiff C.

*A double-money award to cover both months, badly hit by adverse weather.
†Not awarded due to bad weather.

Team of the Year
1983-84: Widnes
1984-85: Hull K.R.
1985-86: Halifax
1986-87: Wigan

	1983-84 First Division	1984-85 First Division	1985-86 First Division	1986-87 First Division
Aug./ Sept.	Bradford N.	Hull K.R.	Hull K.R.	St. Helens
Oct.	Hull K.R.	St. Helens	Wigan	Wigan
Nov.	Widnes	Featherstone R.	Oldham	Warrington
Dec.	Leeds	Halifax	Wigan	Warrington
Jan.	Hull	Hull K.R.	Widnes	Wigan
Feb.	Castleford	Wigan	†	Halifax
Mar.	Wigan	Wigan	St. Helens	Leigh
Apr./ May	St. Helens	St. Helens	Warrington	Halifax

	Second Division	Second Division	Second Division	Second Division
Aug./ Sept.	Barrow	Mansfield M.	Wakefield T.	Sheffield E.
Oct.	Halifax	Carlisle	Rochdale H.	Doncaster
Nov.	Swinton	Dewsbury	Leigh	Hunslet
Dec.	Batley	Batley	Blackpool B.	Rochdale H.
Jan.	Barrow	Batley	Doncaster	Swinton
Feb.	Hunslet	Bramley	†	Whitehaven
Mar.	Huddersfield	Dewsbury	Batley	Doncaster
Apr./ May	Blackpool B.	Swinton	Leigh	Hunslet

Derek Bote, the Second Division's top try scorer in action for Swinton, Daily Mirror — Lada Cars Second Division Team of the Month for January 1987.

STONES BITTER – DAILY STAR STARMEN AWARDS

Introduced in 1982-83, the scheme was sponsored by Stones Bitter and promoted by the *Daily Star*. The Man of the Match for each team in every Stones Bitter Championship and Second Division game is awarded a rating out of 10. The top pollster in the Championship received £1,000 and a trophy, with £500 and a trophy being presented to the top Second Division player.

Championship
1982-83	Harry Pinner (St. Helens)
1983-84	John Woods (Leigh)
1984-85	Ellery Hanley (Bradford N.)
1985-86	Deryck Fox (Featherstone R.)
1986-87	Deryck Fox (Featherstone R.)

Second Division
1982-83	Graham Beale (Keighley)
1983-84	John Wolford (Hunslet)
1984-85	Graham Steadman (York)
1985-86	Dean Carroll (Carlisle)
1986-87	Billy Platt (Mansfield M.)

1986-87 FINAL TABLES
Stones Bitter Championship
Deryck Fox (Featherstone R.)	104
Keith Mumby (Bradford N.)	80
John Lyons (Wakefield T.)	73
Ellery Hanley (Wigan)	66
Paul Harkin (Hull K.R.)	56
Kurt Sorensen (Widnes)	56
Peter Smith (Featherstone R.)	56
Gordon Smith (Hull K.R.)	54
Graham Eadie (Halifax)	54

Second Division
Billy Platt (Mansfield Marksman)	70
Paul Shuttleworth (Dewsbury)	68
John Cogger (Runcorn H.)	60
Alan Platt (Hunslet)	55
Les Holliday (Swinton)	53
Simon Wilson (Batley)	51
Steve Langton (Carlisle)	46

WALLACE ARNOLD – SUNDAY MIRROR ENTERTAINER AWARDS

Introduced for the first time in 1986-87, the scheme was sponsored by Wallace Arnold and promoted by the Sunday Mirror.

Each month an adjudged player was chosen as Entertainer of the Month to receive a Wallace Arnold holiday voucher for £250. The Entertainer of the Year was awarded a £1,000 holiday voucher, the 1987 winner being Great Britain skipper and the game's top try scorer, Ellery Hanley.

Entertainer of the Month
Sept.	Henderson Gill (Wigan)
Oct.	Phil Ford (Bradford N.)
Nov.	Neil Holding (St. Helens)
Dec.	Garry Schofield (Hull)
Jan.	Shaun Edwards (Wigan)
Feb.	Graham Eadie (Halifax)
Mar.	David Noble (Doncaster)
Apr./May	Ellery Hanley (Wigan

Entertainer of the Year
1987:	Ellery Hanley (Wigan)

TRAVELEADS TOP FAN AWARD

The third Traveleads Top Fan award as Rugby League's official Supporter of the Year was presented to Stock Exchange worker Bob Evans.

The 36-year-old Londoner won a £4,000 Canadian holiday for two for a fortnight, in conjunction with Wardair.

The former Aldershot FC soccer fan had watched only one televised 13-a-side match before being converted with the birth of Fulham in 1980.

The inaugural winner in 1985 was Doncaster fan Mrs Joan Martin, the 1986 recipient being Oldham stalwart, 81-year-old Eddie Elson.

REFEREES

REFEREES' HONOURS 1986-87

Silk Cut Challenge Cup final:
John Holdsworth

John Player Special Trophy final:
John Holdsworth

Stones Bitter Premiership final:
Kevin Allatt

Second Division Premiership:
John McDonald

Grunhalle Lager Lancashire Cup final:
Jim Smith

John Smiths Yorkshire Cup final:
John McDonald

Australia v New Zealand (3):
Robin Whitfield

France v Australia (2):
Fred Lindop

Rodstock War of the Roses:
John McDonald

Okells Charity Shield:
Fred Lindop

SENIOR REFEREES 1986-87

KEVIN ALLATT (Southport)
Date of birth: 29.12.42
Grade Two: 1970-71
Grade One: 1972-73
Premiership Trophy 1986-87
Lancashire Cup 1983-84
Lancashire v Yorkshire 1975-76

MICK BEAUMONT (Huddersfield)
Date of birth: 27.6.40
Grade Two: 1973-74
Grade One: 1977-78
Lancashire v Cumbria 1979-80

GEOFF BERRY (Batley)
Date of birth: 26.4.54
Grade Two: 1981-82
Grade One: 1983-84

ALEX BOWMAN (Whitehaven)
Date of birth: 20.9.56
Grade One: 1986-87

DAVE CARTER (Widnes)
Date of birth: 29.11.55
Grade One: 1984-85

STEVE CROSS (Hull)
Date of birth: 23.3.50
Grade One: 1986-87

DEREK FOX (Wakefield)
Date of birth: 2.1.39
Grade Two: 1977-78
Grade One: 1980-81
Lancashire v Cumbria 1981-82
Wales v England 1984-85

STEPHEN HAIGH (Ossett)
Date of birth: 5.4.45
Grade Two: 1980-81
Grade One: 1983-84

CLIFF HODGSON (Maryport)
Date of birth: 18.10.40
Grade Two: 1978-79
Grade One: 1983-84

JOHN HOLDSWORTH (Kippax)
Date of birth: 25.1.47
Grade Two: 1979-80
Grade One: 1980-81
Challenge Cup 1986-87
John Player Trophy 1985-86, 1986-87
Premiership Trophy 1980-81
Lancashire Cup 1982-83, 1985-86
Wales v England 1980-81
Cumbria v Yorkshire 1981-82
France v Great Britain Under-24s 1982-83

PAUL HOUGHTON (Warrington)
Date of birth: 1.10.51
Grade One: 1985-86

JOHN KENDREW (Castleford)
Date of birth: 22.4.50
Grade Two: 1982-83
Grade One: 1983-84

GERRY KERSHAW (Easingwold)
Date of birth: 24.10.43
Grade Two: 1969-70
Grade One: 1970-71
Challenge Cup 1980-81
Lancashire Cup 1980-81
Floodlit Trophy 1973-74
John Player Trophy 1973-74
Wales v England 1981-82
Wales v Australia 1982-83
France v Great Britain Under-24s 1981-82
Lancashire v Yorkshire 1971-72
Lancashire v Cumbria 1972-73
Cumbria v Other Nationalities 1974-75
Cumbria v Lancashire 1978-79, 1980-81

FRED LINDOP (Wakefield)
Date of birth: 20.7.38
Grade Two: 1966-67
Grade One: 1967-68
Great Britain v Australia, 3 Tests 1967-68
France v Great Britain 1968-69
1970 World Cup:
Great Britain v Australia
Great Britain v France
Great Britain v New Zealand
Great Britain v Australia (Final)
Wales v France 1974-75
1975 World Championship:
France v Wales
New Zealand v Australia (at Auckland)
Wales v France
Wales v England 1977-78
Great Britain v New Zealand 1980-81
Australia v New Zealand (2) 1982
France v Australia (2) 1986
Great Britain Under-24s v Australia 1978-79
France v Great Britain Under-24s 1979-80, 1983-84
France v Great Britain Under-21s 1985-86
Premiership Trophy 1976-77, 1982-83, 1985-86
Challenge Cup 1969-70, 1979-80, 1981-82 (+replay)
Floodlit Trophy 1967-68, 1972-73
John Player Trophy 1974-75, 1978-79, 1981-82
Lancashire Cup 1967-68, 1974-75
Yorkshire Cup 1984-85
Capt. Morgan Trophy 1973-74
Cumbria v Lancashire 1973-74
Lancashire v Other Nationalities 1974-75
Lancashire v Yorkshire 1981-82
War of the Roses 1985-86
Charity Shield 1986-87

JOHN McDONALD (Wigan)
Date of birth: 7.10.37
Grade Two: 1974-75
Grade One: 1975-76
Second Division Premiership 1986-87
Yorkshire Cup 1986-87
Floodlit Trophy 1978-79
Yorkshire v Cumbria 1978-79, 1981-82
War of the Roses 1986-87

JOHN MEAN (Leyland)
Date of birth: 12.11.39
Grade Two: 1975-76
Grade One: 1983-84

BRIAN SIMPSON (Manchester)
Date of birth: 23.6.44
Grade One: 1985-86

JIM SMITH (Halifax)
Date of birth: 2.3.44
Grade Two: 1977-78
Grade One: 1983-84
Lancashire Cup 1986-87

KEN SPENCER (Warrington)
Date of birth: 29.8.47
Grade Two: 1974-75
Grade One: 1983-84

RAY TENNANT (Castleford)
Date of birth: 7.4.49
Grade One: 1985-86

FRANK TICKLE (St. Helens)
(Date of birth: 26.10.45
Grade One: 1984-85

PAUL VOLANTE (Batley)
Date of birth: 30.6.52
Grade One: 1983-84

ROBIN WHITFIELD (Widnes)
Date of birth: 26.11.43
Grade Two: 1979-80
Grade One: 1980-81
Challenge Cup 1982-83, 1985-86
Yorkshire Cup 1981-82
France v Australia (2) 1982-83
New Zealand v Australia 1983
Australia v New Zealand (3) 1986
Yorkshire v Lancashire 1981-82

*Robin Whitfield, former full back with Barrow,
Huyton and Widnes.*

THE ALLIANCE

SLALOM LAGER ALLIANCE

FINAL TABLES 1986-87

FIRST DIVISION

	P.	W.	D.	L.	Dr.	FOR Gls.	FOR Trs.	FOR Pts.	Dr.	AGAINST Gls.	AGAINST Trs.	AGAINST Pts.	Pts.
Wigan	24	17	0	7	0	83	123	658	1	47	71	379	34
Warrington W.	24	16	1	7	4	100	126	708	2	50	61	346	33
Widnes	24	16	0	8	2	87	108	608	3	62	79	443	32
St. Helens	24	16	0	8	3	79	106	585	3	68	85	479	32
Castleford	24	15	0	9	5	78	87	509	1	66	79	449	30
Hull K.R.	24	15	0	9	7	78	77	471	2	60	86	466	30
Leeds	24	10	1	13	1	80	96	545	2	78	86	502	21
Hull	24	10	1	13	0	52	73	396	3	73	72	437	21
Salford	24	10	0	14	2	60	77	430	4	68	72	428	20
Halifax	24	9	2	13	3	53	68	381	2	64	94	506	20
Leigh	24	9	0	15	1	69	75	439	3	82	98	559	18
Barrow	24	6	3	15	0	43	63	338	0	93	122	674	15
Wakefield T.	24	3	0	21	0	51	54	318	2	102	128	718	6

SECOND DIVISION

	P.	W.	D.	L.	Dr.	FOR Gls.	FOR Trs.	FOR Pts.	Dr.	AGAINST Gls.	AGAINST Trs.	AGAINST Pts.	Pts.
Swinton C.	26	26	0	0	2	110	154	838	6	27	41	224	52
Hunslet	26	21	1	4	5	92	114	645	3	42	42	255	43
Whitehaven	26	19	0	7	7	105	130	737	3	57	68	389	38
Bradford N.	26	17	2	7	7	85	103	589	8	45	58	330	36
Oldham	26	15	0	11	1	92	105	605	7	61	60	369	30
York	26	14	1	11	4	73	90	510	4	59	77	430	29
Featherstone R.	26	11	1	14	8	54	74	412	4	85	89	530	23
Workington T.	26	11	0	15	6	54	76	418	5	70	86	489	22
Huddersfield P.	26	10	1	15	7	46	68	371	5	80	101	569	21
Batley	26	10	1	15	2	58	48	310	3	71	94	521	21
Carlisle P.	26	9	2	15	11	56	61	367	8	70	87	496	20
Bramley	26	5	1	20	5	36	40	237	6	79	88	516	11
Keighley	26	5	0	21	5	55	63	367	2	111	149	820	10
Dewsbury	26	4	0	22	0	38	42	244	6	97	128	712	8

1986-87 RESULTS

FIRST DIVISION

Home: / Away:	Barrow	Castleford	Halifax	Hull	Hull K.R.	Leeds	Leigh	St. Helens	Salford	Wakefield T.	Warrington W.	Widnes	Wigan
Barrow	—	12-10	22-22	8-8	30-12	12-8	26-6	16-44	16-18	18-20	22-22	18-36	12-10
Castleford	60-10	—	18-12	14-12	23-16	18-12	34-30	48-12	14-8	21-14	28-24	20-28	29-22
Halifax	16-2	10-29	—	18-22	16-18	6-6	37-24	16-8	21-12	34-8	24-26	13-4	30-10
Hull	48-4	14-18	22-6	—	20-5	18-14	20-12	22-32	24-14	30-10	18-29	22-20	16-24
Hull K.R.	24-22	34-2	70-8	13-10	—	18-6	18-16	35-24	18-16	19-10	21-20	7-28	24-22
Leeds	58-6	18-29	32-4	16-8	28-13	—	42-12	8-50	36-14	42-24	16-20	22-34	40-4
Leigh	28-8	18-14	13-6	16-6	14-16	24-36	—	44-6	16-24	20-16	30-14	20-18	12-42
St. Helens	32-6	19-16	20-10	16-8	48-6	28-1	32-10	—	41-28	42-16	8-23	28-14	6-38
Salford	18-26	24-6	34-10	26-6	2-22	30-10	11-18	16-7	—	36-10	20-13	22-0	10-26
Wakefield T.	8-16	6-34	18-20	2-36	10-18	6-40	24-22	18-26	20-14	—	8-36	20-22	16-30
Warrington W.	82-12	34-0	12-18	52-0	16-10	40-24	44-2	64-0	30-13	38-2	—	29-2	6-14
Widnes	52-10	28-12	42-18	30-4	31-18	48-22	31-16	8-38	20-8	46-13	14-24	—	32-20
Wigan	24-4	32-2	34-16	48-2	44-16	36-8	34-16	8-18	18-12	58-12	38-10	14-20	—

1986-87 RESULTS

SECOND DIVISION

Home: / Away:	Batley	Bradford N.	Bramley	Carlisle-Penrith	Dewsbury	Featherstone R.	Huddersfield	Hunslet	Keighley	Oldham	Swinton C.	Whitehaven	Workington T.	York
Batley	—	4-20	20-24	22-32	8-4	8-0	26-12	2-18	32-6	18-22	4-20	20-16	34-13	19-16
Bradford N.	23-4	—	22-8	36-10	17-12	22-12	48-6	22-24	46-0	23-4	4-22	27-13	16-15	26-2
Bramley	2-14	6-18	—	6-6	10-6	7-6	10-27	2-26	22-10	4-22	1-36	8-13	18-3	20-22
Carlisle-Penrith	*	20-38	13-4	—	32-0	6-4	8-40	13-25	42-4	24-4	25-29	8-17	7-1	21-24
Dewsbury	34-4	8-42	24-18	4-10	—	6-42	8-18	0-22	16-14	18-20	0-24	16-70	16-22	16-12
Featherstone R.	25-6	25-25	34-12	24-20	16-14	—	22-10	10-42	25-22	17-12	8-50	12-15	8-12	13-40
Huddersfield	8-10	5-5	12-7	49-7	11-10	14-21	—	4-20	16-12	8-10	19-32	15-4	24-7	26-12
Hunslet	26-10	10-17	16-0	38-6	22-0	40-10	4-9	—	56-4	24-16	9-10	22-10	40-12	22-2
Keighley	8-16	14-28	39-26	20-10	34-10	17-58	26-8	18-32	—	12-30	18-34	16-27	19-12	6-32
Oldham	40-0	10-0	28-0	23-16	56-0	44-6	42-8	10-13	62-8	—	16-24	8-21	50-4	16-22
Swinton C.	46-22	32-4	36-6	34-7	48-6	36-0	62-0	22-4	42-4	34-6	—	18-0	16-12	34-4
Whitehaven	68-4	24-20	42-12	32-3	52-6	12-14	44-16	20-16	66-18	34-12	14-38	—	34-14	42-18
Workington T.	22-6	6-39†	20-4	10-9	40-0	14-0	46-0	12-26	36-18	16-12	23-24	4-21	—	24-10
York	26-2	16-6	1-0	8-22	48-10	24-0	26-6	8-8	36-0	25-12	8-35	24-26	38-18	—

*Not played, Carlisle-Penrith awarded the points. †Abandoned after 63 minutes, result standing.

Mud soaked Hull celebrate their 12-0 Slalom Lager Alliance 1987 Challenge Cup victory over Hull K.R.

Slalom Lager Alliance 1986-87 First Division Champions, Wigan.

SLALOM LAGER ALLIANCE CHALLENGE CUP 1987

First Round

Bradford N.	22	Bramley	14
Carlisle-Penrith		Keighley	

Tie awarded to Carlisle-Penrith

Castleford	23	Halifax	16
Dewsbury	6	Salford	24
Featherstone R.	10	Oldham	4
Huddersfield P.	7	Hull K.R.	18
Hunslet	24	St. Helens	36
Whitehaven	0	Warrington W.	30
Widnes	14	York	1
Wigan	6	Swinton C.	10
Workington T.	12	Batley	18

Byes: Barrow, Hull, Leeds, Leigh, Wakefield T.

Second Round

Castleford		Warrington W.	

Tie awarded to Castleford

Featherstone R.	22	Carlisle-Penrith	18
Hull		Widnes	

Tie awarded to Hull

Leeds	34	Batley	5
St. Helens	8	Hull K.R.	8
Salford	14	Leigh	18
Swinton C.	32	Bradford N.	8
Wakefield T.	14	Barrow	9

Replay

Hull K.R.	10	St. Helens	2

Third Round

Featherstone R.	15	Wakefield T.	13
Hull	30	Leigh	8
Hull K.R.	7	Leeds	6
Swinton C.	30	Castleford	7

Semi-Finals

Featherstone R.	14	Hull K.R.	32
Hull	30	Swinton C.	16

Final

Hull K.R.	0	Hull	12

LANCASHIRE COUNTY CHALLENGE SHIELD 1986-87

First Round

Barrow	46	Salford	6
Oldham	35	Warrington W.	24
Swinton C.	32	Carlisle-Penrith	6
Workington T.	22	Widnes	40

Byes: Leigh, St. Helens, Whitehaven, Wigan

Second Round

Leigh	36	Barrow	18
Swinton	26	Wigan	14
Whitehaven	6	St. Helens	38
Widnes	41	Oldham	22

Semi-Finals

Leigh	8	Widnes	22
St. Helens	15	Swinton	14

Final

St. Helens	16	Widnes	20

YORKSHIRE SENIOR COMPETITION CHALLENGE CUP 1986-87

First Round

Batley	22	Featherstone R.	10
Bradford N.	12	Halifax	4
Bramley	6	Hull	20
Cutsyke (Castleford)	0	Castleford	28
Dewsbury	22	Wakefield T.	20
Huddersfield P.	36	Leeds	18
Hunslet	26	Keighley	20
York	22	Hull K.R.	14

Second Round

Castleford	58	Bradford N.	6
Huddersfield P.	30	Dewsbury	0
Hull	26	Batley	10
Hunslet	40	York	12

Semi-Finals

Castleford	13	Huddersfield P.	0
Hunslet	24	Hull	10

Final

Hunslet	8	Castleford	18

COLTS

COLTS LEAGUE

FINAL TABLES 1986-87

FIRST DIVISION

	P.	W.	D.	L.	Dr.	FOR Gls.	FOR Trs.	FOR Pts.	Dr.	AGAINST Gls.	AGAINST Trs.	AGAINST Pts.	Pts.
Hull	20	17	1	2	3	52	88	459	2	40	33	214	35
St. Helens	19	14	1	4	1	66	82	461	5	37	47	267	29
Wigan	17	11	0	6	4	54	78	424	2	32	44	242	22
Featherstone R.	20	10	2	8	3	39	59	317	7	44	55	315	22
Wakefield T.	19	10	0	9	5	39	45	263	4	25	40	214	20
Castleford	20	9	2	9	9	53	64	371	1	48	74	393	20
Hull K.R.	20	9	0	11	5	47	67	367	1	43	60	327	18
Leeds	20	9	0	11	2	37	55	296	6	45	67	364	18
Barrow	19	6	2	11	3	43	34	225	3	44	62	339	14
Bradford N.	20	5	0	15	2	36	51	278	7	68	80	463	10
Halifax	20	3	0	17	2	30	34	198	1	70	95	521	6

● Leigh withdrew on 17th November 1986.

SECOND DIVISION

	P.	W.	D.	L.	Dr.	FOR Gls.	FOR Trs.	FOR Pts.	Dr.	AGAINST Gls.	AGAINST Trs.	AGAINST Pts.	Pts.
Hunslet	20	16	1	3	1	86	129	689	2	24	37	198	33
Doncaster	19	15	0	4	0	89	133	710	1	28	48	249	30
York	18	13	1	4	1	67	117	603	1	46	51	297	27
Leigh	14	8	0	6	0	39	68	350	3	28	61	303	16
Dewsbury	18	5	0	13	2	25	52	260	3	41	88	437	10
Huddersfield B.	19	5	0	14	2	18	55	258	2	68	104	554	10
Sheffield E.	22	2	0	20	6	14	18	106	0	103	183	938	4

● Leigh joined on 17th November 1986.

COLTS CHAMPIONSHIP ROLL OF HONOUR

1975-76	Wigan
1976-77	Bradford N.
1977-78	Bradford N.
1978-79	Hull K.R.
1979-80	Oldham
1980-81	Hull
1981-82	Hull
1982-83	Hull
1983-84	Castleford

	Division One	Division Two
1984-85	Wakefield T.	St. Helens
1985-86	Wigan	Leigh
1986-87	Wigan	Hunslet

COLTS LEAGUE

1986-87 RESULTS

FIRST DIVISION

Home \ Away	Barrow	Bradford N.	Castleford	Featherstone R.	Halifax	Hull	Hull K.R.	Leeds	Leigh	St. Helens	Wakefield T.	Wigan
Barrow	—	14-24	6-6*	7-6	24-0	8-21	13-10			12-20	10-12	1-28
Bradford N.	12-14	—	22-19	8-9	18-6	4-18	10-11	4-22	32-5	14-18	22-18	12-22
Castleford	22-12	29-18	—	15-20	23-8	11-30	22-20	28-4	70-2	50-2	16-2	34-24
Featherstone R.	10-10	28-12	15-15	—	10-11	28-12	18-25	36-12		18-16	13-8	6-18
Halifax	14-30	30-36	16-26	18-20	—	8-18	2-8	5-0		14-26	4-20	16-50
Hull	11-6	28-14	38-6	26-18	42-2	—	28-9	32-12	60-0	14-20	18-4	34-0
Hull K.R.	4-8	36-4	38-6	10-38	44-12	8-14	—	27-4	84-2	25-16	16-22	40-8
Leeds	32-2	17-14	20-18	22-0	20-26	18-26	40-12	—		8-36	6-4	10-1
Leigh withdrew on 12.11.86			12-62	18-18	19-32	10-54			—			4-82
St. Helens	42-18	38-12	28-10	22-0	40-2	14-14	36-8	14-5		—	15-4	14-19
Wakefield T.	31-0	24-6	24-1	8-18	16-0	6-9	18-14	9-6	26-4	14-34	—	13-6
Wigan		62-12	30-8	40-6	50-4	18-26	8-2	40-4				—

*Abandoned after 25 minutes

SECOND DIVISION

*four-pointer

Home \ Away	Dewsbury	Doncaster	Huddersfield	Hunslet	Leigh	Sheffield E.	York
Dewsbury	—	18-10 8-46	20-16 12-18	0-36*		22-8 20-2	17-22
Doncaster	54-8	—	60-14 64-8	24-16 14-20	48-12*	72-0 52-8	30-20 24-22
Huddersfield	18-10	7-32	—	4-46*		12-8 34-9	8-26 22-32
Hunslet	22-6 52-13	6-34	47-4 42-4	—	52-2	74-0 58-0	16-16 62-26
Leigh joined on 17.11.86	60-12 30-12 30-0		52-15	38-24	—	62-0*	12-48
Sheffield E.	1-76 11-6	6-46 12-68	12-8 4-38	0-60 4-44	12-26	—	4-60 4-36
York		42-24 22-8	46-6 32-22	9-22	32-4 48-22	64-0	—

COLTS CHALLENGE CUP 1987

Preliminary Round

Doncaster	26	Leigh	22
Halifax	16	Castleford	16

Replay

Castleford	32	Halifax	10

First Round

Barrow	32	Hunslet	6
Castleford	21	Wigan	14
Doncaster	18	Bradford N.	18
Featherstone R.	58	Sheffield E.	0
Hull K.R.	18	Wakefield T.	6
Leeds	14	Hull	18
St. Helens	70	Huddersfield B.	6
York	40	Dewsbury	0

Replay

Bradford N.	18	Doncaster	20

Second Round

Barrow	26	York	24
Castleford	14	Hull	22
Doncaster	8	Featherstone R.	15
Hull K.R.	3	St. Helens	8

Semi-Finals

Featherstone R.	10	Barrow	16
St. Helens	22	Hull	16

Final at Wigan

St. Helens	48	Barrow	6

COLTS CHALLENGE CUP ROLL OF HONOUR

1976

Wigan	24	Hull K.R.	12
at Wigan			

1977

Hull K.R.	15	St. Helens	13
at Leeds			

1978

Castleford	19	Wakefield T.	10
at Leeds			

1979

Hull	17	Widnes	17
at Bradford			
Replay			
Hull	22	Widnes	14
at Wakefield			

1980

Leeds	25	Widnes	14
at Wigan			

1981

Hull	32	Castleford	17
at Leeds			

1982

Hull	19	Hull K.R.	16
at Leeds			

1983

Hunslet	11	Hull K.R.	3
at Hull K.R.			

1984

Castleford	24	Hull	11
at Hull K.R.			

1985

Wakefield T.	23	Bradford N.	10
at Leeds			

1986

St. Helens	16	Wigan	16
at St. Helens			
Replay			
Wigan	18	St. Helens	9
at Wigan			

1987

St. Helens	48	Barrow	6
at Wigan			

The Jim Challinor Memorial Trophy for the Man-of-the-Match in the Final:

1977	Steve Crooks (Hull K.R.)
1978	Paul Bastow (Castleford)
1979	Gary Peacham (Hull)
1980	Ian Mackintosh (Leeds)
1981	Lee Crooks (Hull)
1982	Tracey Lazenby (Hull K.R.)
1983	Andrew Tosney (Hunslet)
1984	Dean Mountain (Castleford)
1985	Billy Conway (Wakefield T.)
1986	Richard Russell (Wigan)
1987	Mark Lee (St. Helens)

COLTS PREMIERSHIP 1987

First Round

| Hull | 20 | Wakefield T. | 6 |
| St. Helens | 12 | Wigan | 38 |

Final at Wigan

| Wigan | 19 | Hull | 12 |

COLTS PREMIERSHIP ROLL OF HONOUR

1976
| Hull K.R. | 26 | Wakefield T. | 12 |

at Swinton
1977
| Bradford N. | 29 | Hull K.R. | 15 |

at Swinton
1978
| Wakefield T. | 23 | Hull K.R. | 20 |

at Swinton
1979
| Hull | 17 | Hull K.R. | 9 |

at Huddersfield
1980
| Oldham | 21 | Leeds | 13 |

at Swinton
1981
| Hull K.R. | 27 | Hull | 21 |

at Leeds
1982
| Hull | 19 | Hull K.R. | 11 |

at Leeds

1983
| Hull | 34 | Leigh | 5 |

at Leeds
1984
| Leeds | 24 | Hull | 8 |

at Leeds
1985
| Hull K.R. | 18 | Wakefield T. | 8 |

at Elland Road, Leeds
1986
| Wigan | 21 | Hull K.R. | 6 |

at Elland Road, Leeds
1987
| Wigan | 19 | Hull | 12 |

at Wigan

The Dave Valentine Memorial Trophy for the Man-of-the-Match in the Final:

1977	Paul Harkin (Bradford N.)
1978	David Wandless (Wakefield T.)
1979	Kevin Hickman (Hull K.R.)
1980	Andrew Mackintosh (Leeds)
1981	Malcolm Beall (Hull K.R.)
1982	Shaun Patrick (Hull)
1983	Andrew Kamis (Hull)
1984	Paul Medley (Leeds)
1985	Paul Speckman (Hull K.R.)
1986	Jeff Bimpson (Wigan)
1987	Lee Jackson (Hull)

1987 Colts Premiership winners, Wigan.

COLTS INTERNATIONALS

7th February, 1987   **Toulouse**

GREAT BRITAIN 0   **FRANCE 0**

Chris Bibb (Featherstone R.)	1.
Shaun Barrow (St. Helens)	2.
Steve Barnett (Bradford N.)	3.
Richard Russell (Wigan)	4.
Eddie Riddlesden (Halifax)	5.
Shaun Irwin (Castleford)	6.
Mark Bailey (St. Helens)	7.
Ian Lucas (Wigan)	8.
Martin Dermott (Wigan), Capt.	9.
Tim Street (Wigan)	10.
Chris Harrison (Hull K.R.)	11.
Ian Gildart (Wigan)	12.
Paul Jones (St. Helens)	13.
Craig Rogers (Wigan)	14.
Dennis Betts (Wigan)	15.
Andrew Collier (Leigh)	16.

Eric Costes (Albi)
Michel Fraczkiewickz (Albi)
Eric Vergniol (U.S.V.)
David Fraisse (Entraygues)
Thierry Matter (S.O.A.)
Alain Carriere (F.C.L.)
Romel Zenon (Chatullon), Capt.
Pierre Flovie (XIII Catalan)
Alain Charayron (Limoux)
Joel Roux (Entraygues)
George Granjean (F.C.L.)
Bruno Alibert (Albi)
Henri Bonnafous (Albi)
Didier Foulquier (Valdecagne)
Pierre Giudicelli (Carpentras)
Eric Ascencio (A.S.C)

Substitutions:
Betts for Harrison (61 min.)
Collier for Bibb (66 min.)
Manager: Harry Jepson
Coach: Geoff Lyon

Substitution:
Ascencio for Charayron (47 min.)
Half-time: 0-0
Referee: John Holdsworth (Kippax)

21st March, 1987   **St. Helens**

GREAT BRITAIN 10   **FRANCE 0**

Andrew Collier (Leigh)	1.
Shaun Barrow (St. Helens)	2.
Steve Barnett (Bradford N.)	3.
Ikram Butt (Leeds)	4.
Eddie Riddlesden (Halifax)	5.
Shaun Irwin (Castleford)	6.
Roy Southernwood (Castleford), Capt.	7.
Ian Lucas (Wigan)	8.
Ken Hill (Castleford)	9.
Tim Street (Wigan)	10.
Chris Harrison (Hull K.R.)	11.
Dennis Betts (Wigan)	12.
Paul Jones (St. Helens)	13.
Mark Bailey (St. Helens)	14.
Richard Kerman (Hull)	15.
Mark Lee (St. Helens)	16.

Eric Costes (Albi)
Michael Fraczkiewickz (Albi)
Eric Vergniol (U.S.V.)
David Fraisse (Entraygues)
Thierry Matter (S.O.A.)
Alain Carriere (F.C.L.)
Romel Zenon (Chatullon)
George Granjean (F.C.L.)
Regis Astencio (Carcassonne)
Joel Roux (Entraygues)
Patrick Jammes (Limoux)
Bruno Alibert (Albi)
Jacques Moliner (Albi)
Frederick Mas (Entraygues)
Didier Foulquier (Valdecagne)
Claude Courset (Lezignan)

T: Butt, Southernwood
G: Betts
Substitutions:
Bailey for Riddlesden (28 min.)
Kerman for Jones (63 min.)
Lee for Street (63 min.)
Manager: Harry Jepson
Coach: Geoff Lyon

Substitutions:
Mas for Jammes (25 min.)
Courset for Alibert (73 min.)
Half-time: 4-0
Referee: Bernard Agati (Toulouse)

COLTS COUNTY CHAMPIONSHIP

19th November, 1986 Leigh

LANCASHIRE 28 | | YORKSHIRE 8

LANCASHIRE 28		YORKSHIRE 8
Phil Price (St. Helens)	1.	Chris Bibb (Featherstone R.)
Shaun Barrow (St. Helens)	2.	Terry Swinney (Hull K.R.)
Richard Russell (Wigan)	3.	Steve Barnett (Bradford N.)
Phil Ball (Wigan)	4.	Richard Kay (Hull K.R.)
Alan Burrows (St. Helens)	5.	Eddie Riddlesden (Halifax)
Craig Rodgers (Wigan)	6.	Shaun Irwin (Castleford)
Mark Bailey (St. Helens), Capt.	7.	Roy Southernwood (Castleford), Capt.
Ian Lucas (Wigan)	8.	Chris Harrison (Hull K.R.)
Mark Lee (St. Helens)	9.	Ken Hill (Castleford)
David O'Toole (Leigh)	10.	Paddy Khan (Hull)
Dennis Betts (Wigan)	11.	Richard Kerman (Hull)
Ian Gildart (Wigan)	12.	Paul Worthy (Leeds)
Paul Jones (St. Helens)	13.	Martin Fleming (Bradford N.)
Carl Buxton (Wigan)	14.	Paul Delaney (Leeds)
Austin Donnechan (St. Helens)	15.	Sunny Nickle (Hunslet)

T: Lucas, Burrows, Rodgers, Jones, Donnechan, Barrow
G: Price, Russell
Substitutions:
Donnechan for O'Toole (20 min.)
O'Toole for Donnechan (65 min.)
Coach: Eric Chisnall (St. Helens)
Half-time: 14-2

T: Irwin

G: Bibb (2)
Substitutions:
Nickle for Khan (68 min.)
Delaney for Kay (70 min.)
Coach: David Redfearn (Bradford N.)
Referee: Phil Houghton (Warrington)

12th May, 1987 Wakefield

YORKSHIRE 24		LANCASHIRE 6
Carl Hale (Featherstone R.)	1.	Phil Ball (Wigan)
Anthony Sullivan (Hull K.R.)	2.	John O'Neill (St. Helens)
Grant Anderson (Castleford)	3.	Jason Diamond (St. Helens)
Ikram Butt (Leeds)	4.	Tony Hall (Leigh)
Daniel Beach (Featherstone R.)	5.	Ian Pickervance (St. Helens)
Neil Roebuck (Bradford N.)	6.	Phil Price (St. Helens)
Stephen Blowers (Hull)	7.	Shaun Devine (St. Helens)
Darren Webb (Hunslet)	8.	Stephen Dunbar (Wigan)
Kenneth Hill (Castleford)	9.	Shaun Bannister (Wigan)
David McAreavey (Hull K.R.)	10.	Lee Chisnall (St. Helens)
Martyn Smithson (Leeds)	11.	Ian Gildart (Wigan)
Sonny Nickle (Hunslet)	12.	Dennis Betts (Wigan)
Gary Price (Wakefield T.)	13.	Mike Forshaw (Wigan)
Lee Jackson (Hull)	14.	Tony Greenall (St. Helens)
David Amann (Leeds)	15.	David Bates (St. Helens)

T: Sullivan (3), Price, Anderson
G: Roebuck (2)
Substitutions
Jackson for Smithson (54 min.)
Amann for McAreavey (54 min.)
Coach: David Redfearn (Bradford N.)
Referee: Jim Smith (Halifax)

T: Bannister
G: Devine
Substitution:
Greenall for Diamond (70 min.)
Coach: Eric Chisnall (St. Helens)
Half-time: 12-0

POT POURRI

DIARY OF LANDMARKS

1895 August 29th... the beginning. The Northern Rugby Football Union formed at St. George's Hotel, Huddersfield, following the breakaway from the English RU by 21 clubs who wanted to pay players for taking time off work to play.
September 7th... season opens with 22 clubs.
Joseph Platt appointed Rugby League Secretary.

1897 April 24th... Batley won the first Northern Union — later Rugby League — Challenge Cup final.
Line-out abolished and replaced by punt from touch.
All goals to be worth two points.

1898 Professionalism allowed but players must be in full-time employment.

1899 Scrum if player cannot release the ball after a tackle.

1901 Punt from touch replaced by 10-yard scrum when ball is carried into touch.

1902 Two divisions introduced.
Punt from touch abolished completely.
Touch-finding rule introduced with the ball having to bounce before entering touch.

1905 Two divisions scrapped.
Lancashire and Yorkshire County Cup competitions inaugurated.

1906 Thirteen-a-side introduced, from traditional 15.

1907 Play-the-ball introduced.
First tour — New Zealand to England. The tour party were RU 'rebels'.
First Top Four play-off for championship.

1908 Australia and New Zealand launch Rugby League.
First Australian tour of England.

1910 First British tour of Australia and New Zealand.

1915 Competitive rugby suspended for duration of First World War.

1919 Competitive rugby resumed in January.

1920 John Wilson appointed Rugby League Secretary.

1922 Title of Northern Rugby Football Union changed to Rugby Football League.
Goal from a mark abolished.

1927 First radio broadcast of Challenge Cup Final — Oldham v. Swinton at Wigan.

1929 Wembley staged its first RL Challenge Cup final — Wigan v. Dewsbury.

1932 London exhibition match under floodlights at White City — Leeds v. Wigan.

1933 France staged its first Rugby League match — an exhibition between England and Australia in Paris.
London Highfield, formerly Wigan Highfield, became capital's first Rugby League team, also first to play regularly under floodlights.

1934 A French squad made a short tour of England before Rugby League was officially launched in France.

1935 European Championship introduced, contested by England, France and Wales.

1939 Second World War. Emergency war-time competitions introduced.

1945 War-time emergencies over.
Bill Fallowfield appointed Rugby League Secretary.

1946 First all-ticket match — Hull v. Hull K.R.

1948 King George VI became first reigning monarch to attend Rugby League match — Wigan v. Bradford Northern Cup final at Wembley.
First televised match — at Wembley — but shown only in London area.
Wembley's first all-ticket final.
International Board formed.

1949 Welsh League formed.

1950 Italian squad made brief tour of England.

1951	First televised match in the North — Britain v. New Zealand at Swinton. First floodlights installation by Northern club, Bradford Northern.
1952	First nationally televised Challenge Cup final — Workington Town v. Featherstone Rovers.
1954	First World Cup competition, staged in France.
1955	London staged series of televised floodlit matches for the Independent Television Association Trophy. Welsh League disbanded.
1956	Sunday rugby for amateurs permitted by the Rugby Football League.
1962	Two divisions reintroduced, with Eastern and Western Divisions also formed.
1964	Substitutes allowed for injuries, but only up to half-time. Two division and regional leagues scrapped. One league system with Top-16 play-off for championship.
1965	BBC-2 Floodlit Trophy competition began with regular Tuesday night series. Substitutes allowed for any reason up to and including half-time. English Schools Rugby League formed.
1966	Four-tackle rule introduced for Floodlit Trophy competition in October, then for all games from December.
1967	First Sunday fixtures played, two matches on December 17th.
1969	Substitutes allowed at any time. University Rugby League Association formed.
1971	John Player Trophy competition launched.
1972	Six-tackle rule introduced. Timekeepers with hooter system to signal end of match introduced. Colts League formed.
1973	Two divisions re-introduced. March 4th... British Amateur Rugby League Association formed.
1974	Drop goal value halved to one point. Had been reduced earlier in international matches. David Oxley appointed Rugby League Secretary. David Howes appointed first full-time Public Relations Officer to the Rugby Football League. National Coaching Scheme launched.
1975	Premiership Trophy competition launched.
1976	Differential penalty introduced for technical scrum offences.
1977	County Championship not held for first time since 1895, excluding war years. Anglo-Australian transfer ban agreed.
1978	Papua New Guinea admitted as full members of International Board.
1981	Rugby League Professional Players' Association formed.
1982	County Championship scrapped.
1983	January 1st... Sin bin introduced. Try value increased to four points. Handover after sixth tackle introduced, among several other new or amended laws following meeting of International Board. Anglo-Australia transfer ban lifted.
1984	Alliance League introduced in reserve grade reorganisation.
1985	First Charity Shield match played in Isle of Man. War of the Roses launched on Lancashire v. Yorkshire county of origin basis. Relegation-promotion reduced to three down, three up.
1986	Relegation-promotion altered for one year only to four down, two up to provide a 14-strong First Division for the 1987-88 season.
1987	Division Two Premiership Trophy competition launched.

DISCIPLINARY RECORDS

This sub-section is a compilation of sendings off and disciplinary verdicts for first team players.

The following information is based on the workings of the League's Disciplinary Committee which meets twice-monthly during a season.

DISMISSALS .... A review

The following is a review of the number of first team players sent off in each season since 1980-81.

— indicates where a club was not in existence.

	1986-87	1985-86	1984-85	1983-84	1982-83	1981-82	1980-81
Barrow	4	3	6	2	2	2	2
Batley	7	3	3	3	4	3	2
Blackpool B.	4	5	4	3	3	2	1
Bradford N.	2	4	0	3	3	11	6
Bramley	3	3	2	3	2	0	2
Bridgend	—	—	4	6	2	7	—
Carlisle	3	2	3	8	4	3	—
Castleford	1	3	1	5	4	7	4
Dewsbury	3	4	4	2	5	10	3
Doncaster	2	4	1	10	2	4	2
Featherstone R.	0	0	3	1	1	9	2
Fulham	6	5	4	6	8	3	3
Halifax	2	1	5	3	4	3	3
Huddersfield B.	4	4	4	4	2	3	3
Hull	5	5	2	3	4	3	4
Hull K.R.	4	8	2	5	4	13	5
Hunslet	1	2	4	3	1	4	0
Keighley	7	8	7	0	3	3	5
Leeds	1	2	4	0	3	5	5
Leigh	2	1	1	3	2	6	3
Mansfield M.	6	3	3	—	—	—	—
Oldham	3	6	5	5	3	8	4
Rochdale H.	1	3	4	9	1	7	1
Runcorn H.	3	12	5	5	3	3	2
St. Helens	3	0	4	3	3	2	1
Salford	5	6	5	5	6	3	1
Sheffield E.	3	6	4	—	—	—	—
Southend I.	—	—	3	3	—	—	—
Swinton	3	2	2	0	4	1	2
Wakefield T.	5	6	7	5	2	6	2
Warrington	6	6	1	6	5	10	6
Whitehaven	2	3	3	6	2	4	3
Widnes	4	5	6	7	4	3	6
Wigan	3	3	2	2	3	5	7
Workington T.	5	9	5	4	3	3	2
York	3	2	1	4	2	3	3
Totals	**116**	**139**	**124**	**137**	**104**	**159**	**95**

Sheffield Eagles forward, Derek Bridgeman... sending off sufficient punishment.

DISCIPLINARY ANALYSIS 1986-87

The following is a club-by-club disciplinary record for last season, showing the players sent off in first team matches and the findings of the League's Disciplinary Committee.

The committee's verdict is featured in the brackets after the player's name, each number indicating the match ban imposed. SOS stands for sending off sufficient and NG for not guilty. A suspension reduced or increased on appeal is shown as follows, 6 to 4.

The sin bin suspensions were imposed under the totting-up system where two points were issued for a 10-minute temporary dismissal and one point for a five-minute period off the field. A one-match ban was imposed when the running total reached six points.

SB indicates in brackets the number of one-match bans imposed under the sin bin totting-up system. It does not include a record of players' sin bin dismissals which have not reached the six-point total. The sin bin has operated only for technical offences and verbal abuse of match officials since 1984-85 season.

OC indicates in brackets the number of one-match bans imposed under the official caution totting-up system, one match for each pair of cautions in the same year or season.

* indicates where video evidence was submitted. The 1984-85 season was the first time video action other than official BBC or ITV tapes could be offered in evidence. In 1986-87 the committee considered video evidence in 27 individual cases, two more than during 1985-86. Four cases were considered by the committee after viewing a video, the player not having been dismissed.

Club	Total sent off	Dismissed Player	Sin Bins/ Official Cautions
Barrow	4	S. Carter (SOS), Kay (SOS), Maguire (4), Gittins (4)	
Batley	7	Carroll (2), Williams (2,3), Speight (2), McLeary (2), Hartley (4), Reed (2)	
Blackpool B.	4	Grundy (2), Ganley (3,4), Howarth (2)	
Bradford N.	2	Fleming (8), Fairbank (2)	Hill (1OC)
Bramley	3	Bowman (3 to 2), Burgoyne (2), Schaumkell (2)	
Carlisle	3	Duffy (3), K. Green (2), Kirkby (4)	
Castleford	1	England (*2 to SOS)	
Dewsbury	3	Garner (SOS), Squires (2), Broxholme (2)	
Doncaster	2	Timson (2,4)	
Fulham	6	O'Brien (2), Rampling (SOS), Knight (3), Haggath (2), O'Doherty (SOS), Mills (2)	Milla (1OC)
Halifax	2	Dickinson (*2 to SOS), Beevers (SOS)	
Huddersfield B.	4	J. Johnson (4), Hirst (3), Fitzpatrick (4), Knight (SOS)	
Hull	5	S. Crooks (4 to 3), Dannatt (*2), Dick (6,4), L. Crooks (2)	

Hull K.R.	4	Ema (4), Watkinson (*3 to NG), Kelly (2), Broadhurst (*4)	
Hunslet	1	Skerrett (4)	
Keighley	7	Goodier (6), Hawksworth (4), Turner (6), Proctor (NG, 3 to NG, 6), Roe (NG)	
Leeds	1	Moorby (*SOS)	Kevin Rayne (1OC)
Leigh	2	Henderson (1), Schubert (*2)	
Mansfield M.	6	Leary (4), Hooper (SOS), Sanderson (4), Hough (SOS), Whitehead (2), Chadwick (4)	
Oldham	3	Hobbs (*NG), Topliss (SOS), Sanderson (*SOS)	Sanderson (1OC)
Rochdale H.	1	Williams (2)	
Runcorn H.	3	Prescott (4), Fraser (2), McAllister (2)	
St. Helens	3	Haggerty (4), Platt (NG), Jarvis (2)	
Salford	5	Glynn (1), O'Loughlin (*NG), Pendlebury (*4), Fletcher (2), Bloor (*3 to 1)	
Sheffield E.	3	Bridgeman (SOS), Cholmondeley (4), Gamson (4)	
Swinton	3	Cassidy (*NG), Wilson (2), M. Holliday (4)	
Wakefield T.	5	Cocks (4), Conway (1), Evans (SOS,4), Mallinder (4)	Lyons (1SB)
Warrington	6	Boyd (*2), Cullen (2), Tamati (*2), Bishop (*2), Humphries (*2), Johnson (*NG)	
Whitehaven	2	Hall (6), Burney (*NG)	
Widnes	4	Sorensen (*4), S. O'Neill (*SOS,*SOS), P. Hulme (*2)	
Wigan	3	Roberts (*4 to NG), West (*2), Goodway (*SOS)	
Workington T.	5	Rea (2), Mawson (2), Bailey (2), Sullivan (2), Denny (*SOS)	
York	3	Willey (4), Hughes (4), Strutt (2)	

● In addition, the Disciplinary Committee carried out four 'trials by video', calling up players who had not been dismissed after viewing video tapes. Roy Haggerty, of St. Helens, was given sending off sufficient, Swinton duo Gary Ainsworth and John Allen two and four matches respectively, and Doncaster's Mark Roache, a severe reprimand.

SPONSORSHIP

This updated sub-section is a record of the sponsorship programme under the control of the Rugby
Football League.

Sponsorship has developed into a major subject
in the last decade and is now one of Rugby League's
biggest sources of income.

In addition to the League's sponsorship programme, the individual clubs also enter deals for
sponsorship of jerseys, kit, matches, man of the
match and match ball.

SPONSORSHIP PROGRAMME 1986-87

The following is a compendium of sponsorship activities controlled by the Rugby Football League for
the season 1986-87.

Competitions:

Silk Cut Challenge Cup	£150,000	
Stones Bitter Championship and Premiership	£120,000	
Whitbread Trophy Bitter Tests	£ 85,000	
John Player Special Trophy	£ 85,000	
Okells Charity Shield	£ 5,000	
Rodstock War of the Roses	£ 3,000	
		£448,000

Awards:

Greenalls Man of Steel Awards	£ 9,000	
Daily Mirror/Lada Cars Teams of the Month and Year	£ 5,000	
Greenall Whitley/Sunday People Supreme Awards and Top Scorers	£ 4,000	
Traveleads Top Fan	£ 3,500	
Sunday Mirror/Wallace Arnold Entertainer Awards	£ 3,000	
Daily Star/Stones Bitter Star Men	£ 1,000	
		£ 25,500

Miscellaneous:	£ 40,000
GRAND TOTAL	£513,500

COMPETITION SPONSORSHIP

The following is a review of sponsorship of the game's major competitions.

SILK CUT CHALLENGE CUP

	Prel.	1st	2nd	3rd	S.F.	R.U.	Winners	Development Fund	Total
	£	£	£	£	£	£	£	£	£
1979	—	750	1,160	2,000	3,555	6,555	12,555	4,500	60,000
1980	—	750	1,160	2,000	3,555	6,555	12,555	19,500	75,000
1981	—	750	1,160	2,000	3,555	6,555	12,555	29,500	85,000
1982	1,000	1,000	1,400	2,400	4,325	8,000	14,555	30,000	100,000
1983	1,000	1,000	1,400	2,400	4,325	8,000	14,555	40,000	110,000
1984	1,000	1,000	1,400	2,400	4,325	8,000	14,555	48,000	120,000
1985	1,100	1,100	1,500	2,500	4,500	9,000	16,000	47,600	130,000
1986	1,100	1,100	1,500	2,500	4,500	9,000	16,000	57,600	140,000
1987	1,200	1,200	1,650	2,750	4,500	9,000	16,000	58,200	150,000

● Sponsored by State Express 1979-84.

JOHN PLAYER SPECIAL TROPHY

	Prel.	1st	2nd	3rd	S.F.	R.U.	Winners	Development Fund	Total
	£	£	£	£	£	£	£	£	£
1971-72	—	—	—	—	1,000	2,500	5,000	—	9,500
1972-73	—	150	300	450	1,000	2,500	5,000	—	16,100
1973-74	—	150	300	450	1,000	2,500	5,000	—	16,100
1974-75	—	150	300	450	1,000	2,500	5,000	—	16,100
1975-76	—	300	450	600	1,500	3,000	6,000	—	22,800
1976-77	—	400	550	700	1,500	3,000	6,000	—	25,600
1977-78	—	450	600	750	1,750	3,500	8,000	—	30,000
1978-79	—	550	700	900	1,750	3,500	8,000	—	33,000
1979-80	—	600	800	1,000	2,000	4,000	8,500	—	36,500
1980-81	—	600	800	1,000	2,000	4,000	8,500	3,500	40,000
1981-82	700	700	900	1,175	2,500	4,500	9,000	7,000	50,000
1982-83	700	700	900	1,175	2,500	5,000	10,000	10,500	55,000
1983-84	700	700	900	1,175	2,500	5,000	10,000	15,500	60,000
1984-85	750	750	1,000	1,500	2,500	5,000	10,000	20,000	75,000
1985-86	750	750	1,000	1,500	2,750	5,500	11,000	26,000	80,000
1986-87	800	800	1,100	1,700	3,000	6,000	12,000	26,200	85,000

STONES BITTER

	Championship winners	R.U.	2nd Division winners	R.U.	Premiership winners	R.U.	2nd Division Premiership winners	R.U.	Development Fund	Total
	£	£	£	£	£	£	£	£	£	£
1980-81	6,000	—	3,000	—	4,000	—	—	—	42,000	55,000
1981-82	10,000	—	6,000	—	6,000	—	—	—	48,000	70,000
1982-83	12,000	—	7,000	—	7,000	—	—	—	54,000	80,000
1983-84	12,000	—	7,000	—	7,000	—	—	—	59,000	85,000
1984-85	13,000	—	9,000	—	8,000	—	—	—	60,000	90,000
1985-86	13,000	—	9,000	—	8,000	—	—	—	65,000	95,000
1986-87	20,000	8,000	10,000	4,000	9,000	3,500	4,000	1,500	60,000	120,000

● Sponsored by Slalom Lager from 1980-86

YORKSHIRE CUP

	Sponsor	Winners	Total
		£	£
1972	Esso	800	4,000
1973	Esso	1,500	6,000
1974	Esso	1,400	6,000
1975	Esso	1,200	6,000
1976	Esso	1,200	6,000
1977	Esso	1,600	8,000
1978	Esso	2,000	9,000
1979	Esso	2,000	9,500
1980	Websters Brewery	2,750	13,000
1981	Websters Brewery	3,000	14,000
1982	Websters Brewery	2,500	15,000
1983	Philips Video	2,500	15,000
1984	Philips Video	2,500	15,000
1985	John Smiths	2,500	5,000
1986	John Smiths	2,500	12,500

GRUNHALLE LAGER LANCASHIRE CUP

	Winners	Total
	£	£
1976	1,000	4,000
1977	1,500	5,000
1978	1,800	5,500
1979	1,900	6,000
1980	2,530	10,000
1981	2,700	11,000
1982	3,000	11,500
1983	3,200	12,500
1984	3,400	13,250
1985	3,400	13,250
1986	4,300	17,000

● Sponsored by Burtonwood Brewery 1976-85

INTERNATIONAL

Great Britain v Australia Tests 1978
Forward Chemicals: £17,500

Great Britain v Australia Tests 1982
Dominion Insurance: £40,000

Great Britain v France Tests 1983
Dominion Insurance: £5,000

Great Britain v France Tests 1984
Dominion Insurance: £5,000

Great Britain Tour 1984
Modern Maintenance Products: £100,000

Great Britain 1985-86
Whitbread Trophy Bitter: £85,000

Great Britain 1986-87
Whitbread Trophy Bitter: £85,000

ATTENDANCES

CLUB ATTENDANCE REVIEW

The following is a review of clubs' home attendances for league matches from 1978-87.

The main figure is the individual club's average gate for league games during that season. The figure in brackets indicates an upward or downward trend compared with the previous season.

Also indicated is the division the club competed in that season, i.e.

1 — First Division, 2 — Second Division.

Club	78-79	79-80	80-81	81-82	82-83	83-84	84-85	85-86	86-87
Barrow	1 2988 (+556)	2 3143 (+155)	1 4065 (+922)	1 4162 (+97)	1 3852 (−310)	2 3218 (−450)	1 2728 (−490)	2 1926 (−802)	1 2664 (+738)
Batley	2 915 (+56)	2 1330 (+415)	2 1329 (−1)	2 1052 (−277)	2 916 (−136)	2 864 (−52)	2 1015 (+151)	2 930 (−85)	2 744 (−186)
Blackpool B.	2 1237 (+579)	1 1576 (+339)	2 684 (−892)	2 768 (+84)	2 679 (−89)	2 625 (−54)	2 555 (−70)	2 534 (−21)	2 475 (−59)
Bradford N.	1 5651 (−1585)	1 6236 (+585)	1 6105 (−131)	1 5816 (−289)	1 4920 (−896)	1 5316 (+386)	1 4251 (−1065)	1 3975 (−276)	1 4312 (+337)
Bramley	2 1208 (−854)	2 1204 (−4)	2 1050 (−154)	2 928 (−122)	2 809 (−119)	2 759 (−50)	2 858 (+99)	2 831 (−27)	2 737 (−94)
Bridgend	—	—	—	2 2008 —	2 854 (−1154)	2 581 (−273)	2 510 (−70)	—	—
Carlisle	—	—	—	2 2950 —	1 1924 (−1026)	2 752 (−1172)	2 986 (+244)	2 618 (−368)	2 789 (+171)
Castleford	1 3672 (−175)	1 3714 (+42)	1 4612 (+898)	1 3791 (−821)	1 3548 (−243)	1 4288 (+740)	1 3217 (−1071)	1 3701 (+430)	1 4758 (+1057)
Dewsbury	2 1474 (−686)	2 1552 (+78)	2 1377 (−175)	2 1048 (−329)	2 779 (−269)	2 706 (−73)	2 995 (+189)	1 1819 (+824)	2 669 (−1150)
Doncaster	2 619 (−192)	2 428 (−191)	2 628 (+200)	2 556 (−72)	2 441 (−115)	2 255 (−186)	2 266 (+11)	2 689 (+423)	2 1543 (+854)
Featherstone R.	1 2661 (−897)	2 2301 (−360)	1 3007 (+706)	1 2806 (−201)	1 2647 (−159)	1 3032 (+385)	1 2541 (−491)	1 2320 (−221)	1 2606 (+286)
Fulham	—	—	2 6096 —	1 4321 (−1775)	2 2688 (−1633)	1 2238 (−450)	2 949 (−1289)	2 817 (−132)	2 684 (−133)
Halifax	2 2314 (+975)	2 2969 (+655)	1 4090 (+1121)	2 2818 (−1272)	1 2270 (−548)	2 1254 (−1016)	1 3497 (+2243)	1 4944 (+1447)	1 4891 (−53)
Huddersfield B.	1 2533 (+397)	2 1654 (−879)	2 1769 (+115)	2 1185 (−584)	2 776 (−409)	2 699 (−77)	2 905 (+206)	2 678 (−227)	2 524 (−154)
Hull	2 6853 (+1741)	1 10021 (+3168)	1 11711 (+1690)	1 13190 (+1479)	1 11525 (−1665)	1 10679 (−846)	1 8525 (−2154)	1 6245 (−1280)	1 5538 (−707)
Hull K. R.	1 5945 (+593)	1 6953 (+1008)	1 8904 (+1951)	1 8723 (−181)	1 7379 (−1344)	1 6966 (−413)	1 6715 (−215)	1 4855 (−1860)	1 4651 (−204)
Hunslet	2 1469 (−626)	1 1718 (+249)	2 921 (−797)	2 744 (−177)	2 1195 (+451)	2 1338 (+143)	1 2246 (+908)	2 722 (−1524)	1 1050 (+338)

Club	78-79	79-80	80-81	81-82	82-83	83-84	84-85	85-86	86-87
Keighley	2 1594 (−391)	2 1593 (−1)	2 1612 (+19)	2 1576 (−36)	2 1085 (−491)	2 734 (−351)	2 822 (+88)	2 685 (−137)	2 445 (−240)
Leeds	1 5161 (−378)	1 6681 (+1520)	1 5934 (−747)	1 5599 (−335)	1 5893 (+294)	1 6542 (+649)	1 7330 (+788)	1 6928 (−402)	1 6393 (−535)
Leigh	1 3319 (−108)	1 4418 (+1099)	1 4498 (+80)	1 5939 (+1441)	1 4617 (−1322)	1 4434 (−183)	1 3822 (−612)	2 2710 (−1112)	1 4232 (+1522)
Mansfield M.	—	—	—	—	—	—	2 1020 —	2 487 (−553)	2 368 (−119)
Oldham	2 1207 (−578)	2 2367 (+1160)	1 3220 (+853)	1 2395 (−825)	1 3721 (+1326)	1 4138 (+417)	1 4562 (+424)	1 4333 (−229)	1 3915 (−418)
Rochdale H.	1 1689 (−287)	2 1210 (−479)	2 1149 (−61)	2 888 (−261)	2 619 (−269)	2 538 (−81)	2 542 (+4)	2 1267 (+725)	2 877 (−390)
Runcorn H.	2 599 (+264)	2 238 (−161)	2 270 (+32)	2 385 (+115)	2 224 (−161)	2 172 (−52)	2 509 (+337)	2 363 (−146)	2 331 (−35)
St. Helens	1 5658 (+148)	1 5577 (−81)	1 4934 (−643)	1 4862 (−72)	1 4543 (−319)	1 4656 (+113)	1 7336 (+2680)	1 6022 (−1314)	1 7341 (+1391)
Salford	1 4100 (−33)	1 4846 (+746)	1 3458 (−1388)	2 2404 (−1054)	2 1928 (−476)	1 2399 (+471)	2 1795 (−604)	1 2520 (+725)	1 2826 (+306)
Sheffield E.	—	—	—	—	—	—	2 885 —	2 698 (−187)	2 708 (+10)
Southend Invicta	—	—	—	—	—	2 731 —	2 216 (−515)	—	—
Swinton	2 1331 (−149)	2 1509 (+178)	2 1935 (+426)	2 1567 (−368)	2 1314 (−253)	2 1077 (−237)	2 1590 (+513)	1 2706 (+1116)	2 1622 (−1084)
Wakefield T.	1 4068 (+265)	1 4559 (+491)	1 4814 (+255)	1 3716 (−1098)	2 2344 (−1372)	1 3483 (+1139)	2 1568 (−1915)	2 1714 (+146)	1 2637 (+923)
Warrington	1 5194 (+991)	1 5122 (−72)	1 4917 (−205)	1 3838 (−1079)	1 3824 (−14)	1 4059 (+235)	1 3801 (−258)	1 3618 (−183)	1 4172 (+554)
Whitehaven	2 1364 (+475)	2 1761 (+397)	2 2733 (+972)	1 2710 (−23)	2 1742 (−968)	1 1639 (−103)	2 1540 (−99)	2 1878 (+333)	2 1800 (−78)
Widnes	1 6751 (−737)	1 6143 (−608)	1 5306 (−837)	1 5485 (+179)	1 4703 (−782)	1 4687 (−16)	1 4266 (−421)	1 4019 (−247)	1 3840 (−179)
Wigan	1 4505 (−1039)	1 4665 (+160)	2 4693 (+28)	1 5497 (+804)	1 7426 (+1929)	1 7479 (+53)	1 10056 (+2577)	1 12515 (+2459)	1 12732 (+217)
Workington T.	1 2155 (−567)	1 1834 (−321)	1 2188 (+354)	2 1969 (−219)	1 1470 (−499)	2 934 (−536)	1 920 (−14)	2 702 (−218)	2 653 (−49)
York	2 3265 (+77)	1 3934 (+669)	2 3827 (−107)	1 3677 (−150)	2 1685 (−1992)	2 1215 (−470)	2 1528 (+313)	1 2828 (+1300)	2 1520 (−1380)

COMPETITION ATTENDANCE REVIEW

		78-79	79-80	80-81	81-82	82-83	83-84	84-85	85-86	86-87
FIRST DIVISION	Total	990,728	1,169,956	1,226,428	1,264,520	1,113,915	1,140,548	1,137,195	1,100,329	1,162,666
	Av.	4,128	4,875	5,110	5,268	4,641	4,752	4,738	4,585	4,844
SECOND DIVISION	Total	330,830	302,345	420,994	403,652	321,226	279,673	266,730	310,311	217,552
	Av.	1,817	1,661	2,005	1,484	1,181	914	953	1,014	863
LEAGUE TOTALS (1st & 2nd)	Total	1,321,558	1,472,301	1,647,422	1,668,172	1,435,141	1,420,221	1,403,925	1,410,640	1,380,218
	Av.	3,123	3,489	3,661	3,258	2,803	2,601	2,700	2,584	2,805
R.L. CUP	Av.	9,257	10,370	9,993	11,388	8,355	8,399	8,497	8,280	6,965
JOHN PLAYER	Av.	4,427	4,314	5,362	5,590	4,219	3,893	4,881	4,232	4,122
PREMIER	Av.	8,502	7,343	11,689	9,454	10,099	8,136	10,115	9,273	15,154
10,000+ (No. of)		12	20	36	36	37	26	27	36	43

20,000-plus crowds . . . . A 10-year review
All matches except the Rugby League Challenge Cup final at Wembley

20,386	Wigan v. St. Helens	RL Cup Round 2	Wigan	27 Feb. 1977
26,447	Britain v. Australia	Second Test	Bradford	5 Nov. 1978
29,627	Britain v. Australia	Third Test	Leeds	18 Nov. 1978
20,775	Bradford N. v. Hull	RL Cup Round 3	Bradford	9 Mar. 1980
29,448	Hull v. Hull K.R.	Premiership final	Leeds	16 May 1981
25,245	Hull v. Hull K.R.	John Player final	Leeds	23 Jan. 1982
21,207	Hull v. Castleford	RL Cup semi-final	Leeds	27 Mar. 1982
41,171	Hull v. Widnes	RL Cup final replay	Elland Rd, Leeds	19 May 1982
26,771	Britain v. Australia	First Test	Hull C. FC	30 Oct. 1982
23,216	Britain v. Australia	Second Test	Wigan	20 Nov. 1982
26,031	Hull v. Castleford	RL Cup semi-final	Elland Rd, Leeds	2 Apr. 1983
20,569	Hull v. Hull K.R.	Division One	Hull	8 Apr. 1983
20,077	St. Helens v. Wigan	RL Cup Round 3	St. Helens	11 Mar. 1984
25,237	Hull v. Hull K.R.	Yorks Cup final	Hull C. FC	27 Oct. 1984
26,074	St. Helens v. Wigan	Lancs Cup final	Wigan	28 Oct. 1984
25,326	Hull v. Hull K.R.	John Player final	Hull C. FC	26 Jan. 1985
20,982	Hull v. Castleford	RL Cup semi-final	Leeds	6 Apr. 1985
20,968	Hull v. Castleford	RL Cup semi-final replay	Leeds	10 Apr. 1985
22,209	Britain v. New Zealand	Third Test	Elland Rd, Leeds	9 Nov. 1985
21,813	Wigan v. St. Helens	Division One	Wigan	26 Dec. 1985
23,866	Hull K.R. v. Leeds	RL Cup semi-final	Elland Rd, Leeds	29 Mar. 1986
32,485	Hull K.R. v. Leeds	RL Cup semi-final replay	Elland Rd, Leeds	3 Apr. 1986
28,252	Wigan v. St. Helens	Lancs Cup semi-final	Wigan	1 Oct. 1986
30,622	Wigan v. Australia	Tour	Wigan	12 Oct. 1986
20,180	Oldham v. Wigan	Lancs Cup final	St. Helens	19 Oct. 1986
50,583	Britain v. Australia	First Test	Manchester U. FC	25 Oct. 1986

(continued)

30,808	Britain v. Australia	Second Test	Elland Rd, Leeds	8 Nov. 1986
20,169	Britain v. Australia	Third Test	Wigan	22 Nov. 1986
21,214	St. Helens v. Wigan	Division One	St. Helens	26 Dec. 1986
21,144	Warrington v. Wigan	John Player final	Bolton W. FC	10 Jan. 1987
20,355	Wigan v. St. Helens	Division One	Wigan	17 Apr. 1987
22,457	Wigan v. Halifax	Premiership semi-final	Wigan	10 May 1987
38,756	Warrington v. Wigan	Premiership final	Manchester U.FC	17 May 1987

1986-87 ANALYSIS

FIRST DIVISION

Total attendance 1,162,666
Average 4,844

Compared with the corresponding 1985-86 figures of 1,100,329 and 4,585, there was an increase of 5.65 per cent.

Wigan topped the gates chart for the third successive season, further increasing their average gate to 12,732. Of their 15 Stones Bitter Championship fixtures at Central Park, 13 attracted five-figure gates.

A total of 10 clubs recorded increased gates during the season, promoted Leigh adding an average 1,522 per league match and title runners-up St. Helens 1,319 a game.

SECOND DIVISION

Total attendance 217,552
Average 863

The Second Division average gate fell below the four-figure mark, a 17.5 per cent decrease taking the figure to 863 per match.

Third-placed Whitehaven topped the gate chart with an average turn out of 1,800, despite an annual decrease of 78 per game.

Doncaster recorded the biggest upswing, more than doubling their average league gate to 1,543, the third highest. Increases were also recorded by champions Hunslet, Carlisle and Fulham.

LEAGUE CHAMPIONSHIP

Aggregate 1,380,218
Average 2,805

The average attendence for the 34 clubs competing in the 1986-87 two-division set up rose by 8.5 per cent compared with the previous season's average of 2,584.

SILK CUT CHALLENGE CUP

A total of 271,654 spectators watched the 1987 tournament which included a six-tie preliminary round and two replays. The average gate for the 39 ties was 6,965, an 18.8 per cent decrease on the 1986 return of 8,280. The traditional top attendance was the Wembley gate of 91,267, with only six other matches attracting five-figure turn outs.

JOHN PLAYER SPECIAL TROPHY

The 1986-87 competition attracted a total of 144,256 fans for the 35 ties, an average of 4,122. Compared with the previous campaign's average of 4,232, this was an annual decrease of 2.6 per cent.

STONES BITTER PREMIERSHIP

The end of season top-eight tournament attracted a massive 63.4 per cent increase in support, boosted by a record final gate of 38,756 at Old Trafford, Manchester. The seven ties pulled in a total of 106,076 spectators, an average of 15,154 per match. The comparative figures for 1986 were 64,909 and 9,273.

SECOND DIVISION PREMIERSHIP

The first-ever Second Division tournament featured six ties staged on club grounds and the final as the first part of a new style doubleheader at Manchester United's soccer stadium. The six ties provided an average gate of 2,060, while more than 22,000 were at Old Trafford for the kick off of the Second Division Premiership final, the ultimate return being 38,756.

GRUNHALLE LAGER LANCASHIRE CUP

After annual increases of 77 per cent in 1984-85 and five per cent in 1985-86, the last campaign attracted a further upward swing of 19.5 per cent. The 15 ties were attended by a total of 108,756 fans, an average gate of 7,250, compared with the previous season's figures of 91,007 and 6,067.

JOHN SMITHS YORKSHIRE CUP

The 1986-87 tournament featured a two-tie preliminary round and a replay, the 18 matches attracting a total attendance of 68,104 for an average gate of 3,784. The previous competition's figures were 72,886 and 4,555, giving an annual decrease of 20.3 per cent.

FIVE-FIGURE CROWDS

There was a total of 43 gates topping the 10,000-mark during the 1986-87 season — the best for several years. As per tradition, the top attendance was at Wembley for the Halifax-St. Helens Silk Cut Challenge Cup final which attracted 91,267 spectators.

Gates of 30,000-plus were attracted to four other top games, highlighted by a record British Test gate at Old Trafford, Manchester; a Premiership final record turn out, again at Old Trafford; and a record tour match attendance, on the opening day of the Kangaroo tour at Wigan.

Seven other 20,000-plus attendances were recorded during the season, including two other Tests, the Lancashire Cup final and the John Player Special Trophy final.

Top gate takers Wigan staged the most five-figure attendances with 20 at Central Park, including 13 in the Stones Bitter Championship. Central Park also staged the third Whitbread Trophy Bitter Test and the Silk Cut Challenge Cup semi-final between Leigh and St. Helens, both five-figure gates.

The five-figure gates were divided into the following categories:

League 17
Tour (incl. Tests) 8
Challenge Cup 7
Premiership Trophy 4
John Player Special Trophy 3
Lancashire Cup 3
Yorkshire Cup 1

FIRST DIVISION

	1986-87 Average	Annual Difference
Wigan	12732	(+ 217)
St. Helens	7341	(+1319)
Leeds	6393	(− 535)
Hull	5538	(− 707)
Halifax	4891	(− 53)
Castleford	4758	(+1057)
Hull Kingston Rovers	4651	(− 204)
Bradford Northern	4312	(+ 337)
*Leigh	4232	(+1522)
Warrington	4172	(+ 554)
Oldham	3915	(− 418)
Widnes	3840	(− 179)
Salford	2826	(+ 306)
*Barrow	2664	(+ 738)
*Wakefield Trinity	2637	(+ 923)
Featherstone Rovers	2606	(+ 286)

* Promoted 1985-86

SECOND DIVISION

	1986-87 Average	Annual Difference
Whitehaven	1800	(− 78)
*Swinton	1622	(−1084)
Doncaster	1543	(+ 854)
*York	1520	(−1308)
Hunslet	1050	(+ 338)
Rochdale Hornets	877	(− 390)
Carlisle	789	(+ 171)
Batley	744	(− 186)
Bramley	737	(− 94)
Sheffield Eagles	708	(+ 10)
Fulham	684	(− 133)
*Dewsbury	669	(−1150)
Workington Town	653	(− 49)
Huddersfield Barracudas	524	(− 154)
Blackpool Borough	475	(− 59)
Keighley	445	(− 240)
Mansfield Marksman	368	(− 119)
Runcorn Highfield	331	(− 35)

*Relegated 1985-86

EXTINCT CLUBS

The 1986-87 season was marked by the major move of Blackpool Borough from the Fylde coast to Wigan to share Springfield Park with the town's soccer club.

Formed in 1954, Blackpool were facing extinction with crippling six-figure ground safety improvements at their Borough Park ground and were forced to play most of their 1987 Second Division fixtures at the neighbouring Blackpool FC soccer stadium.

At a Rugby League Council meeting of 15th May, it was agreed by 22 votes to 11 to allow Borough's new 13-man board of directors to move the club to Wigan despite strong protests from Wigan and Leigh clubs.

The new Blackpool board was chaired by Mike Marsland, the leader of a consortium which had failed to introduce Rugby League to Stockport a year earlier.

Southend Invicta and Bridgend, who had their membership suspended at the start of the 1985-86 campaign, again failed to reappear, Southend being taken into liquidation.

The years from 1980 to 1984 had been the most expansive for the game in this country since the early part of the century. The introduction of Fulham, Cardiff City, Carlisle, Kent Invicta, Mansfield Marksman and Sheffield Eagles brought the total of senior clubs in 1984-85 to 36 ... the largest League membership since 1902-03.

In that first ever period of two divisions, 36 clubs were split equally into two leagues. Since then the lowest number of clubs in peacetime was 25 between 1914 and 1922.

Of the 22 clubs who formed the first Northern Rugby Football League following the split with the English Rugby Union in 1895, seven are no longer in existence. Thirty-one more have come and gone.

In recording the number of extinct clubs, some distinction must be made between the early fatalities in the code's formative years and the many expansion attempts that followed. Some of the early victims were clubs leaving the English Rugby Union and not strong enough to compete in the new major leagues, but continued at a lower level.

After 1895-96 the major leagues were the Lancashire and Yorkshire Senior Competitions until there was another change in 1901-02. Then there was a total of 41 senior clubs ... 14 in the NRL, 13 in the LSC and 14 in the YSC.

The following season, 1902-03, staged the first era of two divisions and it is from then that a more meaningful appraisal can be made of the clubs who have dropped out.

Clubs who departed before that eventful season were two founder members in **Tyldesley** and **Liversedge**, plus **Leeds Parish Church, Heckmondwike, Altrincham, Radcliffe, Goole** and **Sowerby Bridge.**

Wales was an immediate target for expansion and in 1908-09 there were six clubs in the Northern Rugby League ... Merthyr Tydfil, Ebbw Vale, Mid-Rhondda, Treherbert, Barry and Aberdare. By 1912 there was none.

Attention was focussed on London in the 1930s with Acton and Willesden, and Streatham and Mitcham, having brief existences. Mention must also be made of London Highfield, who began as Wigan Highfield and progressed through a change of Liverpool titles to the present day Runcorn Highfield.

Wigan Highfield entered the League in 1922 and had one season as London Highfield in 1933-34. This venture was promoted by a group of London businessmen with home games played at White City under floodlights on a Saturday night. It was a fair success to begin with, but flopped when crowds dwindled during the winter. For 'home' matches the team caught a Friday evening train from Wigan and returned on Saturday night. The following season the club became Liverpool Stanley.

THE SURVIVORS

Changes of title, or the death of one club to be immediately replaced by another, can also cause confusion. Bradford Northern and Hunslet are two other clubs who have survived changes. See the CLUBS section for details.

Castleford had a senior club between 1896 and 1906, but the present club did not enter the League until 1926-27. Other clubs which have survived since becoming members after

1901-02 are:

Featherstone Rovers (1921-22), Huyton (1922-23), Workington Town (1945-46), Whitehaven (1948-49), Doncaster (1951-52), Blackpool Borough (1954-55), Fulham (1980-81), Carlisle (1981-82), Mansfield Marksman and Sheffield Eagles, both launched in 1984-85.

FORMER CLUBS

The following is a list of clubs who have dropped out of the League since 1902-03. County references are the old boundaries.

First season	Club	Last season
1895-96	Manningham *(Yorkshire)*	1902-03
	Stockport *(Cheshire)*	1902-03
	Brighouse Rangers *(Yorkshire)*	1905-06
	Runcorn *(Cheshire)*	1914-15
	Broughton Rangers *(Lancashire)*	
	Changed to Belle Vue Rangers in 1946-1947	1954-55
1896-97	*Morecambe *(Lancashire)*	1905-06
	Holbeck *(Yorkshire)*	1903-04
1899-1900	Millom *(Cumberland)*	1905-06
1901-02	Birkenhead Wanderers *(Cheshire)*	1904-05
	Lancaster *(Lancashire)*	1904-05
	Normanton *(Yorkshire)*	1905-06
1902-03	South Shields *(Durham)*	1903-04
1903-04	Pontefract *(Yorkshire)*	1906-07
1906-07	Liverpool City *(Lancashire)*	1906-07
1907-08	Merthyr Tydfil *(Wales)*	1910-11
	Ebbw Vale *(Wales)*	1911-12
1908-09	Aberdare *(Wales)*	1908-09
	Barry *(Wales)*	1908-09
	Mid-Rhondda *(Wales)*	1908-09
	Treherbert *(Wales)*	1909-10
1910-11	Coventry *(Warwickshire)*	1912-13
1918-19	St. Helens Recreation *(Lancashire)*	1938-39
1926-27	Pontypridd *(Wales)*	1927-28
1928-29	Carlisle City *(Cumberland)*	1928-29
1935-36	Acton and Willesden *(London)*	1935-36
	Streatham and Mitcham *(London)*	1936-37
1936-37	Newcastle *(Northumberland)*	1937-38
1951-52	Cardiff *(Wales)*	1951-52
1981-82	Cardiff City *(Wales)*	
	Changed to Bridgend in 1984-85	1984-85
1983-84	Kent Invicta *(Kent)*	
	Changed to Southend Invicta *(Essex)* in 1984-85	1984-85

*Dropped out of League for two seasons 1899-1901

FIXTURES

STONES BITTER CHAMPIONSHIP 1987-88

SUNDAY, 30th AUGUST, 1987

Castleford	v.	St. Helens
Hull K.R.	v.	Swinton
Leeds	v.	Leigh
Salford	v.	Bradford N.
Warrington	v.	Hunslet
Widnes	v.	Halifax
Wigan	v.	Hull

SUNDAY 6th SEPTEMBER, 1987

Bradford N.	v.	Widnes
Halifax	v.	Warrington
Hull	v.	Salford
Hunslet	v.	Leeds
Leigh	v.	Castleford
St. Helens	v.	Hull K.R.
Swinton	v.	Wigan

SUNDAY, 20th SEPTEMBER, 1987

Bradford N.	v.	Leeds
Halifax	v.	Leigh
Hull	v.	Widnes
Hunslet	v.	Swinton
Salford	v.	Hull K.R.
Warrington	v.	St. Helens
Wigan	v.	Castleford

SUNDAY, 27th SEPTEMBER, 1987

Castleford	v.	Warrington
Hull K.R.	v.	Halifax
Leeds	v.	Salford
Leigh	v.	Wigan
St. Helens	v.	Bradford N.
Swinton	v.	Hull
Widnes	v.	Hunslet

SUNDAY, 4th OCTOBER, 1987

Bradford N.	v.	Swinton
Halifax	v.	St. Helens
Hull	v.	Leigh
Hunslet	v.	Castleford
Salford	v.	Widnes
Warrington	v.	Hull K.R.
Wigan	v.	Leeds

SUNDAY, 11th OCTOBER, 1987

Halifax	v.	Bradford N.
Hull K.R.	v.	Wigan
Leeds	v.	Hull
Leigh	v.	Hunslet
Swinton	v.	Warrington

SUNDAY, 18th OCTOBER, 1987

Castleford	v.	Leeds
Hunslet	v.	Salford
St. Helens	v.	Leigh
Warrington	v.	Bradford N.
Widnes	v.	Hull K.R.
Wigan	v.	Halifax

SUNDAY, 25th OCTOBER, 1987

Bradford N.	v.	Hull K.R.
Hull	v.	Castleford
Salford	v.	St. Helens
Widnes	v.	Swinton

SUNDAY 1st NOVEMBER, 1987

Castleford	v.	Wigan
Halifax	v.	Salford

Hull K.R.	v.	Warrington
Hunslet	v.	Hull
Leigh	v.	Widnes
Swinton	v.	Leeds

SUNDAY, 8th NOVEMBER, 1987

Bradford N.	v.	Leigh
Hull K.R.	v.	Hunslet
Leeds	v.	St. Helens
Salford	v.	Hull
Warrington	v.	Halifax
Widnes	v.	Castleford

SUNDAY, 29th NOVEMBER, 1987

Castleford	v.	Bradford N.
Halifax	v.	Widnes
Hull	v.	Warrington
Hunslet	v.	Wigan
Leigh	v.	Leeds
St. Helens	v.	Salford
Swinton	v.	Hull K.R.

SUNDAY, 6th DECEMBER, 1987

Bradford N.	v.	Halifax
Hull K.R.	v.	St. Helens
Leeds	v.	Castleford
Salford	v.	Hunslet
Warrington	v.	Swinton
Widnes	v.	Hull
Wigan	v.	Leigh

SUNDAY, 13th DECEMBER, 1987

Castleford	v.	Salford
Halifax	v.	Wigan
Hull	v.	Leeds
Hunslet	v.	Bradford N.
Leigh	v.	Hull K.R.
St. Helens	v.	Warrington
Swinton	v.	Widnes

BOXING DAY, SATURDAY, 26th DECEMBER, 1987

Leeds	v.	Halifax

SUNDAY, 27TH DECEMBER, 1987

Bradford N.	v.	Hull
Hull K.R.	v.	Castleford
Hunslett	v.	Leigh
Salford	v.	Swinton
Wigan	v.	St. Helens
Widnes	v.	Warrington

1988

NEW YEAR'S DAY, 1st JANUARY, 1988

Bradford N.	v.	Castleford
Halifax	v.	Swinton
Leeds	v.	Hunslet
Leigh	v.	Salford
Warrington	v.	Wigan

SUNDAY, 3rd JANUARY, 1988

Hull	v.	Hull K.R.
St. Helens	v.	Widnes

SUNDAY, 10th JANUARY, 1988

Castleford	v.	Hull
Hull K.R.	v.	Salford
Hunslet	v.	Warrington
St. Helens	v.	Leeds

Swinton v. Halifax
Widnes v. Leigh
Wigan v. Bradford N.

SUNDAY, 17th JANUARY, 1988
Bradford N. v. St. Helens
Halifax v. Hull K.R.
Hull v. Hunslet
Leeds v. Widnes
Leigh v. Swinton
Salford v. Wigan
Warrington v. Castleford

SUNDAY, 24th JANUARY, 1988
Castleford v. Leigh
Hull K.R. v. Leeds
Hunslet v. Halifax
St . Helens v. Hull
Swinton v. Bradford N.
Widnes v. Salford
Wigan v. Warrington

SUNDAY, 7th FEBRUARY, 1988
St. Helens v. Halifax
Warrington v. Leeds

FRIDAY, 19th FEBRUARY, 1988
Salford v. Castleford

SUNDAY, 21st FEBRUARY, 1988
Bradford N. v. Warrington
Halifax v. Hunslet
Hull v. Swinton
Leeds v. Hull K.R.
Leigh v. St. Helens
Widnes v. Wigan

SUNDAY, 28th FEBRUARY, 1988
Castleford v. Widnes
Hull K.R. v. Bradford N.
St. Helens v. Hunslet
Swinton v. Leigh
Warrington v. Hull
Wigan v. Salford

SUNDAY, 6th MARCH, 1988
Castleford v. Swinton
Hull v. Bradford N.
Hunslet v. St. Helens
Leigh v. Halifax
Salford v. Leeds
Wigan v. Hull K.R.

SUNDAY, 13th MARCH, 1988
Bradford N. v. Wigan
Halifax v. Hull
Hull K.R. v. Widnes
Leeds v. Warrington
St. Helens v. Castleford
Salford v. Leigh
Swinton v. Hunslet

SUNDAY, 20th MARCH, 1988
Bradford N. v. Salford
Castleford v. Halifax
Hull v. Wigan
Hunslet v. Hull K.R.
Swinton v. St. Helens
Warrington v. Leigh
Widnes v. Leeds

SUNDAY, 27th MARCH, 1988
Castleford v. Hunslet
Hull v. St. Helens
Leeds v. Swinton
Leigh v. Bradford N.
Salford v. Warrington
Wigan v. Widnes

GOOD FRIDAY, 1st APRIL, 1988
Halifax v. Castleford
Hull K.R. v. Hull
Leeds v. Bradford N.
St. Helens v. Wigan
Swinton v. Salford
Warrington v. Widnes

EASTER MONDAY, 4th APRIL, 1988
Bradford N. v. Hunslet
Castleford v. Hull K.R.
Halifax v. Leeds
Leigh v. Warrington
Widnes v. St. Helens
Wigan v. Swinton

SUNDAY, 10th APRIL, 1988
Hull v. Halifax
Hull K.R. v. Leigh
Hunslet v. Widnes
Leeds v. Wigan
Swinton v. Castleford
Warrington v. Salford

SUNDAY, 17TH APRIL, 1988
Leigh v. Hull
St. Helens v. Swinton
Salford v. Halifax
Widnes v. Bradford N.
Wigan v. Hunslet

2ND DIVISION FIXTURES

SUNDAY, 30th AUGUST, 1987
Barrow v. Featherstone R.
Bramley v. Batley
Dewsbury v. Working T.
Doncaster v. York
Fulham v. Sheffield E.
Huddersfield B v. Springfield B.
Keighley v. Mansfield M.
Rochdale v. Runcorn H.
Wakefield v. Carlisle
Whitehaven v. Oldham

WEDNESDAY 2nd SEPTEMBER, 1987
Bramley v. Doncaster
Dewsbury v. Runcorn H.
Fulham v. Batley
Mansfield M. v. Sheffield
Oldham v. Keighley
Rochdale H. v. Springfield B.
Wakefield v. Barrow
York v. Featherstone R.

SUNDAY, 6th SEPTEMBER, 1987
Carlisle v. Doncaster
Dewsbury v. Wakefield
Featherstone R. v. Whitehaven
Keighley v. York
Mansfield M. v. Batley
Oldham v. Bramley

Runcorn H.	v.	Fulham
Sheffield E.	v.	Rochdale
Springfield B.	v.	Barrow
Workington T.	v.	Huddersfield B.

WEDNESDAY, 9th SEPTEMBER, 1987

Bramley	v.	Dewsbury
Carlisle	v.	Keighley
Doncaster R.	v.	Batley
Huddersfield B.	v.	Fulham
Springfield B.	v.	Mansfield M.
Whitehaven	v.	Wakefield T.

SUNDAY, 20th SEPTEMBER, 1987

Barrow	v.	Sheffield
Batley	v.	York
Carlisle	v.	Workington T.
Featherstone R.	v.	Rochdale H.
Fulham	v.	Keighley
Huddersfield B.	v.	Dewsbury
Oldham	v.	Springfield B.
Runcorn H.	v.	Mansfield M.
Wakefield T.	v.	Bramley
Whitehaven	v.	Doncaster

SUNDAY, 27th SEPTEMBER, 1987

Bramley	v.	Featherstone R.
Doncaster	v.	Oldham
Keighley	v.	Barrow
Mansfield M.	v.	Wakefield T.
Rochdale H.	v.	Carlisle
Sheffield E.	v.	Whitehaven
Springfield B.	v.	Huddersfield B.
Workington T.	v.	Fulham
York	v.	Runcorn H.

SUNDAY, 4th OCTOBER, 1987

Barrow	v.	Rochdale
Batley	v.	Keighley
Featherstone R.	v.	Mansfield M.
Fulham	v.	Doncaster
Huddersfield B.	v.	Oldham
Runcorn H.	v.	Workington T.
Wakefield T.	v.	Dewsbury
Whitehaven	v.	Springfield B.

WEDNESDAY, 7th OCTOBER, 1987

Sheffield E.	v.	Bramley

SUNDAY 11th OCTOBER, 1987

Bramley	v.	Fulham
Dewsbury	v.	Huddersfield B.
Doncaster	v.	Barrow
Mansfield M.	v.	York
Oldham	v.	Sheffield E.
Rochdale H.	v.	Whitehaven
Springfield B.	v.	Carlisle
Workington T.	v.	Batley

SUNDAY, 18th OCTOBER, 1987

Barrow	v.	Runcorn H.
Batley	v.	Doncaster
Carlisle	v.	Oldham
Fulham	v.	Featherstone R.
Huddersfield B.	v.	Mansfield M.
Keighley	v.	Workington T.
Sheffield E.	v.	Wakefield T.
Whitehaven	v.	Bramley
York	v.	Springfield B.

SUNDAY, 25th OCTOBER, 1987

Dewsbury	v.	Fulham
Doncaster	v.	Mansfield M.
Featherstone R.	v.	Carlisle
Huddersfield B.	v.	Batley
Oldham	v.	Barrow
Rochdale H.	v.	Sheffield E.
Springfield B.	v.	Keighley
Wakefield T.	v.	Whitehaven
Workington T.	v.	York

SUNDAY, 1st NOVEMBER, 1987

Batley	v.	Workington T.
Carlisle	v.	Bramley
Keighley	v.	Oldham
Mansfield M.	v.	Dewsbury
Rochdale H.	v.	Doncaster
Runcorn H.	v.	Springfield B.
Sheffield E.	v.	Featherstone R.
Whitehaven	v.	Barrow
York	v.	Huddersfield B.

SUNDAY, 8th NOVEMBER, 1987

Batley	v.	Runcorn H.
Bramley	v.	York
Featherstone R.	v.	Dewsbury
Huddersfield	v.	Carlisle
Sheffield E.	v.	Mansfield M.
Springfield B.	v.	Rochdale H.
Wakefield T.	v.	Fulham

SUNDAY, 29th NOVEMBER, 1987

Barrow	v.	Whitehaven
Dewsbury	v.	Featherstone R.
Doncaster	v.	Wakefield T.
Keighley	v.	Batley
Rochdale H.	v.	Bramley
Runcorn H.	v.	Huddersfield B.
Sheffield E.	v.	Fulham
Springfield B.	v.	York
Workington T.	v.	Oldham

SUNDAY, 6th DECEMBER, 1987

Batley	v.	Sheffield E.
Bramley	v.	Mansfield M.
Carlisle	v.	Runcorn H.
Featherstone R.	v.	Barrow
Fulham	v.	Workington T.
Huddersfield B.	v.	Keighley
Oldham	v.	Doncaster
Wakefield T.	v.	Rochdale
York	v.	Dewsbury

SUNDAY, 13th DECEMBER, 1987

Barrow	v.	Oldham
Dewsbury	v.	Bramley
Doncaster	v.	Featherstone R.
Keighley	v.	Fulham
Mansfield M.	v.	Huddersfield B.
Rochdale H.	v.	Wakefield T.
Runcorn H.	v.	Batley
Sheffield	v.	York
Springfield B.	v.	Whitehaven
Workington T.	v.	Carlisle

SUNDAY 20th DECEMBER, 1987

Batley	v.	Springfield B.
Bramley	v.	Barrow
Carlisle	v.	Sheffield E.
Huddersfield	v.	Workington T.

Wakefield T.	v.	Mansfield M.
Whitehaven	v.	Rochdale H.
York	v.	Keighley

SATURDAY, 26th DECEMBER, 1987

Batley	v.	Dewsbury
Carlisle	v.	Barrow
Doncaster	v.	Sheffield E.
Featherstone R.	v.	Wakefield T.
Keighley	v.	Springfield B.
Oldham	v.	Rochdale H.
Workington T.	v.	Whitehaven
York	v.	Bramley

SUNDAY, 27th DECEMBER, 1987

| Mansfield M. | v. | Runcorn H. |

NEW YEAR'S DAY FRIDAY, 1st JANUARY, 1988

Dewsbury	v.	Batley
Runcorn H.	v.	Keighley
Wakefield T.	v.	Featherstone R.
Whitehaven	v.	Carlisle
York	v.	Doncaster

SUNDAY, 3rd JANUARY, 1988

Barrow	v.	Workington T.
Bramley	v.	Sheffield E.
Mansfield M.	v.	Fulham
Rochdale H.	v.	Huddersfield B.
Springfield B.	v.	Oldham

SUNDAY, 10th JANUARY, 1988

Batley	v.	Wakefield T.
Carlisle	v.	Springfield B.
Doncaster	v.	Bramley
Huddersfield B.	v.	York
Fulham	v.	Runcorn H.
Keighley	v.	Rochdale H.
Manfield M.	v.	Featherstone R.
Oldham	v.	Whitehaven
Sheffield E.	v.	Barrow
Workington T.	v.	Dewsbury

SUNDAY, 17th JANUARY, 1988

Barrow	v.	Huddersfield B.
Bramley	v.	Carlisle
Dewsbury	v.	Mansfield M.
Featherstone R.	v.	Doncaster
Rochdale H.	v.	Workington T.
Runcorn H.	v.	Oldham
Springfield B.	v.	Fulham
Whitehaven	v.	Keighley
York	v.	Sheffield E.

SUNDAY 24th JANUARY, 1988

Batley	v.	Featherstone R.
Doncaster	v.	Dewsbury
Fulham	v.	York
Huddersfield B.	v.	Whitehaven
Keighley	v.	Runcorn H.
Mansfield M.	v.	Bramley
Oldham	v.	Wakefield T.
Sheffield E.	v.	Carlisle
Workington T.	v.	Springfield B.

SUNDAY, 7th FEBRUARY, 1988

Barrow	v.	Keighley
Carlisle	v.	Huddersfield B.
Dewsbury	v.	Doncaster
Featherstone R.	v.	Fulham

| Runcorn H. | v. | Rochdale H. |
| Wakefield T. | v. | Batley |

SUNDAY, 21st FEBRUARY, 1988

Batley	v.	Huddersfield B.
Doncaster	v.	Carlisle
Featherstone R.	v.	Oldham
Fulham	v.	Bramley
Mansfield M.	v.	Keighley
Rochdale H.	v.	Barrow
Springfield B.	v.	Dewsbury
Wakefield T.	v.	Sheffield E.
Whitehaven	v.	Runcorn H.
York	v.	Workington T.

SUNDAY, 28th FEBRUARY, 1988

Carlisle	v.	Wakefield T.
Dewsbury	v.	York
Doncaster	v.	Fulham
Huddersfield B.	v.	Rochdale H.
Keighley	v.	Whitehaven
Oldham	v.	Featherstone R.
Runcorn H.	v.	Barrow
Sheffield E.	v.	Batley
Workington T.	v.	Mansfield M.

SUNDAY, 6th MARCH, 1988

Barrow	v.	Springfield B.
Batley	v.	Bramley
Fulham	v.	Huddersfield B.
Mansfield	v.	Doncaster
Oldham	v.	Workington T.
Rochdale H.	v.	Keighley
Runcorn H.	v.	York
Sheffield E.	v.	Dewsbury
Whitehaven	v.	Featherstone R.

SUNDAY, 13th MARCH, 1988

Bramley	v.	Oldham
Carlisle	v.	Rochdale H.
Dewsbury	v.	Keighley
Doncaster	v.	Whitehaven
Featherstone R.	v.	Sheffield E.
Fulham	v.	Wakefield T.
Springfield B.	v.	Batley
Workington T.	v.	Runcorn H.
York	v.	Mansfield M.

SUNDAY, 20th MARCH, 1988

Barrow	v.	Bramley
Batley	v.	Fulham
Keighley	v.	Carlisle
Mansfield M.	v.	Workington T.
Oldham	v.	Huddersfield B.
Rochdale H.	v.	Featherstone R.
Runcorn H.	v.	Dewsbury
Wakefield T.	v.	Doncaster
Whitehaven	v.	Sheffield E.

SUNDAY, 27th MARCH, 1988

Bramley	v.	Wakefield T.
Carlisle	v.	Featherstone R.
Dewsbury	v.	Springfield B.
Doncaster	v.	Rochdale H.
Fulham	v.	Mansfield M.
Huddersfield B	v.	Barrow
Runcorn H.	v.	Whitehaven
Sheffield E.	v.	Oldham
Workington T.	v.	Keighley
York	v.	Batley

GOOD FRIDAY 1st APRIL, 1988

Barrow	v.	Carlisle
Keighley	v.	Huddersfield B.
Rochdale H.	v.	Oldham
Springfield B.	v.	Runcorn H.
Wakefield T.	v.	York
Whitehaven	v.	Workington T.

SUNDAY, 3rd APRIL, 1988

Featherstone R.	v.	Batley
Mansfield M.	v.	Springfield B.
Sheffield E.	v.	Doncaster

EASTER MONDAY, 4th APRIL, 1988

Bramley	v.	Rochdale H.
Carlisle	v.	Whitehaven
Fulham	v.	Dewsbury
Oldham	v.	Runcorn H.
Workington T.	v.	Barrow
York	v.	Wakefield T.

SUNDAY, 10th APRIL, 1988

Batley	v.	Mansfield M.
Featherstone R.	v.	Bramley
Keighley	v.	Dewsbury
Runcorn H.	v.	Carlisle
Springfield B.	v.	Workington T.
Wakefield T.	v.	Oldham
Whitehaven	v.	Huddersfield B.
York	v.	Fulham

SUNDAY, 17th APRIL, 1988

Barrow	v.	Wakefield T.
Bramley	v.	Whitehaven
Dewsbury	v.	Sheffield E.
Featherstone R.	v.	York
Fulham	v.	Springfield B.
Huddersfield B.	v.	Runcorn H.
Oldham	v.	Carlisle
Workington T.	v.	Rochdale H.